Social Behaviour and Experience

Multiple perspectives

Social Behaviour and Experience

Multiple perspectives

Edited by Hedy Brown and Richard Stevens
at The Open University

Hodder and Stoughton
in association with
The Open University Press

ISBN 0 340 20458 3 Boards
ISBN 0 340 20459 1 Paper

Second impression 1978

Printed and bound in Great Britain for
Hodder and Stoughton Educational,
a division of Hodder and Stoughton Ltd,
Mill Road, Dunton Green, Sevenoaks, Kent,
by Hazell Watson & Viney Ltd, Aylesbury, Bucks

Contents

Section 8 Person perception

Section 9 Man's experience of the world

Section 10 Beliefs and attitudes

Section 11 Communication

Acknowledgments

The editors and publisher wish to thank the following for permission to reprint the articles in this book:
Academic Press Inc. (London) Ltd for 'Stipulations and construction in the social sciences' (reprinted from *The Context of Social Psychology*, edited by J. Israel and H. Tajfel, 1972, pp. 123–6, 129–31 and 192–6); Professor E. N. Barker and S. Karger AG for 'Communicating and attaining knowledge in psychology' (reprinted from *Interpersonal Development*, **2** (1972), pp. 154–63); Professor Karl Weick and The American Psychological Association for 'A specialist in unnoticed causes' (reprinted from *American Psychologist*, **24** (1969), pp. 990–8, copyright © 1969 by The American Psychological Association); Professor Duane Schultz and Basil Blackwell for 'Behaviour and experience' (reprinted from *Journal of the Theory of Social Behaviour*, 2 October 1971); Penguin Books Ltd for 'The biological and the social' (reprinted from *Reconstructing Social Psychology*, edited by N. Armistead, 1974, pp. 234–8); Professor Anne Anastasi and The American Psychological Association for 'The influence of hereditary factors on behaviour' (reprinted from *Psychological Review*, **65** (1958), pp. 197–208, copyright © 1958 by The American Psychological Association); New Science Publications for 'Sex differences: biological and social interactions' (reprinted from *New Scientist: The weekly review of science and technology*, 21 November 1974); Dr L. Erlenmeyer-Kimling, Dr L. F. Jarvik and The American Association for the Advancement of Science for 'Genetics and intelligence' (reprinted from *Science*, **142** (1963), pp. 1477–9, copyright © 1963 by The American Association for the Advancement of Science); Duke University Press for A. H. Buss *et al.*, 'The inheritance of temperaments' (reprinted by permission from *Journal of Personality*, **41** (1973), pp. 513–24); Professor I. Eibl-Eibesfeldt and Holt, Rinehart and Winston Inc. for 'The ethology of man' (reprinted from *Ethology: The biology of behaviour*, 1970, pp. 398–455 © 1970); Macmillan Publishing Co. Inc. for 'Language: the system and its acquisition' (reprinted from *Social Psychology* by Roger Brown, 1965, pp. 246–50, copyright © 1965 by The Free Press); the MIT Press for 'A biological perspective of language' (reprinted from *New Directions in the Study of Language*, edited by E. H. Lenneberg, 1964, pp. 65–88, by permission of The MIT Press, Cambridge, Massachusetts); Professor Beatrice T. Gardner and The American Association for the Advancement of Science for 'Teaching sign language to a chimpanzee' (reprinted from *Science*, **165** (1969), pp. 664–72, copyright © 1969 by The American Association for the Advancement

of Science) and 'Early signs of language in child and chimpanzee' (reprinted from *Science*, 187 (1975), pp. 752–3, copyright © 1975 by The American Association for the Advancement of Science); Macmillan Publishing Co. Inc. for 'What is a social fact?' (reprinted from *Rules of Sociological Method* by E. Dürkheim, copyright 1935 by George E. G. Catlin, renewed 1966 by Sarah A. Solovay, John H. Mueller and George E. G. Catlin); Cambridge University Press for 'The institution as an environment for development' (reprinted from *The Integration of the Child into a Social World*, edited by M. P. M. Richards, 1974, pp. 137–52); Professor Stanley Milgram and The American Association for the Advancement of Science for 'The experience of living in cities' (reprinted from *Science*, 167 (1970), pp. 1461–8, copyright © 1970 by The American Association for the Advancement of Science); The British Psychological Society for 'Early social behaviour and the study of reciprocity' (reprinted from *Bulletin of the British Psychological Society*, 27 (1974), pp. 209–16); Albert Bandura and The American Psychological Association for 'Transmission of aggression through imitation of aggressive models' (reprinted from *Journal of Abnormal and Social Psychology*, 63 (1961), pp. 575–82, copyright © 1961 by The American Psychological Association); Routledge and Kegan Paul Ltd for 'The moral judgment of the child' (reprinted from *The Moral Judgment of the Child* by Jean Piaget (trans. by M. Gabain), 1932); Ziff-Davis Publishing Co. for 'The child as a moral philosopher' (reprinted from *Psychology Today* magazine, September 1973, copyright © 1973 by Ziff-Davis Publishing Company, all rights reserved); Constable and Co. Ltd for 'A theory of personality and behaviour' (reprinted from *Client-Centred Therapy* by Carl R. Rogers, 1965, pp. 482–524); Stanford University Press for 'The problem of relevance in the study of person perception' (reprinted from *Person Perception and Interpersonal Behaviour*, edited by R. Tagiuri and L. Petrullo, 1958, with the permission of the publishers, Stanford University Press: copyright © 1958 by The Board of Trustees of the Leland Stanford Junior University); Professor Paul Ekman, Dr Wallace V. Friesen and The American Psychological Association for 'Constants across cultures in the face and emotion' (reprinted from *Journal of Personality and Social Psychology*, 17 (1971), number 2, pp. 124–9, copyright © 1971 by The American Psychological Association); Cambridge University Press for 'Cultural influences in the perception of people: the case of Chinese in America' (reprinted from *British Journal of Social and Clinical Psychology*, 4 (1965), pp. 110–13); The New School for Social Research for 'The small life-worlds of modern man' (reprinted from *Social Research*, 7 (1970), number 4, pp. 580–96); John Wiley and Sons Inc. for 'The journalist' (reprinted from *Craft and Consciousness: Occupational*

Technique and the Development of World Images by J. Bensman and R. Lilienfeld, 1973, pp. 207–32, copyright © 1973 by Joseph Bensman and Robert Lilienfeld); Penguin Books Ltd for 'Time and deterioration' (reprinted from *Psychological Survival* by Stanley Cohen and Laurie Taylor, 1972, pp. 86–104); John Wiley and Sons Inc. for 'the adjustive functions of attitudes' (reprinted from *Opinions and Personality* by M. Brewster Smith, J. S. Bruner and R. W. White, 1956, pp. 39–44); Professor Robert E. Lane for 'Needs served by ideas: an interpreted appraisal' (reprinted from *Political Thinking and Consciousness*, 1969, pp. 31–46); Professor Nevitt Sanford for 'The F scale and the authoritarian personality' (reprinted from *Psychology of Personality: six modern approaches*, edited by J. McCary, 1956, pp. 266–77); Plenum Publishing Corporation for 'The effects of changes in roles on the attitudes of role occupants' (reprinted from *Human Relations*, 12 (1956), pp. 385–402); Professor Jerome S. Bruner and Edicom NV for 'Communicative intentions' (reprinted from *Cognition* (Journal of Cognitive Psychology), in press); Basil Bernstein and Mouton Publishing for 'Social class, language and socialization' (reprinted from *Class, Codes and Control: Volume I*, 1971, pp. 143–69); Dr William Labov for 'The logic of nonstandard English' (reprinted from *Georgetown Monographs on Language and Linguistics*, 22 (1969), pp. 1–31); Cambridge University Press for 'Non-verbal communication in human social interaction' (reprinted from *Non-verbal Communication*, edited by R. Hinde, 1972, pp. 243–69); Professor Darwyn E. Linder, Dr Elliot Aronson and Academic Press Inc. for 'Gain and loss of esteem as determinants of interpersonal attractiveness' (reprinted from *Journal of Experimental Social Psychology*, 1 (1965), pp. 156–71); André Deutsch Ltd for 'Games people play' (reprinted from *Games People Play* by Eric Berne, 1966, pp. 33–9, 44–56); George Allen and Unwin Ltd for 'The theory of love' (reprinted from *The Art of Loving* by Erich Fromm, 1962, pp. 13–21); Tavistock Publications Ltd for 'Experiences in groups' (reprinted from *Experiences in Groups* by W. R. Bion, 1961, pp. 41–58); Macmillan Publishing Co. Inc. for 'The violent gang as a near group' (reprinted from *The Violent Gang* by Lewis Yablonsky, 1962, pp. 243–54, copyright © 1962 by Lewis Yablonsky); Dr A. P. Sealy for 'The jury: decision-making in a small group'; Elihu Katz and The University of Chicago Press for 'Communication research and the image of society' (reprinted from *American Journal of Sociology*, 65 (1960), number 5); Professor Morris Janowitz, Professor Edward A. Shils and The Public Opinion Quarterly for 'The impact of allied propaganda on Wehrmacht solidarity' (reprinted from *Public Opinion Quarterly*, 12 (1948), pp. 280–315); Victor Gollancz Ltd for 'Reeducation: Dr Vincent' (reprinted from *Thought Reform and the Psy-*

chology of Totalism by Robert J. Lifton, 1961, pp. 19–31); and Plenum Publishing Corporation for 'Conformity and independence – a psychological analysis' (reprinted from *Human Relations*, **12** (1959), pp. 99–120).
logical analysis' (reprinted from *Human Relations*, **12** (1959), pp. 99–120); also Professor Urie Bronfenbrenner for 'A theoretical perspective for research in human development' (reprinted from H. P. Dreitzel (ed.), *Childhood and Socialization*, 1973, Macmillan Publishing Co. Inc.).

General Introduction

It is our belief that no single theory or method is sufficient in itself to achieve the most effective understanding at present possible of social behaviour and experience. Knowledge is a construction. The differing values, assumptions and methods of researchers in this area have generated varied theories and results though, on examination, these very often turn out to be complementary rather than contradictory. The papers in this collection therefore range widely in their origins and approach – hence the subtitle *Multiple Perspectives*. They are drawn not only from the field of social psychology but also from developmental, experimental and clinical psychology, from ethology and sociology. They include both theoretical analyses and research reports. The book has been specifically compiled for the use of students taking the Open University third level course in *Social Psychology* (D 305) although we hope that it will also have more general appeal. It follows the approach and structure of the course.

The excerpts in section 1 focus on epistemological considerations. What is a theory? How can we best investigate and make sense of social behaviour and experience? Sections 2–7 then proceed to explore their foundations. The articles in section 2, for example, consider the nature and extent of genetic influences on human behaviour. This aspect is also discussed in section 3, which looks specifically at language. Language is a key feature of human social interaction, yet without the appropriate genetic endowment it would be impossible to acquire and use it. A child is, of course, born into and grows up in an existing society. The emphasis shifts, therefore, in section 4 to the social and physical milieu. Section 5 looks at socialization, the process by which the child becomes a characteristic member of his society. The interaction of biological and social influences is then explored in two rather different ways. Section 6 adopts a cognitive perspective to explain moral development. It centres on the work of Piaget, which emphasizes that the development of thinking depends not only on the ideas a child is exposed to but also on his cognitive processing capacity, the latter being itself dependent on physiological maturation. Section 7 is concerned with the problems which arise because of conflict between organismic needs and a person's self-concept, which often reflects, to a large extent, the demands and values of others.

The readings go on to explore different aspects of adult social experience and behaviour. Section 8 looks at the process of person perception. The studies included here emphasize the tradition of experimental psychology. In contrast, section 9, which takes up the theme of man's experience of the world, illustrates the way in which phenomenologists approach a related area in a very different way. Section 10 addresses itself to a subject of perennial interest to social psychologists – attitudes. The focus of the final sections then widens to embrace interaction between individuals and within groups. The papers in section 11, for example, examine communication and, in section 12, aspects of personal relationships. These articles again are representative of very different theoretical and methodological traditions. The nature of group dynamics and experience is the topic of section 13, the papers illustrating the approaches of the psychoanalytically orientated clinician, the observer of delinquent groups and the experimental social psychologist. Finally, section 14 centres on the theme of persuasion and coercion, that is on deliberate attempts to influence and change people.

Brief introductions are provided for each section. These are designed both to comment on papers contained there and to link them with other sections.

The papers and excerpts in this book have been chosen in close consultation with our colleagues who are concerned with us in the planning and writing of the Open University Course in *Social Psychology*. Whilst we take responsibility for the content of this volume we would like to express our appreciation and acknowledge our indebtedness to Marian Annett, Judith Greene, Alan Elms, Ronald Fletcher, Jeannette Murphy, Ilona Roth, Philip Sealy, Laurie Taylor and Derek Wright for their suggestions and comments. We should also like to express our gratitude to Marsaili Cameron and Jeff Harvey for editorial assistance and to Margaret Stickland, Maureen Woodcock and Pat Vasiliou for unfailing forbearance and efficiency in providing secretarial support.

Hedy Brown
Richard Stevens

May 1975

Section 1
Studying social behaviour and experience

Introduction

All of us, most of the time, are engaged in the observation and interpretation of social behaviour and experience. We develop ideas and explanations about why people feel and behave in the way that they do. If we have occasion to compare our ideas, however, as when two people talk about a third, such explanations are often found to be different and sometimes contradictory. Disciplines like social psychology and sociology which are concerned with the systematic study of social behaviour and experience present a not dissimilar picture. Many very different and often seemingly contradictory theories and explanations coexist. A learning theorist, for example, asked why a particular individual has developed a phobia about policemen, will give a very different account from the explanation a psychoanalyst would put forward. The methods used to obtain the data or observations on which theories are based also differ radically. One investigator will restrict himself entirely to experimentation; another to observations of behaviour; yet a third to introspection and interpretation of the introspective accounts of others. There is not even agreement as to what constitutes the legitimate subject matter for study. Many psychologists argue that because introspection is difficult to quantify and express in operational terms, it is not valid as the subject matter of a 'science'. Others, in contrast, hold that people's accounts of their own experience offer the most important means of understanding their behaviour. In order to help you appreciate the reasons for this babel of conflicting voices, the first two papers take a brief excursion into epistemology. In other words, they focus on what constitutes knowledge and how it is acquired and communicated.

The first extract is by a sociologist, Joachim Israel. The key point of his paper is that all knowledge is *constructional*. Theories and research results do not mirror reality, they reconstruct it. A description or explanation constitutes an interaction between the person formulating it and certain aspects of his experience. It will be as much a product of him as it will be of the phenomena he is investigating. It will depend on his assumptions and his values. These will determine not only his interpretation but also the problem he chooses to investigate in the first place and the research methods he uses. They will influence the concepts and 'language' in which the results are formulated and communicated to others. The variety of theories and explanations produced by different investigators is not, therefore, a matter of surprise. It is an inevitable consequence of the process of investigation. There is no 'reality' except as experienced by and therefore influenced by a cognizer.

In the second extract, E. N. Barker considers the different forms or 'modes' in which knowledge may be conceived and expressed. In particular, he sees studies of human behaviour and experience as forming a continuum ranging from the relatively unformulated apprehension of everyday experience, through attempts to measure specific variables more precisely, to efforts at relating these variables in the form of constructs, theories and specific hypotheses. He points out that increased rigour and precision of formulation may well be accompanied by sacrifice of richness and subtlety. Barker concludes that the most productive approach is to investigate on all levels and not to exclude any; to allow each to enrich and illuminate the other.

The brief extract by Karl Weick is written from a very different standpoint. It is included here because Weick points out that even from within the confines of one paradigm where there is a good deal of common ground and shared assumptions, there may still arise the impression of fragmentation. In the case of experimental social psychology for example, fragmentation occurs because of the nature of the research process. In order to subject a problem to experimental investigation, it has to be split up into manageable proportions. So, Weick argues, each experimental social psychologist tends to be a specialist in a narrow area. No one individual investigates the whole of social behaviour. For Weick, therefore, knowledge of social behaviour is inevitably a collective social product rather than the province of any one individual or research project.

The import of these three papers is to argue in different ways for the need to take a multi-perspective view. To gain the most effective understanding of social behaviour and experience, we should take into consideration different perspectives, approaches and data. These make varied, but by no means necessarily contradictory, contributions. Two explanations may be different, for example, because they are focusing on different problems, or investigating the same phenomena in rather different ways or at different levels of analysis. They may even be expressing similar ideas in different terms. One of the functions of the course for which this set of readings has been prepared is to contrast and relate the contributions that different approaches make; to see how far they are complementary, tautologous or contradictory. Theories or explanations which are mutually exclusive are, we suggest, rarer than is often presumed.

Both the concluding papers advocate that two approaches often considered in isolation complement each other and are best interrelated. Duane Schultz points out that explanations construed in terms of observed behaviour on the one hand and in terms of the experience of the behaving individual on the other, have often been regarded as incompatible. He argues the opposite. Both need to be taken into account. They are not mutually exclusive. The one illuminates the other. In the final paper, Martin Richards, lecturer in social psychology at Cambridge University, argues the need to take into account both the social and the biological nature of man – again aspects which have, on occasion, been regarded as oppositional rather than complementary and interdependent. Both must be considered and related to each other in any fully effective explanation of why people behave and experience in the way that they do.

1 Stipulations and construction in the social sciences

Joachim Israel

The nature of stipulative statements in social psychological and sociological theory

In all common-sense notions of a psychological or sociological kind certain assumptions about the nature of Man and the nature of society are implicit. Managers of factories have certain views about what motivates workers to work; school teachers have definite ideas about the capacities of their pupils; architects 'know' the needs of people living in urban areas. Politicians tell us not only about Man's natural capacities and motivations ('without competition, no progress' or 'if you increase taxes too much, you counteract the willingness to work') but also about the nature of society and of functional prerequisites for a society to survive. These common-sense notions not only reflect private biases; they also reflect stipulative assumptions on a pre-scientific level concerning Man and society which in fact may form the basis for social organization. Take one example: the use of punching-clocks at factory entrances reflects assumptions about the willingness of workers to go to the factory, i.e. about their basic motivation for working. These assumptions often function as self-fulfilling prophecies thus creating behaviour in accordance with what is assumed. This confers upon them not only the status of empirical statements but of *verified* empirical statements.

The situation which we find at a pre-scientific common-sense level does not differ too much from the situation we find when we move into the realm of social science. One example is the area in which 'scientific theories' are applied for the management of people. Psychiatry and psychiatric treatment provide obvious examples. Thus the treatment of psychoses in closed mental hospitals may be based on certain diagnoses, which are derived from psychiatric theories. These diagnoses then may lead to a certain type of treatment, which in turn is to a large degree responsible for the behaviour predicted by the previous diagnosis. Scheff (1966) put forward an hypothesis that inmates in mental institutions are rewarded if they play the

---

ISRAEL, JOACHIM (1972) 'Stipulations and Construction in the Social Sciences' in Israel, Joachim and Tajfel, Henri (eds), *The Context of Social Psychology. A Critical Assessment* London, Academic Press, 123–126, 129–131, 192–196.

role assigned to them by psychiatrists and hospital staff and punished if they attempt to return to conventional roles. Thus, the patient's self-concept is brought into agreement with the diagnosis.

It seems that theories which have a direct application, such as those in psychiatry or criminology, operate with postulates which are similar to the common-sense notions of a psychological and sociological kind. The same, however, holds true for social science theories which can be located on a higher level of abstraction.

At least *three types of stipulative statements* can be distinguished in these theories. They are: assumptions concerning (1) *the nature of Man, including the nature of knowledge which Man has*, (2) *the nature of society*, and (3) *the nature of the relationship between Man and society*. . . .

The statements concerning the nature of the phenomena to which I refer do not have the status of final explanations but of initial conditions. They are of a stipulative kind. They can be expressed in alternative ways. They are chosen (not necessarily consciously) and empirical theories are derived from them.

My main thesis is that these stipulative statements have regulative functions. They determine the type of empirical theories which are developed and these theories affect the research strategy used. Thus, the S–R model developed by behaviourism gives rise to theories which in turn are tested by experimental methods limited by these theories. Behaviouristic learning theories using rats and pigeons in experimental situations cannot be applied to the study of cognitive learning. However, the concept of 'cognitive learning' may already have been excluded by the postulative assumptions made about phenomena with which theories deal and which precede the development of empirical theories.[1]

The content of the stipulative statements to be found in psychological and sociological theories concerns the nature of Man, the nature of knowledge, the nature of society and finally the nature of the relationship between Man and society. These statements may often be interrelated in a theoretical system. In addition, such statements enter into empirical theories and are usually not clearly differentiated from descriptive statements. In fact, they are usually formulated as descriptive statements, thus veiling their true nature which is that of normative statements. These statements have a regulative function. They determine the content of empirical theories and, together with formal methodological rules, influence the procedures of

1 When I mention 'preceding' stipulative assumptions, I do not refer to temporary sequences. It may be that these postulative assumptions are formulated, if at all explicitly formulated, after empirical observations are carried out in order to give empirical theories a firm basis to stand upon. But once selected, they have regulative functions.

scientific research, which themselves affect the theory. They can be relatively 'freely' chosen among alternative sets of stipulative systems. Different sets of stipulative systems will give rise to different empirical theories. The choice of stipulative systems is in turn influenced by value-statements.

To summarize: The statements discussed above are normative since the assumptions to be made concerning the nature of Man and society are stipulated. They are also normative in the sense that they can be replaced by alternative stipulations.

An example is provided by the stipulative assumptions concerning Man which are often used in economics. It is clear that 'economic Man' is not a descriptive but a normative concept. Man is stipulated to be rational in the sense that his economic behaviour is guided by a striving for maximization of his utility, i.e. he chooses among available modes of behaviour that which provides highest utility. Rational choice presupposes also that he has knowledge of all relevant alternative modes of behaviour, as well as their specific utility value. In addition, a rational choice presupposes that Man has absolute knowledge of the total market, i.e. complete knowledge of all goods and prices. Sometimes it is also required that he should know the strategies available to other people with whom he interacts since the utility of his own behaviour may be dependent on others' behaviour. [...]

Piaget and Skinner – two psychologists representing opposing views

To a majority of psychologists, problems of epistemology are located outside the domain of their scientific interest and enquiry. One of the most outstanding exceptions is Jean Piaget, who has dealt with these problems in his own research and who has advised psychologists that 'they should certainly consider epistemological questions as legitimate problems of their interests' (Furth 1969, p. vii). Piaget's theory of knowledge can be summarized in the following way: (1) He considers epistemological problems from a genetic point of view, splitting the question 'What is knowledge?' into two questions, namely, 'How does knowledge develop?' and 'What is the role of the subject in the process of the development of knowledge?' (2) Answering the second question, he considers knowledge as the relation between the subject and the object: 'A thing in the world is not an object of knowledge until the knowing organism interacts with and constitutes it as an object.' (Furth, op. cit., p. 19.)

Thus in these terms 'knowledge' becomes an activity, a process; in this process the subject partly constructs the object. To understand fully the consequences of this position it will be useful to elaborate briefly upon

Piget's concept of knowledge, and the theory of the development of knowledge.

Piaget assumes that knowledge develops in stages which follow a constant order of succession (Inhelder 1962). Each stage is characterized by the attainment of a certain structure following a period of development. A structure is an organization of elements within the biological organism which responds to the external environment; and the development of a structure is a consequence of an inner organizing activity and of factors extrinsic to the organism: 'A reaction of an organism is therefore not merely a response to an outside stimulation, but is always and at all levels also the response of the underlying structure within the organism.' (Furth op. cit., p. 13.) Hence, in order to respond to outside stimulation, the organism must have a certain, even if only primitive, structure, which in turn is influenced by extrinsic factors. This dialectical principle is underpinned by the concepts of 'assimilation' and 'accommodation'. Knowledge, being an exchange between an organism and its environment, leads to the incorporation of external stimuli into an existing structure; this process of integrating external stimuli with an existing structure is called 'assimilation'. Accommodation is an outgoing process directed towards objects or some state of the surrounding world; in this outgoing process an existing structure is applied to a new situation. Through the process of assimilation the new elements are incorporated into the structure, differentiating it and developing it. . . . To summarize: knowledge is a *relation* of interchange between the structure of a biological organism and its surrounding environment. Through this relation the environment and 'what it means to the subject' is shaped and reshaped and the environment affects, differentiates and develops the existing structure within the organism.

Now let us consider a completely different ontological view concerning knowledge, by comparing the viewpoint developed by Piaget with the one developed by Skinner. According to Skinner, 'science insists that action is initiated by forces impinging upon the individual' (1955, p. 53). This statement *stipulates* an epistemological position implying the view that the subject is a passive recipient of (mainly external) stimuli. Thus, according to Skinner, stimuli impinging upon the subject are independent variables whereas the actions of the subject are viewed as dependent variables. The relationship between the independent and the dependent variables can be formulated in terms of causal laws; this excludes Piaget's theory in which the relationship between subject and object is one of reciprocal interchange. Piaget's viewpoint does not only reject the concept of the passive subject, but also substitutes one-sided causal relations by feed-back processes, cumulative interchange, etc. This makes the question of what is an independent and what is a dependent variable appear to be of the same quality as the one concerning the hen and the egg.

Let us for a moment return to Skinner's statement quoted above. As it is formulated in descriptive terms, it is presented as a theoretical statement. Also, a non-critical reader may take it as a true statement, i.e. one which has been proved. I suggest that it is a stipulation and in this I agree with Copeland (1964): 'The view that the individual is always controlled exclusively by forces in his external environment, instead of being a scientific assertion, is simply the result of Skinner's *choice as to what ought* [my italics] to be emphasized.' (p. 170.)

The next question then becomes: What is the basis of choice? In general we can say that choices are based upon preferences and preferences in turn represent values. Let me here just state one of the consequences of this interpretation: the epistemological position taken clearly stands out as a metaphysical stipulation prior to, and guiding, empirical research. Such stipulations will influence the research strategy, e.g. the way experiments are set up. And this restricts the selection of problems. Thus Koch (1965) concluded: '["Neobehaviourism" through its concern with] *general* laws of behaviour based on intensive analysis of animal learning in a few standard situations, [has] fled the subtler fluxions (not to mention certain obvious hard facts of human function) so vigorously that these matters were all but forgotten.' (p. 30.) He adds that psychologists in their aspirations to be methodologically cautious have neglected relevant problems (the same could be said of sociologists). . . .

The 'constructional' approach

. . . empirical theories partly 'construct' that which they deal with. Let us recollect the two senses in which we previously used the word 'construction': that is '*conferring meaning*' and '*bringing about*'.

A theory of society 'confers meaning' by the very fact that it precedes the collection of data,[2] and that it influences procedures of empirical science (e.g. observational methods) and thereby determines which data can be obtained. Furthermore, when data are 'interpreted' and 'scientific knowledge' is obtained, 'meaning is conferred' again, but this time on the data collected. Only theories make data relevant. The interpreted data in turn affect and reorganize the original theory.

Those who cherish the notion that a theory 'reflects' reality usually

2 This is also the case even if theories are not explicitly formulated as in the type of empirical research, which calls itself 'purely descriptive'. Implicit theoretical notions are always present, however primitive they may be.

assume that reality 'forces itself' in one way or another upon a theory and that organization, systematization or classification of data is 'inherent in the nature' of reality. Consequently, they consider empirical data as influencing theory, but tend to reject the idea of the converse effect, i.e. that a theory should be able to affect reality.

The main problem of an empirical science thinking in terms of a theory 'reflecting' or 'mirroring' reality then becomes the development of reliable instruments and methods which would be able to 'reflect' reality in a valid way.

In the 'constructional' approach the relationship between theory and reality is *mutual*. Theories organize data; theories confer meaning upon them. Nevertheless data cannot be arbitrarily organized: theories have to take into account the 'structure of reality'. The concept of 'structure', therefore, has a different place in the so-called reflectional approach than in the so-called constructional approach. . . .

One main fallacy in the 'reflectional' approach is the underlying assumption that data are considered to be objective in the sense of being independent of the subject collecting them. This illusion is upheld by the emphasis on 'objective' methods of data collection. Although these methods may in some sense be 'objective', the data collected by them are not independent but dependent on theories. In addition, even if procedures are 'objective', that which is collected by them may to a large extent be 'constructed' in the sense of being 'made up' by the procedures themselves: the answers received depend upon the questions asked. [. . .]

We can now summarize. For several reasons I wish to reject the notion of theories 'reflecting' or 'mirroring' reality. Theories not only organize and systematize data, but also interpret them. The moment we interpret data we must abandon the idea that they 'mirror' or 'reflect' reality. Consequently, I maintain that theories assign meaning to reality through the interpretation of data collected in social scientific enquiry. However, it is not only the social scientist who confers meaning upon social reality; other people do the same in their everyday life. Therefore one task of social science is to discover the meaning people assign to reality; but at the same time social scientists must be aware that when they try to interpret the meaning which people in general assign to social reality, they may confer a new meaning upon the meaning which social facts have acquired in daily language.

W. I. Thomas' well-known thesis states that if people define a situation as real, it will be real in its consequences. This applies to the activity of scientists as well as to those of people in their daily lives.

What are the consequences of the fact that meaning has been conferred upon social reality? The answer brings us to the second sense in which social science 'constructs' reality, namely to the way in which it 'brings it about'. Let me take an example. Economics has traditionally considered air and water as utilities which can be used freely. Consequently the pollution of water and air has not been included when computing production costs. This has undoubtedly contributed to the immense social problem that pollution has become. Thus social science, by means of its concepts and theories, may 'bring about' directly or indirectly, by influencing politics or the conceptions of people, the social world it studies.

There is a second sense in which the social sciences can 'bring about' facts through their theories: by functioning as self-fulfilling prophecies, when the very prediction arrived at on the basis of theories concerning certain phenomena can create these phenomena or alternatively prevent their future existence. [...]

References

COPELAND, J. W. (1964) 'Philosophy disguised as science', *Philosophy of Science*, 31, 168–72.

FURTH, H. G. (1969) *Piaget and Knowledge* (with a foreword by J. Piaget) Englewood Cliffs, N.J., Prentice-Hall.

INHELDER, B. (1962) 'Some aspects of Piaget's genetic approach to cognition', in Kessen, W. and Kuhlman, C. (eds) *Thought in the Young Child, Monographs of the Society for Research in Child Development*, 27, no. 2.

KOCH, S. (1965) 'Psychology and emerging conceptions of knowledge as unitary', in Wann, T. W. (ed.) *Behaviourism and Phenomenology* Chicago, University of Chicago Press.

SCHEFF, T. (1966) *Being Mentally Ill* Chicago, Aldine.

SKINNER, B. F. (1955–6) 'Freedom and the control of man', *American Scholar*, 25, 47–65.

2 Communicating and attaining knowledge in psychology

E. N. Barker

Scientific language and experiential referents

There are many ways to define a word. In science, a theoretical term is sometimes entirely defined by its relations to other terms in the theoretical system. The word is defined only by other words. It is assumed that it is necessary for at least some of these 'other words' to be defined by something else than words – some concrete perception. Another way to define a term in science is to ask the reader to keep in mind the referent of the word and then to describe the antecedent, concomitant, and subsequent events to this referent. This is a definition of the event pointed to by the word, by giving a complete description of the events which 'cause it', 'go along with it', and which are 'caused by it'. This kind of definition is seldom attained in science, although it is an ultimate goal. A third way of defining words in science is sometimes called the 'operational definition', that is, a relatively complete specification of the procedures one would follow to measure the occurrence of the event in question. These procedures are sometimes quite complicated, requiring refined tools of technology and delicate manoeuvring, and are sometimes a simple 'pointing' to the simple perception, e.g., 'when the needle jumps to the number 10 on the scale'. In principle, they are the same.

Let us look at the ways words are defined in another, supposedly completely different, context. Is the language of poetry so different in its methods of defining words? Yes and no. The technique of defining a term by other terms is sometimes used. The technique of describing preceding, covarying, and succeeding events is sometimes used. Probably the most characteristic is a technique which is somewhat analogous to the 'operational definition'. The poem *evokes* the referent for the term here and now! The poem may do this by rearousing a memory of a similar past experience of the reader. The poem may do this by a subtle use of words, and word combinations, which 'create' a new, immediate, experiential state by tapping particular clusters of associations never before combined in just that

BARKER, E. N. (1972) 'Communicating and attaining knowledge in psychology', from 'Humanistic psychology and scientific method' in *Interpersonal Development*, vol. 2, 154–63.

way. The poet can 'point' to the referent for his term by a sort of 'triangulation' by the use of metaphor. He may say 'my love is like a red, red rose', evoking the associations to 'red, red roses'. He may go on to say that my love is also like b, and c, and d, and e. That gestalt of the qualities which are common to a red, red rose, and b, and c, and d, and e, is the referent for his term 'my love'.

This is admittedly a much more complex task than telling a person to look for 'the needle-jump to 10 on the scale'. The poet cannot be as sure that the phrase 'my love' evokes 'his' experience in others as the experimenter can be sure that the phrase 'needle jumps to 10' evokes 'his' experience in others. It is *not* that the experience the poet communicates is necessarily more complex – it may be just as 'simple', or 'pure' as the other experience. The difference is in the lack of a specific agreed-upon term, 'a handle' for his referent as compared to the experimenter's. Those of us who are interested in phenomenological theory and research are having to face some of the same problems which the poet faces in communicating about the variable which interests him, and for which there is, as yet, no specific term. While these problems are exceedingly difficult ones, I believe they are resolvable – at least to the extent that we, as scientists, can gain a much greater understanding of many of the so-called 'soft' topics.

'Public' statements

There is a widespread view that the languages of science and of the humanities are basically different – that scientific statements are 'meaningful' while a much higher proportion of statements made by a scholar in the humanities, or by a poet, or in everyday language, are 'meaningless' statements. 'Meaningfulness' refers here to the testability of a statement due to the clear definition of the referents of the terms, and the clear statement of the relations of the terms to each other. Thus, scientific statements imply predictions which can be tested, because agreement can be achieved among persons as to precisely what the implied prediction is. Now there is a sense in which much of the above is true. What is invalid is the sharp dichotomy which is drawn between languages. Let us examine the issue further to see if scientific statements are unique.

Scientific statements have a 'directing' function. They give the reader – the reader who has the appropriate background – directions for having a particular experience or perception. They tell him how to set up the conditions within which he will observe a particular class of events (the predicted ones). In other words, a theoretical proposition is a summary of the instructions necessary for duplicating the essential features of an experiment, so that the reader may observe for himself the predicted outcome which is the basis for the relationship expressed and the scientific 'law'. A scientific statement implies, 'If you will obtain conditions x, y, and z, then you will experience (see, hear, feel) thus!' But is this so unique?

Many poetic statements also imply, 'If you will place yourself in the conditions indicated, then you will experience thus!' There is a rich, virtually untapped, store of hypotheses about man in these statements in the arts and the humanities. Other poetic statements imply, 'If you will immerse yourself in these images and sounds which *create* certain conditions, then you will, now, in the moment, experience thus!' (Of course, the use of poetry as an example is arbitrary. The same would hold for a novel, or a play, or a dance, or a piece of sculpture.)

Now there is a sense in which it is true that scientific language generally is more explicit in describing the conditions and the experience to be expected. The poem does not describe in discursive symbols the experience which it is predicting. If it could be described, in its totality, discursively – the art of poetry would not be necessary. A poem is concerned with a sort of experience which, at this time in history, can be communicated best by non-discursive symbols. One could say, 'But some people will understand the "directions" of the poem and have the experience, and others will not.' But this is also to some extent true with scientific statements. Some will be able to understand the terms describing conditions and the predicted experience and some will not. There is another sense in which the poem describes the conditions and experience much *more* exactly than the scientific statement. One of the criticisms of scientists, by artists, is the scientist's 'sloppy' use of words, whereas the poet is highly disciplined in the precise usage of terms to describe or evoke a particular shading of experience.

There is another difference which is not a necessary one but which is rather an unfortunate result of psychologists generally concentrating on peripheral areas of human concern; that is, that the experience predicted or created by poems is generally of greater human concern, at greater depth, that it has greater transforming power, and more existential meaning to the reader.

The artistic expression which produces a new experience has the scientific benefit of providing new perceptions for us, i.e., new variables which have potential value for an understanding of man. Of course, the value of art stands, whether or not its newly generated perceptions are picked up by science. Most of us would agree that the enlarged experience, the new dimensions in meaning given by art have a value in themselves – some people would say, have a kind of 'truth' – which is at least equal to the value of expressions of scientific truth.

The idea of the psychologists who eagerly took over some of the concepts from operationism, was that a science should be absolutely 'public'. . . . What does 'public' mean? It seems to mean that we know relatively well how to teach another person to have the experience (perception) in question. It is true that statements may be ordered from vague and ineffective directions or shapers of the other person's experience, to precise, specific, effective directions for having the experience. However, this is a continuum. There are no sharp breaks between the publicness of statements in psychology as compared to chemistry, or between many statements in everyday language and statements in physics, or even between many statements in poetry and other statements in science.

I would guess that one of the most important and fruitful areas which should be investigated by psychology is this process of 'defining' – of inter-personal 'teaching', that is, of how we teach another person to have a perception which we want him to have. Communication only occurs when we are successful in directing, or shaping, or influencing, or teaching, the other person to have something close to the experience (cognition, perception, feeling) which we have in mind. Research in this area would have important implications for inter-personal relations, communication, education, psychotherapy, and maybe most important, it might shed light on the old questions of the 'meaning of meaning' in philosophy.

As I understand it, the basic problem in philosophy of science concerns the concept of 'meaning' – the cognitive meaning (more correctly, the experiential meaning) of statements. The operationist's solution to the problem was to define a statement entirely by the physical procedures necessary to check it. Although I suspect that this solution will always be a useful part of the definition of meaning, when it is carried to its extreme it has been found to be too limiting in the process of studying man and nature. If it is true that the meaning of a statement can be defined by the *experience* which it makes possible for the listener, then psychology could have as much to offer in building a psychologically valid base for epistemology and philosophy of science, as philosophy has to offer psychology in building its epistemological base. [. . .]

Let us examine more closely the continuum of 'loose' language, to 'natural' language, to 'tight' language.

Modes of attaining and communicating knowledge

Let us imagine a continuum such as illustrated in figure 1. A mystic simply *has* experience and generally feels no compulsion to attempt to communicate it to others. An artist, for example, a poet, has the function of evoking

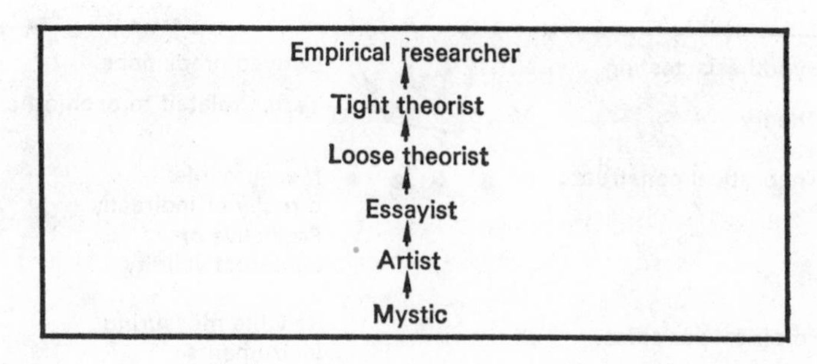

Fig. 1

raw, fresh, experience in his reader. Moving up the continuum, an essayist sometimes will, in prose, try roughly to indicate an experience and describe its relation to other experiences, that is, to other events.

Moving up still further, a more rigorous sort (the 'loose theorist') may try to define the previous terms more precisely (more commonly) so that others may know more certainly whether they agree or disagree with the proposition stated, or if they have experienced the same processes or events. Then, a 'tight theorist' may try to define each term (or a sufficient number) by the procedures which would be necessary for agreement in measuring them, and he would relate the terms to each other. A scientific theory has now been constructed – a theory which implies predictions which can be tested by the researcher.

In this sequence one can see the increasing possibility of interpersonal agreement, which is the usual meaning of 'scientific' or 'objective'. One can also see that the process will often entail some shrinkage of the 'original' experience, i.e., its original completeness, it unverbalizable richness, has to some extent been abstracted or summarized. Only the events which can be 'caught' by the existing 'net' of defined words and operations and instruments can now be herded into the area of formal scientific discourse. The goal of the humanistic psychologist-researcher is to reduce the shrinkage by increasing the 'net' of defined words and operations in certain directions.

One can see that each of these people supports the other. Each of them gives the other one the opportunity for a richer and many-sided view of the world. Actually, these people – 'the mystic, the poet, the essayist, the theorist, the researcher' – are often *not* different people, but simply different aspects within us. At different moments we are simply experiencers ('mystics') or metaphorical expressers, or roughly discursive, or tight

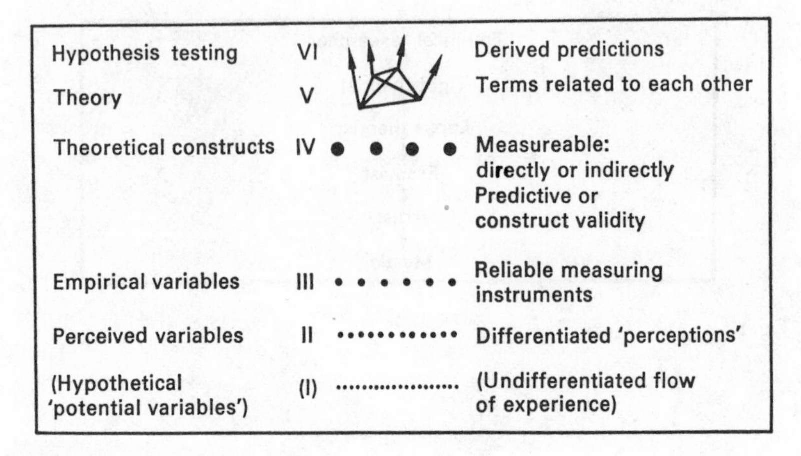

Fig. 2

thinkers, or empirical testers. And each of these sides of ourselves, in a true sense, feeds all the others – is *essential* for the vitality of the others.

For convenience, let us continue to discuss them as though they were different people who use different ways of communicating. The poet-essayist tends to do two things in his communication. First, he says, 'Notice this!' If he is successful, he differentiates for us new dimensions in our experience. Secondly, he often implies 'if . . . then' statements. Both these functions can be extremely useful to the theorist and to the researcher in furthering his work. Each, then, tends to develop ways to teach others how to discriminate the variable reliably and how to translate the implied 'if . . . then' statement into definite predictions under specified conditions. The persons at the top of the scale also serve a similar function for those at the bottom. They can say, as a result of theory construction and research, 'Notice this!' and differentiate new dimensions of experience for the mystic-poet-essayist.

Let us now look at a similar, but not identical, sort of continuum. The process of increasing scientific knowledge may be visualized as a pyramid composed of six levels, as in figure 2.

The first level is hypothetical and might be called the 'potential variables'. It is composed of those stimuli to which we organismically react, which are registered, but of which we do not become aware. Some of these can be raised to awareness and thus move to the second level simply by having our attention called to them, while others require particular conditions for us to 'notice' them.

The second level could be labelled the 'experiential variables' or simply our 'perceptions'. This is composed of all of the things, events, processes, qualities, aspects, of the world which we have differentiated in our experience. If we become interested in one of these perceptions, or a cluster of them, we may take the trouble to communicate to another person that which constitutes this perception or variable. If we go to enough trouble we may be able to train or 'teach' other persons to 'see what we see'. We are then at level three, which we might call the 'empirical variables' or the 'reliable measuring instruments'. At this level would be included the counting of bar presses, the taking of a person's temperature, reliable rating scales, scores on reliable attitude scales, etc. The jump from level two to level three requires that we train other persons to differentiate the same way that we do – to put the same group of stimuli into a class with an agreed-upon label. Level three can contain an infinite number of reliably measured variables. However, as theorists we are interested only in those variables which seem to be potentially powerful in explaining or predicting the realm of events which concern us. Therefore, we take certain variables or combinations of variables from level three. We call these our 'theoretical variables', at level four.

Level four can be added to with the aid of certain formal devices. For example, we may use techniques of factor-analysis to find clusters of variables from level three, in order to form a smaller number of theoretical variables at level four. However, in general, the jump from level three to level four is done in a more 'creative, intuitive, armchair' manner. Level four is made up of the variables which we consider the necessary and sufficient ones to understand the area of interest. However, a mere array of variables is of no use. The variables must be related systematically to each other. When this has been done, we reach level five, that of 'theory'. Depending upon the level of refinement in the area of concern, this 'theory' may be quite explicit and 'tight' or it may be quite vague and mostly implied. However, whether implicit or explicit, from this formulation come guesses as to the relationship of our variables to other measurable events, that is predictions or hypotheses, which takes us to level six.

Depending upon the outcomes of these tests of predictions, we may make slight modifications in the theory at level five, or go back to level three to construct new theoretical variables for level four, which we can bring into the theory at level five. Or we may go all the way back to the 'raw data', that is to level two, to begin again.

The move from level two to level three, from the 'perceptions' to the reliable measuring instruments, while requiring ingenuity, is not a mysterious procedure. It simply requires teaching others how to 'count' that which we are 'counting'. Also, the step from level five, the theory, to level six, the hypotheses, is relatively clear-cut. However, it must be evident that the movement between all the other levels is essentially an unformal, creative process for which there are no known rules.

Different psychologists have interests which lead them to concentrate on work at different levels in this pyramid. This is healthy. Work is needed on all of the levels for a vital science. In general, the so-called 'learning theorists' tend to work from levels four to five, and five to six, and back again. The current 'self-theorists' more often move down to the work of building from level two to three, and three to four, before they can begin the hypothesis testing at level six. In the field of personality many of the apparent moves from level one to level two, which feed new possibilities for variables to the researchers, tend to come from the applied clinicians.

One reason for some of the fruitless and obstructive controversy and competition within psychology is a kind of snobbery about the presumed merits of working on one or another level. Many of us in phenomenological psychology are convinced that some of the most important work to be done is between levels one and four. We are not at all convinced that the variables which psychology now has at levels three and four are likely to be fruitful ones. In general, in the psychological journals, one might get the impression that no work went on, or was necessary, below level four. This is misleading, and, if it were true, would lead to an increasingly sterile science.

The move up to level three is a particularly important one for many of us. Let us examine this 'move' in more detail.

Developing new variables

When a person has a new idea, it is simply a new construction of the world (if we like it we call it 'an insight'). However, if one can communicate this idea, this new differentiation of experience, to at least one other person, it becomes public and, in a sense, 'objective'. Let us consider an example: One evening at home, I was musing about a particular patient I was seeing. I got the idea that this woman could be placed into a class of persons I have known. I had only a vague sense of what qualities defined this class. I interrupted my wife from her reading and asked her if she had ever noticed the 'faculty wife syndrome'. (At this stage in defining for oneself a new differentiation, one often gives an 'incorrect' label, in order simply to have a 'handle' for the class.) I told her that I could think of four women who had these characteristics: She tends to wear medium priced suits, often tweed. She often wears clothes which are a little out of style in an attempt to economize, and for the same reason her hair is often not arranged very attractively. She is obviously bright, but has not used her intelligence for a long time, and it only shows occasionally in rather bright, bitter, hostile remarks. She seems to have lost some feminine quality and to be awkward in her femaleness. She often began some advanced graduate work and then quit upon marriage in order to help support her husband through school. Once her children are along in school she often takes a subordinate job which clearly is no challenge for her. She is overinvolved in her husband's success. She often gets into a rather messy affair in her late thirties. There is a brittle quality to her; her laugh is unpleasant to hear.

On hearing the description, my wife nodded and indicated an immediate recognition of the type. On further discussion she added several other qualities such as: This kind of woman is often a repressed snob; that is, she wants very much to have social prestige but is too ambivalent to try directly to achieve it. She is generally politically liberal, but not really committed. She is often interesting to talk to because she keeps up her reading of current books. There is a great deal of 'undercover' anger at men and especially at her husband. She is ridiculously compliant and submissive to him at times, but often also shows signs of being contemptuous of him, and of men generally.

Now this new differentiation (for us) was simply an isolated half-hour of conversation and was not pursued further. It did not seem 'interesting': that is, these qualities did not seem to generalize to many people as a cluster; it did not seem to be an important variable or group of variables, and it seemed to overlap syndromes about which we already know something, e.g., the authoritarian syndrome. This is an example of a new construction of the world which (for me, at this time) did not seem worthwhile to pursue. However, it illustrates the beginning of a private perception becoming a public one, and theoretically it could have become the basis for further, objective research.

How can one know if a new idea has been communicated to another? We feel some certainty that it has been communicated if the other person can derive an unsaid part of the statement from the part which was said (an example would be my wife's adding of other elements to the cluster that I recognized immediately as belonging there). We also feel some confidence that we have communicated if the other person can hear the implied 'if . . . then' statement, and if he seems to know how to follow directions and to have the experience. In the example given, the implication was 'if you find a person with characteristics a, b, c, then you will find also x, y, and z'. As we discussed it, other predictions became evident. 'If you treat this person in such and such a manner, she will react in such and such a manner.'

To take another example of the transition from the private to the relatively public: Erich Fromm, at some point, made a new differentiation in his experience which he labelled the 'sado-masochistic character'. I would assume that at first the idea was rather vague to him, but he thought about it and began to define just what made up this new category in his thinking. Upon describing this character in a book, other people who 'got the idea' began to refine and modify the original definition. After a number of intervening steps, the California group (Adorno, and others) noticed that some of their findings seemed to fit Fromm's concepts. They then made more explicit the 'if . . . then' statements implied in Fromm's formulation. Out of this was developed a research instrument (the F scale). Then a much greater number of people could have the experience of following the directions of the 'if . . . then' statements to see if the predictions were confirmed. At about this point most scientists would say that Fromm's private idea had finally become public. Some persons with a narrow definition of science would say that this is still at the level of sytematic observation, rather than controlled experimentation, and that as yet we still do not know operationally what the term 'authoritarian' really means. My point here is that the continuum from absolutely private to relatively public (there is no 'absolute public' pole) contains no sharp breaks, and the process we call investigating, or studying, or science, can be aided by work at any point on this continuum.

3 A specialist in unnoticed causes

Karl Weick

Something of the scope of the social psychologist's work is implied in the phrase, *specialist* in unnoticed causes. The word specialist implies that the social psychologist has narrow interests, and in one sense this is true. The twist is that each social psychologist specializes in novel narrow areas. The novelty of this specialization occurs because he makes unique combinations of ideas and methods; the narrowness in this specialization occurs because he studies these novel combinations in depth. Although this is a fairly neutral way to characterize what the social psychologist does, in practice this fact of his existence produces a great deal of negative reaction among colleagues and laymen. A close second to the complaint that social psychology belabours the obvious, is the complaint that it contains a hodgepodge of bits and pieces of information that are largely unrelated. Not many social psychologists would disagree with this characterization, but they would take sharp issue with the judgment that this is bad and reduces the relevance of social psychology for contemporary life.

In fact I would argue that the social psychologist has every right to express warranted arrogance over this state of his field. There are several reasons why the fragmentary quality of social psychology can be viewed as evidence of the vigour of the field.

The subject matter in which social psychologists are interested is complex and messy, and the only way one can register and represent that complexity is to think and talk in imprecise ways. But that occurs only at the first stage of inquiry. Once the researcher has represented the complexity, then he selects the most promising question to ask. When you select a specific question you lay aside much of the complexity you have registered, thus the question is fragmentary. The question is a fragment of all that you initially thought about, but the fragment may also contain some of the more important properties of that representation. Fragments, in other words, can be consequential.

But there are other more important points that are implicit in the fact of novel narrow specialization. Social psychology appears to be one of the most interdisciplinary of the social sciences. But, if it is viewed this way there is a lethal seduction involved. The seduction involves the belief that

---

WEICK, KARL (1969) 'A specialist in unnoticed causes' from 'Social psychology in an era of social change' in *American Psychologist*, vol. 24, 990–8.

one head, one person, can make the bridge between different areas and that one head can make the integration. In other words, the facts that social psychology has to offer are assumed to be the property of single actors. If one views social psychology this way and conducts his professional life accordingly, he is doomed to failure and frivolousness for the simple reason that the locus of scientific knowledge is social, not solitary. The locus of scientific knowledge in social psychology is not in individual minds, rather it is a collective social product that is only imperfectly represented in any one mind. What is known is represented only imperfectly and incompletely in the work of any one scientist. This being the case, the more accurate description of a comprehensive social psychology is that it consists of 'collective comprehensiveness through overlapping patterns of unique narrowness' (Campbell, 1969, p. 1). Thus, for any one scholar the best he can hope for is to find some area neglected by others into which he inserts his inevitably incomplete competence. The resulting science can be portrayed by the analogy of fish scales (Campbell, 1969); each scale is narrow, novel in that it covers a new area, yet it overlaps with adjacent scales. It is the *set* of scales, not individual scales that constitute what is known. Viewed from this perspective, the fact that social psychology is fragmentary takes on a different cast. It is not unified, but it will never be unified if one chooses to find this unity by quizzing individuals. Their knowledge is incomplete and imperfect, but, as long as this knowledge is about combinations neglected by others, the work is important.

This point about the fragmentary quality of social psychology can be viewed from another perspective. To focus the point consider this statement: *Reality is a metaphor*. As a practising social psychologist, my hunch is that the statement is largely true, and, if so, then it recasts rather sharply what the meaning is of the bits and pieces of social psychology. To see this, think of the common way in which science is characterized. The characterization typically goes that the paths to an understanding of nature may be infinite and characterized by unique problems, but that all of these paths lead to '*a* goal, *an* understanding of *one* nature' (Holton, 1965, p. xxii). Stated in another way, 'These two connected [themes] of unlimited outer accessibility and delimited inner meaning can be vaguely depicted by the device of a maze having in its outer walls innumerable entrances, through each of which one can hopefully reach, sooner or later, the one mystery which lies at the centre' (p. xxiii). Now comes a disturbing possibility that renders fragments more significant. Returning to the maze analogy, Holton remarks,

> But another possibility has suggested itself more and more insistently; that at the inner-most chamber of the maze one would find *nothing*. . . . From a

suitable distance, we cannot soundly claim that the historic development of science has proved nature to be understandable in a unique way, as distinct from documentable, manipulable, predictable within limits, or technically exploitable. What has happened is that the ground of the unknown has continually been shifted, the allegory has continually changed (p. xxiii).

The relevance of these comments for how to do social psychology can now be made clear. It seems plausible that doing research in such a way that one tries to reduce the fragmentary nature of knowledge and increase integration will be self-defeating. The reason for this is that unity of knowledge may be a fiction. It may be impossible to enhance the unity of knowledge by one's research simply because unity is unattainable. This also argues that novel narrow specialization is not necessarily detrimental if assessed against the criterion of integration. While specialization may increase the likelihood that 'revealed' knowledge will be fragmentary, this says nothing about whether specialization is responsible for slowing the unification of science. It will not slow unification any more than other activities because unification is not a realistic goal anyway. If a scientist says 'I'm confused' or 'I can't choose between these alternatives' this may not be a limitation of himself or of his work. Instead, that simply may be the way things are. Once an observer takes seriously the view that events may be disjunctive, constantly changing, and characterized by uncertainty, then he views scientific work differently. If a scientist says that he is confused rather than certain, this could mean that he is *more* rather than less aware of what is happening in the object of his inquiry.

Thus social psychologists are not apologetic for their fragments because they assume that omniscience is a collective rather than solitary product, they know that every answer raises new questions they never wanted to ask, they know that uncertainties shift but retain a constant size, and they know that rather than the discovery of truth, it is more accurate to portray their work as the gradual emancipation of knowledge from errors. [. . .]

References

CAMPBELL, D. T. (1969) 'Ethnocentrism of disciplines and the fish-scale model of omniscience' in Sherif, M. (ed.) *Problems of interdisciplinary relationships in the social sciences* Chicago, Aldine.

HOLTON, G. (1965) 'Introduction to the issue "Science and culture"', *Daedalus*, 94, v–xxix.

4 Behaviour and experience

Duane Schultz

Just as it is now recognized that bias and distortion can be introduced into the laboratory by the experimenter effect, it is also becoming clear that our data can be biased by the 'subject effect' (Schultz, 1969b). This subject biasing effect is introduced, in part, by the subject's active participation in terms of his perception of the experimental situation. Kelman (1967), Orne (1962), and Schultz (1969a, 1969b), among others, have discussed much disquieting data which strongly suggest that the subject in an experiment actively tries to interpret the experimental situation and makes his behavioural responses in accordance with his perception.

> Whether his perception is accurate or not is secondary to the fact that he is not a passive responder to the situation. He is an active participant in it, and this very activity changes the nature of the situation for him. His world, then, is not simply what the experimenter defines and presents to him. No matter how thoroughly we attempt to control and standardize the experimental situation, it is, in fact, neither controlled nor standardized to the subject. The resulting situation is one that is not intended and, more importantly, not known to the experimenter (Schultz, 1969a, p. 222).

. . . The subject is an acting, participating, defining, and perceiving element in our data collection, and not simply a passive, reacting object. In the experimental situation, the responses are being determined (or at least influenced or modified) by the experiencing person, the human subject. Our experiments do involve experience as dependent on the experiencing person, whether or not we recognize or like it. . . .

Polanyi (1958) commented that 'as human beings, we must inevitably see the universe from a centre lying within ourselves. Any attempt rigorously to eliminate our human perspective from our picture of the world must lead to absurdity' (p. 3).

Toward an 'experiential behaviourism'

Since the subject's experience of the experimental situation is already an integral part of our research process, might we not secure more valid data

---

SCHULTZ, DUANE (1971) 'Behaviour and experience' from 'Psychology: a world with man left out' in *Journal of Theory of Social Behaviour*, vol. 1, no. 2, 99–107.

by recognizing and including this experience in our interpretation of his behaviour? The argument here is not for a return to the exclusive use of introspection nor for the discarding of the experimental–behavioural approach to psychology. What is suggested is the mutual compatibility, utility, and sheer necessity of combining both experiential and behavioural knowledge in psychological research. How can we understand the behaviour without understanding the behaver?

Instructive use can be made of an analogous situation in modern physics which faced, earlier in this century, a situation involving the apparent mutual exclusiveness of two approaches to its subject matter. Physicists had arrived at a 'choice point' between the opposing wave and corpuscular (or particle) theories. Briefly, the situation was this: the older particle theory accounted for a wide range of physical phenomena, but not all of them; the wave theory, on the other hand, could explain those phenomena not accounted for by the particle theory, but not the data which the particle theory could explain. As Matson (1964) described it: 'both formulations persisted in remaining valid for some observations, but invalid for others; each failed where the other was successful' (p. 148).

The solution, advanced by Niels Bohr as the principle of complementarity, was to accept the validity of both theories or approaches. Bohr suggested that a full explanation of physical phenomena required the application of both approaches – not simultaneously to the same phenomenon, but successively in order to explain the total range of physical phenomena. They are mutually exclusive and therefore cannot both be used at the same time. 'They are like the two faces of an object that never can be seen at the same time but which must be visualized *in turn*, however, in order to describe the object completely' (Broglie, 1953, p. 218, italics ours).

Matson (1964) discussed what J. Robert Oppenheimer called the 'immense evocative analogy' that can be made between complementarity in physics and the situation in contemporary psychology. His discussion takes place within the framework of the mutually exclusive approaches of deterministic and mechanistic causation, on the one hand, and the search for purposes, reasons, and understanding on the other – in more general terms, behaviourism versus humanistic psychology. Behaviouristic psychology seeks causes for behaviour but shuns attempts of humanistic psychology to understand the behaviour. As Polanyi (1951) noted:

> The most important pair of mutually exclusive approaches . . . is formed by the alternative interpretations of human affairs in terms of causes [behaviourism] and reasons [humanistic psychology]. You can try to represent human actions completely in terms of their natural causes. . . . If you carry

> this out and regard the actions of men, including the expression of their convictions, wholly as a set of responses to a given set of stimuli, then you obliterate any grounds on which the justification of those actions or convictions could be given or disputed . . . the two approaches – in terms of causes and reasons – mutually exclude each other (p. 22).

Matson (1964) argued that the existence of these two mutually exclusive approaches does not mean that natural science approaches to the study of behaviour should be abandoned, nor does it imply that the search for understanding alone is sufficient for psychology.

> The point is rather that the two alternative perspectives or frames of reference are *complementary*: i.e., mutually exclusive if applied simultaneously but mutually 'tolerant' if considered as opposite sides of the same coin – differing faces of the same reality (Matson, 1964, p. 152).

Since both causes and reasons are necessary for the thorough understanding of human behaviour, we must utilize both the subject's overt behavioural responses, and his reported experiences of the experimental situation, in order to fully account for his laboratory behaviour. Neither set of data is sufficient by itself, but, taken together, they can yield a meaningful, complete, and more valid science of behaviour. It is argued, then, that both experiential and behavioural data must be obtained and that this is justified both on philosophical and empirical grounds. [. . .]

References

BROGLIE, L. DE (1953) *The revolution in physics* New York, Noonday Press.

KELMAN, H. (1967) 'Human use of human subjects: The problem of deception in social psychological experiments', *Psychological Bulletin*, **67**, 1–11.

MATSON, F. (1964) *The broken image* New York, George Braziller.

ORNE, M. (1962) 'On the social psychology of the psychological experiment: With particular reference to demand characteristics and their implications', *American Psychologist*, **17**, 776–83.

POLANYI, M. (1951) *The logic of liberty* Chicago, University of Chicago Press.

POLANYI, M. (1958) *Personal knowledge* Chicago, University of Chicago Press.

SCHULTZ, D. P. (1969a) 'The human subject in psychological research', *Psychological Bulletin*, **72**, 214–28.

SCHULTZ, D. P. (1969b) 'The "subject effect" in psychology.' Paper presented at the annual meeting of the Southeastern Psychological Association, New Orleans, Louisiana.

5 The biological and the social

Martin Richards

Social psychology is being reconstructed. It is my aim to argue that if these attempts at rebuilding are to be successful, they must take account of both the social *and* the biological nature of man. To do this I will use a discussion of early development and socialization as illustration.

Social scientists have had a longstanding prejudice against biological views of man which has been fed and justified by numerous misleading doctrines about human nature that have arisen from the theories of the biologists. The identification and analysis of these has become a major theme in the history of science (e.g. Young, 1973) and I have only space to mention a few of the more obvious.

The false translation of theories about evolution into Social Darwinism was but one phase in a long tradition which has used organismic analogies for society. In this particular version, the notion of natural selection was used to justify, and make seem inevitable, social divisions within society and the exploitation of man by man. Here, as so often seems to be the case, the biological analogy was not used to explore or analyse the structure of society or the processes acting within it but simply as a justification of a *status quo*. This same process may be found in the attempts to see cultural and social differences between individuals or groups of people as an inevitable product of biological differences, a tradition that runs from nineteenth-century anthropology through to the current debate about the heritability of IQ (Richardson, Spears and Richards, 1972). Here, as well as a misunderstanding about the social nature of social action, there is a misconception about the role of genetic differences in the development of individual characteristics. Those that have argued in this way have not understood that epigenetic processes specify means and not ends, and that therefore genes do not *determine* anything.

Another widespread biologism is obvious in 'explanations' of human action that involve postulating a series of innate drives or instincts. Theories of this kind gloss over all problems about the meaning of behaviour (see Becker, 1972) which they see as being immanent in particular configurations of muscle movements. So behaviour is not distinguished from action and such accounts are unable to cope with fundamental

---

RICHARDS, MARTIN (1974) 'The biological and the social' in Armistead, N. (ed.) *Reconstructing Social Psychology* Harmondsworth, Penguin, 234–8.

questions about intention, the self or self-consciousness.

A final vice that should be mentioned is the use, or rather over-use, of accounts of animal behaviour in discussions of our own species. If these arguments are not based on both a full biological understanding and an appreciation of the social world constructed by man, they will always tend to reduce man to a complex animal–machine. They will underplay the species-specificity of our own behaviour and so ignore the human attributes of language, self-reflection and social communication (Bernal and Richards, 1973).

In a justified attempt to save their concerns from a reduction to biologisms of these and other varieties, many social scientists have moved in the other direction and have constructed entirely social theories of social action and it is this tendency I hope to counteract. Any complete account of man must be able to come to terms with both his social and his biological natures.

A human infant is born with a predisposition to become both adult (Trevarthen, 1972) and social (Berger and Luckman, 1967). Given both the biological structure of the infant and the social world in which he lives and which is necessary for his survival, a social adult will be formed during development. If the biological structure of the infant did not play an essential role in this process, any living organism should serve. But, of course, we find that attempts to rear even our closest biological relatives, the great apes, as children fail to produce people. Similarly, deprived of human companions, a human infant will not become a person. In order to understand socialization, the process whereby an infant born into a society becomes a full adult member, we must analyse the contribution of biological structure to the process. What is it about an infant that allows him to become a person?

One of the first things to notice about a human infant is his inability to survive on his own and so his absolute dependence on other members of his society which will last for several years (Bruner, 1972). During this time, even his most basic biological needs (for food, for warmth) can only be satisfied by the active intervention of others. So the essence of socialization becomes communication, for it is only insofar as other adults perceive and understand an infant's needs that these can be met (Macmurray, 1961, especially chapter 2). From birth onwards, adults are involved in a process of interpreting an infant's behaviour. It is through these interpretations, the actions of adults towards him, that an infant is able to perceive the consequences of his activities, and this allows him to develop an intentional structure for his own activities. Through this process, his behaviour becomes intentional action. This is a line of theoretical speculation which is grounded in the philosophical work of G. H. Mead (Morris, 1934; Strauss, 1956; Miller, 1973). Until recently, this work has largely been ignored by developmental and social psychologists and much more detailed theoretical analysis and empirical research is required before we can get beyond the most general statements. But its great advantage and potentiality lies in the fact that it opens the way to a truly human view of social development which may be married with an adequate theory of developmental biology.

However, there are some areas where our knowledge of development is already sufficient for us to see some of the details of the processes by which the social and the biological interact with one another.

The infant's biological structure provides a selectivity in the perceptual processes so that attention is focused on features that form part of adult communication modes and therefore allow the formation of agreed channels for communication between adult and infant.[1] From an early age one can observe rudimentary dialogue between infant and adult in which there seems to be agreement about how communication is to be effected even if the nature of what has to be communicated is little more than a mutual acknowledgement that there is another person there. Infants selectively attend to faces. This seems so natural to us adults that we seldom pause to consider either the complexity of organization that makes this possible or the enormous importance of this biological preadaptation for socialization and the richness of the face as a source of information about a person's state. Another example of this kind of preadaptation is the infant's preference for speech-like sounds. This provides a structure in (and of) the world for the infant; he does not have to begin from scratch trying to classify all sounds as if they all might have biological and social importance for him. Through this adaptation he is led towards relevant sounds and so into an agreed channel of communication which will culminate in the acquisition of language and his entry into his linguistic community.

To establish communication one needs not only agreed channels or modes, but also rules about the temporal use of the channels. Recent observational studies of infants have shown that their behaviour is structured in time and that they are very sensitive to the timing of the alternations and reciprocations of their social partners in communication episodes. Within the first few weeks of life, they come to expect that responses will arrive at particular points in sequences and, if they do not, the sequence may well be cut short. Abilities of this kind are, of course, essential before speech may be developed as a mode of communication, and yet again

1 This is described in much greater detail elsewhere (Richards, 1974).

the indications are that they are made possible by the existence of a human biological structure.

The fundamental role of these biological preadaptations to social life can easily be appreciated if you perform a thought experiment on yourself. First fix in your mind a picture of an infant – say a nine-month-old. Picture his social actions, his powers of communication and understanding, his abilities to make his intentions known to other people. Then consider how these might have developed taking a traditional view of the infant as a creature which is essentially a *tabula rasa*, with a few reflexes and the rest of his behaviour a series of random movements. Add to this the postulates of any stimulus–response learning ('behaviour') theory. Then explain how the infant grows up into the nine-months-old you pictured at the beginning. . . . Of course, it won't work. Even if one assumes an enormously structured environment, a glorified conditioning laboratory constructed with the sole purpose of ensuring the learning of a vast array of specific attributes, it still does not seem possible. But even that is ruled out. Observation of the environments of infants provide no evidence that parents systematically respond to their children in the ways that are required by learning theory. No; the infant must play a major role in structuring and organizing his own environment and learning particular things about it, and clearly he is endowed with a biological nature that makes this possible.

However, this biological endowment does not determine outcomes – it provides means and not ends. Human development would not be possible without a social world. This is something that is missed by theorists who argue that the infant is a social being and that his behaviour patterns such as crying and smiling constitute social behaviour. Implicit in this view is the idea that the behaviour pattern determines its own social meaning (as it is seen as the determinant of the adult's response to the infant). In contrast to this, I would argue that the infant's behaviour pattern is of biological origin but it is made social by its recognition and interpretation by adults. Its meaning is negotiated by those who interact with the infant.

This difference is much more than a quibble, because if one believes that a behaviour pattern arrives with a ready-made meaning, there is no room left for the development of autonomy and self-reflection by the infant. Furthermore, the infant's signals (his crying, smiling, and so on) would become a kind of biological imperative and any adult who failed to respond to them would have to be regarded as biologically as well as socially deficient. Of course, these infant signals are not randomly associated with his internal states and conditions. Nobody seems to regard smiling as a signal of discomfort nor is crying seen as a sign of contentment. But in responding to the infant's signals an adult must interpret them, decide what they mean and what, if anything, is to be done about them. As cross-cultural studies have demonstrated, these interpretations vary across society and embody each culture's belief system.

In this discussion I have deliberately concentrated on some of the features of the earliest stages in the process of socialization, because it is here that the role of biological structure is perhaps clearest. But all the later stages rest on these beginnings. Often this is forgotten, and accounts of socialization emphasize later childhood and the role of school and other institutions. If these alone are considered it is easy to provide a superficially complete account without mentioning biological structure. However, this only touches the surface of the matter because, though a child may change while a member of a school, the total of such changes do not together make up the whole of socialization. These one-sided accounts take as unproblematic the formation of a person and merely consider the rather superficial processes that result from participation in particular social institutions. The central issue in the problem of socialization is the formation of a person.

In this brief essay I have only had space to sketch out a few points of an extremely complex area, but I hope I have established two things. That theories in social psychology must take account of man's biological structure: without this they are incomplete or, worse still, they will tend to drift off, unanchored, in an endless sea of social definitions. And that biological considerations need not lead to reductionism or to any denial of the social nature of social life.

Given the fragmentation of our academic life, in both research and teaching, into the various disciplines, it is extremely difficult to find positions from which to bring together those things that are traditionally kept in isolation. Here, I think, social psychology is ideally placed, and in its reconstruction the way is open to build a viewpoint that will cut across traditional tendencies and provide a holistic vision of man.

References

BECKER, E. (1972) *The Birth and Death of Meaning* Penguin.

BERGER, P. L. and LUCKMAN, T. (1967) *The Social Construction of Reality* Allen Lane The Penguin Press, Penguin, 1971.

BERNAL, J. F. and RICHARDS, M. P. M. (1973) 'What can the zoologist tell us about human development?' in Barnett, A. S. (ed.) *Ethology and*

Development Little Clinic Clubs in Developmental Medicine, no. 47, Spastics Society and Heinemann.

BRUNER, J. S. (1972) 'The uses of immaturity' in Coelho, G. V. and Rubinstein E. A. (eds) *Social Change and Human Behavior* National Institute of Mental Health.

MACMURRAY, J. (1961) *Persons in Relation* Faber.

MILLER, D. L. (1973) *George Herbert Mead: Self, Language and the World* University of Texas Press.

MORRIS, C. W. (ed.) (1934) *G. H. Mead: Mind, Self and Society* University of Chicago Press.

RICHARDS, M. P. M. (1974) 'The first steps in becoming social' in Richards, M. P. M. (ed.) *The Integration of a Child into a Social World* Cambridge University Press.

RICHARDSON, K., SPEARS, D., and RICHARDS, M. P. M. (eds) (1972) *Race, Culture and Intelligence* Penguin.

STRAUSS, A. (ed.) (1956) *The Social Psychology of George Herbert Mead* University of Chicago Press.

TREVARTHEN, C. B. (1972) 'Behavioural embryology' in Carterette, E. C., and Friedman, M. P. (eds) *The Handbook of Perception* Academic Press.

YOUNG, R. M. (1973) 'The human limits of nature' in Miller, J. (ed.) *The Limits of Human Nature* Penguin.

Section 2
The genetic framework

Introduction

The papers in section 2 focus on the questions of how and to what extent genetic factors influence human social behaviour. Genes control the production of proteins which, in turn, play a considerable role in determining both anatomical development and physiological functioning. The biochemical blueprint provided by the genotype distinguishes one species from another. Also, because nearly all genotypes are different in some respect it helps to give rise to individual variations among members of the same species.

The first point to note is that any relationship between genes and behaviour is inevitably complex. As Gottesman (1966) has pointed out

> Needless to say, the gene to behaviour pathway involves a very complex chain of events (*cf* Fuller and Thompson 1960, Meissner 1965).
>
> There are no genes for behaviour. The genes exert their influence on behaviour through their effects at a more molecular level of organization. Enzymes, hormones and neurons mediate the path between the genes and those psychosocial aspects of behaviour termed personality. Even the latter complications have been compounded by discoveries in molecular genetics involving the concepts of *regulator* and *operator genes* (e.g. the work of Jacob and Monod (1961)) that influence the sequential activation of well-established *structural gene* potential throughout the life of an organism. Henceforth formulations in behavioural genetics will have to reckon with the fact that genetic variation in individual differences may arise from alterations in structural genes, either qualitative or quantitative or by activation or inhibition of regulator genes, also qualitative or quantitative.

Eysenck also has remarked 'heredity can only influence bodily structures and not mental functioning, except insofar as mental functioning and behaviour are themselves determined by the physiological, neurological and hormonal constitution of the individual' (Eysenck 1967). Eysenck has suggested, in fact, specific ways in which genes may influence certain aspects of physiological functioning which, in conjunction with a variety of environmental influences, may then predispose a person to tend to react in a characteristic way. He has attempted to account for individual differences in, for example, introversion/extraversion and emotionality in this way. However, there is little hard evidence on this topic. The precise means by which genetic factors may influence behaviour remain obscure. Not only is genetic influence complex and indirect but it can affect social behaviour in rather different ways. Anne Anastasi briefly reviews a selection of these in the first extract.

A second important point is that the behaviour we observe is always a phenotype – that is, the outcome of the complex interaction of genetic and environmental factors. The way in which these interrelate is the subject of the paper by Archer and Lloyd. Social and biological influences affect each other. The effect of neither can be judged in isolation from the other. They interact from the moment of conception. The nature and extent of the influence each exerts will be modified not only by other concomitant influences but also by their previous interactive effects on the development of that individual. The implication of their argument is, then, that genetic and environmental factors cannot be regarded as additive but only as interactive and in relation to each other.

Ideally, of course, we should study the processes of interaction or, as Anastasi has expressed it, the 'how' of heredity and environment. This is more easily said than done. In fact, the majority of studies of genetic effects on human social behaviour have tended instead to extract a relatively crude measure of heredity on the basis of inferences from observations of the way patterns of behaviour and performance interrelate among people of varying genetic relationships. The paper by Erlenmeyer-Kimling and Jarvik for example, summarizes the results of fifty-two studies of this kind on intelligence test scores. They reveal a remarkable consistency, suggesting that genetic factors do play some role in behaviour of this type. Even such a seemingly clear-cut pattern as this is open to reinterpretation. This paper has recently been subjected to intensive analysis by Kamin (1974). There is no space here to review his criticisms in detail, but a brief comment is appropriate. Many of the differences and correlations observed, Kamin argues, may be due entirely to environmental effects. Identical twins are likely to be reared more similarly than fraternal twins and this could explain the higher correlations found between their IQ scores. There is likely to be some similarity in the homes to which separated siblings are allocated. This, rather than genetic influence, may be the factor generating the low correlation found between their scores. The fact that there is a higher correlation between the scores of separated twins than between separated siblings, Kamin suggests, is merely an artifact of the way IQ tests are constructed: scores between people of the same age being more reliably comparable than scores between people of different ages. Some of Kamin's arguments are rather tenuous. His assertion that bias by Erlenmeyer-Kimling and Jarvik in the selection of results and studies significantly influences the patterns shown is also somewhat unconvincing. However, he does demonstrate the problem of separating out the variables involved and the difficulty of drawing firm conclusions from the data in this area.

The paper by Buss, Plomin and Willerman provides an illustration of a twin study, a widely used method for attempting to evaluate genetic influence on behaviour. The investigation contrasts the correlation between characteristics of monozygotic or identical twins (who originate from one egg and who therefore have essentially identical genotypes) with that between characteristics of dizygotic or fraternal twins (who originate from two separately fertilized eggs and who therefore share some genetic characteristics but to no greater extent than normal siblings). The problems involved in an investigation of this kind are well brought out in the paper; first, for example, the problem of defining and finding an effective measure of the behaviour in question; secondly, the problem of evaluating the possible effects on the results of environmental, methodological and other extraneous factors. The conclusions which can be drawn, however, can only be tentative. The measures used were based on mothers' reports of their children's behaviour and are not necessarily reliable. The heritability indices also are only relatively crude measures. They give some idea as to whether the possibility of genetic influence is worth bearing in mind but provide only a rough indication of the likely extent of its effects.

This study, however, is one of a number which have suggested that genetic factors do influence some aspects of personality. Evidence that both introversion/extraversion and emotionality may have some genetic basis has been reported (see, for example, Shields 1962, Jinks and Fulker 1970). Several studies have indicated that genetic factors contribute to the development of schizophrenia (e.g. Rosenthal 1970) and are probably involved in psychotic depression (e.g. Gottesman 1965) and anxiety (Gottesman 1966). It is quite clear though, as we would expect, that environment is also important in all these cases. Note as well that for by far the majority of measurable and observable aspects of personality, there is no evidence of any genetic contribution at all.

The first four studies all essentially deal with the contribution of genetic factors to individual differences in behaviour. In contrast, the final extract in this section by Irenäus Eibl-Eibesfeldt argues that certain behaviours which characterize man as a species are genetically based and have developed due to their adaptive utility in the course of evolution. A number of claims have been made that complex behaviour patterns such as aggression and territoriality have a similar basis (e.g. Lorenz 1967, Ardrey

1967). Such theses tend to rest on inference and analogy and lack both empirical and logical support. Eibl-Eibesfeldt's claims are on the whole more modest and better documented but his argument is based on a fusion of assertion, illustration, argument by analogy with other species and attempts to identify universal patterns of human behaviour across cultures. As such it remains fairly speculative. Noting that a behaviour pattern occurs in many and diverse cultures does not in itself prove that it is innate. An alternative reason for its universality could be that it is a function of experiences which are common to people in all cultures. In several of the cases that Eibl-Eibesfeldt discusses, it should be borne in mind that other explanations are possible. He views, for example, the use of penis amulets as a ritualized remnant of what was once adaptive behaviour. A psychoanalyst would provide a very different and no less plausible explanation.

The comments above indicate the difficulty of making substantive statements about the relationship between genetic factors and behaviour. Any effects heredity may have will be indirect and in complex interaction with environmental influences. Studies in this area are best regarded as suggestive rather than conclusive. The section does make the point, however, that the possibility, at any rate, of a genetically based contribution to some aspects of social behaviour should not be ignored.

References

ARDREY, R. (1967) *The territorial imperative. A personal enquiry into the animal origins of property and nations* London, Collins.

EYSENCK, H. J. (1967) 'The biological basis of personality' in Eysenck, H. J. and Eysenck, S. B. (eds) *Personality structure and measurement* London, Routledge and Kegan Paul.

GOTTESMAN, I. I. (1965) 'Personality and natural selection' in Vandenberg, S. G. (ed.) *Methods and goals in human behaviour* London, Academic Press.

GOTTESMAN, I. I. (1966) 'Genetic variance in adaptive personality traits', *Journal of Child Psychology and Psychiatry*, 7, 199–208.

JINKS, J. L. and FULKER, D. W. (1970) 'A comparison of biometrical genetical, MAVA and the classical approaches to the analysis of human behaviour', *Psychological Bulletin*, 73, 311–49.

KAMIN, L. (1974) *The Science and Politics of IQ* Potomac, Maryland, Lawrence Erlbaum Associates Publishers.

LORENZ, K. (1967) *On aggression* London, Methuen.

ROSENTHAL, D. (1970) *Genetic theory and abnormal behaviour* New York, McGraw Hill.

SHIELDS, J. (1962) *Monozygotic twins brought up apart and brought up together* London, Oxford University Press.

6 The influence of hereditary factors on behaviour

Anne Anastasi

If we examine some of the specific ways in which hereditary factors may influence behaviour, we cannot fail but be impressed by their wide diversity. At one extreme, we find such conditions as phenylpyruvic amentia and amaurotic idiocy. In these cases, certain essential physical prerequisites for normal intellectual development are lacking as a result of hereditary metabolic disorders.

A somewhat different situation is illustrated by hereditary deafness, which may lead to intellectual retardation through interference with normal social interaction, language development, and schooling. In such a case, however, the hereditary handicap can be offset by appropriate adaptations of training procedures. It has been said, in fact, that the degree of intellectual backwardness of the deaf is an index of the state of development of special instructional facilities. As the latter improve, the intellectual retardation associated with deafness is correspondingly reduced.

A third example is provided by inherited susceptibility to certain physical diseases, with consequent protracted ill health. If environmental conditions are such that illness does in fact develop, a number of different behavioural effects may follow. Intellectually, the individual may be handicapped by his inability to attend school regularly. On the other hand, depending upon age of onset, home conditions, parental status, and similar factors, poor health may have the effect of concentrating the individual's energies upon intellectual pursuits. The curtailment of participation in athletics and social functions may serve to strengthen interest in reading and other sedentary activities. Concomitant circumstances would also determine the influence of such illness upon personality development. And it is well known that the latter effects could run the gamut from a deepening of human sympathy to psychiatric breakdown.

Finally, heredity may influence behaviour through the mechanism of social stereotypes. A wide variety of inherited physical characteristics have served as the visible cues for identifying such stereotypes. These cues thus lead to behavioural restrictions or opportunities and – at a more subtle level

---

ANASTASI, ANNE (1958) 'The influence of hereditary factors on behaviour' from 'Heredity, environment and the question "How?"' in *Psychological Review*, vol. 65, no. 4, 197–208.

– to social attitudes and expectancies. The individual's own self concept tends gradually to reflect such expectancies. All of these influences eventually leave their mark upon his abilities and inabilities, his emotional reactions, goals, ambitions, and outlook on life.

The geneticist Dobzhansky (1950) illustrates this type of mechanism by means of a dramatic hypothetical situation. He points out that, if there were a culture in which the carriers of blood group AB were considered aristocrats and those of blood group O labourers, then the blood-group genes would become important hereditary determiners of behaviour (p. 147). Obviously the association between blood group and behaviour would be specific to that culture. But such specificity is an essential property of the causal mechanism under consideration.

More realistic examples are not hard to find. The most familiar instances occur in connection with constitutional types, sex, and race. Sex and skin pigmentation obviously depend upon heredity. General body build is strongly influenced by hereditary components, although also susceptible to environmental modification. That all these physical characteristics may exert a pronounced effect upon behaviour within a given culture is well known. It is equally apparent, of course, that in different cultures the behavioural correlates of such hereditary physical traits may be quite unlike. A specific physical cue may be completely unrelated to individual differences in psychological traits in one culture, while closely correlated with them in another. Or it may be associated with totally dissimilar behaviour characteristics in two different cultures.

It might be objected that some of the illustrations which have been cited do not properly exemplify the operation of hereditary mechanisms in behaviour development, since hereditary factors enter only indirectly into the behaviour in question. Closer examination, however, shows this distinction to be untenable. First it may be noted that the influence of heredity upon behaviour is always indirect. No psychological trait is ever inherited as such. All we can ever say directly from behavioural observations is that a given trait shows evidence of being influenced by certain 'inheritable unknowns'. This merely defines a problem for genetic research; it does not provide a causal explanation. Unlike the blood groups, which are close to the level of primary gene products, psychological traits are related to genes by highly indirect and devious routes. Even the mental deficiency associated with phenylketonuria is several steps removed from the chemically defective genes that represent its hereditary basis. Moreover, hereditary influences cannot be dichotomized into the more direct and the less direct. Rather do they represent a whole 'continuum of indirectness', along which are found all degrees of remoteness of causal links.

The examples already cited illustrate a few of the points on this continuum.

It should be noted that as we proceed along the continuum of indirectness, the range of variation of possible outcomes of hereditary factors expands rapidly. At each step in the causal chain, there is fresh opportunity for interaction with other hereditary factors as well as with environmental factors. And since each interaction in turn determines the direction of subsequent interactions, there is an ever-widening network of possible outcomes. If we visualize a simple sequential grid with only two alternatives at each point, it is obvious that there are two possible outcomes in the one-stage situation, four outcomes at the second stage, eight at the third, and so on in geometric progression. The actual situation is undoubtedly much more complex, since there will usually be more than two alternatives at any one point.

In the case of the blood groups, the relation to specific genes is so close that no other concomitant hereditary or environmental conditions can alter the outcome. If the organism survives at all, it will have the blood group determined by its genes. Among psychological traits, on the other hand, some variation in outcome is always possible as a result of concurrent circumstances. Even in cases of phenylketonuria, intellectual development is influenced by diet and by type of care and training available to the individual. That behavioural outcomes show progressive diversification as we proceed along the continuum of indirectness is brought out by the other examples which were cited. Chronic illness *can* lead to scholarly renown or to intellectual immaturity; a mesomorphic physique *can* be a contributing factor in juvenile delinquency or in the attainment of a college presidency! Published data on Sheldon somatotypes provide some support for both of the latter outcomes. [...]

Reference

DOBZHANSKY, T. (1950) 'The genetic nature of differences among men' in Persons, S. (ed.) *Evolutionary Thought in America* New Haven, Yale University Press, 86–155.

7 Sex differences: biological and social interactions

John Archer and Barbara Lloyd

Profound changes in our understanding of the nature of behavioural sex differences have taken place in the past hundred years. Freud challenged the notion that masculinity and femininity were divinely ordained and explained sex role development in terms of identification. Basically his approach was mechanistic and he believed that biology was destiny. The Freudian view of the universality of the Oedipal complex was quickly challenged by anthropologists eager to demonstrate that the family dynamics which Freud described were limited to the middle class Viennese milieu which he and his patients shared.

Psychologists measured affective behaviour and intellectual functioning and produced systematic, quantitative evidence of male-female differences for which cultural learning explanations were often offered. In the 1950s the heated heredity–environment controversies of earlier decades appeared to be resolved by a general recognition that neither biological nor cultural explanations were adequate in themselves to explain development. Nevertheless, classic studies such as Jerome Kagan and Howard Moss's longitudinal analysis of aggression, dependence, independence and achievement relied heavily on learning to account for the failure to find predictive value in early measures of dependence in boys and aggression in girls. The necessity to learn adult norms of sex-appropriate behaviour was invoked to account for discontinuities in development, and biological factors were merely mentioned speculatively. A socialization account was similarly central to the theory which Herman Witkin and his colleagues proposed to explain differences in cognitive style. Towards the end of the 1960s there were renewed attempts to explain these same differences from a biological perspective; the first of these was the theory of Donald Broverman and his associates on hormonally-produced differences in activation and inhibition in the central nervous system. Thus, although consensus emerged on the need to consider both biological and social variables to account for the development of sex differences, explanatory arguments still leaned on one or the other set of variables.

Clearly, a more complex model which gives more equal weight to both

---

ARCHER, JOHN and LLOYD, BARBARA (1974) 'Sex roles: biological and social interactions' in *New Scientist*, 21 November.

sources of influence is required. An interactionist approach, which we present here, describes the effort to account for the complex relationship between biological and social factors which occurs as the result of repeated feedback by their action and reaction on one another. In considering genetic and environmental influences on behaviour, an interactionist interpretation would view the genotype (the genetic base) as providing a flexible plan, but not a fixed blueprint, for the developmental process. The final outcome would be determined by interaction with environmental conditions prevailing at each successive moment in the process.

The interactionist model is complex and may fail to produce an easily comprehensible explanation. Instead, a popular approach has been to acknowledge the importance of both social and biological factors, but to draw upon the explanatory power of one while virtually ignoring the other. Typical of the recent resurgence of biological interpretations is Corinne Hutt's article in *New Scientist* (1974, **62**, p. 405). She began by acknowledging that 'Biology and culture are different aspects of a continuous process or interaction . . .' and concluded the same paragraph with an additive model in which 'the social environment may accentuate or attenuate differences between individuals'.

Here, we shall attempt to identify and clarify the issues which make an interactionist explanation difficult for both the theorist and researcher to maintain consistently. In seeking to understand the difficulties encountered, it is useful to consider both the content and the structure of the interactionist model. By content we refer to the different scientific disciplines which must contribute to the analysis, while the structure refers to the formal relationships between the variables.

An understanding of the aetiology of sex differences which takes account of both biological and social factors must be an interdisciplinary enterprise. No single researcher can be expected to have had training and experience encompassing a wide enough variety of sciences. One solution is for investigators to work in multidisciplinary teams. Team research can supply some of the answers, but it is still worth considering the special problems involved when social scientists employ biological findings, and biologists use the results from the social sciences.

Material reality

Tremendous advances have been made in bio-chemistry, genetics and endocrinology in recent years. For example, the presence of the Barr body in a slide of cells taken from a simple smear of buccal tissue allows positive identification of a genetic female; testosterone administered before a female rat is four days old prevents oestrus cycling at maturity even with hormone replacement in adulthood. It is hardly surprising that the psychologist or anthropologist is struck by the apparent certainty which biological research produces. In an epistemological sense, the data with which the biological scientist works offer material reality while their own behavioural variables are difficult to specify and measure. Perhaps it is this appearance of material reality which makes explanations of sex differences primarily in terms of the biological sciences so attractive.

Even when biological evidence is drawn from behavioural studies there are pitfalls for the social scientist to overcome. Data which are drawn from observations on animals are frequently interpreted in terms of concepts derived from human behaviour (aggression, fear and dominance for example). By applying a common label to behavioural results from animal and human subjects, the inference that there is a causal similarity between the two sets of data can become an unquestioned starting point for further theorizing. The apparent close correspondence between animal and human sex differences in aggression obscures diversity in the observational basis of the comparison: the animal findings rely on measures of initial attack, threat displays, or duration and outcome of fighting, whereas the human evidence includes teachers' ratings of assertiveness, self-evaluation on questionnaires and willingness to administer strong electric shocks to peers in a laboratory setting.

The biological scientist who turns to social science data is generally unimpressed by the explanatory power of the theories he encounters. Thus the anthropologist's view that differences in behaviour reflect different positions of the sexes in the social structure, or the sociologist's interpretation of similar behavioural data as reflecting group pressures or power relationships, may be ignored by the biologist.

Central to an understanding of an interactionist model is the concept of feedback. First, we shall discuss the simple form of feedback loop; then we will go on to show how a series of interrelated feedback loops extended in time can illustrate features of the interaction between organism and environment in development.

When discussing sex hormones we have to consider not only how they affect behaviour, but how behaviour affects the hormones. The large number of studies showing influences in the former direction have been drawn upon extensively in biologically based theories of sex differences, whereas those showing the influence of behaviour on hormones are seldom remarked upon. There is, however, increasing evidence that such influences are important. Thus, R. M. Rose and his co-workers found that defeat of a male rhesus monkey by another male led to a rapid and pronounced fall in plasma testosterone levels, showing that not only does the male hormone influence aggression but that the outcome of aggressive encounters influences the male hormone levels. R. M. Rose also found that a two or threefold increase in testosterone occurred when males were given access to a receptive female.

Social environment can also influence female sex hormones. Synchronization of menstrual cycles was investigated by M. K. McClintock in an all-women's college: she found increasing synchrony in women who spent most time together and longer cycles for women having little contact with men. Contact with the opposite sex led to a shortening of these cycles.

These examples from research on behaviour and sex hormones illustrate one important component of the interactionist model: that there is a two-way and not a one-way influence between the variables. Figure 1 summarizes the position diagrammatically, contrasting this feedback loop with a simpler one which recognizes sex hormone effects on behaviour but not the reverse.

The feedback loop is also applicable to the relationship between physical characteristics and the social environment. Behaviour can be influenced indirectly by the way in which the individual appears to others in the social group. Peter Marler found that by painting the breast of a female chaffinch red, males would treat the female as if she were a male, and subsequently her behaviour changed accordingly so that she became as aggressive as males.

Organism and its environment

So far we have discussed how social and biological influences produce mutual reactions which can be represented by a simple feedback model. These interactions are of a relatively restricted nature and cover short periods of time. To appreciate fully the complexity of interactions which are involved in the aetiology of sex differences we must view development as a series of such simple feedbacks, but involving more complex features and being greatly extended in time. Thus we proposed a continuous series of feedbacks between the organism and its environment throughout life.

Figure 2a illustrates the interactive model, in diagrammatic form, showing how the organism and its environment continually influence one another in a two-way process of action and reaction. $A \rightarrow A_n$ and $B \rightarrow B_n$ represent the organism and environment at each successive stage of the interaction. A and B are the initial states, which are successively changed to A_1 and B_1, A_2 and B_2, and so on during development. Thus a succession of changes occurs so that the contribution of the original state

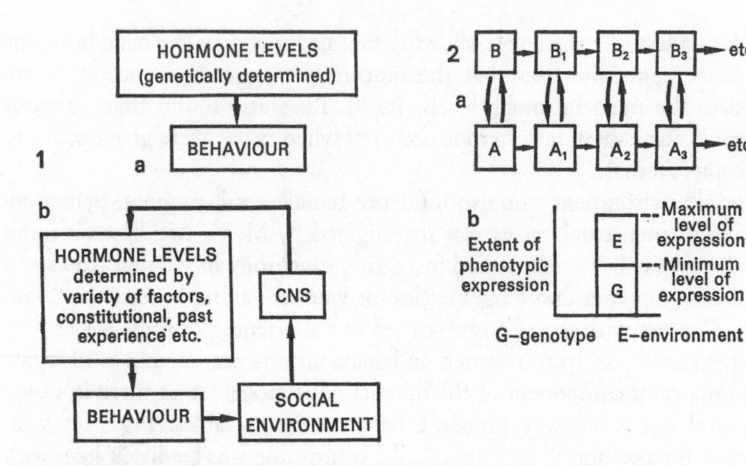

Fig. 1a Simple model of hormonal/behavioural relationships.
Fig. 1b Interactionist model of hormonal/behavioural relationships.

Fig. 2a Interactive model of genotype/environment interaction.
Fig. 2b Simple (additive) model of genotype/environment interaction.

of the organism (A) and the various environmental factors ($B \rightarrow B_n$) cannot be separated as each depends on the state of the other at each successive stage. Figure 2b shows for comparison an additive model which treats genotype and environment as though they were building blocks to be placed one on top of the other.

It is important to consider the implications of these considerations for understanding the development of sex differences. With an additive model (figure 2b) the mathematical relationships between biological and social factors are straightforward: they can only exert a summating or suppressing effect on one another. It is clear how certain misleading concepts and ideas are derived from such a model: for example, that one can refer to the separate influence of genetic and environmental factors, that one can ignore one and consider only the other, that there are limits imposed on characters by genetic factors, and that culture merely amplifies or attenuates what is already there.

In contrast, such misleading concepts and conclusions would not be derived from an interactionist model (figure 2a). Here we have instead of simple addition or subtraction the possibility of a variety of different mathematical relationships between the interacting influences. Some of these may be expressed easily in words whereas others would require detailed mathematical notation.

One of the simplest forms of interaction involves suppression of one influence by the other. A well-known example from animal behaviour is that of 'social inertia' in chickens described by A. M. Guhl. Typically, testosterone treatment of males induces an increase in aggression when the bird is matched with a stranger but this increase is not observed in the chicken's usual social setting where it is assumed to be overridden by habits developed in relation to the peck order.

Other types of relatively simple interactions include the facilitation of one influence by a second which acting in isolation would have been without effect on behaviour. Research on animal behaviour again provides an example. A. R. Lumia and co-workers either injected pigeons lowest in the dominance hierarchy with testosterone, or conditioned them to peck more dominant birds, or gave them a combination of both treatments. Male hormone alone was insufficient to increase aggression but aggression could be increased by conditioning. However, a much greater increase in aggression is produced in pigeons given hormones and conditioning. The extent of this increase could not have been predicted from knowledge of the simple treatment effects.

Parental influence on IQ

These examples describe the interaction of two relatively straightforward and circumscribed variables over a short period of time: to illustrate such simple principles, we relied on laboratory studies of hormonal influences in animals. When considering the continuous interaction between biological and environmental factors occurring throughout human development, such simple models as suppression and facilitation are rarely adequate. In these cases we may be not only unable to predict the extent of the outcome of the interaction, but also unable to predict its direction. Thus many studies of psychological sex differences in human development reveal correlations with opposite signs for the sexes: more maternal protection producing higher IQs in girls but less maternal protection yielding higher IQs in boys. Similar effects have been found for IQ and childhood anxiety and dependency. The processes involved in such interactions cannot readily be understood on the basis of either biological sex or degree of maternal protection, anxiety, or dependence alone but only by the interaction of both in development. To achieve such an understanding, we have to move from a statistical approach to a fuller consideration of continuing development.

Julia Sherman has suggested that a slower general development, later development of talking, and more powerful musculature in boys, interact with the parental responses to these characteristics and produce adult sex differences in spatial and linguistic skills whose origins are to be understood only by considering the combination of influences, any one being insufficient in itself.

In a similar vein, Nicholas Blurton-Jones and M. G. Konner in their discussion of sex differences in the behaviour of London and Bushman children point out that the initial tendency for boys to cry more than girls may interact with the mother's response to the crying in a way which amplifies and extends the original sex difference producing more far-reaching consequences for other forms of behaviour. Thus later behavioural differences may result whose forms could not be predicted readily on the basis of knowledge of only one or the other of the original factors involved.

These two examples suggest possible ways in which biological and cultural factors could interact over a period of time during development to produce sex differences, the source of which could not be characterized in terms of its 'inherited' or 'learnt' components, nor could it be considered as being determined by one or other of these components.

Rarely do we have the opportunity to study an entirely developmental sequence so that the interplay of the many different sources of biological and environmental influences can be fully observed in context. The scarcity of such studies makes John Money's reports of his clinical experiences at the psychohormonal research Unit at Johns Hopkins Hospital all the more important and illuminating.

One of the most dramatic cases involved one of a pair of male identical twins whose penis was accidentally ablated during circumcision in his seventh month. Ten months after the accident the parents decided with medical advice to reassign the child's sex, and gave him a female name, clothing and hair style. When the child was 21 months old surgery was begun at Johns Hopkins Hospital to construct female genitalia. Further plastic surgery would be necessary as well as hormone replacement therapy as the child reached maturity. The child has been brought back to Hopkins for six annual visits during which her progress has been assessed and her parents given counselling. The child's mother is very sensitive to the different needs of her son and daughter and John Money's account contains colourful anecdotal material of sex differences in child training practices. Although generally feminine in her behaviour, the girl's boyish traits include abundant physical energy and high activity levels but her mother tries to shape these in sex appropriate directions. This case is very unusual but is useful in suggesting the complexity of the processes which do eventually produce the clear differentiation of the sexes which has tempted theorists to overemphasize either the biological or the social learning factors.

From this discussion it follows that a developmental approach is necessary to allow adequate study of the more complex forms of interaction which determine adult sex differences. Such an approach must emphasize a two-way process rather than either socialization acting upon the child or the innate expression of the child's nature.

8 Genetics and intelligence

L. Erlenmeyer-Kimling and L. F. Jarvik

Nomothetic psychological theories have been distinguished by the tendency to disregard the individual variability which is characteristic of all behaviour. A parallel between genetic individuality and psychologic individuality has rarely been drawn because the usual assumption has been, as recently noted by Hirsch,[1] that the organisms intervening between stimulus and response are equivalent 'black boxes', which react in uniform ways to given stimuli.

While behaviour theory and its analytic methods as yet make few provisions for modern genetic concepts, the literature contains more information than is generally realized about the relationship between genotypic similarity and similarity of performance on mental tests. In a search for order among the published data on intellectual ability, we have recently summarized the work of the past half century.[2] By using the most commonly reported statistical measure, namely, the correlation coefficient, it has been possible to assemble comparative figures from the majority of the investigations.

Certain studies giving correlations had to be excluded from this compilation for one of the following reasons: (i) type of test used (for example, achievement tests, scholastic performance, or subjective rating of intelligence); (ii) type of subject used (for example, mental defectives); (iii) inadequate information about zygosity diagnosis in twin studies [3] (iv) reports on too few special twin pairs.

The 52 studies [2] remaining after these exclusions yield over 30 000 correlational pairings [4] for the genetic relationship categories shown in figure 1. The data, in aggregate, provide a broad basis for the comparison of genotypic and phenotypic correlations. Considering only *ranges* of the observed measures, a marked trend is seen towards an increasing degree of intellectual resemblance in direct proportion to an increasing degree of genetic relationship, regardless of environmental communality.

Furthermore, for most relationship categories, the *median* of the empirical correlations closely approaches the theoretical value predicted on the basis of genetic relationship alone. The average genetic correlation between parent and child, as well as that between siblings (including dizygotic

ERLENMEYER-KIMLING, L. and JARVIK, L. F. (1963) 'Genetics and intelligence: a review' in *Science*, vol. 142, 1477–9.

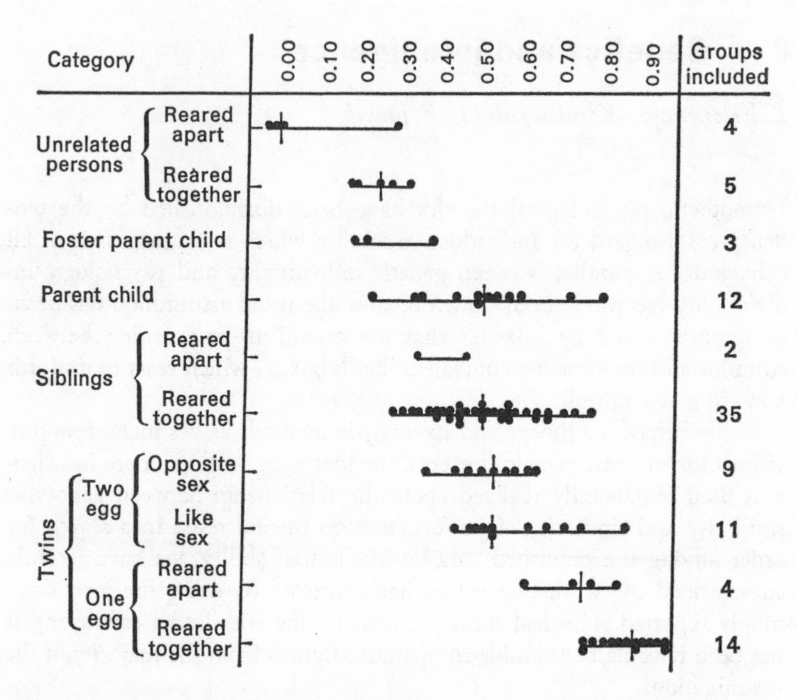

Fig. 1 Correlation coefficients for 'intelligence' test scores from 52 studies. Some studies reported data for more than one relationship category; some included more than one sample per category, giving a total of 99 groups. Over two-thirds of the correlation coefficients were derived from IQs, the remainder from special tests (for example, Primary Mental Abilities). Midparent–child correlation was used when available, otherwise mother–child correlation. Correlation coefficients obtained in each study are indicated by dark circles; medians are shown by vertical lines intersecting the horizontal lines which represent the ranges.

twins) is 0·50. The median correlations actually observed on tests of intellectual fuctioning are: 0·50 for parent–child, 0·49 for siblings reared together, and 0·53 for dizygotic twins, both the opposite-sex and like-sex pairs. Although twins are presumably exposed to more similar environmental conditions than are siblings spaced apart in age, the correlations for mental ability do not indicate a sizeable difference between the groups. Since only two studies dealt with siblings reared *apart*, it is possible to state only that the reported correlations for that group fall within the range of values obtained for siblings reared together and exceed those for unrelated children living *together*.

For unrelated persons in a large random-mating population, the theoretical genetic correlation is usually considered to be zero; for smaller populations, or those that deviate substantially from panmixia, however, the genetic correlation between presumably unrelated individuals in fact may be considerably higher. The observed median for unrelated persons reared apart is −0·01. Medians for unrelated individuals reared together (children reared in the same orphanage or foster home from an early age) and for the foster parent–child group are 0·23 and 0·20, respectively. The relative contributions made by environmental similarity and sample selection to these deviations from zero are still to be analysed.

At the other end of the relationship scale, where monozygotic twins theoretically have 100 per cent genetic correlation, medians of the observed correlations in intellectual functioning are 0·87 for the twins brought up together, and 0·75 for those brought up apart.[5] The correlations obtained for monozygotic twins reared together are generally in line with the intra-individual reliabilities of the tests. The median for the separated twins is somewhat lower, but clearly exceeds those for all other relationship groups.

In further reference to twin studies, our survey[2] shows that mean intra-pair differences on tests of mental abilities for dizygotic twins generally are between 1½ to 2 times as great as those between monozygotic twins reared together. Such a relationship appears to hold also for the upper age groups, as suggested by a longitudinal study of senescent twins.[6]

Taken individually, many of the 52 studies reviewed here are subject to various types of criticism (for example, methodological). Nevertheless, the overall orderliness of the results is particularly impressive if one considers that the investigators had different backgrounds and contrasting views regarding the importance of heredity. Not all of them used the same measures of intelligence (see caption, figure 1), and they derived their data from samples which were unequal in size, age structure, ethnic composition, and socio-economic stratification; the data were collected in eight countries on four continents during a time span covering more than two generations of individuals. Against this pronounced heterogeneity, which should have clouded the picture, and is reflected by the wide range of correlations, a clearly definitive consistency emerges from the data.

The composite data are compatible with the polygenic hypothesis which is generally favoured in accounting for inherited differences in mental ability. Sex-linkage is not supported by these data (for example, under a hypothesis of sex-linkage the correlations for like-sex dizygotic twins should be higher than those for opposite-sex twins), although the possible effects of sex-linked genes are not precluded for some specific factors of ability.

We do not imply that environment is without effect upon intellectual functioning; the intellectual level is *not* unalterably fixed by the genetic constitution. Rather, its expression in the phenotype results from the patterns laid down by the genotype under given environmental conditions. Two illustrations of the 'norm of reaction' concept in relation to intellectual variability are seen in early total deafness and in phenylketonuria. Early deafness makes its stamp upon intellectual development, in that it lowers IQ by an estimated 20 score points.[7] Phenylketonuria is ordinarily associated with an even greater degree of intellectual impairment. However, early alteration of the nutritional environment of the affected child changes the phenotypic expression of this genetic defect.[8] Individual differences in behavioural *potential* reflect genotypic differences; individual differences in behavioural *performance* result from the nonuniform recording of environmental stimuli by intrinsically nonuniform organisms.

References and notes

1 HIRSCH, J. (1963) *Science*, **142**.

2 This material was included in a report presented at the XVII International Congress of Psychology, Washington, D.C., 1963, by L. Erlenmeyer-Kimling, L. F. Jarvik, and F. J. Kallmann.

3 This survey does include reports on opposite-sex (hence dizygotic) twin pairs from these studies.

4 Correlational pairings refer to the number of individual pairs used in deriving the correlation coefficients. Some investigators constructed a large number of pairings on the basis of a relatively small number of individuals. Altogether, we have been able to identify the following minimum numbers: twins, 3134 pairs (1082 monozygotic and 2052 dizygotic); sibs apart, 125 pairs plus 131 individuals; sibs together, 8288 pairs plus 7225 individuals; parent–child, 371 pairs plus 6812 individuals; fosterparent–child, 537 individuals; unrelated apart, 15,086 pairings, unrelated together, 195 pairings plus 287 individuals.

5 Correlational data are now available on 107 separated pairs of monozygotic twins from four series:

NEWMAN, H. H., FREEMAN, F. N. and HOLZINGER, K. J. (1937) *Twins: A Study of Heredity and Environment* Chicago, University of Chicago Press.

CONWAY, J. (1958) *British Journal of Statistical Psychology,* **11**, 171.

JUEL-NIELSEN, N. and MOGENSON, A., cited by E. Strömgren (1962) in Kallmann, F. J. (ed.) *Expanding Goals of Genetics in Psychiatry* New York, Grune and Stratton, 231.

SHIELDS, J. (1962) *Monozygotic Twins Brought Up Apart and Brought Up Together* London, Oxford University Press.

6 JARVIK, L. F. and FALEK, A. (1963) *Journal of Gerontology,* **18**, 173.

7 SALZBERGER, R. M. and JARVIK, L. F. (1963) in Rainer, J. D. et al. (eds) *Family and Mental Health Problems in a Deaf Population* New York, N. Y. State Psychiatric Institute.
8 HOMER, F. A., STREAMER, C. W., ALEJANDRINO, L. L., REED, L. H. and IBBOTT, F. (1962) *New England Journal of Medicine*, 266, 79.

9 The inheritance of temperaments

Arnold H. Buss, Robert Plomin and Lee Willerman

Although there is some disagreement about details, most psychologists accept the definition of temperament given by Allport (1961): '*Temperament refers to the characteristic phenomena of an individual's nature, including his susceptibility to emotional stimulation, his customary strength and speed of response, the quality of his prevailing mood, and all the peculiarities of fluctuation and intensity of mood, these being phenomena regarded as dependent on constitutional make-up, and therefore largely hereditary in origin*' (p. 34). Which aspects of personality should be called temperaments? The answer is determined by the basis of selection, and we suggest three criteria.

First, the personality dispositions should have adaptive value and therefore have an evolutionary history. Any inherited tendency must have survived natural selection, which means that it must have been useful in individual survival, breeding, and the rearing of the next generation. Any disposition that is seen not only in man but also in primates (or perhaps even mammals) must surely have some adaptive value.

Second, the personality dispositions should be present early in life and show some stability during childhood. This is not to deny the importance of socialization and other environmental factors that shape the child's personality. Nevertheless, the child's innate tendencies should presumably modify the impact of life experiences so that his native individuality shines through the overlay of learned tendencies. Otherwise temperaments would contribute little or nothing to adult personality.

Third, there should be evidence that the dispositions are inherited. Inherited differences in temperaments have been clearly established in animals; and dogs, for example, can be bred to be excitable, calm, ferocious, and so on. The question is whether similar inherited tendencies are present in man.

On the basis of these three criteria, we selected four temperaments that also meet Allport's definition: *emotionality* – the level of arousal, which corresponds roughly to intensity of reaction; *activity* – the sheer amount of response output; *sociability* – the tendency to approach others; and *impulsivity* – quickness of response. These four temperaments may be

BUSS, A. H., PLOMIN, R. and WILLERMAN, L. (1973) 'The inheritance of temperaments' in *Journal of Personality*, vol. 41, 513–24.

seen in primates and in such social mammals as dogs, and a strong case has been made for their adaptive aspects (Diamond 1957). Thus they make sense from an evolutionary perspective.

There is also evidence that they are present early in life. Thomas et al. (1968) traced nine personality dispositions from infancy through late childhood. Some of their dependent variables would appear to be determined largely by training: rhythmicity, for example, which involves such behaviours as regular feeding hours. Most of their variables, however, were closely related to the four temperaments listed above, except that Thomas et al. (1968) used slightly different definitions for some of the dispositions. Thus their variable of *approach–withdrawal* included moving towards or away from both persons and objects, whereas our *sociability* is restricted to moving towards or away from persons. On the other hand, they defined activity as we do. Their findings provide evidence consistent with one of the criteria of temperaments: appearance early in life and stability in childhood. Other longitudinal research has also yielded evidence bearing on the four temperaments, but differences in definition suggest caution in interpreting the data.

A similar problem confronts any attempt to draw conclusions from genetic studies of twins. There is evidence concerning the four temperaments in previous research (see Scarr 1969, Vandenberg 1967 and Mittler 1971), but there were variations in the behaviour sampled and the way terms were defined. Thus the research on the inheritance of the four temperaments has generally been positive, but it must be interpreted with caution. What seems to be needed is a study that focuses directly on the four temperaments that meet the criteria outlined above and that provides evidence about their heritability. This was the goal of the present research.

Method

The inheritance of personality dispositions in man is studied almost exclusively with the twin method. This method relies on the fact that monozygotic twins are identical genetically, whereas dizygotic (fraternal) twins have only half their genes in common – as do siblings born at different times. If monozygotic twins are significantly more alike in a trait than dizygotic twins, it follows that the characteristic has an inherited component.[1]

1 This inference rests on the assumption that families do not treat identical twins more alike than they do fraternal twins. If the two kinds of twins were treated differently, the results of a twin study would be questionable. Of course, if the extent of such differences were known, it would be possible to separate them from variance due to the genotype. This issue will be dealt with in the Discussion section.

A questionnaire was constructed that consisted of twenty items, five items for each temperament. Each item was rated on a scale of one (a little) to five (a lot). Thus for each temperament the scores had a possible range of five to twenty-five. The items and a factor analysis of the items are presented below.

Mothers of 127 pairs of white, same-sexed twins completed the mailed temperament questionnaire on their children. The mothers – members of Mothers of Twins Clubs in eight states (Colorado, Illinois, Iowa, Minnesota, New Jersey, Oregon, South Dakota, and Virginia) had an average educational level of one year in college. The average age of the twins was 55 months and they ranged in age from four months to sixteen years. Zygosity of the twins was determined without knowledge of the personality scale findings, using a questionnaire modified from Nichols and Bilbro (1966). The original questionnaire yielded 93 per cent accuracy of diagnosis as compared with serological techniques. This procedure classified 78 pairs as monozygotic and 50 pairs as dizygotic. Of the monozygotic twins, 38 pairs were male and 40 were female; 32 dizygotic twins were male and 18 were female. There is an unusual shortage of dizygotic twin girls, which seems to occur in Twins Clubs generally (as estimated by the National Organization of Mothers of Twins Clubs) and our sample merely reflects this distribution. The zygosity of the total membership of the Mothers of Twins Clubs as given by registration lists breaks down as follows: monozygotic males, 28 per cent; monozygotic females, 30 per cent; dizygotic males, 23 per cent; and dizygotic females, 19 per cent. In our sample the comparable per cents are: monozygotic males, 30 per cent; monozygotic females, 31 per cent; dizygotic males, 25 per cent; and dizygotic females, 14 per cent. There is no obvious explanation of why there are fewer dizygotic twin girls – theoretically, they should comprise 25 per cent of the population of same-sexed twins – but neither is there a basis for assuming that the shortage would bias the findings.

Factor analyses

The items on the inventory were intercorrelated and factor analysed for boys and girls separately, using Kaiser's orthogonal Varimax rotation (Harmon 1967). The items and the factor loadings are presented in table 1, along with the intraclass correlations for monozygotic and dizygotic twins.[2]

2 These correlations are included so that the reader can better understand the heritability of the four scales (temperaments), data that are presented in table 2. The correlations for the items provide a basis for constructing a personality measure using heritability as the criterion for selecting items.

For both boys and girls, four factors accounted for the majority of systematic variance, and these factors were essentially the four temperaments. Thus for each scale, at least three of the five items assigned to the scale a priori loaded highest on the appropriate factor; and for some scales four or five items loaded appropriately.

There were some discrepancies between a priori assignment and the outcome of the factor analysis. For example, for both genders, the item 'Child cannot sit still long' loaded on both the Activity and Impulsivity factors. Nevertheless, the factor analysis was generally consistent with the a priori assignment of items. The factorial picture is somewhat clearer for boys than for girls. Thus, for boys, the Impulsivity items were factorially the purest, whereas for girls these items also loaded in the Emotionality factor. Perhaps mothers are more upset by girls' impulsive behaviour and tend to equate it with emotionality, whereas they accept impulsivity in boys as something to be expected.

Estimates of heritability

The intraclass correlations for monozygotic and dizygotic twins are presented in table 2. Though based on variances associated with the correlations, the *F* ratios furnish estimates of the reliability of the difference between each pair of correlations, and the *H* statistic is a rough index of heritability.[3] In computing these correlations, we used both a priori scales and scales derived from the factor analysis; there was essentially no difference in the outcome, and therefore table 2 contains correlations based on the a priori scales.

The correlations are clearly higher for monozygotic twins than for dizygotic twins, and the difference is significant in all but one comparison. The exception is for impulsivity in girls, where the correlation for dizygotic twins is substantially higher than the other seven correlations for dizygotic twins. Clearly, there is no genetic component for impulsivity in girls as measured in this study. A possible explanation may be found in the data in table 1, which reveal that for girls impulsivity items also load on the emotionality factor. Perhaps impulsivity needs to be assessed differently in girls than in boys.

3 The heritability statistic, Holzinger's *H*, is commonly used to provide an estimate of the proportion of the variance accounted for by genetic factors. *H* can be computed from the following formula:

$$H = \frac{r_{mz} - r_{dz}}{1 - r_{dz}}$$

The significance level of the *H* statistic is the same as the significance of the *F* ratio between the DZ within-pair variance and the MZ within-pair variance.

Table 1 Items, factor loadings,* and item intraclass correlations of the EASI Temperament Survey

A priori scale assignment	*Boys* *factor loadings* EMO	ACT	SOC	IMP	*correlations* MZ	DZ	*Girls* *factor loadings* EMO	ACT	SOC	IMP	*correlations* MZ	DZ
Emotionality												
Child cries easily	0·76				0·56	0·10	0·75				0·47	0·23
Child has a quick temper	0·61				0·34	0·10	0·48				0·40	0·70
Child gets upset quickly	0·86				0·64	0·10	0·67				0·66	0·00
Child is easily frightened	0·56				0·58	0·11	0·55		0·44		0·70	0·00
Child is easy-going or happy-go-lucky	—0·57	0·51			0·46	0·00					0·38	0·00
Activity												
Child is off and running as soon as he wakes up in the morning		0·80			0·88	0·41		0·83			0·86	0·00
Child is always on the go		0·73			0·48	0·02		0·68			0·72	0·01
Child cannot sit still long		0·58		0·55	0·76	0·25		0·53		0·54	0·65	0·27
Child prefers quiet games such as colouring or block play to more active games					0·77	0·00					0·21	0·03
Child fidgets at meals and similar occasions				0·40	0·67	0·38		0·31		0·72	0·68	0·31

Table 1 *cont.*

A priori scale assignment	*Boys*						*Girls*					
	factor loadings				*correlations*		*factor loadings*				*correlations*	
	EMO	ACT	SOC	IMP	MZ	DZ	EMO	ACT	SOC	IMP	MZ	DZ
Sociability												
Child makes friends easily			0·82		0·74	0·26			0·81		0·47	0·00
Child likes to be with others			0·77		0·61	0·27			0·60		0·29	0·05
Child tends to be shy			—0·43		0·57	0·10			—0·73		0·51	0·00
Child is independent					0·58	0·25					0·44	0·24
Child prefers to play by himself rather than with others			—0·62		0·55	0·10					0·73	0·46
Impulsivity												
Learning self-control is difficult for the child				0·79	0·75	0·55	0·42			0·45	0·83	0·69
Child tends to be impulsive				0·68	0·81	0·00	0·35			0·79	0·68	0·39
Child gets bored easily				0·49	0·83	0·13	0·70				0·49	0·59
Child learns to resist temptation easily				—0·67	0·72	0·35				—0·52	0·70	0·52
Child goes from toy to toy quickly				0·63	0·82	0·44	0·35			0·66	0·83	0·62

*Only factor loadings greater than .30 are listed.

Table 2 Intraclass correlations, standard errors, *F* values, and heritabilities of the EASI Temperament Survey

	Boys						*Girls*					
	monozygotic *38 pairs*		dizygotic *32 pairs*				monozygotic *40 pairs*		dizygotic *18 pairs*			
	r_1	SE	r_1	SE	*F*	*H*	r_1	SE	r_1	SE	*F*	*H*
Emotionality	0·63	*0·13*	0·00	*0·18*	2·00†	0·63	0·73	*0·11*	0·20	*0·24*	4·04†	0·66
Activity	0·87	*0·08*	0·17	*0·18*	4·53†	0·84	0·71	*0·11*	0·14	*0·25*	4·80†	0·66
Sociability	0·63	*0·13*	0·25	*0·18*	2·66†	0·51	0·53	*0·14*	0·20	*0·24*	2·17*	0·41
Impulsivity	0·90	*0·07*	0·17	*0·18*	4·69†	0·88	0·85	*0·08*	0·78	*0·15*	1·97	0·32

* $p < 0·05$.
† $p < 0·01$.

The remaining correlations in table 2 argue strongly for a genetic component in the four temperaments. The trend is for heritability in boys to be somewhat higher than in girls; note that the *H* statistic is higher for boys than for girls in three of the four temperaments. The gender differences vary from one temperament to the next, and the standard errors suggest caution in interpreting them; nevertheless, higher heritability in boys than in girls has been found previously in research on personality dispositions (Nichols 1965).

The age of the twins varied over a 15 year range, with the distribution piled up at the younger end. In the interest of greater homogeneity within groups, the distribution was split at the mean – 55 months of age – and intraclass correlations were computed for the younger and older groups separately. These data, which should reveal age trends, are presented in table 3.

For emotionality all the correlations increase over age, which suggests that environmental influences are operating to make the twins more alike. For the other three temperaments, the correlations tend to drop over age, which suggests the possibility of environmental influences that act divergently on the twins. These trends must be regarded with caution, especially in light of the small *Ns*, but future research on heritability might profit from an examination of age trends.

Discussion

Methodological issues

The possibility must be considered that the results of this research might be accounted for by methodological factors. For example, there was a shortage of dizygotic twin girls, which reflected the distribution found in Twin Clubs nationally. If this smaller *N* had introduced systematic bias, the correlations for dizygotic girls would be different from those of dizygotic boys. Examination of table 2 reveals that the correlations for dizygotic girls are similar to those of dizygotic boys, with the exception of impulsivity (as noted above, impulsivity in girls may be different from impulsivity in boys). In brief, there appears to be no systematic bias due to the smaller *N* for dizygotic girls.

The data might also be explained by the fact that each mother rated both of her twins. Thus there might have been a halo effect, resulting in a tendency to rate the twins as more alike than they really are. Such a halo effect would have led to high correlations for *both* kinds of twins; in light

Table 3 Breakdown by age (over and under 55 months): Intraclass correlations, F values, and heritabilities of the EASI Temperament Survey

	Boys				*Girls*			
	Correlations				*Correlations*			
	MZ	DZ			MZ	DZ		
under 55 months:	*26 pairs*	*19 pairs*			*28 pairs*	*10 pairs*		
over 55 months:	*12 pairs*	*13 pairs*	F	H	*12 pairs*	*8 pairs*	F	H
Emotionality								
under 55 months:	0·55	0·00	1·60	0·55	0·71	0·00	3·95*	0·71
over 55 months:	0·87	0·46	5·67*	0·76	0·81	0·38	6·35*	0·69
Activity								
under 55 months:	0·91	0·47	2·93*	0·83	0·68	0·58	—	0·24
over 55 months:	0·73	0·00	4·47*	0·73	0·70	0·00	9·24*	0·70
Sociability								
under 55 months:	0·76	0·42	4·43*	0·72	0·59	0·36	2·03	0·36
over 55 months:	0·42	0·00	1·70	0·42	0·22	0·00	2·75	0·22
Impulsivity								
under 55 months:	0·92	0·38	1·70	0·87	0·78	0·88	1·23	—
over 55 months:	0·86	0·00	4·40*	0·86	0·88	0·65	4·85*	0·66

* $p < 0{\cdot}01$.

of the generally low correlations for dizygotic twins, the notion of a halo effect must be rejected.

But perhaps the mothers of monozygotic twins, knowing them to be identical, rated them as being more alike than the mothers of dizygotic twins. Two kinds of evidence argue against this possibility. First, previous research on personality dispositions has yielded similar differences between monozygotic and dizygotic twin correlations when there were no ratings by the mother – as in self-report and observational research. If heritability is found both with and without mothers' ratings, the results cannot be attributed to mothers' ratings.

Second, Scarr (1966) examined the ratings and childrearing practices of mothers who were wrong about the zygosity of their twins. The actual zygosity was found to have more effect on the ratings and childrearing practice than on the (incorrect) zygosity assumed by the mother. Thus the present data cannot be explained by the mothers' knowledge of their twins' zygosity.

Environmental effects

The results of this research argue strongly for a genetic component in the four temperaments, but the data also suggest environmental effects. A genetic component can be inferred only when there is higher correlation for monozygotic twins than for dizygotic twins. But, if the difference between these correlations is either too small or too large, an environmental effect must be inferred.

Consider impulsivity in girls: the correlations for both monozygotic and dizygotic twins are high, and, in light of the standard errors, they should be regarded as roughly equivalent (see table 2). In the absence of a difference between correlations, the high correlations must both be attributed to environmental effects. Presumably, there are (mainly familial) influences that tend to make the twins more alike, hence the high correlations.

Now consider impulsivity in boys and several other temperaments in both genders, where the differences between the monozygotic and dizygotic correlations are very large. The problem is this: if there is a genetic component as shown by a high monozygotic correlation, the genetic component should also be reflected in a lower but substantial dizygotic correlation. Presumably, the same genetic determinants that act on monozygotic twins should also act on dizygotic twins, although the effect would of course be weaker. But note in the extreme case of impulsivity for boys that the monozygotic correlation is 0·90 and the dizygotic correlation is

0·17 (see table 2). This difference is too great to be explained on genetic grounds alone (Loehlin 1969). It must be assumed that environmental influences have acted to make the monozygotic twins more alike, the dizygotic twins less alike, or both. Thus the data argue strongly not only that the four temperaments are in some degree inherited but also that they are in some degree altered by socialization.

This conclusion is strengthened by the age trends (see table 3). The correlations for emotionality for both kinds of twins rose from early to late childhood, suggesting that environmental influences were pushing the twins together. On the other hand, the correlations for activity and sociability decreased sharply from early to late childhood, suggesting that environmental influences were causing divergence between the twins. Thus age trends in heritability offer a wealth of information about genetic–environmental interaction, and clearly what is needed is longitudinal research on personality in twins.

The gender differences are also intriguing. We noted earlier that impulsivity differs sharply in boys and girls, both in factor loadings and heritability. This and the other less striking gender differences have both theoretical and methodological implications. Theoretically, personality dispositions might show a different inheritance in boys than in girls; moreover, the way the components of personality are organized (regardless of their origin) might be different in the two genders. Methodologically, the implication is clear that not only should the data of boys and girls be analysed separately, but it might be necessary to use different ways of assessing personality in the two genders.

Implications

The temperaments may be used to account for behaviour that is difficult to explain solely on the basis of environmental variables. If the following examples are speculative, the hypotheses are susceptible to empirical verification.

Combinations of temperaments may be a sufficient explanation of certain kinds of persons. The hyperkinetic child moves around too much and cannot control his behaviour; he is both high active and high impulsive. The person who would like to be with others but is too shy represents a combination of high sociability and high emotionality, and the psychopath, who has trouble in delaying gratification and in learning to avoid punishment, might owe his difficulties to a combination of high impulsivity and low emotionality.

Temperaments may account for a bad fit between the person and the job, or between the child and socialization practices. A high sociable person would be as badly maladjusted to a job as forest ranger as would a low sociable person to being a hostess or master of ceremonies. A high impulsive child surely has considerable difficulty growing up in middle class culture, with its demands for delay of gratification and resistance to temptation.

Finally, consider the impact of children on their parents during development. As Bell (1968) has pointed out, psychologists have given too much weight to parental contributions to socialization: the child affects the parents' behaviour just as much as they affect the child's behaviour. A high active child may elicit 'damping' behaviour from his parents; a low active child may elicit stimulation from his parents. The developmental interaction between a low-to-moderate sociable child and moderate-to-high sociable parents is intriguing. Presumably, the parents would initially approach the infant often and would be disappointed at the child's relative lack of reciprocity. They would gradually lower the frequency of contacts with the child until some balance comfortable to parents and child was achieved. Thus the child would at least partially determine the parent–child interaction. Nevertheless, if a psychologist observed the family when the child was older, he would probably conclude that the child's low level of social responses was *caused* by the relatively infrequent approach responses of the parents. This hypothetical example illustrates how temperaments can help us to understand personality development. Most psychologists would agree that personality is the end product of an interaction between a child's initial endowment and socialization practices. The notion of temperaments offers a handle for the first part of the interaction.

Summary

Four inherited tendencies are suggested for humans: emotionality, activity, sociability, and impulsivity. A questionnaire assessing them was completed by mothers of 127 pairs of monozygotic and dizygotic twins. There was a clear genetic component for both genders, but it was stronger in boys than in girls. The impact of the environment was strongly suggested by the patterning of the correlations and by age trends in the correlations. Several implications were stated about the role of temperaments in the organization of personality and its development.

References

ALLPORT, G. W. (1961) *Pattern and Growth in Personality* New York, Holt, Rinehart and Winston.

BELL, R. Q. (1968) 'A reinterpretation of the direction of effects in studies of socialization', *Psychological Review*, **75**, 81–95.

DIAMOND, S. (1957) *Personality and Temperament* New York, Harper and Brothers.

HARMAN, H. (1967) *Modern Factor Analysis* Chicago, University of Chicago Press.

LOEHLIN, J. (1969) 'Psychological genetics' in Cattell, R. (ed.) *Handbook of Modern Personality Theory* New York, Aldine Publishing Company.

MITTLER, P. (1971) *The Study of Twins* New York, Penguin Books.

NICHOLS, R. C. (1965) 'The resemblance of twins in personality and interests' *National Merit Scholarship Corporation Research Reports*, **2**, 1–23.

NICHOLS, R. C. and BILBRO, W. C. (1966) 'The diagnosis of twin zygosity' *Acta Genetica,* **16**, 265–75.

SCARR, S. (1966) 'Environmental bias in twin studies.' Paper presented at the Second International Conference on Human Behavior Genetics, University of Louisville.

SCARR, S. (1969) 'Social introversion–extraversion as a heritable response', *Child Development,* **40**, 823–32.

THOMAS, A., CHESS, S., and BIRCH, H. (1968) *Temperament and Behavior Disorders in Children* New York, New York University Press.

VANDENBERG, S. (1967) 'Hereditary factors in normal personality traits' in Wortis, J. (ed.) *Recent Advances in Biological Psychiatry*, vol. 7, New York, Plenum Press.

10 The ethology of man

Irenäus Eibl-Eibesfeldt

Since Darwin we know that one key to the understanding of human behaviour lies in his phylogenetic development – in the process of how man came to be what he is. We have already made the observation that behaviour mechanisms owing their adaptiveness to phylogenetic processes also determine human behaviour sequences. This instinctive basis of human behaviour has been recognized by many anthropologists, psychologists and other scholars, but it has just as frequently been more or less radically denied by others (R. Bilz 1940, 1944; B. Berelson and G. A. Steiner 1964). [...]

We have presented the facts that compel us to accept the existence of phylogenetic adaptations in the behaviour of animals, and we have demonstrated that these adaptations are present in the form of fixed action patterns, internal motivating mechanisms, innate releasing mechanisms, releasers, and innate learning dispositions. We are now ready to examine to what extent similar adaptations also preprogramme human behaviour and to what degree they are still adaptive today, in the sense that they function in the service of the preservation of the species.

Fixed action patterns and their release in infants

The newborn human being is equipped with a number of functional behaviour patterns (A. Peiper 1951, 1953). . . . Some behaviour patterns, which serve the function of food intake, are phylogenetically quite old, and the human infant shares them with many other mammals. First we may list the rhythmic searching movements for the nipple, a turning of the head left and right, which may occur spontaneously or following a touch of the mouth region (H. F. R. Prechtl and W. M. Schleidt 1950). The seeking behaviour ends when the infant gets the nipple into the mouth and when the lips close firmly around it. This rhythmic seeking of the breast is observed only during the first days after birth. It is soon replaced by an orientated search for the breast: When the mouth region is touched the infant turns towards the stimulus object, orienting in space so that he

---

EIBL-EIBESFELDT, I. (1970) 'The ethology of man' in *Ethology: the biology of behavior* (trans. Klinghammer, E.) New York, Holt, Rinehart and Winston, 398–455.

or she can get hold of it.[...]

A characteristic reaction of the newborn infant is the grasping reflex with the hand. If one touches the palm of the infant's hand the fingers close firmly around the object and, as H. F. R. Prechtl (1955) has shown by motion picture analysis, in an ordered sequence of finger movements. This reflectoric grasping is especially strong during sucking. Quantitative investigations show that children react especially to hair. The grasping reflex undoubtedly served originally the purpose of holding on to the mother's fur. This reflex is often considered a rudiment because man no longer possesses fur and therefore the reflex is thought to be no longer functional. The behaviour does not seem to have completely lost its function, however; one can observe how small infants sleep close to their mother's body and how they hold on to her clothing. The hand-grasp reflex is so strongly developed in premature babies that they are able to hang on to a stretched-out clothesline. This capacity is lost later, which is an indication of a beginning rudimentation.

Swimming movements can be released in infants that are a few weeks old by placing them into the water in a prone position and merely holding them up at their chin. They paddle in a coordinated fashion with their hands and legs. The behaviour disappears at 3 to 4 months.

One can also release walking and crawling behaviour in the newborn child. A newborn infant on its stomach will commence to perform crawling movements by moving the diagonally opposed limbs (Kreuzgang). If one supports the infant and places the feet on to a firm plane it will begin to walk and place one leg before the other (A. Peiper 1953, H. F. R. Prechtl 1955)....

As examples of expressive behaviour in newborn infants we can list crying and smiling. The first is a kind of 'lost call'; a child can be easily quieted by picking it up or by imitating the presence of the mother by appropriate models. The primary function of the smile seems to be to appease. According to the legend, Cypselos, who later became the ruler of Corinth, was spared by those ordered to kill him while still a baby when he smiled at them. It is a fact that the smile releases delight in the mother, even those who initially were indifferent, and aids in the establishment of a strong emotional tie. The time of its first occurrence varies. Sometimes it can be observed in newborn or even prematurely born infants.... R. A. Spitz and K. M. Wolf (1946) were able to release a smile in 3- to 6-month-old children by presenting them scarecrow faces and distorted grimaces as well as a normal human face. Within this wide spectrum everything was smiled at that was placed over the bed. R. Ahrens (1953) followed up the development of the recognition of mimic expressions.

Until the onset of the second month eye-sized, well-defined, contrasting spots on a square or round two-dimensional plate, representing a cardboard model of a head, release smiling better than a painted face or a rectangular bar on the same background. It makes no difference whether the pair of dots is presented in a parallel or vertical position or whether three pairs of dots are shown. One dot alone, on the other hand, is ineffective.

Around the second month of life dots presented in a horizontal plane in front of the infant's face are more effective than if they are presented vertically, and soon the child pays attention to the entire area around the eyes but not to the lower part of the face. This is included gradually towards the third month. At 4 months of age the child reacts to the movements of the mouth, without differentiating all details; it is not until the fifth month that the broadening of the mouth specifically releases smiling, and this is especially true for the 6-month-old child. The effectiveness of models then decreases. The child clearly distinguishes between models and faces of adults, but it does not understand the mimic expressions of smiling until it is 7 to 8 months old, when it reacts appropriately to a laughing person.

Behaviour of children born blind or deaf-blind

With respect to the question of innate components in human behaviour the behaviour of children born blind or deaf-blind is most informative. We have here the accidental experiments of nature which can be assessed as deprivation experiments. From this point of view J. Thompson (1941) studied the expressions of blind and blind-born children and compared them with those of seeing children. The results support and supplement the observations cited in the preceding section. Smiling, laughing, and crying, also the expressions of anger, pouting, fear, and sadness, looked the same in blind-born children, although they could not have imitated anyone. Blind-born children did, however, smile less as time went on in comparison with seeing children or those who had become blind later; no comparable decrease in crying was noted. In smiling a certain social feedback must play a role, which has yet to be investigated. When this feedback is missing the behaviour atrophies somewhat. [. . .]

As part of a still continuing investigation I filmed the laughing and smiling of a 7-year-old deaf-blind born girl and a 5-year-old boy who otherwise had no mental impairment. The motor patterns of laughing corresponded in all details to those of normal children. These two deaf-blind children threw back their heads during high-intensity laughing in a fashion typical for normal children and they also opened their mouths (plates 1a and b). The rhythmic sounds are very clear, but their laughing is somewhat restrained, more like a giggle. The girl also showed a number of typical expressive movements, for example, crying. When angry she stomped with her feet. She rejects by shaking her head or by pushing away with her hand, when she also shakes the hand. If she stumbles she extends both hands forward. When taken on her caretaker's lap or shoulders, she liked to cuddle against him. This girl, who gave a very alert impression, especially when actively exploring her environment with her hands, is able to distinguish strange persons from familiar ones by sniffing briefly at the presented hand. Strangers are pushed away, a gesture that is often accompanied by turning the head away. This behaviour is similar, with the exception of the sniffing, to that of healthy children. In short, a whole array of even quite complex behaviour patterns, which are typical for human beings, have developed also in the deaf-blind and are therefore present as phylogenetic adaptations. Some characteristics of social behaviour developed, even contrary to the educational efforts, such as, for example, the fear of strangers. Similarly, in a boy of the same institution who is approaching puberty now, certain aggressive inclinations developed and needed to be curbed by education. [...]

A number of complex expressive behaviour patterns, such as coquettish embarrassment, cannot be seen in the deaf-blind. This may be due to lack of relevant experience or to the fact that the channels which usually receive such perceptions are closed in these children....

Some results of the comparative method in the study of human behaviour

The observations on blind and deaf-blind people allow only limited statements to be made about human behaviour. Such people lack the more complex behaviour sequences which are normally released by visual and auditory signals. The question of if and how much in complex human behaviour is inborn may be answered by the comparison of behaviour in individuals of different cultures. If one can demonstrate communalities in expressions and gestures, then we may conclude that they derived from a common inherited root, especially the more specific the behaviour patterns concerned are and the more widespread their occurrence in people of different ecology and cultural and racial background as well, and, again, because man is extremely inclined to culturally mould and change behaviour in a relatively short time, as the evolution of language clearly demonstrates. [...]

A method that was developed by H. Hass and which we tested in various parts of the world in photographing people without their awareness overcomes all these difficulties (I. Eibl-Eibesfeldt and H. Hass 1959, 1966, 1967). An attachment that is mounted before the normal lens of the camera and contains a mirror prism makes it possible to film to the side. With this technique it was possible to photograph people even from close distances without their awareness. . . .

For later analysis it is especially important to have a record of what the subject did just prior to and after the filming. We strive, therefore, to understand the behaviour within the context of the situation and the sequence in which it takes place, in the same way as it is necessary in motivational analysis of animal behaviour to avoid subjective interpretations afterwards. In some cases it is possible to cause the releasing stimulus situation. When we were filming, curious onlookers would often gather around us, and we experimented with them without their being aware of it. By handing such a person a small box out of which popped a cloth snake when it was opened, we obtained the unrehearsed expression of fright. By casually looking at a person one can release greeting and sometimes even flirting behaviour.

Until now we have primarily filmed in Europe, Kenya, Tanzania, Uganda, India, Siam, Bali, Hong Kong, New Guinea, Japan, Samoa, the United States, Mexico, Peru, and Brazil. We were especially interested in mother–child behaviour, flirting, greeting, praying, and begging behaviour, and we obtained many film records without the subjects' awareness. . . .

Although the work is still in progress, we have filmed enough to say that some of the more complex human expressions can be traced back to the superposition of a few fixed action patterns which do not seem to be culturally determined. To give just one example, we found agreement in the smallest detail in the flirting behaviour of girls from Samoa, Papua, France, Japan, Africa (Turcana and other Nilotohamite tribes) and South American Indians (Waika, Orinoko).

The flirting girl at first smiles at the person to whom it is directed and lifts her eyebrows with a quick, jerky movement upward so that the eye slit is briefly enlarged. This most probably inborn greeting with the eyes is quite typical. Flirting men show the same movement of the eyebrow, which can also be observed during a friendly greeting between members of the same sex. After this initial, obvious turning towards the person, in the flirt there follows a turning away. The head is turned to the side, sometimes bent towards the ground, the gaze is lowered, and the eyelids are dropped (plate 2). Frequently, but not always, the girl may cover her face with a hand and she may laugh or smile in embarrassment. She continues to look at the partner out of the corners of her eyes and sometimes vacillates between looking at and an embarrassed looking away.

Here we already find that the superposition of a few invariable components (intention movements of turning towards someone, responsiveness, and turning away) yields a relatively complex and variable expression. The assertion of R. L. Birdwhistell (1963, 1966) that there are no culturally independent expressions and that everything is learned is disproved by these results.

The comparative investigation of greeting behaviour in people from different cultures showed additional agreement, even in the smallest details. During a friendly greeting over a distance the greeting person smiles, and if he is in an especially good mood will lift the eyebrows in the manner previously described, and then nod the head (plate 3). I filmed this behaviour even in stone age Papuans, who had only recently come into contact with government patrols (I. Eibl-Eibesfeldt 1968).

Wide agreement is also found in many other expressions. Thus arrogance and disdain are expressed by an upright posture, raising of the head, moving back, looking down, closed lips, exhaling through the nose – in other words through ritualized movements of turning away and rejection. When enraged, people bare their teeth at the corners of the mouth.

With respect to gestures one also finds many agreements among peoples of different cultures. Bowing everywhere seems to be a gesture of submission, for example, during greeting or if one approaches a high-ranking person or in praying (T. Ohm 1948). Differences apply only to the extent; we may nod, while a Japanese bows very low. In triumph and when we are enthusiastic we throw up the arms. Members of the most varied cultures greet by raising the open hand (plate 4). If one man wants to impress another – to display – it is again done quite similarly in different peoples by an erect posture, mean facial expression, and frequently with an artificial enhancement of the body size and width of the shoulders. The only different is in the means to achieve this expression in the various cultures. Some men place feathered crowns on their heads, others fur caps made of bear hide, another displays with weapons and colourful dress – the principle remains the same. When we are angry we become indignant, that is, we jump up into an intention movement for attack, make fists, and may even bang the table, which is a redirected attack behaviour. When angry we may stomp with a foot, an intention of attack which among Europeans is especially found in small, uncontrolled children; adults usually suppress it. I saw the same gesture in an angry Bantu boy. It remains to be investigated to what degree the gestures of approval or disapproval have an innate basis. Many races indicate a general 'no' by shaking the head, closing the mouth, some by showing the tongue (ritualized spitting out; see plate 5), and they say 'yes' by nodding their heads. Darwin points out that the first act of saying 'no' (disapproving) in children is the rejection of food, by turning the head to the side from the breast or a spoon. One could think of a shaking-off movement.

The blind and deaf girl who was discussed earlier shook her head when she did not want to eat, and also when she refused something, for example, an invitation to play. These facts – that people also say 'no' with different gestures, for example, a Sicilian by laying back his head – do not argue against Darwin's interpretation. We know that innate behaviour patterns can be suppressed by training. One would like to know whether a rejecting shaking of the head is also used, for example, in Sicilian children.

It is possible that several primary forms of saying 'no' exist, such as rejection or disapproval, and that people in different cultures accept one or the other by convention. One movement of rejection can be traced from the intention of turning away. In saying 'no' a Greek, for example, lifts his head with a jerk backward, at the same time lowering his eyelids and often raising one or both hands with the open palms showing to the opponent. This behaviour can be observed in northern Europe as a gesture of emphatic refusal ('for heaven's sake'). It is also very similar to the posture of arrogance. Sometimes instead of lifting the head backward we can observe a turning-to-the-side movement. Another widespread gesture of refusal or no is head shaking, and sometimes one can observe a rejecting form of shaking the hand, which may be a ritualized shaking off.

Nodding was derived according to Darwin from an intention movement to eat. Another possible interpretation is given by H. Hass (1968), who says that nodding could be taken as an intention movement to bow, as a ritualized gesture of submission, so to speak. When expressing agreement one does submit to the will of another. . . .

If the accounts are correct, the kiss is not found everywhere. In spite of this, however, one might think of it as a kind of ritualized feeding derived from the care-of-young behaviour system which has been taken over as one of the expressions of tenderness. In this connection the accounts of L. v. Hörmann (1912) are of special interest, in reference to the behaviour of the inhabitants of the Hinterzillertal (mountain valley in Austria). It is the custom there to chew pine resin, which gradually changes into a viscous mass that is no longer sticky and is changed from one cheek into the other and sometimes is visible from the corners of the mouth (Flenken). 'When chewing pitch the same custom, that of mutual exchanging of the wad prevails, as is also done with chewing tobacco. Among lovers this exchange plays an important role' (L. v. Hörmann 1912 : 99).[1] The boy exposes a piece

1 Hörmann previously reported that in the Zillertal, Pustertal, and Pinzgau (regions of Austria) the exchange of chewing tobacco is an expression of friendship between men. Acceptance of a chewed piece of tobacco by a girl is proof of love returned.

Fig. 1 Smiling and laughing in chimpanzee. (After pictures by N. Kohts 1935.)

of pitch from between his teeth and invites the girl to pull it out with her teeth, an attempt that the boys try to prolong as a kind of love play. When the dancing partner responds to this invitation of the boy, it is a sign of her interest and affection and even more.

Not only the comparison of people from different cultures, but also comparisons with animals can be very revealing. In addition to true homologies, there are many analogies. Chimpanzees show a smile that is quite similar to the human smile (N. Kohts 1935; see also figure 1).

Of old inheritance is our threat posture, which is expressed by rolling our arms inward in the shoulders, and during which the hair erectors on the shoulders and back contract, although we no longer have any fur. We experience this contraction only as a shudder. In chimpanzees, which assume the same posture, the hair becomes erect and their outline is enlarged (K. Lorenz 1943)....

A very curious display behaviour of many primates, including man, was pointed out by D. W. Ploog and others (1963) and W. Wickler (1966c)....

Vervet monkeys, baboons, and many other monkeys have been observed where several males sit at the periphery of their group 'on guard'.... W. Wickler has discovered that this behaviour is directed against neighbouring troops. The 'guards' always sit with their backs to their own group and display their male genitals prominently, which in these animals are very conspicuously coloured. When a strange conspecific approaches the penis becomes erect and in some species it is moved rhythmically. This behaviour is a display that serves to mark the territory. Interestingly enough, the same behaviour could be demonstrated in man. Some Papuan tribes emphasize their masculinity by artificial means (figure 2). In some male dresses of Europe this region is still emphasized today by decorative embroideries.

On the Nicobar Islands and on Bali I saw fetishes with an erect penis which are used to ward off ghosts (I. Eibl-Eibesfeldt and W. Wickler 1968).

W. Wickler called attention to stone columns in ancient Greece with a man's head and a penis that were used as property markers. Phallic 'guardians' carved in wood or stone can be discovered in Romanesque churches (in Lorch, West Germany, and St. Remy, France). In modern

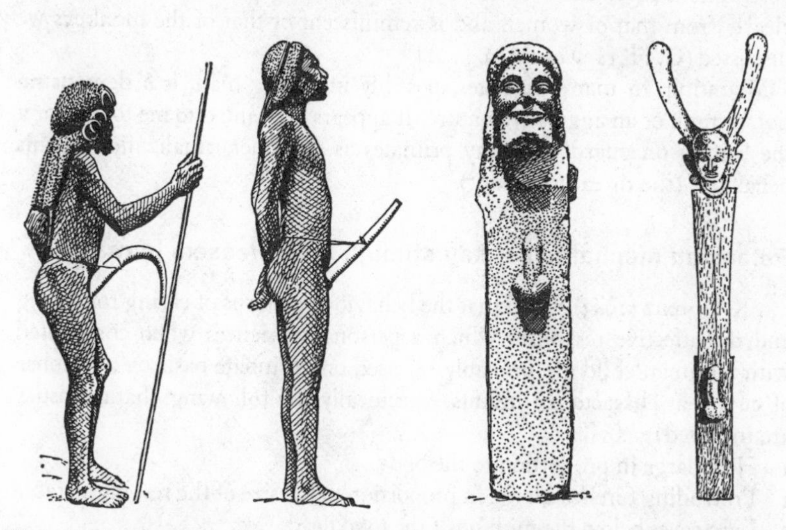

Fig. 2 Genital display in man. Left: two Papuans from Kogume on the Konca river; to the right: Herme of Siphnos (490 BC), 66 cm high, Athens, National Museum; right: house guardian (Siraha) of the natives on the Island of Nias. The man-high figures are still in use. In the Greek statue the beard is emphasized as a male symbol; in beardless peoples the male head ornaments are emphasized. (From W. Wickler 1966.)

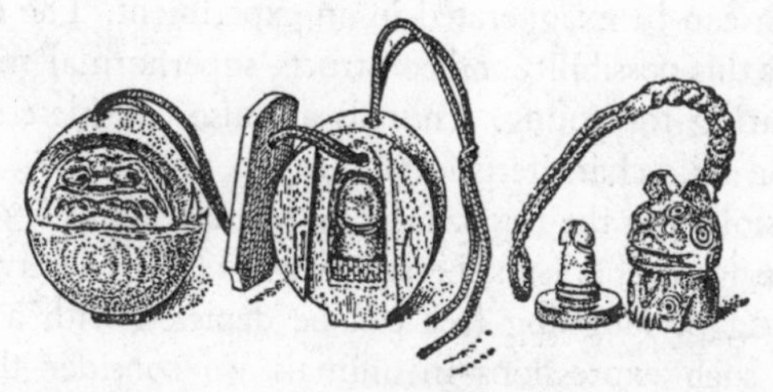

Fig. 3 Amulets which the author acquired in Japan (Tagata Temple) that are intended to protect the wearer. One amulet shows a threatening face on its front. By removing a cover on the back a golden penis becomes visible. The cover is inscribed with the words: To protect against traffic accidents. The threatening face and phallus are repeatedly found elements in figures which are meant to offer protection against demons.

Japan phallic amulets are still used, for example, to protect against car accidents (figure 3). In the Museum of Linz (Austria) one finds amulets that depict male sexual organs. It is possible that pathological exhibitionism can be traced back to a drive to display. This hypothesis is supported by the observations of J. H. Schultz (1966). The sitting position of men differs clearly from that of women and is reminiscent of that of the monkeys we discussed (G. H. Hewes 1957). [...]

Mounting, in many primates, possibly including man, is a demonstration of rank of an aggressive nature. It appears warranted to me to interpret the 'sitting on guard' of many primates as a further ritualization of this behaviour (the threat to mount).

Releasing mechanisms, key stimuli, and releasers in man

... K. Lorenz (1943) stated that the behaviour patterns of caring for young and the affective responses which a person experiences when confronted with a human child are probably released on an innate basis by a number of cues that characterize infants. Specifically the following characteristics are involved:

1 Head large in proportion to the body.
2 Protruding forehead large in proportion to the size of the rest of the face.
3 Large eyes below the midline of the total head.
4 Short, thick extremities.
5 Rounded body shape.
6 Soft-elastic body surfaces.
7 Round, protruding cheeks.

B. Hückstedt (1965) demonstrated experimentally that the rounded forehead and the relatively large brain case are important characteristics of 'cuteness' which can be exaggerated in an experiment. The doll and film industry utilizes this possibility and constructs 'supernormal' models to elicit behaviour of caring for young. Animals are also considered cute if they have some of the child characteristics (figure 4)....

It is also possible that the understanding of expressions is given a priori by innate releasing mechanisms, because we are easily deceived by simple models. A crying or laughing face can be depicted with a few strokes. When we see such expressions in animals we consider them friendly (Mandarin ducks), arrogant (camel), or daring (eagle), although this has nothing to do with the actual mood of the particular animal (figure 5). Finally, the automatic reactions to the expressions of another person argue for innate releasing mechanisms that determine a response to an expression. We already mentioned the disarming smile. [...]

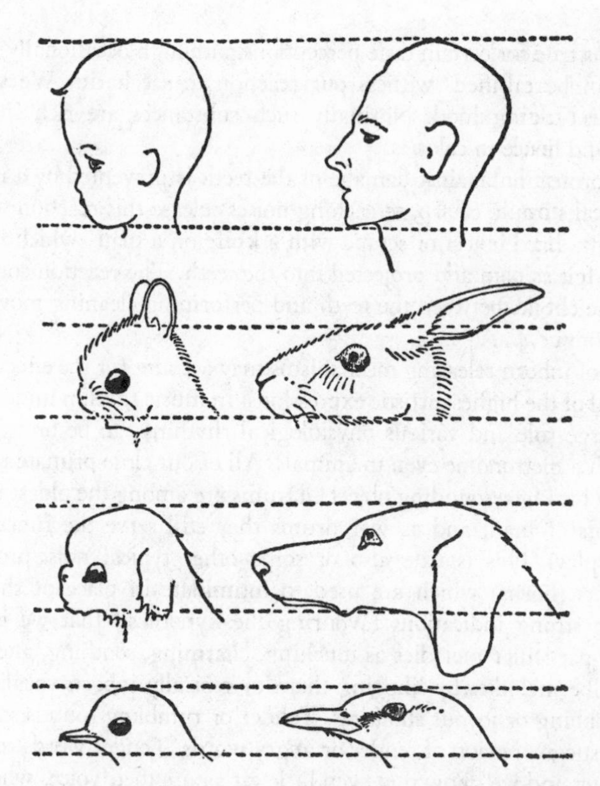

Fig. 4 'Baby' schema of man. Left: head proportions that are generally considered to be 'cute'; right: adult forms, which do not activate the drive to care for the young (brood care). (From K. Lorenz 1943.)

The advertising industry uses our readiness to respond to sexual releasers to attract our attention and to direct it to the actual message. [. . .]

We know only very little about releasing stimuli of other senses. With respect to odours we cited the investigations of J. LeMagnens, who found that girls and women can smell musk substances when they are sexually mature which men cannot perceive, unless they have received estrogen injections. R. v. Krafft-Ebing (1924) reported the case of a young man who sexually aroused peasant girls by wiping their perspiring brows after a dance with a handkerchief that he had carried in his armpit. In Mediterranean countries forms of dancing exist where men dance around their female partners while waving a kerchief. It is said that in some areas it has also been carried previously in their armpits. It seems likely that certain pleasant as well as disgusting odours are reacted to on a primary basis; the same seems true for certain taste perceptions, although occasionally the key stimuli can be falsified, witness our reaction to saccharin. We seem to prefer sweet-tasting food. Normally such substances are rich in carbohydrates and hence in calories.

. . . A protection against damage of the teeth is prevented by a reaction to acoustical stimuli. Sharp, screeching noises release this reaction whether we bite on a hard object or scrape with a knife on a plate, which in some persons is felt as pain and projected into the teeth. The reaction consists of pulling the cheeks between the teeth and performing cleaning movements with the tongue. [. . .]

A basis of inborn releasing mechanisms may account for the effectiveness and appeal of the highest artistic expressions. In music rhythm undoubtedly plays a large role and various physiological rhythms can be brought into phase with a metronome even in animals. All of our close primate relatives display by hitting resounding objects. Drums are among the oldest musical instruments of man, and as war drums they still serve the functions of threat display. This is true also of some other typical noise-producing instruments (horns) which are used to intimidate in place of shouting. There are strong indications favouring the hypothesis that we innately recognize particular melodies as touching, charming, soothing, and so on. We describe melodies by likening them to typically inborn vocalizations such as sobbing or joyous shouting. Tender or rumbling sounds stand for the linguistic expression of tender or angry words. Tender words resemble higher notes and we know that even little girls raise their voices when they

Fig. 5 Many people misunderstand a camel's expression. Man has an innate releasing mechanism which responds to the relative position of the camel's eyes to his nose; only in man does this mean an 'arrogant turning away'. We therefore consider the camel to be an aloof animal. In the eagle the bony ridge above the eyes is seen as a wrinkling of the forehead. Together with the pulled-back corners of the mouth the expression is one of 'proud decisiveness'. (From K. Lorenz 1956.)

talk to a little baby. The shrill vocalizations of an angry person are universally understood and we find them uncomfortable. [...]

When we examine our music we discover that composers use these key stimuli intuitively to evoke various emotions in the listener – think for a moment of the rumbling drums of Beethoven's Fifth Symphony. The releasing stimuli are artfully encoded and lose much of their flashy obtrusiveness, which is a characteristic of popular music that is largely produced for commercial purposes. Because of this coding of key stimuli it also takes awhile before one is able 'to listen one's self into the music', so to speak. By the artistic manipulation of the releasing stimuli the composer can create and dissolve tensions in the listener. The highs and lows of emotional experiences are touched in an ever-changing pattern that cannot be experienced in everyday life. This heightening of experiences is perhaps one of the most important effects of music. It is most certainly not the only component of artistic, musical creation, but it seems to be a substantial one. ...

Inborn releasing mechanisms also seem to determine our need for cover and unobstructed vision into the distance. Persons who have had no fateful experiences with others or with predatory animals occupy corner and wall tables first in a restaurant, the tables in the centre last. Children feel comfortable in niches and like to build such cover when they play. [...]

Quite remarkable finally is K. Lorenz's view (1943) that a number of releasing stimulus situations which affect our ethical value judgments are outlined by innate releasing mechanisms. In the art and literature of all peoples there are recurring themes, sensational clichés: loyalty of friends, manly courage, love of homeland, love of wife or husband, love of children and parents – all are the noble basic motives of human actions that we follow from an inner disposition. They are the basic themes (Leitmotive) of literature and the theatre from the ancient world to this day. We are gripped by the account of the friend who sacrifices himself for his fellow, and we identify with the hero of the legend or the western movie who liberates and protects the innocent girl or helpless child. ...

I do not imply that we have to follow every 'inner' value judgment. We mentioned that animals carry along historic burdens – structure that evolved during phylogeny – which by the changing environmental situations have become maladaptive. The appendix in man, which caused many deaths in former centuries, is one example. In the same way we can consider some of our preprogrammed ethical 'values' as being outdated. We mentioned, for example, that there is a strong conformity pressure in groups of men, and outsiders are reacted to strongly, a pattern found all over the world – even in recent times. Throughout history people have reacted emotionally against deviants and minorities, and demagogues justified this as a 'sound popular instinct'. Needless to say, this is maladaptive. We have furthermore reached a level of consciousness that makes us realize that those different from us are nonetheless basically the same and that the diversity constitutes the particular beauty of mankind. We have therefore to curb our archaic intolerance by encouraging this level of consciousness and taking advantage of our deeply rooted drive to bond. [...]

We have sketched a rough framework into which human social behaviour has been placed by phylogenetic adaptation. These adaptations consist less of rigid behaviour patterns and more of innate motivations and learning dispositions. We mentioned drumming and the phallic display as examples. Both dispositions are probably basic drives and innate releasing mechanisms – adaptations on the receptor side that allow the recognition of the biologically adequate signal and thus shape the activity of people in principle. The detachment of these territorial displays from rigid motor patterns allows, however, a greater range of expression. Man does not need to sit guard the way other primates do but may carve statues instead and thus create symbols. Learning dispositions allow a wider range of freedom. Despite a basic similarity, this leads to a multiplicity of cultural modifications of human social behaviour, where each culture and subculture developed their rites in diverging ways. Once formed, they are as rigid as phylogenetically developed rites. Just as the phylogenetically evolved rites of animals control the inborn motivations, so cultural rites do this in man, and for this reason they are just as important for an orderly life together in groups (K. Lorenz 1966). To gloss over them as just so much 'cultural whitewash' – as a sort of superficial varnish – is basically wrong. Our inborn mechanisms are insufficient to control our drives. They became secondarily reduced during the course of phylogenesis and were replaced by cultural control patterns. This is a gain in adaptive modifiability, because various patterns of culture could be developed that made possible the exploitation of various habitats. An Eskimo does require different patterns for the control of his sexual or aggressive impulses from a modern city dweller of central Europe or the United States. Cultural control patterns can also be changed more quickly along with a change in living conditions, but in all cases they are indispensable for social communal life and man is, as A. Gehlen aptly remarked in this case, a cultural creature by nature.

The cultural rites are probably often developed upon the basis of innate learning dispositions. To examine these questions along ethological lines is a most attractive task for us in the future. We recall the greeting ceremonies, which contain basic components despite the multiplicity of expressions, which all serve the function of appeasement. This holds for the various forms of making presents when entering a strange house, making an inaugural visit, and so on, and for the various forms of symbolic submission such as bowing, concealment of aggression-releasing characteristics, removal of weapons and armour, and similar behaviour. However, in a greeting there is also a distinct display component. One shows the partner who one is, and a firm handshake is already a mutual taking stock of one another, one could say a ritualized tournament, and it is distinctly unpleasant when the other presents his hand in such a way that one cannot properly return his grip when shaking hands. Greetings with displays are seen during state visits. The gun salute is a form of ritualized aggression; it is a demonstration just like the parade of troops in honour of the guest. However, that these forms of greeting are also intended to be friendly is shown by presentation of arms. The response of the greeted person also follows according to rules that have not been investigated further. If he is of high rank and the greeter of lower rank, the former may place his arm protectively around the shoulder or symbolically on the head of the greeter. Persons of equal rank frequently put their arms around each other. [...]

References

AHRENS, R. (1953) 'Beitrag zur Entwicklung des Physiognomie- und Mimikerkennens', *Z. Exptl. Angew. Psychol.*, **2**, 412–54, 599–633.

BERELSON, B. and STEINER, G. A. (1964) *Human Behavior* New York, Harcourt.

BILZ, R. (1940) *Pars pro toto: Ein Beitrag zur Pathologie menschlicher Affekte* Leipzig, Thieme.

BIRDWHISTELL, R. L. (1963) 'The kinesis level in the investigation of the emotions' in Knapp, P. H. (ed.) *Expressions of the Emotions in Man* New York, International University Press.

BIRDWHISTELL, R. L. (1966) 'Communications without words' in Alexandre, P. (ed.) *L'Aventure Humaine* Paris.

EIBL-EIBESFELDT, I. (1968) 'Zur Ethologie des menschlichen Grussverhaltens, I: Beobachtungen an Balinesen, Papuas und Samoanern nebst vergleichenden Bemerkungen', *Z. Tierpsychol*, **25**, 727–44.

EIBL-EIBESFELDT, I. and EIBL-EIBESFELDT, E. (1968) 'Die Parasitenabwehr der Minima-Arbeiterinnen der Blattschneiderameise *Atta cephalotes*', *Z. Tierpsychol.*, **24**, 279–81.

EIBL-EIBESFELDT, I. and HASS, H. (1959) 'Erfahrungen mit Haien', *Z. Tierpsychol.*, **16**, 733–46.

EIBL-EIBESFELDT, I. and HASS, H. (1968) 'Zum Projekt einer ethologisch orientierten Untersuchung menschlichen Verhaltens', *Mitt. Max-Planck-Ges.*, **6**, 383–96.

EIBL-EIBESFELDT, I. and HASS, H. (1967) 'Neue Wege der Humanethologie', *Homo*, **18**, 13–23.

EIBL-EIBESFELDT, I. and WICKLER, W. (1968) 'Die ethologische Deutung einiger Wächterfiguren auf Bali', *Z. Tierpsychol.*, **25**, 719–26.

GEHLEN, A. (1940) *Der Mensch, seine Natur und seine Stellung in der Welt* Berlin.

GEHLEN, A. (1956) *Urmensch und Spätkultur* Bonn.

HASS, H. (1968) *Wir Menschen* Wien, Molden.

HEWES, G. H. (1957) 'The anthropology of posture', *Sci. Am.*, **196**, no. 2, 123–32.

HÖRMANN, L. V. (1912) 'Genuss- und Reizmittel in den Ostalpen, eine volkskundliche Skizze', *Z. Deut. Oesterr. Alpenver*, **43**, 78–100.

HÜCKSTEDT, B. (1965) 'Experimentelle Untersuchungen zum "Kindchenschema" ', *Z. Exptl. Angew. Psychol.*, **12**, 421–50.

KOHTS, N. (1935) 'Infant ape and human child (instincts, emotions, play, habits)', *Sci. Mem. Mus. Darwinianum*, **3** (with Russian and English summaries).

KRAFFT-EBING, R. V. (1924) *Psychopathia sexualis, 17th edition* Stuttgart.

LORENZ, K. (1943) 'Die angeborene Formen möglicher Erfahrung', *Z. Tierpsychol.*, **5**, 235–409.

LORENZ, K. (1966) 'Stames – und kulturgeschichtliche Ritenbildung', *Mitt. Max-Planck-Ges.*, **1**, 3–30 and *Naturwiss. Rundschau*, **19**, 361–70.

OHM, T. (1948) *Die Gebetsgebärden der Völker und das Christentum.*

PEIPER, A. (1951) 'Instinkt und angeborenes Schema beim Säugling', *Z, Tierpsychol.*, **8**, 449–56.

PEIPER, A. (1953) 'Schreit- und Steigbewegungen beim Neugeborenen', *Arch. Kinderheilkde.*, **147**, 135.

PLOOG, D. W., BLITZ, J. and PLOOG, F. (1963) 'Studies on social and sexual behaviour of the squirrel monkey (*Saimiri sciureus*)', *Folia Primat.*, 29–66.

PRECHTEL, H. F. R. and SCHLEIDT, W. M. (1950) 'Auslösende und steuernde Mechanismen des Sangaktes', *Vergleich. Physiol.*, **32**, 256–62.

PRECHTL, H. F. R. (1955) 'Die Entwicklung der frühkindlichen Motorik, I–III', *Wiss. Filme, C 651, C 652, C 653* Göttingen (Inst. wiss. Film).

SCHULTZ, J. H. (1966) *Organstörungen und Perversionen im Liebesleben* Munich, E. Reinhardt.

SPITZ, R. A. and WOLF, K. M. (1946) 'The smiling response: a contribution to the ontogenesis of social relations', *Gen. Psychol. Monogr.*, **34**, 57–125.

THOMPSON, J. (1941) 'Development of facial expression of emotion in blind and seeing children', *Arch. Psychol. N. Y.*, **264**, 1–47.

WICKLER, W. (1966c) 'Ursprung und biologische Deutung des Genital präsentierens männlicher Primaten', *Z Tierpsychol.*, **23**, 422–37.

Section 3
Language

Introduction

Language is of unique interest to anyone concerned with social behaviour. It is a key feature of human interaction and the medium by which the most complex information can be conveyed. It is of critical importance in the transmission of cultural influence and in our learning about the world around us. It is very much a human attribute. On present evidence, only one other species – chimpanzees – has shown any real capacity for communicating by language and this has been achieved only after intensive training and at a relatively rudimentary level. Other species can communicate, of course, but not by means of language. Language has certain key characteristics. Roger Brown discusses these in the first extract in this section. As he also points out, both biological factors and learning opportunities appear to be essential for the development of language occur.

The biological propensities necessary for language acquisition provide the theme of the second paper by Eric Lenneberg. This paper was first published in 1964, and some aspects of it are now outdated. The statement 'there is no evidence that any nonhuman form has the capacity to acquire even the most primitive stages of language development' (p. 91) is belied by the papers by Gardner and Gardner included as the final contributions in this section. Nevertheless, Lenneberg's argument is of value. Although language is clearly not species-specific as he supposed, his argument that language acquisition does depend on a specific and genetically influenced form of neural organization is not undermined by the Gardners' results. And after all, chimpanzees are among the species most closely related phylogenetically to man.

The two papers by Gardner and Gardner are reports of their fascinating efforts to teach sign language to chimpanzees. The first paper is particularly interesting for the details it provides of decisions that had to be made about the procedures used in setting up and developing the research programme. It also throws into relief something of the nature of the achievements involved when a child acquires language skills. Since this paper was published, Washoe has continued to acquire more symbols and has displayed a capacity to both comprehend and use spontaneously more complex and often original constructions. Although she is not now with the Gardners, she is still a research subject. She has been placed with other chimpanzees who have also been taught sign language and the interactions between them are being studied. The Gardners themselves are continuing their research work with other subjects and with modified procedures. Their most recent work is described in the second paper.

The papers in this section focus on certain aspects of language only – in particular its key characteristics and biological basis. They should be read in conjunction with section 11 on Communication. The contributions there emphasize for example, that the precise form a language takes and the different meanings ascribed to an utterance, even among speakers of what is ostensibly the same language, are very much dependent on social influence and context. They also make the point that language itself is but one component of human communication.

11 Language: the system and its acquisition

Roger Brown

Every known human society has a language and no animal society has one. This is not to say that animals do not communicate with one another. The male stickleback is able to communicate his claim on a territory and his readiness to defend its boundaries. The worker honeybee can communicate to other workers the location of a nectar source, the distance of the source from the hive and the source's direction. Chimpanzees in the wild employ gestures and calls to summon, threaten and alert one another (Goodall 1963). Most animal species have some means of communication. What they do not have is the technology of communication called language.

Language is defined by certain design features (Hockett 1958) which taken together make it possible for a creature with limited powers of discrimination and a limited memory to transmit and understand an infinite variety of messages, and to do this in spite of noise and distraction. If we imagine ourselves to have been assigned the task of designing a communication system that will transmit infinitely many meanings, we will see something of the value of the features that define language.

We might undertake to provide a brief unique sound for each message or meaning. Suppose the message were the one that English encodes as *She is preparing dinner*. It would be easy enough to provide a single distinctive grunt or whistle for this total message. That is the way communication problems are solved among the animals. However, we cannot solve them so in our system. The number of messages to be communicated is very greatly in excess of the number of distinct sounds humans can identify.

We would do better to design on the phonemic principle which is the principle all languages follow. This means beginning with a stock of elementary sounds which are called *phonemes* in descriptive linguistics. Phonemes are, for the most part, vowels and consonants, and they correspond roughly to the letters of an alphabetic writing system. Phonemes are not themselves meaningful; they are semantically empty. No language uses very many. The range in the languages of the world is from about fifteen to about eighty-five, with English using forty-five. Probably the number

---

BROWN, ROGER (1965) 'Language: The system and its acquisition' in *Social Psychology* New York, The Free Press, 246–50.

is small because it is advantageous to use only sounds that can be easily produced and identified. By making sequential arrangements of the phonemes, larger units, very much more numerous than the elementary ones, can be constructed. The larger units are called *morphemes* in descriptive linguistics and are similar to, but not the same as, words. With forty-five phonemes one can build the 100,000 or so morphemes of an ordinary college dictionary of American English without making any sequence very long. Morphemes are not semantically empty; each one has a meaning.

We might build our stock of morphemes by combining the elementary sounds in all possible ways up to some limit of length. If the morphemes used up all possible combinations of phonemes, then a change of a single phoneme, any single vowel or consonant, would always constitute a new morpheme. The transmission and identification of morphemes in such a language would be a precarious business. Any elementary error, such as might easily be caused by noise or distraction, would result in the reception of an unintended morpheme and so of an unintended meaning. Natural languages never do use all possible combinations of phonemes. There are always restraints on combination. English, for example, sometimes uses a cluster of consonants to begin a morpheme, but the language does not permit every conceivable cluster to be used in this way. Of the many thousand possible combinations of one, two, or three consonants, fewer than one hundred are actually employed. As a consequence of such restraints a message may be considerably distorted without being mistakenly identified. If we saw *Shx is pxeparxing dinnxr* we probably would know what was intended. This is, in part, because the combinations with *x* do not constitute English morphemes. They would be morphemes if all possible combinations were used.

From our 45 phonemes, let us imagine that we have created 100,000 morphemes. By some estimates highly educated people learn to recognize and understand as many as this, though it is a rare person who *produces* more than about 10,000 different ones (Miller 1951). These are large numbers but something short of the infinite set of messages the system is required to be able to convey. The number of distinct signals can be enormously increased, indeed infinitely increased, if we will allow the creation of morpheme sequences, the creation of sentences. In twenty years or so of life, humans do well to learn to produce and understand 100,000 morphemes or words. How do they ever become competent to produce and understand an infinite number of sentences? The relation between a word or morpheme and its meaning is arbitrary and so has to be memorized. Knowledge that *dinner* is the name of a certain meal does not enable anyone to guess the meaning of the word *preparing*. However, the relation between a sentence and its meaning is not arbitrary in this way. Sentences are built by rule. If anyone knows the meaning of the constituent morphemes of *She is preparing dinner* and knows also certain rules concerning subject–object relations and the formation of the present tense and progressive aspect, he can work out the sense of the sentence. The meanings of sentences can in general be derived from the meanings of the morphemes, in conjunction with knowledge of grammatical constructions and the meanings of these constructions. There is not an infinite variety of morphemes or of grammatical constructions but only of the sentences that can be derived from both together.

The design features of our communications system may be summarized and generalized as follows: Fewer than one hundred sounds which are individually meaningless are compounded, not in all possible ways, to produce some hundreds of thousands of meaningful morphemes, which have meanings that are arbitrarily assigned, and these morphemes are combined by rule to yield an infinite set of sentences, having meanings that can be derived. All of the systems of communication called languages have these design features. [...]

Not every human brain is adequate for the acquisition of a language. Total mass may play some role. Nowhere in the world does the newborn infant begin at once to imitate the speech it hears. Children everywhere in the world start to babble recognizable vowels and consonants some time in the first year and begin to produce words early in the second year. By about the middle of the second year they start to make two-word sentences. By the end of the third year children use a large part of the basic grammatical apparatus of the local language. Lenneberg believes that this worldwide timetable is governed by biological development.

The neonate's brain is likely to weigh about as much as the brain of a full-grown chimpanzee. It is not until three years that the child's brain approximates adult norms in size, weight, and fissuration. In addition to the growth of the brain there are peripheral biological developments that contribute to a readiness for speech. With the end of the nursing period the suckling pads in the cheeks of the infant are absorbed and his oral cavity takes on a shape more like that of the adult. By the end of the first year he usually acquires some front teeth which provide articulatory surfaces for the tongue in the production of such dental consonants as the initial sound in *thin*.

Biology is critical for language acquisition but learning opportunities also matter. It occasionally happens that a child is discovered living in isolation, hidden away in an attic or cellar, usually an illegitimate child, fed quickly and surreptitiously by its mother. One such child, Isabelle, was found in a house in Ohio, secluded from contact with everyone but a deaf-mute mother (Davis 1940). Isabelle was six and a half at the time of her rescue and had apparently been isolated since birth. She had no speech and made only a croaking noise. Isabelle was given good care and training, and, in a week's time, began to vocalize. Two years after rescue, at the age of eight and a half, it is reported that Isabelle's speech could not easily be distinguished from the speech of other children of the same age (Davis 1947). Human children, like Isabelle, who live outside of any speech community, do not invent language, but require a community to provide it.

Learning opportunities may also be responsible for the fact that working-class children lag behind middle-class children on almost any index of speech development (Templin 1957). Irwin has shown, for instance, that middle-class children talk more and produce a greater variety of vowels and consonants from about eighteen months on. This difference may be partly a matter of innate ability since there are consistent IQ differences favouring children of higher SES. However, Irwin (1960) has shown that learning opportunities are also important. In order to increase the amount of speech exposure in the homes of working-class families he induced the mothers of a group of children from thirteen to thirty months of age to read to them daily for a period of fifteen minutes from illustrated baby books. A second group of children of comparable ages in working-class homes in which no systematic stimulation occurred served as the control. After the age of eighteen months the experimental group was significantly superior in the frequency with which speech sounds were produced.

Beginning at about eighteen to twenty-four months maturation and learning opportunities ordinarily come together in a way that makes it possible to acquire a system for the communication of an infinite variety of messages. What are the uses of such a system? The obvious uses are the social ones. Information that one person possesses can be delivered to others who do not have it but could use it. This kind of transmission is possible between generations as well as among contemporaries, and so, with the emergence of language, life experiences begin to be cumulative. Some animal species are able to transmit a small amount of lore across generations; chiefly knowledge of waterholes, feeding places, and the habits of enemies (Wynne-Edwards 1962). But most of what the aged anthropoid knows perishes with him. The young chimpanzee starts life, as he did millennia ago, from scratch. [...]

References

DAVIS, K. (1940) 'Extreme social isolation of a child', *American Journal of Sociology*, **45**, 554–65.

DAVIS, K. (1947) 'Final note on a case of extreme social isolation', *American Journal of Sociology*, **52**, 432–7.

GOODALL, JANE (1963) 'My life among wild chimpanzees', *National Geographic*, **124**, no. 2, 272–308.

HOCKETT, C. F. (1958) *A course in modern linguistics* New York, Macmillan.

IRWIN, O. C. (1960) 'Language and communication' in Mussen, P. H. (ed.) *Handbook of research methods in child development* New York, Wiley.

MILLER, G. A. (1951) *Language and Communication* New York, McGraw-Hill.

TEMPLIN, MILDRED C. (1957) *Certain language skills in children: Their development and interrelationships* Minneapolis, University of Minnesota Press.

WYNNE-EDWARDS, V. C. (1962) *Animal dispersion in relation to social behaviour* Edinburgh and London, Oliver and Boyd.

12 A biological perspective of language

Eric H. Lenneberg

The relevance of biology

At first it may seem as if biology had little to add to our knowledge of speech and language beyond the general and somewhat vague comparison of human communication with animal communication. I would like here to raise the question of whether there might not be biological endowments in man that make the human forms of communication uniquely possible for our species.

The chief reasons for suspecting such specific biological propensities for our ability to acquire language are these:

1 *Anatomic and physiologic correlates.* There is increasing evidence that verbal behaviour is related to a great number of morphological and functional specializations such as oropharyngeal morphology (DuBrul, 1958); cerebral dominance (Ajuriaguerra 1957, Mountcastle 1962); specialization of cerebrocortical topography; special coordination centres (or foci) for motor speech; specialized temporal pattern perception; special respiratory adjustment and tolerance for prolonged speech activities; and a long list of sensory and cognitive specializations prerequisite for language perception.[1]

2 *Developmental schedule.* The onset of speech is an extremely regular phenomenon, appearing at a certain time in the child's physical development and following a fixed sequence of events, as if all children followed the same general 'strategy' from the time they begin to the period at which they have mastered the art of speaking (Lenneberg 1964, Morley 1957, Weir 1962). The first things that are learned are principles – not items: principles of categorization and pattern perception. The first words refer to classes, not unique objects or events. The sounds of language and the configuration of words are at once perceived and reproduced according to principles; they are patterns in time, and they never function as randomly strung up items. From the beginning, very general principles of

1 More detailed treatment of this and the following point may be found in my book, *The Biological Foundation of Language*, 1967, New York, John Wiley.

LENNEBERG, ERIC H. (1964) 'A biological perspective of language' in Lenneberg, Eric H. (ed.) *New Directions in the Study of Language* Cambridge, Massachusetts, MIT Press, 65–88.

semantics and syntax are manifest. Even if the maturational scale as a whole is distorted through retarding disease, the order of developmental milestones, including onset of speech, remains invariable (Lenneberg, Nichols and Rosenberger 1964). Onset and accomplishment of language learning do not seem to be affected by cultural or linguistic variations.

3 *Difficulty in suppressing language.* The ability to learn language is so deeply rooted in man that children learn it even in the face of dramatic handicaps. Congenital blindness has no obvious effect on word acquisition even though there is only a small fraction of words whose referents can be defined tactually. Congenital deafness has a devastating effect on the vocal facilitation for speech, yet presentation of written material enables the child to acquire language through a graphic medium without undue difficulties. Children suffering from gross and criminal parental neglect, or who have parents who have no spoken language whatever, as in the case of adult congenitally deaf parents, may nevertheless learn to speak with only a minimal delay, if any, according to research now in progress.

4 *Language cannot be taught.* There is no evidence that any nonhuman form has the capacity to acquire even the most primitive stages of language development. The vocalization skills and the behavioural responses to verbal commands that we find in a few species can be shown to bear merely a superficial resemblance to human verbal behaviour. In each case it can be demonstrated that their behaviour is based on fundamentally different principles from those in humans. The difference is not merely a quantitative one but apparently a qualitative one (Lenneberg 1962b). No one has demonstrated that a subhuman form can acquire the principles of speech perception in terms of phonemic analysis, of understanding the syntactic structure of a sentence, or imparting the total semantic domain of any word, be it concrete or abstract.

5 *Language universals.* Although language families are so different, one from the other, that we cannot find any historical connection between them, every language, without exception, is based on the same *universal principles* of semantics, syntax and phonology. All languages have words for relations, objects, feelings and qualities, and the semantic differences between these denotata are minimal from a biological point of view. According to a number of modern grammarians (Chomsky 1957, Greenberg 1963, Hartmann 1961, Hjelmslev 1953) working quite independently of each other, syntax of every language shows some basic, formal properties, or, in other words, is always of a peculiar algebraic type. Phonologically, all languages are based on a common principle of phonematization even though there are phonemic divergences.

Language universals are the more remarkable as the speakers live in vastly different types of cultures ranging from an essentially neolithic type to the highly complex cultural systems of Western civilization. Further, language and its complexity is independent of racial variation. It is an axiom in linguistics that any human being can learn any language in the world. Thus, even though there are differences in physical structure, the basic skills for the acquisition of language are as universal as bipedal gait.

Owing to these considerations, it becomes plausible to hypothesize that language is a species-specific trait, based on a variety of biologically given mechanisms. Our task for the future is to discover and describe these mechanisms in greater detail than has been attempted so far.

This formulation poses three major problems which I shall now attempt to deal with:

1 Is uniqueness of behaviour or form acceptable in the light of evolution?
2 Is there evidence for a genetic basis of language propensity?
3 Is language propensity a simple consequence of a general increase in 'intellectual capacity', or must we assume some 'language-specific' correlates?

Uniqueness of species characteristics

The discovery of a unique behavioural trait in a species need not mystify us, first, because we have been made aware by ethologists that speciation affects not only anatomy but also behaviour, and that there are countless species with unique behaviour patterns, and second, because uniqueness is to be expected from the evolutionary process itself.

There are two main processes in evolution: (1) cladogenesis, i.e. the process of branching out into newer and newer species; and (2) anagenesis or phyletic evolution, i.e. the process by which an entire species gradually undergoes change over time. If a given species fails to split up into isolated populations for a long period of time (or if only one of the newly resulting species survives), an animal with relatively unique traits will emerge. If the species has undergone anagenetic evolution, it will further deepen the gap between itself and its next of kin. According to Dobzhansky (1962), man's recent history is marked primarily by anagenesis; extinction of more closely related species has also taken place, as shown in figure 1.

The fact that man communicates with man is not a unique zoological phenomenon. Most animals have inter- and intraspecies communication systems, and among mammals there is usually vocal communication. However, the behavioural traits of animal communication cannot be ordered like a genetic tree and the phylogenetic relations among vertebrates, de-

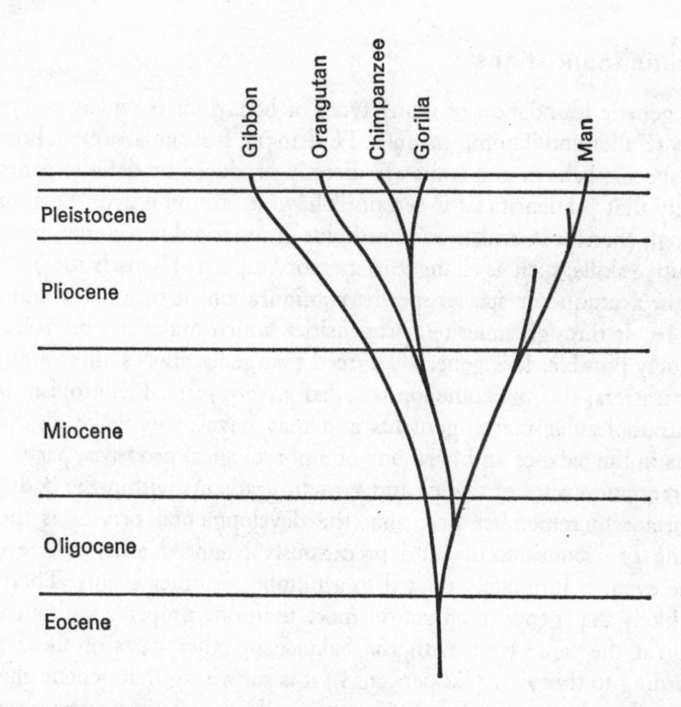

Fig. 1 Schema of the evolution of the *Hominoidea.*

rived from comparative morphology, are not reflected in the taxonomy of their communication behaviour. Many species have evolved highly specialized communication systems, such as the honeybee, many bird species, and dolphins. Neither these systems nor a dog's response to human commands represent primitive stages of human communication. Nor is there evidence that the communication of monkeys and apes constitutes a gradual approximation towards language. The empirically determined primitive beginnings of language in man (in the 18-months-old infant or in feeble-minded individuals) are behaviourally very different from the signals that animals emit for each other. Many animal communication systems are probably evolutionary offshoots, as is man's, and cross-species comparisons must be carried out with great caution.

Genetic foundations

The genetic foundation of many types of behaviour is widely recognized today (Fuller and Thompson 1960, Hall 1951). It is not assumed, however, that specific behavioural traits are directly produced by definite genes, but merely that propensities for certain behaviour are inherited. This may be through changes in sensitivity thresholds or inherited perceptual, motor, or cognitive skills, such as changes in memory capacity (Rensch 1954). Nevertheless, a unique or species-specific configuration of thresholds and skills may result through inherited propensities which make specific behaviour uniquely possible. It is generally agreed that genes always affect a number of characters; this phenomenon is called *pleiotropism*. Pleiotropism is due to intramolecular rearrangements and may have in its wake disarrangements in the balance and harmony of embryological processes, particularly differentiation rates of tissues and growth gradients within the body. It is important to remember here that the developmental process is the unfolding of a continuously and precariously balanced affair where every single event is intimately related to a number of other events. Therefore, it is likely that genes often act on more than one property without interfering at the same time with the balance in other parts of the system. According to this view (Caspari 1958), it is surprising that genetic changes are possible that are confined, phenotypically, to relatively circumscribed phenomena or, to put it differently, that, despite the frequent small changes that occur in the genotype, many characteristics of a species remain so completely stable.

Caspari explains the resistance of many characteristics to genetic change by postulating a gradient of 'protection' against pleiotropic action. Thus, certain traits may be better established or more deeply rooted than others. Those that are well established tend to remain unaffected, even if genetic change has brought about thorough transfiguration of form and function in an individual. If, on the other hand, a given trait is not well protected, it is liable to change whenever there is any genetic disturbance interfering with the original state of balance. This is called polygenic inheritance, i.e. many different gene actions are capable of bringing about a given condition. Fertility is an example of polygenic inheritance in that it is very easily altered; most mutations are likely to affect it.

How do these concepts apply to language? The familial occurrence of language disabilities has been observed since the beginning of medicine. In recent years many reliable and careful studies have been published (Drew 1956, Eustis 1947, Gallagher 1950, Hallgren 1950, Luchsinger 1959, Orton 1930, Pfaendler 1960), and the entire literature has been reviewed

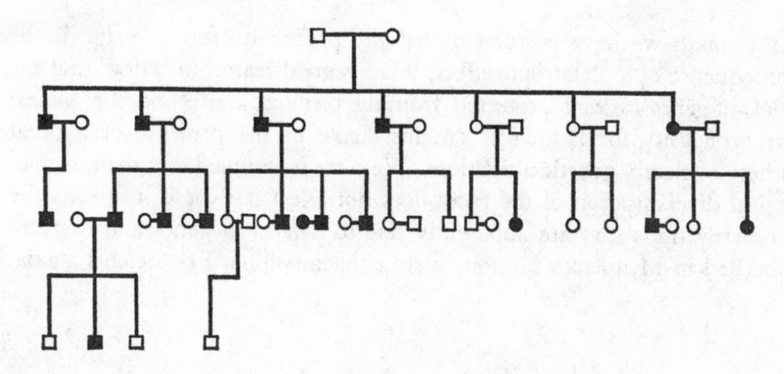

Fig. 2 Pedigree of a family with hereditary specific language disability. Circles are females; squares are males. Presence of trait is shown as solid symbols. (Brewer 1963.)

by Brewer (1963). On the basis of a carefully controlled and objective investigation of an entire family with congenital language disability (fig. 2), Brewer concludes that 'specific language disability is a dominant, sex-influenced, or partially sex-linked trait with almost complete penetrance'. In cases such as Brewer's there is never a total absence of language but merely a combination of certain deficits, including markedly delayed onset of speech, poor articulation persisting into the teens, poorly established hand preference, marked reading difficulties, either complete inability or marked difficulty for acquisition of second languages. Intelligence is usually not affected.

More direct evidence for the genetic basis of language comes from the work of Moorhead, Mellman, and Wenar (1961) who have made chromosome counts of a family in which a mother (fig. 3) and four of her five children had a chromosomal abnormality associated with varying degrees of mental retardation and a striking failure of speech development. The father and a fifth sibling had a normal chromosome picture and were not affected behaviourally. Unfortunately, chromosome studies are too recent a development to have produced a large literature as yet. But it may be expected that in at least some families with specific language disability chromosome studies will eventually become available.

An important question that arises, especially from the Moorhead et al. study, is whether *any* chromosome abnormality is likely to lower intelligence and interfere with language. This is definitely not so. Some chromosome abnormalities are associated with somatic deficits without affecting intelligence, and other chromosome abnormalities affect intelligence but not necessarily language.

Although we have postulated that the propensity for language is the consequence of a pleiotropic effect, there is good reason to believe that the relevant genes are well 'protected' from the pleiotropic effect of other genes; the propensity for language remains stable in the presence of a great variety of clearly genetic alterations. We have mentioned that the morphological diversification of the races does not affect it. Nor is it affected by the many traits that are apparently due to defects in genes and that are inherited in Mendelian fashion, such as haemophilia, Friedreich's ataxia,

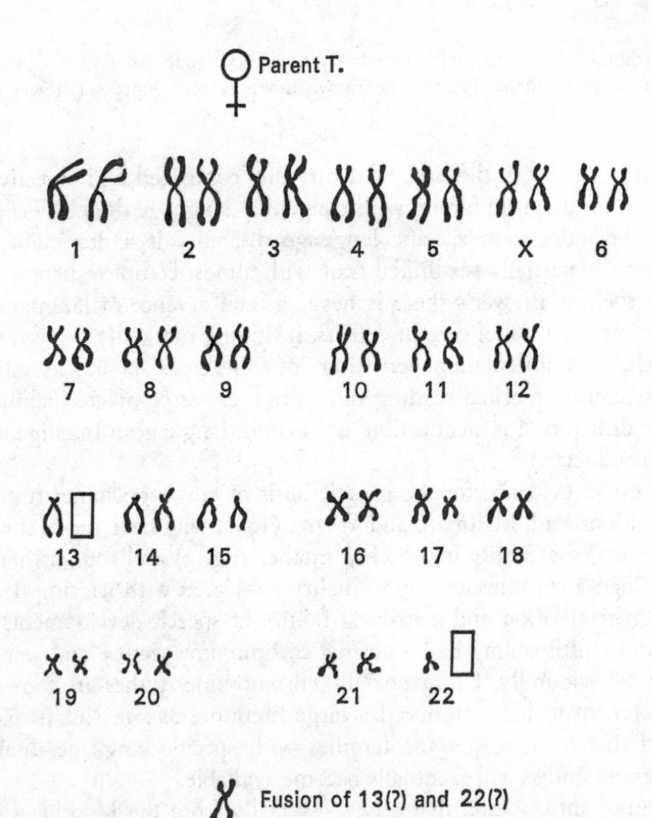

Fig. 3 Abnormal chromosome picture of woman with low intelligence and disproportionately poor speech and language. She gave birth to four children with similar chromosomal and clinical abnormalities. There is an unmatched chromosome which is interpreted as a fusion of missing chromosomes 13 and 22. Approximate enlargement 1200X. (From Moorhead et al. 1961.)

Huntington's chorea, etc. Thus the inheritance for the propensity of language deficits is not polygenic.

On the other hand, there is an inherited error of metabolism producing a disease known as histidinaemia which has in its wake a very high incidence of specific disturbance of language development in children, often without affecting their intelligence or other behavioural traits (Ghadimi, Partington, and Hunter 1961, 1962, Auerbach et al. 1962).

This is the extent of our evidence to date. It poses the interesting question whether proof of language disturbance on a genetic basis is also evidence for the genetic basis of language *ability*. Perhaps so, but more work will have to be done before we can be relatively certain. In any event, evolution and genetics appear to be relevant to the general study of verbal behaviour.

General or specific capacity

Nothing is gained by labelling the propensity for language as *biological* unless we can use this insight for new research directions – unless more specific correlates can be uncovered. At the present time we are merely able to pinpoint certain biological problems and thereby to reopen some questions about language that were falsely thought to have been answered. For instance, it is often assumed that the propensity for language is simply a reflection of man's great non-specific intelligence. And as evidence for a 'phylogenetic increase in intelligence', man's brain-weight/body-weight ratio is cited with the implication that the relative increase in neurons has made a certain level of intellect possible for language development. Both of these assumptions run into serious difficulties.

The definition and measurement of intelligence is difficult enough in our own species. When it comes to comparing different species, it is no longer permissible to talk about intelligence as if it were a single, clear-cut property that can be measured by a single objective instrument so as to yield quantities that are commensurable across species. Attempts have been made to compare across species such functions as memory span (Rensch 1954), peceptual processes (Teuber 1960), problem solving (Köhler 1925), and others. In most of these instances, tasks are administered that are relatively easy for humans and more difficult for animals. On the other hand, tasks have been described in which various animals respond more quickly, with greater accuracy and, in a sense, more efficiently. Thus comparative psychology shows man to have a different mentation from other species and, obviously, a greater capacity to do things human. But we do not have objective and biologically meaningful proof that all mammals are endowed with a homogeneous and nonspecific amount of intelligence and that this amount increases with phylogenetic proximity to man.

Even if species could be compared in terms of general (surplus) intelligence and man could be shown to possess more of this quantity than any other creature, we still could not be certain that his ability for language is the result of, say, general inventiveness. Might it not be possible that language ability – instead of being the consequence of intelligence – is its cause? This has indeed been suggested by such thinkers as Hamann, Herder, W. v. Humboldt, Cassirer, and implied by Hughlings Jackson, Wundt, Whorf, Penfield, and many others before and since them. This proposition, which has been criticized for a number of reasons (Black 1959, Feuer 1953, Greenberg 1954, Lenneberg, 1953, 1954, 1962a, Révész 1954), is important in one respect: it suggests that language might be of greater biological antiquity than the peculiar intellective processes of recent man. Nevertheless, I do not advocate the notion that language is the cause of intelligence because there is no way of verifying this hypothesis. Instead, I would like to propose a *tertium quid*, namely, that the ability to acquire language is a biological development that is relatively independent of that elusive property called intelligence. I see evidence for this view in the fact that children acquire language at a time when their power of reasoning is still poorly developed and that the ability to learn to understand and speak has a low correlation with measured IQ in man. Let me elaborate on this latter point.

In a recent study Lenneberg, Nichols, and Rosenberger (1964) studied the language development of 84 feeble-minded children raised by their own parents in a normal home environment. The basic results are represented diagrammatically in figure 4. IQ figures, as measured by standard instruments, deteriorate with chronological age in the mentally retarded, even though there is objective growth in mental age up to the early teens, after which time mental development is arrested.

Language begins in the same manner in retardates as in the normal population. We found that it is impossible to train a child with, say, mongolism to parrot a complicated sentence if he has not yet learned the underlying principles of *syntax*. However, the general principle underlying *naming* is grasped at once and immediately generalized. Naming behaviour may be observed even in low-grade idiots; only individuals so retarded as to be deficient in stance, gait, and bowel control fail to attain this lowest stage of language acquisition. . . . Children whose IQ is 50 at age 12 and about 30 at age 20 are completely in possession of language though their articulation may be poor and an occasional grammatical mistake may occur.

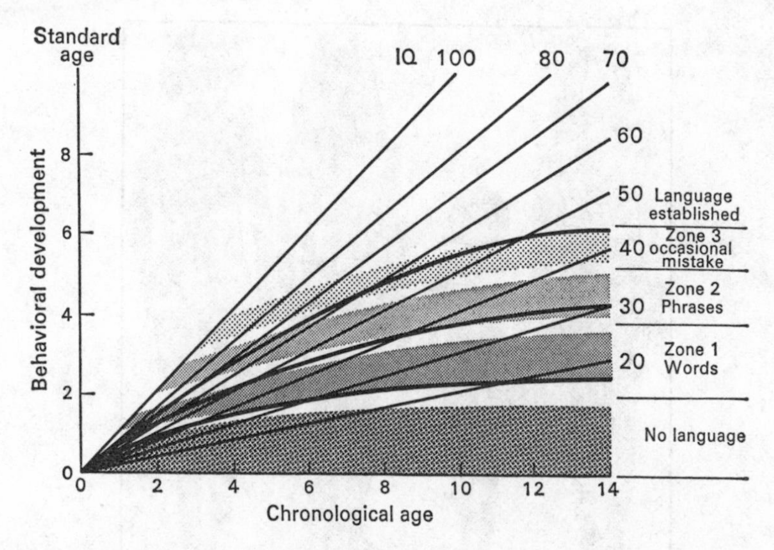

Fig. 4 Relationship between speech development and IQ. The curved lines show empirically determined 'decay rates' of IQ in the mentally retarded. The shadings indicate language development. An individual whose IQ at a given age falls in the dark area at the bottom has no language. If he falls into the lighter areas, he is in one of three stages of language development and will develop further until his early teens, his progress depending upon both his IQ and his age. If he falls into the white area above, he is in full command of language. After age 12 to 13, speech development 'freezes'. (Data based on a follow-up study of 61 mongoloids and 23 children with other types of retarding disease.)

Thus, grossly defective intelligence need not implicate language; nor does the *absence* of language necessarily lower cognitive skills. For instance, congenitally deaf children have in many parts of the world virtually no language or speech before they receive instruction in school. When these preschoolers are given nonverbal tests of concept formation they score as high as their age peers who hear (Furth 1961, Rosenstein 1960, Oléron 1957). From these examples it appears that language and intelligence are to some extent at least independent traits. In order to prove their complete independence it would be necessary to show that there are congenitally aphasic children whose nonverbal intelligence is unimpaired and who are also free from psychiatric disease. Many authorities believe that these cases exist, though in my experience I have not had occasion to examine such a patient. I have, however, studied one child (Lenneberg 1962b) who had a congenital disability for articulation, who could not

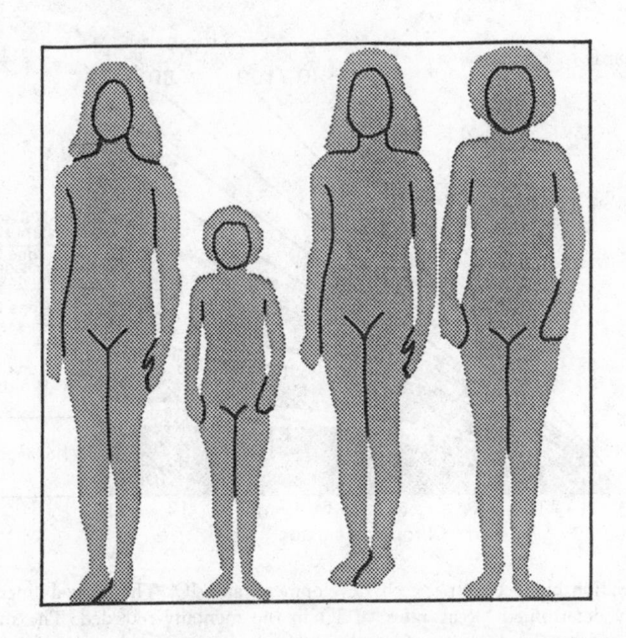

Fig. 5 Left: Body outline of nanocephalic dwarf next to normal girl of same age (9 years); right: the dwarf's outline enlarged to show that bodily proportions are roughly similar to those of the normally developing girl. (Redrawn from Sechel 1960.)

utter any intelligible word, but who did acquire the ability to understand language. Many other similar cases are familiar to me, constituting evidence that there is at least a highly particularly motor skill in man which may be selectively impaired by both discrete lesions and inherited defect.

Let us now return to man's brain-weight/body-weight ratio. Because of our difficulty in defining the phenomenon of intelligence zoologically, we shall circumvent the problem of the relationship of brain size and intellective power. Let us ask directly whether a large brain is the morphological prerequisite for language learning. Would it be possible to learn to understand or to speak a natural language such as English with a brain the size of some nonspeaking animal? The answer is *yes* but only if the individual is of the species *Homo sapiens*. This may sound like a contradiction in terms. Yet there is a clinical condition, first described by the German pathologist Virchow and named by him *nanocephalic dwarfism* (bird-headed dwarfs in the English-speaking world) in which man appears reduced to fairy-tale size. Seckel (1960) has recently described two such dwarfs and has reviewed the scientific literature on thirteen others. He ascribes the condition to a single-locus recessive gene for dwarfish stature without affecting endocrine organs and function. Adult individuals attain a maximum height of 3 feet, and about half of the described patients stand not much higher than 2½ feet at adult age; the shortest adult mentioned measured 23 inches.

Nanocephalic dwarfs differ from other dwarfs in that they preserve the skeletal proportions of normal adults, as illustrated in figure 5; the fully mature have a brain-body weight well within the limits of a young teenager. Yet their head circumference and estimated brain weight barely exceed those of a newborn infant, as shown in figure 6. On microscopic examination these brains have an unremarkable histological appearance; both the size of individual nerve cells and the density of their distribution is within normal limits. Therefore we do not have here miniatured adult brains, but brains that differ very substantially from those of normal

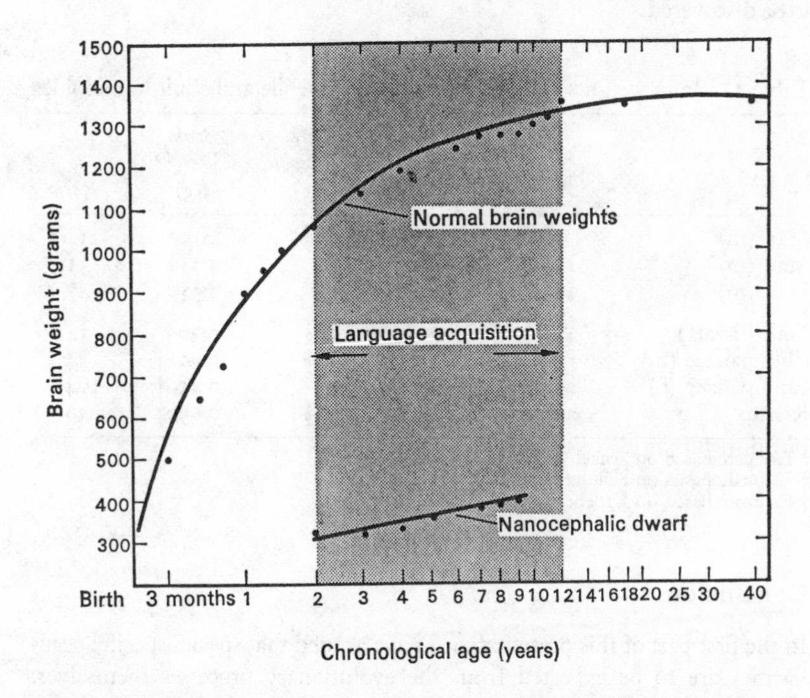

Fig. 6 Children's brain weights determined at autopsy plotted as a function of chronological age (based on data by Coppoletta and Wolbach 1932). Bottom plot: various estimated weights based on repeated measurements of head circumference of patient shown in Fig. 5. The extrapolations were made by comparing autopsied children's head circumference with their brain weight.

adults in the absolute number of cells. Intellectually, these dwarfs for the most part show some retardation, often not surpassing a mental age level of 5 to 6 years. All of them acquire the rudiments of language, including speaking and understanding, and the majority master the verbal skills at least at well as a normal 5-year-old child. From Table 1 it is apparent that neither the absolute nor relative weights of brains and bodies reveal the nature of the relationship between speech and its neurological correlates. Apparently the ability to speak is not dependent upon nonspecific increase in cell number or anything as general as brain-weight/body-weight ratios. Instead of postulating a quantitative parameter as the critical variable for the ability to acquire language, we should look towards much more specific modes of internal organization of neurophysiological processes. At present we do not know what they might be. But man's developmental and maturational history suggests that growth processes and functional lateralization are involved (Lenneberg, in press), the physical nature of which remains to be discovered.

Table 1 Brain weights and body weights of juvenile and adult hominoidea

	Age	*Speech Faculty*	*Body Weight (Kg)*	*Brain Weight (Kg)*	*Ratio*
Man (m)	2½	beginning	13½	1·100	12·3
Man (m)	13½	yes	45	1·350	35
Man (m)	18	yes	64	1·350	47
Man (dwarf)	12	yes	13½	0·400*	34
Chimpanzee (m)	3	no	13½	0·400†	34
Chimpanzee (f)	adult	no	47	0·450†	104
Rhesus	adult	no	3½	0·090‡	40

* Estimate based on Seckel (1960).
† Estimate based on Schultz (1941).
‡ Estimate based on Kroeber (1948).

Conclusion

In the first part of this presentation I have argued that species-specific peculiarities are to be expected from the evolutionary processes themselves. Therefore, language specialization need not mystify us. In the second part I have tried to show that the basis for language capacity might well be transmitted genetically. In the last section I have rejected the notion that man's ability to speak is due to such general properties as an increase in intelligence or a relative increase in the weight of his brain. It seems, rather, as if language is due to as yet unknown species-specific biological capacities.

In conclusion I wish to emphasize that all these considerations serve to establish an hypothesis and to stimulate new directions for research on the nature of man. However, the facts presented do not constitute a theory. Let us hope they will lead to one in the future.

References

AJURIAGUERRA, J. DE (1957) 'Langage et dominance cérébrale', *J. franç. d'Oto-Rhino-Laryngol.*, **6**, 489–99.

AUERBACH, V., DIGEORGE, A., BALDRIDGE, R., TOURTELLOTTE, C., and BRIGHAM, M. (1962) 'Histidinemia: A deficiency in histidase resulting in the urinary excretion of histidine and of imidazolepyruvic acid', *J. Pediatr.*, **60**, 487–97.

BLACK, M. (1959) 'Linguistic relativity: The views of Benjamin Lee Whorf', *Phil. Rev.*, **68**, 228–38.

BREWER, W. F. (1963) 'Specific language disability: Review of the literature and a family study', Honours thesis, Harvard University.

CASPARI, E. (1958) 'Genetic basis of behavior' in Roe, A. and Simpson, G. G. (eds.) *Behavior and evolution* New Haven, Yale University Press.

CHOMSKY, N. (1957) *Syntactic structures* The Hague, Mouton.

COPPOLETTA, J. M., and WOLBACH, S. B. (1932) 'Body length and organ weights of infants and children', *Amer. J. Pathol.*, **9**, 55–70.

DOBZHANSKY, T. (1962) *Mankind evolving* New Haven, Yale University Press.

DREW, A. L. (1956), 'A neurological appraisal of familial congenital word-blindness', *Brain*, **79**, 440–60.

DUBRUL, E. L. (1958) *Evolution of the speech apparatus* Springfield, Illinois, Thomas.

EUSTIS, R. S. (1947) 'The primary etiology of the specific language disabilities', *J. Pediatr.*, **31**, 448–55.

FEUER, L. S. (1953) 'Sociological aspects of the relation between language and psychology', *Phil. Sci.*, **20**, 85–100.

FULLER, J. L., and THOMPSON, W. R. (1960) *Behavior genetics* New York, John Wiley.

FURTH, H. (1961) 'The influence of language on the development of concept formation in deaf children', *J. abnorm. soc. Psychol.*, **63**, 386–9.

GALLAGHER, J. R. (1950) 'Specific language disability: A cause for scholastic failure', *New Engl. J. Med.*, **242**, 436–40.

GHADIMI, H., PARTINGTON, M., and HUNTER, A. (1961). 'A familial disturbance of histidine metabolism', *New Eng. J. Med.*, **265**, 221–4.

GHADIMI, J. R., PARTINGTON, M., and HUNTER, A. (1962) 'Inborn error of histidine metabolism', *Pediatrics*, **29**, 714–28.

GREENBERG, J. H. (1954) 'Concerning influences from linguistic to non-linguistic data' in Hoijer, H. (ed.) *Language in culture* Chicago, University of Chicago Press.

GREENBERG, J. H. (ed.) (1963) *Universals of language* Cambridge, Massachusetts, MIT Press.

HALL, C. S. (1951) 'The genetics of behavior' in Stevens, S. S. (ed.) *Handbook of experimental psychology* New York, John Wiley.

HALLGREN, B. (1950) 'Specific dyslexia (congenital word-blindness)', *Acta psychiatr. neurol. scand.*, Suppl. 65.

HARTMANN, P. (1961) 'Allgemeinste Strukturgesetze' in *Sprache und Grammatik* The Hague, Mouton.

HJELMSLEV, L. (1953) *Prolegomena to a theory of language* Indiana University Publications in Anthropology and Linguistics, Memoir 7, Baltimore, Waverly Press.

KÖHLER, W. (1925) *The mentality of apes* New York, Harcourt, Brace.

KROEBER, A. L. (1948) *Anthropology* New York, Harcourt, Brace.

LENNEBERG, E. (1935) 'Cognition in ethnolinguistics', *Language*, **29**, 463–71.

LENNEBERG, E. (1954) 'A note on Cassirer's *Philosophy of Language*', *Phil. phenomenol. Res.*, **15**, 512–22.

LENNEBERG, E. (1961) 'Language, evolution and purposive behaviour' in Diamond, S. (ed) *Culture in history* New York, Columbia University Press.

LENNEBERG, E. (1962a) 'The relationship of language to the formation of concepts', *Synthèse*, **14**, no. 2/3, 103–9.

LENNEBERG, E. (1962b) 'Understanding language without ability to speak: A case report', *J. abnorm. soc. Psychol.*, **65**, 419–25.

LENNEBERG, E. (1964) 'Speech as a motor skill with special reference to non-aphasic disorders' in Bellugi, U. and Brown, R. (eds) 'The acquisition of language', *Child Developm. Monogr.*, **29**, 115–126.

LENNEBERG, E. (in press) 'Speech development: Its anatomical and physiological concomitants' in Hall, V. E. (ed.) *Speech, language and communication. Brain and Behaviour*.

LENNEBERG, E. H., NICHOLS, I. A., and ROSENBERGER, E. F. (1964) 'Primitive stages of language development in mongolism', *Proc. Assoc. Res. nerv. ment. Disease*, **42**, 119–37.

LUCHSINGER, R. (1959) 'Die Vererbung von Sprach und Stimmstoerungen', *Folia phoniatr.*, **11**, 7–64.

MOORHEAD, P. S., MELLMAN, W. J. and WENAR, C. (1951) 'A familial chromosome translocation associated with speech and mental retardation', *Amer. J. hun. Genet.*, **13**, 32–46.

MORLEY, M. (1957) *The development and disorders of speech in childhood* Baltimore, William and Wilkins.

MOUNTCASTLE, V. B. (ed.) (1962) *Interhemispheric relations and cerebral dominance* Baltimore, Johns Hopkins University Press.

OLDRON, P. (1957) *Recherches sur le developpement mental des sourdes muets* Paris, Centre National de la Recherche Scientifique.

ORTON, S. T. (1930) 'Familial occurrence of disorders in the acquisition of language', *Eugenics*, 3, no. 4, 140–7.

PFAENDLER, U. (1960) 'Les vices de la parole dans l'optique du généticien', *Akt. Probl. der Phoniatr. und Logopaed*, 1, 35–40.

RENSCH, B. (1954) *Neuere Probleme der Abstammungslehre* Stuttgart.

RÉVÉSZ, G. (1954) 'Denken und Sprechen' in Révész, G. (ed.), *Thinking and Speaking: A symposium* Amsterdam, North Holland.

ROSENSTEIN, J. (1960) 'Cognitive abilities of deaf children', *J. Speech Hearing Res.*, 3, 108–19.

SCHULTZ, A. H. (1941) 'The relative size of the cranial capacity in primates', *Amer. J. Anthropol*, 28, 273–87.

SECKEL, H. P. G. (1960) *Birdheaded dwarfs: Studies in developmental anthropology including human proportions* Springfield, Illinois, Thomas.

TEUBER, H. L. (1960) 'Perception' in Field, J., Magoun, H. W. and Hall, V. E. (eds) *Handbook of physiology*, Section 1: Neurophysiology, Vol. III. Washington, D.C. American Physiological Society.

WEIR, R. H. (1962) *Language in the crib* The Hague, Mouton.

13 Teaching sign language to a chimpanzee

R. Allen Gardner and Beatrice T. Gardner

The extent to which another species might be able to use human language is a classical problem in comparative psychology. One approach to this problem is to consider the nature of language, the processes of learning, the neural mechanisms of learning and of language, and the genetic basis of these mechanisms, and then, while recognizing certain gaps in what is known about these factors, to attempt to arrive at an answer by dint of careful scholarship.[1] An alternative approach is to try to teach a form of human language to an animal. We chose the latter alternative and, in June 1966, began training an infant female chimpanzee, named Washoe, to use the gestural language of the deaf. Within the first 22 months of training it became evident that we had been correct in at least one major aspect of method, the use of a gestural language. Additional aspects of method have evolved in the course of the project. These and some implications of our early results can now be described in a way that may be useful in other studies of communicative behaviour. Accordingly, in this article we discuss the considerations which led us to use the chimpanzee as a subject and American Sign Language (the language used by the deaf in North America) as a medium of communication; describe the general methods of training as they were initially conceived and as they developed in the course of the project; and summarize those results that could be reported with some degree of confidence by the end of the first phase of the project.

Preliminary considerations

The chimpanzee as a subject

Some discussion of the chimpanzee as an experimental subject is in order because this species is relatively uncommon in the psychological laboratory. Whether or not the chimpanzee is the most intelligent animal after man can be disputed; the gorilla, or orang-utan, and even the dolphin have their loyal partisans in this debate. Nevertheless, it is generally conceded that chimpanzees are highly intelligent, and that members of this species might be intelligent enough for our purposes. Of equal or greater importance is

---

GARDNER, R. ALLEN and GARDNER, BEATRICE T. (1969) 'Teaching sign language to a chimpanzee' in *Science*, vol. 165, 664–72.

their sociability and their capacity for forming strong attachments to human beings. We want to emphasize this trait of sociability; it seems highly likely that it is essential for the development of language in human beings, and it was a primary consideration in our choice of a chimpanzee as a subject.

Affectionate as chimpanzees are, they are still wild animals, and this is a serious disadvantage. Most psychologists are accustomed to working with animals that have been chosen, and sometimes bred, for docility and adaptability to laboratory procedures. The difficulties presented by the wild nature of an experimental animal must not be underestimated. Chimpanzees are also very strong animals; a full-grown specimen is likely to weigh more than 120 pounds (55 kilograms) and is estimated to be from three to five times as strong as a man, pound-for-pound. Coupled with the wildness, this great strength presents serious difficulties for a procedure that requires interaction at close quarters with a free-living animal. We have always had to reckon with the likelihood that at some point Washoe's physical maturity will make this procedure prohibitively dangerous.

A disadvantage is that human speech sounds are unsuitable as a medium of communication for the chimpanzee. The vocal apparatus of the chimpanzee is very different from that of man.[2] More important, the vocal behaviour of the chimpanzee is very different from that of man. Chimpanzees do make many different sounds, but generally vocalization occurs in situations of high excitement and tends to be specific to the exciting situations. Undisturbed, chimpanzees are usually silent. Thus, it is unlikely that a chimpanzee could be trained to make refined use of its vocalizations. Moreover, the intensive work of Hayes and Hayes[3] with the chimpanzee Viki indicates that a vocal language is not appropriate for this species. The Hayeses used modern, sophisticated, psychological methods and seem to have spared no effort to teach Viki to make speech sounds. Yet in 6 years Viki learned only four sounds that approximated English words.[4]

Use of the hands, however, is a prominent feature of chimpanzee behaviour; manipulatory mechanical problems are their forte. More to the point, even caged, laboratory chimpanzees develop begging and similar gestures spontaneously,[5] while individuals that have had extensive contact with human beings have displayed an even wider variety of communicative gestures.[6] In our choice of sign language we were influenced more by the behavioural evidence that this medium of communication was appropriate to the species than by anatomical evidence of structural similarity between the hands of chimpanzees and of men. The Hayeses point out that human tools and mechanical devices are constructed to fit the human hand, yet chimpanzees have little difficulty in using these devices with great skill.

Nevertheless, they seem unable to adapt their vocalizations to approximate human speech.

Psychologists who work extensively with the instrumental conditioning of animals become sensitive to the need to use responses that are suited to the species they wish to study. Lever-pressing in rats is not an arbitrary response invented by Skinner to confound the mentalists; it is a type of response commonly made by rats when they are first placed in a Skinner box. The exquisite control of instrumental behaviour by schedules of reward is achieved only if the original responses are well chosen. We chose a language based on gestures because we reasoned that gestures for the chimpanzee should be analogous to bar-pressing for rats, key-pecking for pigeons, and babbling for humans.

American sign language

Two systems of manual communication are used by the deaf. One system is the manual alphabet, or finger spelling, in which configurations of the hand correspond to letters of the alphabet. In this system the words of a spoken language, such as English, can be spelled out manually. The other system, sign language, consists of a set of manual configurations and gestures that correspond to particular words or concepts. Unlike finger spelling, which is the direct encoding of a spoken language, sign languages have their own rules of usage. Word-for-sign translation between a spoken language and a sign language yields results that are similar to those of word-for-word translation between two spoken languages: the translation is often passable, though awkward, but it can also be ambiguous or quite nonsensical. Also, there are national and regional variations in sign languages that are comparable to those of spoken languages.

We chose for this project the American Sign Language (ASL), which, with certain regional variations, is used by the deaf in North America. This particular sign language has recently been the subject of formal analysis.[7] The ASL can be compared to pictograph writing in which some symbols are quite arbitrary and some are quite representational or iconic, but all are arbitrary to some degree. For example, in ASL the sign for 'always' is made by holding the hand in a fist, index finger extended (the pointing hand), while rotating the arm at the elbow. This is clearly an arbitrary representation of the concept 'always'. The sign for 'flower', however, is highly iconic; it is made by holding the fingers of one hand extended, all five fingertips touching (the tapered hand), and touching the fingertips first to one nostril then to the other, as if sniffing a flower. While this is an iconic sign for 'flower', it is only one of a number of conventions by which the concept 'flower' could be iconically represented: it is thus arbitrary to some degree. Undoubtedly, many of the signs of ASL that seem quite arbitrary today once had an iconic origin that was lost through years of stylized usage. Thus, the signs of ASL are neither uniformly arbitrary nor uniformly iconic; rather the degree of abstraction varies from sign to sign over a wide range. This would seem to be a useful property of ASL for our research.

The literate deaf typically use a combination of ASL and finger spelling; for purposes of this project we have avoided the use of finger spelling as much as possible. A great range of expression is possible within the limits of ASL. We soon found that a good way to practice signing among ourselves was to render familiar songs and poetry into signs; as far as we can judge, there is no message that cannot be rendered faithfully (apart from the usual problems of translation from one language to another). Technical terms and proper names are a problem when first introduced, but within any community of signers it is easy to agree on a convention for any commonly used term. For example, among ourselves we do not finger-spell the words *psychologist* and *psychology*, but render them as 'think doctor' and 'think science'. Or, among users of ASL, 'California' can be finger-spelled but is commonly rendered as 'golden playland'. (Incidentally, the sign for 'gold' is made by plucking at the earlobe with thumb and forefinger, indicating an earring – another example of an iconic sign that is at the same time arbitrary and stylized.)

The fact that ASL is in current use by human beings is an additional advantage. The early linguistic environment of the deaf children of deaf parents is in some respects similar to the linguistic environment that we could provide for an experimental subject. This should permit some comparative evaluation of Washoe's eventual level of competence. For example, in discussing Washoe's early performance with deaf parents we have been told that many of her variants of standard signs are similar to the baby-talk variants commonly observed when human children sign.

Washoe

Having decided on a species and a medium of communication, our next concern was to obtain an experimental subject. It is altogether possible that there is some critical early age for the acquisition of this type of behaviour. On the other hand, newborn chimpanzees tend to be quite helpless and vegetative. They are also considerably less hardy than older infants. Nevertheless, we reasoned that the dangers of starting too late were much greater than the dangers of starting too early, and we sought the youngest infant we could get. Newborn laboratory chimpanzees are very scarce, and we found that the youngest laboratory infant we could get would be about 2 years old at the time we planned to start the project. It seemed preferable to obtain a wild-caught infant. Wild-caught infants are usually at least 8 to 10 months old before they are available for research. This is because infants rarely reach the United States before they are 5 months old, and to this age must be added 1 or 2 months before final purchase and 2 or 3 months for quarantine and other medical services.

We named our chimpanzee Washoe for Washoe County, the home of the University of Nevada. Her exact age will never be known, but from her weight and dentition we estimated her age to be between 8 and 14 months at the end of June 1966, when she first arrived at our laboratory. (Her dentition has continued to agree with this initial estimate, but her weight has increased rather more than would be expected.) This is very young for a chimpanzee. The best available information indicates that infants are completely dependent until the age of 2 years and semi-dependent until the age of 4; the first signs of sexual maturity (for example, menstruation, sexual swelling) begin to appear at about 8 years, and full adult growth is reached between the ages of 12 and 16.[8] As for the complete life-span, captive specimens have survived for well over 40 years. Washoe was indeed very young when she arrived; she did not have her first canines or molars, her hand-eye coordination was rudimentary, she had only begun to crawl about, and she slept a great deal. Apart from making friends with her and adapting her to the daily routine, we could accomplish little during the first few months.

Laboratory conditions

At the outset we were quite sure that Washoe could learn to make various signs in order to obtain food, drink, and other things. For the project to be a success, we felt that something more must be developed. We wanted Washoe not only to ask for objects but to answer questions about them and also to ask us questions. We wanted to develop behaviour that could be described as conversation. With this in mind, we attempted to provide Washoe with an environment that might be conducive to this sort of behaviour. Confinement was to be minimal, about the same as that of human infants. Her human companions were to be friends and playmates as well as providers and protectors, and they were to introduce a great many games and activities that would be likely to result in maximum interaction with Washoe.

In practice, such an environment is readily achieved with a chimpanzee; bonds of warm affection have always been established between Washoe and her several human companions. We have enjoyed the interaction almost as much as Washoe has, within the limits of human endurance. A number of human companions have been enlisted to participate in the project and relieve each other at intervals, so that at least one person would be with Washoe during all her waking hours. At first we feared that such frequent changes would be disturbing, but Washoe seemed to adapt very well to this procedure. Apparently it is possible to provide an infant chimpanzee with affection on a shift basis.

All of Washoe's human companions have been required to master ASL and to use it extensively in her presence, in association with interesting activities and events and also in a general way, as one chatters at a human infant in the course of the day. The ASL has been used almost exclusively, although occasional finger spelling has been permitted. From time to time, of course, there are lapses into spoken English, as when medical personnel must examine Washoe. At one time, we considered an alternative procedure in which we would sign and speak English to Washoe simultaneously, thus giving her an additional source of informative cues. We rejected this procedure, reasoning that, if she should come to understand speech sooner or more easily than ASL, then she might not pay sufficient attention to our gestures. Another alternative, that of speaking English among ourselves and signing to Washoe, was also rejected. We reasoned that this would make it seem that big chimps talk and only little chimps sign, which might give signing an undesirable social status.

The environment we are describing is not a silent one. The human beings can vocalize in many ways, laughing and making sounds of pleasure and displeasure. Whistles and drums are sounded in a variety of imitation games, and hands are clapped for attention. The rule is that all meaningful sounds, whether vocalized or not, must be sounds that a chimpanzee can imitate.

Training methods

Imitation

The imitativeness of apes is proverbial, and rightly so. Those who have worked closely with chimpanzees have frequently remarked on their readiness to engage in visually guided imitation. Consider the following typical comment of Yerkes[9]: 'Chim and Panzee would imitate many of my acts, but never have I heard them imitate a sound and rarely make a sound peculiarly their own in response to mine. As previously stated, their imitative tendency is as remarkable for its specialization and limitations as for its strength. It seems to be controlled chiefly by visual stimuli. Things which are seen tend to be imitated or reproduced. What is heard is not reproduced. Obviously an animal which lacks the tendency to reinstate auditory stimuli – in other words to imitate sounds – cannot reasonably be expected to talk. The human infant exhibits this tendency to a remarkable degree. So also does the parrot. If the imitative tendency of the parrot could be coupled with the quality of intelligence of the chimpanzee, the latter undoubtedly could speak.'

In the course of their work with Viki, the Hayeses devised a game in which Viki would imitate various actions on hearing the command 'Do this'.[10] Once established, this was an effective means of training Viki to perform actions that could be visually guided. The same method should be admirably suited to training a chimpanzee to use sign language; accordingly we have directed much effort towards establishing a version of the 'Do this' game with Washoe. Getting Washoe to imitate us was not difficult, for she did so quite spontaneously, but getting her to imitate on command has been another matter altogether. It was not until the 16th month of the project that we achieved any degree of control over Washoe's imitation of gestures. Eventually we got to a point where she would imitate a simple gesture, such as pulling at her ears, or a series of such gestures – first we make a gesture, then she imitates, then we make a second gesture, she imitates the second gesture, and so on – for the reward of being tickled. Up to this writing, however, imitation of this sort has not been an important method for introducing new signs into Washoe's vocabulary.

As a method of prompting, we have been able to use imitation extensively to increase the frequency and refine the form of signs. Washoe sometimes fails to use a new sign in an appropriate situation, or uses another, incorrect sign. At such times we can make the correct sign to Washoe, repeating the performance until she makes the sign herself. (With more stable signs, more indirect forms of prompting can be used – for example, pointing at, or touching, Washoe's hand or a part of her body that should be involved in that sign; making the sign for 'sign', which is equivalent to saying 'Speak up'; or asking a question in signs such as 'What do you want?' or 'What is it?') Again, with new signs, and often with old signs as well, Washoe can lapse into what we refer to as poor 'diction'. Of course, a great deal of slurring and a wide range of variants are permitted in ASL as in any spoken language. In any event, Washoe's diction has frequently been improved by the simple device of repeating, in exaggeratedly correct form, the sign she has just made, until she repeats it herself in more correct form. On the whole, she has responded quite well to prompting, but there are strict limits to its use with a wild animal – one that is probably quite spoiled, besides.

Pressed too hard, Washoe can become completely diverted from her original object; she may ask for something entirely different, run away, go into a tantrum, or even bite her tutor.

Chimpanzees also imitate, after some delay, and this delayed imitation can be quite elaborate.[10] The following is a typical example of Washoe's delayed imitation. From the beginning of the project she was bathed regularly and according to a standard routine. Also, from her 2nd month with us, she always had dolls to play with. One day, during the 10th month of the project, she bathed one of her dolls in the way we usually bathed her. She filled her little bathtub with water, dunked the doll in the tub, then took it out and dried it with a towel. She has repeated the entire performance, or parts of it, many times since, sometimes also soaping the doll.

This is a type of imitation that may be very important in the acquisition of language by human children, and many of our procedures with Washoe were devised to capitalize on it. Routine activities – feeding, dressing, bathing, and so on – have been highly ritualized, with appropriate signs figuring prominently in the rituals. Many games have been invented which can be accompanied by appropriate signs. Objects and activities have been named as often as possible, especially when Washoe seemed to be paying particular attention to them. New objects and new examples of familiar objects, including pictures, have been continually brought to her attention, together with the appropriate signs. She likes to ride in automobiles, and a ride in an automobile, including the preparations for a ride, provides a wealth of sights that can be accompanied by signs. A good destination for a ride is a home or the university nursery school, both well stocked with props for language lessons.

The general principle should be clear: Washoe has been exposed to a wide variety of activities and objects, together with their appropriate signs, in the hope that she would come to associate the signs with their referents and later make the signs herself. We have reason to believe that she has come to understand a large vocabulary of signs. This was expected, since a number of chimpanzees have acquired extensive understanding vocabularies of spoken words, and there is evidence that even dogs can acquire a sizable understanding vocabulary of spoken words.[11] The understanding vocabulary that Washoe has acquired, however, consists of signs that a chimpanzee can imitate.

Some of Washoe's signs seem to have been originally acquired by delayed imitation. A good example is the sign for 'toothbrush'. A part of the daily routine has been to brush her teeth after every meal. When this routine was first introduced Washoe generally resisted it. She gradually came to submit with less and less fuss, and after many months she would even help or sometimes brush her teeth herself. Usually, having finished her meal, Washoe would try to leave her high-chair; we would restrain her, signing 'First toothbrushing, then you can go'. One day, in the 10th month of the project, Washoe was visiting the Gardner home and found her way into the bathroom. She climbed up on the counter, looked at our mug full of toothbrushes, and signed 'toothbrush'. At the time, we believed that Washoe understood this sign but we had not seen her use it. She had no reason to ask for the toothbrushes, because they were well within her reach, and it is most unlikely that she was asking to have her teeth brushed. This was our first observation, and one of the clearest examples of behaviour in which Washoe seemed to name an object or an event for no obvious motive other than communication.

Following this observation, the toothbrushing routine at mealtime was altered. First, imitative prompting was introduced. Then as the sign became more reliable, her rinsing-mug and toothbrush were displayed prominently until she made the sign. By the 14th month she was making the 'toothbrush' sign at the end of meals with little or no prompting; in fact she has called for her toothbrush in a peremptory fashion when its appearance at the end of a meal was delayed. The 'toothbrush' sign is not merely a response cued by the end of a meal; Washoe retained her ability to name toothbrushes when they were shown to her at other times.

The sign for 'flower' may also have been acquired by delayed imitation. From her first summer with us, Washoe showed a great interest in flowers, and we took advantage of this by providing many flowers and pictures of flowers, accompanied by the appropriate sign. Then one day in the 15th month she made the sign, spontaneously, while she and a companion were walking towards a flower garden. As in the case of 'toothbrush', we believed that she understood the sign at this time, but we had made no attempt to elicit it from her except by making it ourselves in appropriate situations. Again, after the first observation, we proceeded to elicit this sign as often as possible by a variety of methods, most frequently by showing her a flower and giving it to her if she made the sign for it. Eventually the sign became very reliable and could be elicited by a variety of flowers and pictures of flowers.

It is difficult to decide which signs were acquired by the method of delayed imitation. The first appearance of these signs is likely to be sudden and unexpected; it is possible that some inadvertent movement of Washoe's has been interpreted as meaningful by one of her devoted companions. If the first observer were kept from reporting the observation and from making any direct attempts to elicit the sign again, then it might be possible to obtain independent verification. Quite understandably, we have been more interested in raising the frequency of new signs than in evaluating any particular method of training.

Babbling

Because the Hayeses were attempting to teach Viki to speak English, they were interested in babbling, and during the first year of their project they were encouraged by the number and variety of spontaneous vocalizations that Viki made. But, in time, Viki's spontaneous vocalizations decreased further and further to the point where the Hayeses felt that there was almost no vocal babbling from which to shape spoken language. In planning this project we expected a great deal of manual 'babbling', but during the early months we observed very little behaviour of this kind. In the course of the project, however, there has been a great increase in manual babbling. We have been particularly encouraged by the increase in movements that involve touching parts of the head and body, since these are important components of many signs. Also, more and more frequently, when Washoe has been unable to get something that she wants, she has burst into a flurry of random flourishes and arm-waving.

We have encouraged Washoe's babbling by our responsiveness; clapping, smiling, and repeating the gesture much as you might repeat 'goo goo' to a human infant. If the babbled gesture has resembled a sign in ASL, we have made the correct form of the sign and have attempted to engage in some appropriate activity. The sign for 'funny' was probably acquired in this way. It first appeared as a spontaneous babble that lent itself readily to a simple imitation game – first Washoe signed 'funny' then we did, then she did, and so on. We would laugh and smile during the interchanges that she initiated, and initiate the game ourselves when something funny happened. Eventually Washoe came to use the 'funny' sign spontaneously in roughly appropriate situations.

Closely related to babbling are some gestures that seem to have appeared independently of any deliberate training on our part, and that resemble signs so closely that we could incorporate them into Washoe's repertoire with little or no modification. Almost from the first she had a begging gesture – an extension of her open hand, palm up, towards one of us. She made this gesture in situations in which she wanted aid and in situations in which we were holding some object that she wanted. The ASL signs for 'give me' and 'come' are very similar to this, except that they involve a prominent beckoning movement. Gradually Washoe came to incorporate a beckoning wrist movement into her use of this sign. In Table 1 we refer to this sign as 'come-gimme'. As Washoe has come to use it, the sign is not

Table 1 Signs used reliably by chimpanzee Washoe within 22 months of the beginning of training. The signs are listed in the order of their original appearance in her repertoire (see text for the criterion of reliability and for the method of assigning the date of original appearance).

Signs	*Description*	*Context*
Come-gimme	Beckoning motion, with wrist or knuckles as pivot.	Sign made to persons or animals, also for objects out of reach. Often combined: 'come tickle', 'gimme sweet', etc.
More	Fingertips are brought together, usually overhead. (Correct ASL form: tips of the tapered hand touch repeatedly.)	When asking for continuation or repetition of activities such as swinging or tickling, for second helpings of food, etc. Also used to ask for repetition of some performance, such as a somersault.
Up	Arm extends upward, and index finger may also point up.	Wants a lift to reach objects such as grapes on vine, or leaves; or wants to be placed on someone's shoulders; or wants to leave potty-chair.
Sweet	Index or index and second fingers touch tip of wagging tongue. (Correct ASL form: index and second fingers extended side by side.)	For dessert; used spontaneously at end of meal. Also, when asking for candy.
Open	Flat hands are placed side by side, palms down, then drawn apart while rotated to palms up.	At door of house, room, car, refrigerator, or cupboard; on containers such as jars; and on taps.
Tickle	The index finger of one hand is drawn across the back of the other hand. (Related to ASL 'touch'.)	For tickling or for chasing games.
Go	Opposite of 'come-gimme'.	While walking hand-in-hand or riding on someone's shoulders. Washoe usually indicates the direction desired.
Out	Curved hand grasps tapered hand; then tapered hand is withdrawn upward.	When passing through doorways; until recently, used for both 'in' and 'out'. Also, when asking to be taken outdoors.
Hurry	Open hand is shaken at the wrist. (Correct ASL form: index and second fingers extended side by side.)	Often follows signs such as 'come-gimme', 'out', 'open', and 'go', particularly if there is a delay before Washoe is obeyed. Also, used while watching her meal being prepared.

Table 1 (continued)

Signs	*Description*	*Context*
Hear-listen	Index finger touches ear.	For loud or strange sounds: bells, car horns, sonic booms, etc. Also, for asking someone to hold a watch to her ear.
Toothbrush	Index finger is used as brush, to rub front teeth.	When Washoe has finished her meal, or at other times when shown a toothbrush.
Drink	Thumb is extended from fisted hand and touches mouth.	For water, formula, soda pop, etc. For soda pop, often combined with 'sweet'.
Hurt	Extended index fingers are jabbed toward each other. Can be used to indicate location of pain.	To indicate cuts and bruises on herself or on others. Can be elicited by red stains on a person's skin or by tears in clothing.
Sorry	Fisted hand clasps and unclasps at shoulder. (Correct ASL form: fisted hand is rubbed over heart with circular motion.)	After biting someone, or when someone has been hurt in another way (not necessarily by Washoe). When told to apologize for mischief.
Funny	Tip of index finger presses nose, and Washoe snorts. (Correct ASL form: index and second fingers used; no snort.)	When soliciting interaction play, and during games. Occasionally, when being pursued after mischief.
Please	Open hand is drawn across chest. (Correct ASL form: fingertips used, and circular motion.)	When asking for objects and activities. Frequently combined: 'Please go', 'Out, please', 'Please drink'.
Food-eat	Several fingers of one hand are placed in mouth. (Correct ASL form: fingertips of tapered hand touch mouth repeatedly).	During meals and preparation of meals.
Flower	Tip of index finger touches one or both nostrils. (Correct ASL form: tips of tapered hand touch first one nostril, then the other.)	For flowers.
Cover-blanket	Draws one hand toward self over the back of the other.	At bedtime or naptime, and, on cold days, when Washoe wants to be taken out.
Dog	Repeated slapping on thigh.	For dogs and for barking.
You	Index finger points at a person's chest.	Indicates successive turns in games. Also used in response to questions such as 'Who tickle?' 'Who brush?'

Table 1 (continued)

Signs	*Description*	*Context*
Napkin-bib	Fingertips wipe the mouth region.	For bib, for washcloth, and for Kleenex.
In	Opposite of 'out'.	Wants to go indoors, or wants someone to join her indoors.
Brush	The fisted hand rubs the back of the open hand several times. (Adapted from ASL 'polish'.)	For hairbrush, and when asking for brushing.
Hat	Palm pats top of head.	For hats and caps.
I-me	Index finger points at, or touches, chest.	Indicates Washoe's turn, when she and a companion share food, drink, etc. Also used in phrases, such as 'I drink', and in reply to questions such as 'Who tickle?' (Washoe: 'you'); 'Who I tickle?' (Washoe: 'Me'.)
Shoes	The fisted hands are held side by side and strike down on shoes or floor. (Correct ASL form: the sides of the fisted hands strike against each other.)	For shoes and boots.
Smell	Palm is held before nose and moved slightly upward several times.	For scented objects: tobacco, perfume, sage, etc.
Pants	Palms of the flat hands are drawn up against the body toward waist.	For diapers, rubber pants, trousers.
Clothes	Fingertips brush down the chest.	For Washoe's jacket, nightgown, and shirts; also for our clothing.
Cat	Thumb and index finger grasp cheek hair near side of mouth and are drawn outward (representing cat's whiskers).	For cats.
Key	Palm of one hand is repeatedly touched with the index finger of the other. (Correct ASL form: crooked index finger is rotated against palm.)	Used for keys and locks and to ask us to unlock a door.
Baby	One forearm is placed in the crook of the other, as if cradling a baby.	For dolls, including animal dolls such as a toy horse and duck.
Clean	The open palm of one hand is passed over the open palm of the other.	Used when Washoe is washing, or being washed, or when a companion is washing hands or some other object. Also used for 'soap'.

simply a modification of the original begging gesture. For example, very commonly she reaches forward with one hand (palm up) while she gestures with the other hand (palm down) held near her head. (The result resembles a classic fencing posture.)

Another sign of this type is the sign for 'hurry', which, so far, Washoe has always made by shaking her open hand vigorously at the wrist. This first appeared as an impatient flourish following some request that she had made in signs; for example, after making the 'open' sign before a door. The correct ASL for 'hurry' is very close, and we began to use it often, ourselves, in appropriate contexts. We believe that Washoe has come to use this sign in a meaningful way, because she has frequently used it when she, herself, is in a hurry – for example, when rushing to her nursery chair.

Instrumental conditioning

It seems intuitively unreasonable that the acquisition of language by human beings could be strictly a matter of reiterated instrumental conditioning – that a child acquires language after the fashion of a rat that is conditioned, first, to press a lever for food in the presence of one stimulus, then to turn a wheel in the presence of another stimulus, and so on until a large repertoire of discriminated responses is acquired. Nevertheless, the so-called 'trick vocabulary' of early childhood is probably acquired in this way, and this may be a critical stage in the acquisition of language by children. In any case, a minimal objective of this project was to teach Washoe as many signs as possible by whatever procedures we could enlist. Thus, we have not hesitated to use conventional procedures of instrumental conditioning.

Anyone who becomes familiar with young chimpanzees soon learns about their passion for being tickled. There is no doubt that tickling is the most effective reward that we have used with Washoe. In the early months, when we would pause in our tickling, Washoe would indicate that she wanted more tickling by taking our hands and placing them against her ribs or around her neck. The meaning of these gestures was unmistakable, but since we were not studying our human ability to interpret her chimpanzee gestures, we decided to shape an arbitrary response that she could use to ask for more tickling. We noted that, when being tickled, she tended to bring her arms together to cover the place being tickled. The result was a very crude approximation of the ASL sign for 'more' (see Table I). Thus, we would stop tickling and then pull Washoe's arms away from her body. When we released her arms and threatened to resume tickling, she tended to bring her hands together again. If she brought them back together, we would tickle her again. From time to time we would stop tickling and wait for her to put her hands together by herself. At first, any approximation to the 'more' sign, however crude, was rewarded. Later, we required closer approximations and introduced imitative prompting. Soon, a very good version of the 'more' sign could be obtained, but it was quite specific to the tickling situation.

In the 6th month of the project we were able to get 'more' signs for a new game that consisted of pushing Washoe across the floor in a laundry basket. In this case we did not use the shaping procedure but, from the start, used imitative prompting to elicit the 'more' sign. Soon after the 'more' sign became spontaneous and reliable in the laundry-basket game, it began to appear as a request for more swinging (by the arms) – again, after first being elicited with imitative prompting. From this point on, Washoe transferred the 'more' sign to all activities, including feeding. The transfer was usually spontaneous, occurring when there was some pause in a desired activity or when some object was removed. Often we ourselves were not sure that Washoe wanted 'more' until she signed to us.

The sign for 'open' had a similar history. When Washoe wanted to get through a door, she tended to hold up both hands and pound on the door with her palms or her knuckles. This is the beginning position for the 'open' sign (see Table 1). By waiting for her to place her hands on the door and then lift them, and also by imitative prompting, we were able to shape a good approximation of the 'open' sign, and would reward this by opening the door. Originally she was trained to make this sign for three particular doors that she used every day. Washoe transferred this sign to all doors; then to containers such as the refrigerator, cupboards, drawers, briefcases, boxes, and jars; and eventually – an invention of Washoe's – she used it to ask us to turn on water taps.

In the case of 'more' and 'open' we followed the conventional laboratory procedure of waiting for Washoe to make some response that could be shaped into the sign we wished her to acquire. We soon found that this was not necessary; Washoe could acquire signs that were first elicited by our holding her hands, forming them into the desired configuration, and then putting them through the desired movement. Since this procedure of guidance is usually much more practical than waiting for a spontaneous approximation to occur at a favourable moment, we have used it much more frequently.

Results

Vocabulary

In the early stages of the project we were able to keep fairly complete records of Washoe's daily signing behaviour. But, as the amount of signing behaviour and the number of signs to be monitored increased, our initial attempts to obtain exhaustive records became prohibitively cumbersome. During the 16th month we settled on the following procedure. When a new sign was introduced we waited until it had been reported by three different observers as having occurred in an appropriate context and spontaneously (that is, with no prompting other than a question such as 'What is it?' or 'What do you want?'). The sign was then added to a checklist in which its occurrence, form, context, and the kind of prompting required were recorded. Two such checklists were filled out each day, one for the first half of the day and one for the second half. For a criterion of acquisition we chose a reported frequency of at least one appropriate and spontaneous occurrence each day over a period of 15 consecutive days.

In Table 1 we have listed 30 signs that met this criterion by the end of the 22nd month of the project. In addition, we have listed four signs ('dog', 'smell', 'me', and 'clean') that we judged to be stable, despite the fact that they had not met the stringent criterion before the end of the 22nd month. These additional signs had, nevertheless, been reported to occur appropriately and spontaneously on more than half of the days in a period of 30 consecutive days. An indication of the variety of signs that Washoe used in the course of a day is given by the following data: during the 22nd month of the study, 28 of the 34 signs listed were reported on at least 20 days, and the smallest number of different signs reported for a single day was 23, with a median of 29.[12]

The order in which these signs first appeared in Washoe's repertoire is also given in Table 1. We considered the first appearance to be the date on which three different observers reported appropriate and spontaneous occurrences. By this criterion, 4 new signs first appeared during the first 7 months, 9 new signs during the next 7 months, and 21 new signs during the next 7 months. We chose the 21st month rather than the 22nd month as the cutoff for this tabulation so that no signs would be included that do not appear in Table 1. Clearly, if Washoe's rate of acquisition continues to accelerate, we will have to assess her vocabulary on the basis of sampling procedures. We are now in the process of developing procedures that could be used to make periodic tests of Washoe's performance on samples of her repertoire. However, now that there is evidence that a chimpanzee can acquire a vocabulary of more than 30 signs, the exact number of signs in her current vocabulary is less significant than the order of magnitude – 50, 100, 200 signs, or more – that might eventually be achieved.

Differentiation

In Table 1, column 1, we list English equivalents for each of Washoe's signs. It must be understood that this equivalence is only approximate, because equivalence between English and ASL, as between any two human languages, is only approximate, and because Washoe's usage does differ from that of standard ASL. To some extent her usage is indicated in the column labelled 'Context' in Table 1, but the definition of any given sign must always depend upon her total vocabulary, and this has been continually changing. When she had very few signs for specific things, Washoe used the 'more' sign for a wide class of requests. Our only restriction was that we discouraged the use of 'more' for first requests. As she acquired signs for specific requests, her use of 'more' declined until, at the time of this writing, she was using this sign mainly to ask for repetition of some action that she could not name, such as a somersault. Perhaps the best English equivalent would be 'do it again'. Still, it seemed preferable to list the English equivalent for the ASL sign rather than its current referent for Washoe, since further refinements in her usage maye be achieved at a later date.

The differentiation of the signs for 'flower' and 'smell' provides a further illustration of usage depending upon size of vocabulary. As the 'flower' sign became more frequent, we noted that it occurred in several inappropriate contexts that all seemed to include odours; for example, Washoe would make the 'flower' sign when opening a tobacco pouch or when entering a kitchen filled with cooking odours. Taking our cue from this, we introduced the 'smell' sign by passive shaping and imitative prompting. Gradually Washoe came to make the appropriate distinction between 'flower' contexts and 'smell' contexts in her signing, although 'flower' (in the single-nostril form) (see Table 1) has continued to occur as a common error in 'smell' contexts.

Transfer

In general, when introducing new signs we have used a very specific referent for the initial training – a particular door for 'open', a particular hat for 'hat'. Early in the project we were concerned about the possibility that signs might become inseparable from their first referents. So far, however, there has been no problem of this kind: Washoe has always been able to transfer her signs spontaneously to new members of each class of referents. We have already described the transfer of 'more' and 'open'. The sign for 'flower' is a particularly good example of transfer, because flowers occur in so many varieties, indoors, outdoors, and in pictures, yet Washoe uses the same sign for all. It is fortunate that she has responded well to pictures of objects. In the case of 'dog' and 'cat' this has proved to be important because live dogs and cats can be too exciting, and we have had to use pictures to elicit most of the 'dog' and 'cat' signs. It is noteworthy that Washoe has transferred the 'dog' sign to the sound of barking by an unseen dog.

The acquisition and transfer of the sign for 'key' illustrates a further point. A great many cupboards and doors in Washoe's quarters have been kept secure by small padlocks that can all be opened by the same simple key. Because she was immature and awkward, Washoe had great difficulty in learning to use these keys and locks. Because we wanted her to improve her manual dexterity, we let her practise with these keys until she could open the locks quite easily (then we had to hide the keys). Washoe soon transferred this skill to all manner of locks and keys, including ignition keys. At about the same time, we taught her the sign for 'key', using the original padlock keys as a referent. Washoe came to use this sign both to name keys that were presented to her and to ask for the keys to various locks when no key was in sight. She readily transferred the sign to all varieties of keys and locks.

Now, if an animal can transfer a skill learned with a certain key and lock to new types of key and lock, it should not be surprising that the same animal can learn to use an arbitrary response to name and ask for a certain key and then transfer that sign to new types of keys. Certainly, the relationship between the use of a key and the opening of locks is as arbitrary as the relationship between the sign for 'key' and its many referents. Viewed in this way, the general phenomenon of transfer of training and the specifically linguistic phenomenon of labelling become very similar, and the problems that these phenomena pose for modern learning theory should require similar solutions. We do not mean to imply that the problem of labelling is less complex than has generally been supposed; rather, we are suggesting that the problem of transfer of training requires an equally sophisticated treatment.

Combinations

During the phase of the project covered by this article we made no deliberate attempts to elicit combinations or phrases, although we may have responded more readily to strings of two or more signs than to single signs. As far as we can judge, Washoe's early use of signs in strings was spontaneous. Almost as soon as she had eight or ten signs in her repertoire, she began to use them two and three at a time. As her repertoire increased, her tendency to produce strings of two or more signs also increased, to the point where this has become a common mode of signing for her. We, of course, usually signed to her in combinations, but if Washoe's use of combinations has been imitative, then it must be a generalized sort of imitation, since she has invented a number of combinations, such as 'gimme tickle' (before we had ever asked her to tickle us), and 'open food drink' (for the refrigerator – we have always called it the 'cold box').

Four signs – 'please', 'come-gimme', 'hurry' and 'more' – used with one or more other signs, account for the largest share of Washoe's early combinations. In general, these four signs have functioned as emphasizers, as in 'please open hurry' and 'gimme drink please'.

Until recently, five additional signs – 'go', 'out', 'in', 'open' and 'hear-listen' – accounted for most of the remaining combinations. Typical examples of combinations using these four are, 'go in' or 'go out' (when at some distance from a door), 'go sweet' (for being carried to a raspberry bush), 'open flower' (to be let through the gate to a flower garden), 'open key' (for a locked door), 'listen eat' (at the sound of an alarm clock signalling meal-time), and 'listen dog' (as the sound of barking by an unseen dog). All but the first and last of these six examples were inventions of Washoe's. Combinations of this type tend to amplify the meaning of the single signs used. Sometimes, however, the function of these five signs has been about the same as that of the emphasizers, as in 'open out' (when standing in front of a door).

Towards the end of the period covered in this article we were able to introduce the pronouns 'I-me' and 'you', so that combinations that resemble short sentences have begun to appear.

Concluding observations

From time to time we have been asked questions such as, 'Do you think that Washoe has language?' or 'At what point will you be able to say that Washoe has language?' We find it very difficult to respond to these questions because they are altogether foreign to the spirit of our research. They imply a distinction between one class of communicative behaviour that can be called language and another class that cannot. This in turn implies a well-established theory that could provide the distinction. If our objectives had required such a theory, we would certainly not have been able to begin this project as early as we did.

In the first phase of the project we were able to verify the hypothesis that sign language is an appropriate medium of two-way communication for the chimpanzee. Washoe's intellectual immaturity, the continuing acceleration of her progress, the fact that her signs do not remain specific to their original referents but are transferred spontaneously to new referents, and the emergence of rudimentary combinations all suggest that significantly more can be accomplished by Washoe during the subsequent phases of this project. As we proceed, the problems of the subsequent phases will be chiefly concerned with the technical business of measurement. We are now developing a procedure for testing Washoe's ability to name objects. In this procedure, an object or a picture of an object is placed in a box with a window. An observer, who does not know what is in the box, asks Washoe what she sees through the window. At present, this method is limited to items that fit in the box; a more ingenious method will have to be devised for other items. In particular, the ability to combine and recombine signs must be tested. Here, a great deal depends upon reaching a stage at which Washoe produces an extended series of signs in answer to questions. Our hope is that Washoe can be brought to the point where she describes events and situations to an observer who has no other source of information.

At an earlier time we would have been more cautious about suggesting that a chimpanzee might be able to produce extended utterances to communicate information. We believe now that it is the writers – who would predict just what it is that no chimpanzee will ever do – who must proceed with caution. Washoe's accomplishments will probably be exceeded by another chimpanzee, because it is unlikely that the conditions of training have been optimal in this first attempt. Theories of language that depend upon the identification of aspects of language that are exclusively human must remain tentative until a considerably larger body of research with other species becomes available.

References and notes

1 See, for example, LENNEBERG, E. H. (1967) *Biological Foundations of Language* New York, Wiley.
2 BRYAN, A. L. (1963) *Current Anthropology*, 4, 297.

3 HAYES, K. J. and HAYES, C. (1951) *Proceedings of the American Philosophical Society*, **95**, 105.

4 HAYES, K. J. (personal communication) Dr Hayes also informed us that Viki used a few additional sounds which, while not resembling English words, were used for specific requests.

5 YERKES, R. M. (1943) *Chimpanzees* New Haven, Yale University Press.

6 HAYES, K. J. and HAYES, C. (1955) in Gavan, J. A. (ed.) *The Non-Human Primates and Human Evolution* Detroit, Wayne University Press, p. 110.
KELLOGG, W. N. and KELLOGG, L. A. (1967) *The Ape and the Child* New York, Hafner.
KELLOGG, W. N. (1968) *Science*, **162**, 423.

7 STOKOE, W. C., CASTERLINE, D. and CRONEBURG, C. C. (1965) *A Dictionary of American Sign Language* Washington D.C., Gallaudet University Press.
MCCALL, E. A. (1965) Thesis, University of Iowa.

8 GOODALL, J. (1965) in DeVore, I. (ed.) *Primate Behaviour* New York, Holt, Rinehart and Winston, p. 425.
RIOPELLE, A. J. and ROGERS, C. M. (1965) in Schrier, A. M., Harlow, H. F. and Stollnitz, F. (eds) *Behaviour of Nonhuman Primates* New York, Academic Press, p. 449.

9 YERKES, R. M. and LEARNED, B. W. (1925) *Chimpanzee Intelligence and Its Vocal Expression* Baltimore, William and Wilkins, p. 53.

10 HAYES, K. J. and HAYES, C. (1952) *Journal of Comparative Physiological Psychology*, **45**, 450.

11 WARDEN, C. J. and WARNER, L. H. (1928) *Quarterly Review of Biology*, **3**, 1.

12 The development of Washoe's vocabulary of signs is being recorded on motion-picture film. At the time of this writing, thirty of the thirty-four signs listed in Table 1 are on film.

14 Early signs of language in child and chimpanzee

R. Allen Gardner and Beatrice T. Gardner

The exposure of children to their native language begins at birth, and most theories of language acquisition assume that the exposure during the earliest years is particularly significant. What evidence there is on this point is, at best, indirect. Long-term negative effects of an impoverished linguistic environment can be demonstrated for children reared in orphanages during the first years of life.[1] Favourable effects of early exposure to language – in this case, sign language – can also be demonstrated by comparing deaf children of deaf parents with deaf children of hearing parents on tests of the ability to speak, read, or write English.[2] Moreover, with the recently developed techniques for recording behaviour of neonates, it has been shown that the human infant is responsive to characteristics of adult speech, such as segmentation and the distinction between phonemes, within a month of birth.[3] It seems likely that the beneficial effects of early exposure to language can also be demonstrated in attempts to teach language to animals.

Project Washoe was the first attempt to teach sign language to a chimpanzee. Washoe was about 11 months old when her training in American Sign Language (Ameslan) began. Within 51 months, she had acquired 132 signs of Ameslan, as determined by criteria for reliable usage developed during the research.[4] As with humans using words, Washoe used her signs for classes of referents rather than for particular objects or events, and used signs in combinations.[5] Brown,[6] Klima and Bellugi,[7] and other investigators of child language have commented on the many ways in which Washoe's acquisition of sign language parallels the acquisition of spoken language by children, as, for example, in Washoe's generalization of the meaning of signs, in the gradual increase in length of her sign combinations, and in the types of semantic relations expressed by early combinations. Thus, Project Washoe demonstrated that Ameslan is a suitable medium of communication for a chimpanzee, and that, given a suitable medium, a significant level of two-way communication could be achieved. Since then, several chimpanzees in several laboratories have acquired a vocabulary of signs,[8] and it is appropriate to pose questions about indi-

---

GARDNER, R. ALLEN and GARDNER, BEATRICE T. (1975) 'Early signs of language in child and chimpanzee' in *Science*, vol. 187, 752–53.

vidual differences, about limits, and about the effectiveness of different methods of teaching sign language. In our current project of teaching sign language to several chimpanzees, we are capitalizing upon our experience in the research with Washoe by improving key features of procedure, and we plan to maintain these more favourable conditions until the subjects reach intellectual maturity. In this way, we can come much closer to describing the highest level of two-way communication that can be achieved by chimpanzees taught a form of human language.

One of the significant improvements in procedure is that several fluent signers, including deaf persons and persons who have deaf parents, are research personnel in the current project. These 'native speakers' of Ameslan provide far more adequate models of the language than those we provided for Washoe.

Another improvement is that the exposure of subjects to Ameslan begins 1 or 2 days after birth. Chimpanzee Moja was born at the Laboratory of Experimental Medicine and Surgery in Primates, Tuxedo Park, N.Y., on 18 November 1972 and arrived in our laboratory on the next day. Chimpanzee Pili was born at Yerkes Regional Primate Research Center, Atlanta, Ga., on 30 October 1973 and arrived in our laboratory on 1 November.

No special difficulties were encountered in maintaining the infants in good health. Their care is similar to that of the human infant; around-the-clock feedings, diapering, inoculations, sanitary precautions such as sterilization of bottles, and so on. In addition, we provided the infants with body contact whenever they were awake. Within a few weeks, the infants appeared responsive to the activities of their human companions, which included a great deal of signing. Even in the earliest months, the infants were attentive and alert. They could grasp toys, imitate actions such as blowing kisses or peekaboo, and differentiate their usual companions from strangers.

Both Moja and Pili started to make recognizable signs when they were about 3 months old. In Project Washoe, we kept track of new signs by noting spontaneous and appropriate use of the sign. The day that the third of three observers reported appropriate and spontaneous occurrence was taken as the date of the appearance of the new sign in the vocabulary. By this criterion, Moja's first four signs (*come-gimme, go, more,* and *drink*) appeared during her 13th week of life. Similarly Pili's first sign appeared during his 14th week of life, and he had a four-sign vocabulary (*drink, come-gimme, more* and *tickle*) by his 15th week. The first four signs met the three-observer criterion within a few days of each other for both subjects. At the age of 6 months, Moja's vocabulary consisted of 15 signs, and Pili's of 13 signs. By contrast, Washoe's exposure to sign language did not begin until she was nearly 1 year old, and the effective start of the exposure was further delayed because the research participants were only beginning to learn Ameslan. After 6 months of exposure, Washoe's vocabulary consisted of the signs *come-gimme* and *more*.

In the early stages of Project Washoe, we developed a procedure to determine when a new sign had become a reliable item in the chimpanzee's vocabulary. After the third report of a new sign, the sign was added to a checklist. Each day thereafter, the first person to observe Washoe using a sign on the checklist entered a description of its form and context. As the criterion for deciding the sign had become reliable, we chose a period of 15 consecutive days during which at least one appropriate and spontaneous use of the sign had been recorded.[5]

These 15-day records for the present study show that, even at this early stage, signs were being used, not as mechanical routines, but with variations in form and in appropriate variations of a basic context. For example, in the set of reports on Pili's use of *tickle* during 14 to 28 February 1974, two kinds of context were described. Usually, Pili signed for continuation of tickling when his companion stopped tickling him momentarily or stopped and asked questions such as, *What we play now?* But in two reports, Pili initiated tickling with his sign. Pili also used another of his early signs, *more*, to request continuation of tickling during this period. But *more* was recorded in several contexts in which *tickle* did not occur, as when we had taken away Pili's water bottle after a bout of drinking or had stopped games other than tickling, such as covering and uncovering Pili's face with a scarf. In forming *tickle*, Pili drew the index finger over the back of his other hand or the back of his companion's hand about equally often. Moja also used both her own body and corresponding parts of the addressee's body as the place for making *tickle* and other early signs; this variation in form has been reported for Washoe and for very young deaf children.[4]

Fouts[8] reported that an infant female, Salome, used the sign *food* during her fourth month. While the age at which chimpanzees produce their first signs seems early compared to that for first words of humans, it is not very discrepant from the age at which the first signs appear in humans. There are parental reports of first signs between the fifth and sixth month for children exposed to sign language.[2] Possibly, signs are easier to make than words; more likely it is easier for a parent to recognize the infant's poor approximation to a sign than his poor approximation to a spoken word.

We consider the early appearance of signs to be an important confirmation of two major procedural improvements in the current project; the exposure of subjects of fluent Ameslan signers and the exposure to language from birth. Of course, it is not the size of the early vocabulary per se that is significant but what this promises in terms of further development under the more favourable conditions for the acquisition of sign language.

References and notes

1 MUSSEN, P. H. (1963) *The Psychological Development of the Child* Englewood Cliffs, Prentice-Hall.

2 MINDEL, E. D. and VERNON, M. (1971) *They Grow in Silence: The Deaf Child and his Family* Silver Spring, Md., National Association of the Deaf; SCHLESINGER, H. S. and MEADOW, K. P. (1972) Berkeley, University of California Press.

3 CONDON, W. S. and SANDER, W. L. (1974), *Science*, **183**, 99; EIMAN, P. D. SIQUELAND, E. R., JUSCZYK, P., VIGORITO, J. (1971) *ibid.* **171**, 303.

4 GARDNER, R. A. and GARDNER, B. T. (1972) in Chauvain, R. (ed.) *Modeles Animaux du Comportement Humain* Paris, Centre National de la Recherche Scientifique.

5 GARDNER, R. A. and GARDNER, B. T. (1969) *Science*, **165**, 664; GARDNER, B. T. and GARDNER, R. A. (1971) in Schrier, A. M. and Stollnitz, F. (eds.) *Behavior of Nonhuman Primates* New York, Academic Press; (in press) in Pick, A. (ed.) *Minnesota Symposium on Child Psychology*, (vol. 8), Minneapolis, University of Minnesota Press.

6 BROWN, R. (1970) *Psycholinguistics: Selected Papers by Roger Brown* New York, Free Press; (1973) *A First Language* Cambridge, Mass., Harvard University Press.

7 KLIMA, E. and BELLUGI, U. (1970) in Miller, G. A. (ed.) *Forum Series on Psychology and Communication* Washington, D.C., Voice of America.

8 FOUTS, R. S. (1973) *Science Year: World Book Science Annual, 1974*, p. 34, Chicago, Field.

Section 4
The social framework

Introduction

In this section we are changing our level of analysis from the biological and psycho-biological to the social.

We are setting the scene by asking in our first extract: What is a social fact? This excerpt is taken from Emile Dürkheim's *Rules of Sociological Method*. In this book Dürkheim, writing in the 1890s, was concerned to show that sociology has a status independent of psychology and that there is a distinctive category of facts, the social, existing outside and apart from the individual. Thus, beliefs, laws and customs whose source is society are seen as imposing constraints on the individual's thinking, feeling and acting. Dürkheim writes: 'It is generally accepted today, however, that most of our tendencies are not developed by ourselves but come to us from without. How can they become part of us except by imposing themselves upon us?'

People tend to think that they make their own choices and decisions, from entering marriage to committing suicide, from taking advantage of educational opportunities to choosing a job and spending their earnings. The strength and explanatory utility of sociological analysis rests on its ability to point to social patterns and regularities – Dürkheim's social facts – behind such apparently entirely personal actions.

In the articles which follow we are pursuing, from different points of view, not so much these social facts per se but the ways in which they come to have a meaning for the individual and provide a framework which influences and structures his life. We do not see the social environment (or, indeed, the physical or built environment) as imposing themselves on the individual; rather are we concerned with the interaction between the environment and the individual. 'The social framework' in which social behaviour must be understood ranges from social groupings and institutions to the artifacts and technology of a society. We are born into a world made up not only of other people but of edifices and structures, and these become part of our psychological environment, influencing our feelings of security and personal identity.

By way of example, therefore, we are looking next at different kinds of institutions and the effects they may have on the development of the children growing up in them. Thus, in our second article, Barbara and Jack Tizard discuss the implications of their own and other research and show that institutions, which differ in organizational structure from each other and in the training and attitudes of staff, provide distinct social and psychological climate and experiences, the effects of which can be traced in the child's progress and personality.

Finally, we are focusing on more global aspects of the social framework, man's urban experience. We do so not because cities are the universal environment of man, but rather because this is the predominant Western milieu today. Our third article is an extract from Stanley Milgram's 'The experience of living in cities' (first published in 1970). Milgram does not subscribe uncritically to the often expressed view that cities have pathological effects on man. Instead, he takes as his starting point the 'external' social facts of city life, so often described by sociologists as the size, density and heterogeneity of the population, and discusses how they come to be transmuted into psychological facts. Milgram explores how the individual experiences and adapts to the 'sensory overload' life in a large city entails. He describes the development of defensive norms of non-involvement such as the screening of sensory stimuli, the lack of civility or, more seriously, the lack of social responsibility in crisis situations, often described as 'bystander apathy'. He further reviews experimental work on vandalism and on the extent to which people are prepared to help strangers. These studies throw some light on differences in small town and large city living.

15 What is a social fact?

Emile Dürkheim

There is in every society a certain group of phenomena which may be differentiated from those studied by the other natural sciences. When I fulfil my obligations as brother, husband, or citizen, when I execute my contracts, I perform duties which are defined, externally to myself and my acts, in law and in custom. Even if they conform to my own sentiments and I feel their reality subjectively, such reality is still objective, for I did not create them; I merely inherited them through my education. How many times it happens, moreover, that we are ignorant of the details of the obligations incumbent upon us, and that in order to acquaint ourselves with them we must consult the law and its authorized interpreters! Similarly, the church-member finds the beliefs and practices of his religious life ready-made at birth; their existence prior to his own implies their existence outside of himself. The system of signs I use to express my thought, the system of currency I employ to pay my debts, the instruments of credit I utilize in my commercial relations, the practices followed in my profession, etc., function independently of my own use of them. And these statements can be repeated for each member of society. Here, then, are ways of acting, thinking, and feeling that present the noteworthy property of existing outside the individual consciousness.

These types of conduct or thought are not only external to the individual but are, moreover, endowed with coercive power, by virtue of which they impose themselves upon him, independent of his individual will. Of course, when I fully consent and conform to them, this constraint is felt only slightly, if at all, and is therefore unnecessary. But it is, nonetheless, an intrinsic characteristic of these facts, the proof thereof being that it asserts itself as soon as I attempt to resist it. If I attempt to violate the law, it reacts against me so as to prevevn my act before its accomplishment, or to nullify my violation by restoring the damage, if it is accomplished and reparable, or to make me expiate it if it cannot be compensated for otherwise.

In the case of purely moral maxims, the public conscience exercises a check on every act which offends it by means of the surveillance it exercises over the conduct of citizens, and the appropriate penalties at its disposal. In many cases the constraint is less violent, but nevertheless it always

---

DÜRKHEIM, EMILE (1897) 'What is a social fact?' from Chapter 1 in *Rules of Sociological Method* New York, Free Press edition, 1950.

exists. If I do not submit to the conventions of society, if in my dress I do not conform to the customs observed in my country and in my class, the ridicule I provoke, the social isolation in which I am kept, produce, although in an attenuated form, the same effects as a punishment in the strict sense of the word. The constraint is nonetheless efficacious for being indirect. I am not obliged to speak French with my fellow-countrymen nor to use the legal currency, but I cannot possibly do otherwise. If I tried to escape this necessity, my attempt would fail miserably. As an industrialist, I am free to apply the technical methods of former centuries; but by doing so, I should invite certain ruin. Even when I free myself from these rules and violate them successfully, I am always compelled to struggle with them. When finally overcome, they make their constraining power sufficiently felt by the resistance they offer. The enterprises of all innovators, including successful ones, come up against resistance of this kind.

Here, then, is a category of facts with very distinctive characteristics: it consists of ways of acting, thinking, and feeling, external to the individual, and endowed with a power of coercion, by reason of which they control him. These ways of thinking could not be confused with biological phenomena, since they consist of representations and of actions; nor with psychological phenomena, which exist only in the individual consciousness and through it. They constitute, thus, a new variety of phenomena; and it is to them exclusively that the term 'social' ought to be applied. And this term fits them quite well, for it is clear that, since their source is not in the individual, their substratum can be no other than society, either the political society as a whole or some one of the partial groups it includes, such as religious denominations, political, literary, and occupational associations, etc. On the other hand, this term 'social' applies to them exclusively, for it has a distinct meaning only if it designates exclusively the phenomena which are not included in any of the categories of facts that have already been established and classified. These ways of thinking and acting therefore constitute the proper domain of sociology. It is true that, when we define them with this word 'constraint', we risk shocking the zealous partisans of absolute individualism. For those who profess the complete autonomy of the individual, man's dignity is diminished whenever he is made to feel that he is not completely self-determinant. It is generally accepted today, however, that most of our ideas and our tendencies are not developed by ourselves but come to us from without. How can they become a part of us except by imposing themselves upon us? This is the whole meaning of our definition. And it is generally accepted, moreover, that social constraint is not necessarily incompatible with the individual personality. [...]

16 The institution as an envi[illegible] development

Jack and Barbara Tizard

In industrial societies the proportion of children who are [illegible] in residential institutions during the whole, or for substantial pa[illegible] of their childhood is considerable. King (1970) has estimated that out of a population of 11·5 million children under the age of sixteen years in England and Wales in 1963, there were 146,500 who were 'deprived of a normal home life'. Of these approximately 78,000 were 'deprived' children in the care of local authorities or voluntary agencies and a further 15,000 were 'protected' children in foster homes for reward or adoption. Delinquent children in approved schools or remand homes numbered over 10,000, and handicapped children in special boarding schools nearly 24,000. A further 19,000 handicapped children were in hospitals or mental subnormality units. In all, they amounted to 1·3 per cent of the child population.

Though very substantial numbers of children are admitted to temporary care by local authorities and voluntary agencies because of mother's confinement or some family crisis, the very great majority of children actually in care at any one time are long-stay cases who have been away from home for more than six months. On 31 March 1963 long-stay cases made up 93 per cent of the total in residence (Packman 1968).

Nearly half of all children admitted to the care of local authorities and voluntary organizations are boarded out in private families, but the remainder live in residential institutions, as do the great majority of handicapped and delinquent children classified by King (1970) as deprived of a normal home life. In 1963, and indeed today, the total number of such children in long-stay institutional care must have been 80,000–90,000, many of whom would spend the whole of their childhood in establishments staffed by paid professional staff and organized in a manner very different from that of an ordinary home or foster home (King, Raynes and Tizard 1971, Tizard and Tizard 1971).

The numbers of children in such institutions have remained much the

---

TIZARD, JACK and TIZARD, BARBARA (1974) 'The institution as an environment for development' in Richards, M. P. M. (ed.) *The integration of the child into a social world* Cambridge, Cambridge University Press, 137–52.

...during the last few years. Thus in March 1970 there were 78,274 ...ildren in the care of local authorities or voluntary organizations, as compared with 78,025 in 1963. Of these children 5500 were under two, and 10,700 were aged two to four years.

Residential care of this sort has a long history; it serves a necessary social function in providing for the needs of children who are destitute, in physical or moral danger, or otherwise deprived of normal family care. From a social viewpoint therefore residential establishments serving the needs of children are important institutions.

Because patterns of upbringing in residential institutions are inevitably different from those found in a normal family, or in a foster home, residential institutions also offer opportunities to the investigator to explore the effects of different environmental circumstances upon the development of children. Furthermore, because such places contain numbers of children under one roof, and because they are more open to public scrutiny than are private households, they are convenient as well as important places to study. Little systematic study has however been made of them.

The present paper is concerned primarily with factors affecting the development of young children in long-stay residential care, but reference is made to other types of residential institution in order to put the topic in context. Short-stay care is not discussed.

Institutions have a bad name

Residential children's homes, unlike prisons, concentration camps, barracks and some other types of residential establishment, are benevolent rather than punitive or coercive in intention. In spite of this they have a bad name, and there is virtually no type of children's institution except the kibbutz which has not at some time been the subject of recurring public scandal. Thus, in London during the eighteenth century, 80 per cent of children under three admitted to the care of certain workhouses died within a year (Pinchbeck and Hewitt 1969). Things were admittedly no different elsewhere for pauper children: in 1763 the parish of St James, Westminster, resorted to paying a bonus of a guinea to foster mothers whose foster children survived the first year of life. Conditions in workhouses during the nineteenth century remained 'Dickensian'; and even as late as the end of the Second World War the plight of children in workhouses and barrack type children's homes shocked the Curtis Committee (1946) which investigated the care of children deprived of normal home life. During the last decade in England, public inquiries have been held to examine and report on the ill-treatment of children in approved schools, mental subnormality hospitals, and some boarding schools. The bleakness of life in children's hospitals has also been a subject of unfavourable report (Platt 1959, Oswin 1971).

England is not alone in this respect. Bowlby (1951) summarized much of the comparative literature from other countries. More recently Wolfensberger (1969), Blatt (1967, 1969), and others in the United States have presented graphic accounts of institutional neglect of the mentally handicapped in that country. The situation affecting infants and children in residential institutions in Italy is currently a major public scandal, and it would not be difficult to find examples of ill-treatment or neglect in most, if not all, countries.

It is not only, or indeed not especially, children's institutions which have earned themselves a bad name. Residential institutions for adults have an even more dubious status, portrayed and analyzed by Goffman (1961) in his memorable essay on total institutions. Today, perhaps even more than in the past, public attitudes are strongly opposed to institutional care for the handicapped, the weak or the dependent – so much so that the question is often asked as to whether all forms of institutional life, for adults as well as for children, are not inevitably harmful. Many social workers, psychiatrists and staff in Local Authority welfare departments, appear to think they are. However as Titmuss (1961) has pointed out, when we criticize institutions it is always the bad ones we point to – the Poor Law institution, the old-fashioned asylum, not the public school or the Oxford College.

Changes in policy

Attempts to reduce the numbers of children admitted to residential care have led to a major review, during the last fifteen years, of alternatives open to those concerned with public policy for deprived and handicapped children. It has been shown that better 'preventive' social case work with families, coupled with much more adequate personal social services for people living in their own homes, can sometimes prevent family breakdown and, more often, make it possible for families to cope with children at home in times of crisis (Heywood 1965, Fitzherbert 1967, Schaffer and Schaffer 1968). Even severely handicapped children who would otherwise require hospital or institutional care can usually be looked after at home if adequate services are made available (Tizard 1964). However, the development of domiciliary services has been slow, and the number of deprived children in care per 1000 of the population under eighteen has remained almost constant since 1966.

Attempts to increase the number of foster home placements have been scarcely more successful; the proportion of children in care who are boarded out has remained at about 48 per cent for some years. Hence residential institutions remain with us. During the last twenty years however they have changed remarkably. One of the major reforms here has been the almost total replacement of large children's communities, frequently housed in barrack-type institutions, by smaller, scattered homes. Today, in southern England, it is difficult to find residential children's establishments (except hospitals and schools) which contain more than thirty children. Public policy favours siting the small children's homes in residential areas rather than in disused manor houses or abandoned farmhouses deep in the country. Where conditions permit it, homes which contain more than six to eight children are subdivided into smaller family groups, each of which has its own staff of houseparents. Children normally attend ordinary schools, and efforts are made to keep children in close contact with relatives, to encourage visiting, and visits home. Child care officers with a social work training are responsible for case work with parents and children.

Equally great changes have taken place in establishments for the care of infants and preschool children. Residential nurseries have been thoroughly reorganized. They are better staffed and much better equipped. Efforts are made to retain links with parents and to foster outside contacts which provide breadth of experience for the children. Normally, children under the age of about nine months are cared for in a special baby nursery, but as soon as possible they are moved into small mixed age units of about six children, each with its own staff of trained nursery nurses and helpers. Increasingly, children are being kept in residential nurseries until they are six to eight years of age, in order to avoid a sudden break at the time of starting school. Some authorities are able to dispense with residential nurseries altogether, by putting even the youngest children in all age homes so that a subsequent move becomes unnecessary, and from their earliest years they will have opportunities to mix with older children.

By no means all children's institutions achieve what are regarded as good standards of child care. The organization of mental subnormality hospitals and of some long-stay units for other types of handicapped children in general compares very unfavourably with that of children's homes for 'ordinary' children deprived of normal home life. Institutions dealing with delinquent children also differ in other ways from ordinary children's homes. But here too changes have occurred and new developments (e.g. in the provision of small boarding homes for mentally retarded children, and 'community homes' for difficult and delinquent children) are occurring.

The enormous changes in child care policy which have occurred during the last twenty years are unfortunately less well known to those not professionally concerned with it than are the defects of old-fashioned institutions and the scandals that still make the headlines about those that remain repressive or inadequate. Rather than discuss these further, it is more useful to turn to questions of current concern; how suitable *can* a children's home be as a place for children to grow up in? More generally, what differences in development are likely to be found in children growing up in a modern child-oriented institution, as compared with similar children growing up in their own homes?

The complexity of the problem

The care of children presents problems which are different from, and more complex than, those of adults. Children are more vulnerable than adults both to physical and mental trauma, the effects of which are likely to be longer lasting or even irreversible. They are more defenceless than adults, poor witnesses in a Court of Law and totally dependent upon adults for help and protection. They are also *developing* creatures whose needs change rapidly with age and vary according to their genetic and environmental history. A discussion of the effects of institutional upbringing on children has therefore to take account of the age, handicaps and length of stay of the children in residence, the type and quality of the care provided in the institution, the alternatives actually or in principle available for children not able to be brought up in their own homes, and, above all, the consequences for the child and for the family of leaving the child at home. Most of the classical studies of institutional care have not done this: they have been insufficiently specific and analytical. Nearly all of them were carried out in institutions which were overcrowded, meanly provided for and understaffed; and conditions in these have been compared with those that obtain in ordinary families, close knit, stable, reasonably well housed and economically secure. The indictment of institutional neglect is entirely justified, but it is misleading to generalize about institutional upbringing on the basis of findings obtained only in establishments which are poor and bleak.

A comparative study of institutions

Our own approach has been concerned with attempts to analyze, measure, and account for differences between institutions, and to show how these differences affect the development of children growing up in them. We start from the observation that residential institutions caring for the same type of inmate differ widely one from another, and that in particular establishments characteristic patterns of function tend to remain relatively constant over long periods of time, despite changes in staff and inmate population. Our viewpoint is that an institution tends to function in one way rather than another not simply because of personal factors associated with particular individuals, or idiosyncratic circumstances, but because of the characteristics of its organization. Thus individual units belonging to a particular class of institutions (e.g. small residential hostels) tend to resemble each other more than they resemble members of another class (e.g. large hospitals) irrespective of whether the inmate population is normal or retarded and irrespective of the personality of the various staff members.

If it is true that the characteristics of institutions remain more or less constant over substantial periods of time, practices which differentiate one establishment from another and which impinge on the children who are resident should result in differences in the way in which children in long-term care develop. This is especially true because the residential institutions are encompassing institutions, in that the child's environment is almost entirely circumscribed by the institution in which he lives. Hence the child's world is very largely shaped by the adults who care for him.

The object of our studies has been to explore the implications of this argument, using objective and reliable indicators which would permit the testing of specific hypotheses and admit of replication. Taking a particular inmate population, e.g. severely retarded children, we have selected for study a number of institutions which differ markedly in their mode of organization. A systematic study was then made of the quality and frequency of interactions between staff and children in the different establishments.

The next step was to attempt to relate differences in staff–child interactions to the characteristics of the organization in which the staff worked, using scales to measure those organizational aspects which were considered relevant.

Thirdly, systematic studies were made of individual children to see whether any effects of differing patterns of upbringing could be discovered. Relations were thus sought between three kinds of data: observations of staff–child interactions, measures of organization, and assessment of the children's development.

A full description of the mental subnormality studies has been published (King, Raynes and Tizard 1971). They comprised field studies of a large number of different mental subnormally and child care units, and a detailed observational survey of mental subnormality hospitals and small hostels all caring for severely or profoundly retarded children. Large and characteristic differences, measured by an objective Child Management Scale, were found in child care practices, as between small hostels in which child care practices were strongly *child oriented* on the one hand, and mental subnormality hospitals where child care practices were *institution oriented*. The evidence suggested that differences in child care practices were not due to differences in the handicaps of the children.

Child care practices varied with the size of the institution and the size of the child care units in which the children lived, but differences in unit size did not seem able to account for differences in child management patterns. Nor could differing child care practices be ascribed to differences in assigned staff ratios, though in child oriented units more staff were available in peak periods (i.e. at such times as getting up and breakfast time, and at the end of the day) whereas in institution oriented units staffing was neither increased during peak units nor decreased during those periods of the day in which there was less for them to do.

The organizational structure of child oriented and institution oriented units was very different and it was this which appeared to be the principal determinant of differences in patterns of child care. In child oriented units the person in charge had very much greater responsibility to make decisions about matters which affected all aspects of the unit's functioning. Perhaps because they were accorded greater autonomy, senior staff in those establishments tended to share their responsibilities with their junior colleagues; role differentiation was reduced (e.g. senior staff were more often engaged in child care than were their counterparts in institution oriented units who spent far more time on administration and even domestic work, and far less time in child care). Staff stability was also much greater in child oriented units, partly because staff were not moved from one unit to another to meet crises in units which were short staffed, partly because students in training were not moved about in order to 'gain experience'. Role performance also differed. In child oriented units staff were more likely to involve the children in their activities. They spoke to them more often, and were more 'accepting' of them, and less often 'rejecting'. Junior staff tended to behave in ways similar to those in which the head of the unit acted.

Though the social organization of the institution appeared to be largely responsible for the differences in staff behaviour which we observed, the nature of staff training also seemed important. Trained nurses were in general less child oriented than were staff with child care training. They were more authoritarian, and when the person in charge was a nurse the unit tended to be characterized by sharp role differentiation.

Mentally handicapped children in units which were child care oriented were significantly more advanced in feeding and dressing skills, and in speech, than were those in institution oriented units. Though no very adequate study was made of other personality characteristics of the children, fewer of those in child oriented institutions appeared to be psychiatrically disturbed.

Upbringing in residential nurseries

Our mental subnormality studies left many questions unanswered. Furthermore, mental subnormality institutions have some special characteristics which mark them off from institutions responsible for the care of normal children. In a later series of investigations, which are still continuing, more detailed studies have therefore been made of the manner in which young normal children living in group care are being brought up in modern child oriented nurseries. Differences in child care practices in different institutions are being examined and attempts made to assess their consequences for the children.

The nurseries we have studied do not present gross organizational differences of the kind found amongst institutions for the retarded. None the less pilot studies indicated that there were important differences in the way in which they were organized, and suggested that these would be likely to affect the quality of staff talk and behaviour, and hence the level of language development of the children. It was therefore decided to examine, as in the mental subnormality studies, relationships between three sets of data. The first set, obtained from records and by interview, was concerned with organizational structure in the nurseries; the second, obtained through direct observation using time-sampling techniques, measured the 'verbal environment' of the children; the third, obtained through formal psychological testing, comprised measures of both verbal and non-verbal development. An earlier inquiry (described below) had shown two-year-olds in residential nurseries to be somewhat backward in language, and we wished to ascertain whether or not language retardation increased as the children got older. Language development may be regarded as one indicator of general social development, and all the healthy two to five-year-old children in the thirteen nursery groups which were intensively studied were tested with the Reynell Developmental Language Scales, and the non-verbal scale of the Minnesota Preschool Scale.

Results

The results indicated the fruitfulness of the approach and threw some light on general problems of institutional upbringing in nurseries which maintained high standards of physical and social care (Tizard et al. 1972).

Though all nurseries were divided into mixed age groups of six children, differences in organizational structure were apparent. The autonomy of the nursery group appeared to be of especial importance: in some nurseries the nurse in charge had almost as much freedom as a foster-mother to run her unit as she wished. In these groups also the children were allowed a great deal of freedom. At the other extreme, there were some nurseries in which the nursery matron exercised a dominating role over all the nursery groups. In these, the nurse in charge of a group had little authority, and her tasks were so well defined that someone else could easily take her place. Most decisions not made on an entirely routine basis were referred to the matron, and the freedom of both nurse and child was very limited. Thus the children were not allowed to leave the group room unattended and the nurse would have to ask permission to take the children for a walk or to turn on the television set.

In the more autonomous groups considerable efforts were made to broaden the children's experiences. Special excursions, e.g. to the cinema, zoo, or sea-side, occurred at least as often as in a contrast group of London working-class families, and ordinary social experiences, e.g. shopping, visits to cafés, bus and train trips, were nearly as frequent. The lower the autonomy of the group, the more restricted were the child's experiences. Differences between groups in various characteristics of organizational structure were assessed on quantitative scales. Differences in scale scores were strongly associated with differences in patterns of staff–child interaction. In the least centrally organized groups the staff spent more time talking, reading and playing to the children, and doing things with them in which the children were rated as 'active' rather than 'passive'. The quality (but *not* the amount, which was high in all nurseries) of staff talk to the children also differed. Staff in nursery groups which had most autonomy offered more informative talk, spoke in longer sentences, gave fewer negative commands, and were more likely to explain themselves when they told the child to do something, than were those in the institutionally oriented groups. Thus the linguistic, as well as the general, social environment differed subtly but substantially among the nurseries.

The differences were related to specific differences in the children's attainments. In non-verbal intelligence the mean scores of children in nurseries with differing autonomy did not differ: the mean was 104·9. In verbal attainments however there were marked differences. The mean verbal comprehension score of the three nursery groups which had the highest autonomy was 114·9, 1·5 standard deviations higher than those in the three most institutionally oriented groups – a difference in mean scores equivalent to that found between the verbal comprehension scores of ordinary children of professional families growing up in their own homes, and children of manual workers. The mean language expression score in the same three nurseries was 100·0, 0·5 standard deviations higher than those in the most institutionally oriented.

In all nursery groups the analysis of staff talk indicated that older children tended to be spoken to more frequently than the younger ones. There were no significant differences between the institutions in this respect. It was noteworthy therefore that the older children scored significantly *higher* rather than lower in the verbal comprehension test: thus the hypothesis that institutional children become progressively more retarded in language as they get older was not confirmed. Inasmuch as linguistic attainments are indicators of the social and intellectual adequacy of the environment, this set of nurseries could be said to have attained good standards of care; the best of them were very good indeed. The language studies supported our general belief that the nurseries provided a less adequate environment for some of the younger children, but from the age of 2½ the children scored well above the population means. Since most of the children came from lower working-class parentage it is likely that their cognitive development was more advanced than it would have been had they remained in their own family.

Institutions and the development of personality

Bowlby's (1951) highly influential monograph presented an extensive body of data in support of his thesis that institutional upbringing almost always led to dire consequences. It was plain, he said, that when deprived of maternal care 'the child's development is almost always retarded – physically, intellectually, and socially – and that symptoms of physical and mental illness may appear . . . retrospective and follow-up studies make it clear that some children are gravely damaged for life. This is a sombre conclusion which must be regarded as established' (p. 15).

Later studies, including our own, have shown that these conclusions were too sweeping. We have been able to show that the level of language development depends very much on the characteristics of the institution: in the best residential nurseries the children we studied were not only healthy but intellectually normal, linguistically advanced, and exposed to a near-normal range of general experiences. No study was made of personality development, and we have no evidence of the ways in which differences in institutional environment affect this variable. However, in an ongoing study we are comparing the all-round development of a group of young children who have spent virtually the whole of their lives in good nursery care with others from a similar nursery environment who between the ages of two and four years were adopted or restored to their parents. A contrast group of London working-class children living at home forms part of the study.

In the first stage of the study thirty children admitted to residential nurseries before the age of four months were examined at the time of their second birthday (Tizard and Joseph 1970, Tizard and Tizard 1971). Compared to the contrast group of London children living at home, the institution children were found to be slightly backward in speech and verbal intelligence, and to be somewhat more fearful of a stranger and of separation from a familiar adult. Fewer had achieved bowel and bladder control. Thumb and finger sucking were more common among them, sleep disturbances less so. There was evidence of a relationship between the extent of the children's timidity and the paucity of their previous experience with strangers. Gross disturbances were rare: withdrawn, apathetic or depressed children were not encountered.

A major area of difference between the nursery and home children lay in their relationships with their caretakers. Most of the home two-year-olds showed a marked preference for their mother; they tended to follow her about the house, and to be upset if she left the house without them. However, few of them were disturbed if she left the room. Such relationships result from a close family structure where the mother is the principal if not the sole caretaker and is almost always accessible to the child. By contrast, in the residential nurseries which we studied large numbers of different staff cared for each child, and because of scheduled off-duty hours and study leave particular staff members were by no means always accessible to the child. Moreover, following an adult round the house was not allowed in most nurseries. The attachments of the children were not surprisingly diffuse – although all showed preferences between adults – most children were described as showing attachment to anyone they knew well, that is they tended to cry when any staff they knew well left the room, and to run to be picked up when any familiar staff entered the room. Their behaviour was thus not only more indiscriminate but more immature than that of the home children.

The question arises as to whether deviance in attachment behaviour at twenty-four months is reversible, and if not whether it presages subsequent deviance in personality development. Bowlby (1969) in his recent monumental study of affective development maintains that harmonious social and emotional development is dependent upon the early development of attachment behaviour to a specific adult. He describes in convincing detail the ontogeny of attachment behaviour in human infants, and draws extensively upon animal studies to argue that attachment behaviour serves a biological, protective function, and that primates deprived of the usual mothering experience develop abnormally. So impressed was Bowlby by the bias of a child to attach himself especially to one person, and also by the far-reaching implications of this attachment, that he coined a special term, monotropy, to describe it.

With respect to reversibility, it seems probable that in this as in many other respects human behaviour is more modifiable by experience than animal behaviour. In our study of four-and-a-half-year-old children who had been adopted or restored to their parents from an institution after the age of two we found that in most cases close attachments *had* developed. On the other hand, many of the children who remained in the institution showed markedly deviant attachment behaviour by the age of four and a half; their nurses tended to complain either that they 'didn't care about anyone' or that they would 'follow anyone who took an interest in them'. A number of these children also showed behaviour disturbances, as did some of the children living at home. The analysis of the data is not yet complete, but the evidence suggests that rather different behaviour patterns characterize institutional, adopted, and restored children. Continued institutional care appears to be associated with a particular kind of deviant behaviour.

Two further relevant questions are whether the development of normal attachment behaviour is possible within an institutional setting, and whether some deviant forms of attachment behaviour are compatible with healthy personality development. It is by no means certain how far Bowlby is generalizing about human development from a study of the nuclear Western family. In other societies extended families have existed, and these may develop here in the future; in these the care of children is shared among a number of loving adults. In such circumstances it is possible that healthy development may occur in the absence of specific attachments. However present-day children's institutions differ from such extended families in a number of respects, most of which are related to the professionalism of the staff. Unlike members of a family, staff work limited hours, and have personal and professional needs which in modern society result in fairly frequent job changes. Multiple caretaking is combined with instability of care. The staff are therefore likely to protect themselves and the children by keeping emotional relationships cool, reasoning that difficulties would be created for themselves and the children if the children demanded the care of a particular nurse. Indeed very often the institution will be organized to prevent the development of specific attachments – each child will be cared for by any of the staff on duty, rather than assigning the care of specific children to specific staff. In this way, because care is impersonal, less attempt is made to reduce the number of caretakers or their constant turnover.

Changes in staff are an inevitable feature of modern institutions: however it is possible to organize institutions in such a way that the number of caretakers per child is drastically reduced by assigning the care of specific children to specific staff members, with one or two regular deputies for off duty hours. In these circumstances much closer attachments are likely to develop, but at the risk of a series of almost inevitable bereavements. We found a number of examples in our study of prolonged and marked grief reactions in young children following the departure of their nurses. Thus whilst attempts to mimic a nuclear family within an institutional setting are feasible, they are likely to result in a different pattern of disturbance for the child. Multiple caretaking, changes of caretaker, and impersonal care are features of most but not all institutions, and would seem likely to produce deviant personality development. Unfortunately, the alternative solutions for many deprived children may be unfavourable in other respects – e.g. foster home care may be both impersonal and unstable, whilst the child's own family may be hostile, unstable or neglectful.

Discussion

It should by now be apparent that the title of this chapter needs restating; institutions are many and diverse, and their effects on development may be benign or malignant. In the studies outlined above, and reported in detail elsewhere, an attempt has been made to show that important aspects of the institutional environment can usefully be measured, and that the factors responsible for these aspects can be assessed, as can their effects on children's development. It thus becomes possible in principle to specify the kinds of institutional environment likely to promote different kinds of development, and the kinds of organizational structure in which staff are most likely to produce such environments.

This has already been done to some extent in regard to physical and cognitive (including linguistic) development. Evidence about the effects of different child care patterns upon personality development is less satisfactory – partly because few useful measures of social and emotional development exist, partly because no *systematic* comparative studies of residential institutions for young children have been carried out to examine the complex interactions which presumably influence the personality development of children brought up in differing environments. Neither our own studies, nor those of other research workers, have systematically explored these problems. There is a wealth of data to show that poor institutional child care practices have adverse effects upon children; and a number of long-term follow-up studies indicate that children exposed to such conditions in early childhood are more likely to be disturbed or delinquent in adolescence and adult life. However the interpretation of long-term follow up data poses formidable problems, in that information about the quality of the early environment is usually sketchy, and because a high proportion of the children who are neglected or ill-treated at one point in their lives are likely to continue to live in highly unsatisfactory circumstances.

A further, practical point weakens the use that can be made of longitudinal data by those concerned with child care policy: institutions themselves are liable to have changed so much before their long-term consequences for children become manifest that inferences drawn for current practice from primary data which relate to conditions existing fifteen to thirty years ago must be treated with circumspection.

However it would not seem impossible to carry out studies designed explicitly to measure the 'emotional climate' of institutions serving the needs of young children, to explore the organizational arrangements which facilitate different types of staff–child interaction, and to assess the effects of these upon the children's emotional well-being. Only when this is done will it be possible to assess the effects of different strategies at present advocated as being likely to overcome or mitigate the consequences of discontinuities of institutional upbringing. In our own mental subnormality studies for example we found it possible to rate the quality of observed staff–child interactions very reliably, using a simple three-fold classification (accepting, tolerating and rejecting). In the nursery studies it was found that staff in different nursery groups differed greatly in the *quality* of their verbal exchanges with the children, as well as in the continuity, and the nature, of their relations with them. These differences were related to differences in patterns of nursery organization, and were likely to have affected the children's behaviour. The study of two-year-old children showed that there were significant differences in attachment behaviour and in responses to strangers between those in nurseries and a constant group living at home, and the longitudinal studies in progress throw light on short-term consequences of particular patterns of care, and particular changes in patterns of care.

However indicators such as we have used require further development. The most difficult problems are likely to be encountered not in developing further measures of organizational structure, or of the emotional 'tone' of staff–child interactions, but in quantifying differences in child behaviour. To date, most psychological research concerned with non-cognitive aspects of behaviour during the preschool years has dealt with behavioural pathology. But gross pathology is uncommon in good modern nurseries; and the most rewarding studies in the future are likely to be those which explore differing rates of social and emotional development in children of different age groups, and those which relate differences in children's behaviour in different nursery settings to particular qualities of the nursery environments. Our own studies lead us to believe that behavioural ratings by staff are likely to be too unreliable to be useful for this type of comparative study. Instead, one must rely on direct observation, and clinical and experimental examination of individual children.

The conceptual and technical problems of devising such procedures are of central importance to developmental psychology. And inasmuch as our concern is with environmental determinants of behaviour, comparative research carried out in institutions offers unique opportunities in which to study the development of children in settings in which environmental and hereditary influences are not hopelessly confounded.

References

BLATT, B. (1967) *Christmas in Purgatory: a photographic essay in mental retardation* Boston, Allyn and Bacon.

BLATT, B. (1969) 'Purgatory' in Kugel, R. B. and Wolfensberger W. (eds) *Changing Patterns in Residential Services for the Mentally Retarded* Washington, D.C., President's Panel on Mental Retardation.

BOWLBY, J. (1951) *Maternal Care and Mental Health* Geneva, W.H.O.

BOWLBY, J. (1969) *Attachment and Loss*, vol. 1, *Attachment* London, Hogarth Press.

CURTIS, M. (1946) *Report of the Care of Children Committee* London, H.M.S.O., Cmd. 6922.

FITZHERBERT, K. (1967) *West Indian Children in London*, Occas. Papers on Soc, Admin. no. 19, London, G. Bell.

GOFFMAN, E. (1961) *Asylums: Essays on the Social Situation of Mental Patients and Other Inmates* New York, Doubleday.

HEYWOOD, J. S. (1965) *Children in Care: the Development of the Service for the Deprived Child* London, Routledge and Kegan Paul.

KING, R. D. (1970) 'A Comparative Study of Residential Care for Handicapped Children', Unpublished Ph.D. thesis, Univ. of London.

KING, R. D., RAYNES, N. V. and TIZARD, J. (1971) *Patterns of Residential Care: Sociological Studies in Institutions for Handicapped Children* London, Routledge and Kegan Paul.

OSWIN, M. (1971) *The Empty Hours: a Study of the Weekend Life of Handicapped Children in Institutions* London, Allen and Lane.

PACKMAN, J. (1968) *Child Care: Needs and Numbers* London, George Allen and Unwin.

PLATT, H. (1959) *Report of the Committee: The Welfare of Children in Hospital* Ministry of Health Central Health Services Council, London, H.M.S.O.

PINCHBECK, I. and HEWITT, M. (1969) *Children in English Society*, vol. 1, *From Tudor Times to the Eighteenth Century* London, Routledge and Kegan Paul.

SCHAFFER, H. R. and SCHAFFER, E. B. (1968) *Child Care and the Family* Occas. Papers on Soc. Admin. no. 25, London, G. Bell.

TITMUSS, R. (1961) Cited by J. K. Wing (1962) in 'Institutionalism in mental hospitals', *Brit. J. soc. clin. Psychol*, 1, 38–51.

TIZARD, J. (1964) *Community Services for the Mentally Handicapped* London, Oxford Univ. Press.

TIZARD, B. and JOSEPH, A. (1970) 'The cognitive development of young children in residential care', *J. Child Psychol. Psychiat.*, 11, 177–86.

TIZARD, J. and TIZARD, B. (1971) 'The social development of two-year-old children in residential nurseries' in Schaffer, H. R. (ed.) *The Origins of Human Social Relations* London, Academic Press.

TIZARD, B., COOPERMAN, O., JOSEPH, A. and TIZARD J. (1972) 'Environmental effects on language development: a study of young children in long-stay residential nurseries', *Child Development*, 43, 337–58.

WOLFENSBERGER, W. (1969) 'The origin and nature of our institutional models' in Kugel, R. B. and Wolfensberger, W. (eds) *Changing Patterns in Residential Services for the Mentally Retarded* Washington, D.C., President's Panel on Mental Retardation.

17 The experience of living in cities

Stanley Milgram

> When I first came to New York it seemed like a nightmare. As soon as I got off the train at Grand Central I was caught up in pushing, shoving crowds on 42nd Street. Sometimes people bumped into me without apology; what really frightened me was to see two people literally engaged in combat for possession of a cab. Why were they so rushed? Even drunks on the street were bypassed without a glance. People didn't seem to care about each other at all.

This statement represents a common reaction to a great city, but it does not tell the whole story. Obviously cities have great appeal because of their variety, eventfulness, possibility of choice, and the stimulation of an intense atmosphere that many individuals find a desirable background to their lives. Where face-to-face contacts are important, the city offers unparalleled possibilities. It has been calculated by the Regional Plan Association[1] that in Nassau County, a suburb of New York City, an individual can meet 11,000 others within a 10-minute radius of his office by foot or car. In Newark, a moderate-sized city, he can meet more than 20,000 persons within this radius. But in midtown Manhattan he can meet fully 220,000. So there is an order-of-magnitude increment in the communication possibilities offered by a great city. That is one of the bases of its appeal and, indeed, of its functional necessity. The city provides options that no other social arrangement permits. But there is a negative side also, as we shall see.

Granted that cities are indispensable in complex society, we may still ask what contribution psychology can make to understanding the experience of living in them. What theories are relevant? How can we extend our knowledge of the psychological aspects of life in cities through empirical inquiry? If empirical inquiry is possible, along what lines should it proceed? In short, where do we start in constructing urban theory and in laying out lines of research?

Observation is the indispensable starting point. Any observer in the streets of midtown Manhattan will see (i) large numbers of people, (ii) a high population density, and (iii) heterogeneity of population. These three factors need to be at the root of any sociopsychological theory of city life, for they condition all aspects of our experience in the metropolis. Louis Wirth,[2] if not the first to point to these factors, is nonetheless the soci-

---

MILGRAM, STANLEY (1970) 'The experience of living in cities' in *Science*, vol. 167, 1461–8.

ologist who relied most heavily on them in his analysis of the city. Yet, for a psychologist, there is something unsatisfactory about Wirth's theoretical variables. Numbers, density, and heterogeneity are demographic facts but they are not yet psychological facts. They are external to the individual. Psychology needs an idea that links the individual's *experience* to the demographic circumstances of urban life.

One link is provided by the concept of overload. This term, drawn from systems analysis, refers to a system's inability to process inputs from the environment because there are too many inputs for the system to cope with, or because successive inputs come so fast that input *A* cannot be processed when input *B* is presented. When overload is present, adaptations occur. The system must set priorities and make choices. *A* must be processed first while *B* is kept in abeyance, or one input may be sacrificed altogether. City life, as we experience it, constitutes a continuous set of encounters with overload, and of resultant adaptations. Overload characteristically deforms daily life on several levels, impinging on role performance, the evolution of social norms, cognitive functioning, and the use of facilities.

The concept has been implicit in several theories of urban experience. In 1903 George Simmel[3] pointed out that, since urban dwellers come into contact with vast numbers of people each day, they conserve psychic energy by becoming acquainted with a far smaller proportion of people than their rural counterparts do, and by maintaining more superficial relationships even with these acquaintances. Wirth[2] points specifically to 'the superficiality, the anonymity, and the transitory character of urban social relations'.

One adaptive response to overload, therefore, is the allocation of less time to each input. A second adaptive mechanism is disregard of low-priority inputs. Principles of selectivity are formulated such that investment of time and energy are reserved for carefully defined inputs (the urbanite disregards the drunk sick on the street as he purposefully navigates through the crowd). Third, boundaries are redrawn in certain social transactions so that the overloaded system can shift the burden to the other party in the exchange; thus, harried New York bus drivers once made change for customers, but now this responsibility has been shifted to the client, who must have the exact fare ready. Fourth, reception is blocked off prior to entrance into a system; city dwellers increasingly use unlisted telephone numbers to prevent individuals from calling them, and a small but growing number resort to keeping the telephone off the hook to prevent incoming calls. More subtly, a city dweller blocks inputs by assuming an unfriendly countenance, which discourages others from initiating contact. Additionally, social screening devices are interposed between the individual and environmental inputs (in a town of 5000 anyone can drop in to chat with the mayor, but in the metropolis organizational screening devices deflect inputs to other destinations). Fifth, the intensity of inputs is diminished by filtering devices, so that only weak and relatively superficial forms of involvement with others are allowed. Sixth, specialized institutions are created to absorb inputs that would otherwise swamp the individual (welfare departments handle the financial needs of a million individuals in New York City, who would otherwise create an army of mendicants continuously importuning the pedestrian). The interposition of institutions between the individual and the social world, a characteristic of all modern society, and most notably of the large metropolis, has its negative side. It deprives the individual of a sense of direct contact and spontaneous integration in the life around him. It simultaneously protects and estranges the individual from his social environment.

Many of these adaptive mechanisms apply not only to individuals but to institutional systems as well, as Meir[4] has so brilliantly shown in connection with the library and the stock exchange.

In sum, the observed behaviour of the urbanite in a wide range of situations appears to be determined largely by a variety of adaptations to overload. I now deal with several specific consequences of responses to overload, which make for differences in the tone of city and town.

Social responsibility

The principal point of interest for a social psychology of the city is that moral and social involvement with individuals is necessarily restricted. This is a direct and necessary function of excess of input over capacity to process. Such restriction of involvement runs a broad spectrum from refusal to become involved in the needs of another person, even when the person desperately needs assistance through refusal to do favours, to the simple withdrawal of courtesies (such as offering a lady a seat, or saying 'sorry' when a pedestrian collision occurs). In any transaction more and more details need to be dropped as the total number of units to be processed increases and assaults an instrument of limited processing capacity.

The ultimate adaptation to an overloaded social environment is to totally disregard the needs, interests, and demands of those whom one does not define as relevant to the satisfaction of personal needs, and to develop highly efficient perceptual means of determining whether an individual falls into the category of friend or stranger. The disparity in the treatment of friends and strangers ought to be greater in cities than in towns; the time allotment and willingness to become involved with those who have no personal claim on one's time is likely to be less in cities than in towns.

Bystander intervention in crises

The most striking deficiencies in social responsibility in cities occur in crisis situations, such as the Genovese murder in Queens. In 1964, Catherine Genovese, coming home from a night job in the early hours of an April morning, was stabbed repeatedly, over an extended period of time. Thirty-eight residents of a respectable New York City neighbourhood admit to having witnessed at least a part of the attack, but none went to her aid or called the police until after she was dead. Milgram and Hollander, writing in *The Nation*,[5] analyzed the event in these terms:

> Urban friendships and associations are not primarily formed on the basis of physical proximity. A person with numerous close friends in different parts of the city may not know the occupant of an adjacent apartment. This does not mean that a city dweller has fewer friends than does a villager, or knows fewer persons who will come to his aid; however, it does mean that his allies are not constantly at hand. Miss Genovese required immediate aid from those physically present. There is no evidence that the city had deprived Miss Genovese of human associations, but the friends who might have rushed to her side were miles from the scene of her tragedy.
>
> Further, it is known that her cries for help were not directed to a specific person; they were general. But only individuals can act, and as the cries were not specifically directed, no particular person felt a special responsibility. The crime and the failure of community response seem absurd to us. At the time, it may well have seemed equally absurd to the Kew Gardens residents that not one of the neighbours would have called the police. A collective paralysis may have developed from the belief of each of the witnesses that someone else must surely have taken that obvious step.

Latané and Darley[6] have reported laboratory approaches to the study of bystander intervention and have established experimentally the following principle: the larger the number of bystanders, the less the likelihood that any one of them will intervene in an emergency. Gaertner and Bickman[7] of The City University of New York have extended the bystander studies to an examination of help across ethnic lines. Blacks and whites, with clearly identifiable accents, called strangers (through what the caller represented as an error in telephone dialling), gave them a plausible story of being stranded on an outlying highway without more dimes, and asked the stranger to call a garage. The experimenters found that the white callers had a significantly better chance of obtaining assistance than the black callers. This suggests that ethnic allegiance may well be another means of coping with overload: the city dweller can reduce excessive demands and screen out urban heterogeneity by responding along ethnic lines; overload is made more manageable by limiting the 'span of sympathy'.

In any quantitative characterization of the social texture of city life, a necessary first step is the application of such experimental methods as these to field situations in large cities and small towns. Theorists argue that the indifference shown in the Genovese case would not be found in a small town, but in the absence of solid experimental evidence the question remains an open one.

More than just callousness prevents bystanders from participating in altercations between people. A rule of urban life is respect for other people's emotional and social privacy, perhaps because physical privacy is so hard to achieve. And in situations for which the standards are heterogeneous, it is much harder to know whether taking an active role is unwarranted meddling or an appropriate response to a critical situation. If a husband and wife are quarrelling in public, at what point should a bystander step in? On the one hand, the heterogeneity of the city produces substantially greater tolerance about behaviour, dress, and codes of ethics than is generally found in the small town, but this diversity also encourages people to withhold aid for fear of antagonizing the participants or crossing an inappropriate and difficult-to-define line.

Moreover, the frequency of demands present in the city gives rise to norms of noninvolvement. There are practical limitations to the Samaritan impulse in a major city. If a citizen attended to every needy person, if he were sensitive to and acted on every altruistic impulse that was evoked in the city, he could scarcely keep his own affairs in order.

Willingness to trust and assist strangers

We now move away from crisis situations to less urgent examples of social responsibility. For it is not only in situations of dramatic need but in the ordinary, everyday willingness to lend a hand that the city dweller is said to be deficient relative to his small-town cousin. The comparative method must be used in any empirical examination of this question. A commonplace social situation is staged in an urban setting and in a small town – a situation to which a subject can respond by either extending help or withholding it. The responses in town and city are compared.

One factor in the purported unwillingness of urbanites to be helpful to strangers may well be their heightened sense of physical (and emotional) vulnerability – a feeling that is supported by urban crime statistics. A key

Table 1. Percentage of entries achieved by investigators for city and town dwellings (see text)

Experimenter	*Entries achieved (%)*	
	*City**	*Small town†*
Male		
No. 1	16	40
No. 2	12	60
Female		
No. 3	40	87
No. 4	40	100

* Number of requests for entry, 100.
† Number of requests for entry, 60.

test for distinguishing between city and town behaviour, therefore, is determining how city dwellers compare with town dwellers in offering aid that increases their personal vulnerability and requires some trust of strangers. Altman, Levine, Nadien, and Villena [8] of The City University of New York devised a study to compare the behaviours of city and town dwellers in this respect. The criterion used in this study was the willingness of householders to allow strangers to enter their home to use the telephone. The student investigators individually rang doorbells, explained that they had misplaced the address of a friend nearby, and asked to use the phone. The investigators (two males and two females) made 100 requests for entry into homes in the city and 60 requests in the small towns. The results for middle-income housing developments in Manhattan were compared with data for several small towns (Stony Point, Spring Valley, Ramapo, Nyack, New City, and West Clarkstown) in Rockland County, outside of New York City. As Table 1 shows, in all cases there was a sharp increase in the proportion of entries achieved by an experimenter when he moved from the city to a small town. In the most extreme case the experimenter was five times as likely to gain admission to homes in a small town as to homes in Manhattan. Although the female experimenters had notably greater success both in cities and in towns than the male experimenters had, each of the four students did at least twice as well in towns as in cities. This suggests that the city–town distinction overrides even the predictably greater fear of male strangers than of female ones.

The lower level of helpfulness by city dwellers seems due in part to recognition of the dangers of living in Manhattan, rather than to mere indifference or coldness. It is significant that 75 per cent of all the city respondents received and answered messages by shouting through closed doors and by peering out through peepholes; in the towns, by contrast, about 75 per cent of the respondents opened the door.

Suppporting the experimenters' quantitative results was their general observation that the town dwellers were noticeably more friendly and less suspicious than the city dwellers. In seeking to explain the reasons for the greater sense of psychological vulnerability city dwellers feel, above and beyond the differences in crime statistics, Villena [8] points out that, if a crime is committed in a village, a resident of a neighbouring village may not perceive the crime as personally relevant, though the geographic distance may be small, whereas a criminal act committed anywhere in the city, though miles from the city-dweller's home is still verbally located within the city; thus, Villena says, 'the inhabitant of the city possesses a larger vulnerable space'.

Civilities

Even at the most superficial level of involvement – the exercise of everyday civilities – urbanites are reputedly deficient. People bump into each other and often do not apologize. They knock over another person's packages and, as often as not, proceed on their way with a grumpy exclamation instead of an offer of assistance. Such behaviour, which many visitors to great cities find distasteful, is less common, we are told, in smaller communities, where traditional courtesies are more likely to be observed.

In some instances it is not simply that, in the city, traditional courtesies are violated; rather the cities develop new norms of noninvolvement. These are so well defined and so deeply a part of city life that *they* constitute the norms people are reluctant to violate. Men are actually embarrassed to give up a seat on the subway to an old woman; they mumble 'I was getting off anyway', instead of making the gesture in a straightforward and gracious way. These norms develop because everyone realizes that, in situations of high population density, people cannot implicate themselves in each others' affairs, for to do so would create conditions of continual distraction which would frustrate purposeful action.

In discussing the effects of overload I do not imply that at every instant the city dweller is bombarded with an unmanageable number of inputs, and that his responses are determined by the excess of input at any given instant. Rather, adaptation occurs in the form of gradual evolution of norms of behaviour. Norms are evolved in response to frequent discrete experiences of overload; they persist and become generalized modes of responding.

Overload on cognitive capacities: anonymity

That we respond differently towards those whom we know and those who are strangers to us is a truism. An eager patron aggressively cuts in front of someone in a long movie line to save time only to confront a friend; he then behaves sheepishly. A man is involved in an automobile accident caused by another driver, emerges from his car shouting in rage, then moderates his behaviour on discovering a friend driving the other car. The city dweller, when walking through the midtown streets, is in a state of continual anonymity vis-à-vis the other pedestrians.

Anonymity is part of a continuous spectrum ranging from total anonymity to full acquaintance, and it may well be that measurement of the precise degrees of anonymity in cities and towns would help to explain important distinctions between the quality of life in each. Conditions of full acquaintance, for example, offer security and familiarity, but they may also be stifling, because the individual is caught in a web of established relationships. Conditions of complete anonymity, by contrast, provide freedom from routinized social ties, but they may also create feelings of alienation and detachment.

Empirically one could investigate the proportion of activities in which the city dweller or the town dweller is known by others at given times in his daily life, and the proportion of activities in the course of which he interacts with individuals who know him. At his job, for instance, the city dweller may be known to as many people as his rural counterpart. However when he is not fulfilling his occupational role – say, when merely travelling about the city – the urbanite is doubtless more anonymous than his rural counterpart.

Limited empirical work on anonymity has begun. Zimbardo [9] has tested whether the social anonymity and impersonality of the big city encourage greater vandalism than do small towns. Zimbardo arranged for one automobile to be left for 64 hours near the Bronx campus of New York University and for a counterpart to be left for the same number of hours near Stanford University in Palo Alto. The licence plates on the two cars were removed and the hoods were opened, to provide 'releaser cues' for potential vandals. The New York car was stripped of all movable parts within the first 24 hours, and by the end of 3 days was only a hunk of metal rubble. Unexpectedly, however, most of the destruction occurred during daylight hours, usually under the scrutiny of observers, and the leaders in the vandalism were well-dressed, white adults. The Palo Alto car was left untouched.

Zimbardo attributes the difference in the treatment accorded the two cars to the 'acquired feelings of social anonymity provided by life in a city like New York', and he supports his conclusions with several other anecdotes illustrating casual, wanton vandalism in the city. In any comparative study of the effects of anonymity in city and town, however, there must be satisfactory control for other confounding factors: the large number of drug addicts in a city like New York; the higher proportion of slum-dwellers in the city; and so on.

Another direction for empirical study is investigation of the beneficial effects of anonymity. The impersonality of city life breeds its own tolerance for the private lives of the inhabitants. Individuality and even eccentricity, we may assume, can flourish more readily in the metropolis than in the small town. Stigmatized persons may find it easier to lead comfortable lives in the city, free of the constant scrutiny of neighbours. To what degree can this assumed difference between city and town be shown empirically? Judith Waters,[10] at The City University of New York, hypothesized that avowed homosexuals would be more likely to be accepted as tenants in a large city than in small towns, and she dispatched letters from homosexuals and from normal individuals to real estate agents in cities and towns across the country. The results of her study were inconclusive. But the general idea of examining the protective benefits of city life to the stigmatized ought to be pursued.

Role behaviour in cities and towns

Another product of urban overload is the adjustment in roles made by urbanites in daily interactions. As Wirth has said[2] 'Urbanites meet one another in highly segmental roles. . . . They are less dependent upon particular persons, and their dependence upon others is confined to a highly fractionalized aspect of the other's round of activity.' This tendency is particularly noticeable in transactions between customers and individuals offering professional or sales services. The owner of a country store has time to become well acquainted with his dozen-or-so daily customers, but the girl at the checkout counter of a busy A & P, serving hundreds of customers a day, barely has time to toss the green stamps into one customer's shopping bag before the next customer confronts her with his pile of groceries.

Meier, in his stimulating analysis of the city,[4] discusses several adaptations a system may make when confronted by inputs that exceed its capacity to process them. Meier argues that, according to the principle of competition for scarce resources, the scope and time of the transaction shrink as customer volume and daily turnover rise. This, in fact, is what is meant by the 'brusque' quality of city life. New standards have developed in cities con-

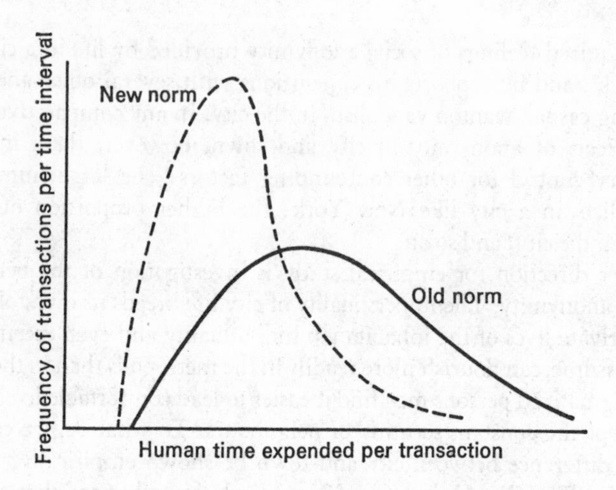

Fig. 1 Changes in the demand for time for a given task when the overall transaction frequency increases in a social system. (From Meier 1962.)

cerning what levels of services are appropriate in business transactions (see figure 1).

McKenna and Morgenthau,[11] in a seminar at The City University of New York, devised a study (i) to compare the willingness of city dwellers and small-town dwellers to do favours for strangers that entailed expenditure of a small amount of time and slight inconvenience but no personal vulnerability, and (ii) to determine whether the more compartmentalized, transitory relationships of the city would make urban salesgirls less likely than small-town salesgirls to carry out, for strangers, tasks not related to their customary roles.

To test for differences between city dwellers and small-town dwellers, a simple experiment was devised in which persons from both settings were asked (by telephone) to perform increasingly onerous favours for anonymous strangers.

Within the cities (Chicago, New York, and Philadelphia), half the calls were to housewives and the other half to salesgirls in women's apparel shops; the division was the same for the 37 small towns of the study, which were in the same states as the cities. Each experimenter represented herself as a long-distance caller who had, through error, been connected with the respondent by the operator. The experimenter began by asking for simple information about the weather for purposes of travel. Next the experimenter excused herself on some pretext (asking the respondent to 'please hold on'), put the phone down for almost a full minute, and then picked it up again and asked the respondent to provide the phone number of a hotel or motel in her vicinity at which the experimenter might stay during a forthcoming visit. Scores were assigned the subjects on the basis of how helpful they had been. McKenna summarizes her results in this manner:

> People in the city, whether they are engaged in a specific job or not, are less helpful and informative than people in small towns; . . . People at home, regardless of where they live, are less helpful and informative than people working in shops.

However, the absolute level of cooperativeness for urban subjects was found to be quite high, and does not accord with the stereotype of the urbanite as aloof, self-centred, and unwilling to help strangers. The quantitative differences obtained by McKenna and Morgenthau are less great than one might have expected. This again points up the need for extensive empirical research in rural–urban differences, research that goes far beyond that provided in the few illustrative pilot studies presented here. At this point we have very limited objective evidence on differences in the quality of social encounters in city and small town.

But the research needs to be guided by unifying theoretical concepts. As I have tried to demonstrate, the concept of overload helps to explain a wide variety of contrasts between city behaviour and town behaviour: (i) the differences in role enactment (the tendency of urban dwellers to deal with one another in highly segmented, functional terms, and of urban sales personnel to devote limited time and attention to their customers); (ii) the evolution of urban norms quite different from traditional town values (such as the acceptance of noninvolvement, impersonality, and aloofness in urban life); (iii) the adaptation of the urban dweller's cognitive processes (his inability to identify most of the people he sees daily, his screening of sensory stimuli, his development of blasé attitudes towards deviant or bizarre behaviour, and his selectivity in responding to human demands); and (iv) the competition for scarce facilities in the city (the subway rush; the fight for taxis; traffic jams; standing in line to await services). I suggest that contrasts between city and rural behaviour probably reflect the responses of similar people to very different situations, rather than intrinsic differences in the personalities of rural and city dwellers. The city is a situation to which individuals respond adaptively. [. . .]

References and notes

1 *New York Times* (15 June 1969).
2 WIRTH, L., *Amer. J. Soc.*, 44, 1 (1938). Wirth's ideas have come under heavy criticism by contemporary city planners, who point out that the city is broken down into neighbourhoods, which fulfil many of the functions of small towns. See, for example, H. J. Gans, *People and Plans: Essays on Urban Problems and Solutions* (Basic Books, New York, 1968); J. Jacobs, *The Death and Life of Great American Cities* (Random House, New York, 1961); G. D. Suttles, *The Social Order of the Slum* (Univ. of Chicago Press, Chicago, 1968).
3 SIMMEL, G., *The Sociology of Georg Simmel*, K. H. Wolff, (ed.) (Macmillan, New York, 1950) [English translation of G. Simmel, *Die Grossstadte und das Geistesleben Die Grossstadt* (Jansch, Dresden, 1903)].
4 MEIER, R. L., *A Communications Theory of Urban Growth* (M.I.T. Press, Cambridge, Mass., 1962).
5 MILGRAM, S. and HOLLANDER, P., *Nation*, 25, 602 (1964).
6 LATANÉ, B. and DARLEY, J., *Amer. Sci.*, 57, 244 (1969).
7 GAERTNER, S. and BICKMAN, L. (Graduate Center, The City University of New York), unpublished research.
8 ALTMAN, D., LEVINE, M., NADIEN, M. and VILLENA, J. (Graduate Center, The City University of New York), unpublished research.
9 ZIMBARDO, P. G., paper presented at the Nebraska Symposium on Motivation (1969).
10 WATERS, J. (Graduate Center, The City University of New York), unpublished research.
11 MCKENNA, W. and MORGENTHAU, S. (Graduate Center, the City University of New York), unpublished research.

Section 5
Socialization

Introduction

Human infants are born helpless and thus dependent on others for survival. Lacking language, culture and moral values at birth, they must acquire these in the societies into which they are born. The concept of socialization refers broadly to all the processes through which the individual becomes a member of his society. This simple definition hides a great many controversies as to the nature of these processes and their precise outcomes. In our first article, Rudolf Schaffer discusses some of the basic changes which have taken place in the conception of the socialization process. In particular, the author shows that recent knowledge of the complex endogenous abilities of infants have forced us to think in terms of the *interaction* between parent and infant rather than in terms of the parent moulding the child.

Some of these new insights have evolved from the observation and video-taping of mother–child interactions. The subsequent frame-by-frame analysis of the video recording reveals, among other things, that it is often the baby which initiates a behaviour sequence (looking at a toy, for instance), and that the mother follows the child's gaze. Schaffer, therefore, in discussing synchronization and reciprocity of behaviour may be said to move from empirical observation to theory.

A great deal of work by psychologists, however, starts with a theoretical statement and research is then undertaken to find empirical support for the theory or hypothesis put forward. A series of experiments may, of course, not vindicate a particular hypothesis in which case the theorist would change the formulation of the expected relationships and conduct new experiments or observations. In this sense, too, observation may be seen to lead to theory.

Our second article by Albert Bandura, Dorothea Ross and Sheila A. Ross is in this hypothetico-deductive tradition. It is reprinted here as an example of careful experimentation in a laboratory setting on how and under what circumstances and to what extent children in the laboratory imitate aggressive behaviour. The notion that learning takes place through imitation and reinforcement belongs to the theoretical apparatus of *social-learning theory*. This approach focuses on the relationship between a stimulus (for instance, viewing a film in which a model behaves in an aggressive manner) and the response (the imitation of the observed behaviour). It is the stimulus which is seen as eliciting the response. Socialization, in this theoretical perspective, is conceptualized as influences impinging on the child from the environment and, typically, in experiments the child is the subject and the experimenter sets the scene. However, doubt as to the appropriateness of the assumption of uni-directional influences has already been raised in our first article in this section. In our third article, Urie Bronfenbrenner questions once more the validity of such an approach, in terms of developing a theoretical framework and of the uses and applicability of the findings. He sets out the criteria he considers necessary for an adequate model of the socialization process. His article is included here particularly also because it stresses dimensions neglected in laboratory-based psychological research. A plea is made to extend the study of socialization processes from two-person systems to include interactions among several family members or in the peer-group and to locate such interactions in the social structures and institutions of society. The article by Tizard and Tizard (1947) we included in the previous section is an example of the impact of institutions as socializing agents.

Three articles on socialization can only provide an introduction to such a wide ranging subject of interest to many social sciences. The focus here has been on childhood socialization, but socialization is a lifelong process and many articles elsewhere in this Reader are concerned, implicitly at any rate, with processes and outcomes of socialization.

18 Early social behaviour and the study of reciprocity

H. R. Schaffer

It is often said that the study of early social behaviour lags well behind the study of early cognitive behaviour. A quick check through some of the recent numbers of the developmental journals confirms this, though it also shows that it is becoming increasingly difficult to make this classification. This is partly because of the growing interest in subjects like language development which seem to belong to both categories and partly because of an increasing tendency to blur the distinction between the two fields and concern oneself with, for example, cognitive processes underlying social behaviour or the social context of cognition.

However this may be, there is no doubt about the liveliness of the social area. This is attested perhaps not so much by the sheer quantity of studies as by the fairly drastic changes in approach which one now finds there. It is about these that I want to talk.

Probably the most basic change refers to our conception of the socialization process itself. It is a change which is reflected in the definitions of this concept. Only a few years ago these were couched entirely in terms of what parents, or society generally, did to the young child, referring to the way in which he was 'moulded' into an effective participant or to the manner in which his behaviour was 'shaped' by his social environment. Emphasis, that is, was entirely on the external influence impinging on the child, and as for the child himself, he tended to be seen as a sort of formless blob of clay that was merely the passive recipient of those external forces, and the final shape that he assumed, therefore, could be ascribed entirely to the characteristics that others had decided he should assume.

More recent definitions see socialization as something rather more complex than clay-moulding. Take Peter Kelvin's (1970, 1971) discussion as one example. Socialization, according to him, refers to the process whereby the social environment becomes reasonably predictable to the individual and where the individual becomes reasonably predictable to those others who constitute the environment. The basic criterion for assessing socialization is whether this mutual predictability has been achieved. In this way the essentially two-way or interactive nature of socialization is brought out

---

SCHAFFER, H. R. (1974) 'Early social behaviour and the study of reciprocity' in *Bulletin of the British Psychological Society*, vol. 27, 209–16.

into the open, for without it the conduct of social interaction would be far from smooth.

Now the former, unidirectional view influenced a large number of studies in the 1950s and early 1960s, of which the series conducted by Sears and his colleagues is probably the best known. Their attempt to correlate parental practices with subsequent child behaviour appeared wholly praiseworthy at the time; the outcome, however, has proved disappointing. We see this in particular in the study by Yarrow et al. (1968), in which an attempt was made to replicate some of the Sears et al. (1957) findings on the relationship between parental characteristics and child characteristics – an attempt which by and large failed. As Yarrow et al. conclude in their book: 'The compelling legend of maternal influences on child behaviour that has evolved does not have its roots in solid data, and its decisive verification remains in many respects a subject for future research.' And again: 'We are still searching for the specific conditions in the child's cumulative experience with his parents that evoke, strengthen and modify his behaviour. The questions of child rearing have not yielded easily to scientific study.' A similar conclusion is reached by, amongst others, Cairns (1972): 'Child rearing studies have shown that the processes by which parents influence their children's behaviour are considerably more complex than was first assumed to be the case. Summary variables like maternal warmth and dependency were selected because it seemed likely that concepts at this level of abstraction would yield stable antecedent–consequent relations. That expectation has not for the most part been confirmed.'

There are, no doubt, many reasons for this state of affairs, but it seems likely that one of the main factors was the tendency to concentrate on what parents did to their children and to pay no attention to the possibility that even the very youngest child is no formless blob of clay, that his behaviour is organized in a particular manner from the beginning, and that he has an individuality of his own that determines how he responds to parental treatment and even determines the nature of this treatment itself. The nature of the young child, that is, was not really considered.

And yet, in recent years we have begun to learn a great deal about the psychological nature of even very young children – indeed one could say that there has been something of a switch from the study of the experience-giving parent to that of the experiencing infant. The study of infant behaviour has probably become one of the major growth points in developmental psychology in recent years, and there is now an increasing body of data available on this topic. We have looked at the infant's ability to attend to and perceive events occurring in his environment; we have examined the extent to which he can retain and be influenced by his previous experiences; and we have learned something about the manner in which he forms his first social relationships, begins to imitate others, and starts using language. From these data it has become clear that the baby, psychologically speaking, is a far more competent organism than we originally gave him credit for, and as a result our concept of what an infant is has changed markedly: we do not discuss him any more in such purely negative terms as the 'blooming, buzzing confusion' with which William James once characterized the baby's consciousness, nor do we see him merely as an assembly of reflexes or as random mass activity. We see him rather as a being with considerable powers to gather and process information from his surroundings even in the earliest weeks of life, and though his capabilities are obviously limited by adult standards his orientation and responsiveness to the environment are nevertheless a marked feature from the beginning of life.

However, this does not mean that the infant is just a passive absorber of experience, that he is affected by every stimulus that his caretakers expose him to. On the contrary, it seems that from the start he is already structured in such a way that he will help to determine his own experience, and the adults who care for him must take into account and respect the particular kind of inherent mental organization with which he arrives in the world.

Take as an example what is often regarded as the first truly social response, the smile. Smiling has generally been described as an essentially elicited response, which appears from about 6 or 8 weeks on and is found only when the relevant stimulus (usually the human face) is presented. More recently, however, Emde and Harrison (1972) have established that smiling as a spontaneous, non-elicited activity can be seen from birth on. It appears in regular rhythms, takes place in bursts rather like spontaneous sucking, occurs with an average density of 11 smiles per 100 minutes no matter where it is observed in the feeding cycle or the 24-hour cycle, and is generally found in association with particular EEG patterns and specific arousal states. It bears, in short, all the hall-marks of an endogenously organized response which becomes evident only if the investigator is prepared to stand back and observe what happens when the child is left to his own devices. As long as it was believed that an infant's responses appear only when the experimenter happens to let loose on him a stimulus and that on all other occasions the baby was more or less inert, a partial and somewhat misleading view of the response system was obtained. In due course endogenous smiling diminishes and by the fifth or sixth month it becomes a rarity. By that time smiling has become closely linked to certain classes of environmental stimuli, and it is this transition from an endogenous to an exogenous pattern that must be of interest to students of the socialization process.

The same applies to that other powerful social signalling system, the crying response. We know from the work of Wolff (1969) that the cry is essentially a high-frequency micro-rhythm, regulated by apparently endogenous brain mechanisms and arranged as an auditory pattern involving quite complex time sequences. Wolff has shown that there are at least three distinct patterns, and that mothers generally have no difficulty in distinguishing them. The pain cry, in particular, has arousing properties that the other two do not have and will ensure that the mother takes prompt action. It seems, therefore, that quite different information is carried by these patterns, that they act as signals to the child's caretakers, and that by their means the baby is already capable of determining to some extent when and how much attention he obtains. What we know very little about so far is how this endogenously regulated, reflexive behaviour becomes converted into an instrumental response which the child uses intentionally and in the full anticipation of bringing about some effect on the social environment. That this transition has taken place by about the end of the first year is clear, but how it occurs is a very important problem to be solved by future work.

The extent to which a child is capable of determining the parent's behaviour is perhaps most easily seen from examining the influence of individual difference factors that exist in children from the beginning. Let it first of all be asserted that these can exist from the beginning: children do not come into the world like a lot of cigarettes, exactly alike in size, shape, weight, colour, and the propensity to induce ill-health in all those coming into contact with them. Indeed one of the earliest signs of individuality is to be found by examining once again the crying response, where individual differences in the duration of the various sequences of the response and in the intervals between them have been found, so that a mother is likely to respond differently to different babies. This point is made best by referring to the pathological extreme, namely the finding that brain-damaged infants may show quite irregular crying patterns, presumably because of injury to the endogenous mechanism which controls this response. Under these circumstances the signalling capacity of the baby will, of course, be adversely affected, with considerable implications for the mother's ability to care for the child. The end-product that we are likely to see then is a disturbed mother–child relationship, which up till now has only too often been ascribed to faulty mothering. The onus, that is, tends to be put entirely on the parent – a view clearly based on the conception of the child as a blob of clay.

Just what it is that each child brings with him to an interaction situation is still very much in need of definition. A certain amount of attention has been given to a number of so-called intrinsic reaction patterns such as activity level, where individual differences are said to persist from birth, to show stability across situations as well as over age, and to exert a marked influence on maternal behaviour. Unfortunately, the work involved in isolating these characteristics is still very great and has up till now frequently yielded ambiguous or controversial results. Take as an example sex differences in early behaviour. It seems very reasonable to expect these and they are indeed frequently reported. Unfortunately when one goes through these reports no clear picture emerges. Together they add up to a picture of contradictions and ambiguities that makes one wonder whether any differences reported may not simply be due to a replication failure. Take, for example, a study reported some time ago by Watson (1969) on the early dependence on different sensory channels of boys and girls respectively. This was based on an operant conditioning study in which either visual or auditory reinforcement was administered to three-month-old infants. Conditioning, it was found, could be accomplished for the boys only if lights were used for reinforcement, whereas for the girls only sound was effective. This is a very fascinating and intriguing finding, but before we change all our child rearing and educational practices for the two sexes accordingly let us just note that the same author more recently repeated this study (Ramey and Watson, 1972) and, sad to say, failed to replicate his earlier findings.

Parents have certain characteristics; children have certain characteristics, and in some way synchronization of the two sets of forces must take place. Let me illustrate. As part of an intensive investigation of mother–infant interaction that he is carrying out, Richards (1971) has reported on some film sequences he obtained of mothers and babies smiling at each other – just that. But when he then carried out frame-by-frame analysis he found two things: first, the infant's behaviour in this situation goes through a definite sequence: he would, for example, be quietly attentive while the mother smiled, he would then gradually become more and more active, pumping himself up as it were, and at the point of maximum 'pumpedupness' he would pause a moment – and then he would smile. And the other thing Richards found was that what the mother did during this time had to be carefully phased to the infant's behaviour. For example, it was important that at the point of maximum 'pumpedupness' the mother for her part should stop all activity, giving the infant time, so to speak, to smile. If she did not do so, if instead she continued to bombard the infant with stimuli in an unphased fashion, then the child would become tense and fretful and eventually begin to cry instead of smile.

This example seems to me useful for three reasons: first, because it provides us with a good illustration of the interactive nature of the behaviour of mother and child; second because it emphasizes the importance of timing in this interaction; and third because it draws attention to the usefulness of micro-analytic techniques. I would like to say something about each one of these three points.

As to the first, it needs to be stressed that any relationship is after all a two-way process, a kind of ping-pong game where the move of each partner is to some extent dictated by the previous move of the other partner. The trouble is that psychology has in the past tended to neglect this two-way flow and instead concentrated on artificially isolated one-way units. Reports on social behaviour in laboratory situations will, for example, provide details of the number of times a child made physical contact with his mother and yet say nothing about how the mother responded to such contacts, in what way the nature of her response in turn impinged on the child, how this affected his further responsiveness to her, and so forth. Sequential analysis of dyadic behaviour has been undertaken by a number of ethologists working with such varied species as hermit crabs and rhesus monkeys but has so far been applied only very rarely to the study of early human interaction. Where it has been undertaken, on the other hand, some intriguing observations have already been unearthed such as, for instance, the very high percentage of mother–baby interaction sequences that are initiated by the baby, not by the adult partner. The same applies to the terminating of such sequences: once again a baby is surprisingly capable of dismissing the adult from his presence.

There are also now available some fascinating, detailed descriptions of precisely how mothers behave in a face-to-face interaction situation with their babies. Most mothers under these conditions show what would be regarded as highly deviant behaviour if it occurred vis à vis another adult; the slowed tempo of speech, the highly repetitive nature of vocalizations, the grossly exaggerated nature of facial expression and of gesture – all these look like supernormal stimuli which Stern (1974) has suggested mothers adopt in order to match the infant's limited tolerance of stimulus change. It has also been shown (again by Stern) that the duration of the mother's gazes at her infant is very much longer than that found in a comparable situation with another adult, approaching only that found between two lovers. Again, whatever the explanation, we have some useful descriptive data here to show just what is involved in that otherwise rather elusive term 'mothering'.

Take another example: we are just now watching the behaviour of mothers and babies sitting opposite each other, in an attempt to get at some interactional parameters and also to see how far an infant's behaviour is dependent on particular kinds of maternal input. One phenomenon struck us repeatedly, and though I must emphasize the still tentative nature of the data it is relevant to mention it here. This refers to the turn-taking nature of mother's and baby's vocalizations. It seems that the two rarely vocalize simultaneously and that their vocal interchange therefore has almost a conversational flavour. Now the 'speaker-switch' phenomenon has been described by George Miller as one of the universals of social interaction, and it has been suggested that it reflects a limit on information processing in that one cannot simultaneously speak and listen. If this phenomenon can indeed be established in young infants it may seem to suggest another characteristic which the child brings with him to the interaction situation as part of his endogenous equipment which paves the way for social interaction. But let us just note that before we can reach such a conclusion we must take cognizance of the alternative explanation, namely that the switching is entirely due to the mother letting herself be paced by the infant. According to this view his vocalization bursts take little account of such external happenings as the mother's speech, are determined instead by various internal factors, and it is then left entirely to the mother to fill in the pauses. What one then observes is a synchronization of the two sets of responses which in fact does not yet reflect true reciprocity. That can come about only when the infant, as much as the mother, becomes sensitive to the effects of his responses on the other person and can adjust his behaviour accordingly.

Now both this example and the observation by Richards to which I referred earlier highlight the second point I want to emphasize, namely the increasing concern with timing and sequence relationships as opposed to the use of summary quantitative indices. What seems to matter about 'successful' mother–infant interaction (if I may use so evaluative a term) is above all the temporal integration of the two partners' responses, and when we talk, say, about a mother's sensitivity it is often this temporal characteristic that we have in mind.

Let me give you an example referring to some other work we have in hand just now. Most studies examining dyadic processes have the two partners interacting directly with one another in a face-to-face situation, and then concentrate on mutual gazing, vocal interchange, and so on. But while the face-to-face situation is clearly important and for the understanding of interaction has – dare I say it – face value, one should not forget that an enormous amount of interactive behaviour is indirect, in the sense that it takes place via some object or feature of the environment to which both partners give simultaneous attention, and it may well be that this applies particularly to very young children, in whom visual and manipulative exploration of the environment accounts for a substantial part of their daily activities and where verbal interchange does not yet play a substantial role.

With this in mind, we have been observing the responses of mothers and babies to a novel environment, with particular reference to the way in which the visual behaviour of the two is synchronized. They are brought to a small observation room in our laboratory, where the baby sits on the mother's knee and we videotape from behind a one-way window. The room is bare except for a number of large, brightly coloured and prominently placed toys. What we then see is a good example of the fact that it can be the baby's behaviour that elicits the mother's response and not always and necessarily the other way round. If we examine the looking behaviour of the couple we find that the baby looks at the various toys in turn, and that the mother then closely and often most sensitively visually follows him. In other words, she will keep an eye on the baby, find him looking in a particular direction, and then also look there. In this way mother and baby share by visual means an interest in some feature of the environment – an interest that is instigated by the baby but that shows interactional synchrony thanks to the mother's activity. The mother, moreover, does not only visually follow but may also elaborate on what the baby is looking at by pointing and, in particular, by verbal means – naming the object, talking about it and so on, and in this way linking word to action. All this may be trite were it not, in the first place, for the opportunity offered to examine timing relationships in the interaction and, in the second place, for the common view that the baby's behaviour is always somehow passively elicited by the mother – analogous to the following response of the young gosling. It seems on the contrary that, in this sense at least, a mother may follow the baby.

It is also interesting to note in this situation that when the mother then tries to take the initiative and attempts to draw the baby's attention to a toy he is not looking at she tends to be singularly unsuccessful – at any rate in the younger of the two age groups we are looking at, namely around 5 months. Again it seems one can get interactional synchrony without true reciprocity.

There are, of course, questions to be answered as to how situation-specific such observations are, but then the more detailed one's data (and in this situation we have found the most useful time unit for data analysis to be one tenth of a second) the more specific they are bound to be. On the other hand, statements about temporal relationships often do require micro-analytic work and especially so when one deals with something as fleeting as looking behaviour.

This brings us to the third point I wanted to discuss, namely the usefulness of providing descriptive data at a very detailed level. We have relied for too long on techniques that at the end of a 30-minute period of observation merely yield the statement '5', referring to some point on a rating scale describing one or another aspect of mother or child behaviour. The mother's behaviour in the situation I have just described, for instance, obviously has something to do with the variable 'maternal sensitivity', but instead of imposing this on the data we let the data give rise to the construct. The same move away from summary constructs applies, of course, to child behaviour. Instead of, for instance, treating attachment as a 'thing' that is measured by some single index, there is an attempt to describe and analyse the actual dyadic interaction sequences on which this construct is based. The situation is somewhat analogous to that which we have faced in relation to intelligence: conceived first as a unitary 'thing' described by just one index, interest subsequently shifted to the cognitive processes that underlie it.

This is not to argue, of course, that either one of these approaches is right and the other one is wrong; they may both be useful in answering certain kinds of questions and may thus be complementary. And yet there may also be situations where they provide apparently conflicting results, as for example in the definition of what constitutes maternal deprivation. On the one hand this has been regarded as an *insufficiency of maternal care*, emphasizing, that is, the quantitative aspect of the situation. On the other hand it can be thought of as an *unresponsiveness to the child's signals*, emphasizing in this case the timing relationship and seeing the child as deprived because of the lack of contingency between his behaviour and events in his social environment, even though quantitatively the interaction may not be at all unusual. The former interpretation has in fact received most attention because the institutions described so graphically by people like Spitz clearly did provide an insufficiency of care. However, the more typical residential institution of today, with its noise and bustle and large numbers of children and even of staff, is probably much better characterized by lack of responsiveness to individual signals, by lack of contingency relationships, and by such other features as refer to the absence of proper timing in the interaction between the child and his caretakers. What is more, this is not just a matter of interpretation; it is also a matter of the kind of remedial action one takes in this situation. Studies come to mind here which attempted to rectify the condition of institutionalized infants by giving them a daily dosage of extra stimulation and which thus illustrate very clearly the 'blob of clay' or 'tabula rasa' conception of the infant on whom environmental stimulation is imposed arbitrarily, without regard to the state and condition of the infant, his willingness to engage in social interaction, his own ability to lead such interaction, or the effect that any one stimulation episode may be seen to produce. In short, the 'problem of the match', as Hunt once referred to it, is discounted, and yet it is surely precisely with this that any remedial effort should start.

Indeed, it may well be argued that one of the main reasons why so many of the early Operation Headstart efforts failed was just this sort of philosophy – namely the belief that one can rectify a condition of deprivation merely by adding something called enrichment willy-nilly to a child's experience without first asking whether in fact the child can assimilate such an addition. And it is therefore hardly surprising to find that some of the more recent efforts to deal with the cultural deprivation syndrome have been much less ambitious in terms of numbers and much more ambitious in terms of the effort put into the diagnosis of each individual case and the design of remedial action geared to that particular child. It is also significant that some of these much more promising efforts take into account the child's baseline experience and, instead of taking him away from his natural environment for a few hours a day, giving him books and attempting to foster conceptual thought and then returning him to a home where none of these things are valued, attention is now being paid to attempts to bridge the gap between home and school and in particular to involve the parents in one way or another. Here too then we have an example of the way in which the child is acknowledged to be an active rather than a passive partner in his own upbringing.

One of the dangers of an arbitrary imposition of stimulation lies in its static nature. It does not change, that is, with the child's response to the stimulation and the relationship remains therefore a unidirectional one. Probably the best example we have of such one-way traffic comes from Harlow's well-known work on contact comfort. The models to which Harlow's infant monkeys clung so fondly may have provided contact comfort, and this clearly served an important purpose at the time, but they were unable to participate in the to-and-fro, hither and thither, ping-pong type of pattern that characterizes truly dyadic behaviour, and as adults the animals brought up in this way then turned out to be quite incapable of entering into the subtleties of interpersonal relationships. It is also worth remembering that Harlow showed that only 20 minutes daily play with peers prevented the infant from developing such pathology.

Unfortunately, not all examples from other species are equally helpful in understanding human development, and in the past our lack of data on the social behaviour of young children has sometimes led to quite unjustified extrapolation.

The imprinting phenomenon is probably the most obvious example of this temptation – partly because it has been so vividly described and illustrated. It immediately conjures up the picture of that bearded professor of zoology crawling through some Austrian meadow followed by a string of adoring ducklings, and there are indeed many who have succumbed to the temptation and simply explained the formation of the first human bond as 'imprinting'. Quite apart from the fact that imprinting is a descriptive and not an explanatory term it also disregards the behavioural dissimilarities of the species involved. Anderson (1972), for example, studied the following response of children between one and three in a London park. Coming from the imprinting literature one might well think that one would find children trailing behind their mothers at a nicely fixed distance as though being pulled by an invisible string on the chick-in-runway model. What Anderson in fact found was a great variety of modes of interaction, not one of which approximated the invisible-string pattern. Human beings, it seems, are not like chicks – at least not those observed in experimental settings.

It is, incidentally, worth noting that Anderson's study is one of the surprisingly few that is concerned with walking children rather than with sitting down children. It is a curious fact (confirmed by yet another quick check through the developmental journals) that the majority of investigations have their pre-school subjects sitting firmly and safely in chairs that they are prohibited to leave in case their attention strays from the levers and buttons and pictures and three-mountain model landscapes confronting them. Yet any pre-school child that I have ever come into contact with seems to spend 90 per cent of its waking life rushing through space, and I cannot help wondering why we, in our capacity as psychologists, are not rushing after him. The sitting down child is surely a highly unusual phenomenon compared with the running, jumping, walking child, and it is surely the latter kind whose study would bring us much nearer to the real life organism.

Maybe we have here one indication of the considerable gap that is still evident between child psychology and child rearing – between the orientation and interests and data of developmental psychologists on the one hand and the needs and interests of the main consumers in the applied situation, namely parents, on the other hand. There are many who have striven hard to bridge this gap. But child psychology as a whole has, at least until quite recently, had very little to say to parents that could be used by them in the bringing up of their children. Go through one of the popular baby books like Dr Spock's and see how little of the material provided there owes its existence to the findings of psychology; or, conversely, go through one of the conventional developmental textbooks and see what a small proportion of its material is orientated to an applied situation. There are no doubt many reasons for this gap, but one factor appears to be the lack of a firm basis of descriptive data. In this connection it is interesting to note that Feshbach (1970), in his review of aggression in the Carmichael *Manual*, spends about 100 pages carefully summarizing the many studies which in recent years have examined this topic under laboratory conditions and is then forced to conclude: 'The most obvious hiatus and, in many respects, the most important, is the absence of descriptive, normative data bearing on the development of aggression. Of particular interest are the patterns of aggression and the transformation in these patterns that occur during the period from birth to the child's fifth year . . . A detailed longitudinal analysis focusing on the emergence of the different facts of aggression, coupled with cross-sectional sampling of aggressive behaviours during this age period, would provide the normative data necessary for the formulation of an adequate theoretical description of this development.'

We can none of us be under any illusion as to our ignorance regarding such details of young children's social behaviour. But by getting away from misleading models, by getting behind summary constructs to the reality of interactive behaviour, and by acknowledging the two-way nature of the relationship, we should at least be setting out in the right direction.

References

ANDERSON, J. W. (1972) 'Attachment behaviour out of doors', in Blurton Jones, N. (ed.) *Ethological Studies of Child Behaviour* Cambridge University Press.

CAIRNS, R. B. (1972) 'Attachment and dependency: a psychological and social-learning synthesis' in Gewirtz, J. L. (ed.) *Attachment and Dependency* Washington, D.C., V. H. Winston.

EMDE, R. N. and HARRISON, R. J. (1972) 'Endogenous and exogenous smiling systems in early infancy', *J. child Psychiat*, **11**, 177–200.

FESHBACH, S. (1970) 'Aggression', in Mussen, P. H. (ed.) *Carmichael's Manual of Child Psychology, 3rd ed.* New York, Wiley.

KELVIN, P. (1970) *The Bases of Social Behaviour* New York, Holt, Rinehart and Winston.

KELVIN, P. (1971) 'Socialization and conformity', *J. child Psychol. Psychiat.*, **12**, 211–22.

RAMEY, C. T. and WATSON, J. S. (1972) 'Nonsocial reinforcement of infant vocalization', *Dev. Psychol.* **6**, 538.

RICHARDS, M. P. M. (1971) 'Social interaction in the first weeks of human life', *Psychiat., Neurol., Neurochir.*, 74, 35–42.

SEARS, R. R., MACCOBY, E. E. and LEVIN, H. (1957) *Patterns of Child Rearing* Evanston, Row, Peterson.

STERN, D. N. (1974) 'Mother and infant at play' in Lewis, M. and Rosenblum, L. (eds) *The Origins of Behaviour I* New York, Wiley.

WATSON, J. S. (1969) 'Operant conditioning of visual fixation in infants under visual and auditory reinforcement', *Dev. Psychol.*, 1, 508–16.

WOLFF, P. H. (1969) 'The natural history of crying and other vocalizations in early infancy' in Foss, B. M. (ed.) *Determinants of Infant Behaviour IV* London, Methuen.

YARROW, M. R., CAMPBELL, J. D. and BURTON, R. V. (1968) *Child Rearing: An Inquiry into Research and Methods* San Francisco, Jossey-Bass.

19 Transmission of aggression through imitation of aggressive models

Albert Bandura, Dorothea Ross and Sheila A. Ross

A previous study, designed to account for the phenomenon of identification in terms of incidental learning, demonstrated that children readily imitated behaviour exhibited by an adult model in the presence of the model (Bandura and Huston 1961). A series of experiments by Blake (1958) and others (Grosser, Polansky, and Lippitt 1951; Rosenblith 1959; Schachter and Hall 1952) have likewise shown that mere observation of responses of a model has a facilitating effect on subjects' reactions in the immediate social influence setting.

While these studies provide convincing evidence for the influence and control exerted on others by the behaviour of a model, a more crucial test of imitative learning involves the generalization of imitative response patterns to new settings in which the model is absent.

In the experiment reported in this paper children were exposed to aggressive and non-aggressive adult models and were then tested for amount of imitative learning in a new situation in the absence of the model. According to the prediction, subjects exposed to aggressive models would reproduce aggressive acts resembling those of their models and would differ in this respect both from subjects who observed nonaggressive models and from those who had no prior exposure to any models. This hypothesis assumed that subjects had learned imitative habits as a result of prior reinforcement, and these tendencies would generalize to some extent to adult experimenters (Miller and Dollard 1941).

It was further predicted that observation of subdued nonaggressive models would have a generalized inhibiting effect on the subjects' subsequent behaviour, and this effect would be reflected in a difference between the nonaggressive and the control groups, with subjects in the latter group displaying significantly more aggression.

Hypotheses were also advanced concerning the influence of the sex of model and sex of subjects on imitation. Fauls and Smith (1956) have shown that preschool children perceive their parents as having distinct preferences regarding sex appropriate modes of behaviour for their children. Their

---

BANDURA, A., ROSS, D. and ROSS, S. A. (1961) 'Transmission of aggression through imitation of aggressive models' in *Journal of Abnormal and Social Psychology*, vol. 63, no. 3, 575–82.

findings, as well as informal observation, suggest that parents reward imitation of sex appropriate behaviour and discourage or punish sex inappropriate imitative responses, e.g., a male child is unlikely to receive much reward for performing female appropriate activities, such as cooking, or for adopting other aspects of the maternal role, but these same behaviours are typically welcomed if performed by females. As a result of differing reinforcement histories, tendencies to imitate male and female models thus acquire differential habit strength. One would expect, on this basis, subjects to imitate the behaviour of a same-sex model to a greater degree than a model of the opposite sex.

Since aggression, however, is a highly masculine-typed behaviour, boys should be more predisposed than girls towards imitating aggression, the difference being most marked for subjects exposed to the male aggressive model.

Method

Subjects

The subjects were 36 boys and 36 girls enrolled in the Stanford University Nursery School. They ranged in age from 37 to 69 months, with a mean age of 52 months.

Two adults, a male and a female, served in the role of model, and one female experimenter conducted the study for all 72 children.

Experimental design

Subjects were divided into eight experimental groups of six subjects each and a control group consisting of 24 subjects. Half the experimental subjects were exposed to aggressive models and half were exposed to models that were subdued and nonaggressive in their behaviour. These groups were further subdivided into male and female subjects. Half the subjects in the aggressive and nonaggressive conditions observed same-sex models, while the remaining subjects in each group viewed models of the opposite sex. The control group had no prior exposure to the adult models and was tested only in the generalization situation.

It seems reasonable to expect that the subjects' level of aggressiveness would be positively related to the readiness with which they imitated aggressive modes of behaviour. Therefore, in order to increase the precision of treatment comparisons, subjects in the experimental and control groups were matched individually on the basis of ratings of their aggressive behaviour in social interactions in the nursery school.

The subjects were rated on four five-point rating scales by the experimenter and a nursery school teacher, both of whom were well acquainted with the children. These scales measured the extent to which subjects displayed physical aggression, verbal aggression, aggression towards inanimate objects, and aggressive inhibition. The latter scale, which dealt with the subjects' tendency to inhibit aggressive reactions in the face of high instigation, provided a measure of aggression anxiety.

Fifty-one subjects were rated independently by both judges so as to permit an assessment of interrater agreement. The reliability of the composite aggression score, estimated by means of the Pearson product-moment correlation, was 0·89.

The composite score was obtained by summing the ratings on the four aggression scales; on the basis of these scores, subjects were arranged in triplets and assigned at random to one of two treatment conditions or to the control group.

Experimental conditions

In the first step in the procedure subjects were brought individually by the experimenter to the experimental room and the model who was in the hallway outside the room, was invited by the experimenter to come and join in the game. The experimenter then escorted the subject to one corner of the room, which was structured as the subject's play area. After seating the child at a small table, the experimenter demonstrated how the subject could design pictures with potato prints and picture stickers provided. The potato prints included a variety of geometrical forms; the stickers were attractive multicolour pictures of animals, flowers and western figures to be pasted on a pastoral scene. These activities were selected since they had been established, by previous studies in the nursery school, as having high interest value for the children.

After having settled the subject in his corner, the experimenters escorted the model to the opposite corner of the room which contained a small table and chair, a tinker toy set, a mallet, and a 5-foot inflated Bobo doll. The experimenter explained that these were the materials provided for the model to play with and, after the model was seated, the experimenter left the experimental room.

With subjects in the *nonaggressive condition*, the model assembled the tinker toys in a quiet subdued manner totally ignoring the Bobo doll.

In contrast, with subjects in the *aggressive condition*, the model began by assembling the tinker toys but after approximately a minute had elapsed, the model turned to the Bobo doll and spent the remainder of the period aggressing towards it.

Imitative learning can be clearly demonstrated if a model performs sufficiently novel patterns of responses which are unlikely to occur independently of the observation of the behaviour of a model and if a subject reproduces these behaviours in substantially identical form. For this reason, in addition to punching the Bobo doll, a response that is likely to be performed by children independently of a demonstration, the model exhibited distinctive aggressive acts which were to be scored as imitative responses. The model laid Bobo on its side, sat on it and punched it repeatedly in the nose. The model then raised the Bobo doll, picked up the mallet and struck the doll on the head. Following the mallet aggression, the model tossed the doll up in the air aggressively and kicked it about the room. This sequence of physically aggressive acts was repeated approximately three times, interspersed with verbally aggressive responses such as, 'Sock him in the nose. . . .', 'Hit him down. . . .', 'Throw him in the air. . . .', 'Kick him. . . .', 'Pow. . . .', and two nonaggressive comments, 'He keeps coming back for more' and 'He sure is a tough fella'.

Thus in the exposure situation, subjects were provided with a diverting task which occupied their attention and at the same time insured observation of the model's behaviour in the absence of any instructions to observe or to learn the responses in question. Since subjects could not perform the model's aggressive behaviour, any learning that occurred was purely on an observational or covert basis.

At the end of 10 minutes, the experimenter entered the room, informed the subject that he would now go to another game room, and bid the model goodbye.

Aggression arousal

Subjects were tested for the amount of imitative learning in a different experimental room that was set off from the main nursery school building. The two experimental situations were thus clearly differentiated; in fact, many subjects were under the impression that they were no longer on the nursery school grounds.

Prior to the test for imitation, however, all subjects, experimental and control, were subjected to mild aggression arousal to insure that they were under some degree of instigation to aggression. The arousal experience was included for two main reasons. In the first place, observation of aggressive behaviour exhibited by others tends to reduce the probability of aggression on the part of the observer (Rosenbaum and deCharms, 1960). Consequently, subjects in the aggressive condition, in relation both to the nonaggressive and control groups, would be under weaker instigation following exposure to the models. Second, if subjects in the nonaggressive condition expressed little aggression in the face of appropriate instigation, the presence of an inhibitory process would seem to be indicated.

Following the exposure experience, therefore, the experimenter brought the subject to an anteroom that contained these relatively attractive toys: a fire engine, a locomotive, a jet fighter plane, a cable car, a colourful spinning top, and a doll set complete with wardrobe, doll carriage and baby crib. The experimenter explained that the toys were for the subject to play with but, as soon as the subject became sufficiently involved with the play material (usually in about 2 minutes), the experimenter remarked that these were her very best toys, and that she did not let just anyone play with them, and that she had decided to reserve these toys for the other children. However, the subject could play with any of the toys that were in the next room. The experimenter and the subject then entered the adjoining experimental room.

It was necessary for the experimenter to remain in the room during the experimental session; otherwise a number of the children would either refuse to remain alone or would leave before the termination of the session. However, in order to minimize any influence her presence might have on the subject's behaviour, the experimenter remained as inconspicuous as possible by busying herself with paper work at a desk in the far corner of the room and avoiding any interaction with the child.

Test for delayed imitation

The experimental room contained a variety of toys including some that could be used in imitative or non-imitative aggression, and others that tended to elicit predominantly nonaggressive forms of behaviour. The aggressive toys included a 3-foot Bobo doll, a mallet and peg board, two dart guns, and a tether ball with a face painted on it which hung from the ceiling. The nonaggressive toys, on the other hand, included a tea set, crayons and colouring paper, a ball, two dolls, three bears, cars and trucks, and plastic farm animals.

In order to eliminate any variation in behaviour due to mere placement of the toys in the room, the play material was arranged in a fixed order for each of the sessions.

The subject spent 20 minutes in this experimental room during which time his behaviour was rated in terms of predetermined response categories by judges who observed the session through a one-way mirror in an adjoining observation room. The 20-minute session was divided into 5-second intervals by means of an electric interval timer, thus yielding a total number of 240 response units for each subject.

The male model scored the experimental sessions for all 72 children. Except for the cases in which he served as model, he did not have knowledge of the subjects' group assignments. In order to provide an estimate of interscorer agreement, the performances of half the subjects were also scored independently by a second observer. Thus one or the other of the two observers usually had no knowledge of the conditions to which the subjects were assigned. Since, however, all but two of the subjects in the aggressive condition performed the model's novel aggressive responses while subjects in the other conditions only rarely exhibited such reactions, subjects who were exposed to the aggressive models could be readily identified through their distinctive behaviour.

The responses scored involved highly specific concrete classes of behaviour and yielded high interscorer reliabilities, the product-moment coefficients being in the 0·90s.

Response measures

Three measures of imitation were obtained:

Imitation of physical aggression: This category included acts of striking the Bobo doll with the mallet, sitting on the doll and punching it in the nose, kicking the doll, and tossing it in the air.

Imitative verbal aggression: Subject repeats the phrases 'Sock him', 'Hit him down', 'Kick him', 'Throw him in the air', or 'Pow'.

Imitative nonaggressive verbal responses: Subject repeats 'He keeps coming back for more', or 'He sure is a tough fella'.

During the pretest, a number of the subjects imitated the essential components of the model's behaviour but did not perform the complete act, or they directed the imitative aggressive response to some object other than the Bobo doll. Two responses of this type were therefore scored and were interpreted as partially imitative behaviour.

Mallet aggression: Subject strikes objects other than the Bobo doll aggressively with the mallet.

Sits on Bobo doll: Subject lays the Bobo doll on its side and sits on it, but does not aggress towards it.

The following additional nonimitative aggressive responses were scored:

Punches Bobo doll: Subject strikes, slaps, or pushes the doll aggressively.

Nonimitative physical and verbal aggression: This category included physically aggressive acts directed towards objects other than the Bobo doll and any hostile remarks except for those in the verbal imitation category; e.g. 'Shoot the Bobo', 'Cut him', 'Stupid ball', 'Knock over people', 'Horses fighting, biting'.

Aggressive gun play: Subject shoots darts or aims the gun and fires imaginary shots at objects in the room.

Rating were also made of the number of behaviour units in which subjects played nonaggressively or sat quietly and did not play with any of the material at all.

Results

Complete imitation of models' behaviour

Subjects in the aggression condition reproduced a good deal of physical and verbal aggressive behaviour, resembling that of the models, and their mean scores differed markedly from those of subjects in the nonaggressive and control groups who exhibited virtually no imitative aggression (see Table 1).

Since there were only a few scores for subjects in the nonaggressive and control conditions (approximately 70 per cent of the subjects had zero scores), and the assumption of homogeneity of variance could not be made, the Friedman two-way analysis of variance by ranks was employed to test the significance of the obtained differences.

The prediction that exposure of subjects to aggressive models increases the probability of aggressive behaviour is clearly confirmed (see Table 2). The main effect of treatment conditions is highly significant both for physical and verbal imitative aggression. Comparison of pairs of scores by the sign test shows that the obtained overall differences were due almost entirely to the aggression displayed by subjects who had been exposed to the aggressive models. Their scores were significantly higher than those of either the nonaggressive or control groups, which did not differ from each other (Table 2).

Imitation was not confined to the model's aggressive responses. Approximately one-third of the subjects in the aggressive condition also repeated the model's nonaggressive verbal responses while none of the subjects in either the nonaggressive or control groups made such remarks. This difference, tested by means of the Cochran Q test, was significant well beyond the 0·001 level (Table 2).

Table 1 Mean aggression scores for experimental and control subjects

Response category	*Experimental groups*				*Control groups*
	Aggressive		*Nonaggressive*		
	F Model	*M Model*	*F Model*	*M Model*	
Imitative physical aggression					
Female subjects	5·5	7·2	2·5	0·0	1·2
Male subjects	12·4	25·8	0·2	1·5	2·0
Imitative verbal aggression					
Female subjects	13·7	2·0	0·3	0·0	0·7
Male subjects	4·3	12·7	1·1	0·0	1·7
Mallet aggression					
Female subjects	17·2	18·7	0·5	0·5	13·1
Male subjects	15·5	28·8	18·7	6·7	13·5
Punches Bobo doll					
Female subjects	6·3	16·5	5·8	4·3	11·7
Male subjects	18·9	11·9	15·6	14·8	15·7
Nonimitative aggression					
Female subjects	21·3	8·4	7·2	1·4	6·1
Male subjects	16·2	36·7	26·1	22·3	24·6
Aggressive gun play					
Female subjects	1·8	4·5	2·6	2·5	3·7
Male subjects	7·3	15·9	8·9	16·7	14·3

Table 2 Significance of the differences between experimental and control groups in the expression of aggression

Response category	χ^2_r	*Q*	*p*	*Comparison of pairs of treatment conditions*		
				Aggressive vs. Nonaggressive *p*	*Aggressive vs. Control* *p*	*Nonaggressive v. Control* *p*
Imitative responses						
Physical aggression	27·17		<0·001	<0·001	<0·001	0·09
Verbal aggression	9·17		<0·02	0·004	0·048	0·00
Nonaggressive verbal responses		17·50	<0·001	0·004	0·004	*ns*
Partial imitation						
Mallet aggression	11·06		<0·01	0·26	*ns*	0·005
Sits on Bobo		13·44	<0·01	0·018	0·059	*ns*
Nonimitative aggression						
Punches Bobo doll	2·87		*ns*			
Physical and verbal	8·96		<0·02	0·026	*ns*	*ns*
Aggressive gun play	2·75		*ns*			

Partial imitation of models' behaviour

Differences in the predicted direction were also obtained on the two measures of partial imitation.

Analysis of variance of scores based on the subjects' use of the mallet aggressively towards objects other than the Bobo doll reveals that treatment conditions are a statistically significant source of variation (Table 2). In addition, individual sign tests show that both the aggressive and the control groups, relative to subjects in the nonaggressive condition, produced significantly more mallet aggression, the difference being particularly marked with regard to female subjects. Girls who observed nonaggressive models performed a mean number of 0·5 mallet aggression responses as compared to mean values of 18·0 and 13·1 for girls in the aggressive and control groups, respectively.

Although subjects who observed aggressive models performed more mallet aggression ($M=20{\cdot}0$) than their controls ($M=13{\cdot}3$), the difference was not statistically significant.

With respect to the partially imitative response of sitting on the Bobo doll, the overall group differences were significant beyond the 0·01 level (Table 2). Comparison of pairs of scores by the sign test procedure reveals that subjects in the aggressive group reproduced this aspect of the models' behaviour to a greater extent than did the nonaggressive ($p=0{\cdot}018$) or the control ($p=0{\cdot}059$) subjects. The latter two groups, on the other hand, did not differ from each other.

Nonimitative aggression

Analyses of variance of the remaining aggression measures (Table 2) show that treatment conditions did not influence the extent to which subjects engaged in aggressive gun play or punched the Bobo doll. The effect of conditions is highly significant ($\chi^2{}_r=8{\cdot}96$, $p < 0{\cdot}02$), however, in the case of the subjects' expression of nonimitative physical and verbal aggression. Further comparison of treatment pairs reveals that the main source of the overall difference was the aggressive and nonaggressive groups which differed significantly from each other (Table 2), with subjects exposed to the aggressive models displaying the greater amount of aggression.

Influence of sex of model and sex of subjects on imitation

The hypothesis that boys are more prone than girls to imitate aggression exhibited by a model was only partially confirmed. *t* tests computed for subjects in the aggressive condition reveal that boys reproduced more imitative physical aggression than girls ($t=2{\cdot}50$, $p<0{\cdot}01$). The groups do not differ, however, in their imitation of verbal aggression.

The use of nonparametric tests, necessitated by the extremely skewed distributions of scores for subjects in the nonaggressive and control conditions, preclude an overall test of the influence of sex of model per se, and of the various interactions between the main effects. Inspection of the means presented in Table 1 for subjects in the aggression condition, however, clearly suggests the possibility of a Sex × Model interaction. This interaction effect is much more consistent and pronounced for the male model than for the female model. Male subjects, for example, exhibited more physical ($t=2{\cdot}07$, $p<0{\cdot}05$) and verbal imitative aggression ($t=2{\cdot}51$, $p<0{\cdot}05$), more non-imitative aggression ($t=3{\cdot}15$, $p<0{\cdot}025$), and engaged in significantly more aggressive gun play ($t=2{\cdot}12$, $p<0{\cdot}05$) following exposure to the aggressive male model than the female subjects. In contrast, girls exposed to the female model performed considerably more imitative verbal aggression and more non-imitative aggression than did the boys (Table 1). The variances, however, were equally large and with only a small *N* in each cell the mean differences did not reach statistical significance.

Data for the nonaggressive and control subjects provide additional suggestive evidence that the behaviour of the male model exerted a greater influence than the female model on the subjects' behaviour in the generalization situation.

It will be recalled that, except for the greater amount of mallet aggression exhibited by the control subjects, no significant differences were obtained between the nonaggressive and control groups. The data indicate, however, that the absence of significant differences between these two groups was due primarily to the fact that subjects exposed to the nonaggressive female model did not differ from the controls on any of the measures of aggression. With respect to the male model, on the other hand, the differences between the groups are striking. Comparison of the sets of scores by means of the sign test reveals that, in relation to the control group, subjects exposed to the nonaggressive male model performed significantly less imitative physical aggression ($p=0{\cdot}06$), less imitative verbal aggression ($p=0{\cdot}002$), less mallet aggression ($p=0{\cdot}003$), less non-imitative physical and verbal aggression ($p=0{\cdot}03$), and they were less inclined to punch the Bobo doll ($p=0{\cdot}07$).

While the comparison of subgroups, when some of the overall tests do not reach statistical significance, is likely to capitalize on chance differences, nevertheless the consistency of the findings adds support to the interpretation in terms of influence by the model.

Nonaggressive behaviour

With the exception of expected sex differences, Lindquist (1956) Type III analyses of variance of the nonaggressive response scores yielded few significant differences.

Female subjects spent more time than boys playing with dolls ($p < 0.001$), with the tea set ($p < 0.001$), and colouring ($p < 0.05$). The boys on the other hand, devoted significantly more time than the girls to exploratory play with the guns ($p < 0.01$). No sex differences were found in respect to the subjects' use of the other stimulus objects, i.e. farm animals, cars, or tether ball.

Treatment conditions did produce significant differences on two measures of nonaggressive behaviour that are worth mentioning. Subjects in the nonaggressive condition engaged in significantly more nonaggressive play with dolls than either subjects in the aggressive group ($t=2.67$, $p < 0.02$), or in the control group ($t=2.57$, $p < 0.02$).

Even more noteworthy is the finding that subjects who observed nonaggressive models spent more than twice as much time as subjects in aggressive condition ($t=3.07$, $p < 0.01$) in simply sitting quietly without handling any of the play material.

Discussion

Much current research on social learning is focused on the shaping of new behaviour through rewarding and punishing consequences. Unless responses are emitted, however, they cannot be influenced. The results of this study provide strong evidence that observation of cues produced by the behaviour of others is one effective means of eliciting certain forms of responses for which the original probability is very low or zero. Indeed, social imitation may hasten or short-cut the acquisition of new behaviours without the necessity of reinforcing successive approximations as suggested by Skinner (1953).

Thus subjects given an opportunity to observe aggressive models later reproduced a good deal of physical and verbal aggression (as well as nonaggressive responses) substantially identical with that of the model. In contrast, subjects who were exposed to nonaggressive models and those who had no previous exposure to any models only rarely performed such responses.

To the extent that observation of adult models displaying aggression communicates permissiveness for aggressive behaviour, such exposure may serve to weaken inhibitory responses and thereby to increase the probability of aggressive reactions to subsequent frustrations. The fact, however, that subjects expressed their aggression in ways that clearly resembled the novel patterns exhibited by the models provides striking evidence for the occurrence of learning by imitation.

In the procedure employed by Miller and Dollard (1941) for establishing imitative behaviour, adult or peer models performed discrimination responses following which they were consistently rewarded, and the subjects were similarly reinforced whenever they matched the leaders' choice responses. While these experiments have been widely accepted as demonstrations of learning by means of imitation, in fact, they simply involve a special case of discrimination learning in which the behaviour of others serves as discriminative stimuli for responses that are already part of the subject's repertoire. Auditory or visual environmental cues could easily have been substituted for the social stimuli to facilitate the discrimination learning. In contrast, the process of imitation studied in the present experiment differed in several important respects from the one investigated by Miller and Dollard in that subjects learned to combine fractional responses into relatively complex novel patterns solely by observing the performance of social models without any opportunity to perform the models' behaviour in the exposure setting, and without any reinforcers delivered either to the models or to the observers.

An adequate theory of the mechanisms underlying imitative learning is lacking. The explanations that have been offered (Logan, Olmsted, Rosner, Schwartz and Stevens 1955, Maccoby 1959) assume that the imitator performs the model's responses covertly. If it can be assumed additionally that rewards and punishments are self-administered in conjunction with the covert responses, the process of imitative learning could be accounted for in terms of the same principles that govern instrumental trial-and-error learning. In the early stages of the developmental process, however, the range of component responses in the organism's repertoire is probably increased through a process of classical conditioning (Bandura and Huston 1961, Mowrer 1950).

The data provide some evidence that the male model influenced the subjects' behaviour outside the exposure setting to a greater extent than was true for the female model. In the analyses of the Sex × Model interactions, for example, only the comparisons involving the male model yielded significant differences. Similarly, subjects exposed to the nonaggressive male model performed less aggressive behaviour than the controls, whereas comparisons involving the female model were consistently nonsignificant.

In a study of learning by imitation, Rosenblith (1959) has likewise found male experimenters more effective than females in influencing childrens' behaviour. Rosenblith advanced the tentative explanation that the school setting may involve some social deprivation in respect to adult males which, in turn, enhances the male's reward value.

The trends in the data yielded by the present study suggest an alternative explanation. In the case of a highly masculine-typed behaviour such as physical aggression, there is a tendency for both male and female subjects to imitate the male model to a greater degree than the female model. On the other hand, in the case of verbal aggression, which is less clearly sex linked, the greatest amount of imitation occurs in relation to the same-sex model. These trends together with the finding that boys in relation to girls are in general more imitative of physical aggression but do not differ in imitation of verbal aggression, suggest that subjects may be differentially affected by the sex of the model but that predictions must take into account the degree to which the behaviour in question is sex-typed.

The preceding discussion has assumed that maleness–femaleness rather than some other personal characteristics of the particular models involved, is the significant variable – an assumption that cannot be tested directly with the data at hand. It was clearly evident, however, particularly from boys' spontaneous remarks about the display of aggression by the female model, that some subjects at least were responding in terms of a sex discrimination and their prior learning about what is sex appropriate behaviour (e.g. 'Who is that lady? That's not the way for a lady to behave. Ladies are supposed to act like ladies. . . .' 'You should have seen what that girl did in there. She was just acting like a man. I never saw a girl act like that before. She was punching and fighting but no swearing'). Aggression by the male model, on the other hand, was more likely to be seen as appropriate and approved by both the boys ('Al's a good socker, he beat up Bobo. I want to sock like Al.') and the girls ('That man is a strong fighter, he punched and punched and he could hit Bobo right down to the floor and if Bobo got up he said, "Punch your nose." He's a good fighter like Daddy.').

The finding that subjects exposed to the quiet models were more inhibited and unresponsive than subjects in the aggressive conditions, together with the obtained difference on the aggression measures, suggests that exposure to inhibited models not only decreases the probability of occurrence of aggressive behaviour but also generally restricts the range of behaviour emitted by the subjects.

'Identification with aggressor' (Freud 1946) or 'defensive identification'

(Mowrer 1950), whereby a person presumably transforms himself from object to agent of aggression by adopting the attributes of an aggressive threatening model so as to allay anxiety, is widely accepted as an explanation of the imitative learning of aggression.

The development of aggressive modes of response by children of aggressively punitive adults, however, may simply reflect object displacement without involving any such mechanism of defensive identification. In studies of child training antecedents of aggressively antisocial adolescents (Bandura and Walters 1959) and of young hyperaggressive boys (Bandura 1960), the parents were found to be nonpermissive and punitive of aggression directed towards themselves. On the other hand, they actively encouraged and reinforced their sons' aggression towards persons outside the home. This pattern of differential reinforcement of aggressive behaviour served to inhibit the boys' aggression towards the original instigators and fostered the displacement of aggression towards objects and situations eliciting much weaker inhibitory responses.

Moreover, the findings from an earlier study (Bandura and Huston 1961), in which children imitated to an equal degree aggression exhibited by a nurturant and a non-nurturant model, together with the results of the present experiment in which subjects readily imitated aggressive models who were more or less neutral figures suggest that mere observation of aggression, regardless of the quality of the model–subject relationship, is a sufficient condition for producing imitative aggression in children. A comparative study of the subjects' imitation of aggressive models who are feared, who are liked and esteemed, or who are essentially neutral figures would throw some light on whether or not a more parsimonious theory than the one involved in 'identification with the aggressor' can explain the modelling process.

Summary

Twenty-four preschool children were assigned to each of three conditions. One experimental group observed aggressive adult models; a second observed inhibited non-aggressive models; while subjects in a control group had no prior exposure to the models. Half the subjects in the experimental conditions observed same-sex models and half viewed models of the opposite sex. Subjects were then tested for the amount of imitative as well as nonimitative aggression performed in a new situation in the absence of the models.

Comparison of the subjects' behaviour in the generalization situation revealed that subjects exposed to aggressive models reproduced a good deal of aggression resembling that of the models, and that their mean scores differed markedly from those of subjects in the nonaggressive and control groups. Subjects in the aggressive condition also exhibited significantly more partially imitative and nonimitative aggressive behaviour and were generally less inhibited in their behaviour than subjects in the nonaggressive condition.

Imitation was found to be differentially influenced by the sex of the model with boys showing more aggression than girls following exposure to the male model, the difference being particularly marked on highly masculine-typed behaviour.

Subjects who observed the nonaggressive models, especially the subdued male model, were generally less aggressive than their controls.

The implications of the findings based on this experiment and related studies for the psychoanalytic theory of identification with the aggressor were discussed.

References

BANDURA, A. (1960) 'Relationship of family patterns to child behaviour disorders', *Progress Report, Stanford University, Project No. M-1734* United States Public Health Service.

BANDURA, A. and HUSTON, ALETHA C. (1961) 'Identification as a process of incidental learning', *Journal of Abnormal and Social Psychology*, 63, 311–18.

BANDURA, A. and WALTERS, R. H. (1959) *Adolescent aggression* New York, Ronald.

BLAKE, R. R. (1958) 'The other person in the situation' in Tagiuri, R. and Petrullo, L. (eds) *Person perception and interpersonal behavior* Stanford, California, Stanford University Press, pp. 229–42.

FAULS, LYDIA B. and SMITH, W. D. (1956) 'Sex role learning of five-year-olds', *Journal of Genetic Psychology*, 89, 105–17.

FREUD, ANNA (1946) *The ego and the mechanisms of defense* New York, International University Press.

GROSSER, D., POLANSKY, N. and LIPPITT, R. (1951) 'A laboratory study of behavior contagion', *Human Relations*, 4, 115–42.

LINDQUIST, E. F. (1956) *Design and analysis of experiments* Boston, Houghton Mifflin.

LOGAN, F., OLMSTED, O. L., ROSNER, B. S., SCHWARTZ, R. D. and STEVENS, C. M. (1955) *Behavior theory and social science* New Haven, Yale University Press.

MACCOBY, ELEANOR E. (1959) 'Role-taking in childhood and its consequences for social learning', *Child Development*, 30, 239–52.

MILLER, N. E. and DOLLARD, J. (1941) *Social learning and imitation* New Haven, Yale University Press.
MOWRER, O. H. (ed.) (1950) 'Identification: A link between learning theory and psychotherapy' in *Learning theory and personality dynamics* New York, Ronald, pp. 69–94.
ROSENBAUM, M. E. and DECHARMS, R. (1960) 'Direct and vicarious reduction of hostility', *Journal of Abnormal and Social Psychology*, **60**, 105–11.
ROSENBLITH, JUDY F. (1959) 'Learning by imitation in kindergarten children', *Child Development*, **30**, 69–80.
SCHACHTER, S. and HALL, R. (1952) 'Group-derived restraints and audience persuasion', *Human Relations*, **5**, 397–406.
SKINNER, B. F. (1953) *Science and human behavior* New York, Macmillan.

20 A theoretical perspective for research on human development

Urie Bronfenbrenner

This is a presumptuous paper. In relatively brief compass, it purports to demonstrate that the scientific model typically employed for research on human development is critically impoverished – both theoretically and empirically; it then proceeds to present a new theoretical model alleged to be more adequate to the task.

I approach this rash endeavour from the peculiarly narrow perspective of my own discipline – scientific psychology. I use the term 'narrow' advisedly. As we know, psychology borrowed its reasearch model from the more prestigious physical and biological sciences. Precisely because that model was designed to isolate physical and biological phenomena in their pure form, it is psychologically sterile.

I contend that the much-prized model of the experimental psychologist, as it is usually applied, is impoverished in at least four major respects:

First, it is ordinarily limited to a two-person system involving, or at least confining attention to one experimenter and one child – the latter typically – and significantly – referred to as a 'subject'.

The term 'subject' reflects the second major restriction. The process taking place between experimenter and child is ordinarily conceived of as unidirectional; that is, one is concerned with the effect of the experimenter's behaviour on the child, and not the reverse.

Third, this second participant in the system, the experimenter, is usually a stranger, nine times out of ten a graduate student, whose prior relationship to the child is nonexistent, or if existent, trivial in character.

Fourth, and most important of all, the two-person system exists, or is treated as if it existed, in isolation from any other social context that could impinge on or encompass it.

These four features so common in our experiments are hardly characteristic of the situations in which children actually develop. Thus in the family, the day care centre, preschool, play group, or school classroom:

1 There are usually more than two people.
2 The child invariably influences those who influence him.

BRONFENBRENNER, URIE (1973) 'A theoretical perspective for research on human development' in Dreitzel, H. P. (ed.) *Childhood and Socialization* London, Collier-Macmillan, 337–63.

3 The other participants are not strangers but persons who have enduring and differing relationships with the child.
4 Finally, the behaviour of all these persons is profoundly affected by other social systems in which these same persons participate in significant roles and relationships, both vis-à-vis the child and each other.

If all this be true, then much of our research is off the mark. We are using a theoretical model which is *ecologically invalid*. By ruling out of consideration the very phenomena that we most need to study, the model commits us to a science that is puny and trivial in comparison with the true nature of the processes which it purports to study. And we continue to employ this model in the mistaken belief that it constitutes our only hope for scientific legitimacy.

But, as we all know, times are changing, and, at least in child development, illegitimacy is on the rise. As a result, there is some hope of a new theoretical perspective.

In attempting to lay out the basic dimensions of that perspective, I make no claim to originality. Rather I have sought to consolidate and make explicit developments that are reflected, often only by implication, in scattered writings and researches, often on seemingly unrelated problems. In the interests of brevity, I shall identify the research evidence on which I have drawn only by reference rather than detailed description.[1]

To turn to the model itself. What properties must it have if it is to meet the major requirements already outlined?

Reciprocality

First and foremost, the model must be conceived as a two-way system, in which the behaviour of each participant both affects and is affected by the behaviour of the others. Thus, in a laboratory experiment, one would have to be concerned not only with changes in the child's response as a function of the behaviour of an experimenter but also with the reverse; that is, the effects on the experimenter of the behaviour of the child. The same consideration would apply to studies of other socialization systems such as parent and child, teacher and child, the child in the group, etc.

The importance of reciprocality as a defining property of any adequate model for the socialization process has been recognized in theoretical discussions (e.g., Bronfenbrenner 1968, Gewirtz 1969a, 1969b, Rheingold 1969a), but in research practice the principle has been more honoured in the breech than in the observance. For example, only a very few studies have analyzed mother–infant interaction as a reciprocal system (e.g. S. M.

1 A more extended discussion of some of these studies appears in Bronfenbrenner (1972).

Bell 1971, Gewirtz and Gewirtz 1965, Moss 1967), and none, to this writer's knowledge has examined interaction between infant and experimenter as a two-way process.

The property of reciprocality implies two important corollary principles which have received some attention in empirical work.

1 *The child as stimulus*. The child is to be viewed not merely as a reactive agent but as an instigator of behaviour in others. To use the language of Kurt Lewin, the child has 'demand characteristics' which tend to evoke certain patterns of response in others. Thus a young baby's 'cuteness', and even more clearly its cry, invite, indeed almost compel a reaction from persons in its immediate environment. An adequate research model must take into account the almost inevitable impact of such demand characteristics on others, including the experimenter.

The role of the child as a stimulus and instigator of response has been stressed by a number of developmental psychologists, especially R. Q. Bell (1968, 1971). There are also a few direct studies of the phenomenon as manifested in the relation between mother and infant (S. M. Bell 1971, Gewirtz and Gewirtz 1969, Moss 1967, Moss and Robson 1968), but only the last is based on systematic analysis of the actual sequence of mother–infant interaction in a substantial sample (54 pairs). Nevertheless, all four studies show striking evidence for the predominance of infant-initiated over mother-initiated behaviour in the first year of life. This writer has not been able to find any studies of this phenomenon for later ages.

As illustrated by Moss's research (1967), focusing attention on the child as a stimulus also brings to light the role of genetic and constitutional factors in giving both impetus and direction to the socialization process. Thus Moss argues persuasively from his data that the greater 'soothability' of female versus male infants in the first weeks of life sets in motion a more rapidly converging pattern of mutual reinforcement and attachment which contributes to the emergence of sex differences in early language development and social relationships.

2 *The child as a socializing agent*. The potency of the child as a stimulus takes on added significance in any situation involving protracted interaction between the child and another person. For, over a period of time, not only does the adult produce lasting changes in the behaviour of the child, but *vice versa*. In other words, not only does the mother, or other consistent caregiver, train the child, but *the child also trains the mother*, a phenomenon of considerable importance for human development not only in terms of science but also of social policy on day care, children's institutions, etc.

The role of the child as a socializing agent has been emphasized by a number of writers (R. Q. Bell 1968, 1971, Rheingold 1969a), and Richard Bell (1968) has reinterpreted the findings of a large number of researches on socialization as possibly reflecting the influence of the child on the adult. But a search for direct studies of the phenomenon has proved unsuccessful. Despite considerable emphasis on the theoretical importance of this effect and some inferential evidence in support of its existence, as yet there appears to be no systematic investigation specifically focusing on and documenting the way in which a child, through such processes as reinforcement and modelling, produces enduring changes in the behaviour of an adult, such as a parent, teacher, or – wonder of wonders – an experimenter.

In the absence of studies of this kind, it appears desirable to suggest some research designs which would make possible the analysis of socialization as a reciprocal process. Here are two examples of research currently under way.

a) *The effects of actual and attributed sex on adult–infant interaction.* James Garbarino [2] has proposed an experiment for testing directly some of the hypotheses on the genesis of sex differences in child rearing derived by Moss from his observational study (1967). The experiment employs the technique of cross-labelling developed by Condry and Garbarino, in which infants of each sex are identified by false names, with half of the girls being given boy's names and *vice versa.* Using a group of volunteer student caretakers, Garbarino proposes to examine the development of sex differences in the treatment of children as a joint function of actual and attributed sex. He hypothesizes that, even when the infants are cross-labelled, patterns of behaviour associated with their actual sex will evoke differential response from the caretaker in terms of such variables as response to crying, talking to the infant, and, in particular, the frequency of responses contingent upon the infant's behaviour.

b) *The impact of the child's initiative on mother–child interaction.* Bonny Parke [2] has designed an experiment to gauge the effect of the child's initiative in shaping the course of mother–child interaction. Working with a sample of preschool children she asks the mother to present the child with a story picture-book under two different sets of instructions. In one, the mother is asked to look at the story with the child 'the way you usually do'. In the other, the mother is told that the primary interest is in what about the book attracts the interest of the child; therefore the mother is to let the child take the initiative. The dependent variables relate differences in pattern of mother–child interaction instigated by the two sets of instructions, with particular reference to the relative frequency of reciprocal

2 Graduate student, Department of Human Development and Family Studies, New York State College of Human Ecology, Cornell University, Ithaca, New York.

reinforcement, imitation, and alternation from one participant to the other.

Both of these examples illustrate an important feature that distinguishes the present research designs from those traditionally employed in socialization studies. In the latter, the independent variable is typically the behaviour of an adult and the dependent variable the behaviour of the child. In the present examples, both adult and child behaviours are analyzed as dependent variables. The independent variable in each case is some systematic variation in the ecological situation – in the first example, actual *v.* attributed sex of the child; in the second, an instruction influencing the extent to which the child is permitted some initiative in the interactive process.

A second distinctive feature of the research designs here proposed is that the dependent variables cannot be confined to the behaviours of the adult and child as separate individuals, but must describe properties of their interaction in a two-person reciprocal system. Thus it would not be sufficient to compute measures based on the frequency with which the mother engages in an action vis-à-vis the child or *vice versa*. One needs in addition indices which reflect the interdependency between behaviours of the two participants; for example, *the probability that an act of A is directly followed by an act of B, and vice versa*, or the number of *alternations* in action between A and B per unit of time. In computing such measures it would be important to take special note of *reciprocations in kind* (e.g. smile followed by smile) or *within the same modality* (e.g. vocalization followed by vocalization) as distinguished from non-imitative sequences (e.g. vocalization followed by eye contact). Finally, and most importantly, attention must be given to *convergence* phenomena, such as increased rates of alternation or homologous response over time, which would reflect the development and strengthening of a reciprocal system.

Role specification

A second requirement of an ecologically valid model is that the roles of other participants besides the child be specified and systematically examined as independent variables. Two types of roles are usefully distinguished. First, there are the persons who play specific and enduring roles in the child's life, such as mother, father, old brother, teacher, friend, etc. G. H. Mead (1934) coined the term '*significant other*' to designate this special kind of special relationship, and we shall follow his usage. A second type, presumably derived from the first, involves more *generalized roles*, such as male adult, female adult, older child, younger child, etc.

1 *Significant others*. It is a sobering fact, that whether from the point of view of science or social policy, in terms of direct observation and systematic

study, we know more about the impact on the child of an unidentified stranger, who happens to serve as an experimenter, than of the child's own parents, family members, and other close associates. Although direct observational and experimental studies of mother–infant interaction during the first two years of life have shown a gratifying increase over the past decade (e.g. Foss 1961, 1963, 1965, 1969, Kagan 1971, Lewis 1969), analogous investigations for children three years of age and older are still comparatively rare. There are a few observations of mother–child interaction in preschoolers (Baldwin 1947, Caldwell et al. 1970, Hilton 1967, Lasko 1954, Mussen and Parker 1965, Rothbart 1971), most of them focusing on the issue of differences in the socialization of first *v.* later born children. But beginning with the school age child, virtually all the research on mother–child relationships still relies on far from adequate verbal reports.[3]

As for father–child interaction, direct observational or experimental investigations are extremely rare. Recently, two studies have appeared reporting the behaviour of fathers towards infants in the first year of life (Ban and Lewis 1971, Rebelsky and Hanks 1971). The findings indicate that, although American fathers spend only 10 to 20 minutes a day attending to a child under one year of age, they nevertheless have an impact on the infant's response, particularly with respect to more distal interactions such as eye contact and vocalization. With the exception of these two researches, this writer has been unable to find any direct studies of father–child interaction until adolescence (Strodtbeck 1958, Rosen and D'Andrade 1959), and both of these investigations are limited to boys.

Even more conspicuous than the absence of the father in research on child rearing is the absence of any other representative from the child's world besides his parents. For example, the effect on the child of interaction with his siblings, both older and younger, is virtually unexamined except in occasional clinical case studies. Even more striking is the complete exclusion of adult relatives. A search of the abstracts failed to reveal a single study of the role of such figures as grandmothers, grandfathers, uncles, or aunts, at least in Western countries. Perhaps investigators are prepared to assume that, in our modern mobile society with its shrunken nuclear family, such persons can no longer play a meaningful role in the lives of children. If so, then at least we should expect some attention to the principal agent who has taken their place as parent substitute – the ubiquitous member of every American family containing young children – the *baby-sitter*. But again the research annals are silent on the subject. To be sure, there is a growing literature on the reaction of the young child to a stranger (e.g., Morgan and Ricciuti 1969, Rheingold 1969b, Schaffer 1966, Wahler

3 A notable exception is Rosen and D'Andrade's (1959) ingenious experimental study.

1967) but, to date, attention has been limited to the immobilizing, anxiety producing impact of the initial encounter with no follow-up on the subsequent course of interaction of repeated contact over longer periods of time.

In summary, if we are to judge by the research literature, only if and when the child enters nursery, preschool, or school can other people besides parents significantly influence his life, and even these persons are limited to teachers and peers operating within an educational setting. The extended family, the informal peer group, older and younger children, other adults, the street, the neighbourhood – all of these have remained outside the pale of direct investigation as agents affecting or *affected by* the developing child.

2 *Generalized roles.* This possibility that the young child may be differentially and significantly responsive to persons not only as particular individuals but as possessors of more generalized characteristics such as sex, age, or social background, has also been largely overlooked. Part of the reason derives from a scientific tradition which defines the experimenter as a neutral nonentity excluded from substantive consideration in the experimental design. Significantly referred to only as E, bereft of age, sex, or social identity, he is treated as if he were an interchangeable part of the research apparatus, like a light bulb. In point of fact, of course, the experimenter is not just anybody, but always someone of a particular age, sex, and social background. And in the few studies that have taken such factors into account, the evidence indicates that they can be of considerable importance. For example, differences in child's response associated with the sex of the stimulus person have been reported in the first year of life (Kagan and Lewis 1965) and, in Soviet research, even within the first three months. Differences in test performance as a function of race of examiner have been documented for both Negro and White children from the first grade onward (Abramson 1969, Katz, Henchy, and Allen 1968, Kennedy and Vega 1965, Sattler 1966, Turner 1971). It appears likely that similar differences would be found in responsiveness to reinforcement, modelling, and other social influence techniques not only in terms of the race of the experimenter but also his ethnic and social class background as reflected in speech pattern, gestures, attire, etc. The further demonstration of such experimenter effects would have obvious and important implications for the interpretation of the ethnic and social class differences in performance so commonly found in research literature.

Several studies reporting experimenter effects indicate the development, by preschool age, of a complex pattern of interaction between the sex of the examiner and the sex of the child (Bandura et al. 1961, Cieutat 1965, Fryrear and Thelen 1969, Gewirtz 1954, Gewirtz and Baer 1958, May 1966, Stevenson 1961, Stevenson and Allen 1964, Stevenson and Knights 1964). In general, performance appears to be enhanced when the child is presented with a model of the same sex and is reinforced by a person of the opposite sex, who also reinforces the model. The reader will note that this fairly intricate set of specifications defines a rather familiar and indeed universal structure in human societies – *the nuclear family*. The pattern also calls attention to an additional essential requirement for an ecologically valid model for the socialization process. The model must be expandable from a two-person to a three-person system and beyond. This expansion, in turn, introduces new structural properties which add complexity and richness to the socialization process and its products.

Two-person v. n-person systems

Expanding the socialization system to include more than two people increases opportunity for both role differentiation and reciprocal response. To take the classical example of a three-person system – the nuclear family, we have within it the possibility of differential allocation of parental roles between father and mother, and, now, instead of only one dyadic relationship, a total of three – mother with child, father with child, and mother and father. In each of these, patterns of reciprocal socialization take place which may duplicate, complement, or even contradict each other, with profound consequences not only for the behaviour and development of the child but also of the two adults in their roles as parents, and of the nuclear family as a total system.

The special structural and functional characteristics of the nuclear family as a *triad* have been discussed from a broad theoretical perspective (Parsons and Bales 1955) but empirical work has been largely confined to examining the role of such factors in the genesis of psychiatric disorders (Ackerman and Babrens 1956, Alkire 1969, Farber and Jenné 1963. Goldstein et al. 1968, Henry 1956, Kohn and Clausen 1956, Lidz et al. 1958). Except for indirect evidence from the now extensive research of the effects of father absence (summarized in Biller 1970 and Herzog and Sudia 1970), there appears to be only one study focusing explicitly on the effects of varying patterns of parental role differentiation on development in normal children (Bronfenbrenner 1961a, 1961b, 1961c). The results indicated that adolescents showing the highest degree of leadership and dependability tended to come from families in which parental roles were differentiated, with some division between father and mother in the spheres of discipline and affection. Since the results of this investigation were based on correlations between questionnaire responses and sociometric data, the findings are yet to be confirmed by an observational study. They receive some indirect support, however, from the interpretation of their experimental results offered by Rosen and D'Andrade (1959).

The father–mother–child triad is clearly not the only ecologically important example of a three-person socialization system. Another is provided by the mother in simultaneous interaction with a first and second child. Unfortunately, none of the existing studies of differences in socialization of first *v.* later borns (Baldwin 1947, Lasko 1954, Hilton 1967, Rothbart 1971) has actually employed a three-person model. The observations focus on the behaviours of mother with each child separately, so that the interplay among all three parties, especially between the two children, is overlooked. Also, these investigations have concerned themselves with only one parent – the mother. Inclusion of the father of course produces a four-person system, with a geometric increase in the number of possible reciprocal relationships. Nor, from an ecological point of view, are the important participants limited to parents and children. Conceivably they might also include a grandparent, babysitter, teacher, etc. In terms of research strategy, however, it would probably be wise to assess the role of such ancillary participants first in triadic situations involving parent, child, and third party.

It should be recognized that the three- or more-person system provides opportunity not only for role differentiation but other configurational features that are foreclosed in only a two-person interaction. For example, with a third person present, there is the possibility of vicarious reinforcement or imitation in which the child, or adult, does not himself participate but is susceptible to what Bandura (1962, 1965, 1969) has called observational learning. Finally, a three- or n-person model permits the occurrence and analysis of a phenomenon of the greatest importance for socialization processes that has thus far received little systematic study: *the influence of a third party on the pattern of reciprocal interaction between the other two.*

Second-order effects

Ordinarily, research on socialization is confined to what might be called *first-order effects* – the direct impact of one person on the behaviour of another. But the pattern of interaction between two people, such as mother and child, can also be profoundly affected by third parties. Thus both mother and child may act differently towards each other in the presence of the father, younger child, or stranger. This is what is meant by a *second-order effect.*

The author has been able to find only one example of the systematic study of such second-order effects in the research literature. Though the context is a rather specialized one, the results are dramatic. I refer to the ingenious series of experiments by Rheingold (1969b) documenting the effect of the mother's presence on the young child's reaction to a stranger. Although when left alone with an unfamiliar person, ten-month-old infants exhibited considerable emotional distress, the appearance of the mother not only appeared to allay the fear of the stranger but instigated vocalization and exploratory behaviour. It is as if the presence of the mother served as a catalyst enabling other kinds of interaction to occur.

Within the family system itself, the potency and magnitude of second-order effects are reflected in the now voluminous literature on the impact of father absence (see above) and birth order differences (summarized in Clausen 1965), but direct evidence for the phenomenon is almost completely lacking. What is needed are observational and experimental studies of the changes that occur in patterns of interaction as a function of the presence or participation of the third party. Such a formulation points to the need, for example, of studying the effects of father absence not solely in broken families, but, more importantly, in families that are intact, and in terms of the father's influence not only on the child but on the mother and the mother–child dyad. Conversely, we can now envision a new aspect to the study of maternal behaviour: the impact of the mother on the father–child relationship. For example, are there any consistent differences in the behaviour of father with child as a function of the presence or absence of the mother? Or, to consider a less obvious second-order effect, does consistent reliance on a babysitter have any systematic influence on the mother–child relationship, or the capacity of the child to relate to other adults?

It is important to recognize that the source for a second-order effect is not limited to another human being. For example, the recent research and discussion on the role of early stimulation in infancy has led to the development of new types of baby equipment. Thus a brochure recently received in the mail describes a 'cognition crib' equipped with a tape recorder that can be activated by the sound of the infant's voice. In addition, frames built into the sides of the crib permit insertion of 'programmed play modules for sensory and physical practice'. The modules come in sets of six, which the parent is 'encouraged to change' every three months so as to keep pace with the child's development. Since 'faces are what an infant sees first', 'six soft plastic faces . . . adhere to the window', including a distorted face of the type so often included in recent studies of perceptual development in infants. Other modules include mobiles (among them a 'changing faces mobile'), a crib aquarium, and 'ego building mirrors'.

Quite apart from the effectiveness of such devices for accelerating the infant's cognitive development, one may ask what influence they have on adult–infant interaction. Are they likely to increase the frequency, say, of picking up the infant, reciprocal eye contact, vocalization, or lead to its reduction?

At an older age level, an analogous issue of second-order effects arises with respect to television. Much of recent research and public concern about television in the lives of children focuses on the influence of TV violence. But perhaps an even more important phenomenon, both scientifically and socially, is the effect of television in reducing social interaction. As the author has written elsewhere (Report on Forum 15, 1970): 'The primary danger of television lies not so much in the behaviour it produces as the behaviour it prevents – the talks, the games, the family festivities and arguments through which much of the child's learning takes place and his character is formed.' It is this impact of television on the socialization processes within the family that needs to be investigated.

The role of television in changing patterns of interaction within the family points to the most potent form of second-order effect, one in which the external agent is not a single individual, but another ecological system that impinges on or encompasses the system in which the direct socialization is taking place.

Experimental human ecology

Perhaps the best documented example of a second-order effect at the level of ecological settings rather than individuals is the influence of social class on socialization practices and outcomes (for a recent summary see Hess 1970). Subsequently, Tulkin, Kagan and others (Kagan 1971, Lewis and Wilson 1973, Tulkin 1970, Tulkin and Kagan 1970) have identified reliable class differences in mother–infant interaction within the first year of life. Ecological differences of even larger order are of course found in cross-cultural studies (for a recent summary see Levine 1970). But the difficulty with most investigations of this kind is that they shed little light on the processes through which cultural or class values come to affect child rearing practices, or *vice versa*. Clearly the connection is mediated through particular social structures and institutions in the society, such as schools, neighbourhoods, places of work, and the like. An instructive example is provided by a recent observational study of mother–child interaction in Japan (Caudill and Weinstein 1969). Utilizing Miller and Swanson's (1958) distinction between entrepreneurial and bureaucratic job settings, Caudill and Weinstein found that wives of independent business men were more likely to talk to, rock, and stimulate their babies than wives of a matched group of salaried personnel. The latter mothers were content to look, and remain passive.

Second-order effects at an older age level are demonstrated in Bronfenbrenner's study (1970b) of matched groups of Soviet children attending day schools and boarding schools. Consistent with the hypothesis of the study, children reared primarily in a single socialization setting (the peer collective in the boarding school) differed from those exposed to two somewhat divergent contexts (peer collective at school, family at home). Children brought up in boarding schools subscribed more strongly to culturally approved values and showed greater conformity to social pressures in their immediate environment.

In the foregoing examples, variation in ecological settings is observed as it occurs in society. But the full import of ecological systems for the development of both science and social policy is to be sought not in experiments of nature but in experiments of man – that is, through *the deliberate design, systematic manipulation and scientific analysis of new ecological settings that can affect primary socialization processes*. We refer to this approach as *experimental human ecology*.

There are few examples of this kind of experimentation in the research literature, but the few that do exist testify to its power and its promise. The most familiar is Skeels' (1966) remarkable follow-up study of two groups of mentally retarded, institutionalized children who constituted the experimental and control groups in an experiment he had initiated thirty years earlier (Skeels, Undegraff, Wellmann and Williams 1938, Skeels and Dye 1939). When the children were three years of age, thirteen of them were placed in the care of female inmates of a state institution for the mentally retarded with each child being assigned to a different ward. The control group was allowed to remain in the original – also institutional – environment, a children's orphanage. During the formal experimental period, which averaged a year and a half, the experimental group showed a gain in IQ of 28 points, whereas the control group dropped 26 points. Upon completion of the experiment, it became possible to place the institutionally-mothered children in legal adoption. Thirty years later, all thirteen children in the experimental group were found to be self-supporting, all but two had completed high school, with four having one or more years of college. In the control group, all were either dead or still institutionalized. Skeels concludes his report with some dollar figures on the amount of taxpayers' money expended to sustain the institutionalized group, in contrast to the productive income brought in by those who had been raised initially by mentally deficient women in a state institution.

In seeking to explain the early gains shown by the children placed on the wards, Skeels calls attention to facts like the following. In each instance, one of the inmates in effect adopted the infant and became its mother; in addition, the entire ward was caught up in activities on behalf of 'our baby'. New clothes and playthings appeared, and the children were lavished with attention. Also, the several wards began to compete with each other in terms of whose baby was developing most rapidly.

All of these developments derive, however, from a deliberately-contrived ecological change – the restructuring of a social system in such a way as to maximize adult–child interaction.

A number of authorities have expressed serious scepticism about Skeels' dramatic results. Several of the crucial methodological issues raised by McNemar (1940) in his critique of Skeels' early work have in fact been refuted by the follow-up study and its clear demonstration that the early dramatic differences were not ephemeral either in their magnitude or durability. More recently, Jensen (1969) has called Skeels' work into question not on grounds of fact but of interpretation. Substantial gains in IQ, such as those reported by Skeels, he asserts, can be expected only in severely deprived children, whereas 'typical culturally disadvantaged children are not reared in anything like the degree of sensory and motor deprivation that characterize, say, the children of the Skeels study'.

In response to this criticism one need only point to a growing body of well-designed researches documenting significant and substantial gains in IQ and related measures for samples clearly representative of disadvantaged families (Gray and Klaus 1970, Hodges et al. 1967, Karnes et al. 1970, Palmer 1972, Schaefer 1969a, Schaefer and Aaronson 1972, Weikart 1969). Of particular significance, in terms of second-order ecological effects, is the study by Karnes, which involved no work directly with the children themselves but only with their mothers. Fifteen mothers, all but one of them Negro, from economically depressed neighbourhoods, attended weekly two-hour meetings over a 15-month period. The project provided transportation and costs of baby-sitters for the mothers' initially 12 to 24-month-old infants. During the meetings,

> . . . mothers in disadvantaged families were provided a sequential educational program to use at home in stimulating the cognitive and verbal development of their children and were instructed in principles of teaching which emphasized positive reinforcement. In addition to these child-centered activities, a portion of each meeting was devoted to mother-centered goals related to fostering a sense of dignity and worth as the mother demonstrated self-help capabilities within the family setting and the community at large. (p. 926)

Two types of control groups were employed – one consisting of children of similar family background,[4] the other of siblings of the experimental children, who had been tested previously at similar ages prior to the mother's enrolment in the training programme. At the end of the 15 month period, when the children averaged three years of age, the experimental group showed a 16 point gain in IQ over their matched controls and a 28 point gain over their own siblings, cared for in the same home by the same mother prior to her exposure to the programme.

The rather powerful implications of this experiment are well summarized by the authors.

> The 16-point Binet IQ difference between the infants whose mothers worked with them at home and the control infants nearly equals the 17-point Binet IQ difference between the experimental and control subjects in the Schaefer study, where the educational intervention was carried out by college graduates who served as tutors, visiting the child at home for 1 hour a day, 5 days a week, over a 21-month period. . . . Since at-home intervention by mothers can be budgeted at a fraction of the cost of tutorial intervention, the direction for further research in preventive programs of very early intervention seems clear. Further, programs which train the mother to serve as the agent for intervention hold potential for developing her self-help capabilities, and sense of personal worth, pivotal factors in effecting broader changes within the disadvantaged family. Not only may the mother represent the ideal agent for fostering an improved school prognosis for the young disadvantaged child, but through group interaction she may extend this sense of responsibility for infant, self and family to the wider community in which they live.[5] (p. 934)

Results paralleling those of Karnes are reported in a recent study by Levenstein (1970). Working once a week with a group of mothers of 2 to 3-year-olds from low income families, Levenstein demonstrated the use of books and toys as a means of stimulating mother–child interaction. Over a seven month period, the children showed a mean IQ gain of 17 points.

In the light of Karnes' and Levenstein's findings, it is noteworthy that of the more conventional intervention programmes, in which the child is worked with directly, those showing lasting effects have involved a strong

4 The children were matched on family size, working status of mother, mother's birthplace, mother's education, presence of father or father surrogate, and welfare status.

5 The authors note in this connection that at a local meeting called to discuss the possibility of establishing a parent–child centre in the community, twelve of the fifteen mothers attended 'and were in fact the only persons indigenous in the neighbourhood in attendance'.

component of parent involvement (Gray and Klaus 1970,[6] Weikart 1969). Despite substantial gains at the end of the programme, follow-up studies in other group intervention projects report gradual attenuation of differences between the experimental and control groups, with no significant effects after two or three years (Hodges et al. 1967, Palmer 1972, Schaefer, personal communication). And even before the dramatic effects of his tutorial intervention programme had 'washed out' at the end of two years, Schaefer (1969b) had concluded from a review of the literature: 'Evidence that mean IQ scores increase during intensive stimulation and decrease after such stimulation is terminated (is) cited as supporting family centred programmes.' Additional results consistent with this conclusion come from the growing body of research on the effects of parent participation on the child's capacity to profit from intervention programmes (Gilmer 1969, Grotberg 1969, Hoffman, Jordan and McCormick 1971, Strickland 1967, Weikart and Lambie 1968, Willmon 1969).

Such findings provide post hoc support for a general principle that guided the design and development of the Head Start programme. Early in its deliberations, the Planning Committee of Project Head Start, of which this writer was privileged to be a member, stressed in its statements and memoranda to Government officials that the immediate objective of the programme should be to effect positive changes *not* in the child himself (e.g. gain in IQ) but in his enduring environment in home, neighbourhood, and community. The former, we emphasized, were easily achieved, but likely to be short-lived; only the latter could give promise for continuing psychological development.

As the foregoing statements imply, ecological intervention as a strategy both for the scientific analysis and enhancement of human development can not be limited to the establishment of preschool or parent education programmes. The principle applies to the full range of ecological systems that directly or indirectly impinge on the world of the child and those immediately concerned with his welfare. For example, this author has argued elsewhere (Bronfenbrenner 1972) that the key to an understanding of socialization in contemporary American society, and the Western world generally, lies in the phenomenon of segregation by age, and the alienation which such segregation produces. This segregation, in turn, is the unintended consequence of developments in many different aspects of contemporary life. A host of factors conspire to isolate children from the rest of society. The fragmentation of the extended family, the separation of residential and business areas, the disappearance of neighbourhoods, super-

6 Gray and Klaus also found positive changes in the younger siblings of the target child, additional evidence of the power of second-order effects.

markets, zoning ordinances, occupational mobility, commuting, child labour laws, the abolishment of the apprentice system, consolidated schools, television, the decay of public transportation, separate patterns of social life for different age groups, the working mother, the delegation of child care to specialists – all these manifestations of progress operate to decrease opportunity and incentive for meaningful contact between children and persons older, or younger, than themselves.

Ecological changes are crucial not only for the solution of urgent social problems. They are also critical for the further development of adequate theory and research on the process of human development. It is the central thesis of this paper that most of the environmental variance in human capacities, motivations, and behaviour derives not from first-order socialization effects within family, classroom, or peer group, but from the second-order impact of other institutions in the society, such as the world of work, public transportation, or the structure of neighbourhoods. Moreover, instead of attempting to study these in the scientifically confounded and, nowadays, often socially disintegrated form in which nature, or – more accurately – society gives them to us, we should endeavour to create new ecological arrangements designed simultaneously both to solve pressing social problems and to test important theoretical propositions.

I close with a few examples of possible research designs for such an experimental human ecology.[7]

1 A study currently under way is based on an adaptation of a Soviet pattern in which business organizations 'adopt' groups of school children and establish relationships of mutual visiting, help, and interest in each other's work (Bronfenbrenner 1970a). Such a programme has been introduced in a New England community. The parents of the children are not directly involved, but changes are being assessed in the attitudes of parents towards their children and children towards their parents.

2 A related design involves giving older children some responsibility for the young in the primary grades. They are to escort the younger children to and from school, teach them games, help them with schoolwork, etc. Dependent variables include changes in the older children's school performance, career plans, reading interests, views on child rearing, and behaviour at home.

3 An educational programme is set up for couples expecting their first child. Both husband and wife must volunteer to be included but only one spouse is selected (on a random basis). After completion of the programme and arrival of the child, observations are made of mother–infant interaction.

7 The practical, programmatic, and public policy aspects of these proposals are discussed in Bronfenbrenner (1972).

Higher frequency of reciprocal response is predicted for mothers whose husbands attended the programme than for the mothers who attended themselves.

4 A large business firm employing working mothers is persuaded to introduce, in selected departments, an option of part-time employment. Mothers volunteer for this option with the understanding that both the experimental and control group would be selected from among the volunteers. To compensate for the Hawthorne effect, the control group receives some other fringe benefit, such as longer vacation periods. The dependent variables in the study relate to changes in patterns of interaction within the family and their effects on child behaviour and development.

5 Two comparable low-cost housing projects are selected which differ in that one of them has shops and services within easy walking distance, the other involves a trip by car or bus. The dependent variable is the amount of time parents and other adults spend in interaction with school age children and the consequent effects on the children's behaviour and performance both in and out of school.

Hopefully such investigations would have a beneficial effect simultaneously in two domains. They would contribute to making human beings more human – both in research and in reality.

References

ABRAMSON, T. (1969) 'The influence of examiner race on first-grade and kindergarten subjects' Peabody Picture Vocabulary Test scores', *Journal of Educational Measurements*, 6, 241–6.

ACKERMAN, N. W. and BEHRENS, M. L. (1956) 'A study of family diagnosis', *American Journal of Orthopsychiatry*, 26, 66–78.

ALKIRE, A. A. (1969) 'Social power and communication, within families of disturbed and non-disturbed preadolescents', *Journal of Personality and Social Psychology*, 13, 335–49.

BALDWIN, A. L. (1947) 'Changes in parent behavior during pregnancy', *Child Development*, 18, 29–39.

BAN, P. L. and LEWIS, M. (1971) 'Mothers and fathers, girls and boys: Attachment behavior in the one-year-old'. Paper presented at the Meetings of the Eastern Psychological Association, New York.

BANDURA, A. (1962) 'Social learning through imitation' in Jones, M. R. (ed.) *Nebraska Symposium on Motivation 1962* Lincoln, University of Nebraska Press, pp. 211–69.

BANDURA, A. (1965) 'Vicarious processes: A case of no trial learning' in Berkowitz, L. (ed.) *Advances in Experimental Social Psychology, Vol. II* New York, Academic Press, pp. 1–55.

BANDURA, A, (1969) 'A social learning-theory of identificatory processes' in Goslin, D. A. (ed.) *Handbook of Socialization Theory and Research* Chicago, Rand McNally, pp. 213–62.

BANDURA, A., ROSS, P. and ROSS, S. (1961) 'Transmission of aggression through imitation of aggressive models', *Journal of Abnormal and Social Psychology*, **62**, 570–82.

BELL, R. Q. (1968) 'A reinterpretation of the direction of effects in studies of socialization', *Psychological Review*, **75**, 81–95.

BELL, R. Q. (1971) 'Stimulus control of parent or caretaker behaviour by offspring', *Developmental Psychology*, **4**, 63–72.

BELL, S. M. (1971) 'The effectiveness of various maternal responses as terminators of crying: Some developmental changes and theoretical implications'. Paper presented at the Meeting of the Society for Research in Child Development, Minneapolis.

BILLER, H. B. (1970) 'Father-absence and the personality development of the male child, *Developmental Psychology*, **2**, 181–201.

BRONFENBRENNER, U., (1961a) 'Some familial antecedents of responsibility and leadership in adolescents', in Petrullo, L. and Bass, B. L. (eds) *Leadership and Interpersonal Behavior* New York, Holt, Rinehart and Winston, pp. 239–71.

BRONFENBRENNER, U. (1961b) 'Toward a theoretical model for the analysis of parent-child relationships in a social context' in Glidewell, J. C. (ed.) *Parental Attitudes and Child Behavior* Springfield, Illinois, Charles C. Thomas, pp. 90–109.

BRONFENBRENNER, U. (1961c) 'The changing American child – A speculative analysis', *Merrill-Palmer Quarterly*, **7**, 73–84.

BRONFENBRENNER, U. (1968) 'Early deprivation: A cross-species analysis' in Levine S. and Newton G. (eds) *Early Experience and Behavior* Springfield, Illinois, Charles C. Thomas, pp. 627–764.

BRONFENBRENNER, U. (1970a) *Two Worlds of Childhood: U.S. and U.S.S.R.* New York, Russell Sage Foundation.

BRONFENBRENNER, U. (1970b) 'Reaction to social pressure from adults versus peers among Soviet day school and boarding pupils in the perspective of an American sample', *Journal of Personality and Social Psychology*, **18**, 179–89.

BRONFENBRENNER, U. (1972) 'Developmental research and public policy' in Romanyshyn, J. M. (ed.) *Social Science and Social Welfare* New York, Council on Social Work Education.

CALDWELL, B. M., WRIGHT, C. M., HONIG, A. S. and TANNENBAUM, J. (1970) 'Infant day care and attachment', *American Journal of Orthopsychiatry*, **3**, 397–412.

CAUDILL, W. and WEINSTEIN, H. (1969) 'Maternal care and infant behavior in Japan and America', *Psychiatry*, **32**, 12–43.

CIEUTAT, V. J. (1965) 'Examiner differences with Stanford-Binet IQ', *Perceptual and Motor Skills*, **20**, 317–18.

CLAUSEN, J. A. (1965) *Family size and birth order as influences upon socialization and personality: Bibliography and abstracts* New York Social Science Research Council.

FARBER, B. and JENNÉ, W. C. (1963) 'Family organization and parent-child communication: Parents and siblings of a retarded child', *Monographs of the Society for Research in Child Development*, **28**, no. 7.

FOSS, B. M. (1961, 1963, 1965, 1969) *Determinants of Infant Behaviour, Volumes I–IV* London, Methuen.

FRYREAR, L. L. and THELEN, M. H. (1969) 'The effect of sex of model and sex of observer on the imitation of affectionate behaviour', *Developmental Psychology*, **1**, 298.

GEWIRTZ, H. B. and GEWIRTZ, J. L. (1969) 'Caretaking settings, background events, and behaviour differences in four Israeli child-rearing environments: Some preliminary trends' in Foss B. M. (ed.) *Determinants of Infant Behaviour, IV* London, Methuen, pp. 229–95.

GEWIRTZ, J. L. (1954) 'Three determinants of attention seeking in young children', *Monographs of the Society for Research in Child Development*, **19**, no. 59.

GEWIRTZ, J. L. (1969a) 'Mechanisms of social learning: Some roles of stimulation and behavior in early human development' in Goslin, D. A. (ed.) *Handbook of Socialization Theory and Research* Chicago, Rand McNally, pp. 57–212.

GEWIRTZ, J. L. (1969b) 'Levels of conceptual analysis in environment-infant interaction research', *Merrill-Palmer Quarterly of Behavior and Development*, **15**.

GEWIRTZ, J. L. and BAER, D. M. (1958) 'The effect of brief social deprivation on behaviors for a social reinforcer', *Journal of Abnormal and Social Psychology*, **56**, 49–56.

GEWIRTZ, J. L. and GEWIRTZ, H. B. (1965) 'Stimulus conditions, infant behaviors, and social learning in four Israeli child rearing environments: A preliminary report illustrating differences in environment and behaviour between the only and "the youngest" child' in Foss B. M. (ed.) *Determinants of Infant Behaviour, III* London, Methuen, pp. 161–84.

GILMER, B. R. (1969) 'Intra-family diffusion of selected cognitive skills as a function of educational stimulation'. Nashville, Tennessee: George Peabody College for Teachers, DARCEE Paper and Reports, 3:1.

GOLDSTEIN, M. J., LEWIS, L. J., RODNICK, E. H., ALKIRE, A. and GOULD, E. (1968) 'A method for studying social influence and coping patterns within families of disturbed adolescents', *Journal of Nervous and Mental Diseases*, **147**, 233–51.

GRAY, S. W. and KLAUS, R. A. (1970) 'The early training project: A 7th Year Report', *Child Development*, **41**, 909–24.

GROTBERG, E. H. (1969) *Review of research – Project Head Start, 1965–1969* Washington, D.C., Research and Evaluation Office, Project Head Start, OEO Pamphlet 6108–13.

HENRY, A. F. (1956) 'Family role structure and self-blame', *Social Forces*, 35, 34–8.

HERZOG, E. and SUDIA, C. E. (1970) *Boys in fatherless families* Washington D.C., Office of Child Development.

HESS, R. D. (1970) 'Social class and ethnic influences upon socialization' in Mussen, P. H. (ed.) *Carmichael's Manual of Child Psychology, Vol. II* New York, John Wiley, pp. 457–557.

HILTON, I. (1967) 'Differences in the behavior of mothers toward first- and later-born children', *Journal of Personality and Social Psychology*, 7, 282–90.

HODGES, W. L., MCCANDLESS, B. R. and SPIKER, H. H. (1967) *The development and evaluation of a diagnostically based curriculum for pre-school psychosocially deprived children. Final Report University of Indiana Project No. 50350* Washington, D.C., U.S. Office of Education.

HOFFMAN, D. B., JORDAN, J. S. and MCCORMICK, F. (1971) *Parent participation in pre-school day care* Atlanta, Georgia, Southeastern Educational Laboratory.

JENSEN, A. R. (1969) 'How much can we boost IQ in scholastic achievement?' *Harvard Educational Review*, 39, 1–123.

KAGAN, J. (1971) *Change and continuity in infancy* New York, Wiley

KAGAN, J. and LEWIS, M. (1965) 'Studies of attention in the human infant', *Merrill-Palmer Quarterly*, 11, 95–127.

KARNES, M. B., TRESKA, J. A., HODGINS, A. S. and BADGER, E. D. (1970) 'Educational intervention at home by mothers of disadvantaged infants', *Child Development*, 41, 925–35.

KATZ, I., HENCHY, T., and ALLEN, H. (1968) 'Effects of race of tester, approval–disapproval, and need on Negro children's learning', *Journal of Personality and Social Psychology*, 8, 38–42.

KENNEDY, W. A. and VEGA, M. (1965) 'Negro children's performance on discrimination test as a function of examiner, race, and verbal incentive', *Journal of Personality and Social Psychology*, 2, 839–43.

KOHN, M. L. and CLAUSEN, J. A. (1956) 'Parental authority behavior and schizophrenia,' *American Journal of Orthopsychiatry*, 26, 297–313.

LASKO, J. K. (1954) 'Parental behavior toward first and second children', *Genetic Psychology Monographs*, 49, 97–137.

LEVENSTEIN, P. (1970) 'Cognitive growth in preschoolers through verbal interaction with mothers', *American Journal of Orthopsychiatry*, 40, 426–32.

LEVINE, R. A. (1970) 'Cross-cultural study of child psychology' in Mussen, P. H. (ed.) *Carmichael's Manual of Child Psychology, Vol. II* New York, John Wiley, pp. 359–614.

LEWIS, M. (1969) 'A developmental study of information processing within the first three years of life: Response decrement to a redundant signal', *Monographs of the Society for Research in Child Development*, 34, no. 133.

LEWIS, M. and WILSON, C. D. (1973) 'Infant development in lower class American families', *Human Development*.

LIDZ, T., CORNELISON, A., TERRY, D., and FLECK, S. (1958) 'Intrafamiliar environment of the schizophrenic patient: VI. The transmission of irrationality', *Archives of Neurology and Psychiatry*, **79**, 305–16.

MAY, J. G. (1966) 'A developmental study of imitation', *Dissertation Abstracts*, **26**, 6852–3.

MCNEMAR, Q. (1940) 'A critical examination of the University of Iowa Studies of Environmental Influences upon the IQ', *Psychological Bulletin*, **37**, 63–91.

MEAD, G. H. (1934) *Mind, Self and Society* Chicago, University of Chicago Press.

MILLER, D. R. and SWANSON, G. E. (1958) *The changing American parent* New York, Wiley.

MORGAN, G. A. and RICCIUTI, H. N. (1969) 'Infants' responses to strangers during the first year' in Foss, B. M. (ed.) *Determinants of Infant Behaviour, IV* London, Methuen, pp. 253–72.

MOSS, H. A. (1967) 'Sex, age, and state as determinants of mother–infant interaction', *Merill-Palmer Quarterly*, **13**, 19–36.

MOSS, H. A. and ROBSON, K. S. (1968) 'The role of protest behavior in the development of the mother–infant attachment'. Paper presented at the Meeting of the American Psychological Association, San Francisco.

MUSSEN, P. H and PARKER, A. L. (1965) 'Mother nurturants and girls' incidental imitative learning', *Journal of Personality and Social Psychology*, **2**, 94–7.

PALMER, F. H. (1972) 'Minimal intervention at age 2 and 3 and subsequent intellective changes' in Parker, R. K. (ed.) *The Preschool in Action* Boston, Allyn and Bacon.

PARSONS, T. and BALES, R. F. (1955) *Family socialization and interaction process* Glencoe, Illinois, Free Press.

REBELSKY, F. and HANKS, C. (1971) 'Father's verbal interactions with infants in the first three months of life', *Child Development*, **42**, 63–8.

Report of Forum 15 (1970) White House Conference on Children.

RHEINGOLD, H. L. (1969a) 'The social and socializing infant' in Goslin, D. A. (ed.) *Handbook of Socialization Theory and Research* Chicago, Rand McNally, pp. 779–90.

RHEINGOLD, H. L. (1969b) 'The effect of a strange environment on the behaviour of infants' in Foss, B. M. (ed) *Determinants of Infant Behaviour, IV* London, Methuen, pp. 137–66.

ROSEN, B. C. and D'ANDRADE, R. (1959) 'The psychosocial origins of achievement motivation', *Sociometry*, **22**, 185–218.

ROTHBART, M. K. (1971) 'Birth order and mother–child interaction in an achievement situation', *Journal of Personality and Social Psychology*, **17**, 113–20.

SATTLER, J. M. (1966) 'Statistical reanalysis of Canady's "The effect of 'rapport' on the IQ": A new approach to the problem of racial psychology', *Psychological Reports*, **19**, 1203–6.

SCHAEFER, E. S. (1969a) 'A home tutoring program', *Children*, 16, 59–61.

SCHAEFER, E. S. (1969b) 'The need for early and continuing education'. Paper presented at the 136th Annual Meeting of the American Association for the Advancement of Science, Washington, D.C.

SCHAEFER, E. S. and AARONSON, N. (1972) 'Infant education research project: Implementation and implications of a home tutoring program' in Parker, R. K. (ed.) *The Preschool in Action* Boston, Allyn and Bacon.

SCHAFFER, H. R. (1966) 'The onset of fear of strangers and the incongruity hypothesis', *Journal of Child Psychology and Psychiatry*, 7, 95–106.

SKEELS, H. M. (1966) 'Adult status of children with contrasting early life experience', *Monographs of the Society for Research in Child Development*, 31, no. 105.

SKEELS, H. M., UNDERGRAFF, R., WELLMAN, B. L. and WILLIAMS, H. N. (1938) 'A study of environmental stimulation: An orphanage preschool project', *University of Iowa Studies in Child Welfare*, 15, no. 4.

SKEELS, H. M. and DYE, H. B. (1939) 'The study of the effects of differential stimulation on mentally retarded children', *Proceedings and Addresses of the American Association of Mental Deficiency*. 44, 114–36.

STEVENSON, H. W. (1961) 'Social reinforcement with children as a function of CA, sex of E, and sex of S', *Journal of Abnormal and Social Psychology*, 63, 147–54.

STEVENSON, H. W. and ALLEN, S. (1964) 'Adult performance as a function of sex of experimenter and sex of subject', *Journal of Abnormal and Social Psychology*, 68, 214–16.

STEVENSON, H. W. and KNIGHTS, R. M. (1964) 'Social reinforcement with normal and retarded children as a function of pretraining, sex of E, and sex of S', *Journal of Experimental Child Psychology*, 1, 248–55.

STRICKLAND, J. H. (1967) 'The effect of a parent education program in the language development of underprivileged kindergarten children', *Dissertation Abstracts*, pp. 1633a–1634a.

STRODTBECK, F. L. (1958) 'Family interaction, values, and achievement' in McClelland, D. C., Baldwin, A. L., Bronfenbrenner, U., and Strodtbeck, F. L., *Talent and Society* New York, Van Nostrand, pp. 135–94.

TULKIN, S. R. (1970) 'Mother-infant interaction in the first year of life: An inquiry into the influences of social class'. Unpublished doctoral dissertation, Harvard University.

TULKIN, S. R. and KAGAN, J. (1970) 'Mother–child interaction: Social class differences in the first year of life', *Proceedings of the 78th APA Annual Convention*, pp. 261–2.

TURNER, C. (1971) 'Effects of race of tester and need for approval on children's learning', *Journal of Educational Psychology*, 62, 240–4.

WAHLER, R. G. (1967) 'Infant social attachments: Reinforcement theory, interpretation, and investigation', *Child Development*, 38, 1079–88.

WEIKART, D. P. (1969) *Ypsilanti Carnegie Infant Education Project. Progress*

Report Ypsilanti, Michigan, Ypsilanti School Department of Research and Development.

WEIKART, D. P. and LAMBIE, D. (1968) 'Preschool intervention through a home teaching project'. Paper presented at the American Educational Research Association, Ypsilanti, Michigan, Ypsilanti Public Schools.

WILLMON, B. (1969) 'Parent participation as a factor in the effectiveness of Head Start Programs', *Journal of Educational Research*, **62**, 406–10.

Section 6
Moral development – a cognitive perspective

Introduction

Most of the major theories of personality development or socialization have addressed themselves to the problem of how the growing child develops a sense of morality or a conscience which monitors his behaviour or thoughts and feelings. However, the key issues have been defined in rather different terms by different theorists. Thus Piaget sees the child as a moral philosopher, increasingly capable of making more sophisticated moral judgments. Freud focused on the experience of guilt when a conflict exists between the superego, the ego and the id. Learning theorists conceptualize this problem neither in terms of cognitive development and judgment nor in terms of affect (guilt) but in terms of conformity to social norms.

In this section of the book we are concerned only with one of these perspectives, Piaget's cognitive–developmental approach to socialization. The basic assumption underlying it is that all action which is in some degree conscious and intentional is shaped by 'cognitive structures', and that these structures develop through a succession of stages in childhood and adolescence. What this means is that, however impulsive and emotionally driven such an action may appear, there is always an element of more or less implicit and inarticulate reasoning behind it, and that the character of this reasoning, its logic and frame of reference, changes with age in one direction rather than any other. As the underlying mode of reasoning changes, so does the behaviour that reasoning shapes and directs. The most direct way of getting at the underlying reasoning structures is to study the answers children give to carefully designed questions; but what is important is not only the content of their replies, which is heavily conditioned by cultural influences, but their form and reasoning, which is mainly determined by the level of development their cognitive structures have reached.

Piaget is the principle architect of cognitive–developmental theory. His primary concern has always been with the development of cognitive structures in the areas of concept development and problem solving. However he has devoted one early monograph, *The moral judgment of the child*, to such development in the area of socialization. The first paper in this section consists of a series of extracts from this work. It should be emphasized that in this monograph Piaget was making a tentative and provisional exploration of the field, and his findings should in no way be regarded as definitive. Nevertheless, his study has served as the major stimulus for subsequent work, and it is the necessary starting point for the student.

Since the monograph was published in 1932, a number of investigators have sought to replicate his findings, and in the main they have been substantiated. Many important advances have come from the work of Lawrence Kohlberg, the author of our second paper. He undertook a much more thorough study of moral reasoning than did Piaget by following the development of a large group of boys over many years and also exploring the validity of Piaget's approach by research in other cultures. As a result he has considerably revised and extended Piaget's original work, though staying very much within the kind of theoretical interpretation that Piaget evolved.

21 The moral judgment of the child

Jean Piaget
(Excerpts chosen and linked by Derek Wright)

All morality consists in a system of rules, and the essence of all morality is to be sought for in the respect which the individual acquires for these rules.

Piaget's book is divided into four sections. The first studies the development of children's behaviour in regard to the game of marbles and of their consciousness of the nature of the rules of that game. The second deals with children's attitudes and thoughts in relation to stealing and lying. The third examines the issues of punishment, responsibility and justice as the child sees them. The fourth section is theoretical.

Piaget's method was in general that of 'clinical interrogation'. He would question children in such a way as to bring them to face problems about morality they had never had to face before and which were often beyond their capacity to cope with adequately. Piaget's purpose in doing this was to probe behind the child's superficial responses and gain some insight into the basic logic of his thinking. The subjects were Swiss children varying in age from about four to twelve. Piaget does not report his results systematically, nor does he clearly separate empirical findings from theoretical discussion. Instead, he offers illustrative examples of what he claims are his main findings, and throughout the book these are embedded in theoretical discussions in which he progressively develops his own particular conceptual framework. His main purpose is to reveal the ways in which the child's moral judgment and thinking change with age.

The rules of the game

Piaget's general procedure was to get the child to explain the game to him, then play the game with the child, and in the process question him about the rules, how they originated, whether they could be changed, and so on.

Now, the rules of the game of marbles are handed down, just like so-called moral realities, from one generation to another, and are preserved solely by the respect that is felt for them by individuals. The sole difference is that the relations in this case are only those that exist between children. . . .

With regard to game rules, there are two phenomena which it is particularly easy to study: first, the *practice* of rules, i.e. the way in which

PIAGET, JEAN (1932) from *The moral judgment of the child* (trans. Gabain, M.) London, Routledge and Kegan Paul.

children of different ages effectively apply rules; second, the *consciousness* of rules, i.e. the idea which children of different ages form of the character of these game rules, whether of something obligatory and sacred or of something subject to their own choice, whether of heteronomy or autonomy....

From the point of view of the practice or application of rules four successive stages can be distinguished.

A first stage of a purely *motor* and *individual* character, during which the child handles the marbles at the dictation of his desires and motor habits. This leads to the formation of more or less ritualized schemas, but since play is still purely individual, one can only talk of motor rules and not of truly collective rules.

The second may be called *egocentric* for the following reasons. This stage begins at the moment when the child receives from outside the example of codified rules, that is to say, some time between the ages of two and five. But though the child imitates this example, he continues to play either by himself without bothering to find play-fellows, or with others, but without trying to win, and therefore without attempting to unify the different ways of playing. In other words children of this stage, even when they are playing together, play each one 'on his own' (everyone can win at once) and without regard for any codification of rules. This dual character, combining imitation of others with a purely individual use of the examples received, we have designated by the term Egocentrism.

A third stage appears between seven and eight, which we shall call the stage of incipient *cooperation*. Each player now tries to win, and all, therefore, begin to concern themselves with the question of mutual control and of unification of the rules. But while a certain agreement may be reached in the course of one game, ideas about the rules in general are still rather vague. In other words, children of seven to eight who belong to the same class at school and are therefore constantly playing with each other, give, when they are questioned separately, disparate and often entirely contradictory accounts of the rules observed in playing marbles.

Finally between the years of eleven and twelve, appears a fourth stage, which is that of the *codification of rules*. Not only is every detail of procedure in the game fixed, but the actual code of rules to be observed is known to the whole society. There is remarkable concordance in the information given by children of ten to twelve belonging to the same class at school when they are questioned on the rules of the game and their possible variations.

These stages must of course be taken only for what they are worth. It is convenient for the purposes of exposition to divide children up into age-classes or stages, but the facts present themselves as a continuum which cannot be cut up into sections. This continuum, moreover, is not linear in character, and its general direction can only be observed by schematizing the material and ignoring the minor oscillations which render it infinitely complicated in detail. So that ten children chosen at random will perhaps not give the impression of a steady advance which gradually emerges from the interrogatory put to the hundred odd subjects examined by us at Geneva and Neuchâtel.

If, now, we turn to the consciousness of rules we shall find a progression that is even more elusive in detail, but no less clearly marked if taken on a big scale. We may express this by saying that the progression runs through three stages, of which the second begins during the egocentric stage and ends towards the middle of the stage of cooperation (nine to ten), and of which the third covers the remainder of this cooperating stage and the whole of the stage marked by the codification of rules.

During the first stage, rules are not yet coercive in character, either because they are purely motor, or else (at the beginning of the egocentric stage) because they are received, as it were, unconsciously, and as interesting examples rather than as obligatory realities.

During the second stage (apogee of egocentric and first half of cooperating stage) rules are regarded as sacred and untouchable, emanating from adults and lasting for ever. Every suggested alteration strikes the child as a transgression.

Finally during the third stage, a rule is looked upon as a law due to mutual consent, which you must respect if you want to be loyal but which it is permissible to alter on the condition of enlisting general opinion on your side.

The correlation between the three stages in the development of the consciousness of rules and the four stages relating to their practical observance is of course only a statistical correlation and therefore very crude. But broadly speaking the relation seems to us indisputable. The collective rule is first something external to the individual and consequently sacred to him; then, as he gradually makes it his own, it comes to that extent to be felt as the free product of mutual agreement and an autonomous conscience. And with regard to practical use, it is only natural that a mystical respect for laws should be accompanied by a rudimentary knowledge and application of their contents, while a rational and well-founded respect is accompanied by an effective application of each rule in detail.

There would therefore seem to be two types of respect for rules corresponding to two types of social behaviour. This conclusion deserves to be closely examined, for if it holds good, it should be of the greatest value to the analysis of child morality. One can see at once all that it suggests in regard to the relation between child and adult. Take the insubordination of the child towards its parents and teachers, joined to its sincere respect for the commands it receives and its extraordinary mental docility. Could not this be due to that complex of attitudes which we have observed during the egocentric stage and which combines so paradoxically an unstable practice of the law with a mystical attitude towards it? And will not cooperation between adult and child, in so far as it can be realized and in so far as it is facilitated by cooperation between children themselves, supply the key to the interiorization of commands and to the autonomy of the moral consciousness? [...]

> In short, then, the early morality is characterized by a sense of mystical authority behind rules together with considerable instability in their application, and this is associated with relations of *unilateral respect* for adults and others, their policy of *constraint* towards the child, and the child's own *egocentrism*. The later morality is characterized by the interiorizing of rules, a sense of their relativity and dependence upon mutual agreement, together with a meticulous obedience to them, and this is associated with relations of *mutual respect* with adults and peers and growth out of egocentricity.

Egocentrism in so far as it means confusion of the ego and the external world, and egocentrism in so far as it means lack of cooperation, constitute one and the same phenomenon. So long as the child does not dissociate his ego from the suggestions coming from the physical and from the social world, he cannot cooperate, for in order to cooperate one must be conscious of one's ego and situate it in relation to thought in general. And in order to become conscious of one's ego, it is necessary to liberate oneself from the thought and will of others. The coercion exercised by the adult on the older child is therefore inseparable from the unconscious egocentrism of the very young child...

There is, in our opinion, the same relation between mutual respect and autonomy as between unilateral respect and egocentrism...

As the child grows up, the prestige of older children diminishes and he can discuss matters more and more as an equal and has increasing opportunities (beyond the scope of suggestion, obedience or negativism) of freely contrasting his point of view with that of others. Henceforward he will not only discover the boundaries that separate his self from the other person, but will learn to understand the other person and be understood by him....

Mutual respect is, in a sense, the state of equilibrium towards which unilateral respect is tending when differences between child and adult, younger and older are becoming effaced....

The great difference between constraint and cooperation or between unilateral respect and mutual respect, is that the first imposes beliefs and rules which are ready made and to be accepted *en bloc*, while the second only suggests a method – a method of verification and reciprocal control in the intellectual field, of justification and discussion in the domain of morals....

Adult constraint and moral realism

In this and the succeeding sections Piaget investigates 'theoretical moral judgment as opposed to that which occurs in actual experience'. In other words he studies the child's response to hypothetical moral problems presented in story form. He sees this kind of verbal response as related to the child's actual behaviour through the principle of *conscious realization*. 'We have often noted that in the intellectual field the child's verbal thinking consists of the progressive coming into consciousness, or conscious realization of schemas that have been built up by action.' There is therefore a 'time lag' between the level of thought at which the child acts and the expression of the same level of thought in articulated verbal discussion.

First of all, however, Piaget develops the concept of *moral realism*, which he holds to characterize the moral thinking of the younger child.

We shall therefore call moral realism the tendency which the child has to regard duty and the value attaching to it as self-subsistent and independent of the mind, as imposing itself regardless of the circumstances in which the individual may find himself.

Moral realism thus possesses at least three features. In the first place, duty, as viewed by moral realism, is essentially heteronomous. Any act that shows obedience to a rule or even to an adult, regardless of what he may command, is good; any act that does not conform to rules is bad. A rule is therefore not in any way something elaborated or even judged and interpreted by the mind; it is given as such, ready made and external to the mind. It is also conceived of as revealed by the adult and imposed by him. The good, therefore, is rigidly defined by obedience.

In the second place, moral realism demands that the letter rather than the spirit of the law shall be observed. This feature derives from the first. Yet it would be possible to imagine an ethic of heteronomy based on the spirit of the rules and not on their most hard and fast contents. Such an attitude would already have ceased to be realist; it would tend towards rationality and inwardness. But at the outset of the moral evolution of the child, adult constraint produces, on the contrary, a sort of literal realism of which we shall see many examples later.

In the third place, moral realism induces an objective conception of responsibility. We can even use this as a criterion of realism, for such an attitude towards responsibility is easier to detect than the two that precede it. For since he takes rules literally and thinks of good only in terms of obedience, the child will first evaluate acts not in accordance with the motive that has prompted them but in terms of their exact conformity with established rules. [...]

> In the first empirical part of this section, Piaget studies objective versus subjective responsibility in relation to clumsiness and stealing. His procedure is to present pairs of stories to the child and to ask which of the two children involved is the naughtier and why. In one story a child accidentally causes a lot of damage while trying to be helpful or steals something relatively valuable for entirely unselfish reasons, and in the other the child accidentally causes less damage while trying to do something wrong or steals something of less value for entirely selfish reasons. Objective responsibility occurs when the amount of damage done or the value of the object stolen is given primacy in the child's judgment, subjective responsibility when the motive or intention is given primacy. The methodological error in Piaget's procedure should be noted: he should really have held constant the consequence and varied intention, or held intention constant and varied consequence while as it is these two variables are confounded.

We obtained the following results. Up to the age of ten, two types of answer exist side by side. In one type actions are evaluated in terms of material result and independently of motives; according to the other type of answer motives alone are what counts. It may even happen that one and the same child judges sometimes one way, sometimes the other. Besides, some stories point more definitely to objective responsibility than others. In detail, therefore, the material cannot be said to embody stages properly so called. Broadly speaking, however, it cannot be denied that the notion of objective responsibility diminishes as the child grows older. We did not come across a single definite case of it after the age of ten. In addition, by placing the answers obtained under ten into two groups defined by objective and subjective responsibility . . . we obtained seven as the average age for objective responsibility and nine as the average age for subjective responsibility. Now we were unable to question children under six with any profit because of the intellectual difficulties of comparison. . . .

What explanation can we give of these facts? The objective conception of responsibility arises, without doubt, as a result of the constraint exercised by the adult. But the exact meaning of this constraint has still to be established, because in cases of theft and clumsiness it is exercised in a rather different form from what appears in cases of lying. For in some of the cases we have been examining it is quite certain that adults, or some adults, apply their own sanctions, whether 'diffused' (blame) or 'organized' (punishment), in accordance with the rules of objective responsibility. The average housewife (most of the children we examined came from very poor districts) will be more angry over fifteen cups (broken) than over one, and independently, up to a point, of the offender's intentions. Broadly speaking, then, one may say that it is not only the externality of the adult command to the child's mind that produces the effects we are discussing, it is the example of the adult himself. In cases of lying, on the other hand, we shall find that it is almost entirely in spite of the adult's intention that objective responsibility imposes itself upon the child's mind . . .

How, then, does subjective responsibility appear and develop within the limited domain we are analyzing at present? There is no doubt that by adopting a certain technique with their children, parents can succeed in making them attach more importance to intentions than to rules conceived as a system of ritual interdictions. Only the question is, whether this technique does not involve perpetually taking care not to impose on their children any duties properly so called, and placing mutual sympathy above everything else? It is when the child is accustomed to act from the point of view of those around him, when he tries to please rather than obey, that he will judge in terms of intentions. So that taking intentions into account presupposes cooperation and mutual respect. Only those who have children of their own know how difficult it is to put this into practice. Such is the prestige of parents in the eyes of the very young child, that even if they lay nothing down in the form of general duties, their wishes act as law and thus give rise automatically to moral realism. . . . In order to remove all traces of moral realism, one must place oneself on the child's own level, and give him a feeling of equality by laying stress on one's own obligations and one's own deficiencies. . . . In this way the child will find himself in the presence, not of a system of commands requiring ritualistic and external obedience, but of a system of social relations such that everyone does his best to obey the same obligations, and does so out of mutual respect. [. . .]

The remainder of this section is concerned with the child's ideas about lying. 'Our interrogatory bore mainly upon the three following points: definition of a lie, responsibility as a function of the lie's content, responsibility as a function of its material consequences.' In other words: (a) what is a lie? (b) to what extent is the literal deviation from the truth taken as the indication of its gravity, e.g. fantasy contrasted with an intentional, plausible lie? and (c) is a well-intentioned mistake with relatively serious consequences worse than an intentional lie without serious consequences?

In regard to (a) Piaget again finds three stages emerging:

The most primitive and, at the same time, from our present point of view, the most characteristic definition we were able to find was a purely realistic one: a lie is 'a naughty word'. Thus the child, while perfectly well acquainted with a lie when he meets one, identifies it completely with the oaths or indecent expressions which one is forbidden to use. . . .

It should be noted in the first place that no mere verbal confusion is at work here. The child who defines a lie as being a 'naughty word' knows perfectly well that lying is not speaking the truth. He is not, therefore, mistaking one thing for another, he is simply identifying them one with another by what seems to us a quaint extension of the word 'lie'. . . .

A more advanced definition of lies which remains the usual one until fairly late (between six and ten on the average) consists simply in saying, 'A lie is something that isn't true.' But the mere words here must not deceive us, and we must get at the implicit notions which they conceal. We have seen how difficult it is for the child to give an adequate definition of the notions he uses owing to his inability to realize them consciously. In order, therefore, to know the meaning of the definition we have just given we must ascertain whether the child confuses lying with every kind of inaccuracy (especially with mistakes) or whether he implicitly considers a lie to have been told only when someone intentionally betrays the truth. . . . The interrogatory shows that children of five to seven, while perfectly aware of the shade of difference between an intentional act and an involuntary mistake, do not tend to stress this distinction at all, and often, on the contrary, group both facts under the same name of 'a lie'. . . .

Let us turn to the third type of definition, or correct definition of lies: any statement that is intentionally false is a lie. Not till about the age of ten to eleven do we find this definition in an explicit form. [. . .]

We need not quote in detail Piaget's report of the answers to questions (b) and (c). Briefly, the young child uses the criteria of literal degree of departure from the truth, even when this involves a wholly unrealistic fantasy, and sheer amount of damage done in judging the badness of a lie, whereas the older child focuses on the degree of selfish intentionality.

In discussing these results Piaget has some interesting observations to make.

The [young] child, owing to his unconscious egocentrism, tends spontaneously to alter the truth in accordance with his desires and to neglect the value of veracity. The rule that one must not lie, imposed by adult authority, will therefore seem all the more sacred in his eyes and will demand all the more 'objective' an interpretation just because it does not in fact correspond with any felt inner need on his part. Hence moral realism and objective responsibility, which stand for an inadequate practical application of the rule. In the second place, in so far as habits of cooperation will have convinced the child of the necessity of not lying, rules will become comprehensible, will become interiorized, and will no longer give rise to any judgments but those of subjective responsibility. . . .

Every thought that enters the head of a child of two to three does so from the first in the form of a belief and not in the form of a hypothesis to be verified. . . .

We may say that up till the age of seven to eight, the child tends spontaneously to alter the truth, that this seems to him perfectly natural and completely harmless, but that he considers it a duty towards adults not to lie, and recognizes that a lie is a 'naughty' action. Moral realism and objective responsibility are the inevitable outcome of so paradoxical a situation. . . .

It is obvious that if the desire for truthfulness does not correspond to something very fundamental in the child's nature, the adult's command, in spite of the nimbus that surrounds it, will always remain external, 'stuck on' as it were, to a mind whose structure is of a different order. For the spirit of such a command could only be understood by experience. One must have felt a real desire to exchange thoughts with others to discover all that a lie can involve. And this interchange of thoughts is from the first not possible between children and adults, because the initial inequality is too great and the child tries to imitate the adult and at the same time to protect himself against him rather than really to exchange thoughts with him. The situation we have described is thus almost the necessary outcome of unilateral respect. [. . .]

As a supplementary question Piaget asked the children why lying is wrong.

The older children of ten to twelve generally invoked against lying reasons which amount to this: that truthfulness is necessary to reciprocity and mutual agreement. . . . The reaction in question implies that truthfulness is necessary because deceiving others destroys mutual trust. . . .

It would seem, then, that the evolution of the answers with age marks a definite progress in the direction of reciprocity. Unilateral respect, the source of the absolute command, taken literally, yields place to mutual respect, the source of moral understanding. We can indeed distinguish three stages in this progress. In the first stage a lie is wrong because it is the object of punishment; if the punishment were removed, it would be allowed. Then a lie becomes something wrong in itself and would remain so even if the punishment were removed. Finally a lie is wrong because it is in conflict with mutual trust and affection. Thus the consciousness of lying gradually becomes interiorized and the hypothesis may be hazarded that it does so under the influence of cooperation. . . .

He again takes up the principle of *conscious realization*.

To realize consciously is not simply to throw into light ideas that have been already fully worked out. Conscious realization is a reconstruction and consequently a new and original construction superimposed upon the constructions already formed by action. As such, therefore, it comes on the scene later than action proper. Hence the time lag noted by Stern, and which we have found in every sphere of child thought. . . . If, then, this moral realism corresponds to something present in the moral activity itself, it is not during those years that we must seek for that something but at a much earlier period. For objective responsibility can perfectly well be discarded long ago at the level of action and yet subsist on the level of theoretical thought. . . . It should be noted that, however averse one may be in education to use any constraint, even moral, it is not possible completely to avoid giving the child commands that are incomprehensible to it. In such cases – which are almost the rule in the traditional form of education based on authority – the mere fact of accepting the command almost invariably provokes the appearance of moral realism. [. . .]

Cooperation and the development of the idea of justice

In this section, Piaget attempts to probe the 'more intimate impulses' of the child's mind, 'social attitudes that do not easily admit of definition in conversations held with the children'. In particular he focuses upon the sense of justice, and does this mainly through questioning about punishment, its nature and justification.

The conclusion which we shall finally reach is that the sense of justice, though naturally capable of being reinforced by the precepts and the practical example of the adult, is largely independent of these influences, and requires nothing more for its development than the mutual respect and solidarity which holds among children themselves. It is often at the expense of the adult and not because of him that the notions of just and unjust find their way into the youthful mind. In contrast to a given rule, which from the first has been imposed upon the child from outside and which for many years he has failed to understand, such as the rule of not telling lies, the rule of justice is a sort of immanent condition of social relationships or a law governing their equilibrium. And as solidarity between children grows we shall find this notion of justice gradually emerging in almost complete autonomy. [...]

Piaget begins by examining the sorts of punishment children think appropriate, and how they justify punishment. His method, as before, consisted of presenting stories and asking questions about them.

Very briefly, the result we shall be led to is the following. Two types of reaction are to be found with regard to punishment. Some think that punishment is just and necessary; the sterner it is, the juster, and it is efficacious in the sense that the child who has been duly chastised will in future do his duty better than others. Others do not regard expiation as a moral necessity; among possible punishments those only are just that entail putting things right, a restoration of the *status quo ante*, or which make the guilty one endure the consequences of his deed; or again, those which consist in a purely reciprocal treatment. Indeed, apart from such non-expiatory penalties, punishment as such is regarded as useless, reproach and explanation being deemed more profitable than chastisement. On the average this second mode of reaction is found more frequently among the older children, while the first is oftener to be found among the little ones. But the first, favoured as it is by certain types of family life and social relationship, survives at all ages and is even to be found in many adults. [...]

This distinction between two attitudes towards punishment, *expiatory punishment* and *punishment by reciprocity* is developed further by Piaget.

There are, in the first place, what we shall call *expiatory punishments*, which seem to us to go hand in hand with constraint and the rules of authority. Take any given rule imposed upon the individual's mind from without, and suppose the individual to have transgressed this rule. Independently even of the indignation and anger that will occur in the group or among those in authority, and which will inevitably be visited upon the transgressor, the only way of putting things right is to bring the individual back to his duty by means of a sufficiently powerful method of coercion and to bring home his guilt to him by means of a painful punishment. Thus expiatory punishment has an arbitrary character, arbitrary in the sense that, in linguistics, the choice of a sign is arbitrary in relation to the thing signified, that is to say, there is no relation between the content of the guilty act and the nature of its punishment. It is all one when a lie has been told whether you inflict corporal punishment on the transgressor or take his toys away from him or condemn him to some school task: all that matters is that a due proportion should be kept between the suffering inflicted and the gravity of the misdeed.

And there are, in the second place, what we shall call *punishments by reciprocity* in so far as they go hand in hand with cooperation and rules of equality. Take any rule that the child accepts from within, that is to say of which he knows that it binds him to his equals by the bond of reciprocity (e.g. not to lie because lying does away with mutual trust). If this rule is violated, there is no need, in order to put things right again, for a painful coercion which will impose respect for the law from without; it will be enough for the breach of the social bond incurred by the transgressor to make its effect felt, in other words, it will be enough if the principle of reciprocity be brought into play. Since the rule is no longer, as before, something imposed from without, something which the individual could dispense with, but on the contrary constitutes a necessary relation between the individual and those around him, it suffices to make plain the consequences following upon the violation of the law in order to make the individual feel isolated and to make him long for a return to normal relations. Censure no longer needs to be emphasized by means of painful punishment: it acts with full force in so far as the measures taken by way of reciprocity make the transgressor realize the significance of his misdeeds. [...]

Piaget provides six examples of punishment by reciprocity. They include making the transgressor suffer his own offence, excluding him from the group, and censure which includes explanation.

He then proceeds to investigate children's attitudes towards *collective responsibility*, when the group is punished for the offences of the few, *immanent justice*, when natural events or 'accidents' following misdeeds are seen as punishments for them, equality and authority, and justice.

[In general the results show] the existence of three great periods in the development of the sense of justice in the child. One period, lasting up to the age of seven to eight, during which justice is subordinated to adult authority; a period contained approximately between eight and eleven, and which is that of progressive equalitarianism; and finally a period which sets in towards eleven to twelve, and during which purely equalitarian justice is tempered by considerations of equity.

The first is characterized by the non-differentiation of the notions of just and unjust from those of duty and disobedience: whatever conforms to the dictates of the adult authority is just. As a matter of fact even at this stage the child already looks upon some kinds of treatment as unjust, those, namely, in which the adult does not carry out the rules he has himself laid down for the children (e.g. punishing for a fault that has not been committed, forbidding what has previously been allowed, etc.). But if the adult sticks to his own rules, everything he prescribes is just. In the domain of retributive justice, every punishment is accepted as perfectly legitimate, as necessary, and even as constituting the essence of morality: if lying were not punished, one would be allowed to tell lies, etc. In the stories where we have brought retributive justice into conflict with equality, the child belonging to this stage puts the necessity for punishment above equality of any sort. In the choice of punishments, expiation takes precedence over punishment by reciprocity, the very principle of the latter type of punishment not being exactly understood by the child. In the domain of immanent justice, more than three-quarters of the subjects under eight believe in an automatic justice which emanates from physical nature and inanimate objects. If obedience and equality are brought into conflict, the child is always in favour of obedience: authority takes precedence over justice. Finally in the domain of justice between children, the need for equality is already felt, but is yielded to only where it cannot possibly come into conflict with authority. For instance, the act of hitting back, regarded by the child of ten as one of elementary justice, is considered 'naughty' by the children of six and seven, though, of course, they are always doing it in practice. (It will be remembered that the heteronomous rule, whatever may be the respect in which it is held mentally, is not necessarily observed in real life.) On the other hand, even in the relations between children, the authority of older ones will outweigh equality. In short, we may say that throughout this period, during which unilateral respect is stronger than mutual respect, the conception of justice can only develop on certain points, those, namely, where cooperation begins to make itself felt independently of constraint. On all other points, what is just is confused with what is imposed by law, and law is completely heteronomous and imposed by the adult.

The second period does not appear on the plane of reflection and moral judgment until about the age of seven or eight. But it is obvious that this comes slightly later than what happens with regard to practice. This period may be defined by the progressive development of autonomy and the priority of equality over authority. In the domain of retributive justice, the idea of expiatory punishment is no longer accepted with the same docility as before, and the only punishments accepted as really legitimate are those based upon reciprocity. Belief in immanent justice is perceptibly on the decrease and moral action is sought for its own sake, independently of reward or punishment. In matters of distributive justice, equality rules supreme. In conflicts between punishment and equality, equality outweighs every other consideration. The same holds good a fortiori of conflicts with authority. Finally, in relations between children, equalitarianism obtains progressively with increasing age.

Towards eleven and twelve we see a new attitude emerge, which may be said to be characterized by the feeling of equity, and which is nothing but a development of equalitarianism in the direction of relativity. Instead of looking for equality in identity, the child no longer thinks of the equal rights of individuals except in relation to the particular situation of each. In the domain of retributive justice this comes to the same thing as not applying the same punishment to all, but taking into account the extenuating circumstances of some. In the domain of distributive justice it means no longer thinking of a law as identical for all but taking account of the personal circumstances of each (favouring the younger ones, etc.). Far from leading to privileges, such an attitude tends to make equality more effectual than it was before. [...]

The two moralities of the child

Most of this last section is given over to a discussion of the work of other writers in relation to Piaget's own theory and findings, in particular Dürkheim, Fauconnet, Bovet and J. M. Baldwin. However, Piaget also reviews his findings and discusses them in relation to society generally.

For we have recognized the existence of two moralities in the child, that of constraint and that of cooperation. The morality of constraint is that of duty pure and simple and of heteronomy. The child accepts from the adult a certain number of commands to which it must submit whatever the circumstances may be. Right is what conforms with these commands; wrong is what fails to do so; the intention plays a very small part in this conception, and the responsibility is entirely objective. But, first parallel with this morality, and then in contrast to it, there is gradually developed a morality of cooperation, whose guiding principle is solidarity and which puts the primary emphasis on autonomy of conscience, on intentionality, and consequently on subjective responsibility. Now it should be noted that though the ethics of mutual respect is, from the point of view of values, opposed to that of unilateral respect, the former is nevertheless the natural outcome of the latter from the point of view of what causes this evolution. In so far as the child tends towards manhood, his relations with the adult tend towards equality. The unilateral respect belonging to constraint is not a stable system, and the equilibrium towards which it tends is no other than mutual respect. It cannot, therefore, be maintained with regard to the child that the final predominance of subjective over objective responsibility is the outcome of antagonistic forces in relation to responsibility in general. Rather is it in virtue of a sort of inner logic that the more evolved follow upon the more primitive forms, though in structure the former differ qualitatively from the latter.

Why, then, in an extremely schematic way, should the same thing not hold good of society? It is no mere metaphor to say that a relation can be established between the individual's obedience to collective imperatives and the child's obedience to adults in general. In both cases the human being submits to certain commands because he respects his elders. Society is nothing but a series (or rather many intersecting series) of generations, each exerting pressure upon the one which follows it, and Auguste Comte was right in pointing to this action of one generation upon another as the most important phenomenon of sociology. Now when we think of the part played by gerontocracy in primitive communities, when we think of the decreasing power of the family in the course of social evolution, and of all the social features that characterize modern civilization, we cannot help seeing in the history of societies a sort of gradual emancipation of individuals; in other words, a levelling up of the different generations in relation to each other. As Dürkheim himself pointed out, one cannot explain the passage from the forced conformity of 'segmented' societies to the organic solidarity of differentiated societies without invoking the diminished supervision of the group over the individual as a fundamental psychological factor. The 'denser' the community, the sooner will the adolescent escape from the direct constraint of his relations and, coming under a number of fresh influences, acquire his spiritual independence by comparing them one with another. The more complex the society, the more autonomous is the personality and the more important are the relations of cooperation between equal individuals. . . .

In conclusion . . . social constraint and cooperation lead to results that do not admit of comparison. Social constraint – and by this we mean any social relation into which there enters an element of authority and which is not, like cooperation, the result of interchange between equal individuals – has on the individual results that are analogous to those exercised by adult constraint on the mind of the child. The two phenomena, moreover, are really one and the same thing, and the adult who is under the dominion of unilateral respect for the 'elders' and for tradition is really behaving like a child. It may even be maintained that the realism of primitive conceptions of crime and punishment is, in certain respects, an infantile reaction. To primitive man, the moral and physical universe are one and the same thing, and a rule is both a law of nature and a principle of conduct. For this reason, crime threatens the very existence of the universe and must be mystically set at naught by a suitable expiation. But this idea of a law that is both physical and moral is the very core of the child's conception of the world; for under the effect of adult constraint the child cannot conceive the laws of the physical universe except in the guise of a certain obedience rendered by things to rules. As to ideas of punishment and expiation, how could they have become so widespread in the adult community if men had not all first been children, and if the child had not been from the very beginning of his mental development respectful towards the decisions of the adult who reprimands and punishes him? Under the effects of social differentiation and cooperation, on the contrary, the individual is less and less dominated by the cult of the past and by the forced conformity that accompanies it. He then becomes really adult, and the infantile traits that mark the conformist spirit make place for the features that are the outcome of cooperation. Thus autonomy of conscience takes the place of heteronomy . . . thus the purely interior responsibility which blames itself for not reaching a certain ideal follows upon the responsibility born of the reactions of the group. It is true that this inner responsibility remains a social phenomenon; unless individuals cooperated, conscience would be ignorant of right and of the sense of guilt. But this is a phenomenon of a different order from that of the facts of constraint, though it constitutes in a fashion the form of equilibrium towards which the whole history of responsibility tends.

22 The child as a moral philosopher

Lawrence Kohlberg

How can one study morality? Current trends in the fields of ethics, linguistics, anthropology and cognitive psychology have suggested a new approach which seems to avoid the morass of semantical confusions, value-bias and cultural relativity in which the psychoanalytic and semantic approaches to morality have foundered. New scholarship in all these fields is now focusing upon structures, forms and relationships that seem to be common to all societies and all languages rather than upon the features that make particular languages or cultures different.

For 12 years, my colleagues and I studied the same group of 75 boys, following their development at three-year intervals from early adolescence through young manhood. At the start of the study, the boys were aged 10 to 16. We have now followed them through to ages 22 to 28. In addition, I have explored moral development in other cultures – Great Britain, Canada, Taiwan, Mexico and Turkey.

Inspired by Jean Piaget's pioneering effort to apply a structural approach to moral development, I have gradually elaborated over the years of my study a typological scheme describing general structures and forms of moral thought which can be defined independently of the specific content of particular moral decisions or actions.

The typology contains three distinct levels of moral thinking, and within each of these levels distinguishes two related stages. These levels and stages may be considered separate moral philosophies, distinct views of the socio-moral world.

We can speak of the child as having his own morality or series of moralities. Adults seldom listen to children's moralizing. If a child throws back a few adult clichés and behaves himself, most parents – and many anthropologists and psychologists as well – think that the child has adopted or internalized the appropriate parental standards.

Actually, as soon as we talk with children about morality, we find that they have many ways of making judgments which are not 'internalized' from the outside, and which do not come in any direct and obvious way from parents, teachers or even peers.

KOHLBERG, LAWRENCE (1968) 'The child as a moral philosopher' in *Psychology Today*, vol. 2, 25–30.

Moral levels

The *preconventional* level is the first of three levels of moral thinking; the second level is *conventional*, and the third *postconventional* or autonomous. While the preconventional child is often 'well-behaved' and is responsive to cultural labels of good and bad, he interprets these labels in terms of their physical consequences (punishment, reward, exchange of favours) or in terms of the physical power of those who enunciate the rules and labels of good and bad.

This level is usually occupied by children aged four to ten, a fact long known to sensitive observers of children. The capacity of 'properly behaved' children of this age to engage in cruel behaviour when there are holes in the power structure is sometimes noted as tragic (*Lord of the Flies*, *High Wind in Jamaica*), sometimes as comic (Lucy in *Peanuts*).

The second or *conventional* level also can be described as conformist, but that is perhaps too smug a term. Maintaining the expectations and rules of the individual's family, group or nation is perceived as valuable in its own right. There is a concern not only with *conforming* to the individual's social order but in *maintaining*, supporting and justifying this order.

The *postconventional* level is characterized by a major thrust towards autonomous moral principles which have validity and application apart from authority of the groups or persons who hold them and apart from the individual's identification with those persons or groups.

Moral stages

Within each of these three levels there are two discernible stages. At the preconventional level we have:

Stage 1. Orientation towards punishment and unquestioning deference to superior power. The physical consequences of action regardless of their human meaning or value determine its goodness or badness.

Stage 2. Right action consists of that which instrumentally satisfies one's own needs and occasionally the needs of others. Human relations are viewed in terms like those of the marketplace. Elements of fairness, of reciprocity and equal sharing are present, but they are always interpreted in a physical, pragmatic way. Reciprocity is a matter of 'you scratch my back and I'll scratch yours' not of loyalty, gratitude or justice.

And at the conventional level we have:

Stage 3. Good-boy – good-girl orientation. Good behaviour is that which pleases or helps others and is approved by them. There is much conformity to stereotypical images of what is majority or 'natural' behaviour. Behaviour is often judged by intention – 'he means well' becomes important for the first time, and is overused, as by Charlie Brown in *Peanuts*. One seeks approval by being 'nice'.

Stage 4. Orientation towards authority, fixed rules and the maintenance of the social order. Right behaviour consists of doing one's duty, showing respect for authority and maintaining the given social order for its own sake. One earns respect by performing dutifully.

At the postconventional level, we have:

Stage 5. A social-contract orientation, generally with legalistic and utilitarian overtones. Right action tends to be defined in terms of general rights and in terms of standards which have been critically examined and agreed upon by the whole society. There is a clear awareness of the relativism of personal values and opinions and a corresponding emphasis upon procedural rules for reaching consensus. Aside from what is constitutionally and democratically agreed upon, right or wrong is a matter of personal 'values' and 'opinion'. The result is an emphasis upon the 'legal point of view', but with an emphasis upon the possibility of *changing* law in terms of rational considerations of social utility, rather than freezing it in the terms of Stage 4 'law and order'. Outside the legal realm, free agreement and contract are the binding elements of obligation. This is the 'official' morality of American government, and finds its ground in the thought of the writers of the Constitution.

Stage 6. Orientation towards the decisions of conscience and towards self-chosen *ethical principles* appealing to logical comprehensiveness, universality and consistency. These principles are abstract and ethical (the Golden Rule, the categorical imperative); they are not concrete moral rules like the Ten Commandments. Instead, they are universal principles of *justice*, of the *reciprocity* and *equality* of human rights, and of respect for the dignity of human beings as *individual persons*.

Up to now

In the past, when psychologists tried to answer the question asked of Socrates by Meno 'Is virtue something that can be taught (by rational discussion), or does it come by practice, or is it a natural inborn attitude?' their answers usually have been dictated, not by research findings on children's moral character, but by their general theoretical convictions.

Behaviour theorists have said that virtue is behaviour acquired according to their favourite general principles of learning. Freudians have claimed that virtue is superego-identification with parents generated by a proper balance of love and authority in family relations.

The American psychologists who have actually studied children's morality have tried to start with a set of labels – the 'virtues' and 'vices', the 'traits' of good and bad character found in ordinary language. The earliest major psychological study of moral character, that of Hugh Hartshorne and Mark May in 1928–1930, focused on a bag of virtues including honesty, service (altruism or generosity) and self-control. To their dismay, they found that there were *no* character traits, psychological dispositions or entities which corresponded to words like honesty, service or self-control.

Regarding honesty, for instance, they found that almost everyone cheats some of the time, and that if a person cheats in one situation, it doesn't mean that he *will* or *won't* in another. In other words, it is not an identifiable character trait, *dis*honesty, that makes a child cheat in a given situation. These early researchers also found that people who cheat express as much or even more moral disapproval of cheating as those who do not cheat.

What Hartshorne and May found out about their bag of virtues is equally upsetting to the somewhat more psychological-sounding names introduced by psychoanalytic psychology: 'superego-strength', 'resistance to temptation', 'strength of conscience', and the like. When recent researchers attempt to measure such traits in individuals, they have been forced to use Hartshorne and May's old tests of honesty and self-control and they get exactly the same results – 'superego strength' in one situation predicts little to 'superego strength' in another. That is, virtue-words like honesty (or superego-strength) point to certain behaviours with approval, but give us no guide to understanding them.

So far as one can extract some generalized personality factor from children's performance on tests of honesty or resistance to temptation, it is a factor of ego-strength or ego-control, which always involves non-moral capacities like the capacity to maintain attention, intelligent task performance, and the ability to delay response: 'Ego-strength' (called 'will' in earlier days) has something to do with moral action, but it does not take us to the core of morality or to the definition of virtue. Obviously enough, many of the greatest evil-doers in history have been men of strong wills, men strongly pursuing immoral goals.

Moral reasons

In our research, we have found definite and universal levels of development in moral thought. In our study of 75 American boys from early adolescence on, these youths were presented with hypothetical moral dilemmas, all deliberately philosophical, some of them found in medieval works of casuistry.

On the basis of their reasoning about these dilemmas at a given age, each boy's stage of thought could be determined for each of 25 basic moral concepts or aspects. One such aspect, for instance, is 'Motive Given for Rule Obedience or Moral Action'. In this instance, the six stages look like this:

1 Obey rules to avoid punishment.
2 Conform to obtain rewards, have favours returned, and so on.
3 Conform to avoid disapproval, dislike by others.
4 Conform to avoid censure by legitimate authorities and resultant guilt.
5 Conform to maintain the respect of the impartial spectator judging in terms of community welfare.
6 Conform to avoid self-condemnation.

In another of these 25 moral aspects, the value of human life, the six stages can be defined thus:

1 The value of a human life is confused with the value of physical objects and is based on the social status or physical attributes of its possessor.
2 The value of a human life is seen as instrumental to the satisfaction of the needs of its possessor or of other persons.
3 The value of a human life is based on the empathy and affection of family members and others towards its possessor.
4 Life is conceived as sacred in terms of its place in a categorical moral or religious order of rights and duties.
5 Life is valued both in terms of its relation to community welfare and in terms of life being a universal human right.
6 Belief in the sacredness of human life as representing a universal human value of respect for the individual.

I have called this scheme a typology. This is because about 50 per cent of most people's thinking will be at a single stage, regardless of the moral dilemma involved. We call our types *stages* because they seem to represent an *invariant developmental sequence*. 'True' stages come one at a time and always in the same order.

All movement is forward in sequence, and does not skip steps. Children may move through these stages at varying speeds, of course, and may be found half in and half out of a particular stage. An individual may stop at any given stage and at any age, but if he continues to move, he must move in accord with these steps. Moral reasoning of the conventional or Stage 3–4 kind never occurs before the preconventional Stage-1 and Stage-2 thought has taken place. No adult in Stage 4 has gone through Stage 6, but all Stage-6 adults have gone at least through 4.

While the evidence is not complete, my study strongly suggests that moral change fits the stage pattern just described. (The major uncertainty is whether all Stage 6s go through Stage 5 or whether these are two alternate mature orientations.)

How values change

As a single example of our findings of stage-sequence, take the progress of two boys on the aspect 'The Value of Human Life'. The first boy Tommy, is asked 'Is it better to save the life of one important person or a lot of unimportant people?' At age 10, he answers, 'all the people that aren't important because one man just has one house, maybe a lot of furniture, but a whole bunch of people have an awful lot of furniture and some of these poor people might have a lot of money and it doesn't look it.'

Clearly Tommy is Stage I: he confuses the value of a human being with the value of the property he possesses. Three years later (age 13) Tommy's conceptions of life's value are most clearly elicited by the question, 'Should the doctor "mercy kill" a fatally ill woman requesting death because of her pain?'. He answers, 'Maybe it would be good to put her out of her pain, she'd be better off that way. But the husband wouldn't want it, it's not like an animal. If a pet dies you can get along without it – it isn't something you really need. Well, you can get a new wife, but it's not really the same.'

Here his answer is Stage 2: the value of the woman's life is partly contingent on its hedonistic value to the wife herself but even more contingent on its instrumental value to her husband, who can't replace her as easily as he can a pet.

Three years later still (age 16) Tommy's conception of life's value is elicited by the same question, to which he replies: 'It might be best for her, but her husband – it's a human life – not like an animal; it just doesn't have the same relationship that a human being does to a family. You can become attached to a dog, but nothing like a human you know.'

Now Tommy has moved from a Stage-2 instrumental view of the woman's value to a Stage-3 view based on the husband's distinctively human empathy and love for someone in his family. Equally clearly, it lacks any basis for a universal human value of the woman's life, which would hold if she had no husband or if her husband didn't love her. Tommy, then, has moved step by step through three stages during the age 10–16. Tommy, though bright (IQ 120), is a slow developer in moral judgment. Let us take another boy, Richard, to show us sequential movement through the remaining three steps.

At age 13, Richard said about the mercy-killing, 'If she requests it, it's really up to her. She is in such terrible pain, just the same as people are always putting animals out of their pain,' and in general showed a mixture of Stage-2 and Stage-3 responses concerning the value of life. At 16, he said, 'I don't know. In one way, it's murder, it's not a right or privilege of man to decide who shall live and who should die. God put life into everybody on earth and you're taking away something from that person that came directly from God, and you're destroying something that is very sacred, it's in a way part of God and it's almost destroying a part of God when you kill a person. There's something of God in everyone.'

Here Richard clearly displays a Stage-4 concept of life as sacred in terms of its place in a categorical moral or religious order. The value of human life is universal, it is true for all humans. It is still, however, dependent on something else, upon respect for God and God's authority; it is not an autonomous human value. Presumably if God told Richard to murder, as God commanded Abraham to murder Isaac, he would do so.

At age 20, Richard said to the same question: 'There are more and more people in the medical profession who think it is a hardship on everyone, the person, the family, when you know they are going to die. When a person is kept alive by an artificial lung or kidney it's more like being a vegetable than being a human. If it's her own choice, I think there are certain rights and privileges that go along with being a human being. I am a human being and have certain desires for life and I think everybody else does too. You have a world of which you are the centre, and everybody else does too and in that sense we're all equal.'

Richard's response is clearly Stage 5, in that the value of life is defined in terms of equal and universal human rights in a context of relativity ('You have a world of which you are the centre and in that sense we're all equal'), and of concern for utility or welfare consequences.

The final step

At 24, Richard says: 'A human life takes precedence over any other moral or legal value, whoever it is. A human life has inherent value whether or not it is valued by a particular individual. The worth of the individual human being is central where the principles of justice and love are normative for all human relationships.'

This young man is at Stage 6 in seeing the value of human life as absolute in representing a universal and equal respect for the human as an individual. He has moved step by step through a sequence culminating in a definition of human life as centrally valuable rather than derived from or dependent on social or divine authority.

In a genuine and culturally universal sense, these steps lead towards an increased *morality* of value judgment, where morality is considered as a form of judging, as it has been in a philosophic tradition running from the analyses of Kant to those of the modern analytic or 'ordinary language' philosophers. The person at Stage 6 has disentangled his judgments of – or language about – human life from status and property values (Stage 1), from its uses to others (Stage 2), from interpersonal affection (Stage 3), and so on; he has a means of moral judgment that is universal and impersonal. The Stage-6 person's answers use moral words like 'duty' or 'morally right', and he uses them in a way implying universality, ideals, impersonality: He thinks and speaks in phrases like 'regardless of who it was', or '. . . I would do it in spite of punishment'.

Across cultures

When I first decided to explore moral development in other cultures, I was told by anthropologist friends that I would have to throw away my culture-bound moral concepts and stories and start from scratch learning a whole new set of values for each new culture. My first try consisted of a brace of villages, one Atayal (Malaysian aboriginal) and the other Taiwanese.

My guide was a young Chinese ethnographer who had written an account of the moral and religious patterns of the Atayal and Taiwanese villages. Taiwanese boys in the 10–13 age group were asked about a story involving theft of food. A man's wife is starving to death but the store owner won't give the man any food unless he can pay, which he can't. Should he break in and steal some food? Why? Many of the boys said, 'He should steal the food for his wife because if she dies he'll have to pay for her funeral and that costs a lot.'

My guide was amused by these responses, but I was relieved: they were of course 'classic' Stage-2 responses. In the Atayal village, funerals weren't such a big thing, so the Stage 2-boys would say, 'He should steal the food because he needs his wife to cook for him.'

This means that we need to consult our anthropologists to know what content a Stage-2 child will include in his instrumental exchange calculations, or what a Stage-4 adult will identify as the proper social order. But one certainly doesn't have to start from scratch. What made my guide laugh was the difference in form between the children's Stage-2 thought and his own, a difference definable independently of particular cultures.

Figures 1 and 2 (see pages 246–7) indicate the cultural universality of the sequence of stages which we have found. Figure 1 presents the age trends for middle-class urban boys in the U.S., Taiwan and Mexico. At age 10 in each country, the order of use of each stage is the same as the order of its difficulty or maturity.

In the United States, by age 16 the order is the reverse, from the highest to the lowest, except that Stage 6 is still little-used. At age 13, the good-boy, middle stage (Stage 3), is not used.

The results in Mexico and Taiwan are the same, except that development is a little slower. The most conspicuous feature is that at the age of 16, Stage-5 thinking is much more salient in the United States than in Mexico or Taiwan. Nevertheless, it *is* present in the other countries, so we know that this is not purely an American democratic construct.

Figure 2 shows strikingly similar results from two isolated villages, one in Yucatan, one in Turkey. While conventional moral thought increases steadily from ages 10 to 16 it still has not achieved a clear ascendency over pre-conventional thought.

Trends for lower-class urban groups are intermediate in the rate of development between those for the middle-class and for the village boys. In the three divergent cultures that I studied, middle-class children were found to be more advanced in moral judgment than matched lower-class children. This was not due to the fact that the middle-class children heavily favoured some one type of thought which could be seen as corresponding to the prevailing middle-class pattern. Instead, middle-class and working-class children move through the same sequences, but the middle-class children move faster and farther.

This sequence is not dependent upon a particular religion, or any religion at all in the usual sense. I found no important differences in the development of moral thinking among Catholics, Protestants, Jews, Buddhists, Moslems and atheists. Religious values seem to go through the same stages as all other values.

Trading up

In summary, the nature of our sequence is not significantly affected by widely varying social, cultural or religious conditions. The only thing that is affected is the *rate* at which individuals progress through this sequence.

Why should there be such a universal invariant sequence of development? In answering this question, we need first to analyze these developing social concepts in terms of their internal logical structure. At each stage, the same basic moral concept or aspect is defined, but at each higher stage this definition is more differentiated, more integrated and more general or universal. When one's concept of human life moves from Stage 1 to Stage 2 the value of life becomes more differentiated from the value of property, more integrated (the value of life enters an organizational hierarchy where it is 'higher' than property so that one steals property in order to save life)

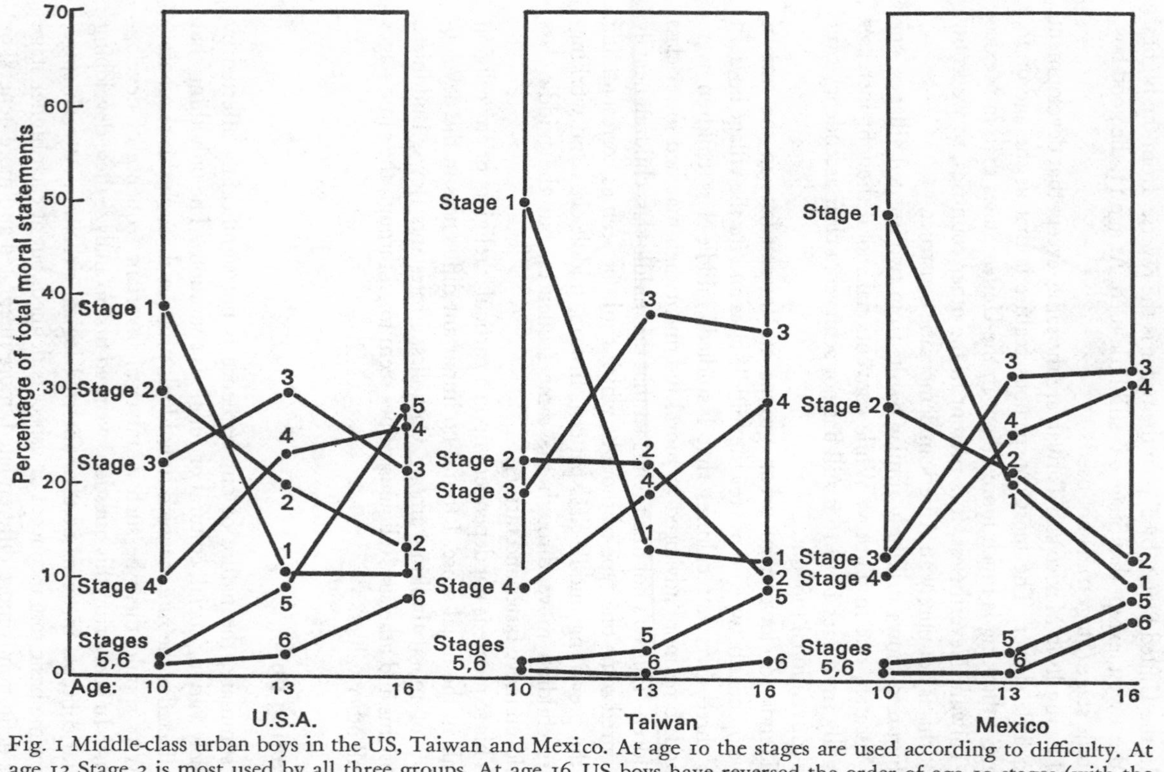

Fig. 1 Middle-class urban boys in the US, Taiwan and Mexico. At age 10 the stages are used according to difficulty. At age 13 Stage 3 is most used by all three groups. At age 16 US boys have reversed the order of age 10 stages (with the exception of 6). In Taiwan and Mexico, conventional (3–4) stages prevail at age 16, with Stage 5 also little used.

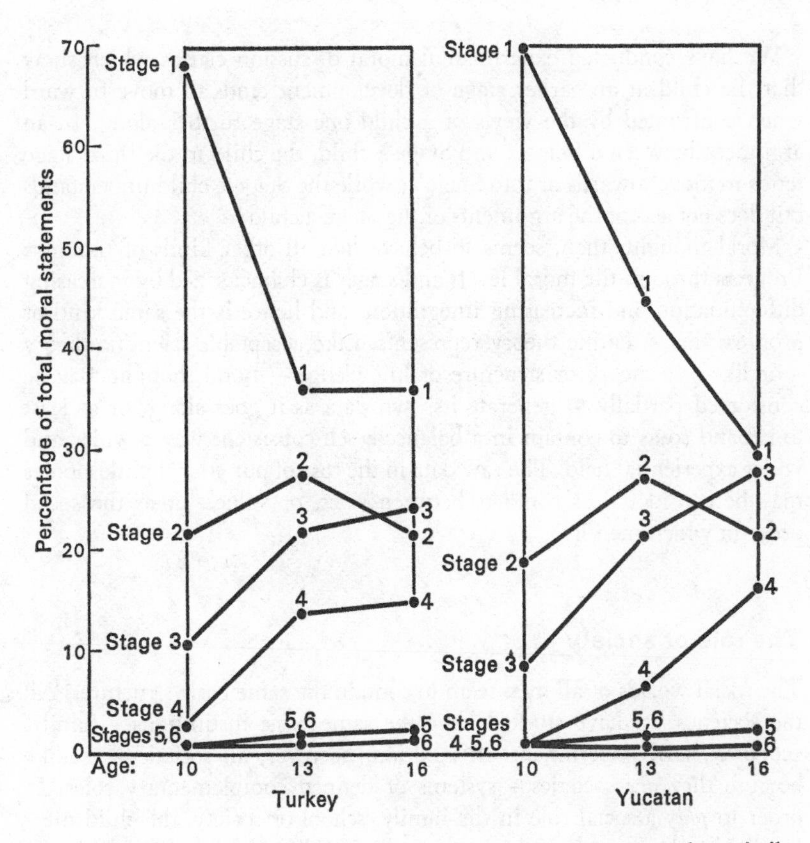

Fig. 2 Two isolated villages, one in Turkey, the other in Yucatan, show similar patterns in moral thinking. There is no reversal of order, and preconventional thought (1–2) does not gain a clear ascendancy over conventional stages at age 16.

and more universalized (the life of any sentient being is valuable regardless of status or property). The same advance is true at each stage in the hierarchy. Each step of development then is a better cognitive organization than the one before it, one which takes account of everything present in the previous stage, but making new distinctions and organizing them into a more comprehensive or more equilibrated structure. The fact that this is the case has been demonstrated by a series of studies indicating that children and adolescents comprehend all stages up to their own, but not more than one stage beyond their own. And importantly, *they prefer this next stage.*

We have conducted experimental moral discussion classes which show that the child at an earlier stage of development tends to move forward when confronted by the views of a child one stage further along. In an argument between a Stage-3 and Stage-4 child, the child in the third stage tends to move towards or into Stage 4, while the Stage-4 child understands but does not accept the arguments of the Stage-3 child.

Moral thought, then, seems to behave like all other kinds of thought. Progress through the moral levels and stages is characterized by increasing differentiation and increasing integration, and hence is the same kind of progress that scientific theory represents. Like acceptable scientific theory – or like *any* theory or structure of knowledge – moral thought may be considered partially to generate its own data as it goes along, or at least to expand so as to contain in a balanced, self-consistent way a wider and wider experiential field. The raw data in the case of our ethical philosophies may be considered as conflicts between roles, or values, or as the social order in which men live.

The role of society

The social worlds of all men seem to contain the same basic structures. All the societies we have studied have the same basic institutions – family, economy, law, government. In addition, however, all societies are alike because they *are* societies – systems of defined complementary roles. In order to *play* a social role in the family, school or society, the child must implicitly take the role of others towards himself and towards others in the group. These role-taking tendencies form the basis of all social institutions. They represent various patternings of shared or complementary expectations.

In the preconventional and conventional levels (Stages 1–4), moral content or value is largely accidental or culture-bound. Anything from 'honesty' to 'courage in battle' can be the central value. But in the higher postconventional levels, Socrates, Lincoln, Thoreau and Martin Luther King tend to speak without confusion of tongues, as it were. This is because the ideal principles of any social structure are basically alike, if only because there simply aren't that many principles which are articulate, comprehensive and integrated enough to be satisfying to the human intellect. And most of these principles have gone by the name of justice.

Behaviouristic psychology and psychoanalysis have always upheld the Philistine view that fine moral words are one thing and moral deeds another. Morally mature reasoning is quite a different matter, and does not really depend on 'fine words'. The man who understands justice is more likely to practice it.

In our studies, we have found that youths who understand justice act more justly, and the man who understands justice helps create a moral climate which goes far beyond his immediate and personal acts. The universal society is the beneficiary.

Section 7
Integration and the concept of self

Introduction

The single contribution in this section consists of excerpts from a book by Carl Rogers on client-centered therapy. It differs in several respects from those included in the Reader so far. It constitutes an attempt to formulate a general theory of personality and behaviour. Rogers essentially adopts a phenomenological or experiential approach; his focus is on the *experience* of an individual. Not only is this of interest in itself but it is seen as the key to understanding behaviour. It has been emphasized in previous sections that biological and social influences on behaviour must be viewed in relation to each other – as operating in interaction. The theory outlined here is very much concerned with the implications of this interaction, particularly as it relates to a person's awareness of self. An individual's self-concept depends not only on his direct experience but also on the evaluations of him made by parents and others. Much of Rogers' theory centres on the problems which arise when a person's self-concept, developed in this way, conflicts with his organismic needs.

The author is widely recognized (one could say revered!) as one of the most influential of American psychologists today. Rogers is first and foremost a clinician. He has very extensive experience of people in the intimate settings of individual and group psychotherapy. It is from this rich source of understanding, as well as from his deep grounding in academic psychology, that his theory springs. In terms of Barker's levels of research investigation, outlined in the extract included in Section 1, his theory is at level four. Rogers has attempted to point to, clarify and differentiate important features of behaviour and experience and to show how they interrelate. He has formulated his propositions with great care and effort at precision. It may serve to draw attention to and clarify aspects of your own experience. This is valuable in itself, of course. Ideally, however, we need to go further and to test formally the propositions put forward. Only research can really demonstrate how far they hold up and rule out the possibility of any bias arising from the fact that his theory has been generated largely by experience of people in therapy. Rogers and his co-workers are well aware of this need and have made many attempts to test specific hypotheses based on his ideas.

There are resemblances in Rogers' theory to psychoanalysis. He himself acknowledges, for example, the similarity of some of the ideas expressed in proposition 11 to the psychoanalytic concept of repression. Like psychoanalysis too, theory is closely interwoven with the practice of therapy. However, Rogers' technique of non-directive therapy is very different from psychoanalytic practice. There is, for example, no attempt at interpretation by the therapist. Rather he acts as a catalyst, a mirror to enable the client himself to bring into his awareness aspects of himself which he has hitherto been unable to symbolize. His task also is to provide the atmosphere of acceptance and non-evaluation which is an essential context for the client to develop fuller integration and understanding of himself.

What is notable about Rogers' approach is his breadth. He is aware not only of the need to ground his theory in intimate interaction with people but also of the need to formulate propositions precisely and to test them where at all possible. In other words, he tries to attain a constant interplay between detailed observation, therapeutic practice, theory construction and hypothesis testing.

23 A theory of personality and behaviour

Carl Rogers

The material which follows is offered as a series of propositions, with a brief explanation and exposition of each proposition. Since the theory is regarded as tentative, questions are raised in regard to various propositions, particularly where it seems uncertain that they adequately account for all the phenomena. Some of these propositions must be regarded as assumptions, while the majority may be regarded as hypotheses subject to proof or disproof....

The propositions

I Every individual exists in a continually changing world of experience of which he is the centre.

It should be recognized that in this private world of experience of the individual, only a portion of that experience, and probably a very small portion, is *consciously* experienced. Many of our sensory and visceral sensations are not symbolized. It is also true, however, that a large portion of this world of experience is *available* to consciousness, and may become conscious if the need of the individual causes certain sensations to come into focus because they are associated with the satisfaction of a need. In other words, most of the individual's experiences constitute the ground of the perceptual field, but they can easily become figure, while other experiences slip back into ground. We shall deal later with some aspects of experience which the individual *prevents* from coming into figure.

An important truth in regard to this private world of the individual is that it can only be known, in any genuine or complete sense, to the individual himself. No matter how adequately we attempt to measure the stimulus – whether it be a beam of light, a pinprick, a failure on an examination, or some more complex situation – and no matter how much we attempt to measure the perceiving organism – whether by psychometric tests or physiological calibrations – it is still true that the individual is the only one who can know how the experience was perceived. I can never know with vividness or completeness how a pinprick or a failure on an examination is experienced by you. The world of experience is for each individual, in a very significant sense, a private world.

ROGERS, CARL (1951) 'A theory of personality and behavior' in *Client-centered Therapy* Boston, Houghton Mifflin, 482–524.

This complete and first-hand acquaintance with the world of his total experience is, however, only potential; it does not hold true of the individual's general functioning. There are many of the impulses which I feel, or the sensations which I experience, which I can permit into consciousness only under certain conditions. Hence my actual awareness of and knowledge of my total phenomenal field is limited. It is still true, however, that potentially I am the only one who can know it in its completeness. Another can never know it as fully as I.

2 The organism reacts to the field as it is experienced and perceived. This perceptual field is, for the individual, 'reality'.

This is a simple proposition, one of which we are all aware in our own experience, yet it is a point which is often overlooked. I do not react to some absolute reality, but to my perception of this reality. It is this perception which for me *is* reality. ...

This proposition could be illustrated from the daily experience of everyone. . . . Two young parents each perceive differently the behaviour of their offspring. The son and daughter have differing perceptions of their parents. And the behaviour in all these instances is appropriate to the reality-as-perceived. This same proposition is exemplified in so-called abnormal conditions as well. The psychotic who perceives that his food is poisoned, or that some malevolent group is out to 'get' him, reacts to his reality-as-perceived in much the same fashion that you or I would respond if we (more 'realistically') perceived our food as contaminated, or our enemies as plotting against us. [...]

While it is not necessary for our purposes to define any absolute concept of reality, it should be noted that we are continually checking our perceptions against one another, or adding them one to another, so that they become more reliable guides to 'reality'. For example, I see some salt in a dish. That, for me at that instant, is reality. If I taste it and it tastes salty, my perception is further confirmed. But if it tastes sweet, my whole interpretation of the situation is changed, and both in seeing and tasting I perceive the material as sugar. Thus each perception is essentially a hypothesis – a hypothesis related to the individual's need – and many of these perceptions are tested and re-tested by experience. . . . Thus the world comes to be composed of a series of tested hypotheses which provide much security. It acquires a certain predictability upon which we depend. Yet mingled with these perceptions, which have been confirmed by a variety of experiences, are perceptions which remain completely unchecked. These untested perceptions are also a part of our personal reality, and may have as much authority as those which have been checked.

That the perceptual field is the reality to which the individual reacts is often strikingly illustrated in therapy, where it is frequently evident that when the perception changes, the reaction of the individual changes. As long as a parent is perceived as a domineering individual, that is the reality to which the individual reacts. When he is perceived as a rather pathetic individual trying to maintain his status, then the reaction to this new 'reality' is quite different.

3 The organism reacts as an organized whole to this phenomenal field.
. . . . Any simple S–R type of explanation of behaviour seems almost impossible. A young woman talks for an hour about her antagonism to her mother. She finds, following this, that a persistent asthmatic condition, which she has not even mentioned to the counsellor, is greatly improved. On the other hand, a man who feels that his security in his work is being seriously threatened, develops ulcers. It is extremely cumbersome to try to account for such phenomena on the basis of an atomistic chain of events. The outstanding fact which must be taken into theoretical account is that the organism is at all times a total organized system, in which alteration of any part may produce changes in any other part. Our study of such part phenomena must start from this central fact of consistent, goal-directed organization.

4 The organism has one basic tendency and striving – to actualize, maintain, and enhance the experiencing organism.
Rather than many needs and motives, it seems entirely possible that all organic and psychological needs may be described as partial aspects of this one fundamental need. . . .

We are talking here about the tendency of the organism to maintain itself – to assimilate food, to behave defensively in the face of threat, to achieve the goal of self-maintenance even when the usual pathway to that goal is blocked. We are speaking of the tendency of the organism to move in the direction of maturation, as maturation is defined for each species. This involves self-actualization, though it should be understood that this too is a directional term. The organism does not develop to the full its capacity for suffering pain, nor does the human individual develop or actualize his capacity for terror or, on the physiological level, his capacity for vomiting. The organism actualizes itself in the direction of greater differentiation of organs and of function. It moves in the direction of limited expansion through growth, expansion through extending itself by means of its tools, and expansion through reproduction. It moves in the direction of greater independence or self-responsibility. Its movement, as Angyal (1941) has pointed out (pp.32–50), is in the direction of an increasing self-government, self-regulation, and autonomy, and away from heteronymous control, or control by external forces. This is true whether we are speaking of entirely unconscious organic processes, such as the regulation of body heat, or such uniquely human and intellectual fuctions as the choice of life goals. Finally, the self-actualization of the organism appears to be in the direction of socialization, broadly defined. [...]

It is our experience in therapy which has brought us to the point of giving this proposition a central place. The therapist becomes very much aware that the forward-moving tendency of the human organism is the basis upon which he relies most deeply and fundamentally. It is evident not only in the general tendency of clients to move in the direction of growth when the factors in the situation are clear, but is most dramatically shown in very serious cases where the individual is on the brink of psychosis or suicide. Here the therapist is very keenly aware that the only force upon which he can basically rely is the organic tendency towards ongoing growth and enhancement. Something of our experience has been summarized by the writer in an earlier paper.

> As I study, as deeply as I am able, the recorded clinical cases which have been so revealing of personal dynamics, I find what seems to me to be a very significant thing. I find that the urge for a greater degree of independence, the desire for a self-determined integration, the tendency to strive, even through much pain, towards a socialized maturity, is as strong as – no, is stronger than – the desire for comfortable dependence, the need to rely upon external authority for assurance ... Clinically I find it to be true that though an individual may remain dependent because he has always been so, or may drift into dependence without realizing what he is doing, or may temporarily wish to be dependent because his situation appears desperate, I have yet to find the individual who, when he examines his situation deeply, and feels that he perceives it clearly, deliberately chooses dependence, deliberately chooses to have the integrated direction of himself undertaken by another. When all the elements are clearly perceived, the balance seems invariably in the direction of the painful but ultimately rewarding path of self-actualization or growth. (1948, p. 218)

... Why must the factors of choice be clearly *perceived* in order for this forward-moving tendency to operate? It would seem that unless experience is adequately symbolized, unless suitably accurate differentiations are made, the individual mistakes regressive behaviour for self-enhancing behaviour. This aspect will be more fully discussed in Proposition 11 and following.

5 Behaviour is basically the goal-directed attempt of the organism to satisfy its needs as experienced, in the field as perceived.

... These needs occur as physiological tensions which, when experienced, form the basis of behaviour which appears functionally (though not consciously) designed to reduce the tension and to maintain and enhance the organism. The need itself is not necessarily consciously experienced; there are seemingly different levels of description. In hunger, for example, stomach contractions occur which ordinarily are not directly experienced. The excitation which is thus set up may be experienced vaguely and below the conscious level, nevertheless bringing about behaviour which is in the direction of food, or it may be symbolized and perceived on the conscious level as hunger. [...]

It is noted that behaviour is postulated as a reaction to the field as perceived. This point, like some of the other propositions, is proved every day in our experience, but is often overlooked. The reaction is not to reality, but to the perception of reality. A horse, sensing danger, will try to reach the safety and security which he perceives in his stall, even though the barn may be in flames. A man in the desert will struggle just as hard to reach the 'lake' which he perceives in a mirage, as to reach a real water hole. At a more complex level, a man may strive for money because he perceives money as the source of emotional security, even though in fact it may not satisfy his need. Often, of course, the perception has a high degree of correspondence with reality, but it is important to recognize that it is the perception, not the reality, which is crucial in determining behaviour. [...]

6 Emotion accompanies and in general facilitates such goal-directed behaviour, the kind of emotion being related to the seeking versus the consummatory aspects of the behaviour, and the intensity of the emotion being related to the perceived significance of the behaviour for the maintenance and enhancement of the organism.

In this goal-seeking effort which is termed behaviour, what is the place of emotion, feeling, emotionalized attitudes? Any brief answer is likely to contain serious inadequacies, yet some framework for our thinking may be supplied by Proposition 6. We may think of emotions as falling primarily into two groups – the unpleasant and/or excited feelings, and the calm and/or satisfied emotions. The first group tends to accompany the seeking effort of the organism, and the second to accompany satisfaction of the need, the consummatory experience. The first group appears to have the effect of integrating and concentrating behaviour upon the goal, rather than having the disintegrating effect which some psychologists have pictured. Thus, in anything but excessive degree, fear accelerates the organization of the individual in the direction of escape from danger, and competitive jealousy concentrates the efforts of the individual to surpass.

The intensity of the emotional reaction appears to vary according to the perceived relationship of the behaviour to the maintenance and enhancement of the organism. Thus if my leap to the curb to escape the oncoming automobile is perceived as making the difference between life and death, it will be accompanied by strong emotion. The reading of another chapter tonight in a new psychology book, a behaviour which is seen as having a slight relationship to my development, will be accompanied by a very mild emotion indeed.

Both these propositions have been worded and discussed as though behaviour always had to do with the maintenance and enhancement of the *organism*. As we shall see in later propositions, the development of the self may involve some modification of this, since behaviour is then often best described as meeting the needs of the self, sometimes as against the needs of the organism, and emotional intensity becomes gauged more by the degree of involvement of the self than by the degree of involvement of the organism. As applied, however, to the infra-human organism, or to the human infant, Propositions 5 and 6 appear to hold.

7 The best vantage point for understanding behaviour is from the internal frame of reference of the individual himself.

It was mentioned in Proposition 1 that the only person who could fully know his field of experience was the individual himself. Behaviour is a reaction to the field as perceived. It would therefore appear that behaviour might be best understood by gaining, in so far as possible, the internal frame of reference of the person himself, and seeing the world of experience as nearly as possible through his eyes. . . . The only way to understand his behaviour meaningfully is to understand it as he perceives it himself, just as the only way to understand another culture is to assume the frame of reference of that culture. When that is done, the various meaningless and strange behaviours are seen to be part of a meaningful and goal-directed activity. . . .

If we could empathically experience all the sensory and visceral sensations of the individual, could experience his whole phenomenal field including both the conscious elements and also those experiences not brought to the conscious level, we should have the perfect basis for understanding the meaningfulness of his behaviour and for predicting his future behaviour. This is an unattainable ideal. . . . For one thing, we are largely limited to gaining an acquaintance with the phenomenal field as it is experienced in consciousness. This means that the greater the area of experience not in consciousness, the more incomplete will be the picture. The more we try to infer what is present in the phenomenal field but not conscious (as in interpreting projective techniques), the more complex grow the inferences until the interpretation of the client's projections may become merely an illustration of the clinician's projections.

Furthermore our knowledge of the person's frame of reference depends primarily upon communication of one sort or another from the individual. Communication is at all times faulty and imperfect. Hence only in clouded fashion can we see the world of experience as it appears to this individual.

We may state the whole situation logically thus:

It is possible to achieve, to some extent, the other person's frame of reference, because many of the perceptual objects – self, parents, teachers, employers, and so on – have counterparts in our own perceptual field, and practically all the attitudes towards these perceptual objects – such as fear, anger, annoyance, love, jealousy, satisfaction – have been present in our own world of experience.

Hence we can infer, quite directly, from the communication of the individual, or less accurately from observation of his behaviour, a portion of his perceptual and experiential field.

The more all his experiences are available to his consciousness, the more is it possible for him to convey a total picture of his phenomenal field.

The more his communication is a free expression, unmodified by a need or desire to be defensive, the more adequate will be the communication of the field. (Thus a diary is apt to be a better communication of the perceptual field than a court utterance where the individual is on trial.)

It is probably for the reasons just stated that client-centred counselling has proved to be such a valuable method for viewing behaviour from the person's frame of reference. The situation minimizes any need of defensiveness. The counsellor's behaviour minimizes any prejudicial influence on the attitudes expressed. The person is usually motivated to some degree to communicate his own special world, and the procedures used encourage him to do so. The increasing communication gradually brings more of experience into the realm of awareness, and thus a more accurate and total picture of this individual's world of experience is conveyed. On this basis a much more understandable picture of behaviour emerges. [. . .]

8 A portion of the total perceptual field gradually becomes differentiated as the self.

Gradually, as the infant develops, a portion of the total private world becomes recognized as 'me', 'I', 'myself'. There are many puzzling and unanswered questions in regard to the dawning concept of the self.

Is social interaction necessary in order for a self to develop? Would the hypothetical person reared alone upon a desert island have a self? Is the self primarily a product of the process of symbolization? Is it the fact that experiences may be not only directly experienced, but symbolized and manipulated in thought, that makes the self possible? Is the self simply the symbolized portion of experience? These are some of the questions which shrewd research may be able to answer.

Another point which needs to be made in regard to the development of a conscious self is the fact that it is not necessarily coexistent with the physical organism. Angyal points out that there is no possibility of a sharp line between organism and environment, and that there is likewise no sharp limit between the experience of the self and of the outside world. Whether or not an object or an experience is regarded as a part of the self depends to a considerable extent upon whether or not it is perceived as within the control of the self. Those elements which we control are regarded as a part of self, but when even such an object as a part of our body is out of control, it is experienced as being less a part of the self. The way in which, when a foot 'goes to sleep' from lack of circulation, it becomes an object to us rather than a part of self, may be a sufficient illustration. Perhaps it is this 'gradient of autonomy' which first gives the infant the awareness of self, as he is for the first time aware of a feeling of control over some aspect of his world of experience. [...]

9 As a result of interaction with the environment, and particularly as a result of evaluational interaction with others, the structure of self is formed – an organized, fluid, but consistent conceptual pattern of perceptions of characteristics and relationships of the 'I' or the 'me', together with values attached to these concepts.

10 The values attached to experiences, and the values which are a part of the self structure, in some instances are values experienced directly by the organism, and in some instances are values introjected or taken over from others, but perceived in distorted fashion, as if they had been experienced directly.

As the infant interacts with his environment he gradually builds up concepts about himself, about the environment, and about himself in relation to the environment. While these concepts are nonverbal, and may not be present in consciousness, this is no barrier to their functioning as guiding principles, as Leeper (unpublished) has shown. Intimately associated with all these experiences is a direct organismic valuing which appears highly important for understanding later development. The very young infant has little uncertainty in valuing. At the same time that there is the dawning awareness of 'I experience', there is also the awareness that 'I like', 'I dislike', 'I am cold, and I disike it', 'I am cuddled and I like it', 'I can reach my toes and find this enjoyable' – these statements appear to be adequate descriptions of the infant's experience, though he does not have the verbal symbols which we have used. . . .

There soon enters into this picture the evaluation of self by others. 'You're a good child', 'You're a naughty boy' – these and similar evaluations of himself and of his behaviour by his parents and others come to form a large and significant part of the infant's perceptual field. Social experiences, social evaluations by others, become a part of his phenomenal field along with experiences not involving others – for example, that radiators are hot, stairs are dangerous, and candy tastes good.

It is at this stage of development, it would seem, that there takes place a type of distorted symbolization of experience, and a denial of experience to awareness, which has much significance for the later development of psychological maladjustment. Let us try to put this in general and schematic terms.

One of the first and most important aspects of the self-experience of the ordinary child is that he is loved by his parents. He perceives himself as lovable, worthy of love, and his relationship to his parents as one of affection. He experiences all this with satisfaction. This is a significant and core element of the structure of self as it begins to form.

At this same time he is experiencing positive sensory values, is experiencing enhancement, in other ways. It is enjoyable to have a bowel movement at any time or place that the physiological tension is experienced. It is satisfying and enhancing to hit, or to try to do away with, baby brother. As these things are initially experienced, they are not necessarily inconsistent with the concept of self as a lovable person.

But then to our schematic child comes a serious threat to self. He experiences words and actions of his parents in regard to these satisfying behaviours, and the words and actions add up to the feeling 'You are bad, the behaviour is bad, and you are not loved or lovable when you behave in this way'. This constitutes a deep threat to the nascent structure of self. The child's dilemma might be schematized in these terms: 'If I admit to awareness the satisfactions of these behaviours and the values I apprehend in these experiences, then this is inconsistent with my self as being loved or lovable.'

Certain results then follow in the development of the ordinary child. One result is a denial in awareness of the satisfactions that were experienced. The other is to distort the symbolization of the experience of the parents. The accurate symbolization would be: 'I perceive my parents as experiencing this behaviour as unsatisfying to them.' The distorted symbolization, distorted to preserve the threatened concept of self, is: '*I* perceive this behaviour as unsatisfying.'

It is in this way, it would seem, that parental attitudes are not only introjected, but what is much more important, are experienced not as the attitude of another, but in distorted fashion, *as if* based on the evidence of one's own sensory and visceral equipment. Thus, through distorted symbolization, expression of anger comes to be 'experienced' as bad, even though the more accurate symbolization would be that the expression of anger is often experienced as satisfying or enhancing. The more accurate representation is not, however, permitted to enter awareness, or if it does enter, the child is anxious because of the inconsistency he is entertaining within himself. Consequently, 'I like baby brother' remains as the pattern belonging in the concept of the self, because it is the concept of the relationship which is introjected from others through the distortion of symbolization, even when the primary experience contains many gradations of value in the relationship, from 'I like baby brother' to 'I hate him!' In this way the values which the infant attaches to experience become divorced from his own organismic functioning, and experience is valued in terms of the attitudes held by his parents, or by others who are in intimate association with him. These values come to be accepted as being just as 'real' as the values which are connected with direct experience. The 'self' which is formed on this basis of distorting the sensory and visceral evidence to fit the already present structure acquires an organization and integration which the individual endeavours to preserve. Behaviour is regarded as enhancing this self when no such value is apprehended through sensory or visceral reactions; behaviour is regarded as opposed to the maintenance or enhancement of the self when there is no negative sensory or visceral reaction. It is here, it seems, that the individual begins on a pathway which he later describes as 'I don't really know myself'. The primary sensory and visceral reactions are ignored, or not permitted into consciousness, except in distorted form. The values which might be built upon them cannot be admitted to awareness. A concept of self based in part upon a distorted symbolization has taken their place.

Out of these dual sources – the direct experiencing by the individual, and the distorted symbolization of sensory reactions resulting in the introjection of values and concepts *as if* experienced – there grows the structure of the self. Drawing upon the evidence and upon clinical experience, it would appear that the most useful definition of the self-concept, or self-structure, would be along these lines. The self-structure is an organized configuration of perceptions of the self which are admissible to awareness. It is composed of such elements as the perceptions of one's characteristics and abilities;

the percepts and concepts of the self in relation to others and to the environment; the value qualities which are perceived as associated with experiences and objects; and the goals and ideals which are perceived as having positive or negative valence. It is, then, the organized picture, existing in awareness either as figure or ground, of the self and the self-in-relationship, together with the positive or negative values which are associated with those qualities and relationships, as they are perceived as existing in the past, present, or future.

It may be worth while to consider for a moment the way in which the self-structure might be formed without the element of distortion and denial of experience. Such a discussion is to some extent a digression, and anticipates a number of the propositions which follow, but it may also serve as an introduction to some of them.

If we ask ourselves how an infant might develop a self-structure which did not have within it the seeds of later psychological difficulty, our experience in client-centred therapy offers some fruitful ideas. Let us consider, very briefly, and again in schematic form, the type of early experience which would lay a basis for a psychologically healthy development of the self. The beginning is the same as we have just described. The child experiences, and values his experiences positively or negatively. He begins to perceive himself as a psychological object, and one of the most basic elements is the perception of himself as a person who is loved. As in our first description he experiences satisfaction in such behaviours as hitting baby brother. But at this point there is a crucial difference. The parent who is able (1) genuinely to accept these feelings of satisfaction experienced by the child, (2) fully to accept the child who experiences them, and (3) at the same time to accept his or her own feeling that such behaviour is unacceptable in the family, creates a situation for the child very different from the usual one. The child in this relationship experiences no threat to his concept of himself as a loved person. He can experience fully and accept within himself and as a part of himself his aggressive feelings towards his baby brother. He can experience fully the perception that his hitting behaviour is not liked by the person who loves him. What he then does depends upon his conscious balancing of the elements in the situation – the strength of his feeling of aggression, the satisfactions he would gain from hitting the baby, the satisfactions he would gain from pleasing his parent. The behaviour which would result would probably be at times social and at other times aggressive. It would not necessarily conform entirely to the parent's wishes, nor would it always be socially 'good'. It would be the adaptive behaviour of a separate, unique, self-governing individual. Its great advantage, as far as psychological health is concerned, is that it would be realistic, based upon an accurate symbolization of all the evidence given by the child's sensory and visceral equipment in this situation. It may seem to differ only very slightly from the description given earlier, but the difference is an extremely important one. Because the budding structure of the self is not threatened by loss of love, because feelings are accepted by his parent, the child in this instance does not need to deny to awareness the satisfactions which he is experiencing, nor does he need to distort his experience of the parental reaction and regard it as his own. He retains instead a secure self which can serve to guide his behaviour by freely admitting to awareness, in accurately symbolized form, all the relevant evidence of his experience in terms of its organismic satisfactions, both immediate and longer range. He is thus developing a soundly structured self in which there is neither denial nor distortion of experience. [...]

11 As experiences occur in the life of the individual, they are either (a) symbolized, perceived, and organized into some relationship to the self, (b) ignored because there is no perceived relationship to the self-structure, (c) denied symbolization or given a distorted symbolization because the experience is inconsistent with the structure of the self.

Let us look first at those experiences which are ignored because they are irrelevant to the self-structure. There are various noises going on at this moment, in the distance. Until they serve my intellectual need of this moment for an example, I am relatively oblivious to them. They exist in the ground of my phenomenal field, but they do not reinforce or contradict my concept of self, they meet no need related to the self, they are ignored. Often there might be doubt as to whether they existed in the phenomenal field at all, were it not for the ability to focus on those experiences when they might serve a need. I walk down a street a dozen times, ignoring most of the sensations which I experience. Yet today I have need of a hardware store. I recall that I have seen a hardware store on the street, although I have never 'noticed' it. Now that this experience meets a need of the self it can be drawn from ground into figure. It is undoubtedly true that the great majority of our sensory experiences are thus ignored, never raised to the level of conscious symbolization, and exist only as organic sensations, without ever having been related in any way to the organized concept of the self or to the concept of the self in relation to the environment.

A more important group of experiences are those which are accepted into consciousness and organized into some relationship with the self-structure either because they meet a need of the self or because they are consistent with the self-structure and thus reinforce it. The client who has a concept of self that 'I just don't feel that I can take my place in society like everybody else' perceives that she hasn't learned from her schoolwork, that she fails when she attempts things, that she does not react normally, and so on. She selects from her many sensory experiences those which fit in with her concept of herself. (Later, when her concept of self changes, she perceives that she has successfully attempted new projects, that she is sufficiently normal to get along.)

Likewise a great many experiences are symbolized because they are related to the needs of the self. I notice a book because it is on a topic I wish to learn about; I perceive neckties when I am preparing to buy one for myself. The infantryman perceives spots of freshly turned dirt in the road when these might indicate the existence of a land mine.

It is the third group of sensory and visceral experiences, those which seem to be prevented from entering awareness, which demand our closest attention, for it is in this realm that there lie many phenomena of human behaviour which psychologists have endeavoured to explain. In some instances the denial of the perception is something rather conscious. The client cited above, whose self-concept was so negative, reports: 'When people tell me they think I'm intelligent, I just don't believe it. I just – I guess I don't want to believe it. I don't know why I don't want to believe it – I just don't want to. It should give me confidence, but it doesn't. I think they just really don't know.' Here she can perceive and accept readily anyone's depreciation of her, because this fits in with her self-concept. Contradictory evaluations however are denied, by selecting and stressing other perceptions, such as that others cannot really know her. This type of more or less conscious denial of perception is certainly a frequent occurrence with everyone.

There is, however, an even more significant type of denial which is the phenomenon the Freudians have tried to explain by the concept of repression. In this instance, it would appear that there is the organic experience, but there is no symbolization of this experience, or only a distorted symbolization, because an adequate conscious representation of it would be entirely inconsistent with the concept of self. Thus, a woman whose concept of self has been deeply influenced by a very strictly moralistic and religious upbringing, experiences strong organic cravings for sexual satisfaction. To symbolize these, to permit them to appear in consciousness, would provide a traumatic contradiction to her concept of self. The organic experience is something which occurs and is an organic fact. But the symbolization of these desires, so that they become part of conscious awareness, is something which the conscious self can and does prevent. The adolescent who has been brought up in an oversolicitous home, and whose concept of self is that of one who is grateful to his parents, may feel intense anger at the subtle control which is being exerted over him. Organically he experiences the physiological changes which accompany anger, but his conscious self can prevent these experiences from being symbolized and hence consciously perceived. Or he can symbolize them in some distorted fashion which is consistent with his structure of self, such as perceiving these organic sensations as 'a bad headache'.

Thus the fluid but consistent organization which is the structure or concept of self, does not permit the intrusion of a perception at variance with it, except under certain conditions which we shall consider later.

It should be noted that perceptions are excluded because they are contradictory, not because they are derogatory. It seems nearly as difficult to accept a perception which would alter the self-concept in an expanding or socially acceptable direction as to accept an experience which would alter it in a constricting or socially disapproved direction. The self-distrusting client cited above has as much difficulty accepting her intelligence as a person with a self-concept of superiority would have in accepting experiences indicating mediocrity. [...]

12 Most of the ways of behaving which are adopted by the organism are those which are consistent with the concept of self.

... As the organism strives to meet its needs in the world as it is experienced, the form which the striving takes must be a form consistent with the concept of self. The man who has certain values attached to honesty cannot strive for a sense of achievement through means which seem to him dishonest. The person who regards himself as having no aggressive feelings cannot satisfy a need for aggression in any direct fashion. The only channels by which needs may be satisfied are those which are consistent with the organized concept of self.

In most instances this channelization does not involve any distortion of the need which is being satisfied. Of the various ways of satisfying the need for food or for affection, the individual selects only those which are consistent with the concept which he has of himself. There are times, however, when the denial of experience, spoken of above, plays a part in this process. For example, a pilot who conceives of himself as a brave and relatively fearless individual is assigned to a mission which involves great risk. Physiologically he experiences fear and a need to escape from this danger. These reactions cannot be symbolized into consciousness, since they would be too contradictory to his concept of self. The organic need, however, persists. He can perceive that 'the engine is not running quite properly', or that 'I am ill and have an upset digestive system', and on these grounds excuse himself from the mission. In this example, as in many others which could be cited, the organic needs exist but cannot be admitted into consciousness. The behaviour which is adopted is such that it satisfies the organic need, but it takes channels which are consistent with the concept of self. Most neurotic behaviour is of this type. In the typical neurosis, the organism is satisfying a need which is not recognized in consciousness, by behavioural means which are consistent with the concept of self and hence can be consciously accepted. [...]

13 Behaviour may, in some instances, be brought about by organic experiences and needs which have not been symbolized. Such behaviour may be inconsistent with the structure of the self, but in such instances the behaviour is not 'owned' by the individual.

In moments of great danger or other emergency stress, the individual may behave with efficiency and ingenuity to meet the needs for safety or whatever other needs exist, but without ever bringing such situations, or the behaviour called forth, to conscious symbolization. In such instances the individual feels 'I didn't know what I was doing', 'I really wasn't responsible for what I was doing'. The conscious self feels no degree of government over the actions which took place. The same statement might be made in regard to snoring or restless behaviour during sleep. The self is not in control, and the behaviour is not regarded as a part of self.

Another example of this sort of behaviour occurs when many of the organically experienced needs are refused admittance to consciousness because inconsistent with the concept of self. The pressure of the organic need may become so great that the organism initiates its own seeking behaviour and hence brings about the satisfaction of the need, without ever relating the seeking behaviour to the concept of self. Thus, a boy whose upbringing created a self-concept of purity and freedom from 'base' sexual impulses was arrested for lifting the skirts of two little girls and examining them. He insisted that he could not have performed this behaviour, and when presented with witnesses, was positive that 'I was not myself'. The developing sexuality of an adolescent boy, and the accompanying curiosity, constituted a strong organic need for which there seemed no channel of satisfaction which was consistent with the concept of self. Eventually the organism behaved in such a way as to gain satisfaction, but this behaviour was not felt to be, nor was it, a part of the self. It was behaviour which was dissociated from the concept of self, and over which the boy exercised no conscious control. [...]

14 Psychological maladjustment exists when the organism denies to awareness significant sensory and visceral experiences, which consequently

are not symbolized and organized into the gestalt of the self-structure. When this situation exists, there is a basic or potential psychological tension.

If we think of the structure of the self as being a symbolic elaboration of a portion of the private experiential world of the organism, we may realize that when much of this private world is denied symbolization, certain basic tensions result. We find, then, that there is a very real discrepancy between the experiencing organism as it exists, and the concept of self which exerts such a governing influence upon behaviour. This self is now very inadequately representative of the experience of the organism. Conscious control becomes more difficult as the organism strives to satisfy needs which are not consciously admitted, and to react to experiences which are denied by the conscious self. Tension then exists, and if the individual becomes to any degree aware of this tension or discrepancy, he feels anxious, feels that he is not united or integrated, that he is unsure of his direction. Such statements may not be the surface account of the maladjustment, such surface account having more often to do with the environmental difficulties being faced, but the feeling of inner lack of integration is usually communicated as the individual feels free to reveal more of the field of perception which is available to his consciousness. Thus, such statements as 'I don't know what I'm afraid of', 'I don't know what I want', 'I can't decide on anything', 'I don't have any real goal' are very frequent in counselling cases and indicate the lack of any integrated purposeful direction in which the individual is moving.

To illustrate briefly the nature of maladjustment, take a familiar picture of a mother whom the diagnostician would term rejecting. She has as part of her concept of self a whole constellation which may be summed up by saying, 'I am a good and loving mother.' This conceptualization of herself is, as indicated in Proposition 10, based in part upon accurate symbolization of her experience and in part upon distorted symbolization in which the values held by others are introjected as if they were her own experiences. With this concept of self she can accept and assimilate those organic sensations of affection which she feels towards her child. But the organic experience of dislike, distaste, or hatred towards her child is something which is denied to her conscious self. The experience exists, but it is not permitted accurate symbolization. The organic need is for aggressive acts which would fulfil these attitudes and satisfy the tension which exists. The organism strives for the achievement of this satisfaction, but it can do so for the most part only through those channels which are consistent with the self-concept of a good mother. Since the good mother could be aggressive towards her child only if he merited punishment, she perceives much of his behaviour as being bad, deserving punishment, and therefore the aggressive acts can be carried through, without being contrary to the values organized in her picture of self. If under great stress, she at some time should shout at her child, 'I hate you', she would be quick to explain that 'I was not myself', that this behaviour occurred but was out of her control. 'I don't know what made me say that, because of course I don't mean it.' This is a good illustration of most maladjustment in which the organism is striving for certain satisfactions in the field as organically experienced, whereas the concept of self is more constricted and cannot permit in awareness many of the actual experiences.

Clinically two somewhat different degrees of this tension are observed. There is first of all the type just illustrated, in which the individual has a definite and organized self-concept, based in part upon the organic experiences (in this case, feelings of affection) of the individual. While this concept of a good mother has been introjected from social contacts, it has also been formed in part from some of the sensations actually experienced by the individual, and has thus become more genuinely her own.

In other instances, the individual feels, as he explores his maladjustment, that he has no self, that he is a zero, that his only self consists of endeavouring to do what others believe he should do. The concept of self, in other words, is based almost entirely upon valuations of experience which are taken over from others and contains a minimum of accurate symbolization of experience, and a minimum of direct organismic valuing of experience. Since the values held by others have no necessary relationship to one's actual organic experiencings, the discrepancy between the self structure and the experiential world gradually comes to be expressed as a feeling of tension and distress. One young woman, after slowly permitting her own experiences to come into awareness and form the basis of her concept of self, puts it very briefly and accurately thus: 'I've always tried to be what the others thought I should be, but now I'm wondering whether I shouldn't just see that I am what I am.'

15 Psychological adjustment exists when the concept of the self is such that all the sensory and visceral experiences of the organism are, or may be, assimilated on a symbolic level into a consistent relationship with the concept of self.

This proposition may be put in several different ways. We may say that freedom from inner tension, or psychological adjustment, exists when the concept of self is at least roughly congruent with all the experiences of the organism. [To use an illustration previously given,] the mother who 'rejects' her child can lose the inner tensions connected with her relationship to her child if she has a concept of self which permits her to accept her feelings of dislike for the child, as well as her feelings of affection and liking.

The feeling of reduction of inner tension is something that clients experience as they make progress in 'being the real me' or in developing a 'new feeling about myself'. One client, after gradually giving up the notion that much of her behaviour was 'not acting like myself' and accepting the fact that her self could include these experiences and behaviours which she had hitherto excluded, expressed her feeling in these words: 'I can remember an organic feeling of relaxation. I did not have to keep up the struggle to cover up and hide this shameful person.' The cost of maintaining an alertness of defence to prevent various experiences from being symbolized in consciousness is obviously great.

The best definition of what constitutes integration appears to be this statement that all the sensory and visceral experiences are admissible to awareness through accurate symbolization, and organizable into one system which is internally consistent and which is, or is related to, the structure of self. Once this type of integration occurs, then the tendency towards growth can become fully operative, and the individual moves in the directions normal to all organic life. When the self-structure is able to accept and take account in consciousness of the organic experiences, when the organizational system is expansive enough to contain them, then clear integration and a sense of direction are achieved, and the individual feels that his strength can be and is directed towards the clear purpose of actualization and enhancement of a unified organism.

One aspect of this proposition for which we have some research evidence, but which could be tested even more clearly, is that conscious acceptance of impulses and perceptions greatly increases the possibility of conscious control. It is for this reason that the person who has come to accept his own experiences also acquires the feeling of being in control of himself. If it seems puzzling that the term 'conscious awareness' should be used almost interchangeably with 'conscious control', perhaps an analogy may be of help in clarification. I am driving my car on an icy pavement. I am controlling its direction (as the self feels itself to be in control of the organism). I desire to swing left to follow the curve of the road. At this point the car (analogous to the physiological organism) responds to physical laws (analogous to physiological tensions) of which I am not aware, and skids, moving in a straight line rather than rounding the curve. The tension and panic I feel are not unlike the tension of the person who finds that 'I am doing things which are not myself, which I cannot control'. The therapy is likewise similar. If I am aware of, and willing to accept all my sensory experiences, I sense the car's momentum forward, I do not deny it, I swing the wheel 'with the skid', rather than around the curve, until the car is again under control. Then I am able to turn left, more slowly. In other words I do not immediately gain my conscious objective, but by accepting all the evidences of experience and organizing them into one integrated perceptual system, I acquire the control by which reasonable conscious objectives can be achieved. This is very parallel to the feeling of the person who has completed therapy. He may have found it necessary to modify his objectives, but any disappointment in this respect is more than compensated by the increased integration and consequent control. No longer are there aspects of his behaviour which he cannot govern. The sense of autonomy, of self-government, is synonymous with having all experiences available to consciousness.

The term 'available to consciousness' in the last sentence is deliberately chosen. It is the fact that all experiences, impulses, sensations are *available* that is important, and not necessarily the fact that they are present in consciousness. It is the organization of the concept of self *against* the symbolization of certain experiences contradictory to itself, which is the significant negative fact. Actually, when all experiences are assimilated in relationship to the self and made a part of the structure of self, there tends to be *less* of what is called 'self-consciousness' on the part of the individual. Behaviour becomes more spontaneous, expression of attitudes is less guarded, because the self can accept such attitudes and such behaviour as a part of itself. Frequently a client at the beginning of therapy expresses real fear that others might discover his real self. 'As soon as I start thinking about what *I* am, I have such a terrible conflict at what I am that it makes me feel awful. It's such a self-depreciation that I hope nobody ever knows it. . . . I'm afraid to act natural, I guess, because I just don't feel as though I like myself.' In this frame of mind, behaviour must always be guarded, cautious, self-conscious. But when this same client has come to accept deeply the fact that 'I am what I am', then she can be spontaneous and can lose her self-consciousness.

16 Any experience which is inconsistent with the organization or structure of self may be perceived as a threat, and the more of these perceptions there are, the more rigidly the self-structure is organized to maintain itself. If the rejecting mother previously mentioned is told that several observers have come to the conclusion that she does reject her child, the inevitable result is that she will, for the moment, exclude any assimilation of this experience. She may attack the conditions of observation, the training or authority of the observers, the degree of understanding they possess, and so forth and so on. She will organize the defences of her own concept of herself as a loving and good mother, and will be able to substantiate this concept with a mass of evidence. She will obviously perceive the judgment of the observers as a threat, and will organize in defence of her own governing concept. The same phenomenon would be observed if the girl who regards herself as utterly lacking in ability received a high score on an intelligence test. She can and will defend her self against this threat of inconsistency. If the self cannot defend itself against deep threats, the result is a catastrophic psychological breakdown and disintegration.

A concise and helpful formulation of the essential elements in threat and defence, as they apply to personality, has been constructed by Hogan (1948a, 1948b). In his summary he lists eight statements as describing the way in which defensive behaviour occurs. These are as follows:

1 Threat occurs when experiences are perceived or anticipated as incongruent with the structure of the self.
2 Anxiety is the affective response to threat.
3 Defence is a sequence of behaviour in response to threat, the goal of which is the maintenance of the structure of the self.
4 Defence involves a denial or distortion of perceived experience to reduce the incongruity between the experience and the structure of the self.
5 The awareness of threat, but not the threat itself, is reduced by the defensive behaviour.
6 Defensive behaviour increases susceptibility to threat in that denied or distorted experiences may be threatened by recurring perceptions.
7 Threat and defence tend to recur again and again in sequence; as this sequence progresses, attention is removed farther and farther from the original threat, but more of experience is distorted and susceptible to threat.
8 This defensive sequence is limited by the need to accept reality. (1948b)

Hogan's theory helps to explain the spread of defensive behaviour in the individual by noting the fact that the more of sensory and visceral experience that is denied symbolization, or given a distorted symbolization, the greater the likelihood that any new experience will be perceived as threatening, since there is a larger false structure to be maintained.

17 Under certain conditions, involving primarily complete absence of any threat to the self-structure, experiences which are inconsistent with it may be perceived, and examined, and the structure of self revised to assimilate and include such experiences.

. . . In therapy of a client-centred form, by means of the relationship and the counsellor's handling of it, the client is gradually assured that he is accepted as he is, and that each new facet of himself which is revealed is also accepted. It is then that experiences which have been denied can be symbolized, often very gradually, and hence brought clearly into conscious form. Once they are conscious, the concept of self is expanded so that they may be included as a part of a consistent total. Thus the rejecting mother, in such an atmosphere, is apt first to admit the perception of her behaviour – 'I suppose that at times it must seem to him that I don't like him' – and then the possibility of an experience inconsistent with self – 'I suppose that at times I *don't* like him' – and gradually the formulation of a broadened concept of self: 'I can admit that I like him and I don't like him and we can still get along satisfactorily.' . . .

If we try to analyze the elements which make possible this reorganization of the structure of self, there would appear to be two possible factors. One is the self-initiated apprehension of the new material. Exploration of experience is made possible by the counsellor, and since the self is accepted at every step of its exploration and in any change it may exhibit, it seems possible gradually to explore areas at a 'safe' rate, and hitherto denied experiences are slowly and tentatively accepted just as a small child slowly and tentatively becomes acquainted with a frightening object. Another factor which may be involved is that the counsellor is accepting towards all experiences, all attitudes, all perceptions. This social value may be introjected by the client, and applied to his own experiences. This last certainly cannot be the major reason, since it is often known to the client that the counsellor is one among a thousand in holding such a value, and that society in general would not accept the client as he is. Nevertheless this introjection of the counsellor attitude may be at least a temporary or partial step towards the client's experiencing of himself as acceptable. [. . .]

A question sometimes raised is that if absence of threat to the self-concept were all that was required, it might seem that the individual could, at any time that he was alone, face these inconsistent experiences. We know that this does happen in many minor circumstances. A man may be criticized for a persistent failing. At the time he refuses to admit this experience at face value, because it is too threatening to his self-organization. He denies the fault, rationalizes the criticism. But later, alone, he rethinks the matter, accepts the criticism as just, and revises his concept of self, and consequently his behaviour, as a result. For experiences which are deeply denied, however, because they are deeply inconsistent with the concept of self, this does not avail. It appears possible for the person to face such inconsistency only while in a relationship with another in which he is sure that he will be accepted.

To leave this discussion with a somewhat simpler example, the child who feels that he is weak and powerless to do a certain task, to build a tower or repair a bicycle, may find, as he works rather hopelessly at the task, that he is successful. This experience is inconsistent with the concept he holds of himself, and may not be integrated at once; but if the child is left to himself he gradually assimilates, upon his own initiative, a revision of his concept of self, that while he is generally weak and powerless, in this respect he has ability. This is the normal way in which, free from threat, new perceptions are assimilated. But if this same child is repeatedly told by his parents that he is competent to do the task, he is likely to deny it, and to prove by his behaviour that he is unable to do it. The more forceful intrusion of the notion of his competence constitutes more of a threat to self and is more forcefully resisted. [...]

18 When the individual perceives and accepts into one consistent and integrated system all his sensory and visceral experiences, then he is necessarily more understanding of others and is more accepting of others as separate individuals.

This proposition has been felt to be true in our clinical therapeutic work, and is now supported by Sheerer's research investigation (1949a, 1949b). It is one of the unexepected findings that have grown out of the client-centred approach. . . .

We find clinically that the person who completes therapy is more relaxed in being himself, more sure of himself, more realistic in his relations with others, and develops notably better interpersonal relationships. One client, discussing the results which therapy has had for her, states something of this fact in these words: 'I am myself, and I am different from others. I am getting more happiness in being myself, and I find myself more and more letting other people assume the responsibility for being selves.'

If we try to understand the theoretical basis upon which this takes place, it appears to be as follows:

The person who denies some experiences must continually defend himself against the symbolization of those experiences.

As a consequence, all experiences are viewed defensively as potential threats, rather than for what they really are.

Thus in interpersonal relationships, words or behaviours are experienced and perceived as threatening, which were not so intended.

Also, words and behaviours in others are attacked because they represent or resemble the feared experiences.

There is then no real understanding of the other as a separate person, since he is perceived mostly in terms of threat or nonthreat to the self.

But when all experiences are available to consciousness and are integrated, then defensiveness is minimized. When there is no need to defend, there is no need to attack.

When there is no need to attack, the other person is perceived for what he really is, a separate individual, operating in terms of his own meanings, based on his own perceptual field.

While this may sound abstruse, it is corroborated by much everyday evidence, as well as by clinical experience. Who are the individuals, in any neighbourhood, or in any group, that inspire confidential relationships, seem able to be understanding of others? They tend to be individuals with a high degree of acceptance of all aspects of self. In clinical experience, how do better interpersonal relationships emerge? It is on this same basis. The rejecting mother who accepts her own negative attitudes towards her child finds that this acceptance, which at first she has feared, makes her more relaxed with her child. She is able to observe him for what he is, not simply through a screen of defensive reactions. Doing so, she perceives that he is an interesting person, with bad features, but also good ones, towards whom she feels at times hostile, but towards whom she also feels at times affectionate. On this comfortable and realistic and spontaneous basis a *real* relationship develops out of her real experiencing, a satisfying relationship to both. It may not be composed entirely of sweetness and light, but it is far more comfortable than any artificial relationship could possibly be. It is based primarily upon an acceptance of the fact that her child is a separate person. [...]

The implications of this aspect of our theory are such as to stretch the imagination. Here is a theoretical basis for sound interpersonal, intergroup and international relationships. Stated in terms of social psychology, this proposition becomes the statement that the person (or persons or group) who accepts himself thoroughly, will necessarily improve his relationship with those with whom he has personal contact, because of his greater understanding and acceptance of them. This atmosphere of understanding and acceptance is the very climate most likely to create a therapeutic experience and consequent self-acceptance in the person who is exposed to it. Thus we have, in effect, a psychological 'chain reaction' which appears to have tremendous potentialities for the handling of problems of social relationships.

19 As the individual perceives and accepts into his self-structure more of his organic experiences, he finds that he is replacing his present value system – based so largely upon introjections which have been distortedly symbolized – with a continuing organismic valuing process.

In therapy, as the person explores his phenomenal field, he comes to examine the values which he has introjected and which he has used as if they were based upon his own experience. (See Proposition 10.) He is dissatisfied with them, often expressing the attitude that he has just been doing what others thought he should do. But what does *he* think he should do? There he is puzzled and lost. If one gives up the guidance of an introjected system of values, what is to take its place? He often feels quite incompetent to discover or build any alternative system. If he cannot longer accept the 'ought' and 'should', the 'right' and 'wrong' of the introjected system, how can he know what values take their place?

Gradually he comes to experience the fact that he is making value judgments, in a way that is new to him, and yet a way that was also known to him in his infancy. Just as the infant places an assured value upon an experience, relying on the evidence of his own senses, as described in Proposition 10, so too the client finds that it is his own organism which supplies the evidence upon which value judgments may be made. He discovers that his own senses, his own physiological equipment, can provide the data for making value judgments and for continuously revising them. No one needs to tell him that it is good to act in a freer and more spontaneous fashion, rather than in the rigid way to which he has been accustomed. He senses, he feels that it is satisfying and enhancing. Or when he acts in a defensive fashion, it is his own organism that feels the immediate and short-term satisfaction of being protected and that also senses the longer-range dissatisfaction of having to remain on guard. He makes a choice between two courses of action, fearfully and hesitantly, not knowing whether he has weighed their values accurately. But then he discovers that he may let the evidence of his own experience indicate whether he had chosen satisfyingly. He discovers that he does not need to *know* what are the correct values; through the data supplied by his own organism, he can experience what is satisfying and enhancing. He can put his confidence in a valuing *process*, rather than in some rigid introjected *system* of values.

Let us look at this proposition in a slightly different way. Values are always accepted because they are perceived as principles making for the maintenance, actualization, and enhancement of the organism. It is on this basis that social values are introjected from the culture. In therapy it would seem that the reorganization which takes place is on the basis that those values are retained which are *experienced* as maintaining or enhancing the organism as distinguished from those which are said by others to be for the good of the organism. For example, an individual accepts from the culture the value, 'One should neither have nor express feelings of jealous aggressiveness towards siblings.' The value is accepted because it is presumed to make for the enhancement of the individual – a better, more satisfied person. But in therapy this person, as a client, examines this value in terms of a more basic criterion – namely, his own sensory and visceral experiences: 'Have I felt the denial of aggressive attitudes as something enhancing myself?' The value is tested in the light of personal organic evidence.

It is in the outcome of this valuing of values that we strike the possibility of very basic similarities in all human experience. For as the individual tests values, and arrives at his own personal values, he appears to come to conclusions which can be formulated in a generalized way: that the greatest values for the enhancement of the organism accrue when all experiences and all attitudes are permitted conscious symbolization, and when behaviour becomes the meaningful and balanced satisfaction of *all* needs, these needs being available to consciousness. The behaviour which thus ensues will satisfy the need for social approval, the need to express positive affectional feelings, the need for sexual expression, the need to avoid guilt and regret as well as the need to express aggression. Thus, while the establishment of values by each individual may seem to suggest a complete anarchy of values, experience indicates that quite the opposite is true. Since all individuals have basically the same needs, including the need for acceptance by others, it appears that when each individual formulates his own values, in terms of his own direct experience, it is not anarchy which results, but a high degree of commonality and a genuinely socialized system of values. One of the ultimate ends, then, of an hypothesis of confidence in the individual, and in his capacity to resolve his own conflicts, is the emergence of value systems which are unique and personal for each individual, and which are changed by the changing evidence of organic experience, yet which are at the same time deeply socialized, possessing a high degree of similarity in their essentials. [...]

References

ANGYAL, A. (1941) *Foundations for a Science of Personality* New York, Commonwealth Fund.

HOGAN, R. (1948a) 'The development of a measure of client defensiveness in a counselling relationship'. Ph.D. thesis, University of Chicago.

HOGAN, R. (1948b) 'The development of a measure of client defensiveness in a counselling relationship'. Ph.D. thesis abstract, University of Chicago.

LEEPER, R. W. (unpublished) 'Cognitive and symbolic processes'.

SHEERER, ELIZABETH T. (1949a) 'An analysis of the relationship between acceptance of and respect for self and acceptance of and respect for others in seven counselling cases'. Ph.D. thesis, University of Chicago.

SHEERER, ELIZABETH T. (1949b) 'An analysis of the relationship between acceptance of and respect for self and acceptance of and respect for others in ten counselling cases,' *Journal of Consulting Psychology*, 13, 169–75.

Section 8
Person perception

Introduction

What do we perceive or know about other individuals? How do we acquire this knowledge, and what consequences does it have? Psychologists have varied widely in their relative emphasis on these aspects of social perception. Here, as elsewhere in social psychology, theoretical orientation shapes methodology. The view expressed by Hastorf, Richardson and Dornbusch in the first article is that attention should be focused upon the relationship of perception to other aspects of behaviour. To this end, the authors suggest that psychologists should study the categories that individuals actually employ in their perception of others, rather than the use they make of categories provided by an experimenter. In this the authors reflect to some extent the phenomenologists' concern with subjective experience, which is well represented in section 9. The use of 'free description' should reveal which categories are *relevant* to the individual. The psychologist can then set about establishing the social variables which may determine this choice of categories, and finally the consequences for the individual's behaviour. The authors mention but underestimate the problem posed by the analysis of free descriptions. The true size of this problem may explain the relative infrequency of such studies in the subsequent literature.

The next two extracts reflect the recently renewed interest in the recognition of emotional expression. A special focus of interest here arises from the work of Darwin (1872). Darwin's evolutionary theory led him to believe that the expression of the basic emotions and their recognition are inherited and universal to all cultures. In an earlier extract Eibl-Eibesfeldt described some of his observations of children born blind and deaf. These children seemed to show many of the same expressions (smiling, frowning, etc.) as normal children, and he concluded that the basis for the complex motor patterns involved must be innate. The claims that expressive behaviour is inherited and that it takes the same form in all cultures are logically distinct, although not always treated as such. Both have been challenged, particularly by those influenced by developments in the field of linguistics and anthropology. Notable among these is Ray L. Birdwhistell, who has argued, partly on the basis of evidence and partly on a priori grounds, against a cultural universalist viewpoint. In 1968 he wrote:

> Insofar as I have been able to determine, just as there are no universal words, no sound complexes, which carry the same meaning the world over, there are no body motions, facial expressions, or gestures which provoke *identical* responses the world over. A body can be bowed in grief, in humility, in laughter, or in readiness for aggression. A 'smile' in one society portrays friendliness, in another embarrassment, and in still another a warning, that, unless tension is reduced, hostility and attack will follow.

In the article by Ekman and Friesen it is argued that the observed cultural differences in expressive behaviour may nonetheless be reconciled with the view that there are universal elements to such behaviour. Distinctive patterns of emotional expression are seen as universal, while the circumstances eliciting these emotions, the rules governing the 'display' of emotions in social settings and the consequences of emotional arousal are said to vary from culture to culture. They report an intriguing study of a preliterate culture in New Guinea as evidence for universal recognition of 'basic' emotions. Clearly, much in this controversy hinges on the type of evidence which is considered relevant, and caution should be adopted in the interpretation of findings.

Whether observed cultural differences in recognition are due to differences in the expressive behaviours themselves, or in the eliciting circumstances, display rules etc., we might expect such differences to be influenced by exposure to a new culture. The last article, by Fong, suggests that exposure to western culture brings about changes in the social perceptions of Chinese people.

References

DARWIN, C. (1872) *The expression of the emotions in man and animals* London, John Murray, reprinted Chicago, University of Chicago Press, 1965.

BIRDWHISTELL, R. L. (1970) *Kinetics and context: essays on body-motion communication* University of Pennsylvania, Penguin University Books, 1973, 34.

24 The problem of relevance in the study of person perception

Albert H. Hastorf, Stephen A. Richardson and Sanford M. Dornbusch

Behavioural scientists have long been interested in the manner in which people perceive one another. This interest stems not only from a concern with perception in general but also from the assumption that differences in interpersonal perception are functionally related to differences in other aspects of interpersonal behaviour. During the past ten years, interest has grown markedly in this area of perceptual research. This has resulted in a spate of studies concerned with the influence of many 'social factors' on perception, with attempts to measure individual differences in the accuracy of predicting ('perceiving') the responses of other people, and with attempts at theories of behaviour that make pointed use of certain perceptual variables.

A thesis of this paper is that behavioural scientists, working in the area of interpersonal perception, have not, so far, met with great success in specifying relationships that help us understand interpersonal behaviour in general. More specifically, there has been little impact of the research in interpersonal perception on our understanding of, and thus ability to predict, in the general field of interpersonal behaviour. Much of the research has had an 'isolationist' aura in that the concern with perceptual variables has led to a lack of concern with other aspects of interpersonal behaviour. It should be pointed out that this somewhat depressing description of the present state of affairs may be rather unfair in that we are dealing with a relatively young area of research interest. One must not expect miracles in less than ten years. It seems apparent, however, that one reason for the lack of carry-over of the perceptual research to the prediction of other aspects of interpersonal behaviour may well be a result of the failure to specify just what the goals are in studying interpersonal perception. Considerable confusion can be found over the question of whether certain studies are pointed at elucidating specific aspects of the perceptual process itself or relating certain resultants of the process to other aspects of social

HASTORF, A. H., RICHARDSON, S. A. and DORNBUSCH, S. M. (1958) 'The problem of relevance in the study of person perception' in Tagiuri, R. and Petrullo, L. (eds) *Person Perception and Interpersonal Behaviour* California, Stanford University Press, 54–61.

behaviour. Confusion between these goals, which are in fact quite distinct, has led to much expenditure of energy on research without a clear focus.

We should like to defend the proposition that studies of interpersonal perception will make more headway if two criteria of relevance are met. These are:

1 Researchers should make more of an attempt to study the perceptual categories that are actually employed by, and thus relevant to, the perceiver under consideration. This is especially important to all those studies concerned with the 'accuracy' of the perception of people. It is now beginning to look as though the early hopes for measuring a 'trait' of social sensitivity by sampling a person's ability to perceive other people on a set of variables selected by the experimenter are doomed to failure (Crow 1954). We urge a shift of focus from the 'trait' approach to the study of how people categorize other people; what are the relevant characteristics of other people?

2 Studies of perception *made by social psychologists* should always have at the forefront the relationship of the perceptual act under consideration to some other aspect of the social behaviour of the perceiver. Our argument is that in the long pull, the helpful empirical studies are those that specifically tie a perceptual act to other aspects of behaviour. It must be relevant to other behaviour. Naturally, this dictum does not apply to those researchers concerned with the perceptual process itself. It might be added that the social psychologist's goal is the understanding and predicting of social behaviour, and that studies designed to merely demonstrate the influence of 'social factors' on perception no longer push us towards that goal.

To develop our thesis, we will first identify three primary and interrelated aspects of perception and then discuss each. These aspects are:

1 What are the *qualities* of experience in social perception? We are interested here in the experiences one has of other people in social situations which are reflected in the verbal categories one employs in talking about other people. Some aspects of human experience such as the perception of colour, timbre, and pitch thus fall outside the scope of our interest.

2 What are the *determinants* of these specific experiences? We use *determinants* in the sense of correlates of these experiences in terms of the variables of social psychology, for example, status, occupation, or certain facets of individual personality. We do not mean *determinant* in the sense that the laboratory experimentalist studying perception uses the term, as a statement of precise position in a mechanistic sequence.

3 What are the *consequences* of a specific perception? This is the crucial point. The social psychologist should be interested in the qualities and

the determinants of experience because he is concerned with the consequences of these experiences for other types of behaviour.

Let us now look at these primary and interrelated problems in greater detail. The need for a greater concern with the qualities of social experience can best be illustrated by those numerous current studies concerned with assessing the sensitivity of an individual to other persons. A wide variety of research techniques has been used but little progress has been made towards producing a valid measure of social sensitivity (Bruner and Tagiuri 1954). The most common method is to ask the subject to predict the attitudes, behaviour, or self-concept of another. The criterion of sensitivity has been the accuracy of these predictions. Many questions have been raised about the psychological meaningfulness of these accuracy scores. A major problem seems to be that subjects' accuracy may vary for each of the kinds of percepts with which the investigator is concerned. In other words, the experimenter has set the categories the subject must employ with little concern for the *relevance* of these to the subject's cognitive map of other people. Subjects are asked to predict the responses of other people to attitude or personality items that may be quite meaningless to the subject. They may even report such feelings as, 'I can't tell you whether he feels aggressive or not, but I can tell you how he feels about quiet people.' In essence, the subject is reporting the nonrelevance of the 'aggressive' category and reporting the relevance of the 'quiet' category. It makes little sense to gather precise, quantitative data on measures of sensitivity when this essential matter of the relevance of the categories or qualities is neglected. It should be noted that self-conscious acts of interpersonal perception during experiments may be markedly more accurate than in everyday life for those very same people who seldom use the categories the experimenter has required them to use. This may well be a reason why accuracy scores on categories selected by the experimenter are not very predictive of other aspects of interpersonal behaviour.

We urge a momentary pause in the search for the 'trait' of sensitivity in order to study the qualities of a person's experience of others in terms of the verbal categories he uses in reporting that experience. The central characteristic of this type of methodology would be the eliciting of free and unrestricted descriptions of other persons. The classes of persons to be described would be specified by the experimenter. One might mention an interesting result of this methodology in simple form as noted by Sarbin (1954). He asked certain members of a class to stand up while others in the class jotted down a few pertinent characteristics of the person standing. A rather striking finding was that women differed from men in that they tended to use 'personality' variables in describing these people, such as 'aggressive' or 'pleasant', whereas men tended to employ 'role' categories, such as 'doctor' or 'chairman', in describing the stimulus people. These data suggest differences between men and women in the way they see people when an experimenter is *not* specifying the terms in which they *should* see them.

Some other important advantages accrue from obtaining free descriptions of how people perceive others. Research in survey-interviewing methodology has shown clearly the problems of communication between the questioner and the person who answers and of analysis in interpreting the meaning of the answer. This suggests a point that has not received sufficient attention in the many studies in which the experimenter imposes lists of personality traits on the subjects, such as the set of perceptual categories to be used in a prediction experiment. To what extent do the labels used to indicate personality traits mean the same thing to the subject as they do to the experimenter and the same thing from one subject to another? When dealing with free descriptions given by the informant, we are not dealing with a set of isolated terms but rather with words which are embedded in a context. The context increases the chance of adequate communication between the experimenter and the subject. Earlier work on forming impressions of personality shows clearly that the sequence with which categories are used has an important effect on social perception (Asch 1946). By obtaining free descriptions, the sequence of categories used is freely determined by the subject and becomes a variable which can be analyzed. An objection to eliciting free descriptions from persons about other people is that some of the significant perceptual variables used by the perceiver may be so habitual that he may not bother to express them verbally. For this reason, a necessary step in this type of research will be to discuss the free descriptions with the perceiver after they have been given; e.g. a person, in describing another, may include a number of inferences. Only later exploration will determine the extent to which the describer is conscious of the evidence on which he bases his inference.

There are a number of conditions which may affect the categories used by a person when giving a free description of another. Some of the more influential factors may be:

1 The describer's definition of the situation when meeting the person he is to describe, e.g. for what purpose is the meeting? how important will this person be to the describer in the future? what is his prior knowledge of the person? The definition of the situation is likely to be most influential for first impressions and occasions when the describer has very limited information about the person to be described.

2 What is the breadth of the social relationship between the describer

and the person to be described? The more narrowly prescribed the relationship, the more particular are the categories likely to be.

3 The cues which the person to be described exhibits. For example, a man who has a prosthesis instead of a hand, by extending a hook instead of a hand on the first meeting, may influence the categories of perception so that they are different from the situation in which the prosthesis does not become apparent for a considerable time.

4 The categories used by the describer may be influenced by his immediate prior experience. Perceptual categories which are not normally brought into play may become manifest under extreme conditions; e.g. in extreme fatigue or anxiety, a describer may use categories expressing racial or ethnic prejudice which, under different circumstances, would not have become evident.

There are a number of problems related to the analysis of the free descriptions: to what extent should the analyst inductively derive the categories from the terms which the describer actually uses and to what extent should the analyst impose higher-level abstract categories on the descriptions? We would suggest that in the initial stages of research, it will be necessary to use more than one level of analysis which will cover both of the approaches we have identified. It will be necessary not only to identify the categories that are used, but also to relate the frequency with which they are used and their sequence. A particularly difficult problem is determining valid grounds upon which to make comparisons between subjects who give free descriptions of others. There is again an interesting parallel between the development of survey-interviewing methodology and the approach to social perception we are advocating. In the early survey questionnaires, the investigators frequently devised the questions without any contact with the people who were to be surveyed and then assumed the questions were understood and the answers were comparable. It is now general practice to conduct a number of exploratory free interviews with a sample of people to be studied. From these exploratory free interviews, information can be gained on the level of discourse, idiom, and colloquialisms used by the persons being studied. Questions which are relevant to the people being studied can then be constructed and worded more meaningfully. What we are suggesting in social perception research is the value of obtaining exploratory free descriptions of other people for determining which categories are relevant to the subjects being studied. Then subsequent studies may impose categories of social perception on subjects with some assurance that they are relevant and meaningful to them.

Some of the determinants of perception (as we have defined 'determinant') can best be suggested by stating some testable questions. For example, is the strength of a person's aspiration to high social status related to his frequency of use of role categories? When a person describes people of superordinate or subordinate positions, how do his categories change? What are the differences in the categories used for first impressions and for persons well known to the perceiver? Do members of religious groups which differ in their teachings as to the proper role of women have corresponding differences in the categories of perception when men from these groups describe women? Sarbin's study of the differences in perceptual categories of men and women in describing persons is, again, suggestive. Here the purpose of the descriptions was left vague. The important variable may have been that, given an unclear definition of the situation, men and women formulate their descriptions of others in terms of categories which from long experience they have found most useful for their usual types of social relationships. It would be interesting to repeat Sarbin's experiment when the describers knew precisely the future relationship in which they were going to be involved with the person they were about to describe, seeing if the differences originally reported still hold.

We are aware of only two studies which have analyzed free descriptions to determine whether systematic differences in perceptual categories are related to determinants: those of Schatzman and Strauss (1955) and Campbell and Radke-Yarrow (1956). The study of Schatzman and Strauss is primarily suggestive of the type of method we propose. They analyzed the descriptions of a disaster by people of widely differing socioeconomic status. Their analysis suggested that lower-class people were prone to describe the disaster only from their own standpoint and in relation to their own activities while middle-class respondents tended to describe the disaster from several points of view. Campbell and Radke-Yarrow asked children in a camp to describe each other. They found the boys were more likely than the girls to describe children in terms of aggressive, rebellious, and nonconforming behaviour. The girls were more likely than the boys to stress nurturant relationships.

So far, we have suggested a number of determinants that might be called sociological. Certainly, a number of personality variables might also be included, especially if one is interested in the fascinating question of what might be called 'the layman's psychodynamics' or, as Bruner and Tagiuri put it, 'implicit theories' of personality.

Let us now turn to the important question of the consequences of interpersonal perception. We have already stated the desirability of separating the goal of understanding the perceptual process from the goal of using perceptual data to predict other aspects of behaviour. In some respects, the study of the categories of interpersonal perception is primarily important as a prerequisite for investigating the vital problem of the extent to which knowledge of perceptual categories will provide us with a tool for understanding interpersonal behaviour in general. In dealing with the consequences of differential perception, our concern is that social psychologists may be too easily satisfied with showing – let us say – differences between upward-mobile and non-upward-mobile people in the categories they employ in perceiving other people. This is clearly important information that is needed. But we want to stress the importance of relating such perceptual differences to other aspects of behaviour. One assumption we are making is that the social psychologist has, perhaps, the best opportunity for the investigation of the perception–behaviour relationship.

Let us mention three studies that seem to be pushing towards investigation of the consequences of differing perceptions. In 1952, Chowdry and Newcomb (1952) published an article dealing with an aspect of the social sensitivity problem in group life. They asked the question: Are leaders more accurate social perceivers than nonleaders? They found differences between the two groups on what they called 'relevant' issues and not on 'nonrelevant' issues. Two years later, Talland (1954) raised a very interesting question as to the relationship found by Chowdry and Newcomb. He demonstrated that leaders play an important role in formulating the opinions they then have to estimate. Let us push this question a little further. Are those people who emerge as leaders especially sensitive to certain opinions of the members, and do they gain the position of leadership by using this capacity, or does the leadership role (a product of many variables) lead to special opportunities for behaviours and perceptions that make it possible for a leader to appear to have special sensitivity? Clearly, this is a simple statement of a complicated problem, but the issue is the need for research that studies the action consequences of differential perceptions in a situation like this. Can we not conceive of ongoing measures of perceptions in a group where we can relate these to behaviour? A research project along this line is at present being carried out in the group behaviour laboratory at Dartmouth, where differential perceptions of individuals prior to group action are being studied; then, following group action, perceptual measures are, again, obtained. Two questions of concern are: Do the 'task' and 'process' specialists perceive the group differentially? Are they accurate in different categories of experience and what are the behavioural consequences of these differences?

Let us take a second example. Thibaut and Riecken (1955) have recently published a pertinent study in this area. They concerned themselves with the determinants of the perception of high and low status among college students. The subject then interacted with one high- and one low-status person, leading to the 'yielding' of the high- and low-status confederates to the opinion of the subject. Two questions arise: how does the subject perceive this yielding and what are the consequences of it? The consequences were measured in terms of changes in the acceptance scores the high- and low-status confederates received from the subject. An important aspect of this study was its attempt to measure some of the consequences of differential perception. Could not more be done even with this situation? What are the consequences of such perceptions on future interactions between these people? What is the impact of this yielding experience on the subject in terms of his future perceptions of other people?

The third example is the previously mentioned paper by Campbell and Radke-Yarrow (1956) in which different perceptual categories were used by children who utilize different types of behaviour in getting information about another person. Some children (whom they called the observer type) proceed in the fashion illustrated by 'I just hanged around him a lot. Tried to diagnose him the way I usually do people. Watched his actions.' The other approach, the provoker type, proceeds as follows: 'We were making bunks. Started talking. We had a couple of wrestling matches – not mad or anything, just testing our strength. I let him throw me just to try him out.'

A number of interesting research problems immediately come to mind in investigating relationships between perceptual categories and behaviour in interpersonal situations; e.g. to what extent can two people known to have very different sets of perceptual categories cooperate and understand each other in working on a common problem in human relationships? Are there any consistent relationships between the use of certain perceptual categories and the occupational role of a person?

Let us make a final comment. The methodology we propose is certainly not a simple one. Obtaining reliable data of this sort is not easy. However, we have done some preliminary work with this method by asking a small number of subjects to give free descriptions of a number of people well known to them. Some of the impressions we have formed from this work are:

1 That people in giving free descriptions of other people consistently use a rather limited number of perceptual categories even when describing very different kinds of people.
2 That there is a strong positive relationship between categories which people use in describing other people and in describing themselves.
3 That a person has a core of generally consistent categories used in

describing all people and a set of more particular categories which depend more on situational factors.

It will be necessary to determine the extent to which these impressions can be upheld by further empirical work. The simplest assumption which can be tested is that a single category of perception enables prediction of a specified type of interpersonal behaviour. To test this relationship, a specific index both of perception and behaviour must be identified. Within this assumption is embedded a second assumption that there is a reasonable degree of consistency in the perceptual categories used. A third embedded assumption is that the relationships between perceptual categories and behaviour are common to a wide range of people. To test the assumption of the relationship between specified perceptual categories and behaviour, it may be more economical to start with measures of behaviour and then predict, or inductively determine, related perceptual categories.

In summary, let us restate our position. The social psychologist must face three interrelated problems in any study of the perception of people: (a) the qualities of experience, (b) their determinants, and (c) the consequences of certain experiences. Major stress needs to be placed on the discovery of people's categorizing schemata and on the action consequences of differential perceptual categories. The period has passed when a social psychologist can be satisfied with demonstrating the role of 'social factors' in perception. He must go on to demonstrate some behavioural consequences of these perceptions. Only then will cognitive variables make a significant contribution to a science of human behaviour.

References

ASCH, S. E. (1946) 'Forming impressions of personality', *J. abnorm. soc. Psychol.*, 41, 258–90.

BRUNER, J. S. and TAGIURI, R. (1954) 'The perception of people' in Lindzey, G. (ed.) *Handbook of social psychology* Cambridge, Mass., Addison-Wesley.

CAMPBELL, J. D. and RADKE-YARROW, MARIAN J. (1956) 'Interpersonal perception and behavior in children'. Paper read at meetings of the American Psychological Association, Chicago.

CHOWDRY, KALMA and NEWCOMB, T. M. (1952) 'The relative ability of leaders and non-leaders to estimate opinions of their own group', *J. abnorm. soc. Psychol.*, 47, 51–7.

CROW, W. J. (1954) 'A methodological study of social perceptiveness.' PhD. thesis, University of Colorado.

SARBIN, T. (1954) 'Role theory' in Lindzey, G. (ed.) *Handbook of social psychology* Cambridge, Mass., Addison-Wesley.
SCHATZMAN, L. and STRAUSS, A. (1955) 'Social class and modes of communication', *Amer. J. Sociol.*, **60**, 329–38.
TALLAND, G. (1954) 'The assessment of group opinion by leaders and their influence on its formation', *J. abnorm. soc. Psychol.*, **49**, 431–4.
THIBAUT, J. and RIECKEN, H. W. (1955) 'Some determinants and consequences of the perception of social causality', *J. Pers.*, **24**, 113–33.

25 Constants across cultures in the face and emotion

Paul Ekman and Wallace V. Friesen

This study addresses the question of whether any facial expressions of emotion are universal. Recent studies showing that members of literate cultures associated the same emotion concepts with the same facial behaviours could not demonstrate that at least some facial expressions of emotion are universal; the cultures compared had all been exposed to some of the same mass media presentations of facial expression, and these may have taught the people in each culture to recognize the unique facial expressions of other cultures. To show that members of a preliterate culture who had minimal exposure to literate cultures would associate the same emotion concepts with the same facial behaviours as do members of Western and Eastern literate cultures, data were gathered in New Guinea by telling subjects a story, showing them a set of three faces, and asking them to select the face which showed the emotion appropriate to the story. The results provide evidence in support of the hypothesis that the association between particular facial muscular patterns and discrete emotions is universal.

Introduction

Prolonged and at times heated controversy has failed to demonstrate whether facial behaviours associated with emotion are universal for man or specific to each culture. Darwin (1872) postulated universals in facial behaviour on the basis of his evolutionary theory. Allport (1924), Asch (1952) and Tomkins (1962, 1963) have also postulated universals in emotional facial behaviour, although each writer offered a different theoretical basis for his expectation. The culture-specific view, that facial behaviours become associated with emotion through culturally variable learning, received support from Klineberg's (1938) descriptions of how the facial behaviours described in Chinese literature differed from the facial behaviours associated with emotions in the Western world. More recently, Birdwhistell (1963) and LaBarre (1947) have argued against the possibility

---

EKMAN, PAUL and FRIESEN, WALLACE V. (1971) 'Constants across cultures in the face and emotion' in *Journal of Personality and Social Psychology*, vol. 17, no. 2, 124–29.

of any universals in emotional facial behaviour, supplying numerous anecdotal examples of variations between cultures.

Ekman (1968) and Ekman and Friesen (1969) considered these contradictory viewpoints within a framework which distinguished between those elements of facial behaviour that are universal and those that are culture-specific. They hypothesized that the universals are to be found in the relationship between distinctive patterns of the facial muscles and particular emotions (happiness, sadness, anger, fear, surprise, disgust, interest). They suggested that cultural differences would be seen in some of the stimuli, which through learning become established as elicitors of particular emotions, in the rules for controlling facial behaviour in particular social settings, and in many of the consequences of emotional arousal.

To demonstrate the hypothesized universal element, Ekman and Friesen (1969) conducted experiments in which they showed still photographs of faces to people from different cultures in order to determine whether the same facial behaviour would be judged as the same emotion, regardless of the observers' culture. The faces were selected on the basis of their conformity to Ekman, Friesen, and Tomkins's (in press) a priori descriptions of facial muscles involved in each emotion. College-educated subjects in Brazil, the United States, Argentina, Chile, and Japan were found to identify the same faces with the same emotion words, as were members of two preliterate cultures who had extensive contact with Western cultures (the Sadong of Borneo and the Fore of New Guinea), although the latter results were not as strong (Ekman, Sorenson and Friesen 1969). Izard (1968, 1969), working independently with his own set of faces, obtained comparable results across seven other culture-language groups.

While these investigators interpreted their results as evidence of universals in facial behaviour, their interpretation was open to argument; because all the cultures they compared had exposure to some of the same mass media portrayals of facial behaviour, members of these cultures might have learned to recognize the same set of conventions, or become familiar with each other's different facial behaviour.

To overcome this difficulty in the interpretation of previous results, it is necessary to demonstrate that cultures which have had minimal visual contact with literate cultures show similarity to these cultures in their interpretation of facial behaviour. The purpose of this paper was to test the hypothesis that members of a preliterate culture who had been selected to insure maximum visual isolation from literate cultures will identify the same emotion concepts with the same faces as do members of literate Western and Eastern cultures.

Method

Subjects

Members of the Fore linguistic–cultural group of the South East Highlands of New Guinea were studied. Until 12 years ago, this was an isolated, Neolithic material culture (Gajdusek 1963, Sorenson and Gajdusek 1966). While many of these people now have had extensive contact with missionaries, government workers, traders, and United States scientists, some have had little such contact. Only subjects who met criteria established to screen out all but those who had minimal opportunity to learn to imitate or recognize uniquely Western facial behaviours were recruited for this experiment. These criteria made it quite unlikely that subjects could have so completely learned some foreign set of facial expressions of emotion that their judgments would be no different from those of members of literate cultures. Those selected had seen no movies, neither spoke nor understood English or Pidgin, had not lived in any of the Western settlement or government towns, and had never worked for a Caucasian (according to their own report). One hundred and eighty-nine adults and 130 children, male and female, met these criteria. This sample comprises about 3 per cent of the members of this culture.

In addition to data gathered from these more visually isolated members of the South Fore, data were also collected on members of this culture who had had the most contact with Westerners. These subjects all spoke English, had seen movies, lived in a Western settlement or government town, and had attended a missionary or government school for more than 1 year. Twenty-three male adults, but no females, met these criteria.

Judgment task

In a pilot study conducted 1 year earlier with members of this same culture, a number of different judgment tasks were tried. The least Westernized subjects could not be asked to select from a printed list of emotion terms the one that was appropriate for a photograph, since they could not read. When the list was repeated to them with each photograph, they seemed to have difficulty remembering the list. Further, doubts remained about whether the meaning of a particular emotion concept was adequately conveyed by translating a single English word into a single South Fore word. Asking the subject to make up his own story about the emotions shown in a picture was not much more successful, although the problems were different. Subjects regarded this as a very difficult task, repeated probes were necessary, and as the procedure became lengthy, subjects became reluctant.

To solve these problems, it was decided to employ a task similar to that developed by Dashiell (1927) for use with young children.[1] Dashiell showed the child a group of three pictures simultaneously, read a story, and told the child to point to the picture in which the person's face showed the emotion described in the story. The advantages of this judgment task in a preliterate culture are that (a) the translator recounts well-rehearsed stories which can be recorded and checked for accurate translation; (b) the task involves no reading; (c) the subject does not have to remember a list of emotion terms; (d) the subject need not speak, but can point to give his answer; and (e) perfect translation of emotion words is not required since the story can help provide connotations.

Emotion stories

With the exception of the stories for fear and surprise, those used in the present study were selected from those which had been most frequently given in the pilot study. Considerable care was taken to insure that each story selected was relevant to only one emotion within the Fore culture, and that members of the culture were agreed on what that emotion was. Since the stories told by the pilot subjects for fear and surprise did not meet these criteria, the authors composed stories for these emotions based on their experience within the culture. The stories used are given below:

Happiness: His (her) friends have come, and he (she) is happy.

Sadness: His (her) child (mother) has died, and he (she) feels very sad.

Anger: He (she) is angry; or he (she) is angry, about to fight.

Surprise: He (she) is just now looking at something new and unexpected.

Disgust: He (she) is looking at something he (she) dislikes; or He (she) is looking at something which smells bad.

Fear: He (she) is sitting in his (her) house all alone, and there is no one else in the village. There is no knife, axe, or bow and arrow in the house. A wild pig is standing in the door of the house, and the man (woman) is looking at the pig and is very afraid of it. The pig has been standing in the doorway for a few minutes, and the person is looking at it very afraid, and the pig won't move away from the door, and he (she) is afraid the pig will bite him (her).[2]

1 Carrol E. Izard brought Dashiell's procedure to our attention. This method has also been used in recent studies of referential communications (e.g. Rosenberg and Gordon 1968).

2 The fear story had to be long in order to eliminate possibilities for anger or surprise being associated with the story.

Pictures and emotions

The six emotions studied were those which had been found by more than one investigator to be discriminable within any one literate culture (cf. Ekman, Friesen and Ellsworth, in press, for a review of findings). The photographs used to show the facial behaviour for each of the six emotions had been judged by more than 70 per cent of the observers in studies of more than one literate culture as showing that emotion. The sample included pictures of both posed and spontaneous behaviour used by Ekman and Friesen (1968), Frijda (1968), Frois-Wittmann (1930), Izard (1968), Engen, Levy and Schlosberg (1957), and Tomkins and McCarter (1964). A total of 40 pictures were used of 24 different stimulus persons, male and female, adult and child. The photographs were prepared as 3×5 inch prints, cropped to show only the face and neck.

Story–photographs trial

A single item consisted of an emotion story, a correct photograph, in which the facial behaviour shown in the photograph was the same as that described in the story, and either one or two incorrect photograph(s). Adult subjects were given two incorrect pictures with each correct picture; children were given only one because of a shortage of copies of the stimuli.

Because of a limitation on the number of available photographs, and upon the subjects' time, not all of the possible pairings of correct and incorrect photographs were tested. Instead, the subjects were presented with some of the presumably more difficult discriminations among emotions. The emotion shown in at least one of the incorrect photographs was an emotion which past studies in literate cultures had found to be most often mistaken for the correct emotion. For example, when *anger* was the emotion described in the story, the incorrect choices included *disgust*, *fear*, or *sadness*, emotions which have been found to be often mistaken for anger. The age and sex of the stimulus persons shown in the correct and incorrect photographs were held constant within any trial.

No one subject was given all the emotion discriminations, because again the stimuli would have been too few and the task too long. Instead, subjects from different villages were required to make some of the same and some different discriminations. Subjects were shown from 6 to 12 sets of photographs, but no picture appeared in more than 1 of the sets shown to any particular subject.[3] A subject's task included making at least three

3 The number of sets of photographs shown varied among villages, because a limited number of photographs were available in this field setting; the need to assure that the three pictures in any one set were comparable (in terms of the configuration of the mouth, the tilt of the head, and the age of the stimulus persons) restricted the number of sets which could be composed for some of the combinations.

different emotion discriminations; the same story was told more than once, with differing correct and incorrect photographs, and often requiring discriminations among differing sets of emotions. For example, the anger story might have been read once with Anger Picture A, Sadness Picture B, and Fear Picture C; the same anger story might have been read again to the same subject, but now with Anger Picture D, Disgust Picture E, and Surprise Picture F.

Procedure

Two-person teams conducted the experiment. A member of the South Fore tribe recruited subjects, explained the task, and read the translated stories; a Caucasian recorded the subjects' responses. Three such teams operated at once within a village; one team with a male Caucasian worked with male adult subjects; the two others with female Caucasians worked with the female adult subjects and the children. In most instances, almost all members of a village participated in the experiment within less than 3 hours.

Considerable practice and explanation was given to the translators. They were told that there was no correct response and were discouraged from prompting. Repeated practice was given to insure that the translators always repeated the stories in the same way and resisted the temptation to embellish. Spot checks with tape recordings and back translations verified that this was successful. The Caucasians, who did know the correct responses, averted their faces from the view of the subject, looking down at their recording booklet, to reduce the probability of an unwitting experimenter bias effect. Data analysis did not reveal any systematic differences in the responses obtained with different translators.

Results

No differences between male and female subjects were expected, and no such differences had been found in the literate culture data. In this New Guinea group, however, the women were more reluctant to participate in the experiment, and were considered by most outsiders to have had less contact with Caucasians than the men. The number of correct responses for each subject was calculated separately for males and females and for adults and children. The t tests were not significant; the trend was in the direction of better performance by women and girls. The data revealed no systematic differences between male and female subjects in the discrimination of particular emotions, or in relation to the sex of the stimulus person shown on the photographs. In the subsequent analyses, data from males and females were combined.

Table I shows the results for the least Westernized adults for each emotion discrimination. Within each row, the percentage of subjects who gave the correct response for a particular discrimination between three emotions was calculated across all subjects shown that particular discrimination, regardless of whether the photographs used to represent the three emotions differed for individual subjects. Within each row, each subject contributed only one response, and thus the sum of responses was derived from independent subjects. However, the rows are not independent of each other. Data from a given subject appear in different rows, depending upon the particular discriminations he was asked to make. If a group of subjects are requested to discriminate the same emotion from the

Table 1 Adult results

Emotion described in the story	*Emotions shown in the two incorrect photographs*	*No. Ss*	*% choosing correct face*
Happiness	Surprise, disgust	62	90†
	Surprise, sadness	57	93†
	Fear, anger	65	86†
	Disgust, anger	36	100†
Anger	Sadness, surprise	66	82†
	Disgust, surprise	31	87†
	Fear, sadness	31	87†
Sadness	Anger, fear	64	81†
	Anger, surprise	26	81†
	Anger, happiness	31	87†
	Anger, disgust	35	69*
	Disgust, surprise	35	77†
Disgust (smell story)	Sadness, surprise	65	77†
Disgust (dislike story)	Sadness, surprise	36	89†
Surprise	Fear, disgust	31	71*
	Happiness, anger	31	65*
Fear	Anger, disgust	92	64†
	Sadness, disgust	31	87†
	Anger, happiness	35	86†
	Disgust, happiness	26	85†
	Surprise, happiness	65	48
	Surprise, disgust	31	52
	Surprise, sadness	57	28[a]

* $p < 0{\cdot}05$.
† $p < 0{\cdot}01$.
[a] Subjects selected the surprise face (67%) at a significant level ($p < 0{\cdot}01$, two-tailed test).

Table 2 Results for children

Emotion described in the story	*Emotion shown in the* one *incorrect photograph*	*No. Ss*	% *choosing the correct face*
Happiness	Surprise	116	87*
	Sadness	25	96*
	Anger	25	100*
	Disgust	25	88*
Anger	Sadness	69	90*
Sadness	Anger	60	85*
	Surprise	33	76*
	Disgust	27	89*
	Fear	25	76*
Disgust (smell story)	Sadness	19	95*
Disgust (dislike story)	Sadness	27	78*
Surprise	Happiness	14	100*
	Disgust	14	100*
	Fear	19	95*
Fear	Sadness	25	92*
	Anger	25	88*
	Disgust	14	100*

$^{*}p \leq 0{\cdot}01$.

same two other emotions more than once, only one randomly chosen response was included in the table.

A binomial test of significance assuming chance performance to be one in three showed that the correct face was chosen at a significant level for all of the discriminations (rows) except that of fear from surprise. Twice, fear was not discriminated from surprise, and once surprise was chosen more often than fear, even though the story had been intended to describe fear. A binomial test assuming chance to be one in two (a more conservative test, justified if it was thought that within a set of three pictures, there may have been one which was obviously wrong) still yielded significant correct choices for all but the fear-from-surprise discriminations.

The results for the most Westernized male adults were almost exactly the same as those reported in Table 1 for the least Westernized male and female adults. The number of correct responses for each subject was calculated; the *t* test showed no significant difference between the most and least Westernized subjects. Again, the only failure to select the correct picture occurred when fear was to be distinguished from surprise.

Table 2 shows the results for the children, tabulated and tested in similar fashion. The children selected the correct face for all of their discriminations. Through an oversight, the one discrimination which the adults could not make, fear from surprise, was not tried with the children. The percentages reported in Table 2 are generally higher than those in Table 1, but this is probably due to the fact that the children were given two photographs rather than three, and chance performance would be 50 per cent rather than about 33 per cent. Six- and 7-year-old children were compared with 14- and 15-year-olds, by the same procedures as described for comparing males and females. No significant differences or trends were noted.

Discussion

The results for both adults and children clearly support our hypothesis that particular facial behaviours are universally associated with particular emotions. With but one exception, the faces judged in literate cultures as showing particular emotions were comparably judged by people from a preliterate culture who had minimal opportunity to have learned to recognize uniquely Western facial expressions. Further evidence was obtained in another experiment, in which the facial behaviour of these New Guineans was accurately recognized by members of a literate culture. In that study, visually isolated members of the South Fore posed emotions, and college students in the United States accurately judged the emotion intended from their videotaped facial behaviour. The evidence from both studies contradicts the view that all facial behaviour associated with emotion is culture-specific, and that posed facial behaviour is a unique set of culture-bound conventions not understandable to members of another culture.[4]

The only way to dismiss the evidence from both the judgment and posing studies would be to claim that even these New Guineans who had not seen movies, who did not speak or understand English or Pidgin, who had never worked for a Caucasian, still had *some* contact with Westerners, sufficient contact for them to learn to recognize and simulate culture-specific, uniquely Western facial behaviours associated with each emotion. While these subjects had some contact with Westerners, this argument

4 If posed behaviour were simply a set of arbitrary conventions, it would be unlikely that the same conventions would be ultilized in the cultures discussed here. That does not, however, imply that posed facial behaviour is identical with spontaneous behaviour. Ekman, Friesen and Ellsworth (in press) have suggested that most posed behaviour is similar in appearance to that spontaneous facial behaviour which is of extreme intensity and unmodulated, although it may still differ in onset, duration and decay time.

seems implausible for three reasons. First, the criteria for selecting these subjects makes it highly improbable that they had learned a 'foreign' set of facial behaviours to such a degree that they could not only recognize them, but also display them as well as those to whom the behaviours were native. Second, contact with Caucasians did not seem to have much influence on the judgment of emotion, since the most Westernized subjects did no better than the least Westernized and, like the latter, failed to distinguish fear from surprise. Third, the women, who commonly have even less contact with Westerners than the men, did as well in recognizing emotions.

The hypothesis that there are constants across cultures in emotional facial behaviour is further supported by Eibl-Eibesfeldt's (1970) films of facial behaviour occurring within its natural context in a number of pre-literate cultures. Evidence of constants in facial behaviour and emotion across cultures is also consistent with early studies which showed many similarities between the facial behaviour of blind and sighted children (Fulcher 1942, Goodenough 1932, Thompson 1941). Universals in facial behaviour associated with emotion can be explained from a number of nonexclusive viewpoints as being due to evolution, innate neural programmes, or learning experiences common to human development regardless of culture (e.g., those of Allport 1924, Asch 1952, Darwin 1872, Huber 1931, Izard 1969, Peiper 1963, Tomkins 1962, 1963). To evaluate the different viewpoints will require further research, particularly on early development.

The failure of the New Guinean adults to discriminate fear from surprise, while succeeding in discriminating surprise from fear, and fear from other emotions, suggests that cultures may not make *all* of the same distinctions among emotions, but does not detract from the main finding that most of the distinctions were made across cultures. Experience within a culture, the kinds of events which typically elicit particular emotions, may act to influence the ability to discriminate particular pairs of emotions. Fear faces may not have been distinguished from surprise faces, because in this culture fearful events are almost always also surprising; that is, the sudden appearance of a hostile member of another village, the unexpected meeting of a ghost or sorcerer, etc.

The growing body of evidence of a pan-cultural element in emotional facial behaviour does not imply the absence of cultural differences in the face and emotion. Ekman (1968) and Ekman and Friesen (1969) have suggested that cultural differences will be manifest in the circumstances which elicit an emotion, in the action consequences of an emotion, and in the display rules which govern the management of facial behaviour in particular social settings. Izard (1969) agrees with the view that there are cultural differences in the antecedent and consequent events, and has also found evidence suggesting differences in attitudes about particular emotions.

References

ALLPORT, F. H. (1924) *Social psychology* Boston, Houghton Mifflin.

ASCH, S. E. (1952) *Social psychology* Englewood Cliffs, N.J., Prentice-Hall.

BIRDWHISTELL, R. L. (1963) 'The kinesic level in the investigation of the emotions' in Knapp, P. H. (ed.), *Expression of the emotions in man* New York, International Universities Press.

DARWIN, C. (1872) *The expression of the emotion in man and animals* London, Murray.

DASHIELL, J. F. (1927) 'A new method of measuring reactions to facial expression of emotion', *Psychological Bulletin*, **24**, 174–5.

EIBL-EIBESFELDT, I. (1970) *Ethology, the biology of behavior* New York, Holt, Rinehart and Winston.

EKMAN, P. (1968) 'Research findings on recognition and display of facial behavior in literate and nonliterature cultures', *Proceedings of the 76th Annual Convention of the American Psychological Association*, **3**, 727 (Summary).

EKMAN, P. and FRIESEN, W. V. (1968) 'Nonverbal behavior in psychotherapy research' in Shlien, J. (ed.) *Research in psychotherapy, Vol. 3*, Washington, D.C., American Psychological Association.

EKMAN, P. and FRIESEN, W. V. (1969) 'The repertoire of nonverbal behavior – Categories, origins, usage and coding', *Semiotica*, **1**, 49–98.

EKMAN, P., FRIESEN, W. V. and ELLSWORTH P. *Emotion in the human face: Guidelines for research and integration of findings* New York, Pergamon Press, in press.

EKMAN, P., FRIESEN, W. V. and TOMKINS, S. S. 'Facial affect scoring technique: A first validity study'. *Semiotica*, in press.

EKMAN, P., SORENSON, E. R. and FRIESEN, W. V. (1969) 'Pan-cultural elements in facial displays of emotions', *Science*, **164**, 86–88.

ENGEN, T., LEVY, N. and SCHLOSBERG, H. (1957) 'A new series of facial expressions', *American Psychologist*, **12**, 264–6.

FRIJDA, N. H. (1968) 'Recognition of emotion' in Berkowitz L. (ed.) *Advances in experimental social psychology* New York, Academic Press.

FROIS-WITTMANN, J. (1930) 'The judgment of facial expression', *Journal of Experimental Psychology*, **13**, 113–51.

FULCHER, J. S. (1942) '"Voluntary" facial expression in blind and seeing children', *Archives of Psychology*, **38**, 272.

GAJDUSEK, D. C. (1963) 'Kuru', *Transactions of the Royal Society of Tropical Medicine and Hygiene*, **57**, 151–69.

GOODENOUGH, F. L. (1932) 'Expression of the emotions in a blind-deaf child', *Journal of Abnormal and Social Psychology*, **27**, 328–33.

HUBER, E. (1931) *Evolution of facial musculature and facial expression* Baltimore, Johns Hopkins Press.

IZARD, C. E. (1968) 'Cross-cultural research findings on development in recognition of facial behavior', *Proceedings of the 76th Annual Convention of the American Psychological Association*, 3, 727 (Summary).

IZARD, C. E. (1969) 'The emotions and emotion constructs in personality and culture research' in Cattell, R. B. (ed.) *Handbook of modern personality theory* Chicago, Aldine Press.

KLINEBERG, O. (1938) 'Emotional expression in Chinese literature', *Journal of Abnormal and Social Psychology*, 33, 517–20.

LABARRE, W. (1947) 'The cultural basis of emotions and gestures', *Journal of Personality*, 16, 49–68.

PEIPER, A. (1963) *Cerebral function in infancy and childhood* New York: Consultants Bureau.

ROSENBERG, S., and GORDON, A. (1968) 'Identification of facial expressions from affective descriptions. A probabilistic choice analysis of referential ambiguity', *Journal of Personality and Social Psychology*, 10, 157–66.

SORENSON, E. R. and GAJDUSEK, D. C. (1966) 'The study of child behavior and development in primitive cultures. A research archive for ethnopediatric film investigations of styles in the patterning of the nervous system', *Pediatrics*, 37 (1, Pt. 2).

THOMPSON, J. (1941) 'Development of facial expression of emotion in blind and seeing children', *Archives of Psychology*, 37, 264.

TOMKINS, S. S. (1962) *Affect, imagery, consciousness. Vol 1. The positive affects* New York, Springer.

TOMKINS, S. S. (1963) *Affect, imagery, consciousness. Vol. 2. The negative affects* New York, Springer.

TOMKINS, S. S. and MCCARTER, R. (1964) 'What and where are the primary affects? Some evidence for a theory', *Perceptual and Motor Skills*, 18, 119–58.

26 Cultural influences in the perception of people: The case of Chinese in America

Stanley L. M. Fong

Summary

The social perception of 336 Chinese college students in America was studied. The results indicate that as the Chinese are becoming progressively removed from their ethnic culture and in greater contact with the host culture, they show an increase in their internalization of the affective–cognitive norms of western culture. However, the Chinese from urban Hong Kong showed a greater degree of internalization than Chinese from other areas of China and even some of the Chinese generations in America.

Introduction

Cultural groups vary widely from one another in their expressive behaviour. As a result, Chinese and Americans, for example, differ in their interpretation of the emotions displayed in photographs of each other (Vinacke 1949, Vinacke and Fong 1955).

It may be hypothesized that as Chinese in America become progressively removed from the influence of Chinese culture and in greater contact with the host culture, they will show an increase in their internalization of western affective–cognitive norms. Thus, they will develop, to a growing extent, a predisposition to perceive as Americans do.

The second hypothesis is that Chinese from modern Asian cities, where western influence has made much inroad, such as Hong Kong, will show a greater degree of internalization than those from rural China or even some of the Chinese reared in America. The basis of this hypothesis is that the Chinese in America have not become assimilated as rapidly as other ethnic minority groups. This state of affairs is partly due to anti-Oriental sentiment, chiefly before World War II, on the one hand, and to the multitude of ethnocentric institutions in the ghettoes, where old-world customs have flourished, on the other (Lee 1960).

FONG, STANLEY L. M. (1965) 'Cultural influences in the perception of people: The case of Chinese in America' in *British Journal of Social and Clinical Psychology*, vol. 4, 110–13.

Method

Subjects

The subjects were 336 Chinese college students in America, ranging from first (i.e. China-born) to fifth generations. There were 158 males and 178 females. The mean age was 21 years. There were 57 China-born subjects; of these, 24 were born or had lived largely in Hong Kong before coming to America. The Hong Kong and the non-Hong Kong Chinese, both of the first generation, were treated separately because of the above expectation of differences between these two groups. The median length of American residence for the Hong Kong group was 4 years; the remaining members of the first generation (i.e. non-Hong Kong) was 9 years (this difference is significant at the 0·05 level).

Personal data form

This form contained actuarial items such as age, sex, generation, citizenship, area of residence, ethnicity of social groups, intimate friends, and proficiency in the Chinese language. The particular sociological indices could be arranged in an order of progressive removal from Chinese culture, such as from first to fifth generation, and so on (see Table 1). In general, the items were presented in multiple-choice form.

Stick figures test

The Stick Figures Test was used to measure the subjects' recognition of the expressive modes of the American culture. The test consisted of a series of forty-three simple line drawings of human-like stick figures, drawn to represent a wide range of expressive states (see examples in Sarbin and Hardyck 1955, Sarbin 1954). The figures varied only in pose or posture in a manner that allowed various emotional and attitudinal states to be attributed to or projected onto them. The subject could therefore base his perceptual response only on gestural and postural cues and was not influenced by any stereotyped attributes of physique, clothing, social status, and ethnic identity. The test, thus, provides no clear cue to the socially 'correct' response. For each figure, the subject was instructed to select one of five adjectives (empirically tailored to each figure) which best described his judgment of the emotion or attitude being expressed. A blank space was also provided for each figure, to be filled in when none of the adjectives adequately described his impressions. For each figure, a modal response (i.e. the most frequently chosen adjective) had been determined from a large Caucasian–American sample of college students (Sarbin and Hardyck 1955). The test score for each Chinese subject was simply the number of stick figures on which he gave the modal Caucasian–American response.

Results

Salient sociological indices of progressive removal which yielded significant results on the Stick Figures Test are presented in Table 1. The Kruskal–Wallis H Test (Siegel 1956) was used to evaluate the significance of the results. For all sociological categories shown, the H Test was significant beyond the 0·05 level. Most important, the various subgroups within each category yielded mean ranks which fell, in almost every instance, exactly in the expected order, i.e. from least to most progressive removal. The results, therefore, supported the hypothesis that the internalization of western norms increases with the progressive removal from the ethnic culture.

Moreover, the Hong Kong group had the second highest mean rank among the various Chinese generations. The evidence, therefore, supported the second hypothesis that the Hong Kong Chinese have internalized western cultural norms to a greater extent than the other first-generation members. But perhaps of equal interest is that their scores were higher than all the American-born generations except for the fifth. Indeed the high scores of the Hong Kong group were closely comparable to Caucasian–American norms, as presented by Hardyck (1957).

The view that cultural forces of western life have altered the affective–cognitive processes of the Chinese is supported by the present study. These positive results contribute to a growing body of evidence indentifying these psychological dimensions which become transformed as acculturation proceeds. It has been observed that the overt facial expressions and mannerisms of Chinese in America undergo change with progressive removal (Adams 1937). Also, Abel and Hsu (1949) found that the nature of emotional control of Chinese alters in favour of the expressiveness and spontaneity indigenous to the American scene. We suggest that the present utilization of purely perceptual stimuli provides an approach to the diffuse study of the acculturation process that minimizes the effects of pressures to conform (to give the socially desirable or 'correct' response, etc.).

Table 1 Mean ranks of Stick Figures Test

Indices of progressive removal	*Mean rank*	*Group size*
Generation		
First	114·0	33
Second	166·7	121
Third	180·3	133
Fourth	166·7	22
Fifth	192·2	3
Hong Kong	186·4	24
	H = 13·4*	336
Residence†		
In China	103·7	36
In Chinatown	138·7	24
Near Chinatown	140·7	64
Away from Chinatown	150·9	38
In white neighbourhood	155·2	124
	H = 11·3*	286‡
Intimate Friends		
China-born	108·6	32
American-born Chinese	145·5	214
Caucasians	160·8	40
	H = 7·6*	286
Ability to speak Chinese		
Can	160·3	238
Cannot	188·2	98
	H = 5·7*	336

* Significant beyond the 0·05 level.
† Where the subject has lived most of his life.
‡ Missing answers or more than one answer for the item of the Personal Data Form led to the omission of a subject from the analysis. This disparity among the total N is due to these omissions.

References

ABEL, T. M. and HSU, F. L. K. (1949) 'Some aspects of personality of Chinese as revealed by the Rorschach test', *Rorschach Res. Exch.*, 13, 285–301.

ADAMS, R. (1937) *Interracial Marriage in Hawaii* New York, Macmillan.

HARDYCK, C. (1957) *Communality: A Definition and Criteria for measurement* (Unpublished manuscript).

LEE, R. H. (1960) *The Chinese in the United States of America* Hong Kong, Hong Kong University Press.

SARBIN, T. R. (1954) 'Role theory' in Lindzey, G. (ed.) *Handbook of Social Psychology*, vol. 1, pp. 223–58, Mass., Allison-Wesley.

SARBIN, T. R. and HARDYCK, C. (1955) 'Conformance in role perception as a personality variable', *Journal Cons. Psychol.*, **19**, 109–11.

SIEGEL, S. (1956) *Nonparametric statistics* New York, McGraw-Hill.

VINACKE, W. E. (1949) 'The judgment of facial expressions by three national-racial groups in Hawaii: I', *Journal of Personality*, **17**, 407–29.

VINACKE, W. E. and FONG, R. W. (1955) 'The judgment of facial expressions by three national-racial groups in Hawaii: II Orient faces', *Journal of Social Psychology*, **41**, 185–95.

Plate 1a Deaf-blind 7-year-old girl, laughing. When fully laughing, she throws her head back, opens her mouth, and laughs audibly, although restrained. (Photograph: I. Eibl-Eibesfeldt.)

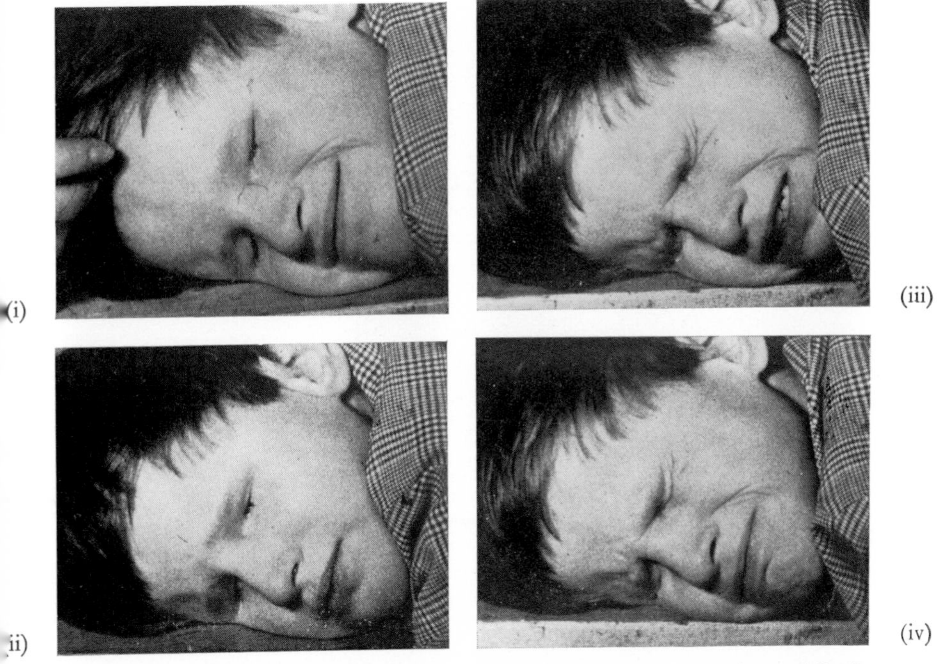

Plate 1b A deaf-blind girl (9 years old). Transition from smiling to weeping and finally to crying. This is the same girl as in Plate 1a.

Plate 2 Flirting Turkana woman (Lorukumu, Kenya) as an example of successive ambivalence. She makes contact with the eyes, laughs, lowers the head (in embarrassment?) and eyelids, and repeats full contact with the eyes. From a slow-motion sequence (48 frames per second). The entire sequence includes 6·04 seconds (290 frames). (Photographs: H. Hass.)

Plate 3 Eyebrow-flash during greeting. Papua, Huri tribe near Tari, New Guinea. The sequence lasts 45 frames. Twenty-six frames after he had started to smile, he began to lift the eyebrows, and 4 frames later they were maximally raised and held so over 7 frames. (Photographs: I. Eibl-Eibesfeldt.)

Plate 4 Left: A Schom Pen (Great Nicobar Island) greets by raising the open hand; right: a woman from Karamojo (Africa) greeting in the same manner. (Photographs: I. Eibl-Eibesfeldt.)

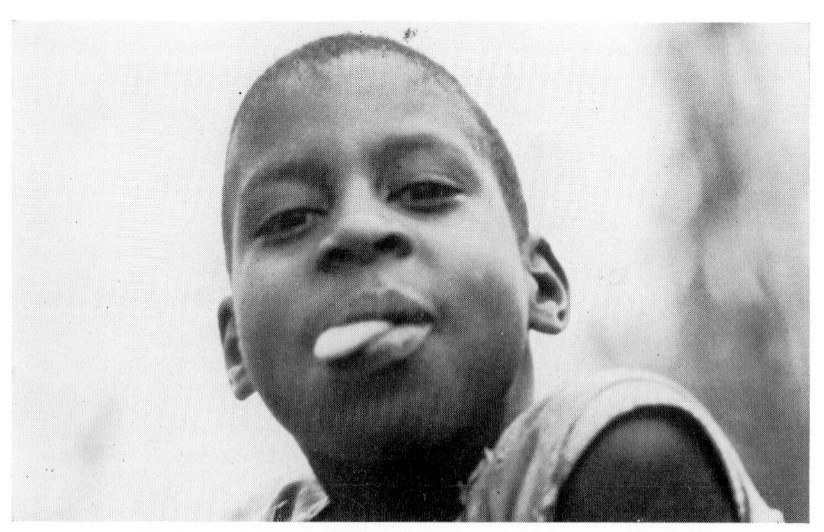

Plate 5 Showing the tongue, a widespread gesture of disdainful rejection, a Negro boy from the Bihamarulu region (Tanzania). (Photograph: I. Eibl-Eibesfeldt.)

Section 9
Man's experience of the world

Introduction

At times, social psychologists seem so concerned with describing and explaining the *processes* by which men acquire their knowledge of the world that they do less than justice to the actual nature of that knowledge as it is experienced by the human being. The following extracts are all concerned with the ways in which we experience the world, with our consciousness of everyday life. They are enquiries into our subjective constructions of the world, and into the ways in which these subjective constructions are influenced by historical, cultural and situational factors.

Benita Luckmann, for example, contrasts traditional and contemporary views of the 'life-world', considering the changes which have occurred over time in our subjective maps of social reality. By contrast, Joseph Bensman and Robert Lilienfeld concentrate more specifically upon the consciousness of life which is generated by one's involvement within a particular craft or occupation. The practice of journalism, they argue, involves the treatment of information about the world in a specialized manner and this in turn induces a particular subjective view of the world and its arrangements. The writers indicate the ways in which the export of this journalistic attitude into other areas of life affects the actual meanings which are ascribed to the activities and operations of a large range of institutions.

The selection on 'Time' is taken from some research conducted by Stanley Cohen and Laurie Taylor into the effects of long-term imprisonment. This represents an even more specific contribution to our understanding of the experience of life in that it focuses upon a single aspect of consciousness as realized in a very particular situation. The passage of time is typically taken for granted in everyday life; we recognize it as a feature of our lives, but it rarely becomes a matter which requires reflection or interpretation. However, for long-term prisoners who face the prospect of spending as long as twenty-five years in prison, time suddenly becomes problematic. The years ahead are not neatly structured in occupational, educational or domestic careers as they are for men outside. Instead, these men have to construct new ways of ordering time and of making time pass.

Each of the articles has a phenomenological basis. Their starting-point is the attitude which individuals hold towards everyday life or towards aspects of everyday life. This is not the scientific or objective attitude in which features of the world are regarded as objectively measurable units, but rather the common-sense or natural attitude in which such features are simply accepted as 'the way the world is'. The three selections show how this sense of the constancy of our subjective experience of the world may be undermined by demonstrations of how such consciousness is influenced by the nature of the society in which we live (Luckmann), by the nature of our occupational involvement in that world (Bensman and Lilienfeld) and by over-confrontation with certain situational predicaments (Cohen and Taylor).

The mode of analysis which is illustrated by these examples simultaneously claims to deal with 'psychological' and 'sociological' features of human existence in that it attempts to construct a relationship between man's consciousness of the world and the nature of his activity within that world. It has much in common with recent developments in cognitive social psychology, particularly those developments which deal with the organization of attitudes and knowledge (cognitive dissonance, cognitive maps) but it may be distinguished from them by the greater emphasis it lays upon the coherence of all subjective experience ('the natural attitude') and by its stress upon the ways in which such subjective constructions of reality are rendered relative by their dependence upon the nature of man's involvement in the world.

27 The small life-worlds of modern man

Benita Luckmann

Husserl speaks of 'our everyday life-world' (*unsere alltaegliche Lebenswelt*) as the world which man experiences at every point of his existence as immediately and simply given.[1] Comprising objects, trees, animals, men, values and goods, it is an intersubjective, i.e. a social world in which man experiences the whole round of his life. It is a world of practical interest to man, a familiar world, a world taken for granted.

The everyday life-world extends indefinitely in space and time. Man's interests, however, focus on '. . . that sector of the world of his everyday life which is within his scope and which is centred in space and time around himself'.[2] Embedded in the *Lebenswelt* which in various degrees of closeness and distance surrounds them as a '. . . darkly perceived horizon of undetermined reality',[3] these sectors of everyday life are only sub-universes of human existence. They are not separate and independent social 'wholes'. In different ways – directly and indirectly – they are connected and bound to larger and still larger 'outside worlds'. Living in his 'small life-worlds', man may perceive the receding horizons of the *Lebenswelt* acutely or dimly. They may represent 'outside worlds' of which his small community appears to be an integral part, as in the case of traditional societies. They may also be conceived of as non-human worlds of animals, ghosts, demons, which surround and threaten or protect the existence of the tribal isolate. In late industrial society the segment of the life-world actually 'inhabited' by man consists of many small worlds. These are located within the 'private' as well as the institutional spheres of existence. Though of different degrees of importance and necessity to man's existence, none of them represents a 'whole' life-world in which all of man's life unfolds. One can rather speak of man's part-time existence in part-time societies. To describe

1 Edmund Husserl, *Ideen zu einer reinen Phaenomenologie und Phaenomenologischen Philosophie*, Vol. 1, The Hague: Martinus Nijhoff, 1950 (First edition 1913), especially §§ 27, 28, 29, 30; and *Krisis der Europaeischen Wissenschaften und die transzendentale Phaenomenologie*, The Hague: Martinus Nijhoff, 1954, especially §§ 9 and 33 ff.

2 Alfred Schutz, *On Multiple Realities*, in *Collected Papers*, The Hague: Martinus Nijhoff, 1962, p. 222.

3 Edmund Husserl: *Ideen, op. cit.*, § 27, p. 58 (my translation).

LUCKMANN, BENITA (1970) 'The small life-worlds of modern man' in *Social Research*, vol. 37, 580–96.

tentatively the multi-dimensional nature of everyday life in contemporary society I shall speak of the small life-worlds of man.

The historically predominant life experience of man has taken place within the more or less well defined limits of small communities. The tribe, the clan, the village, the small town represented kinds of small worlds within which all of man's living was done. Of these small life-worlds with distinct territories, a high degree of self-sufficiency and shared beliefs in what constitutes the good life, man possessed detailed and intimate knowledge. He knew all or most of the other inhabitants as fellow-hunters, chiefs, guardians of the sacred lore, relatives, neighbours, witches, dog catchers, beggars, grocers, etc., whom he encountered in his daily rounds in face-to-face relationships. He knew his own 'pre-ordained' place in the community and could predict the actions and reactions of his fellow-men with considerable certainty. He knew about the 'right order of things' in his community and it 'made sense' to him. He knew that this *right order of existence* to which he was 'attuned'[4] through his life within the community was approved by the gods and should not be disturbed, lest it be destroyed, or he himself cast out, which 'would be like death'.[5] The fears and anxieties originating mainly in the surrounding world of nature, and the conflict situations of his social life notwithstanding, traditional man moved within his small life-world with a certain ease and safety. Acting in accordance with the generally recognized norms and expectations which emanated from the common world view, he participated in a continuity of being which transcended not only his own life but that of his family – in most instances that of his community as well.

While representing separate existential and political units the traditional communities were at the same time parts of larger societies. To these they were connected by stronger or weaker – but always intermediary – links: the feudal landlord who dispensed the justice of the king; the starosta of the mir who collected taxes for the tsar; the distantly related bureaucrat who as a minor official in the capital could intervene in behalf of a deserving cousin; the travelling salesman who told his tall stories of the Babylonian wonders of the city; the visiting opera company which performed the legendary events of the cosmological myths, etc. The filtered knowledge about the larger society was incomplete and fragmentary. In the slow process of passing from one institutional level to the next – on a vertical as well

4 Cf. Eric Voegelin, *Order and History*, Vol. 1.: *Israel and Revelation*, Baton Rouge Louisiana State University Press, 1956, pp. 4, 9.

5 Essence of the answer of a peasant respondent ('tradition-minded') to the question where he would like to live if he could not live in his native village. Reported by Daniel Lerner in *The Passing of Traditional Society*, New York: The Free Press of Glencoe, 1964, p. 25.

as on a horizontal plane – social knowledge, while being absorbed and transformed, was fitted into the already established conceptual framework of the small society. In a reverse but synchronized process the little community was fitted into the plan of the larger society and beyond it into the order of the cosmos or the universal God.

To be sure, life in the communities of traditional society is seen 'looking backwards' as to a 'finished product' – when the actual communities have already disappeared, are disappearing or undergoing fast and dramatic changes. Aristotle, at the imperial court of Alexander the Great, wrote about the 'good life' of the polis after its fall; Redfield wrote about the 'wholeness' and 'homogeneity' of 'folk culture' in Chan Kom when the village had already 'chosen progress'. The classical sociologists (Tönnies, Durkheim, Maine and others), trying to provide systematic presentations of industrial society did so against the backdrop of an ideal-typical construct of traditional society. Other social scientists of different schools of thought and methodological persuasions in trying to make visible and understandable life in communities of pre-literate and classic societies have in most instances presented it in self-sufficient isolation or cosmic harmony: The '. . . small, closely integrated social units . . .'[6] are seen as 'cosmions', 'illuminated with meaning from within',[7] existing '. . . for all the business and pleasure of living'.[8] Very much as a jeweller would lovingly display a precious stone on a velvet tray and in the best of lights, anthropologists and sociologists present traditional small life-worlds against the stated or implied 'urbanism', 'disorganization', 'heterogeneity', or 'segmentation' of modern 'mass' society.

The bi-polar systems of explanation (Gemeinschaft–Gesellschaft; mechanical–organic solidarity, status–contract, sacred–secular, folk–urban, collectivistic-individualistic societies, etc.) explicitly or implicitly point to the loss of unity, meaning, harmony, satisfaction in the transition from traditional to modern life. But theoretical constructs meant to generalize and to compare are not found existing in their 'pure form'. They are not to be confused with the social reality as actually experienced by man living in traditional small communities. There is no doubt that, as for all men, life in traditional societies, too, has had its share of burdens, anxieties and frustrations. The fear of hunger, disease, wild animals, thunder, eclipse,

6 Ralph Linton, *The Study of Man*, New York: D. Appleton-Century Co., 1936, pp. 283–284.
7 Eric Voegelin, *The New Science of Politics*, Chicago: University of Chicago Press, 1952, p. 27.
8 Robert Redfield, 'How Human Society Operates,' in *Man, Culture and Society*. Harry L. Shapiro (ed.), New York: Oxford University Press, 1960, p. 345.

drought, floods; the worries and terrors about mistakes in ritual performances which might not have sufficiently pleased the gods or assuaged the demons; the temptations of the Devil and the wrath of God must have been very real and disruptive experiences of traditional or 'primitive' man. This is not to underestimate the actual structural and cultural differences between traditional and modern societies, nor to minimize the changes in the perception of social reality as more or less meaningful to individual existence.

The intricate and complex processes of industrialization which led to a segmentation, specialization and 'rationalization' of institutions also eroded the beliefs in a cosmological order[9] of traditional societies. Separate institutional spheres acquired a degree of autonomy which permitted them to develop their own 'rationally' founded legitimations and to withdraw, as it were, from a hierarchically interlocked system of representations of society as a whole.[10] The accompanying increased division of labour, the increase in specialized role performances, the diversification of loyalty claims, to mention but a few manifestations of modernization, have accordingly affected the coherence of individual biography as well as the microcosmic character of the small communities. Both have lost their 'wholeness'.[11]

Contemporary man no longer 'naturally'[12] sees himself as a useful and necessary member of a social whole geared into a meaningful plan of existence within the totality of a cosmic or divine order. The transcendence-continuum which in traditional society reached out from the centre of individual life within the community, through the various spatial units of outer society into the encompassing order of the cosmos has been broken. We may speak of a *transcendentia interrupta* which perhaps more than any other single phenomenon of modern life accounts for the 'great feeling of meaninglessness, a search for something to grab hold of, some unifying thing',[13] experienced by modern man.

The separate institutional spheres which appear to function according to their own laws and pursue their own separate goals alternately or in

9 Cf. Voegelin, *Order and History, op. cit.*, Vol. I, pp. 1–52.

10 Cf. among others Ralf Dahrendorf, *Class and Class Conflict in Industrial Society*, London: Routledge & Kegan Paul, 1968, in which he develops the term 'institutional isolation'.

11 Cf. Arnold Gehlen, *Sozialpsychologische Probleme in der industriellen Gesellschaft*, Tübingen: J. C. B. Mohr (Paul Siebeck), 1949.

12 Cf. Max Scheler's concept of the 'relative-natural world view' ('relativnatürliche Weltanschauung'), as developed in *Die Wissenformen und die Gesellschaft*, Bern: Francke, 1960 (First published in 1925).

13 Quoted from an interview reported by Steven V. Roberts in 'The Better Earth', *New York Times Magazine*, March 29, 1970.

combination dominate various parts and particles of man's daily life. Like a Kafkaesque creation, man may try to come to terms with them to get them in his grasp and fight imaginary and losing battles against them in the process. They continue to make compelling demands on him. Yet none of them provides him with knowledge and guidelines for fitting his whole life experience and eventual death into the order of larger society and beyond it. After satisfying the institutional claims, he is left free – a freedom, it would seem, for which in the course of history man has fought persistently and passionately – to pick up the loose strands of his existence and fit them together as best he can.

The domains of freedom interpenetrating the institutionally controlled life of modern man have come to be called his 'private sphere'.[14] A relatively recent dimension of the social structure and of human existence, it is located between and within the institutionally defined 'spheres of interests' and represents a 'no man's land', unclaimed by the powers that be. Within its confines man is free to choose and decide on his own what to do with his time, his home, his body and his gods.

Lacking institutional means [15] to define new cultural goals and thereby to give the uncertainties of his life and the certainty of his death a unity and meaning which could enable him to transcend them, man can turn to the 'idea market' in which industries, ideologies, prophets, cranks and 'beautiful people' compete in their offerings of 'meaning', 'fulfilment', 'happiness', 'oblivion', 'truth' and 'togetherness'. In his socially undirected and uninhibited (though certainly not unlimited) freedom he can choose to 'freak out on Jesus' to satisfy his 'spiritual hunger',[16] to join 'man's most advanced school of the mind' and through Dianetics 'rid himself of unwanted feelings and sensations, and achieve a new enthusiasm towards life'; or to wind up with an 'oom' feeling at Esalen. He can take an 'acid trip' to overcome his loneliness, alienation, mistrust, his 'horrible state of misery',[17] and he can chant with the Soka Gakkai and achieve '. . . a natural high, an essential high, a universal high' (he can also chant for a bass fiddle or a new refrigerator). [18] He can take to the streets 'in a show of

14 Cf. Thomas Luckmann, *The Invisible Religion*, New York: The Macmillan Co., 1967; also, John Kenneth Galbraith, *The Affluent Society*, Cambridge: Houghton Mifflin Co., 1958, esp. Ch. XVIII.

15 Cf. Robert Merton, *Social Theory and Social Structure*, Glencoe: The Free Press, 1959, esp. Ch. IV.

16 From an interview reported by Edward B. Fiske in 'New Youth Groups "Freaked Out" on Jesus', *New York Times*, February 22, 1970.

17 Description of socio-psychological state of youth addicts by Dr. Donald H. Louria, President, New York State Council on Drug Addiction, as reported by Lacey Fosburgh in 'Experts Predict a Flood of Heroin in U.S. Schools', *New York Times*, February 5, 1970.

18 '2,000,000 Americans Attracted to Buddhist Sect', *New York Times*, March 8, 1970.

strength and determination and hope' and 'stay in the streets' where he can be together with others who share his food, his music and his thoughts.[19] He can 'tune in' rather than 'out' to participate in the mysteries of 'The Poetry of the Rock'. He can order the *Whole Earth Catalog* to provide him with 'tools . . . to conduct his own education, find his own inspiration, shape his own environment and share his adventures with whoever is interested'.[20]

With man's innate, biologically founded sociality, his corresponding 'gift' in constructing meaningful social realities,[21] his long historical experience of life in small communities, he proceeds to create within his private sphere and around the various roles he performs a variety of small universes of existence. Choosing and rejecting among the prefabricated parts of the vast array of 'existence kits' offered and available to him, man proceeds to build them into the small existence units which constitute his actual life-worlds. Very tentatively one might say that the construction of small life-worlds takes place on two levels:

1 On the institutional level, where they are built around the specific institutional roles the individual performs. On this level they are limited by the institutionally imposed restrictions.

2 On the level of the 'private sphere' in which (a) life-worlds are being constructed from modern as well as traditional elements of small-world existence patterns, or (b) attempts are being made to create *new* designs for 'whole and lasting communities', using hedonistic, theoretical, 'scientific', but also romanticized historical 'models' of communal life.

The life-round of modern man is not of one piece. It does not unfold within one but within a variety of small 'worlds' which often are unconnected with one another. Within a lifetime – within the round of one day – the individual is alternately, consecutively or simultaneously a participant of variegated groups of communities which, in many instances, he is able to leave at will. He can – at least theoretically – change his job, he can in effect become a member of another social club, political party or church; he can sell or redecorate his house, move into another slum or suburb, divorce his wife and establish a new family. He can adopt a new subcultural style of clothes, appearance, gestures, language, love-making; he can create a new 'image' of himself or buy a new personality from his

19 Invitation leaflet to join the 'Bobby Seale Contingent' in the April 15, 1970 Moratorium against the War in Vietnam in Cambridge, Mass.

20 From an interview reported by Steven V. Roberts in 'Mail Order Catalogue of the Hip becomes National Bestseller', *New York Times*, April 12, 1970.

21 Cf. Peter L. Berger and Thomas Luckmann, *The Social Construction of Reality*, New York: Doubleday & Company, Inc., 1966.

psychoanalyst. Instead of being a full-time member of one 'total and whole' society, modern man is a part-time citizen in a variety of part-time societies. Instead of living within one meaningful world system to which he owes complete loyalty he now lives in many differently structured 'worlds' to each of which he owes only partial allegiance.

Most of modern man's existential universes are *single-purpose communities*.[22] They are built around one specific role of the individual. The definition of this role – which all members of the community perform – is clearly understood and fully accepted. There is no doubt that X is a co-expert on fifteenth-century Mongolian history, even though one might disagree with him on the original meaning of the name and the actual location of the place at which the Chinese General Chu, having been lured deep into Upper Mongolia by Bunyaširis warriors, was defeated in 1410. One's disagreement might be violent. Yet, within the small world of Mongolian studies one does after all speak the same language, one shares the same students, reads the same texts, goes to the same meetings, quarrels over the same footnotes whose paramount importance is not appreciated by anybody else. Other historians and scholars may be concerned with Mongolian history, but in ever decreasing degrees of intensity. Their professional worlds might touch and from time to time overlap in part with one's own. But *they* will always be clearly distinguished from the experts on Mongolia. The highly formalized and routinized kind of interaction which provided 'security' and 'peace of mind' to man in traditional communities may also be found, though of a more limited variety, in the small life-worlds of modern individuals, at least for the duration of their stay in any particular world.

The new existential universities of the private sphere may be *freely chosen* or *deliberately* (though not necessarily reflectively) *constructed*. They are not *given* in the sense in which traditional man is born into a community of 'the living and the dead'. While traditional man takes for granted that he will live and die in the community of his birth, the modern individual can exchange one of his several life-worlds for another without having to fear punishment or repercussions. He may, e.g. exchange his 'food world' for an 'anti-food world', and move from the gourmet club set of his 'graciously living' friends into the 'slim-gym' togetherness of fat ladies who are trying to reduce their 'whole and total' weight of 3875 pounds to that of 3475 in six months of 'mutual friendship, support and

22 Cf. also the concept of 'segmentally rather than totally relevant' reference groups as developed by Ralph H. Turner, 'Reference Groups of Future-Oriented Men', in *Social Forces*, 1955, 34, 130–136.

encouragement'.[23] He cannot, even though supported and driven by the implications of the mobility ethos, move as easily from one job to another. The new small life-worlds, of the private sphere, at least, are interchangeable but not when the 'exchange' creates a conflict with the 'rational' laws of the individual's 'institutional existence'.

Not unlike the traditional communities, the modern life-worlds are *small, comprehensible* and *knowable*. Inside a particular typing pool of this large corporation whose policies do not interest me and whose goals I only vaguely understand, I know the girls with whom I work. I know about their families, their hobbies, their biographies. I know the pool supervisor and the five or ten men whose letters I type. I recognize their voices as they come out of the dictating machine. I connect these voices with the individual people who sit in their cubicles down the hall. I know that X and Y are bachelors worth dressing up for. I know that Z and W always have second thoughts about their formulations and make you retype letters. I know that V's wife always calls at 5 o'clock to check up on her husband, etc. I know where the coffee machine is kept and whom I can meet there when. I know when the man who sells doughnuts and candies comes around. I have that little routine in the ladies' room where I go with the girl from the pool with whom I am friendly; we exchange notes on dates, clothes, plans and the current office gossip. I am equally familiar with the members, the rules, the inadequacies, the intrigues of my tennis club, my local church, the PTA of my children's school. All of them represent some of the small worlds within which my life unfolds and in which I participate for some limited ends. Inside these small worlds I feel quite safe. I feel 'at home'. There are not many uncertainties. Things make sense to me. I understand them.

The 'residence' within these small worlds is not always durable: I get married and quit my job in the typing pool; my husband does not play tennis and I take up golf so we can play together; the children grow older, go to college, I am no longer a member of the PTA, and I have become converted to Catholicism. 'Residence' is frequently of a *temporary* and always of a *migratory* character. The existence of the small worlds themselves is restricted and limited. So is individual participation. The individual is a temporary and part-time member, precisely because he is also a temporary and part-time member of other small life-worlds. The *multi-world existence* of modern man requires frequent 'gear-shifting'. As he moves from one small world into the next, he is faced with at least marginally different expectations, requiring different role performances in concert with different sets of people. The small life-worlds of modern

23 Communication of a friend.

man belong to different 'jurisdictions' and different realms of meaning.[24] They pursue different goals, aim at the attainment of a different 'good', are differently organized, require different forms of behaviour, satisfy different 'needs' of man, make different kinds of demands upon him. Unlike the small communities of traditional society and similar to the autonomous institutional spheres, the small life-worlds never claim the total individual. Modern man lives in a set of small worlds. The connection and cohesiveness among his various life-worlds are provided solely by the biographical coincidence of his memberships.

Man, who creates and improves his small life-worlds, also attempts to arrange and fit them into at least a biographically reasonably meaningful whole. For this purpose he usually singles out one or two which seem of greatest permanence and importance to him. This one, or these few micro-universes will become the nucleus around which his other life-worlds can be arranged. The existence units predestined to constitute the *navel* of the small world clusters of existence are those which traditionally have carried out major functions in fitting the individual for life in society and providing individual existence with a sense of permanence. They are the family and the ecological community. Though of more recent origins, man's work world must also be included.

These three *omphalic* small worlds have undergone and are undergoing significant changes in the process of modernization. Though the family still socializes the young it no longer teaches them clearly defined patterns of behaviour, supported by firm beliefs which would prepare them for life in a correspondingly stable society. In a way one can say that the family socializes its young for the multi-dimensional existence in potential sets of part-time worlds by socializing them into the family itself as an instance of small-world existence – but also by the 'world-openness' of anticipatory socialization. The socialization process is further carried on in some of the other partial universes.

Biologically and economically of vital importance for man's early survival, emotionally the most stable and satisfying life-world, and at the same time the most durable one, the family continues to occupy a central position among the small life-worlds of modern man. This being so, the family is presumed to gratify expectations that in traditional society were the concern of other associations and institutions, but mainly of a multi-generational and extended family. One such expectation is to provide 'fulfilment 'of an almost religious nature to the lives of the marriage partners[25] and by implication a meaningful integration of their multi-world existences. Another

24 Alfred Schutz, *op. cit.*
25 Cf. Thomas Luckmann, *op. cit.*, pp. 112–113.

is the sustenance of a 'transcendence-promise', inherent in the family's procreation and socialization functions, for which, in traditional societies, whole symbolic universes had been created, frequently administered by specialized personnel. These 'societal' burdens placed upon a significantly changed and reduced family may strain its resources and overtax its functional limitations, thereby endangering its very continuity.

The ecological community, like the family, has preserved a number of its traditional functions, though they too have been modified and recast. Even more so than in the case of the family, a vigorous community ideology based on old symbolic associations has survived, at least on the rhetorical level, correspondingly supported by politicians on all levels of government. Though day-to-day decisions of local political institutions are made on 'rational' grounds (the scope and nature of 'rationality' usually being determined by supra-local institutional spheres in which the 'local branch' of government represents but a small constitutive unit) [26] these decisions may be reached and carried out in the traditional political style of the small town – while preserving the latter's old 'small world' character.

A contemporary citizen of a village, small town, faubourg, suburb, quarter or ghetto, decidedly 'modern' in his style of life, 'rational' on the job and in business, 'progressive' in his economic beliefs – and sometimes even in his private morals – may fight with conviction against the removal of an old (and ugly) historical monument which is a traffic hazard to boot. He may vigorously oppose the felling of an old tree which keeps the sunshine out of the nursing home, and the moving in of a new 'dirty' industry which holds the promise of an economic boost for the city's dwindling resources.[27]

The survival of historical landscapes, the 'character of a village', city profiles, old communal rituals [28] may provide a 'sense of community' and continuity which is not warranted by the range of functions performed nor the amount of political control exercised by the ecological communities. The very fact of 'settling down', of buying a house, planting a rose bush, competing with one's neighbours over the least amount of crabgrass in one's lawn or upbraiding the owners of 'uncurbed' dogs on the streets of one's neighbourhood, creates bonds which may make the prospect of moving away something more than just a problem of packing and frantic wives. Even the ghetto of one's childhood which one has left with joy and

26 Cf. Arthur J. Vidich and Joseph Bensman, *Small Town in Mass Society*, Princeton: Princeton University Press, 1958.

27 Cf. Benita Luckmann, *Politik in einer deutschen Kleinstadt*, Stuttgart: Ferdinand Enke, 1970.

28 Cf. W. Lloyd Warner, *The Living and the Dead*, New Haven: Yale University Press, 1959.

shame may be rediscovered as the 'stake' of one's 'black future', because 'Watts is my home'.[29]

The fact that working serves other than strictly economic function is an amply substantiated truism.[30] This holds true for professionals and white-collar workers as well as for managers, craftsmen and tradesmen, the service occupations and the skilled and semi-skilled industrial workers. An overwhelming majority of employed men in a national sample stated, for example, that they would continue working even if by some chance they inherited enough money to live comfortably without work.[31] They explained that they enjoyed working, and also that work kept them occupied, justified their existence and enhanced their self-respect, and that without it they would 'feel lost' and 'go crazy'.[32]

The work ethos internalized along with other values of the Protestant ethic in America,[33] but equally strongly stressed in all other industrializing countries, has been carried over into life patterns of late industrial society. There it fills that part of leisure time – by 'do-it-yourself' occupations and the immersion in 'hobby worlds' – which is not passed 'educationally', 'informatively', 'enjoyably' or 'boringly' in viewing television.[34] Work being a dominant value-theme of industrial society, the rejection of work is analogously experienced as a rejection of society, followed, in turn, by the negative evaluation on the part of the 'working class' of 'bearded do-nothings', 'hairy parasites', etc.

As occupation has become the dominant status indicator for modern man, the work-world has become central for 'establishing' him in many of his other life-worlds in and outside the institutional spheres. A number of professions and occupations also may foster hopes and aspirations for

29 Stanley Saunders, 'I'll Never Leave the Ghetto', *Ebony*, Vol. 20, No. 10, August 1967.

30 Cf. among others in this field Elton Mayo's classical study, *The Social Problems of Industrial Civilization*, Cambridge: Harvard University Press, 1945. Mayo describes the stabilizing influence on members of a clique in the workshop as against the anomic effects of their neighbourhoods.

31 Only among the unskilled workers one half wanted to quit work.

32 The actual withdrawal from the work-world at retirement may, like widowhood, produce reactions of anomie. See Nancy C. Morse and R. S. Weiss, 'The Function and Meaning of Work', in *Man, Work, and Society*, Sigmund Nosow and William H. Form (eds.), New York: Basic Books, Inc., 1962, pp. 29–35; also E. A. Friedmann and R. J. Havighurst, 'Work and Retirement', *Ibid.*, pp. 41–55. Cf. also Pierre Bourdieu, 'Le Désenchantement du Monde: Travail et travailleurs en Algérie', mimeographed monograph of the Centre de Sociologie Européenne, Paris, 1966.

33 The qualities and aspirations of the 'Protestant ethic' imputed to the Puritan settlers seem to be analogous to those guiding the economic activities of Catholic refugees (from former German territories or settlements) forcibly settled in a predominantly Protestant town in Southern Germany at the end of World War II. Cf. Benita Luckmann, *op. cit.* Part I, 6.

34 Television programmes can and do provide bases for fantasy-life worlds which may, in turn, give 'meaning' to one's everyday life.

extending the limits of one's physical existence by books written, students taught, pictures painted, services rendered, 'empires' built, etc.

The omphalic small life-worlds meet basic biological needs and perform equally important social functions. Enhanced by the residual 'traditional prestige' and supported by modern institutional ideologies as well as diffused 'general values' of society, the omphalic life-worlds are viewed as potential carriers of the incoherently articulated values of 'unity', 'meaning' and 'sense of permanence'. At the same time on the level of experimentation the search is on for 'total' and 'lasting' life-worlds, small and universal. This is true particularly among the young who in their confrontations' with existing society have in stages become disappointed, frustrated, disgusted, enraged and estranged from what they designate as a 'meaningless', 'anonymous', 'abstract', 'sick', 'bureaucratic' and 'repressive' society. In a dialectical interplay between 'activism' and 'turning-off' (possibly, but not necessarily involving different sets of people), in alternating phases of 'creative destructionism' [35] and 'dropout', the period of new world construction is ushered in.

While the 'rejection' of the old world is usually marked by nonconventional appearance and manners, offensive speech, the spurning of established morals, etc., its symbolic 'break-down' is played out in acts of violence aimed at the destruction of objects symbolizing modern society: the wrecking of a computer, the burning of banks, the decimation of files, the bombing of corporation office buildings, etc. The 'old world' is also exorcized and 'overcome' through witchcraft, magic, mystical cults – usually of Oriental origin – drug cultures, etc. What follows is the search for 'one's identity', 'one's thing', new and ever newer life-worlds. Everybody is 'running for the woods' and 'taking to the hills'. Communes are sought out or built up: American style, i.e. basically 'religious' and 'tribal' despite the anarchical intentions of their founders; Scandinavian style: promiscuous at first and boring later; 'functional' ones – those mostly conceived by women in cities in order to save money, divide labour, share babies and gain more free time. 'Scientific' communities are being produced 'with available behavioural technology' which should, in the words of the man who has provided the blueprint,[36] make it 'possible for any group of men of goodwill to construct a good life'. Western towns are being resurrected to 'discover things for oneself'; Blacks '. . . build a community

35 Term coined by Michael Bakunin. Cf. his *Gosudarstvennost' i anarkhiya* (Statism and Anarchism), Zürich and Geneva, 1873.

36 From interview of B. F. Skinner by Richard Todd, ' "Walden Two": Three? Many More?', *New York Times Magazine*, March 15, 1970. Cf. also Skinner's book, *Walden Two*, New York: Macmillan Paperbacks, 1962.

of love . . . among blacks', in which '. . . the white man no longer exists'.[37] Ecology is becoming '. . . a whole way of life' which 'gives unity to experience' and some day '. . . might be as important as rock'n'roll'.[38] 'The future is a blank screen you can play your fantasies out on' [39] in '. . . looking for life's reality'.[40]

All this seems to indicate at least two things: 'Life's reality' is something that the traditional systems of meaning transmitted and that the 'big' social institutions of modern society fail to transmit for large numbers of individuals. Modern society does not provide the 'links' for fitting the totality of individual existence into the order of the industrial universe. On the other hand, modern man possesses enclaves of 'freedom' in which he can arrange his private life in almost any way he likes. This does not mean that his private life is solitary; on the contrary. In his quest for 'order and meaning' modern man seems to be creating for himself a small-world existence again in which the complex, bewildering and often frightening outside world is placed more or less effectively in parentheses.

The life of man in modern industrial societies does indeed differ in many important and less important, in obvious and hidden respects from the life of man not only in prehistoric and 'primitive' societies but also in traditional and even early industrial societies. Yet there are some intrinsic continuities in the manner in which he arranges his life or at least in the manner in which he seeks and finds meaning in such arrangements. Modern man continues to live in small worlds which are comprehensible and manageable to him. These small worlds are not 'whole' but partial; they are not life-long but part-time; they are less 'naturally-given' than 'intentionally chosen'; there is no single small world but many of them.

37 Stokely Carmichael, 'Towards Black Liberation', *Massachusetts Review*, Autumn, 1966.
38 From interviews as reported by Steven V. Roberts in: 'The Better Earth', *op. cit.*
39 From an interview of Stewart Brand, creator of Whole Earth Catalog and owner of Whole Earth Truck Store, as reported by Steven V. Roberts, *op. cit.*
40 From an interview of Scott Ross, thirty-year-old former disc jockey turned Pentecostal: 'I went the political route, and then through the drug trip. Others get into meditation or Hare Krishna. We're all looking for life's reality.' *New York Times*, March 1970, 'Many Youths turn to Pentecostals'.

28 The journalist

Joseph Bensman and Robert Lilienfeld

The journalistic attitude is related to the reporting of events by media which have, as one of their central characteristics, periodicity in publication, whether it be a daily newspaper, a weekly or bimonthly journal, or a radio or television programme. The act of reportage is limited. It conveys an image of the world defined within the framework of the reported event and of the periodicity of publication. Thus, time is a major dimension which determines a vast part of that reporting of events which defines and determines an image of the world.

The time feature is not the natural time of the natural man, but, because given the periodicity of publication, is an objective factor, subject to conditions and controls that are external to the psychological conditions of action though they may be incorporated into it. Nor, for the same reasons, does the journalistic attitude assume the objective constant, measured attitude that underlies the scientific attitude.

The externality of time is not the preordained rhythm of a ceremony or ritual, in which submission to the tyranny of time – rhythm – becomes a major aesthetic end. Time, for the journalist, is purely an arbitrary accident of the requirements of publication. It has no inherent rhythm other than the economics of publication and the expectations of readers that publication will occur at given periods. Thus, the journalist must consciously discipline himself to the tyranny of these objective forms of time. Having done so, he may enjoy the aesthetics of completing assignments within the framework of what might otherwise be purely arbitrary and capricious publication dates. Regardless of the completeness of his research and knowledge, he must present a complete story by his deadline. The appearance of completeness of a story, the who, when, where, and how of journalism, resembles the images of a total world as presented in a work of art, so that in this respect the journalist is an artist. The applied artist who works on schedule supplied by others and the performing artist quite often are subject to *the same* time requirements. The requirement, however, that the story appear complete forces the journalist to work for a closure which

---

BENSMAN, JOSEPH and LILIENFELD, ROBERT (1937) 'The journalist' in *Craft and Consciousness: Occupational Technique and the Development of World Images* New York, John Wiley, 207–32.

is not the closure that might have occurred had he not been subject to the time requirements.

A second characteristic of the journalistic attitude is based on the attitude of the journalist to his audience. In the artistic attitude, the truly creative artist, including the painter, the poet, novelist, musician and sculptor, works out his own subjective image of reality, develops it through the use of the objective techniques of his art, and imposes them upon his audience. He creates the standards and the vision by which his work is judged. Of course, the lesser creative artist will work in terms of visions, standards, and techniques which are part of the on-going traditions or styles of his field at a given time.

The journalist, hemmed in by the periodicity of publication, and by the fact that he is selling some kind of media or publication, is forced to anticipate the response of his audience in terms of what the journalist calls newsworthy, or 'human interest'. He must anticipate what will excite, stimulate, and titillate an audience at the time of publication. This means that the flow of his attention must be consistent with the 'natural' flow of attention of his audience. He must drop stories and his interest in events as the events themselves shift either in their dramatic impact on audiences, or in the journalist's estimate of the audience's rhythm of interest.[1]

The cliché that there is nothing as old as yesterday's newspaper is no less true because it is a cliché. For this reason, journalism cannot or does not necessarily have the depth and the timeless quality of art, though in other respects it resembles the image-making of art.

In a third respect, however, journalism has much in common with science and art. One of the characteristics of outstanding journalism is that it results in a transvaluation, at least momentarily, of the natural world. Good journalism takes as its framework the world of everyday assumptions of routine, and the normal expectations of a natural audience, and discovers, through the significant story, the violation of the expectations of everyday life. So, the newsworthy, the dramatic, the 'human interest' aspect of reporting looks either for the dramatic affirmation or the dramatic denial by events of the world of everyday life.

In dramatizing the denial of everyday life by events, the journalist exposes the incongruities between image and reality, the fraud and chicanery behind many façades, and suggests the operation of more essential structures governing the world of appearances. At times, such activities result in a renovation of values which are frequently neglected because they are taken for granted. At other times, the effect of continuous exposures may cause the devaluation of values because they appear to be inoperative. But in both cases, the act of good reporting is something more than reporting;

it is, like art, an act of creation and re-creation. Its effects, while they may be startling at a given time, are likely to be temporary, because the journalist is continuously forced to shift the focus of attention, as even the exposure in a given area becomes routinized, and as the response of his readership shifts.

While the result of such activities may from time to time cause public scandals, the arrest of malefactors, the redesigning of automobiles, the enactment of new legislation, or changes in the sensibilities of audiences, the journalist who lives at the point of the chasm between appearances and reality is likely at a personal level to feel that all appearances are fraudulent, managed or engineered for reasons totally unrelated to the appearances. As a result, his personal attitude may be one of intellectual cynicism, which is not necessarily incongruous with intellectual honesty and the maintenance of high standards of personal ethics.

In presenting these characteristics of the journalistic attitude, we have tended to neglect the simple and more obvious characteristics of technical facility in the handling, arranging, and manipulation of words and symbols, so that taken together they produce for the moment total images of a reality as evoked by an event or story.

Viewed in terms of his technical virtuosity as a craftsman and artisan, the journalist is an information-disseminator. He is able to present images of the world in apparently clear, personalistic, simple and dramatic forms that are not abstract, academic, or complicated. He is likely to look for the *specific* image, illustration, symbol, anecdote, or event that illustrates his point; and having found and presented that symbol, he is likely to allow the symbol or succession of symbols to convey his point without presenting the abstract argument. In his search for the specific, concrete image, he resembles the poet.

This latter aspect, the technical and aesthetic virtuosity of the journalist, not only constitutes his professional and artistic methodology, but constitutes his basis for evaluation and appreciation by others, including other journalists.

The qualities of the journalist as information specialist may be seen under two perspectives. First, that of the social functions of journalism, and the social consequences of journalism; second, the relation of this attitude to intellectual work of all types, including the scientific, the artistic and the scholarly.

The societal settings and social functions of journalism

Journalism as an activity becomes meaningful in various societal settings, which, if these settings were not extant, would not require a journalistic attitude. Thus, journalism is appropriate to only limited kinds of social worlds. In a small society in which all available knowledge is gathered through direct and personal experience, the journalistic attitude would not develop, or would be part of the normal cognitive and perceptual equipment of every individual in this society. This also applies to the extent of differentiation within a society. If all individuals in the society are equipped to understand from direct experience the total range of events and activities in that society, then the normal channels of personal communication would be effective in disseminating information within that society.

When the technical development of a society grows to the point where most of the basic issues and dynamics are too complex, abstract, or removed from the experience of the individuals in the society, there is need for the qualities of personification, dramatization, and the removal of abstraction and complexity from events and issues.[2]

Thus, the journalist becomes necessary as the result of societal developments which coincide with the growth of large-scale civilizations, the increased differentiation within society, and the development of complex administrative, scientific, technical and industrial processes which at an operative level can be understood only by highly trained, experienced professionals.

The journalist, by developing professional competence in one or more of the abstract technical areas in the society, and by combining them with his 'communications skills', makes distant and complex areas of the world available to audiences who are presumed to lack either the experience or the equipment to understand those events and issues directly in their own terms. As a result, he is or seems indispensable to a mass society.

The second aspect of the information function of journalism is related to the uses of information in a large-scale society. Organized groups, business corporations, government agencies, universities, and other large-scale organizations are or become aware that information dissemination is related to their specialized public and private purposes. There is need to employ specialists at dramatization, personalization, simplification, in order to present most effectively the specialized claims of these groups to distant publics. It is no accident, then, that the beginnings of professional propaganda began with the beginnings of professional journalism. The information talents of the journalist develop in response to needs for substitute sources of information when genuine or direct sources of experience are not available. But this situation, in which the individual is not capable or is presumed to be not capable of evaluating issues and events in terms of direct experience, is precisely that situation which makes possible large-scale fraud, charlatanry, and deceit by misdirection. For the conscious manipulation of information becomes possible only when access to genuine information or direct sources of experience is obscured by the complexity of events, issues, technology, size or differentiation in a society.[3]

The development of a complex society provides the opportunity and the motivation, but the misapplication of journalism supplies the means.

Personification, concreteness, comprehensibility

The journalist, like the novelist, in avoiding abstraction and the cold deadness of difficult and abstract themes, seeks to find the image or the personality that embodies the idea, and deals with the image or personality in place of the idea. This enables him to communicate at levels that a large and nonprofessional audience is able to understand. Frequently, the characteristics of the journalistically treated personality begin to transcend that idea. Thus, the personal habits, the love stories, the leisure pursuits, the personal character or lack of it, all overpower that which would make the personality of journalistic interest original.[4]

Thus the journalistic treatment of Albert Einstein would emphasize his eccentricities: his haircut, his hatred of shaving cream, his absent-mindedness, his proclivity for wearing old sweaters, all at the expense of any presentation of his contribution, which is defined as so abstract that allegedly only a dozen men could understand it.[5]

The concreteness and 'comprehensibility' embodied in this form of journalistic treatment results in the 'hero' or the 'star', who symbolizes and personifies, in terms larger than life, a field of endeavour which would otherwise not be salient. Once the attempt is made to make the 'star' salient, the person who is momentarily presented as a star has a fabricated image. The dramatic aspects have to be emphasized; traits are created either in the person himself, so that he is made to resemble his journalistic image, or so that the image is made independent of his genuine characteristics or qualities.[6]

In this sense, journalism not only reports on the operation of appearances, and on realities underlying appearances, but also creates appearances or the appearance of realities.

Journalism in public relations

The manipulator of public opinion, the propagandist, the public relations man, seeks from whatever source is available those individuals whose technical skills, knowledge, and artistry will implement his purposes. The journalist possesses some of these skills, though in modern society he is not too different in these respects from the artist, the intellectual, the researcher, and the academician, who can become, if he desires, available for the same purposes.

Starting with the pure model of the journalist as developed above, a whole subsidiary set of occupations which can be called applied journalism can become available. These include the information functions, that is, the information specialist in large-scale organizations, and primarily as defined by the term in government. In this sense, the information specialist translates the often complex, scientific, abstract procedural documents of quasi-literate technicians into the dramatic, the personal, the concrete imagery characteristic of the essential journalistic model. As an employee of a specialized agency which has vested interests of its own, his job entails the repression of information which is not consistent with those specialized interests, the concealment of weaknesses, of original documents, and their restatement so that the positive interests of the agency are enhanced. In the private sphere, the same function is called public relations; it includes all of the same functions.

The essential devices of dramatization and personification enable both the public and the private agency to attain visibility or salience in a world where the overabundance of information tends to clog all avenues of information.

The journalist must work out dramatic devices. The public relations man, by means of hokum, teasers, and fraudulent stories, gains access to media which allow the favourable story to become visible.

To the extent that journalism makes itself available for such uses, it destroys one of its original basic attributes: that of revealing conflicts between appearances and underlying structures. It reverses this relationship by contributing to the manufacture of appearances, and to a fraudulent public life. The journalist in these roles becomes a modern bureaucratic replacement for the primitive mythmaker. He also becomes, at the bureaucratic level, an ideologist. In his role as educator and purveyor of the thought, values, and screens to thought of others; he is neither a mythmaker nor an ideologist.

When 'public relations' is conducted simultaneously for a vast number of institutions and organizations, the public life of a society becomes so congested with manufactured appearances that it is difficult to recognize any underlying realities.

As a result, individuals begin to distrust all public façades and retreat into apathy, cynicism, disaffiliation, distrust of media and publication institutions. They develop forms of psychological sabotage and rebellion.

At this point the journalist unwittingly often exposes the workings of the public relations man or information specialist, if he operates within a genuine journalistic attitude.

Unfortunately, in a complex society where the sources of information are so varied and numerous, the journalist and his enterprises in their basic news reporting function are frequently forced to accept the press release or handout as a substitute for the genuine legwork that results in journalism as a peculiar art form.[7]

In the above discussion, the journalistic attitude is primarily located in journalism as an occupation, and corruptions of the journalistic attitude are seen in the use of journalism by applied journalists for ends not related to the original ends of journalism. One must not forget that journalism in the original sense of our usage has been a 'habit of mind', a way of viewing the world, and of creating articulate images of it. The point to be made here is that this journalistic habit of mind can become independent of a specific occupation, and can become applied to spheres other than that of journalism itself, or of bureaucratic information control and information manipulation. This is especially true since the social conditions which originally evoked the journalistic attitude are independent of journalism itself. The complexity, differentiation, abstractness, and social distances of modern society force everyone who wishes to communicate with others who do not directly experience the events communicated to do so in manners and styles that flow from the journalistic attitude.

These manners and styles, we have indicated, are the use of drama, personification, concreteness, simplification, imagery, etc.[8]

Journalistic treatment

Journalism serves social functions in the articulation of images of the world of appearances and the appearances of reality. But it also has a set of techniques, which, with professionalization, specialization, and academic development, become fairly objective, and thus teachable. Then, the use of the objective techniques of journalism can become independent of professional journalism in its primary and original sense.

Once this occurs, it is followed by what we call journalistic treatment, in which the methods of journalism – personification, simplification, the quest for imagery along with easy treatment of almost incomprehensible information – are used in nonjournalistic enterprises. Whenever a new idea, institution, technological development, art work or form appears, in a society imbued with highly developed journalistic tradition, these new forms are almost immediately redeveloped, reported, and publicized, within the framework of journalistic treatment.

Modern art, or a new development in modern art, will become within a relatively short period of time, in journalistic form, invested with the glamour, the exoticism, and the chic inherent in a 'hero' or 'star' system. Given the appeal of the journalistic treatment to audiences whose interests have been aroused and jaded by past journalistic treatment, there is a high probability that the new development, if 'taken up' either by journalists or public relations men, or even by sensation-seeking audiences, can have almost instantaneous currency, due both to the form of its treatment, and the media of mass dissemination for such material.

As a result, within the last hundred years, it can be argued that the time interval between the development of a style, a form, an innovation, and its acceptance at a popular level, has been shortened, so that by now, instant acceptance of innovation is often guaranteed, provided the availability of the innovation for journalistic treatment, even before the idea can be properly understood and developed by its protagonists. The individual as worker or innovator is pulled into the world of the stars and of public characters, before he has time to assess, criticize, and develop the innovation.[9] There is a probability that basically good ideas are exhausted or vulgarized before their immanent meaning emerges. In the absence of general ideas, effects may be forced by a wilful experimentalism and sensationalism.

If this is true of innovators, it is even more true of audiences, who must be prepared, if they wish to be *au courant*, to leap from one journalistically created vogue to another, preferably before the high point of each succeeding vogue has been reached. The artist or innovator must risk the danger of becoming outmoded almost before he has done his work. And if he values his recently acquired stardom, he must learn to leave work which becomes passé as new styles replace it. The dangers of journalistically induced success are greater than the dangers of obscurity.[10]

Other forms of journalistic treatment abound. The most frequent form occurs when journalistic treatment combines with academic treatment, in which the journalistic explicator must explain in journalistic terms how work that is independently valuable was really done, or how it can be understood in more simplified and 'basic' terms. This results in the industry of commentaries. But it is not enough for the journalist (or non-journalist who provides journalistic treatment) to amplify, and explain the original work. He must add elements to the original work and to previous commentaries, to justify his present commentary. This results in journalistic 'improvements' of the original work by individuals who are not equipped to do the original work, but who know how to write about it.

As one example, in the field of music one of the largest critical industries is that of writing annotations – explanations of the systems of interpretation of such works as the Beethoven piano sonatas. Thus, for many original compositions, there are a host of editions, each annotated by an inferior musical mind, each introducing his own personal idiosyncrasies, preferences, and personality into his revision of Beethoven's works. In the process, the original annotations by Beethoven were lost or obscured, so that at a later date, a more advanced critical industry was forced to emerge, that of the discovery of the musical work in its original form. It is a tribute to recent musicological scholarship that it has discovered the necessity for removing the barnacles of past journalistic and critical growths.

Journalistic treatment results in a dialectic in which the creation of myths is but a phase. The removal of inaccuracies then becomes a necessary phase of another form of journalistic treatment, which may in turn result in the creation of new myths. In this sense, journalistic myth-making becomes an autonomous process, almost independent of any reality towards which the myth may originally have been related. This autonomous process was most advanced, perhaps during the thirties and forties, in the treatment of Hollywood and the Hollywood stars.

The journalistic attitude outside of journalism

Given the growth of journalistic treatment as an activity apart from journalism per se it becomes necessary to consider the uses of the journalistic attitude by nonjournalists in nonjournalistic situations. Perhaps the simplest form of application of the journalistic attitude is the use of this device by a scholar or expert towards his peers who presumably have the experience, the background, and the technique at levels which do not require the simplifications of the journalistic attitude. Why this should occur so pervasively is not directly perceivable. Perhaps the habits of mind developed from dealing with outgroups become so pervasive that the trained professional presents his own materials to other trained professionals in ways that previously would have been considered inappropriate.

But other factors might be relevant as well. Among these is the technicalization of society to the extent that professional, technical and occupational peers are so distant from each other that one treats them as strangers, as laymen, or as a general public. In addition, even within relatively narrow technical areas, the amount of information to be transmitted is so great that to gain the attention of one's peers requires the development of dramatic devices, which in specialized technical areas necessarily falsifies the data so presented. And, thirdly, the amount of specialization even within a narrow technical area is so great that the specialist does not feel confident that another specialist in a closely related field will be able to understand specialized information in its own terms.

Regardless of the cause, then, the specialist as receiver of information must guard himself against the forms of information which might mislead him, even though he himself, in his dissemination of information, might use the very same forms.

Related to these activities is the journalistic institution of the book review as a means of coping with the immense flow of information to be found in technical and specialized journals. This flow is so great that the academician is often forced to subscribe to reviewing journals, and to engage clipping services and graduate students to provide abstracts, digests, and quotations from unread books, monographs and articles.

Beyond this, the specialist in any area must deal with audiences that do not and cannot have the technical equipment to comprehend his communication in the sense that he himself (hopefully) understands. He must thus become his own journalist.

The physician, for example, has a choice between developing or presenting descriptions of disease which are beyond the comprehension of the layman, or of vulgarizing the description. He may, in vulgarizing it, seek to maintain the essential accuracy of the description, or he may slant the information in order thereby to dramatize himself and the quality of his practice.

If, on the other hand, he presents the data in its original technical complexity, he can do so in order to be accurate but incommunicable, or he can do it in order to evoke the aura of science, complexity, and professional esotericism, and thus magnify and enhance his professional image. In this latter case, the use of the professional mysteries of science in its original complexity can become a public relations device in all the implications of the term. The example of the physician in dealing with the layman is the typical case, in which the complexity of a given field promises opportunity for material and psychological profit-making through either the simplification or the complexity of the specialized worlds of the expert.

Given the size of the various lay audiences for the products and byproducts of specialization, the opportunities for such simplification or manipulation are boundless. Thus, the textbook industry, swollen in size by the number of subcollege and college students, provides vast opportunities for the specialist to simplify his materials so that they can be packaged and sold to neophytes in the field. A successful textbook can provide more material rewards than an entire career of undramatic but serious scholarly or technical work. The problem involved in such work is what level of simplification, dramatization, personification, and so on, is necessary to present the neophyte with a working knowledge of a field.

The journalistic attitude has a dual character. It has a specific attitude towards the material of scholarly work, and a specific attitude towards the audience.[11] The journalistic attitude treats the audience as a consumer: knowledge disseminated should excite, stimulate, titillate, entertain, surprise, and evoke temporary interest, but no effort, on the part of the consumer. A genuine educational attitude must treat the neophyte as a producer, must teach him to handle the complexity of the data of his field in its own terms. When the journalistic attitude becomes part of the process of education, then the would-be producer is treated as a consumer, and his perception of the field is distorted by the importation of dramatic elements into what might be serious, undramatic, persistent, long-term technical work. Disillusion must follow an orientation to work based on the expectation of the drama of work.

More important, the use of the dramatization inherent in the journalistic attitude delays the entry of the neophyte into the work itself, so that it is difficult for him to learn what work is. Again, to repeat a cliché, he learns *about* the work, instead of learning the work.[12]

Ordinarily, genuine learning takes place during the process of working on real problems in real settings. Knowledge is acquired if and when it becomes useful to the worker in the solution of those problems. The salience of a technique or a method, or of information, is immediately perceptible in the light of the ongoing activity. It is never 'theoretical', distant, or 'abstract' because it is never removed from the problem.

However, with the substitution of the consumer's point of view for the producer's point of view, the journalistic presentation of non-journalistic material, with its glamorizing and dramatizing of the activity, puts distance between the image of the work and the work itself, and creates a gap which cannot be closed until problems are confronted in the attempt to solve tnem.

Journalism in intellectual work

Here we would distinguish between two ideal types of creation and dissemination of knowledge: 'self-generated' material, and 'externally generated' material. Externally generated material is developed simply to meet a deadline, to fill up space in a journal, or to fill time, as at a broadcast or popular lecture. Self-generated material includes all those books, art works, and scientific reports which are developed out of concern for immanent empirical or theoretical problems, out of perceptions or improvisations on the part of a writer or artist which are seen by him as promising and requiring further development or investigation, and which are not generated by immediate external pressures. Preoccupation with the material alone generates the work to be done.

A major component of journalistic activity and of the journalistic attitude is the pressure to have something written in time for a deadline, and of sufficient volume to fill the space or the time allotted to it. Thus, to paraphrase Karl Kraus, the journalist must write though he has nothing to say, and the journalist has something to say because he must write.[13] If, under this pressure, it happens that the journalist finds something to say, all is well, but if not, he must then have recourse to various devices.

One such device is to have recourse to that body of material which is, as described above, 'self-generated', and to 'popularize' it; that is, to explain it, 'clarify' it, make it amusing or dramatic. One may go further, and in the process may 'improve' the material by removing from it what one takes to be offensive to an audience, or merely boring, or threatening to one or another interest group. Here, the journalistic attitude actually acts as mediator between two groups. Towards the public, it decides what the public is fit or able to understand; towards the producers of work, it will dictate what may or may not be appropriate for an audience presumed to be rather lightly educated and having a somewhat limited capacity for attention. If this aspect of the journalistic attitude becomes internalized by a producer of self-generated material, he may become induced to shape this material in ways different from those he would have chosen had he not anticipated public responses. Thus, the extent to which the journalistic attitude becomes internalized may serve to distinguish various classes of intellectual work from one another, ranging from speculative philosophical works, works of high art, original theoretical treatises, on one hand, to works of popularization, 'introductions', 'how to' books, anthologies, readers, etc.

The distinction made here between 'self-generated' and 'externally generated' material actually describes the opposite poles of a continuum. At one end stands, in Schutzean terms, the expert, at the other end the journalist or the propagandist. Somewhere in between stands Schutz's model of the well-informed citizen,[14] or Weber's concept of the cultivated layman.

Journalism and propaganda

Part of journalistic treatment is to present arguments for or against a given issue or idea in such a way that the arguments of the advocate can be understood and accepted without access to the complexities of the issue in its original form. Most points of contention in a complex society are dealt with in terms of legalistic, technical, administrative, procedural, and economic complexities. Their substantive merits are not immediately visible, especially as major substantive points will frequently turn on relatively innocuous but abstract legal or technical issues.

The argument at the level of abstraction of the original issue is often difficult to present, especially to a lay public, difficult to understand, difficult to evoke loyalties and passions, even though these arguments may involve the life and growth of major groups and institutions within a society. The journalistic treatment of these issues provides a solution to this problem. The techniques of personification, simplification, imagery, linguistic devices, and the truncated journalistic story can, at its highest point, provide a description of the issue, in which no argument is ever made. The selection of words and the emotional loading of words, the slanting of the treatment of events, the sympathetic or unsympathetic treatment of personalities all constitute the application of journalistic treatment to complex issues. The argument is contained in the form of the treatment of the story, rather than in the argument itself. Argumentativeness, that is, the ideologized form of argument, is frowned upon from this point of view, for the ideological form or the polemic form of the argument alerts the individual to the idea that an argument is about to be presented. This signals him to adopt a critical stance in which the argument is to be subjected to logical or empirical criticism, or simply to emotional resistance. The argumentative form in its essential nature implies that the 'other' should be prepared to resist the argument, and invites him to develop counterarguments. In using these forms of journalistic treatment, the individual is not alerted to the polemic situation, is not warned, alarmed, and invited to use his critical faculties. The argument is presented in such a way that the individual does not know that an argument has been made. If the presentation is successful, he accepts the argument as a series of facts, emotional tones, or as reality. He has been manipulated. This form of journalistic treatment finds its most concentrated expression in 'mood advertising', in magazines like *Time*, and in indirect public relations campaigns. It is for this reason that ideology as a form of disputation has become unfashionable in a world where journalistic treatment replaces ideological or polemic treatment of controversial issues.[15]

Journalism and public relations

The public relations attitude requires a state of continuing innovation. One needs to have a story about something new and exciting occurring within an institution at relatively frequent intervals, so that press releases can be made. Since the routine operation of an efficient institution is not newsworthy, items that are newsworthy have to be manufactured. This means that new programmes, new ideas, new personnel, the employment and application of new technology, machinery, and inventions all evoke the possibility of newsworthy public relations. When public prominence becomes a primary need for an institution, then the rate of innovation must be increased, even though on technical or intrinsic grounds there is no need for innovations. Thus, perfectly good ideas, programmes, and techniques can be instituted even when unnecessary or misapplied. Their use is not intrinsic to the operation but only to the publicity. This is very important when related to considerations of the rate of innovation or change within a society. In a public relations world paralleling the development of innovation in the arts, the use of public relations techniques accentuates the rate of innovation and application beyond what one might expect from the need for such inventions or their usefulness.

Journalists who are insiders in large institutions and who are aware of both the public image and the internal image of the operations of institutions tend to be sceptical regarding the applicability of publicly valued technology to the institutions, such as high-powered computers, team teaching, teaching machines, operations research and linear programming, PERT systems, systems development, and many other similar ideas. This technology may be valuable, but its value becomes suspect because, at least in its early stages, it is highly amenable to public relations treatment.

Under this heading come such developments as the establishment of university chairs at very high salaries, for which an outstanding scholar is hired, primarily to enhance the 'image' of the institution, the establishment of special curricula and education programmes and degrees, new construction of various types, and the establishment of various research institutions.

Applied journalism involves more than the selective presentation of favoured facts and interpretations by means which make the desired story easy and attractive to accept. To convey an effective story from the standpoint of criteria that are independent of the story itself, it may be necessary to withhold information, to alter the facts, to be selective in the release of information, to colour the story, and to provide the proper mood music and nuance. This has sometimes been called 'information management'. It may include the burning of documents, the shredding of papers, the firing of controversial figures, the deflection of issues from the embarrassing to the innovative, and outright falsification. In some cases, when the avoidance of a major scandal seems to be impossible, applied journalism will include the apparent exposure of a minor scandal in the hope that in so doing, the major scandal will be avoided. Furthermore, exposure of a specific contradiction between appearance and reality often has the effect of being an end in itself. The exposure is assumed to be self-remedying, and the action undertaken in light of the exposure may be limited. But since journalism operates most often at the level of the specific concrete case, the exposure of a concrete case, or even of an interlocking series of specific cases, quite frequently results in only the treatment, sometimes temporary, of those cases. The conditions which make the individual cases possible are often left untouched because the habit of mind upon which journalism rests, and which it reinforces, does not go beyond the specific case. The journalist, having operated successfully at the case level, will then go on to other cases, while the vested interest may well concede defeat in a specific case so long as the general condition favourable to their interests remains untouched. Journalism can thus reveal specific, extreme abuses and contradictions between official appearances and underlying realities; but, by itself, it cannot go beyond exposure. To be effective, the journalistic attitude must be transcended; but, of course, such transcendence need not be the task of the journalist: it may well be the task of the 'well-informed citizen'.

Thus the negative aspects of applied journalism include turning the journalistic attitude into its opposite: from the exposure of unseemly facts underlying appearances, it turns itself into the creation of new and intentionally false appearances. But it uses the methods of verisimilitude to do so.

The journalistic treatment of politics

Political leaders can dramatically announce vast changes in policy, even if the change may be that of co-opting the language of the opposition without changing any behaviour that might follow from the policy. The linguistic co-optation may be used to label a policy that has opposite intentions or consequences to that of the language employed. It may include the promotion and removal of officials who symbolize a policy that has become unpopular or controversial, with the change in personnel being used as a substitute for a change in policy. The journalistic personification may involve worldwide travels, publicly celebrated meetings and ceremonies under the eye of the television camera and the press. It produces drama, ceremony, personification and simplification, whether or not there is in fact a change in policy. The immediacy of personification introduced originally by radio with Franklin Delano Roosevelt's fireside chats has been intensified by television, and includes the personification of issues in an aural and visual sense. It results in the attempt to select leaders who can personify policies whether they have policies in fact or not, and who can project images of warmth, sincerity, or masculinity. When these attributes are lacking, journalistic treatment involves the rehearsal, concealment, makeup, face-lifts and other anatomical alterations, and other forms of dramatic projection. As a result, part of the attitude of the performing artist is imported into the journalistic attitude to create newer forms of dramatic journalism.

The use of television, radio, and the film as means of simplification and personification in politics is only a technical advance over similar schemes of journalistic treatment based on different media. The most obvious of the earlier schemes was embodied in the slogan.[16] The slogan as a self-conscious method of political propaganda was developed to its highest point by Lenin during the Iskra period, from 1901 to 1905. The slogan was designed by the communists to embody in simple dramatic and emotional terms the aspirations of the downtrodden masses that were consistent with or could be used by the Communist Party in promoting the revolution.[17] There was an intense struggle among the various factions of the Communist Party as to what slogans (a) reflected the aspirations of the means, and (b) were correct from the standpoint of the revolutionary aspirations of the party. The use of the slogan by the Communist Party reflected an intense hundred-year study of the French Revolution, and the first dramatic political slogan, 'Liberty, Equality, and Fraternity'. The counterrevolution of the Congress of Vienna used an equally terse but not as emotionally powerful slogan, 'Restoration, Legitimacy, and Compensation'.

The intense study of the use of these slogans by the communists was first undertaken by Marx, who was himself, among other things, a journalist ('You have nothing to lose but your chains'). But after the development of this special field of applied politics, the use of the slogan became almost an intrinsic aspect of all politics. The slogan was based on the print media. The development of visual media in part collapses the slogan into the appearance of the man himself.

The presentation

The journalistic attitude, as we have indicated, emerges out of a need for simplicity in a world that is increasingly complex. Part of this complexity is due to technology, or to the increased technology by which society operates, and part is due to the increasing knowledge of the way the world operates; the development of science and research provides an overabundance of information which tends to drown the cultivated laymen (or, in Schutz's terminology, the well-informed citizen), such that even the information at his disposal becomes useless. The journalistic attitude responds by its own dialectic to the very problems it in part creates. For higher journalistic treatment includes the simplification of the presentation and the use of complex statistical devices to present simple dramatic facts and images of facts. These include the use of charts, simple indices, and animation, all aimed at presenting the most complex data in the world in forms that all but an expert in the collection of these materials can understand. This dialectic thus has further consequences: the deciphering of the meaning and basis for simple 'facts' becomes the basis for some of the highest forms of expertise in our world, but so of course is the presentation of these facts.

Journalism and book publishing

The 'migration' of the journalistic attitude out of journalism and into various other fields has been discussed above. Its effects in the publishing of books may be briefly indicated. There are three principal loci of the journalistic attitude in book publishing. A firm may wish to fill out its catalogue in various subject-matter fields, for reasons of competition, and so may commission or generate books which would otherwise not have existed. Textbooks are often generated for this reason. The second principal locus of the journalistic attitude in publishing is frequently located among editors. An editor who receives a manuscript from a subject-matter expert may find that its obscurity and disorganization of style require reordering clarification. In so acting, the editor is following the Schutzean model of the well-informed citizen. But a book editor may follow another model, as described above, namely that of anticipating audience responses to original, controversial, difficult, or otherwise disturbing material, and may in the process truncate, disfigure, or suppress a book entirely. This may be operative especially in the area of translating a major work into English, either from a foreign language or from technical jargon, in the process of which the editor frequently announces his deletion of considerable amounts of material which he has considered as not suitable for the English reading audience. Here, the editor has clearly adopted the journalistic attitude.

The third locus of the journalistic attitude in the field of book publishing lies in the area of reference books. The development of a complex technological world, and with it of journalism in all senses of the term, has led to a need for information about areas and field which an individual cannot be expected to know at first hand. For the 'well-informed citizen' reference books may serve a legitimate purpose, but they may serve journalistic purposes as well, enabling a popularizer, rewrite man, or commentator to assume the mantle of a depth of scholarship he does not possess. The influence of journalism may be shown not only in the proliferation of encyclopedias, textbooks, and reference books, but in the regularity with which they are revised and updated, to the point where they begin to resemble periodicals, even though the developments reported on may be peripheral or of ephemeral interest in a subject-matter field.

At any given point in time in any field of study, the sum total of knowledge in that field is fragmentary and unorganized. A vast number of individuals are working on a series of frequently unrelated problems, others are working in terms of intellectual traditions which are often competing, antagonistic, or anomalous. An accurate summation of knowledge in any field, for those who expect a unified, organized, progressive march of science and knowledge, might prove discrediting to that field. When public relations purposes are first in mind, the presentation of the state of the art or science requires that the field be presented in an orderly, systematic, unified, and dramatic way such that all professionals have two orders of data about their own field: (1) inside knowledge which determines the operative data for the professional in his intramural work; (2) a pseudo-integration of his field, which is presented to laymen, neophytes, the general public, and to outside administrators whose work impinges on the field.

This may appear at times to be necessary. The attempt, however, to treat the pseudo-order as genuine often results in a falsification of the entire field. Furthermore, when a field is full of the conflicts and divergences of approach which is necessarily characteristic of a search for knowledge based upon free inquiry by independent minds, then the problem of orientation to the various approaches within a field is important not only to the public and to the neophyte, but also to the professional. Here, the scholar as intramural journalist operates by defining lines along which an individual can find avenues for the expression of loyalties and commitments. At the same time, the lines define the 'enemies', and, with it, those schools of thought and approaches that are to be ignored, disdained, or accorded low prestige.[18]

Journalism of this nature is necessary for the political organization of any intellectual field, and parallels the use of journalism as a device for controlling and manipulating information by the public relations man and by the information specialists of large bureaucracies.

Journalistic treatment combines with scholarship in other forms as well. The most frequent is that in which the journalistic explicator must explain in popular terms how work that is independently valuable was really done, or how it can be understood in more simplified and 'basic' terms. This, as we have previously indicated, results in the industry of commentaries, in which each commentary on basic work encrusts itself on other commentaries, so that the original idea, which was sufficiently attractive to invite commentaries, gets lost in the total weight of commentaries. But it is not enough for the journalist (or for the non-journalist–scholar providing journalistic treatment) to simplify and explain the original work. He must add elements to the original work and to previous commentaries, to justify his present commentary, frequently 'on the basis of more recent scholarship'. This results in 'improvements' on the original work by individuals who are not equipped to do the original work, but who know how to write about it.

The process of developing critical encrustations on original work by journalists or critics who have not done the original work results in further journalistic camouflage. The journalistic critic, in confronting both the original work and the audiences who know the original work or previous commentaries, must establish credentials to perform surgery upon these earlier stages. Therefore, scholarship, or the appearance of scholarship, becomes an indispensable tool for the journalist–critic. In the light of this predicament, the journalist critic has greater need for such scholarship. Because of this situation, a secondary set of industries has been developed to provide instant scholarship and instant credentials for validating the journalistic enterprise. These involve the use and creation of specialized encyclopedias, almanacs, dictionaries, and reference works, easily cross-referenced and indexed, which all allow the acquisition of the externals of expertise, at little cost of time and energy. To the expert who is not a journalist, knowledge of the same order of technical depth is based upon his total life history in the accumulation of such knowledge. The knowledge is an intrinsic part of him and manifests itself through his work at the moment of work, and not in the autonomous display of erudition. Only a genuine scholar can be simple in the manner of his presentation. There is a special type of scholarly paper whose format is by now fairly standardized, in which the scholar reveals in the course of the paper that he has read the original and every commentary thereon over the course of two thousand years. The amassing citations, especially obscure ones, becomes the exclusive preoccupation of the paper as a work of scholarly erudition. The process reaches its culmination when the display of erudition is so concentrated that it leaves no room for a theme, a hypothesis, or a point.

One conceptual device which has become a major part of the critical industry, and which can be traced back to journalistic usages, is that of the establishment, within a subject-matter field, of a pantheon of the major historical figures of that field. Many a survey of a field for the beginner or for the layman, has the model of a guided tour of the pantheon, in which the leading figures are brought forth, their lives and works briefly sketched using the techniques of personification and simplification, and then their relative merits are established. Thus, one figure will be established in the main section, others in the lesser wings of the pantheon, according to their stature, as established by the critic describing the field. Thus, we will be given ratings of the figures in the field: the greatest and most important, the second after him, the next, and so on. This device of establishing, as though once and for all, the relative merits of the figures in a field, is journalistic in nature, borrowed primarily from the sports pages of the newspapers, in which individual athletes and teams are rated either according to their standings in the season's competition, or on the basis of long-term statistical measures, or according to public opinion polls.

In scholarly work, this results in the use of the biography or the anthology of biographical essays in which the life, glamour, travails and tragedies, the 'agonies and ecstasies' of creative geniuses are presented as a substitute for the great work or thought itself.

The industry of commentaries also serves the political organization of an intellectual field in the problem of according recognition for original or valuable work which originates in an opposing or rival school of thought. If the concepts or findings developed are really indispensable, they can be gradually and anonymously appropriated, and sources for the appropriation can be eventually cited only among scholars of an allied, rather than an opposing, school of thought.

We have presented the development of a phenomenological model of an attitude as related to a specialized kind of treatment of information appropriate to given types of social and societal structures. The journalistic attitude is evoked by the needs for the periodistic presentation of images of the world to distant publics who are unable to comprehend parts of their world in terms of their direct experience. At its best, journalism performs an extremely important function in the creation, re-creation, and re-emphasis of world images. It transvalues the world even in the process of trying to present it.

But the very development of the skills and techniques for manifesting such images demonstrates the possibility of use and abuse by those who would use the journalistic attitude for non-journalistic purposes in a society in which the need for information is so great that, when fulfilled, the fulfilment cancels the need by drowning the public in information.

In addition to the overabundance of information presented to the society at large, one finds that public relations treatment has been imported into most other areas of life, even by those who are not professionally aware of using the journalistic attitude. Thus, when journalistic treatment begins to pervade a great part of the major institutions, and the thinking processes, of a society, the creation of images and appearances becomes an autonomous process in which the institutions, techniques, and methodologies of the society become the product of the attempt to manufacture images.

Thus, the image is no longer a byproduct of the generic and necessary operation of an institution, but a major *raison d'être* of the institution. When this occurs, the activities and operations of the institutions are depleted of their intrinsic meanings, and extrinsic meanings become the only meanings available. If and when this occurs, self-consciousness concerning image-building, that is, the journalistic attitude and journalistic treatment, results in the devaluation of all intrinsic meanings. The articulation of meaning thus becomes a device by which meaning is depleted of its content.

Notes and references

1 *The Sociology of Georg Simmel* translated by Kurt Wolff (1964) New York, Free Press, pp. 185–6. 'The journalist gives content and direction to the opinions of a mute multitude. But he is nevertheless forced to listen, combine, and guess what the tendencies of this multitude are, what it desires to hear and to have confirmed, and whether it wants to be led. While apparently it is only the public which is exposed to *his* suggestions, actually he is as much under the sway of the public's suggestion. Thus, a highly complex interaction (whose two, mutually spontaneous forces, to be sure, appear under very different forms) is hidden here beneath the semblance of the pure superiority of the one element and a purely passive being-led of the other.'

2 Alfred Schutz, in his essay, *The Well-Informed Citizen: An Essay on the Social Distribution of Knowledge*, formulates this problem in a somewhat different but related perspective, in which he constructs three ideal types:

the expert, the man in the street, and the well-informed citizen as three separate forms of social knowledge (see *The Collected Works*, vol. 3, p. 129 *et passim*). The present essay on the journalistic attitude focuses upon certain aspects which Schutz developed only in passing. See also W. LIPPMANN (1925) *The Phantom Public* New York, Harcourt, Brace, p. 42. 'Modern society is not visible to anybody, nor intelligible continuously and as a whole. One section is visible to another section, one series of acts is intelligible to this group and another to that.'

3 LEO GURKO (1953) *Heroes, Highbrows and the Popular Mind* New York, Bobbs-Merrill, p. 236: 'The enormous specialization that accompanied the spread of scientific and technical knowledge broke life up into smaller segments, and made the custodian of each segment increasingly important. In due course this custodian developed into the professional expert, who, by virtue of his total knowledge of a single area (and often total ignorance of everything else), set up shop as middleman between his area and the public at large. His very concentration on a single sphere at the expense of every other kind of knowledge was a strong element in his functioning as an expert.'

4 LEO LOWENTHAL (1956) *Biographies in Popular Magazines*, in William Petersen (ed.) *American Social Patterns* Garden City, N.Y., Doubleday, p. 71. 'A biography seems to be the means by which an average person is able to reconcile his interest in the important trends of history and in the personal lives of other people.' Also pp. 108–10: 'The important role of familiarity in all phenomena of mass culture cannot be sufficiently emphasized. People derive a great deal of satisfaction from the continual repetition of familiar patterns . . . there has never been any rebellion against this fact . . . the biographies repeat what we have always known . . . [The] distance between what an average individual may do and the forces and powers that determine his life and death has become too unbridgeable such that that identification with normalcy, even with Philistine boredom, becomes a readily grasped empire of refuge and escape. . . . By narrowing his focus of attention he can experience the gratification of being confirmed in his own pleasures and discomforts by participating in the pleasures and discomforts of the great. The large and confusing issues on the political and economic realm and the antagonisms and controversies in the social realm – all these are submerged in the experience of being at one with the lofty and great in the sphere of consumption.' See also Lippmann, *op. cit.*, pp. 13–14.

5 ORRIN E. KLAPP (1964) *Symbolic Leaders: Public Dramas and Public Men* Chicago, Aldine, Chap. 8, 'Hero Stuff.' See p. 127 for other props of famous characters: sweaters, spectacles, moustaches, stovepipe hats, etc.

6 EDGAR MORIN (1960) *The Star: An Account of the Star System in Motion Pictures* New York, Grove Press, p. 39. 'The actor does not engulf his role. The role does not engulf the actor. Once the film is over, the actor becomes an actor again, the character remains a character, *but from their union*

is born a composite creature who participates in both, envelops them both: the star. G. Gentilhomme gives an excellent primary definition of the star (in *Comment devenir vedette de cinema*): 'A star appears when the interpreter takes precedence over the character he is playing while profiting by that character's qualities on the mythic level.' Which we might complete: 'and when the character profits by the star's qualities on this same mythic level.' p. 67: 'Possessed by her own myth, the star imposes it on the film universe of which she is the product. Stars demand or refuse roles in the name of their own image. P. Richard Wilm wanted to make only films in which he would be victorious in love; Gabin, before 1939, demanded his death in every film he made.' p. 66: 'The star is in effect subjectively determined by her double on the screen. She is nothing since her image is everything. She is everything since she is this image too.'

7 DANIEL J. BOORSTIN (1962) *The Image, or What Happened to the American Dream* New York, Atheneum, pp. 17–19: '[Our] whole system of public information produces always more "packaged" news, more pseudo-events . . . The common "news releases" which every day issue by the ream from Congressmen's offices, from the President's press secretary, from the press relations offices of businesses, charitable organizations, and universities are a kind of *Congressional Record* covering all American life. To secure "news coverage" for an event, . . . one must issue, in proper form a "release." . . . The release is news pre-cooked, and supposed to keep till needed. . . . The account is written in past tense but usually describes an event that has not yet happened when the release is given out. . . . The National Press Club in its Washington clubrooms has a large rack which is filled daily with the latest releases, so the reporter does not even have to visit the offices which give them out. In 1947 there were about twice as many government press agents engaged in preparing news releases as there were newsmen gathering them in.'

8 ISRAEL GERVER and JOSEPH BENSMAN (1954) 'Towards a Sociology of Expertness' in *Social Forces*, **32**, no. 3, pp. 227–9: '. . . symbolic experts may personify complexities not only for the distant public, but also for insiders under conditions which are sufficiently complex so that these complexities cannot be understood exclusively and immediately in terms of direct participant experience. . . . In many fields of endeavour the symbolic expert is not actually a substantive expert but appears to be one. The symbolic expert is not necessarily a particular living person but may be a complex of traditional evaluations and definitions which become personified . . . such as Rembrandt, Beethoven, Bach, Van Gogh . . . Copernicus and Galileo. . . .' 'The interpretive expert who is attached to the organization publicizes the results and creates and maintains the symbolic expert. Both emphasize the magic of scientific technique to the public at large. Both are likely to pressure the substantive experts for publicly demonstrative results and both are more likely to announce these results before substantive experts would do so.'

9 BERNARD ROSENBERG and NORRIS FLIEGEL (1965) *The Vanguard*

Artist: Portrait and Self-Portrait Chicago, Quadrangle Books, pp. 57–8: '. . . by becoming celebrities too soon, many of the young are deprived of experience. The quiet novitiate, an extended period of steady work without public celebration, toughens and inures a man to success. With adequate pre-conditioning and time to grow he can take it in stride. Young men in a hurry, overambitious to start with, who "click" on the marketplace find it difficult to resist the ballyhoo which envelops them.'

10 *Ibid.*, pp. 194–5: 'To get their work before a sizeable audience, artists feel that they are forced into alien procedures; they must also accept the fact that much of their work will be acquired by aesthetically unappreciative buyers. They are elated when things go otherwise, but there is rarely any expectation that they will. Few can hold out for the "perfect buyer". The size of the purchasing audience often makes it difficult for the painter to know who his "customer" is. The pervasive feeling is that the patron of yesteryear and the collector of yesterday have been replaced by a new and difficult-to-define breed of art consumers – a group whose motivations are at best suspect. Painters seems to accommodate themselves to these realities without excessive rancour. Understandably, they deplore the fact that the buying group . . . is often guided by extraneous considerations.'

11 JOSEPH BENSMAN and ROBERT LILIENFELD (1973) *Craft and Consciousness: Occupational Technique and the Development of World Images* New York, John Wiley, Chapter 1.

12 WILLIAM JAMES (1896) *The Principles of Psychology* New York, Holt, pp. 221–2: 'There are two kinds of knowledge broadly and practically distinguishable: we may call them respectively *knowledge of acquaintance* and knowledge-about. . . . In minds able to speak at all there is, it is true, some knowledge about everything. Things can at least be classed, and the times of their appearance told. But in general, the less we analyze a thing, and the fewer of its relations we perceive, the less we know about it and the more our familiarity with it is of the acquaintance-type. The two kinds of knowledge are, therefore, as the human mind practically exerts them, relative terms. That is, the same thought of a thing may be called knowledge-about it in comparison with a simpler thought or acquaintance with it in comparison with a thought of it that is more articulate and explicit still.' See also the development of this idea made by Robert Park in his essay, 'News as a Form of Knowledge' in Hughes, Everett C., Johnson, Charles S., Masouka, Jitsuichi, Redfield, Robert, and Wirth, Louis (eds) (1955) *The Collected Papers of Robert Ezra Park, Vol. 3* Glencoe, Ill., Free Press, p. 76: 'What are here described as "acquaintance with" and "knowledge-about" are assumed to be distinct forms of knowledge – forms having different functions in the lives of individuals and of society – rather than knowledge of the same kind but of different degrees of accuracy and validity. . . . "Knowledge about" [is] . . . a body of tested and accredited fact and theory. . . . On the other hand, acquaintance with, as I have sought to characterize it, so far as it is based on the slow accumulation of experience

and the gradual accommodation of the individual to his individual and personal world, becomes, as I have said, more and more completely identical with instinct and intuition.' See also Chap. 10, 'News and the Power of the Press'. In journalism as in so many other areas, Park's work is as valuable as it is neglected.

13 KARL KRAUS (1955) *Beim Wort Genommen* Munich, Kösel-Verlag, p. 212. This and many other features of the journalistic attitude were first developed in the polemic and satirical writings of Kraus, e.g. 'A historian is often just a journalist facing backwards' (p. 215).

14 See Schutz, *op. cit.*, pp. 122–3 and 132–3.

15 A byproduct of this process is the development of a special journalistic language which conveys meaning by indirection, and by surrounding familiar words with new emotional connotations to convey meanings opposite to their traditional sense. In addition, new language, spelling, and coinages, elisions, and acronyms are invented. These debase the traditional usages of language, and introduce new forms of barbarisms. They do, however, facilitate the above-described journalistic treatment of events. See, for example, DWIGHT MACDONALD (1962) *Against the American Grain* New York, Random House, pp. 12–13, and the essays, 'The String Untuned', pp. 289ff and 'The Decline and Fall of English', pp. 317ff. See also KARL KRAUS (1960) *Untergang der Welt durch Schwarze Magie* Munich, Kösel-Verlag.

16 See JOSEPH BENSMAN and BERNARD ROSENBERG (1963) *Mass, Class, and Bureaucracy: The Evolution of Contemporary Society* Englewood Cliffs, N.J., Prentice-Hall, pp. 351–4.

17 EDMUND WILSON (1940) *To the Finland Station: A Study in the Writing and Acting of History* Garden City, N.Y., Doubleday (Anchor Books reprint 1953), pp. 383ff.

18 Such practices of modern journalistic scholarship suggest the emergence of a new problem in the study of artistic and intellectual history: the fame of the ephemeral, and the obscuration of original or important work. What is visible on the surface of intellectual life and what is of lasting value are now sharply separated.

29 Time and deterioration

Stanley Cohen and Laurie Taylor

Time as a problem

Time is a much more taken-for-granted element of everyday life than is friendship or privacy. We may periodically reflect upon our inability to manage without friends or privacy, we may talk philosophically about the need to seek new friends or dispense with old ones, and consciously reflect upon the merits of gregariousness and isolation. But behind such thinking and planning time ticks away relatively unobserved and unanalysed. We talk of it chiefly as a resource – we do not have enough of it, we cannot spare any for visits to our relations, we must make some so that we can squeeze in this or that activity. We can turn down any engagement on the grounds that we 'simply have no time' and we can become irritated by those who waste time or have time 'on their hands' without using it.

The association between time and money is hardly surprising in a highly industrialized society in which time wasted is often equivalent to money wasted in the great and continuing race for higher productivity. But there are occasions upon which the daily planning and allocation of intervals, the according of hours, days, and weekends to specific activities, breaks down. The sudden loss of a job, the cancellation of an engagement, removal from occupational time-scheduling by holiday or hospitalization, all provide opportunities for absenting ourselves from the obsession with marked time. It is then that time may become an open landscape rather than a set of pigeon-holes.

On these occasions 'past' and 'future' may have a meaning not in terms of time wasted or potential time to use in the future, but rather as parameters which define the present moment. Time then becomes less of an object in its own right. We then recognize that our past is not simply a pile of spent time, it has a personal meaning and significance. In the same way, the future becomes not simply a set of unfilled hours, but it is seen to hold a determinate position in our present existence. It assures us of the finiteness of life and thereby makes a mockery of the customary use of hours and days as steps towards some final goal. Our memory of the past

---

COHEN, STANLEY and TAYLOR, LAURIE (1972) 'Time and deterioration' in *Psychological Survival* Harmondsworth, Penguin, 86–111.

and our recognition of the end of the future throw into relief our everyday human time-scheduling.

But such speculation is quickly ended for most of us. Life, as we say, catches up with us and we become locked back into the round of activities perhaps even persuading ourselves that only by such a self-conscious immersion can we manage to live at all. There is little consideration for those in our society who continually cast doubt upon the need to use time profitably. Much of the hostility felt towards such groups as hippies in contemporary society, is due to their disdain for conventional notions of time and their tendency to alter time perspectives by experiencing only the present and the immediate. One observer of the hippie subculture, Fred Davis,[1] notes how these groups raise doubts about 'the magically rationalistic faith in converting present efforts to future pay off', how their use of 'happenings' and interest in such ideas as astrology are attempts 'to denude the future of its temporal integrity – its unknowability and slow unfoldingness – by fusing it indiscriminately with present dispositions and sensations'. He goes on:

> The hippies' structureless round-of-day ('hanging loose'), his disdain for appointments, schedules, and straight society's compulsive parcelling out of minutes and hours, are all implicated in his intense reverence for the possibilities of the present and uninterest in the future. Few wear watches and as a colleague who has made a close participant observer study of one group of hippies remarked, 'None of them ever seems to know what time it is.'

Such experiences are, of course, linked in these subcultures with the use of mind-altering drugs and indeed a central claim made by proselytizers for such drugs concerns their properties for wholly altering time perspectives.[2] One subject in an LSD experiment reports: 'One of the grossest distortions was that of time perception. Centuries were lived, yet the minute hand of the watch barely moved. My Rorschach took 200 light years, the longest on record.'[3]

Long-term prisoners do not volunteer like hippies for special time experiences, they are not briefly placed outside the normal routines of life like hospital patients or holiday makers, they have instead been given time as a punishment. But they have been given someone else's time. Their own time has been abstracted by the courts like a monetary fine and in its place they have been given prison time. This is no longer a resource but a controller.

1 Fred Davis (1967), 'Why All of Us May Be Hippies Someday', *Trans-Action*, December 5, 1967.
2 For example, Timothy Leary (1970), *The Politics of Ecstasy*, London, Paladin.
3 Quoted in Sidney Cohen (1970), *Drugs of Hallucination*, London, Paladin, p. 86.

It has to be served rather than used. The men have described the ways in which they repeated their sentences to themselves – 'twenty years', 'thirty years' – in an attempt to understand the nature of their predicament.

Prisoners are, of course, not the only group who are forced to see time as a problem. For most workers, as one observer notes, '. . . Time is what the factory worker sells: not labour, not skill, but time, dreary time. Desolate factory time that passes so slowly compared with the fleeting seconds of the weekend.'[4] An industrial sociologist, Donald Roy, has provided a classic account of how a group of factory machine operatives kept themselves from 'going nuts' in a situation of monotonous work activity by a grim process of fighting against the clock.[5]

But the factory worker's day ends, he goes home, he has weekends and holidays, he will eventually retire. And although his time might indeed have been stolen from him he has not been sentenced to a long period in which he is continually and inevitably plunged into considerations about the meaning of time. A long prison sentence is not, however, a short intermission in the real business of life, it is the real business of life.

In these circumstances it is not surprising that the most frequently used metaphor to describe prison experience is a temporal one: serving a sentence is 'doing time' and the most frequent injunction to inmates is to 'do your time and not let your time do you':

> In prison, time accumulates a new dimension. You try to eat it away rather than enjoy it. If a prisoner is having difficulty with his station, if the days are hopelessly long, he is doing 'hard time'. Instead of asking why another is making life difficult one asks 'why are you cutting into my time?' And a frequent answer when one tells of his troubles is 'do your own time' or 'don't press my time'.[6]

The present and the future

Those who dislike speculation about past and future, can usually see an end to the situation which has induced such reflective breaks in the normal scheduling of life; they can consider plans for when they get out of hospital, or prison, or home on holiday. There are still bills to be paid, visits to relations to be arranged, home-coming parties to be organized during those times when one is absent from the normal run of life. The ordinary tem-

4 Ronald Fraser (ed.) (1968), *Work*, Penguin, vol. I, p. 12.
5 Donald Roy (1959–60), '"Banana Time": Job Satisfaction and Informal Interaction', *Human Organization*, 18.
6 John Rosevear (1970), 'The Fourth Mad Wall' in Ross Firestone (ed.), *Getting Busted*, New York, Douglas Books, p. 234.

poral scheduling of one's affairs is kept in the background of one's mind by the continued operation of such financial, domestic and social matters. When twenty years of one's time is taken away, even these routine matters disappear. The landscape of time, the past and the future, and the actual significance of the present moment insistently occupy the mind. The prisoners in E-Wing found Victor Serge's description of this obsessive state the most accurate.

> The unreality of time is palpable. Each second falls slowly. What a measureless gap from one hour to the next. When you tell yourself in advance that six months – or six years – are to pass like this, you feel the terror of facing an abyss. At the bottom, mists in the darkness.[7]

This unlimited time does not have the same subjective appeal for the prisoners as for the hippie drug user, or the monk or hermit. For as we have said it is not their own time. They did not volunteer for twenty years' self-reflection. And neither do they have a ready-made set of interpretations, a personal ideology to fill the hours of self-reflection. The sophisticated drug-user may be self-consciously using his expanded consciousness of time to construct mental reveries, the hermit and the monk may be conversing with God in their time-free trances, but the long-term prisoner has no such ready-made mystical voyages to take the place of his previous involvement in plans, schedules and routines.

In these circumstances, it is not surprising that the prisoners live for the present – not from some ideological disdain for future planning, but out of necessity. To quote from the experience of one American prisoner: 'You do your time in little daily jerks, living from one microscopic pleasure to the next – from breakfast pancakes to a flash of blue sky. . . . Try it any other way and you'll be pounding the walls, screaming until your lungs give out.'[8] Richard Byrd, isolated in a polar camp, came to the same solution:

> I built a wall between myself and the past in an effort to extract every ounce of diversion and creativeness inherent in my immediate surroundings. Every day I experimented with new schemes for increasing the content of the hours . . . My environment was intrinsically treacherous and difficult but I saw ways to make it agreeable. I tried to cook more rapidly, take weather

7 Victor Serge (1970), *Men In Prison*, London, Gollancz, p. 56. It was not only here that the prisoners found Victor Serge most accurate. In our view, *Men in Prison* is the best existing account of survival and resistance in prisons and we have been consistently stimulated by its insights.

8 J. Godwin (1963), *Alcatraz: 1938–1963*, New York, Doubleday & Co.

> and auroral observations more expertly and do routine things more systematically. Full mastery of the impinging moment was my goal.[9]

In prison, one also has to find ways of 'increasing the content of the hours' but 'mastery of the impinging moment' has a very different meaning for those who – unlike explorers or even short-term prisoners – do not have a clear conception of the future after one survives the treacherous environment. It is all very well to engage in relatively 'meaningless' activities – such as making weather observations – so long as this can be seen as part of a finite period of waiting before release. The long-termer has only the choice between surrendering himself to this meaningless world as a life project or obsessionally thinking about the future – a near certain way of doing hard time.

This discussion leads us to the paradox inherent in the way long-termers deal with the future. In one sense the future is unthinkable. Roy once remarked that, 'If I really thought that I had to do another seventeen years, I'd do myself in.' Other prisoners fight attempts by prison officers to bring home the time factor. Jock said: 'Whenever a screw asks me how long do I think I'll do, I always say, "Oh, about thirty-five years", because then he can get no advantage from the conversation. If I say, "Twenty," he'd say, "Oh no, I think it'll be at least twenty-five." Really I don't know what any of the figures mean.' The paradox arises in that while the men reject attempts by others to raise the subject, or dismiss thoughts about the nature of the future from their own minds, they are also relying upon ideas about a future life outside to sustain themselves through their temporally undifferentiated days.

For without entertaining the prospect of a life beyond the prison, without literally believing in an 'after life', one has to either face the fact that one's life was over at the moment of entering the prison, or that one's life is that existence which takes place within the prison. The concept of 'my life' is an important one in our culture. Young men look ahead to life, old men look back upon it. People talk about their life being behind or ahead of them. In other words we identify life with particular periods of our existence, with the time between youth and old age, that time before prison, the time which is to come after prison. What appears to be totally unacceptable is the idea that one's life is experienced in prison. One may be serving life, but one is not serving 'my life'. This was certainly true for the men we knew and Farber found it to be the case in his interviews with 'Eight Men Whose Chances of Ever Getting Out Are Slight'. His principal generalization was that '*in not a single case of these men whose*

9 Richard Byrd (1938), *Alone*, London, Putnam, p. 109.

chances of ever getting out are negligible is there complete resignation to dying in prison. That most dismal of all platitudes "Where there is life there's hope" takes on a new freshness.'[10] (Italics in original.)

Marking time

In the circumstances, prisoners who have to sustain their lives in some way look around for ways of marking out the passage of the days, ways of differentiating and dividing time. Psychologists and sociologists have paid little attention to the problems which occur for those whose lives are suddenly emptied of time markers in this total way. Perhaps their involvement in a particularly highly scheduled career structure makes them insensitive to the empty formless years which others have to occupy. At least the only major research into such matters was carried out by Julius Roth, a sociologist who suddenly found himself absorbed by the problem of time-scheduling when he was away from academic life and spending time as a patient in a T.B. sanatorium.[11]

Patients who enter such sanatoria are often surprised to find that they are given no exact date for their release. Lack of information over this matter leads to a frantic activity. Doctors, nurses and other patients are repeatedly questioned and quite ambiguous items of information are treated as significant clues. The demand for a timetable leads the patients to bargain with physicians about the nature and extent of their improvement in order that an earlier release date may be negotiated. Roth's principal concern is to indicate how important career timetables are in most areas of life and to demonstrate the concern which arises when the stages which constitute them are ambiguous or non-existent.

This study by Roth brings out the fact that one obvious benchmark, one way of dividing time, which is built into the sanatorium régimes, is the notion of linear progress. One gets better or stronger; one is able to do things one could not do before. But in E-Wing no such reference to linear progress is possible. Criteria for the positive evaluation of one's progress are not built into the system, and there are no progressive stages of reward and punishment. Though parole is a reward somewhat contingent on good behaviour, most of the men we know see its attainment (realistically) as so remote that it hardly functions as a stage of progress. Indeed, the chances of parole can be almost arbitrarily affected by the sudden appearance of a newspaper item on a notorious criminal. The men in the wing saw any

10 Maurice Farber, 'Suffering and Time Perspective of the Prisoner', p. 180.
11 Julius Roth (1962), *Timetables*, Indianapolis, Bobbs-Merrill.

popular reference to them in the Sunday newspapers as setting back even further their chances of remission. They were sophisticated enough to know how much the deliberations of a parole board were eventually influenced by public opinion, despite its avowed concern with the actual individual under consideration.

Unlike the T.B. patients described by Roth, these men have no opportunities for bargaining with the authorities. Their behaviour cannot influence their timetable, there is no room for 'making deals' with their keepers that will help to shorten the stretch or bring an earlier relaxation of restrictions. Unlike hospitals, again, there is nothing in the behaviour of the staff to give the prisoners any clues about when events should occur in the passage of time. The absence and the inscrutability of the Home Office personnel who control a few of the temporal and situational outcomes, are seen as necessary ways of keeping control and preserving security.

The men therefore tend to create stages themselves. They build their own subjective clock in order to protect themselves from the terror of 'the misty abyss'. There are a few achievements which can be used to mark the passage of time. One can engage in mind-building (reading or studying) and in body-building (usually weightlifting). Some of the men talk about an educational career, describing the passage from 'O' levels to 'A' levels to university with an enthusiasm which is rarely found in even those who have a chance of occupationally capitalizing upon the restricted years of specialized study which constitute contemporary secondary education. The significance of weightlifting in this context may be less than we at first thought. It was possible in the wing to find men who agreed that being able to lift extra weights constituted a way of marking out improvements over time, but a somewhat more cynical view came in reply to an article of ours in which we had made this point. An ex-member of the class wrote: 'In my opinion body-building was a bad example because it serves far more potent motives than the need for a concrete progression. Some of the prisoners in question would rather put an inch on their biceps than take a year off their sentence.'

In any case there is a danger in these pursuits of mental and physical targets, for there soon comes a day in which progress is inhibited, in which fewer books are read, fewer essays written and less weights lifted. In normal life we can declare that our interests have declined in such matters and re-invest successfully in foreign travel and golf. For these prisoners the loss of such matters marks the re-entry of unstructured time.

There are other methods of marking time. One can tick off certain fixed, definable periods: days, weeks or months. But this may merely bring home the unreality of time even more forcibly. As Serge writes:

> So as not to lose track of the date, you have to count the days attentively, mark each one with a cross. One morning you discover that there are forty-seven days – or one hundred and twenty, or three hundred and forty-seven! – and that it is a straight path leading backwards without the slightest break: colourless, insipid, senseless. Not a single landmark is visible. Months have passed like so many days; entire days pass like minutes. Future time is terrifying. The present is heavy with torpor.
>
> Each minute may be marvellously – or horribly – profound. That depends to a certain extent on yourself. There are swift hours and very long seconds. Past time is void. There is no chronology of events to mark it; external duration no longer exists.[12]

It is the lack of a chronology of events that is most important in Serge's description. Of course, days come and go, but they do not pass as they do on the outside when one is waiting for an event, simply because they are no longer beads on a wire, or counters on a board. They are not progressively used up as one moves towards a goal. They are isolated entities, existing away from the normal cumulative linear context they inhabit. In Roth's words: 'The life prisoner can look forward to Sunday as a welcome break in a dreary routine, but the succession of Sundays does not lead him anywhere.'[13]

In these circumstances, the external clock may be partially abandoned in favour of such subjective markers as changes in mood or feeling. These may have a reality and a temporal meaning which is lacking in the world of clocks and diaries and calendars. Christopher Burney although writing specifically about solitary confinement, captures this transition:

> Days in prison are distinguishable only by such rare incidents as from time to time make one of them memorable among its fellows. Although I never lost count of the week or of the date, I followed them subconsciously, and life was divided into longer periods, limited by a state of mind or a physical condition; and it was these more personal symbols than sun or moon which marked out the calendar.[14]

Shorter sentences undoubtedly are managed in more orthodox ways: days are crossed off calendars and hours until release are pencilled on all walls. The techniques for conducting such time management become accepted parts of prison folk-lore. Leary recalls noticing that the numbers

12 Victor Serge, *Men in Prison*, pp. 56–7.
13 Julius Roth, *Timetables*, p. 99.
14 Christopher Burney (1952), *Solitary Confinement*, New York, Coward & McCann, p. 23.

pinned to a trustee's wall signifying the date were removed each day but there was no number for the day on which he was looking at the wall. He asked the prisoner why and the reply was: 'in con terminology when you wake up in the morning that day is over'.[15] There were attempts to advocate variations in such techniques to meet the case of long sentences. When Roland arrived in E-Wing he turned to Paul for advice on the structuring of time. 'How am I going to do twenty years?' Paul, on the basis of three years' experience of an equally long sentence, provided the only reassurance he knew: 'It's easy, do it five years at a time.'

There are of course the 'incidents' referred to by Burney which occur in the wing and which break up the dull passage of time. Many of these are, however, unscheduled and it is therefore not possible to look forward to them or prepare for them. The sudden transfer of a man from the wing or the arrival of a new inmate is typically unexpected. Events which occur in this sudden way are deprived of significance. Once again it is easy to forget how important for our existence is the anticipation of such matters in everyday life. The dull Monday morning becomes acceptable because of the promise of an evening out on Thursday, the long winter is bearable because of an anticipated Easter holiday. Each event by itself may be trivial, even dispensable without great psychic cost, but together they constitute a set of inducements which help to move us forward through time.

Donald Roy's factory workers, spending a day of 'infinitesimal cerebral excitation', repetitively clocking a machine, faced similar problems of marking time: the lunch break, occasional trips to the lavatory or drinking fountain, obviously functioned to 'break the day up into digestible parts'. But Roy soon realized that the men were doing more than this, they were creating 'incidents' and in fact much of their informal activity was devoted to deliberately making new time markers and interruptions in the 'day's long grind'. These were not *just* rest pauses or work interruptions or accentuations of progress points in the passage of time – although they performed this latter function better than a clock:

> If the daily series of interruptions be likened to a clock then the comparison might best be made with a special kind of cuckoo clock, one with a cuckoo which can provide variation in its announcements and can create such an interest in them that the intervening minutes become filled with intellectual content. . . . The group interactions thus not only marked off the time; they gave it content and hurried it along.[16]

15 Timothy Leary (1970), *Jail Notes*, New York, Douglas Books, p. 77.
16 Donald Roy, ' "Banana Time": Job Satisfaction and Informal Interaction', p. 162.

The clicker operators called these breaks 'times' and they usually involved the consumption of food or drink: coffee time, peach time, banana time, fish time or coke time. All the themes in the group's interactions, their joking, horseplay, ritualistic conversation provided interaction which captured attention and held interest to make the long day pass.

The routine of E-Wing was so short of events that even our classes became something of an occasion. We were told by the men, quite self-consciously (gently mocking themselves and us at the same time) how they would sometimes make quite elaborate preparations – like 'dressing up' – for our meetings. We were at least outsiders and this they found reassuring. We could pass on in detail the changes in life which were occurring outside, we could interpret changes in the political climate, in drug use, in popular music, in sexual permissiveness. Their ability to assimilate these changes, to approve or accept the widespread use of marihuana or the increased permissiveness of the cinema, provided some type of guarantee that they could rejoin society without too great a strain upon their release. To put it pretentiously, we helped to keep them in gear with external time and in this way provided them with a way of marking time which did not simply refer to the unserved years of their sentence.

But our visits did not of course have the emotional significance or impact of visits from friends and relatives. Such visits were events to be planned for, to be anticipated over days and weeks. Fred Davis talks about the 'accordion effect' that such events produce: a man stretches the time of the event, from the point of its anticipation through to the discussions that follow its occurrence.[17] With more feeling Serge calls these effects 'exultation': the radiant joy at the expectation of recognition by others, and the fact that 'a fifteen-minute visit is enough to fill long days with expectation and long days with meaning afterwards'.

Unfortunately, as we noted in the last chapter, such events may become increasingly rare as the prisoner moves towards the end of his first decade inside. The joy produced by a visit and the structuring of time which its anticipation allows is not enough to overcome the pains of anxiety which a possible break in that relationship induces.[18]

17 Quoted by Kathy Calkins (1970) in 'Time: Perspectives, Marking and Styles of Usage', *Social Problems 17*, 6 (Spring 1970).

18 We should mention in passing one of the solutions some prison reformers and many of the E-Wing men themselves have suggested as a way of alleviating some of the pains associated with very long sentences. This is to introduce some measure of indeterminacy in which the men's release or parole would depend on progress within the prison – 'progress' being assessed by evidence of good behaviour and willingness to change. Experience with such systems, however, suggests that only new temporal problems will result. In California, for example, the Indeterminate Sentence (IS) was introduced for a number of humanitarian

Work and making time pass

Victor Serge described the 'present' in prison as being 'heavy with torpor'. Days do not go past at their conventional pace. However the adoption of new methods of time-scheduling in this ambiguous situation is not the only problem facing the long-termer. It is not just the division of time which concerns him but the *speed* of its passage. How can it be made to go more quickly? The anticipation of visits or the expectation of letters does nothing about increasing the speed at which time goes. Obsessional concern with such future events may even slow time as anyone who has fixedly waited for a kettle to boil will know.

In everyday life we typically make time go by throwing ourselves into occupational activities. We bury ourselves in our work so that we have no time for 'clock-watching'. This method is not much use even to the average prisoner. It is not much use hoping that a man in Parkhurst's 'tag shop' will become involved in his job of sticking metal ends in to the lengths of green string used to keep files together. It is even less reasonable to suppose that men facing twenty years in jail can lose themselves in repairing sewing machines or making mosquito nets – to name two of the jobs provided for E-Wing men. But people faced with such monotonous jobs in the outside world do, of course, cope. One commentator on the workers' struggle to 'cling to the remnants of joy in work' notes that 'it is psychologically impossible to deprive any kind of work of all its positive emotional elements'.[19] The worker will always find *some* meaning, some scope for initiative, play and creative impulse in the activity assigned to him.

We doubt that this is true for long-term prisoners. The culturally defined meanings of work: learning a trade, making something for one's family, financial incentive are gone. Even if prison jobs were interesting, work for a life prisoner has a very peculiar status indeed: if factory workers have to desperately invest jobs with meaning and time markers, then

motives, for example, to allow rehabilitative considerations rather than purely legal retribution to determine the time a man spent inside. The results of this system have been anything but humane, and under these conditions the obsessions with time only increases. To the administrator, time becomes a weapon and means of control. The staff use the impending hearing before the review board as a manipulative device to ensure passivity and obedience to the régime. For the inmate who 'gets a date' of release time acquires a new and positive meaning. But if a date is denied, time perspectives are shattered: the inmate has to restructure his temporal strategies because of the uncertainty, to change his expectations of the future and to employ further frustrating efforts in attempting to discover his fate. (This footnote makes use of unpublished research by Marty Miller on the temporal strategies used by prisoners serving indeterminate sentences in California.)

19 Henri de Man, quoted in Donald Roy, op. cit., p. 160.

prisoners without clear meanings or time markers have to try and find them in the work they are given. So their problem is a double one.

In these circumstances it is not surprising to find that only five men out of the forty-two in the Eccleston sample listed work as a way of making time go faster. Ten of the rest saw no ways at all of solving this problem and the others mentioned hobbies, reading, or private study: activities we would regard in the outside world as leisure. When workshops were introduced into E-Wing in 1968 there were references to the fact that the men had done no work for six months and were becoming lazy. Certainly many of them regarded the introduction of the workshops as an additional punishment rather than as an escape from torpor and this was the main reason for the protest and barricade which immediately followed. An editorial comment at this time admitted that the work that was being offered was not interesting or relevant. The real value of the new workshops was that they would 'occupy idle hands and minds, and perpetuate the idea that work, as opposed to idleness, is a requirement of life'. (*Newcastle Journal.*)

The very use of the word 'work' is misleading in this context. As Erving Goffman observed in *Asylums*:

> In the ordinary arrangements of living in our society, the authority of the work place stops with the worker's receipt of a money payment; the spending of this in a domestic and recreational setting is the worker's private affair and constitutes a mechanism through which the authority of the work place is kept within strict bounds. But to say that inmates of total institutions have their full day scheduled for them is to say that all their essential needs will have to be planned for. Whatever the incentive given for work, then, this incentive will not have the structural significance it has on the outside. There will have to be different motives for work and different attitudes towards it. This is a basic adjustment required of the inmates and of those who must induce them to work.[20]

The absurdity of 'work' within the context of the security wing is perhaps most neatly illustrated by the fact that what is a 'job' in one wing – making soft toys – is offered as a hobby in another.

We always found it difficult to maintain a conversation about work with prisoners in E-Wing. They gave the impression that there were other more important matters to be discussed. What job they were doing at the time made little apparent difference to their feelings about life inside. Once again, we are able to turn to Farber for some interesting confirmation of these findings. With the help of prison officials and prisoners he divided

20 Erving Goffman (1969), *Asylums*, Penguin, p. 10.

up jobs along a good–bad axis and then checked on the relationship between the relative suffering experienced by the prisoners and the quality of the job. There was no link at all. Those with bad jobs suffered no more or less than those with good. He was sufficiently surprised by this result to check up on job satisfaction as well. For perhaps men who had good jobs might *dislike* them and vice versa. But no relationship between degree of job satisfaction and suffering could be found. Farber concludes by saying that 'what would seem to be one of the most important of day-to-day activities bears no relation to suffering. Suffering is related to broader, less immediate aspects of the life situation.'[21]

We have been a little too sweeping, however, in writing off work as a way of speeding up the passage of time. There are a few in prison who feel it to be better than nothing. They admit that it is a self-deception, but claim that there is no alternative. They feel sympathetic to Ivan Denisovich's view: 'How time flew when you were working. That was something he'd often noticed. The days rolled by in the camp – they were over before you could say "knife". But the years never rolled by, they never moved by a second.'[22]

For some time we assumed that these differences in attitude towards the use of work to pass time were idiosyncratic. But behind the cynical view of work may lie a concern about what is involved in passing time in this way. It was the more rebellious members of the group who played down the significance of becoming involved in such activities. In doing this they may have been recognizing the loss of personal autonomy which is involved in fitting oneself to others' schedules. Kathy Calkins, who has conducted a very sensitive investigation into the significance of time in a rehabilitation hospital, reserves the phrase 'time passing' for this particular style of adaptation:

> When time is *passed* (our stress), the patient tends to relinquish a certain amount of control over his own time. Essentially, he fits into the time of others according to their time prescriptions. In this style, the patient voluntarily fills pockets of time outlined by the institution.[23]

For the long-termer to seek to pass time by immersing himself in institutional routines may be to accord some type of legitimacy to the institution. It is to acknowledge that his sentence will be served in accordance with the intentions of the authorities.

21 Maurice Farber in Lewin, K. (ed.), *Studies in Authority and Frustration*, p. 174.
22 Alexander Solzhenitsyn (1968), *One Day in the Life of Ivan Denisovich*, Penguin.
23 Calkins, 'Time: Perspectives, Marking and Styles of Usage', p. 495.

The marking and the passing of time are then major elements in long-term prisoners' lives. Time presents itself as a problem. It is no longer a resource to be used, but rather an object to be contemplated – an undifferentiated landscape which has to be marked out and traversed. Conventional markers cannot be used and neither can one's journey be expedited by recourse to conventional methods. Nevertheless the length of the journey continually preoccupies the mind, for only after it has been made, can life be effectively resumed.

There is another preoccupation for these particular time travellers. As the journey proceeds they are accompanied by a number of growing anxieties. Above all long-term prisoners have to learn to live with a constant fear of deterioration. [. . .]

Section 10
Beliefs and attitudes

Introduction

Beliefs and attitudes denote the ways in which a person makes sense of and responds to the world about him. In some respects, therefore, the papers in this section continue consideration of man's experience of the world. Their concern, however, is not with content – what is actually experienced and believed – but with the nature of the belief process and, in particular, the factors which determine whether one particular set of beliefs or attitudes is adopted rather than another. The contributions here stress the functional nature of beliefs, their consistency or organization and their relationship to both personality and social context. The picture that emerges is that attitudes and beliefs reflect far more the characteristics of the person holding them than the nature of the objects with which they are concerned. This conception of belief systems as functional constructions is reminiscent of Israel's analysis of the nature of scientific theories included in section 1 (see pp. 6–12).

The first two contributions look specifically at the functions that opinions and ideas may serve, a topic which has engaged the attention of several psychologists. The brief extract from the now classic monograph by Smith, Bruner and White, *Opinions and personality*, postulates three essential functions. Lane's longer and more recent contribution is primarily concerned with political ideas. While acknowledging Smith, Bruner and White's account, he suggests a more detailed list. If you compare the two sets you will see that there is a great deal of similarity between them. Each of the functions in the earlier list tends to subsume one or more of the ten more precisely differentiated functions put forward by Lane.

The third extract is taken from an account by Nevitt Sanford of the Authoritarian Personality study. Sanford, along with Adorno, Frenkel-Brunswik, Levinson and others, carried out this seminal research into the psychological basis of prejudice. The project extended over several years and used a variety of techniques ranging from the administration of attitude scales to the analysis of interview and projective test material. Its essential conclusion has been expressed in the phrase 'anti-Semitism has nothing to do with Jews'. Sanford's description of the development of the

F or Authoritarian scale draws heavily on psychoanalytic concepts and indicates how some prejudice may be neither a realistic response to characteristics of the target person nor yet a result of conformity to group or cultural norms, but rather an expression of the personality conflicts and weaknesses of the prejudiced person himself.

In contrast to the previous contributions, the final paper in this section is a report of a 'natural field experiment'. Seymour Lieberman took advantage of naturally occurring events, in this case, changing work roles, to explore the relation between attitudes held and roles played. His results reveal a remarkable consistency between role and belief. When a worker became a foreman, for example, his attitude showed a distinct shift in favour of management and to a more negative view of unions and their policies. If, as happened in some cases, a foreman returned to his role as worker, then his attitudes would tend to revert back accordingly. While acknowledging that the results themselves do not provide an explanation for the attitude shifts observed, Lieberman suggests that the change may have been brought about by the need for the individuals concerned to maintain consistency with either the actions or the reference groups intrinsic to the roles which they played, or both.

The theme which runs in different ways through all these papers is that attitudes and beliefs are not mere reflections of aspects of the world with which an individual comes in contact but rather constructions, coloured and shaped by effort to maintain consistency, not just with related beliefs, but with personal needs and actions, external demands and social context.

30 The adjustive functions of opinion

M. Brewster Smith, Jerome S. Bruner and Robert W. White

... What purpose is served by holding an opinion? Put more technically, the question becomes, 'What adjustive functions of personality are served by the formation and maintenance of an opinion?'

Let us say at the most general level that one's opinions or attitudes serve as mediators between the inner demands of the person and the outer environment – the material, social, and, most immediately, the informational environment of the person. Figures of speech may be misleading, yet we do well to think of a man's attitudes as his major equipment for dealing with reality. This equipment is not a product solely of basic needs and defences nor is it fashioned directly according to the blueprint of the world in which the person finds himself. Nor is it simply borrowed ready-made from the groups to which he belongs or aspires. Something of all of these but not quite any one of them, it is, essentially, an apparatus for balancing the demands of inner functioning and the demands of the environment. One cannot predict a man's opinions by knowledge of his personality alone or of his environment alone. Both must enter into any predictive formula.

It is a mistake to restrict the concepts of attitude and opinion to those predispositions which have as their object the issues of contemporary social and political life. Such restriction overlooks the fact that these attitudes are embedded in larger systems of opinion which mediate between the most compelling pressures of the environment and the most imperious and pervasive needs. ... Look far enough into the origins of any opinion, and one will find not just an opinion but a sample of how the holder of that opinion copes with his world.

Rather than risk later misunderstanding we shall pause for a moment to examine the two meanings that can be attached to 'having an opinion'. Let us say first that one can *hold* an opinion and at the same time reserve option on when and how the opinion should be *expressed*. It is obvious that the two acts serve somewhat different functions. And while we may be inclined to say that the one is freer of constraints than the other – that a man may hold whatever view he likes so long as he is discreet in its expression – it is the better wisdom to attribute an equal lawfulness to each. Only in a most superficial sense is one 'free' to hold whatever opinion he

SMITH, M. B., BRUNER, J. S. and WHITE, R. W. (1956) 'The adjustive functions of opinion' in *Opinions and Personality* New York, Wiley, pp. 39–44.

will. The illusion of free choice of opinion is scarcely borne out by closer analysis of the many inner and outer requirements that limit what a person will find acceptable. 'I can't believe that,' he will say; or, 'What an irresponsible, almost despicable point of view that is!'

Once we have said that there is a lawful determination both in the opinions one holds and in the occasions and circumstances of their expression, we must then go on to say that the same laws do not hold for each. The two must be held separate, for separate but concurrent examination. It is true, of course, that the opinions permissible to express are, under some circumstances, the very opinions one wishes to hold. Or, quite the reverse, the rebel may find himself repelled by popular points of view whose expression savours to him of conformism. Such instances do not cancel the need for separate analysis.

In our discussion of the adjustive functions of opinion we shall make no special effort to incarcerate 'holding' and 'expressing' into separate and purified theoretical categories. They each present somewhat different problems for empirical analysis and we shall, where possible, analyze them separately. Our principal theoretical interest is in the opinions *held* by the individual. It is a crucial but secondary theoretical problem how a man works out the strategy of their expression.[1]

There are three functions served by holding an opinion, and we shall call them *object appraisal*, *social adjustment*, and *externalization*. Let us note briefly the characteristics of each and then return to a more extended discussion of their significance.

Object appraisal

We use this expression in the same sense in which psychoanalysts employ 'reality testing'. The holding of an attitude provides a ready aid in 'sizing up' objects and events in the environment from the point of view of one's major interests and going concerns. In so far as attitudes are predispositions to experience certain classes of objects, to be motivated by them, and to respond to them, it is evident that their existence permits the individual to check more quickly and efficiently the action-relevancy of the events in the environment around him. Presented with an object or event, he may categorize it in some class of objects and events for which a predisposition

1 If one should ask, 'How do you know the opinion held by a person save by its expression?' we shall reply that we know it only in that way. Knowledge of a 'held' opinion is based upon inference from observation of its expression under a variety of special situations – including those highly permissive diagnostic situations in which there is neither gain nor loss to be earned or incurred by expressing one's views.

to action and experience exists. Once thus categorized, it becomes the focus of an already-established repertory of reactions and feelings, and the person is saved the energy-consuming and sometimes painful process of figuring out *de novo* how he shall relate himself to it. If the environmental fact either defies categorization or is categorized in such a way as to bring harmful consequences to the person, new attitudes may be developed or shifts in categorization may occur. In sum, then, attitudes aid us in classifying for action the objects of the environment, and they make appropriate response tendencies available for coping with these objects. This feature is a basis for holding attitudes in general as well as any particular array of attitudes. In it lies the function served by holding attitudes per se. Without them, we should be in the constant throes of determining the relevance of events, of fashioning decisions and of deciding upon actions – all *ab initio*. More specifically, object appraisal is the process whereby the person develops attitudes that are a creative solution to the problems posed by the existence of disparate internal demands and external or environmental demands.

Social adjustment

Opinions can play another role: that of facilitating, disrupting, or simply maintaining an individual's relations with other individuals. It is in this realm particularly that one must take care to distinguish the functions served by holding an opinion and by expressing it, for the strategy of expression is of particular importance in maintaining or cementing one's relationship with what may be called 'membership groups' – the individuals with whom one is in direct contact. Where there is a need to be accepted in the community, one will more readily and more forthrightly express acceptable attitudes while inhibiting or modulating the expression of less approved ones.

The function of social adjustment served by holding an opinion is at once more subtle and more complex. For it is by holding certain views that one identifies with, or, indeed, differentiates oneself from various 'reference groups' within the population. By reference groups we mean here those groups in terms of whose standards the individual judges himself and with which he identifies or feels kinship. They may or may not correspond to the membership groups with which he has face-to-face commerce; moreover, certain reference groups may never be physically present to the individual for interaction. Representative of reference groups are such symbols as 'intellectuals', 'average middle-class Americans', 'decent girls', and so on. The act of holding certain opinions, as Merton (1950), Centers

(1949), Warner (1941) and various others have pointed out, is an act of affiliation with reference groups. It is a means of saying, 'I am like them'.

Reference groups, we shall see, may also play a negative role in opinion functioning. There are groups with which one seeks to reject kinship or identification. Thus, one of our subjects sought as hard to dissociate himself from the bourgeoisie as he sought to associate himself with the *avant-garde* left. When rebelliousness and rejection are prominent features in a man's adjustment, we may expect negative reference groups to play a prominent role in his opinion formation.

Two rather unique kinds of social adjustment can also be achieved by holding opinions of a certain kind. First, one may develop opinions as the expression of a need to be autonomous from others. Such declarations of autonomy – and we must distinguish the term from rebellion – are in a curious backhand way still another mode of identifying oneself with various reference groups. Thus one of our subjects showed a strong need for working out his opinions independently, unswayed by prevailing points of view. This procedure was for him a way of expressing his lack of dependence on others; but it was also a way of identifying with that nebulous category known as 'independent and liberal thinkers'. And second, it is sometimes convenient to indulge hostility towards others by holding opinions that are at odds with prevailing beliefs. If such an adjustment be neurotic in origin, it is nonetheless a form of negativism one occasionally encounters.

The very act of holding an opinion, whatever its nature, may serve the social adjustment of the individual, as Riesman and Glazer (1948) have remarked. Given identification with certain groups – let us take the reference group called 'intellectuals' – the individual feels that he *must* have opinions on certain issues to maintain his sense of identification.

We must not, however, leave a false impression. The underlying motive gratified by holding and expressing opinions that aid our social adjustment is neither a conformity need nor its reverse, a need to rebel. A wide variety of psychological mechanisms is at work, motivating us to relate our destinies to those of the concrete membership groups around us and to those of the more remote reference groups to which we adhere. Requirements of ego defence, dependency needs, drives for autonomy, hostility, drives and status, and many other dynamisms may be involved.

Externalization

It would be all too easy to equate externalization of inner requirements with the classical conceptions of projection and displacement. These two mechanisms are two *examples* of what we mean by externalization. Externalization occurs when an individual, often responding unconsciously, senses an analogy between a perceived environmental event and some unresolved inner problem. He adopts an attitude towards the event in question which is a transformed version of his way of dealing with his inner difficulty. By doing so, he may succeed in reducing some of the anxiety which his own difficulty has been producing.

Perhaps an illustration, a case not included in our study, will clarify the process. An adolescent develops a violent hatred for Fascism, the Nazis, and for Hitler, particularly during the 1930s. Although he is not accepted because of his age, he is aroused to the point of volunteering for the Abraham Lincoln Brigade during the Spanish Civil War. Upon entry of the United States into the War, he volunteers, is rejected, but flings himself into a lather of civilian war activity from which he derives a deep satisfaction.

Whence the tremendous intensity of this attitude? Leaving aside the realities of the situation, the grave threat with which Fascism *did* in fact confront the world and which our subject sensed, why was there such an extraordinarily intense compulsion to do something about his feelings? Analysis reveals in this man a strong and unresolved fear of rejection by powerful figures who can be reached neither through their sympathies nor through their intellect: the figure of an inchoate, powerful, cruel, but basically unreachable force. We need not examine the genesis of this deeply repressed fear. It suffices that it existed. The emergence of Hitler and the Nazis served for the adolescent as a concretization or 'binding' for this fearsome and rejecting figure. Hitler in a unique way could serve as the apotheosis of that figure which could be reached neither by sympathy nor by reason. Energies previously directed at coping with the inner problem could now be liberated and focused on an external object. If anxiety could thereby be reduced, so much the better.

We present this case not only to illustrate externalization but also to show how it differs from run-of-the-mill displacement. Certainly the case illustrates displacement, but that is not all: there are also externalization of affect and externalization of action. An external object is treated in terms relevant to an internal problem: where the internal rejecting figure could not be destroyed by direct assault, the externalized object could become a target for highly energized, creatively destructive planning and action. If the externalization proved an adaptive one, that is partly the good fortune of history and partly the result of adequate object appraisal. The fact that there were active membership groups and palpable reference groups with whom our young man could align himself also helped. [...]

References

CENTERS, R. (1949) *The Psychology of Social Classes* Princeton, Princeton University Press.

MERTON, R. K. and KITT, A. S. (1950) 'Contributions to the theory of reference-group behaviour' in Merton, R. K. and Lazarsfeld, P. F. (eds) *Continuities in Social Research* Glencoe, Illinois, Free Press.

RIESMAN, D. and GLAZER, N. (1948) 'The meaning of opinion', *Public Opinion Quarterly*, 12, 633–48.

WARNER, W. L. and LUNT, P. S. (1941) *The Social Life of a Modern Community* New Haven, Yale University Press.

31 Needs served by ideas: an interpreted appraisal

Robert E. Lane

Each man's concept of human needs reflects his interests, his research, and the general state of working thought on the subject at the time. With more than a glance over the shoulder at Murray, Maslow, and others, let us set out the array of human needs that seem, on reflection, most adequately to account for the political thought, at least of young middle-class men, and perhaps of a much larger group as well. Here they are: (1) cognitive needs: learning, curiosity, understanding; (2) consistency needs: emotional and logical and veridical, the kinds of needs satisfied by the reduction of dissonance; (3) social needs: affiliation, approval, being liked; (4) moral needs, satisfied by the appeasing of conscience and/or by giving the impression of rectitude to others; (5) esteem needs: worth, status, importance; (6) needs for personality integration and identity clarification; (7) needs on occasion (but for everyone at some time) for the expression of aggression: the desire to injure; (8) needs for autonomy, freedom, the removal of constraint, and the experience of choice; (9) the need for self-actualization: development, growth; (10) the need for adequate instrumental guides to reality, object appraisal, and attainment.

1 Cognitive needs

The need to know and understand, which Maslow thinks is an independent basic need, could be interpreted as merely instrumental to such other basic needs as the need for safety or the need to earn a living, somehow, but the evidence seems to be against this instrumental view. There is an independent need to interpret experience, a persistent curiosity, a desire for knowledge, a need for cues in placing oneself in the social universe, defining rights and duties and expectations, reciprocal relations, and more than that, for giving these 'placings' meanings or rationalizations. By classifying things and each other, men add properties to what they see, enlarging its significance, giving themselves cues for proper feelings and perceptions. We say of a certain state that it is a 'dictatorship', suggesting that one should be against it and see the associated acts as restrictive of freedom.

LANE, ROBERT E. (1969) 'Needs served by ideas: an interpreted appraisal' in *Political Thinking and Consciousness* Chicago, Markham, 31–46.

How should one feel? What should one 'see'? The individual seeks cues on these matters. They are, in one sense, the meaning of meaning.

The apothegms and clichés that pass for theory among ordinary citizens (most of us most of the time) gives cues for a 'useless' understanding, an understanding that wants to know *why* in matters that hardly affect us. The child's persistent 'Why?' and the primitive mythologies relating things beyond man's control illustrate this pursuit, this drive. Similarly, as every storyteller and historian knows, men want to know 'what happened next', even in Wonderland, even in ancient Cathay.

At more elevated levels of education and understanding, the pleasure of creating larger intellectual constructs embodies the exercise of a skill, something said to be satisfying in itself.

Murray suggests that there is a need for *play*; is idea manipulation a form of adult play? Is there something in political discussion and thought that satisfies some of the same needs as anagrams and Scrabble? Beyond this, perhaps, *curiosity* is a motive in itself, for that great animal experimenter, Harry Harlow, found that 'monkeys can and do solve mechanical puzzles when no motivation is provided other than the presence of the puzzle'.[1] Harlow believes curiosity is an independent motive. Achievement needs, the need to meet some internalized standard of excellence, may be enlisted in all forms of thought; certainly the construction of a better argument would qualify. Perhaps, too, some quasi-aesthetic sense aroused by an 'elegant' solution, where parsimony combines with logic to give a form of gratification, is at work. There is even a theory that as one goes up the phylogenetic scale, as one moves from primitive to more advanced civilizations, and as a child matures, there is apparent to the observer a development from concrete (taxic or stimulus-bound) thinking to abstract thinking.[2] It is almost as though there were some force in life urging it towards more complicated and more abstract and more useful ideas, ideas with better fit to reality; in Smith, Bruner and White's terms, a force towards better and better 'object appraisal'.

'Cognitive needs' are composite, including, as suggested, (a) a placing or orienting function, which tells both what to see and how to feel and respond, (b) a play function, (c) a curiosity function, (d) an achievement function, (e) some aesthetic functions, and, overall, (f) a security function, all guided by some continued search to make ideas and reality, words and things fit together better.

One might say, too, that one seeks knowledge in order to seek further knowledge, a metacognitive function, for in order to collect new information a person needs, as it were, bins in which to put it, labels to tag it, handles to grasp it with. Men need the concepts appropriate to the information they would acquire. Thus it is that one idea can serve to improve memory and give utility to sensation and observation. Moreover, since ideas draw meaning from other ideas – as when, say, the concept of 'welfare state', through antitheses and discrimination, gives meaning to the concepts 'capitalism' and 'socialism' – learning serves as the basis for further thought and for further learning. Everyone, in a hit-or-miss fashion, engages in a kind of programmed learning, where one thing must precede another to give it meaning and make it usable. So it is with political ideas.

Finally, political ideas, like other kinds, are the means of economizing time and effort, for they give the means for habitual and easy responses . . . One cannot be rethinking these matters all the time; ideological reflexes are essential to daily living. Men are curious for that piece of information that tells them 'the rest', often, paradoxically, stifling further curiosity.

In his list of values, Allport suggests a type of man, 'the theoretical', who is interested in truth and draws his satisfactions from searching for and perhaps finding something he regards as 'true', whatever it may be. Lasswell suggests that one of the eight values of man is enlightenment and another is the employment and enjoyment of a skill. Men not only need to know, they appreciate knowing and knowledge; they value it.

2 The need for consistency and balance

If the mind undertakes this search-and-seizure operation on the world, seeking to know it and give it meaning, however primitive, however minimal, the intake is perception mingled with thought from which concepts or 'cognitions' emerge (to guide further perception). These elements or cognitions must somehow fit together; if they do not, a person is uncomfortable with what he knows, and seeks to readjust the elements so that they do fit together in a way that reduces the strain. 'The existence of nonfitting relations among cognitions,' says Festinger, 'is a motivating factor in its own right,' producing a drive like hunger or avoidance of pain.[3] Broadly speaking, there are three ways in which ideas must fit together: (a) The cognition should fit reality (theories should fit the evidence, effects should follow causes, established expectations should be confirmed); this is termed veridicality. (b) Statements must follow the rules of logic, avoiding fallacies recognized in Western thought [and] contradiction; this is called logical inconsistency. (c) And, in a somewhat different vein, moved by somewhat different but no less strong motivating forces (and one more universally experienced), cognitions should have emotional harmony or balance. . . . The basic idea rests on men's preference to have favoured objects or concepts (like the self) positively related to favoured concepts, qualities, or events (like good looks or success) and disfavoured objects or concepts (like a political opponent) negatively related to similarly disfavoured concepts or qualities. With two concepts each of which may be favoured or disfavoured and related conjunctively or disjunctively to each other, eight combinations are possible, of which half are dissonant or unbalanced and painful. [...]

One often sees the principle at work in ideological discussions. S. M. Lipset, an old socialist and clearly an academic liberal, sets forth a reasonable and persuasive case on the 'authoritarianism' of the working class,[4] a case that, if believed, would create a cognitive dissonance among socialists and communists everywhere: the working class (a favoured concept) is positively related to authoritarianism (a disfavoured attribute), and a howl arises from these quarters. . . . Former Vice President Hubert Humphrey, a historic liberal, supports the American war effort in Vietnam; antiwar liberals, in order to reduce their dissonance, first disbelieved the reports, then attributed them to the requirements of the office ('The real Hubert Humphrey is not for it'), reducing dissonance in two of the ways most commonly employed. Could it be said that Rousseau, clinging to his theory of the goodness of mankind and his democratic inclinations in the face of man's evident fallibility and selfishness, reduced the dissonance by reconceptualizing 'the will of all' into a vague concept of 'the general will', not to be tested by observable vote or decision?

3 Social needs and values

Perhaps . . . one hardly has to stress the ways in which ideas serve men's needs for 'belongingness and love', for 'love and affect', for 'affiliation', so familiar are we with the problems of conformity, of the 'other-directedness' of the 'organization man' and the 'marketing personality'. This 'social adjustment' function is stressed by Smith, Bruner and White, as it is by others who have thought about this problem. It is a feature of many studies of small groups, in which men have adjusted their attitudes towards Russia, their perceptions of the length of a line, the movement of a point of light, the pitch of a tone, so as to fit their ideas in with those of others, even, sometimes, against the clear evidence of their senses. For some men, this is quite conscious – as we shall see, for example, in the case of a young man who says that when he got to college he quickly decided he would have to adopt the prevailing norms of that college because, being Jewish, being from a little-known school, being physically small, and having no real dynamic qualities of his own, he would need to do this in order to get along. But, too, we shall see the opposite: men who become radical in the presence of conservatives and create an image of themselves as 'angry young men' in defiance of the pressures around them. Moreover, since the social functions of ideologies – their functions for society, not the individual – are so often said to be the improvement of interpersonal relations, providing means of cooperative work, improving group morale and solidarity, and rationalizing sacrifices and restraints, it must be the case that political ideologies tend to have these functions for individuals as well. It could not be otherwise.

Yet, of course, political ideas are also partisan, generated and maintained in conflict, organized to support the group interests of contending factions. Thus, at the same time that they serve to improve some interpersonal relations, they must also damage others. One might say that it is their capacity to meet both needs that gives them their power to satisfy; they meet the need for affection and belonging *and* the need to express and legitimize hostile feelings, the antagonisms built up in a life inevitably met with frustrations. The nature of the politics of a society will, in some measure, depend on just this balance of needs served, the need to express love and the need to express hate, the need for consensus and the need for dissensus.

But, as so much contemporary writing tells us, the pattern of conflict in society, like the pattern of association and friendship itself, does not simply separate one man neatly from his opponents and rivals and associate him with his friends and fellow partisans. Rather, he has a number of reference groups, ideal and real, whose opinions differ in such a way that if he adopts one set of ideas to accommodate to a valued group, he threatens to make himself less popular with another.[5] It is at this point of internal conflict that the social adjustment problem becomes interesting, for here the man must devise strategies of thought and evaluation which take into account (a) the importance of an idea to him, (b) the risks of losing the good opinion of some group, (c) the gains promised by ingratiation with another; and in doing this, he must consider not only (d) what these groups believe, but (e) how they value him on other grounds, (f) their likely reaction to disagreement, and (g) what it would cost him in consistency and self-respect if he changed his ideas, or, alternatively, if he changed his group allegiances.[6]

Maslow says that those who have most nearly satisfied their needs for love and belongingness early in life can later, when some question of, say, personal integrity is raised, best do without such evidence of the love of others.[7] Thus needs are, here as elsewhere, complexly related to a person's history of need satisfaction. The social adjustment needs seem to come in an infinite variety of shapes, sizes, and colours, ranging from the 'neurotic need for affection' which Horney says is associated with an inability to give affection in return, through the search for popularity, as a symbol of affection without the real thing, or the need for and fear of intimacy, reflected in several of our cases, to the varieties of altruistic love, some of them reflected in Murray's term 'the need for nurturance', that is, a desire to give help to others. And, as it is expressed in the language of needs, so also, perhaps preeminently, love is a value, the core of religion and morality, not so much in the getting as the giving ('Love thy neighbour', not 'Seek love from thy neighbour'). It is in this form that Allport's list has it: 'The social man prizes other persons as ends, and is therefore himself kind, sympathetic, unselfish';[8] but in Lasswell's list the emphasis is on the value of love received, of affection gained.

It is, I think, in this area of love and hate, affection and its opposite, that the distinction between the intrinsic and the extrinsic properties of ideas is most important. For it is here that a man may gain the affectionate support of his comrades by expressing a philosophy of hate, a situation that must have occurred many times in the barracks and beer halls of Nazi Germany. On the other hand, a person who really loved and trusted his fellow men might, in his pacifism or equalitarianism or civil rights advocacy, alienate his companions, at what cost to himself it would be hard to say. (But, of course, there are pacifists who adopt their views to provoke their parents to anger, and advocates of interracial brotherhood who are filled with anger and hate.) This dual function of ideas, their capacity to move others and to express one's own love–hate impulses through their content, requires the most careful sorting out; but, at least in ambiguous situations where social conventions are somewhat obscure, the matching of content and inner needs is likely to give greater weight to the idea that serves this intrinsic function.

4 Moral needs and values

. . . In referring to moral needs and values here, I intend to cover both guilt and shame, both the propitiation of the conscience and the sense that it is dangerous to violate a conventional moral code. [. . .]

Political ideas are functional for this feature of the human system by their capacity to legitimize, rationalize, moralize a man's own acts of *obedience*, which might otherwise offend his sense of independence; his acts of *aggression*, which otherwise might offend his sense that hostile acts are immoral; his acts of *sacrifice*, which he might otherwise resent, considering them collective depredations against his purse and person; and, of course, his acts of *revolt* against authority, which otherwise might offend a deep-seated inhibition against challenging parental surrogates. In this sense ideologies are indeed the springs of action, the levers whereby ideas prompt movements.

Politics is the area where men seek something for themselves, usually presented at least as something for their group or faction, and probably also as something in the public interest. It is an arena of selfish interests, yet it is the domain where talk of the public interest has its greatest currency, not only as rationalized self-interest, but also, at the official level, because some concept of what is better for more people must enter into the calculations of responsible officials if the polity is to survive. The function of political ideas, then, is not only to help displace private emotions on to public objects and rationalize these in terms of some concept of public interest. Political ideas deal with interests, clearly conscious and fully accepted, and place these within the framework of some overall concept of the general welfare. They relate self to others, and in doing so call on moral codes and conventions to give legitimacy and 'meaning' to political life.

Contrary to popular belief, it is, I think, easier for most men to believe that their positions in society are somehow 'just' or merited than otherwise.[9] It saves them what they most dread, an obligation to attack the foundations of the system, to alienate themselves from the values of the society, to cut themselves off from the nourishing flow of sentiment and solidarity which pours from the established religious and secular authorities. This is true for most men; but some, particularly those isolated from the main cultural stream or bulwarked behind the social barriers divorcing their group from another, or marginal in some way to the main group affiliations, are more relieved to find corrupt the society that dealt them their hands. In either case, the rationale that accounts for a man's place in society is a moral one, and political ideas express these moral sentiments better than almost any others. They fill that need.

5 Esteem needs and values

Somehow self-esteem seems to be bound up with all activity; it seems to be an ingredient of all other needs. Certainly a person's self-esteem hinges on his concept of himself as moral; guilt might be described as the disappointment with the self over the failure to live up to some moral code. Self-love and self-esteem may be validated through the affection of others. Careers are the vehicles of self-esteem. But it has never seemed enough to leave this need as merely the spirited ghost of other needs; it has had to be given a status of its own – as Maslow does with his basic esteem needs, as Rotter does in his use of 'recognition-status' as a basic need, as Crowne and Marlowe do in seeking to measure the approval motive, that is, a fairly widespread 'tendency to avoid self-criticism', and in their test conditions 'to choose self-evaluative statements which . . . portray a stereotypically self-image'.[10]

The relationship between a person's self-esteem and the way he thinks other people perceive him is intimate because, inevitably, over the long haul men do tend to see themselves as others see them. They have, as Robert Burns requested, that gift. It has often been remarked that the problem of self-respect for those who are discriminated against by society, preeminently the American Negro, whose status is flagged by his skin colour for all to see, have great difficulty in achieving that level of self-respect which would enable them to believe in their own capacities and so to utilize them to the full. It is a matter of timing; genuine self-esteem, built with loving care into the structure of the plastic psyche early in life, seems to reduce the craving for evidence of the esteem of others in adulthood. For it is doubt about the self that creates that craving. Just as the Calvinistic code made doubt about one's predestined state of grace a lever for the hard work and striving characteristic of the Puritan ethic, so doubt about one's worth creates the striving for ever refreshed evidence of worth reflected in the deference or plaudits of others, those little reassurances that still the qualms of doubt. Certainty of low worth breeds apathy; doubt breeds striving. As Adler pointed out, a modest inferiority complex is one source of ambition; . . . it is the germ of a politics of status. . . .

Almost everything that one does is freighted in some measure with an increment of self-esteem or a decrement thereof; or, if the act be public, it will imply some change in the esteem of others. How, then, shall we isolate those features of behaviour and thought which are, more than others, expressions of this need? Crowne and Marlowe sought to measure the 'approval motive' by testing people's tendencies on attitude tests to 'fake good', that is, to say they liked or did certain things they thought they ought to like or do, but which in fact people rarely did like or do, and to say they did *not* do certain things that people usually did do, but felt guilty about. This would be one way to measure the need for social approval or respect, the need for the esteem of others.

Another way is to see what aspects of life are stressed in talking about oneself: whether or not a person is paying special attention to 'what other people will think', whether or not an act is fraught with 'loss of face', or, to employ the Greek phrase, with jeopardy to his *philotema*, or to his honour, or to his prestige. Does income buy experience or sensuous gratification, or does it buy esteem? Does a promotion bring opportunity for the exercise of skill or power or opportunity to carry out some pur-

pose, or status and respect? Does achievement satisfy some 'instinct of workmanship' or achievement motive, or does it prove something to others?

There is a third way: ask people to speak directly about their sense of self-esteem. With enough insight, they may say something important about the part it plays in their own lives, the things that diminish it, the way they earn it. These last two methods are the ones I used.

The enjoyment of the exercise of power over others might have its source only in the fruits such power brings, money or the advancement of some goal, but there might be more to it than that. There may be something about imposing one's will over others which, as in the case of Woodrow Wilson, gives satisfaction of a secret, almost intrinsic kind.[11] . . . But there is also wisdom in the common interpretation of the man who 'likes to throw his weight around', acts bossy, or engages in unnecessary show of authority and power. The common interpretation is that this behaviour 'makes him feel big'; it is a restitution to the small man of the sense of bigness he cannot find, unaided, in himself. It is often a feature of the official's desperate search for self-esteem, under the borrowed mantle of government or other institutional authority.

Again the extrinsic facets of political ideas meet men's needs in one way, the intrinsic in another. Men gain, or think they gain, the esteem of others by expressing greater love of their country than another, a greater willingness to sacrifice, a greater appreciation of the founding fathers, or, given a different audience, a greater daring in criticism, a greater sophistication regarding corruption, or, again with a shift in circumstances, a greater knowledge of the way the government works. But the intrinsic satisfactions that come with ideas resonant with the need for esteem are of another character, and are reflected, for example, in a set of ideas that places one's own group at the pinnacle of honour, as when a scholarly political scientist devises a government in which the experts have the greatest authority, or when a philosopher elaborates the reasons why philosophers should be kings. The concept of popular sovereignty is accepted by most people and, I think, helps to keep governments stable because it helps to put the people, their self-esteem flattered, one notch higher in their own eyes.

6 Personality integration and identity formation

If we take a view of men as men, of their human condition, we will find generic conflicts not associated with any special role or cultural situation, for it is the nature of man to oppose one tendency to another, one need against another. . . . Inner conflicts are inevitable; it is the way they are worked out that measures a man's 'wholeness', his health and capacity for fulfilment.

Given this situation, I am surprised to find so little attention to 'personality integration' or 'ego synthesis' in the discussion of motivation, although one can see its shadow in the term 'self-actualization', meaning the realization of a man's potential. . . . Smith, Bruner and White speak of the function of an opinion in externalizing just such inner conflicts as we have in mind, but this is less for the purpose of healing or reducing these conflicts than to express them, to bind them, to contain them, as when a man responds inappropriately to an authority because he is externalizing some long buried hostility to authority arising in his relations with his father.

The most common kinds of disintegration are those arising from six sources: (a) conflicts developing from the repression and maldirection of the sex drives, (b) those emerging from unacceptable hostile and angry feelings, (c) conflicts over tendencies to retain some dependency (irresponsible) status of which one is ashamed or which are inappropriate to one's responsibilities, (d) conflicts over one's posture towards authority and those who embody it, (e) the related but separate conflicts over demands for autonomy and choice in interdependent situations, and (f) the inevitable and ceaseless conflicts over the tendency to indulge the self versus the moralized need to care for and share with others. Then, to extend this harassing list, there are scheduling problems, the weighing of now against tomorrow, combined with the natural conflict created by consideration of the cost, in sacrificed alternatives, of every act, every expenditure, every option chosen. All of these, at every level, involve the overall problem: restraint against indulgence, a defining characteristic of personality.

The resolution of these conflicts with a minimum of repression (that is, the stuffing of some need down into the dark hole of the unconscious, where it rarely sleeps, but rather finds another outlet, illegitimate, uncontrolled by conscious processes of reason) is an important part of the identity-formation process, for such minimum of repression permits a person to describe himself to himself accurately, to know himself in depth. The other most important part of identity formation is the social placing of the self, something we referred to in describing the need to orient oneself in the world, but which here, with the concept turned to reveal another facet, refers to the way in which a man seeks to know what properties are appropriate to himself through knowing what groups he belongs to, what roles he occupies, what cultural traits are indisputably his own. If personality integration is largely self-referential, identity formation is, in addition, inclusive of the self-in-society theme, the understanding of 'who I am' through understanding 'where and what I am'. It is in this way that a man is helped to a party identification by an identification with a social class. . . . A person thus consumes and uses ideas, such as loyalty to party, to fill out his identity, to make it resonant with his image of himself in society, and to reduce the need to account for discrepancies that might, if challenged, bother him. They justify his position in society ('It is lack of education that accounts for my relatively low status'; 'It is hard work that accounts for my being better off than others'), they reduce the 'absurdity' of pain and suffering ('I suffer for a cause: my children will be better off'). Ideas give continuity to life, and identity is a vehicle for self-continuity. To change the language, political ideas contribute to the pattern maintenance of the self by linking the self to an ongoing social purpose, beyond the self, enlarging the self.

7 The expression of aggression

Aggression is behaviour and thought aimed at the injury of an object where the injury is the point of the act.[12] It emerges from anger and may be learned through the usual processes of rewarded effort, or may be imitative, or may be what seems to be the natural outcome of frustration. There are more or less aggressive individuals, and, since group norms vary, more or less aggressive populations; that is, individuals and populations who, although not chronically aggressive, are more easily aroused than others. And, of course, there is a variety of restraints against this mode of expression, especially fear of the consequences and guilt over the violation of a moral inhibition. Yet, in spite of fundamental differences in aggressive feelings and in spite of the power of the restraints, the need to express these feelings is powerful and universal.

Politics invites the expression of aggressive feelings because it is an area of conflict, partisanship, frustration. It is that domain of thought and action where rival interests confront each other, and where rival policies must be 'thrashed out'. There is always an 'opposition', legitimate or otherwise; there are always rival candidates for that scarce resource, power. At the same time, politics is an area of moralized sentiment, as in patriotic songs and verse; it is where expressions of solidarity are quite meaningful; it is where common history is made.

For these two reasons, then, the ubiquity of aggressive feelings and their special relevance to politics and political thought, that I include this need and motive in a basic list.

8 Autonomy and freedom

If we think of the crux of the question of lack of freedom as resting on restraint of choice, and if we include in this restraint three things – lack of opportunity or resources, coercion in its various manifestations, and psychological inhibition or incapacity – we shall have, if not a single meaning, an area of meaning sufficient for our purposes. Is the need for such free choice widespread, intensely felt, basic, that is, developed early and dominant over other needs on occasion? Readers of *Escape from Freedom* may doubt this, but they should recall that Fromm was referring to a setback in a process that he said had been going on for four hundred years.[13] For these times, one might give the need a higher place than for other times. But in all times, I would argue, the child has, year by year, successively broken through restrictive barriers; the adult has been restive over the restrictions over some domains of traditional or expected choice, even in traditional society. It is a strong motive force and one that is so intimately related to problems of authority and its internalized components as to produce internal conflicts and guilt.

And, of course, it is, like aggression, woven into politics, so that hardly a fibre does not imply some theme of governmental restraint, coercion, impediment to 'doing what I want to do'. This is the other side of the concept that government, as the source of frustration, is the instigator of aggressive feelings. Frustration is exactly what we are talking about: the interruption of purposive behaviour. More than that, the relationship of imperialist or colonizing countries to their dependent peoples is fraught with restrictions on the sense of freedom. Whatever they do, because *they* do it, these metropolitan nations are seen as deprivers of freedom, of autonomy. Government is law and law is prescription and restraint, however lightly worn.

There is something more in this relation between the need for autonomy and political thought. Some men work together easily as teams of co-operative and more or less equal partners, while some find the constraints of compromising their own purposes, of dealing with independent personalities, difficult. It is reasonable to suppose that these differences in need for independence of others or need for interrelations with others should find their way into political thought. Almost all utopian philosophies, for example, create images of totally harmonious interacting individuals, and hence the means for reconciling conflict are undervalued and underdeveloped. So devious is the mind, however, that a perverse principle prevails: those utopias are more likely to be invented and accepted by persons who have difficulty in getting along with others. The utopian solution expresses their need for something they cannot achieve now, or, it seems, even in the faction-ridden societies of utopian radicals.

It takes no further argument, I think, to convince one that the need for freedom and autonomy is both a strong and enduring motive and pre-eminently relevant to political thought, realistic or utopian.

9 Self-actualization

After the conflicts are dealt with and contained, if not resolved (because, as we said, it is a condition of life to be torn between competing needs), and after an identity is shaped and made usable in life's struggles, there is that further need to achieve, to be fulfilled and to fulfil oneself, to 'become' something. I am combining here the thoughts of others and synthesizing them under the term Maslow and Rogers employed in a larger sense, 'self-actualization'. . . . Rogers speaks of 'self-actualization' in the following terms; 'Rather than many needs and motives, it seems entirely possible that all organic and psychological needs may be described as partial aspects of . . . one fundamental need.' 'That need,' he says, is 'to actualize, maintain, and enhance the experiencing organism.'[14] While rather vague, this concept means, among other things, self-knowledge, autonomy from external forces, development of various parts of the self. Allport, in a literate and moving essay on *Becoming*, speaks of this concept as follows:

> We maintain . . . that personality is governed not only by the impact of stimuli upon a slender endowment of drives common to the species. Its process of becoming is governed, as well, by a disposition to realize its possibilities, i.e. to become characteristically human at all stages of development. And one of the capacities most urgent is individuation, the formation of an individual style of life that is self-aware, self-critical, and self-enhancing. . . . Becoming is the process of incorporating earlier stages into later; or when this is impossible, of handling the conflict between early and late stages as well as one can.[15]

All of these centre on 'the need to grow', to develop, to employ the teachings of experience in a progressively more fruitful manner. There is something serendipitous in this, something melioristic, but also something recognizable and real.

But is it the kind of need that can be gratified by ideological manipulation, by thought and imagination? Here I would refer the reader to the concepts of human nature in the works of the classical political philosophers. One of the criteria for sorting out these concepts is just this: the educability of mankind, the possibility of growth, the plasticity of a basic material that is not instinct-ridden or inherently aggressive or distrustful. Is it too exotic, then, to believe that, because men populate their vision of the world with creatures like themselves, those who are themselves aware of a self-actualizing need, and not frustrated in this, will think of political man as a self-actualizing developing person, and so will conceive of political systems that promote individuation and growth, giving them that quality of freedom in which this is possible? For John Stuart Mill, the criterion by which a political system is to be judged is this, and only this: the kind of intellectual and moral growth (self-actualization) it produces. Democracy is a better system than any other just for this reason.[16] Through encouraging people to take responsibility for their own and others' destinies, it develops their faculties. And who will deny that Mill himself experienced a dominating need for self-actualization?

10 Instrumental guide to reality

One need merges with another. Earlier I suggested a need to know and understand expressed in self-orientation, curiosity, speculative play, the pleasure of consistency and logical relations, creativity, considering these to be somehow satisfying in themselves, not merely for their usefulness in helping a man to get what he wants. Here I have in mind the usefulness of ideas in helping to get what one wants, a utility criterion, especially since, whatever other needs they satisfy, men must 'make a living', must satisfy some of their economic wants. Maslow lists physiological needs and safety needs; merging these, I am saying here that ideas gratify these needs by guiding men correctly in their groping with nature and society, things, and men. . . . Smith, Bruner and White make 'object appraisal' one of their three functions of opinions, for 'the holding of an attitude provides a ready aid in "sizing up" objects and events in the environment from the point of view of one's major interests and going concerns.'[17] I mean more than appraisal, however; I mean guiding a man in getting the object. It has always seemed to me that the term 'object appraisal' was too passive, possibly because it was developed to deal with opinions on Russia, about which the respondents couldn't do very much, and not about taxes and playgrounds and pensions, all of which are much more important as well as accessible to their own influence for most people.

Notes and references

1 HARLOW, H. F. (1953) 'Mice, monkeys, men and motives', *Psychological Review*, 60, 23–32 (reprinted in McClelland (ed.) *Studies in Motivation*).

2 GOLDSTEIN, K. and SCHEERER, M. (1941) 'Abstracts and concrete behaviour: An experimental study with special tests', *Psychological Monographs*, 53, no. 239.
There are some closely related concepts in Jean Piaget's *The Moral Development of the Child* New York, Free Press, Macmillan, 1965.

3 FESTINGER, LEON (1957) *A Theory of Cognitive Dissonance* Stanford University Press, p. 3.

4 LIPSET, S. M. (1963) *Political Man* Garden City, N.Y., Doubleday Anchor, pp. 87–126.

5 See HYMAN, HERBERT H. and SINGER, E. (eds) (1968) *Readings in Reference Group Therapy and Research* New York, Free Press, Macmillan.

6 For additional theoretical interpretations of conflicting reference groups, see FESTINGER, LEON, 'A theory of social comparison processes', ibid., pp. 123–46.

7 MASLOW, A. H. (1954) *Motivation and Personality* New York, Harper, pp. 89–90.

8 ALLPORT, G. (1937) *Personality* New York, Holt, p. 229.

9 LANE, R. E. (1967) *Political Ideology* New York, Free Press, Macmillan, pp.161–86.

10 CROWNE, D. P. and MARLOWE, D. (1964) *Approval Motive* New York, Wiley, p. 189.

11 GEORGE, ALEXANDER L. and JULIETTE L. (1964) *Woodrow Wilson and Colonel House* New York, Dover.

12 Here, as in the later analysis of aggressive thought, I rely heavily on BERKOWITZ, LEONARD (1962) *Aggression* New York, McGraw-Hill.

13 FROMM, ERICH (1941) *Escape from Freedom* New York, Rinehart.

14 ROGERS, CARL R. (1951) *Client-centered Therapy* Boston, Houghton Mifflin, pp. 487–8.

15 ALLPORT, GORDON W. (1960) *Becoming* New Haven, Yale University Press, pp. 27–128.

16 See especially his *Representative Government* in the Everyman edition (New York, Dutton, 1910), which includes *Utilitarianism* and *On Liberty*, p. 193.

17 SMITH, M. BREWSTER, BRUNER, J. S. and WHITE, R. (1956) *Opinions and Personality*, New York, Wiley, p. 41.

32 The F scale and the authoritarian personality

Nevitt Sanford

The F scale

Although the idea of constructing a scale for measuring potential fascism in the personality appeared at a relatively late stage in these explorations, it still came at a time when the focus of attention was upon anti-Semitism and prejudice. A Likert-type scale for measuring ethnocentrism (E) had been constructed and studied in relation to anti-Semitism (A-S). This scale, which embraced hostility to various intra- and extra-national outgroups as well as the tendency to overestimate and to glorify the ingroup, correlated so highly with anti-Semitism, 0.80, that it seemed reasonable to view this latter as, mainly, a manifestation of general ethnocentrism. Ethnocentrism, in the group's thinking, had become something very general indeed. Not only did it include generalized outgroup rejection and exaggerated ingroup loyalty but also such defects in thinking as stereotypy, rigidity, and rationalization; it was a way of looking at groups and group relations that was, in the long run at least, maladaptive; it had begun to take on the aspect of a fundamental psychological problem.

The high correlation between A-S and E meant that it would be possible to go on studying anti-Semitism without having to rely on the original A-S scale itself. This scale had evoked protests both from a local chapter of the Anti-Defamation League, who considered that the instrument spread anti-Semitism, and from the dean of a graduate school, who objected to 'the pro-Semitic bias' in this research. From whatever point of view it was seen, this scale did tend to bring the matter of prejudice painfully into the open and it was used with reluctance, particularly in groups that included Jews. But the same considerations held for members of other minority groups. The real need was for an instrument that would measure prejudice without appearing to have this aim and without mentioning the name of any minority group.

The idea of the F scale was a product of thinking about the A-S and E scales. An effort was being made to abstract from the A-S and E scale

---

SANFORD, NEVITT (1956) 'The F scale and the authoritarian personality' from 'The Approach of the Authoritarian Personality' in McCary, J. L. (ed.) *Psychology of Personality* New Jersey, Logos Press, 266–77.

items the kinds of psychological dispositions – fears, anxieties, values, impulses – being expressed, the thought being that a systematic covering of this ground might suggest additional E items. There were certain general themes in the item content: e.g., Jews were 'extravagant' or 'sensual' or 'lazy' or 'soft'; or Jews were mysterious, strange, foreign, basically different; or minority groups generally failed to come up to ordinary standards of middle-class morality. It was as if the subject, in agreeing with these scale items, was not so much considering Jews or other minority group members as expressing concern lest other people 'get away' with tendencies which he himself had to inhibit, or anxiety lest he be the victim of strange forces beyond his control, or lest his moral values, already somewhat unstable, be undermined. And since, apparently, items expressing these kinds of preoccupation were agreed with consistently by some subjects regardless of the minority groups involved, would not these subjects agree with such items even though no minority group were mentioned at all? In short, why not have a scale that covered the psychological content of the A-S and E scales but did not appear to be concerned with the familiar phenomena of prejudice? Certainly this fitted in with Leo Loewenthal's memorable if somewhat exaggerated dictum: 'Anti-Semitism has nothing to do with Jews.'

It cannot really be claimed that this notion came as the result of a deliberate quest for an instrument that would be less awkward to administer to groups of varied ethnic backgrounds, although it came at a time when the need for such an instrument was keenly felt and this implication of the new notion was more or less immediately seen. Furthermore, this notion was conceived at a time when the group was prepared to exploit it to the full. Interviews with subjects scoring high on A-S and E had suggested many psychological characteristics of the highly prejudiced subjects, and whereas many of these characteristics had not yet found a place in the A-S or E scales there was no reason why they should not. And now, since attention was going to be directed to items expressing the general outlook of the highly prejudiced individual, it was possible to make use of the vast literature on Nazism and Fascism and, particularly, the ideas represented by Dr Adorno and the Institute for Social Research. Finally, it was possible to make explicit a theoretical assumption which, actually, had been a guide to the group's thinking for some time.

The essence of this assumption was that some of the deeper needs of the personality were being expressed by agreement with prejudiced statements. If this were true, then these needs should express themselves in other ways as well. If, for example, a subject's tendency to attribute weakness to Jews sprang from his own underlying fear of weakness, that fear might also express itself in an over-accent upon his own strength and toughness. Thus, scale items having to do with the supposed weakness of Jews or of other people and items expressing exaggerated strength and toughness would correlate positively in a population of men because agreement with both kinds of items commonly sprang from the same underlying source, fear of weakness. All of us were accustomed to this kind of thinking in terms of levels of functioning in the personality; it had loomed large in earlier work of Frenkel-Brunswik (1942) and of Sanford (1943). It is, of course, essentially psychoanalytic.

Given this way of looking at things, the task became one of imagining what personality needs were commonly expressed in overt prejudice, and then thinking of other surface manifestations of these same needs. The intention was, of course, to gain access to those other manifestations by means of scale items. Here it was possible to make good use of the existing literature on anti-Semitism and Fascism. Fromm (1941), Erikson (1942), Maslow (1932), Chisholm (1946), Reich (1946), Stagner (1936) were among the writers who influenced us the most, although heaviest reliance was on the group's own earlier explorations. The central personality trends which were expected to be most significant were those which emerged from the analysis of clinical material and those which, as hypothetical constructs, seemed best to explain the consistency of response to the A-S and E scales.

Content of the F scale

For every item of the F scale there was a hypothesis or, more usually, several hypotheses stating the nature of its supposed connection with prejudice. And there were hypotheses concerning the relations of these items one to another, theorizing having led the group more and more towards the conceptualization of a *pattern* of personality that predisposed the individual to prejudice and fascism.

Here it seems worth while to go into some detail, for progress in an understanding of authoritarianism will come from the closest involvement with the subtle workings of this and similar trends in the personality.

Conventionalism

First consider the idea of *conventionalism*. It was observed in our conversations with anti-Semitic subjects that most of their accusations against Jews were couched in conventionally moralistic terms. This theme was also pronounced in the original A-S scale items. It may be recalled that Hitler made this same type of accusation when addressing middle-class audiences.

Our thought here was that we were dealing not so much with bad experiences with Jews or with adaptation to a general climate of opinion as with a need to adhere strictly to conventional, middle-class values, a disposition to feel anxious at the sight of or the thought of any violation of these values – something that could be attributed to instability in the individual's own value system. It is important to note that conventionalism refers not merely to conformity with middle-class values but to *rigid* adherence to such values, to an *over*accent upon them and to responsiveness to contemporary *external* social pressure. Items expressive of this trend invited the subject to go *all-out* in his support of conventional values, e.g. 'A person who has bad manners, habits and breeding can hardly expect to get along with decent people.'

Authoritarian submission

Submission to authority, desire for a strong leader, subservience of the individual to the state, had for some time been put forward as important aspects of the Nazi creed. It was thus natural that these themes should be taken into account in a search for the correlates of prejudice. *Authoritarian submission*, as we termed the hypothetical generalized disposition of personality, was conceived of not as a balanced, realistic respect for valid authority but as an exaggerated, emotional need to submit. This seems well represented in the item: 'Every person should have a deep faith in some supernatural force higher than himself to which he gives total allegiance and whose decisions he obeys without question.' Here, as with conventionalism, the individual is assumed to be oriented towards external powers or agencies of control rather than under the direction of a conscience of his own.

Authoritarian aggression

Authoritarian submission is closely related, conceptually, to *authoritarian aggression*. Both attitudes, according to theory, spring from underlying hostility towards ingroup authorities, originally the parents. The individual strives to keep this hostility in check by overdoing in the direction of respect, obedience, gratitude towards the ingroup authorities and by displacing the underlying hostility towards these authorities onto outgroups. This is the most essential connection between authoritarian submission and ethnocentrism. But it appears that the tendency to displace hostility is more general than that seen in the common forms of prejudice; the greatest variety of people and actions are likely to become the objects of condemnation. The connection of this hostility and its original source is seen in the fact that the kinds of things for which the individual would punish other peoples are the same as those for which he was punished or for which he feels in his heart he deserves to be punished. But he has identified himself with the ingroup authorities of his childhood, and found in the tendency to punish wrongdoing in others a safe, and fairly well-sanctioned, outlet for his aggression. The items chosen to represent authoritarian aggression offer the subject a chance to favour condemnation, total rejection, stern discipline or severe punishment as ways for dealing with a variety of people and forms of behaviour; e.g. 'Sex crimes, such as rape and attacks on children, deserve more than mere imprisonment; such criminals ought to be publicly whipped, or worse.'

Anti-intraception

It was common to note in the interviews of more prejudiced subjects, and in some of the A-S and E scale items with which they heartily agreed, disapproval of a free emotional life, of the intellectual or theoretical, of the impractical. These were things they tended to attribute to their outgroups. And there was theory at hand to explain the relations of these attitudes to prejudice and to the personality trends just discussed. The individual who had been forced to repress hostility against his parents and others who appeared to be strong, and who was thus forced into submissiveness which impaired his self-respect, would naturally be required to maintain a narrow range of consciousness. Self-awareness might threaten his whole scheme of adjustment. He could be afraid of genuine feeling because his emotions might get out of control, afraid of thinking about human phenomena because he might, as it were, think the wrong thoughts. The term *anti-intraception* was borrowed from Murray et al (1938). It stands for a general attitude of impatience with and opposition to feelings, fantasies, speculations and other subjective or 'tender-minded' phenomena. A sample item: 'When a person has a problem or worry, it is best for him not to think about it, but to keep busy with more cheerful things.'

Superstition and stereotypy

The narrowness of consciousness just referred to appeared also to be a major source of both *superstition and stereotypy,* two tendencies which loomed large in our early clinical studies of highly prejudiced individuals. Superstitiousness indicates a tendency to shift responsibility from within the individual onto outside forces beyond one's control. It suggests a narrow area within which there is a conscious sense of self-determination, a broad area of unconscious forces which are projected onto the external world, to appear to the individual as mystical or fantastic determinants of his fate. Stereotypy is the tendency to think in rigid, oversimplified categories, in unambiguous terms of black and white, particularly in the realm of psychological or social matters. It was hypothesized that one reason why people, even those who are otherwise 'intelligent', resort to primitive explanations of human events is that so many of the ideas and observations needed for an adequate account are not allowed to enter into the calculations: because they are affect-laden and potentially anxiety-producing they could not be included in the conscious scheme of things. The assumption here is, of course, that many of the common phenomena of prejudice were superstitions or stereotypes. The present task was to devise scale items that would express these tendencies without reference to minority groups, e.g. 'It is entirely possible that this series of wars and conflicts will be ended once and for all by a world-destroying earthquake, flood, or other catastrophe.'

Power and toughness

As suggested above, the state of affairs in which the individual has to submit to powers or agencies with which he is not fully in sympathy leaves him with a nagging sense of weakness. Since to admit such weakness is to damage self-respect, every effort is made to deny it. These include the projection of weakness onto outgroups according to the formula 'I am not weak, they are,' and the use of the mechanism of overcompensation, according to which the individual seeks to present to the world an aspect of *power and toughness*. Accent on the strong–weak, dominant–submissive, leader–follower dimension in human relations is, of course, a familiar feature of the Nazi outlook. In our experience it appeared that the 'power complex' contained elements that were essentially contradictory. Whereas the power-centred individual wants to have power, he is at the same time afraid to seize it and wield it. He also admires power in others and is inclined to submit to it, but is at the same time afraid of the weakness thus implied. A common solution for such a person is to align himself with power figures, thus gratifying both his need to have power and his need to submit. By submitting to power he can still somehow participate in it. The following is a sample of the items designed to represent this theme: 'Too many people today are living in an unnatural, soft way; we should return to the fundamentals, to a more red-blooded, active way of life.'

Destructiveness and cynicism

Although authoritarian aggression provides a very broad channel for the expression of underlying hostile impulses, it seemed that this might not be enough for many of the prejudiced subjects. We supposed that they harboured, as a result of numerous externally imposed restrictions upon the satisfaction of their needs, a great deal of resentment and generalized hostility, and that this would come into the open when it could be justified or rationalized. *Destructiveness and cynicism* was the term for rationalized, ego-accepted aggression, not including authoritarian aggression. Cynicism was regarded as a form of rationalized aggression: one can the more freely be aggressive when he believes that everybody is doing it and, hence, if he wants to be aggressive he is disposed to believe that everybody is similarly motivated, e.g. that it is 'human nature' to exploit and to make war on one's neighbours. It seemed a fairly safe assumption that such undifferentiated aggressiveness could be directed against minority groups with a minimum of external stimulation.

Projectivity

The mechanism just described is, of course, a form of projection. And it will have been noted that this unconscious defensive device has had an important place in our earlier related theory-making, particularly in the discussion of authoritarian aggression and of superstition. Indeed, projection has a crucial role in the whole theory of prejudice as a means for keeping the individual's psychological household in some sort of order. The most essential notion is that impulses which cannot be admitted to the conscious ego tend to be projected onto minority groups – convenient objects. In constructing the F scale, the concern was with a readiness to project, with *projectivity* as a general feature of the personality, considered independently of the object onto which the projection was made. Hence, the items expressive of this tendency were designed to tap any preoccupation with 'evil forces' in the world, with plots and conspiracies, germs, sexual excesses.

Sex

Concern with *sex* seemed to deserve a certain amount of special consideration. Inhibitions in this sphere, and moral indignation with respect to the sexual behaviour of other people, had been noted in the interviews with our prejudiced subjects; sexual immorality was one of the many violations of conventional values which they attributed to minority groups. Ego-alien sexuality was conceived then as a part of the picture of the typical prejudiced person, and included in the F scale were several items having to do with belief in the existence of 'sex orgies' and with the punishment of violators of sex mores.

In summary, there were nine major personality variables which, by hypothesis, were dynamically related to overt prejudice.
1 *Conventionalism*. Rigid adherence to conventional middle-class values.
2 *Authoritarian submission*. Submissive, uncritical attitude towards idealized moral authorities of the ingroup.
3 *Authoritarian aggression*. Tendency to be on the lookout for, and to condemn, reject and punish people who violate conventional values.
4 *Anti-intraception*. Opposition to the subjective, the imaginative, the tender-minded.
5 *Superstition and stereotypy*. The belief in mystical determinants of the individual's fate; the disposition to think in rigid categories.
6 *Power and toughness*. Preoccupation with the dominance–submission, strong–weak, leader–follower dimension; identification with power figures; exaggerated assertion of strength and toughness.
7 *Destructiveness and cynicism*. Generalized hostility, vilification of the human.
8 *Projectivity*. The disposition to believe that wild and dangerous things go on in the world; the projection outward of unconscious emotional impulses.
9 *Sex*. Ego-alien sexuality; exaggerated concern with sexual 'goings on', and punitiveness towards violators of sex mores.

Theory underlying the F scale

In their theoretical work on the F scale the research group leaned heavily upon the concepts of superego, ego and id. It was considered that these features of the personality have characteristic modes of functioning in the ethnocentric subject. As a first approximation, one might say that in the highly ethnocentric person the superego is strict, rigid and relatively externalized, the id is strong, primitive and ego-alien, while the ego is weak and can manage the superego–id conflicts only by resorting to rather desperate defences. But this general formulation would hold for a very large segment of the population and, thus, it is necessary to look more closely at the functioning of these parts of the person in the authoritarian syndrome.

In considering the variables which entered into the theory underlying the F scale, it may be seen that the first three – *Conventionalism, Authoritarian submission*, and *Authoritarian aggression* – all have to do with superego functioning. The accent is upon external reinforcements of strict superego demands, and upon punishment in the name of those authorities to whom the subject has submitted.

Anti-intraception, Superstition and stereotypy, and *Projectivity* may be regarded as manifestations of a relatively weak ego. Anti-intraception involves the primitive defensive mechanisms of repression, denial, keeping things ego-alien. *Superstition* shows an inclination to shift responsibility onto the external world, as if the ego were giving up its attempts to predict and control, while *Stereotypy* is an attempt to deal with complex events by means of oversimplified categories. *Projectivity* is the consistent use of another relatively primitive mechanism of defence.

Power and toughness is another manifestation of ego weakness, involving as it does an over-accent upon the conventionalized aspects of the ego, e.g. the emphasis on 'will power'; but this variable, like *Destructiveness and cynicism*, and *Sex*, also expresses with a minimum of indirectness the activity of id tendencies.

However, superego, ego and id can be separated in this fashion only arbitrarily. In actuality, the functioning of any one of these agencies depends at any moment upon the activities of the other two; and everyday behaviour, expressed attitudes and values, are not readily classifiable as manifestations of superego, ego or id but are to be understood as expressions of the relationships among these agencies. This, at any rate, was the thinking that went into the F scale. Consider the item: 'He is indeed contemptible who does not feel an undying love, gratitude, and respect for his parents.' On the surface, this item expresses authoritarian aggression and authoritarian submission and, hence, might be classified as primarily a superego item. But the theory was that agreement with this extreme statement might well mask an underlying hostility towards the parents. To put this differently, it was hypothesized that unconscious hostility towards the parents was a distinguishing feature of the highly ethnocentric person, and the problem was to determine how this tendency might give itself away in an attitude scale. One answer was through signs of a reaction formation, this mechanism being a common one in the highly ethnocentric person. Thus the present item has to do with an interplay of superego, ego and id: an underlying unconscious, ego-alien tendency, coming mainly from the id, has led to anxiety of punishment (superego) which the ego seeks to ward off or reduce by transforming the forbidden tendency into its opposite. But this is not all. This is merely the authoritarian submission expressed in the item. 'He is indeed contemptible' is authoritarian aggression. The ego must, so to speak, be doubly sure that punishment is avoided and it must see to it that the original id tendency finds some sort of gratification; hence, it joins forces with the punitive agency, imputes the 'badness' to other people who may then be freely aggressed against in good conscience.

Or consider the item: 'The wild sex life of the old Greeks and Romans was tame compared to some of the goings on in this country, even in places where people might least expect it.' Here it is assumed that underlying sexual tendencies, inhibited because of a strict superego, have found through the ego's work some expression in fantasies, which, however, can be enjoyed or tolerated only when other people, and not the self, are the actors and when the fantasies are accompanied by moral indignation.

Now it is not suggested that the whole authoritarian personality structure is somehow embedded in each F scale item. But it is fair to say that theory of the kind just indicated lay behind the writing of each item, and that, according to this theory, the F pattern is a structure whose features are so closely interrelated that a clear expression of one permits quite unreasonable inferences concerning the activity of the others. Perhaps the items just used are among the best for making this point, but all the F scale items should be viewed from this standpoint.

The F scale works as if the superego, ego, id theory were correct, and there is no doubt but that without this theory the scale would not have been constructed. On the other hand, it cannot be claimed that such results as have been obtained could not be explained as well in other terms. [...]

References

CHISHOLM, G. B. (1946) 'The Reestablishment of Peacetime Society,' *Psychiatry*, 9, 3–21.

ERIKSON, E. H. (1942) 'Hitler's Imagery and German Youth', *Psychiatry*, 5, 475–93.

FRENKEL-BRUNSWIK, E. (1942) 'Motivation and Behavior', *Genet. Psychol. Monogr.*, 26, 121–265.

FROMM, E. (1941) *Escape from Freedom* New York, Farrar and Rinehart.

MASLOW, A. H. (1943) 'The Authoritarian Character Structure', *J. soc. Psychol.*, 18, 401–11.

MURRAY, H. A. et al. (1938) *Explorations in Personality* New York, Oxford University Press.

REICH, W. (1946) *The Mass Psychology of Fascism* New York, Orgone-Institute Press.

SANFORD, N., ADKINS, M., COBB, E. and MILLER, B. (1943) 'Physique, Personality and Scholarship', *Monogr. Soc. Res. Child Devel.*, 8, 1–705.

STAGNER, R. (1936) 'Fascist Attitudes: Their Determining Conditions', *J. soc. Psychol.*, 7, 438–54.

33 The effects of changes in roles on the attitudes of role occupants

Seymour Lieberman

Problem

One of the fundamental postulates of role theory, as expounded by Newcomb (1950), Parsons (1951) and other role theorists, is that a person's attitudes will be influenced by the role that he occupies in a social system. Although this proposition appears to be a plausible one, surprisingly little evidence is available that bears directly on it. One source of evidence is found in common folklore. 'Johnny is a changed boy since he was made a monitor in school.' 'She is a different woman since she got married.' 'You would never recognize him since he became foreman.' As much as these expressions smack of the truth, they offer little in the way of systematic or scientific support for the proposition that a person's attitudes are influenced by his role.

Somewhat more scientific, but still not definitive, is the common finding, in many social–psychological studies, that relationships exist between attitudes and roles. In other words, different attitudes are held by people who occupy different roles. For example, Stouffer et al. (1949) found that commissioned officers are more favourable towards the Army than are enlisted men. The problem here is that the mere existence of a relationship between attitudes and roles does not reveal the cause and effect nature of the relationship found. One interpretation of Stouffer's finding might be that being made a commissioned officer tends to result in a person's becoming pro-Army – i.e. the role a person occupies influences his attitudes. But an equally plausible interpretation might be that being pro-Army tends to result in a person's being made a commissioned officer – i.e. a person's attitudes influence the likelihood of his being selected for a given role. In the absence of longitudinal data, the relationship offers no clear evidence that roles were the 'cause' and attitudes the 'effect'.

The present study was designed to examine the effects of roles on attitudes in a particular field situation. The study is based on longitudinal data obtained in a role-differentiated, hierarchical organization. By taking advantage of natural role changes among personnel in the organization, it

---

LIEBERMAN, SEYMOUR (1956) 'The effects of changes in roles on the attitudes of role occupants' in *Human Relations*, vol. 9, 385–402.

was possible to examine people's attitudes both before and after they underwent changes in roles. Therefore, the extent to which changes in roles were followed by changes in attitudes could be determined, and the cause and effect nature of any relationship found would be clear.

Method: Phase 1

The study was part of a larger project carried out in a medium-sized Midwestern company engaged in the production of home appliance equipment. Let us call the company the Rockwell Corporation. At the time that the study was done, Rockwell employed about 4000 people. This total included about 2500 factory workers and about 150 first-level foremen. The company was unionized and most of the factory workers belonged to the union. . . . About 150 factory workers served as stewards in the union, or roughly one steward for every foreman.

The study consisted of a 'natural field experiment'. The experimental variable was a change in roles, and the experimental period was the period of exposure to the experimental variable. The experimental groups were those employees who underwent changes in roles during this period; the control groups were those employees who did not change roles during this period. The design may be described in terms of a three-step process: 'before measurement', 'experimental period', and 'after measurement'.

Before measurement

In September and October 1951, attitude questionnaires were filled out by virtually all factory personnel at Rockwell – 2354 workers, 145 stewards, and 151 foremen. The questions dealt for the most part with employees' attitudes and perceptions about the company, the union, and various aspects of the job situation. The respondents were told that the questionnaire was part of an overall survey to determine how employees felt about working conditions at Rockwell.

Experimental period

Between October 1951 and July 1952, twenty-three workers were made foremen and thirty-five workers became stewards. Most of the workers who became stewards during that period were elected during the annual steward elections held in May 1952. They replaced stewards who did not choose to run again or who were not re-elected by their constituents. In addition, a few workers replaced stewards who left the steward role for one reason or another throughout the year.

The workers who became foremen were not made foreman at any particular time. Promotions occurred as openings arose in supervisory positions. Some workers replaced foremen who retired or who left the company for other reasons; some replaced foremen who were shifted to other supervisory positions; and some filled newly created supervisory positions.

After measurement

In December 1952, the same forms that had been filled out by the rank-and-file workers in 1951 were readministered to:

1 The workers who became foremen during the experimental period (N=23).
2 A control group of workers who did not become foremen during the experimental period (N=46).
3 The workers who became stewards during the experimental period (N=35).
4 A control group of workers who did not become stewards during the experimental period (N=35).

Each control group was matched with its parallel experimental group on a number of demographic, attitudinal, and motivational variables. Therefore, any changes in attitudes that occurred in the experimental groups but did not occur in the control groups could not be attributed to initial differences between them.

The employees in these groups were told that the purpose of the follow-up questionnaire was to get up-to-date measures of their attitudes in 1952 and to compare how employees felt that year with the way that they felt the previous year. The groups were told that, instead of studying the entire universe of employees as was the case in 1951, only a sample was being studied this time. They were informed that the sample was chosen in such a way as to represent all kinds of employees at Rockwell – men and women, young and old, etc. The groups gave no indication that they understood the real bases on which they were chosen for the 'after' measurement or that the effects of changes in roles were the critical factors being examined.[1]

Statistical significance of the results was obtained by the use of chi square. The probability levels that are differentiated in the tables are: less

1 Some of the top officials of management and all of the top officers of the union at Rockwell knew about the nature of the follow-up study and the bases on which the experimental and control groups were selected.

than 0·01, between 0·01 and 0·05, between 0·05 and 0·10, and N.S. (not significant – p is greater than 0·10).

Results: Phase 1

The major hypothesis tested in this study was that people who are placed in a role will tend to take on or develop attitudes that are congruent with the expectations associated with that role. Since the foreman role entails being a representative of management, it might be expected that workers who are chosen as foremen will tend to become more favourable towards management. Similarly, since the steward role entails being a representative of the union, it might be expected that workers who are elected as stewards will tend to become more favourable towards the union. Moreover, in so far as the values of management and of the union are in conflict with each other, it might also be expected that workers who are made foremen will become less favourable towards the union and workers who are made stewards will become less favourable towards management.

Four attitudinal areas were examined: 1) attitudes towards management and officials of management; 2) attitudes towards the union and officials of the union; 3) attitudes towards the management-sponsored incentive system; and 4) attitudes towards the union-sponsored seniority system. The incentive system (whereby workers are paid according to the number of pieces they turn out) and the seniority system (whereby workers are promoted according to the seniority principle) are two areas in which conflicts between management and the union at Rockwell have been particularly intense. Furthermore, first-level foremen and stewards both play a part in the administration of these systems, and relevant groups hold expectations about foremen and steward behaviours with respect to these systems. Therefore, we examined the experimental and control groups' attitudes towards these two systems as well as their overall attitudes towards management and the union.

The data tend to support the hypothesis that being placed in the foreman and steward roles will have an impact on the attitudes of the role occupants. As shown in Tables 1 to 4, both experimental groups undergo systematic changes in attitudes, in the predicted directions, from the 'before' situation to the 'after' situation. In the control groups, either no attitude changes occur, or less marked changes occur, from the 'before' situation to the 'after' situation.

Table 1 Effects of foreman and steward roles on attitudes towards management

	Kind of Change					
	More favourable to management	*No change*	*More critical of management*	*Total*	*N*	*p*
	%	%	%	%		
1 *How is Rockwell as a place to work?*						
New foremen	70	26	4	100	23	N.S.
Control group*	47	33	20	100	46	
New stewards	46	31	23	100	35	N.S.
Control group†	46	43	11	100	35	
2 *How does Rockwell compare with others?*						
New foremen	52	48	0	100	23	0·01–0·05
Control group	24	59	17	100	46	
New stewards	55	34	11	100	35	N.S.
Control group	43	46	11	100	35	
3 *If things went bad for Rockwell, should the workers try to help out?*						
New foremen	17	66	17	100	23	N.S.
Control group	17	66	17	100	46	
New stewards	26	74	0	100	35	N.S.
Control group	14	69	17	100	35	
4 *How much do management officers care about the workers at Rockwell?*						
New foremen	48	52	0	100	23	<0·01
Control group	15	76	9	100	46	
New stewards	29	62	9	100	35	N.S.
Control group	20	80	0	100	35	

* Workers who did not change roles, matched with future foremen on demographic and attitudinal variables in the 'before' situation.

† Workers who did not change roles, matched with future stewards on demographic and attitudinal variables in the 'before' situation.

Table 2 Effects of foreman and steward roles on attitudes towards the union

	Kind of Change					
	More favourable to the union	*No change*	*More critical to the union*	*Total*	*N*	*p*
	%	%	%	%		
5 *How do you feel about labour unions in general?*						
New foremen	30	48	22	100	23	N.S.
Control group*	37	48	15	100	46	
New stewards	54	37	9	100	35	0·1–0·05
Control group†	29	65	6	100	35	
6 *How much say should the union have in setting standards?*						
New foremen	0	26	74	100	23	<0·01
Control group	22	54	24	100	46	
New stewards	31	66	3	100	35	N.S.
Control group	20	60	20	100	35	
7 *How would things be if there were no union at Rockwell?*						
New foremen	9	39	52	100	23	0·01–0·05
Control group	20	58	22	100	46	
New standards	14	86	0	100	35	N.S.
Control group	11	72	17	100	35	
8 *How much do union officers care about the workers at Rockwell?*						
New foremen	22	69	9	100	23	N.S.
Control group	15	78	7	100	46	
New stewards	57	37	6	100	35	0·01–0·05
Control group	26	68	6	100	35	

* Workers who did not change roles, matched with future foremen on demographic and attitudinal variables in the 'before' situation.

† Workers who did not change roles, matched with future stewards on demographic and attitudinal variables in the 'before' situation.

Table 3 Effects of foreman and steward roles on attitudes towards the incentive system

	Kind of Change					
	More favourable to incentive system	*No change*	*More critical of incentive system*	*Total*	*N*	*p*
	%	%	%	%		
9 *How do you feel about the principle of an incentive system?*						
New foremen	57	26	17	100	23	0·01
Control group*	15	52	33	100	46	
New stewards	17	54	29	100	35	N.S.
Control group†	31	40	29	100	35	
10 *How do you feel the incentive system works out at Rockwell?*						
New foremen	65	22	13	100	23	0·5–0·10
Control group	37	41	22	100	46	
New stewards	43	34	23	100	35	N.S.
Control group	40	34	26	100	35	
11 *Should the incentive system be changed?*						
New foremen	39	48	13	100	23	0·01
Control group	11	69	20	100	46	
New stewards	14	63	23	100	35	N.S.
Control group	20	60	20	100	35	
12 *Is a labour standard ever changed just because a worker is a high producer?*						
New foremen	48	43	9	100	23	0·01
Control group	11	74	15	100	46	
New stewards	29	57	14	100	35	N.S.
Control group	26	65	9	100	35	

* Workers who did not change roles, matched with future foremen on demographic and attitudinal variables in the 'before' situation.

† Workers who did not change roles, matched with future stewards on demographic and attitudinal variables in the 'before' situation.

Table 4 Effects of foreman and steward roles on attitudes towards the seniority system

	Kind of Change					
	More favourable to seniority system	*No change*	*More critical of seniority system*	*Total*	*N*	*p*
	%	%	%	%		
13 *How do you feel about the way the seniority system works out here?*						
New foremen	0	65	35	100	23	0·01–0·05
Control group*	20	63	17	100	46	
New stewards	23	48	29	100	35	N.S.
Control group†	9	71	20	100	35	
14 *How much should seniority count during lay-offs?*						
New foremen	9	52	39	100	23	0·05–0·10
Control group	24	59	17	100	46	
New stewards	29	48	23	100	35	N.S.
Control group	29	40	31	100	35	
15 *How much should seniority count in in moving to better jobs?*						
New foremen	17	44	39	100	23	N.S.
Control group	20	54	26	100	46	
New stewards	34	46	20	100	35	0·01–0·05
Control group	17	34	49	100	35	
16 *How much should seniority count in promotion to foreman?*						
New foremen	17	70	13	100	23	N.S.
Control group	15	52	33	100	46	
New stewards	31	35	34	100	35	N.S.
Control group	17	43	40	100	35	

* Workers who did not change roles, matched with future foremen on demographic and attitudinal variables in the 'before' situation.

† Workers who did not change roles, matched with future stewards on demographic and attitudinal variables in the 'before' situation.

Although a number of the differences are not statistically significant, those which are significant are all in the expected directions, and most of the non-significant differences are also in the expected directions. New foremen, among other things, come to see Rockwell as a better place to work compared with other companies, develop more positive perceptions of top management officers, and become more favourably disposed towards the principle and operation of the incentive system. New stewards come to look upon labour unions in general in a more favourable light, develop more positive perceptions of the top union officers at Rockwell, and come to prefer seniority to ability as a criterion of what should count in moving workers to better jobs. In general, the attitudes of workers who become foremen tend to gravitate in a pro-management direction and the attitudes of workers who become stewards tend to move in a pro-union direction.

A second kind of finding has to do with the relative *amount* of attitude change that takes place among new foremen in contrast to the amount that takes place among new stewards. On the whole, more pronounced and more widespread attitude changes occur among those who are made foremen than among those who are made stewards. Using a *p*-level of 0·10 as a criterion for statistical significance, the workers who are made foremen undergo significant attitude changes, relative to the workers who are not made foremen, on ten of the sixteen attitudinal items presented in Tables 1 to 4. By contrast, the workers who are made stewards undergo significant attitude changes, relative to the workers who are not made stewards, on only three of the sixteen items. However, for the steward role as well as for the foreman role, most of the differences found between the experimental and control groups still tend to be in the expected directions.

The more pronounced and more widespread attitude changes that occur among new foremen than among new stewards can probably be accounted for in large measure by the kinds of differences that exist between the foreman and steward roles. For one thing, the foreman role represents a relatively permanent position, while many stewards take the steward role as a 'one-shot' job and even if they want to run again their constituents may not re-elect them. Secondly, the foreman role is a full-time job, while most stewards spend just a few hours a week in the performance of their steward functions and spend the rest of the time carrying out their regular rank-and-file jobs. Thirdly, a worker who is made a foreman must give up his membership in the union and become a surrogate of management, while a worker who is made a steward retains the union as a reference group and simply takes on new functions and responsibilities as a representative of it. All of these differences suggest that the change from worker to foreman is a more fundamental change in roles than the change from worker to steward. This, in turn, might account to a large extent for the finding that, although attitude changes accompany both changes in roles, they occur more sharply among new foremen than among new stewards.

A third finding has to do with the *kinds* of attitude changes which occur among workers who change roles. As expected, new foremen become more pro-management and new stewards become more pro-union. Somewhat less expected is the finding that new foremen become more anti-union but new stewards do not become more anti-management. Among workers who are made foremen, statistically significant shifts in an anti-union direction occur on four of the eight items dealing with the union and the union-sponsored seniority system. Among workers who are made stewards, there are no statistically significant shifts in either direction on any of the eight items having to do with management and the management-sponsored incentive system.

The finding that new foremen become anti-union but that new stewards do not become anti-management may be related to the fact that workers who become foremen must relinquish their membership of the union, while workers who become stewards retain their status as employees of management. New foremen, subject to one main set of loyalties and called on to carry out a markedly new set of functions, tend to develop negative attitudes towards the union as well as positive attitudes towards management. New stewards, subject to overlapping group membership and still dependent on management for their livelihoods, tend to become more favourable towards the union but they do not turn against management, at least not within the relatively limited time period covered by the present research project. Over time, stewards might come to develop somewhat hostile attitudes towards management, but, under the conditions prevailing at Rockwell, there is apparently no tendency for such attitudes to be developed as soon as workers enter the steward role.

Method: Phase 2

One of the questions that may be raised about the results that have been presented up to this point concerns the extent to which the changed attitudes displayed by new foremen and new stewards are internalized by the role occupants. Are the changed attitudes expressed by new foremen and new stewards relatively stable, or are they ephemeral phenomena to be held only as long as they occupy the foreman and steward roles? An unusual set of circumstances at Rockwell enabled the researchers to glean some data on this question.

A short time after the 1952 re-survey, the nation suffered an economic recession. In order to meet the lessening demand for its products, Rockwell, like many other firms, had to cut its work force. This resulted in many rank-and-file workers being laid off and a number of the foremen being returned to non-supervisory jobs. By June 1954, eight of the twenty-three workers who had been promoted to foreman had returned to the worker role and only twelve were still foremen. (The remaining three respondents had voluntarily left Rockwell by this time.)

Over the same period, a number of role changes had also been experienced by the thirty-five workers who had become stewards. Fourteen had returned to the worker role, either because they had not sought re-election by their work groups or because they had failed to win re-election, and only six were still stewards. (The other fifteen respondents, who composed almost half of this group, had either voluntarily left Rockwell or had been laid off as part of the general reduction in force.)

Once again, in June 1954, the researchers returned to Rockwell to re-administer the questionnaires that the workers had filled out in 1951 and 1952. The instructions to the respondents were substantially the same as those given in 1952 – i.e. a sample of employees had been chosen to get up-to-date measures of employers' attitudes towards working conditions at Rockwell and the same groups were selected this time as had been selected last time in order to lend greater stability to the results.

In this phase of the study, the numbers of cases with which we were dealing in the various groups were so small that the data could only be viewed as suggestive, and systematic statistical analysis of the data did not seem to be too meaningful. However, the unusual opportunity to throw some light on an important question suggests that a reporting of these results may be worthwhile.

Results: Phase 2

The principal question examined here was: on those items where a change in roles resulted in a change in attitudes between 1951 and 1952, how are these attitudes influenced by a reverse change in roles between 1952 and 1954?

The most consistent and widespread attitude changes noted between 1951 and 1952 were those that resulted when workers moved into the foreman role. What are the effects of moving out of the foreman role between 1952 and 1954? The data indicate that, in general, most of the 'gains' that were observed when workers became foremen are 'lost' when they become workers again. The results on six of the items, showing the proportions who take pro-management positions at various points in time, are presented in Table 5. On almost all of the items, the foremen who

Table 5 Effects of entering and leaving the foreman role on attitudes towards management and the union

	Workers who became foremen and stayed foremen (N = 12)			*Workers who became foremen and were later demoted (N = 8)*		
	(*W*) *1951*	(*F*) *1952*	(*F*) *1954*	(*W*) *1951*	(*F*) *1952*	(*W*) *1954*
% who feel Rockwell is a good place to work	33	92	100	25	75	50
% who feel management officers really care about the workers at Rockwell	8	33	67	0	25	0
% who feel the union should not have more say in setting labour standards	33	100	100	13	63	13
% who are satisfied with the way the incentive system works out at Rockwell	17	75	75	25	50	13
% who believe a worker's standard will not be changed just because he is a high producer	42	83	100	25	63	75
% who feel ability should count more than seniority in promotions	33	58	75	25	50	38

remain foremen either retain their favourable attitudes towards management or become even more favourable towards management between 1952 and 1954, while the demoted foremen show fairly consistent drops in the direction of re-adopting the attitudes they held when they had been in the worker role. On the whole, the attitudes held by demoted foremen in 1954, after they had left the foreman role, fall roughly to the same levels as they had been in 1951, before they had ever moved into the foreman role.

The results on the effects of moving out of the steward role are less clear-cut. As shown in Table 6, there is no marked tendency for ex-stewards to revert to earlier-held attitudes when they go from the steward role to the worker role. At the same time, it should be recalled that there had not been particularly marked changes in their attitudes when they initially changed from the worker role to the steward role. These findings, then, are consistent with the interpretation offered earlier that the change in roles between worker and steward is less significant than the change in roles between worker and foreman.

A question might be raised about what is represented in the reversal of attitudes found among ex-foremen. Does it represent a positive taking-on of attitudes appropriate for respondents who are re-entering the worker role, or does it constitute a negative, perhaps embittered reaction away from the attitudes they held before being demoted from the foreman role? A definitive answer to this question cannot be arrived at, but it might be suggested that if we were dealing with a situation where a reversion in roles did not constitute such a strong psychological blow to the role occupants (as was probably the case among demoted foremen), then such a marked reversion in attitudes might not have occurred.[2]

One final table is of interest here. Table 7 compares the attitudes of two groups of respondents: 1) the twelve employees who were rank-and-file workers in 1951, had been selected as foremen by 1952, and were still foremen in 1954; and 2) the six employees who were rank-and-file workers in 1951, had been elected as stewards by 1952, and were still stewards in 1954. At each time period, for each of the sixteen questions examined earlier in Tables 1 to 4, the table shows 1) the proportion of foremen or future foremen who took a pro-management position on these questions;

2 There were a number of reactions to demotion among the eight ex-foremen, as obtained from informal interviews with these respondents. Some reacted impunitively (i.e. they blamed uncontrollable situational determinants) and did not seem to be bothered by demotion. Others reacted extrapunitively (i.e. they blamed management) or intrapunitively (i.e. they blamed themselves) and appeared to be more disturbed by demotion. One way of testing the hypothesis that attitude reversion is a function of embitterment would be to see if sharper reversion occurs among extrapunitive and intrapunitive respondents. However, the small number of cases does not permit an analysis of this kind to be carried out in the present situation.

Table 6 Effects of entering and leaving the steward role on attitudes towards management and the union

	Workers who were elected stewards and were later re-elected ($N = 6$)			*Workers who were elected stewards but were not later re-elected* ($N = 14$)		
	(*W*) *1951*	(*S*) *1952*	(*S*) *1954*	(*W*) *1951*	(*S*) *1952*	(*W*) *1954*
% who feel Rockwell is a good place to work	50	0	0	29	79	36
% who feel management officers really care about the workers at Rockwell	0	0	0	14	14	0
% who feel the union should not have more say in setting labour standards	0	17	0	14	14	14
% who are satisfied with the way the incentive system works out at Rockwell	17	17	0	43	43	21
% who believe a worker's standard will not be changed just because he is a high producer	50	50	17	21	43	36
% who feel ability should count more than seniority in promotions	67	17	17	36	36	21

Table 7 Effects of foreman and steward roles over a three-year period: before change in roles, after one year in new roles, and after two–three years in new roles

% who take a pro-management position on the following questions:†	*Before Change in Roles (1951)*			*After 1 Year in New Roles (1952)*			*After 2–3 Years in New Roles (1954)*		
	Workers who became foremen	*Workers who became stewards*	*D%**	*Workers who became foremen*	*Workers who became stewards*	*D%**	*Workers who became foremen*	*Workers who became stewards*	*D%**
Question 1	33	50	−17	92	0	+92	100	0	+100
Question 2	33	33	0	75	33	+42	67	17	+50
Question 3	92	83	+9	100	100	0	100	50	+50
Question 4	8	0	+8	33	0	+33	67	0	+67
Question 5	67	100	−33	67	17	+50	33	17	+16
Question 6	33	0	+33	100	17	+83	100	0	+100
Question 7	8	0	+8	50	0	+50	58	0	+58
Question 8	75	67	+8	75	50	+25	58	17	+41
Question 9	33	83	−50	83	17	+66	83	0	+83
Question 10	17	17	0	75	17	+58	75	0	+75
Question 11	17	17	0	25	0	+25	67	0	+67
Question 12	42	50	−8	83	50	+33	100	17	+83
Question 13	58	50	+8	100	17	+83	100	17	+83
Question 14	33	67	−34	50	17	+33	75	17	+58
Question 15	33	0	+33	58	0	+58	67	0	+67
Question 16	67	33	+34	67	33	+34	67	67	0
No. of Cases	12	6		12	6		12	6	
Mean D%			−0·1			+47·8			+62·4

* Percentage of workers who became foremen who take a pro-management position minus percentage of workers who became stewards who take a pro-management position.
† Question numbers refer to the question numbers of the attitudinal items in *Tables 1* through *4*.

2) the proportion of stewards or future stewards who took a pro-management position on these questions; and 3) the difference between these proportions. The following are the mean differences in proportions for the three time periods:

1 In 1951, while both future foremen and future stewards still occupied the rank-and-file worker role, the mean difference was only – 0·1 per cent, which means that practically no difference in attitudes existed between these two groups at this time. (The minus sign means that a slightly, but far from significantly, larger proportion of future stewards than future foremen expressed a pro-management position on these items.)

2 In 1952, after the groups had been in the foreman and steward roles for about one year, the mean difference had jumped to +47·8 per cent, which means that a sharp wedge had been driven between them. Both groups had tended to become polarized in opposite directions, as foremen took on attitudes consistent with being a representative of management and stewards took on attitudes appropriate for a representative of the union.

3 In 1954, after the groups had been in the foreman and steward roles for two to three years, the mean difference was +62·4 per cent, which means that a still larger gap had opened up between them. Although the gap had widened, it is interesting to note that the changes that occurred during this later and longer 1952 to 1954 period are not as sharp or as dramatic as the changes that occurred during the initial and shorter 1951 to 1952 period.

These findings offer further support for the proposition that roles can influence attitudes. The data indicate that changes in attitudes occurred soon after changes in roles took place. And inside a period of three years those who had remained in their new roles had developed almost diametrically opposed sets of attitudinal positions.

Discussion

A role may be defined as a set of behaviours that are expected of people who occupy a certain position in a social system. These expectations consist of shared attitudes or beliefs, held by relevant populations, about what role occupants should and should not do. The theoretical basis for hypothesizing that a role will have effects on role occupants lies in the nature of these expectations. If a role occupant meets these expectations, the 'rights' or 'rewards' associated with the role will be accorded to him. If he fails to meet these expectations, the 'rights' or 'rewards' will be withheld from him and 'punishments' may be meted out.[3]

3 An earlier discussion of the role concept, with particular reference to its application to the study of complex organizations, is found in Jacobson, Charters and Lieberman (1951).

A distinction should be made between the effects of roles on people's attitudes and the effects of roles on their actions. How roles affect actions can probably be explained in a fairly direct fashion. Actions are overt and readily enforceable. If a person fails to behave in ways appropriate to his role, this can immediately be seen, and steps may be taken to bring the deviant or non-conformist into line. Role deviants may be evicted from their roles, placed in less rewarding roles, isolated from other members of the group, or banished entirely from the social system.

But attitudes are not as overt as actions. A person may behave in such a way as to reveal his attitudes, but he can – and often does – do much to cover them up. Why, then, should a change in roles lead to a change in actions? A number of explanatory factors might be suggested here. The present discussion will be confined to two factors that are probably generic to a wide variety of situations. One pertains to the influence of reference groups; the other is based on an assumption about people's need to have attitudes internally consistent with their actions.

A change in roles almost invariably involves a change in reference groups. Old reference groups may continue to influence the role occupant, but new ones also come into play. The change in reference groups may involve moving into a completely new group (as when a person gives up membership in one organization and joins another one) or it may simply involve taking on new functions in the same group (as when a person is promoted to a higher position in a hierarchical organization). In both situations, new reference groups will tend to bring about new frames of reference, new self-percepts, and new vested interests, and these in turn will tend to produce new attitudinal orientations.

In addition to a change in reference groups, a change in roles also involves a change in functions and a change in the kinds of behaviours and actions that the role occupant must display if he is to fulfil these functions. A change in actions, let us assume, comes about because these actions are immediately required, clearly visible, and hence socially enforceable. If we further assume a need for people to have attitudes that are internally consistent with their actions, then at least one aspect of the functional significance of a change in attitudes becomes clear. A change in attitudes enables a new role occupant to justify, to make rational, or perhaps simply to rationalize his change in actions. Having attitudes that are consistent with actions helps the role occupant to be 'at one' with himself and facilitates his effective performance of the functions he is expected to carry out.

The reference-group principle and the self-consistency principle postulate somewhat different chains of events in accounting for the effects of roles on attitudes and actions. In abbreviated versions, the different chains may be spelled out in the following ways:

1 Reference-group principle: A change in roles involves a change in reference groups . . . which leads to a change in attitudes . . . which leads to a change in actions.
2 Self-consistency principle: A change in roles involves a change in functions . . . which leads to a change in actions . . . which leads to a change in attitudes.

In the former chain, a person's attitudes influence his actions; in the latter chain, a person's actions influence his attitudes. Both chains might plausibly account for the results obtained, but whether either chain, both chains, or other chains is or are valid cannot be determined from the data available. A more direct investigation of the underlying mechanisms responsible for the impact of roles on attitudes would appear to be a fruitful area for further research.

But apart from the question of underlying mechanisms, the results lend support to the proposition that a person's attitudes will be influenced by his role. Relatively consistent changes in attitudes were found both among workers who were made foremen and among workers who were made stewards, although these changes were more clear-cut for foremen than for stewards. The more interesting set of results – as far as role theory in general is concerned – would seem to be the data on the effects of entering and leaving the foreman role. It was pointed out earlier that the foreman role, unlike the steward role, is a full-time, relatively permanent position, and moving into this position entails taking on a very new and different set of functions. When workers are made foremen, their attitudes change in a more pro-management and anti-union direction. When they are demoted and move back into the worker role, their attitudes change once again, this time in a more pro-union and anti-management direction. In both instances, the respondents' attitudes seem to be moulded by the roles which they occupy at a given time.

The readiness with which the respondents in this study shed one set of attitudes and took on another set of attitudes might suggest either that 1) the attitudes studied do not tap very basic or deep-rooted facets of the respondents' psyches, or 2) the character structures of the respondents are such as not to include very deeply ingrained sets of value orientations. Riesman (1950) deals with this problem in his discussion of 'other-directedness' v. 'inner-directedness'. How much the rapid shifts in attitudes observed here reflect the particular kinds of respondents who underwent changes in roles in the present situation, and how much these shifts reflect the national character of the American population, can only be speculated on at the present time.

Summary

This study was designed to test the proposition that a person's attitudes will be influenced by the role he occupies in a social system. This is a commonly accepted postulate in role theory but there appears to be little in the way of definitive empirical evidence to support it. Earlier studies have generally made inferences about the effects of roles on attitudes on the basis of correlational data gathered at a single point in time. The present study attempted to measure the effects of roles on attitudes through data gathered at three different points in time.

In September and October 1951, 2354 rank-and-file workers in a factory situation were asked to fill out attitude questionnaires dealing with management and the union. During the next twelve months, twenty-three of these workers were promoted to foreman and thirty-five were elected by their work group as union stewards. In December 1952, the questionnaires were re-administered to the two groups of workers who had changed roles and to two matched control groups of workers who had not changed roles. By comparing the attitude changes that occurred in the experimental groups with the attitude changes that occurred in their respective control groups, the effects of moving into the foreman and steward roles could be determined.

The results on this phase of the study showed that the experimental groups underwent systematic changes in attitudes after they were placed in their new roles, while the control groups underwent no changes or less marked changes from the 'before' situation to the 'after' situation. The workers who were made foremen tended to become more favourable towards management, and the workers who were made stewards tended to become more favourable towards the union. The changes were more marked among new foremen than among new stewards, which can be probably accounted for by the fact that the change from worker to foreman seems to be a more significant and more meaningful change in roles than the change from worker to steward.

In the months following the second administration of the questionnaire, a number of the workers who had become foremen and stewards reverted to the rank-and-file worker role. Some of the foremen were cut back to non-supervisory positions during a period of economic recession, and some of the stewards either did not run again or failed to be re-elected during the annual steward elections. In June 1954, the questionnaires were once again administered to the same groups of respondents. By comparing the attitude changes that occurred among foremen and stewards who left these roles with the attitude changes that occurred among foremen and stewards who remained in these roles, the effects of moving out of these roles could be assessed.

The results of this phase of the study showed that foremen who were demoted tended to revert to the attitudes they had previously held while they were in the worker role, while foremen who remained in the foreman role either maintained the attitudes they had developed when they first became foremen or moved even further in that direction. The results among stewards who left the steward role were less consistent and less clear-cut, which parallels the smaller and less clear-cut attitude changes that took place when they first became stewards.

The findings support the proposition that a person's role will have an impact on his attitudes, but they still leave unanswered the question of what underlying mechanisms are operating here. A more direct investigation of these underlying mechanisms might comprise a fruitful area for further research.

References

JACOBSON, E., CHARTERS, W. W. Jr. and LIEBERMAN, S. (1951) 'The use of the role concept in the study of complex organizations', *Journal of Social Issues*, 7, no. 3, pp. 18–27.

NEWCOMB, T. M. (1950) *Social Psychology* New York, The Dryden Press (reprinted London, Tavistock Publications Ltd, 1952).

PARSONS, T. (1951) The Social System Glencoe, Illinois, The Free Press (reprinted London, Tavistock Publications Ltd, 1951).

RIESMAN, D (1950) *The Lonely Crowd* New Haven, Yale University Press.

STOUFFER, S. A., SUCHMAN, E. A., DEVINNEY, L. C., STARR, S. A. and WILLIAMS, R. M. Jr. (1949) *The American Soldier: Adjustment During Army Life. Vol. I* Princeton University Press.

WALKER, H. M. and LEV, J. (1953) *Statistical Inference* New York, Henry Holt and Co. Inc.

Section 11
Communication

Introduction

Section 3 laid a basis for a study of language by focusing on its fundamental characteristics and viewing it from a biological perspective. In the first three papers of this section on communication, the emphasis shifts to other aspects of language, in particular variations within and between cultures and the relationship between such variations and social structure.

Effective communication depends on a system of shared assumptions between communicators as to the meaning, significance and appropriateness of utterances. The style of communication a speaker adopts will often reflect not only his individual intentions and characteristics but also his social context, his family, cultural and educational background. It will be characteristic of a speech community. Subcultures, gangs, professions and cliques may all form their own speech communities. Special parlances with their own significance and meaning may evolve for particular roles and groups. So the language of religious ritual differs from that of cocktail party chat and political speech making. Such distinctions may serve not only the function of specialized communication but also to express solidarity, identity and maintain power differentials.

The brief extract from Jerome Bruner emphasizes the point that the intentions of a communicator can only be understood if his message is viewed in the context of the nature of the situation in which it occurs and the conventions of the linguistic community concerned. Communication, as well as language acquisition, takes place in a total context of circumstances, intentions and social interchange. Bruner briefly describes Jakobson's model of communication functions and points out that speech communities may also have conventions as to the appropriateness and, therefore, the meaning and use of particular functions.

In the second extract, the English sociologist, Basil Bernstein, discusses two particular forms of communication style – restricted and elaborated codes. These codes differ not only in their overt form but in the communication function they can best fulfil. A restricted code, for example, facilitates social solidarity, an elaborated code the expression of individual experience. Social context, particularly the pattern of social relationships and experience a person is exposed to in childhood, will be a key determinant of the style he adopts. Problems may arise when communicators who speak the same language do not share the same code. This kind of disjunction, Bernstein points out, is often a feature of the working class child's experience of school.

In the following article Labov warns of the dangers of assuming too much from observations of speakers from different speech communities. He demonstrates, for example, how a child's normal expressiveness may be inhibited in the adult–child interaction of an interview situation. Labov also argues for the need to interpret utterances from within the context of the norms operative for the speech community of the speaker. Viewed in this way, the use of nonstandard English may turn out to communicate more powerfully and expressively than a middle-class verbal style and, in the examples he gives, certainly reveals no deficit in complexity of conceptual thinking.

Human communication does not only take place through language. In the final paper in this section, Michael Argyle, Reader in Social Psychology at the University of Oxford, provides a comprehensive review of research on *non-verbal* communication. He contrasts the distinctive roles played by such forms of communication and considers the primary functions it serves and the information it best conveys. In his paper on the ethology of man included in section 2 of the Reader, Irenäus Eibl-Eibesfeldt made a case that much non-verbal communication should be regarded as a function of innate predispositions developed during the course of evolution. Argyle acknowledges that there is some value in this view but emphasizes also that, as with language, cultural conventions also play a considerable role in determining the meaning which will be assigned to non-verbal expressions. He also points out the value of viewing sequences of non-verbal communication from the standpoints of structural linguistics and social psychology.

The papers in this section serve, in their different ways, to bring out the extraordinary richness and complexity of human communication. They emphasize the need to view communication in its social context and also highlight the methodological difficulties involved both in making effective analyses and drawing appropriate inferences from observations of ongoing communication and in identifying the factors which influence it.

34 Communicative intentions

Jerome S. Bruner

Any study of prelinguistic communication – indeed, any study of language – presupposes an intent to communicate. Linguistics most usually takes intent for granted, but does so at its peril, as we know from the criticisms of philosophers of language. For even in well formed utterances, there may be a marked discrepancy between the intent of the communicator and the syntactic form of the message. The sentence, 'Would you be kind enough to get off of my foot?' is a demand conventionally couched in the interrogative, the convention designed to cloak command in the form of a question in consenting contexts. If it is not heeded, it will usually be followed by, 'Get off my foot, I said!'

In a different context, the reverse procedure is followed. In welcoming, we use the imperative, 'Come in!' not as a command, but a request – to show our commitment to the welcome, perhaps. If the interlocutor fails to comprehend, we revert to the interrogative: 'Won't you please come in?'

Philosophers like Austin (1962), Grice (1968) and Searle (1969) have been particularly insistent on drawing the distinction between the performative or illocutionary functions of utterances, judged by their felicity or efficacy in achieving a behavioural resultant, and the locutionary function, to be judged against such criteria as well-formedness or truth value. Indeed, Austin has insisted that certain utterances can be considered pure performatives, designed only to perform an intended act – such as promising or anointing or officiating, as in, 'I do thee wed.'

Let it be borne in mind, then, that the inference of communicative intent in *any* communicative act is subject to interpretation in the light not only of the message but also the nature of the situation in which it occurs and the conventions that govern such situations in a linguistic community.

Jakobson (1960) proposes that in order to be clear about such matters we bear in mind that any communication can serve and often does serve manifold functions. His scheme for distinguishing these is useful. He represents the communication situation by the conventional diagram, functions being noted by numbers.

BRUNER, J. S. (1975) 'Communicative intentions' from 'From communication to language – a psychological perspective', *Cognition* (in press).

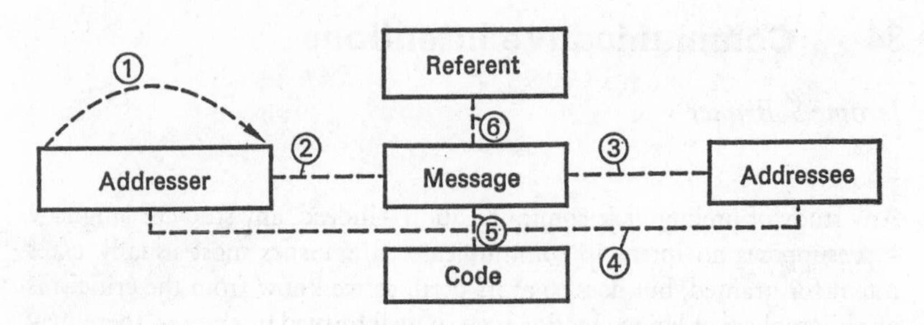

Fig. 1

Function 1 is *expressive* and is made up usually of accompaniments to the addresser's feelings. On a windy, moonlit night in mid-Atlantic, an ordinarily peaceful architect at the helm of a fast-moving sailing yacht on passage was heard to cry in full voice, 'Let loose the hounds of hell!' When asked by his watch-mates what he had in mind, he answered rather sheepishly, that his shout was just an expression of how gloriously he felt. Function 2 is *poetic* and embodies the intent of the addresser to the form or style of the message. 'Hounds of hell' exemplifies the poetic device of paranomasia, inclusion of an element from one term into a neighbouring one. So does 'let loose'. How earth bound would have been the cry 'Release the dogs of hell'? Function 3 is *conative* and is concerned with forming the message in such a way as to produce desired behaviour in the addressee. It encompasses the philosophers' illocutionary force. Function 4 is *phatic* and relates to the maintenance of a channel of communication between addresser and addressee. Its conduct is sometimes governed by standard procedures for ensuring message transmission under noisy conditions: 'What function did you say?' – 'PAPA, HOTEL, ALPHA, TANGO, INDIA, CHARLIE – phatic function.' Function 5 is *metalinguistic* and it serves to explicate, usually by rewrite rules, what is meant by a message through reference to a code: 'Why do you call it *meta*linguistic?' – 'Oh, because it is talk about talk itself.' Function 6 is *referential* and its use is to make clear the referent of a message by clearing up the context for interpreting an utterance: 'What did you mean, in front of the house?' – 'It's right in front of the house, by the wall.'

Any linguistic community has conventions for dealing with the functions of language. So do sub-communities. Scientists follow conventions of appearing to avoid conative, poetic and expressive functions by the use of meticulous declaratives, passive voice, and words of compact rather than diffuse associative value, etc. The sociologist Garfinkel (1963) notes that excessive request for metalinguistic clarification in ordinary discourse is often taken as a sign of hostility or disbelief in one's interlocutor. To be felicitous requires learning a great many such conventions and rituals.

To characterize these conventions Grice (1967–8) invokes conversational postulates that govern discourse, from which rather loose-fitting maxims are derived – maxims of relevance, of quantity, of quality. Speakers in conversation are expected to stick to the point, to give not too little and not too much information about context, to speak the truth as they see it. When they depart from these maxims, it is expected that they will do so in a patterned way, with specific intent – irony, humour, or some effort at manipulation. Obviously, the pre-linguistic child is not under the sway of such maxims. The postulates governing their communication cannot be taken for granted. But we as their tutors in communication very soon learn their conventions and very early try to shape them to those of the adult community. Unfortunately, there are no studies that have investigated the ways in which this is done, although work on social class differences seem to be making a start (Bernstein 1960, Hess and Shipman 1965, Schoggen and Schoggen 1971).

References

AUSTIN, J. L. (1962) *How to do things with words* Oxford University Press.

BERNSTEIN, B. (1960) 'Language and social class', *British Journal of Sociology*, 11, 271–6.

GARFINKEL, H. (1963) 'Trust and stable actions' in Harvey, O. J. (ed.) *Motivation and Social Interaction* New York, Ronald.

GRICE, H. P. (1967–8) 'Utterer's meaning, sentence-meaning, and word-meaning', The William James Lecture Series, Harvard University.

GRICE, H. P. (1968) 'Utterer's meaning, sentence meaning and word meaning', *Foundations of Language*, 4, 225–42.

HESS, R. D. and SHIPMAN, VIRGINIA (1965) 'Early experience and socialization of cognitive modes in children', *Child Development*, 36, 869–86.

JAKOBSON, R. (1960) 'Linguistics and poetics' in Sebeok, T. A. (ed.) *Style in Language* Cambridge, Mass., MIT Press.

SCHOGGEN, M. and P. (1971) 'Environmental forces in the home lives of three-year-old children in three population subgroups', *D.A.R.C.E.E. Papers and Reports*, 5, no. 2 (John Kennedy Center for Research on Education and Human Development, George Peabody College, Nashville, Tennessee).

SEARLE, J. R. (1969) *Speech Acts: An essay in the philosophy of language* Cambridge University Press.

35 Social class, language and socialization

Basil Bernstein

I want first of all to make clear what I am not concerned with. Chomsky, in *Aspects of the Theory of Syntax*, neatly severs the study of the rule system of language from the study of the social rules which determine their contextual use. He does this by making a distinction between competence and performance. Competence refers to the child's tacit understanding of the rule system, performance relates to the essentially social use to which the rule system is put. Competence refers to man abstracted from contextual constraints. Performance refers to man in the grip of the contextual constraints which determine his speech acts. Competence refers to the Ideal, performance refers to the Fall. In this sense Chomsky's notion of competence is Platonic. Competence has its source in the very biology of man. There is no difference between men in terms of their access to the linguistic rule system. Here Chomsky, like many other linguists before him, announces the communality of man; all men have equal access to the creative act which is language. On the other hand, performance is under the control of the social – performances are culturally specific acts, they refer to the choices which are made in specific speech encounters. Thus, according to Hymes, Chomsky indicates the tragedy of man, the potentiality of competence and the degeneration of performance.

Clearly, much is to be gained in rigour and explanatory power through the severing of the relationship between the formal properties of the grammar and the meanings which are realized in its use. But if we are to study speech, *la parole*, we are inevitably involved in a study of a rather different rule system; we are involved in a study of rules, formal and informal, which regulate the options we take up in various contexts in which we find ourselves. This second rule system is the cultural system. This raises immediately the question of the relationship between the linguistic rule system and the cultural system. Clearly, specific linguistic rule systems are part of the cultural system, but it has been argued that the linguistic rule system in various ways shapes the cultural system. This very briefly is the view of those who hold a narrow form of the linguistic relativity hypothesis. I do not intend to get involved in that particular quag-

---

BERNSTEIN, BASIL (1971) from 'Social class, language and socialization' in Abramson, A. S. et al. (eds) *Current Trends in Linguistics* The Hague, Mouton Press.

mire. Instead, I shall take the view that the code which the linguist invents to explain the formal properties of the grammar is capable of generating any number of speech codes, and there is no reason for believing that any one language code is better than another in this respect. On this argument, language is a set of rules to which all speech codes must comply, but which speech codes are realized is a function of the culture acting through social relationships in specific contexts. Different speech forms or codes symbolize the form of the social relationship, regulate the nature of the speech encounters, and create for the speakers different orders of relevance and relation. The experience of the speakers is then transformed by what is made significant or relevant by the speech form. This is a sociological argument because the speech form is taken as a consequence of the form of the social relation or, put more generally, is a quality of a social structure. Let me qualify this immediately. Because the speech form is initially a function of a given social arrangement, it does not mean that the speech form does not in turn modify or even change that social structure which initially evolved the speech form. This formulation, indeed, invites the question: Under what conditions does a given speech form free itself sufficiently from its embodiment in the social structure so that the system of meanings it realizes points to alternative realities, alternative arrangements in the affairs of men? Here we become concerned immediately with the antecedents and consequences of the boundary maintaining principles of a culture or sub-culture. I am here suggesting a relationship between forms of boundary maintenance at the cultural level and forms of speech.

I am required to consider the relationship between language and socialization. It should be clear from these opening remarks that I am not concerned with language, but with speech, and concerned more specifically with the contextual constraints upon speech. Now what about socialization? I shall take the term to refer to the process whereby a child acquires a specific cultural identity, *and* to his responses to such an identity. Socialization refers to the process whereby the biological is transformed into a specific cultural being. It follows from this that the process of socialization is a complex process of control, whereby a particular moral, cognitive and affective awareness is evoked in the child and given a specific form and content. Socialization sensitizes the child to the various orderings of society as these are made substantive in the various roles he is expected to play. In a sense, socialization is a process for making people safe. The process acts selectively on the possibilities of man by creating through time a sense of the inevitability of a given social arrangement, and through limiting the areas of permitted change. The basic agencies of socialization in contemporary societies are the family, the peer group, school and work. It is through these agencies, and in particular through their relationship to each other, that the various orderings of society are made manifest.

Now it is quite clear that given this view of socialization it is necessary to limit the discussion. I shall limit our discussion to socialization within the family, but it should be obvious that the focusing and filtering of the child's experience within the family in a large measure is a microcosm of the macroscopic orderings of society. Our question now becomes: What are the sociological factors which affect linguistic performances within the family critical to the process of socialization?

Without a shadow of doubt the most formative influence upon the procedures of socialization, from a sociological viewpoint, is social class. The class structure influences work and educational roles and brings families into a special relationship with each other and deeply penetrates the structure of life experiences within the family. The class system has deeply marked the distribution of knowledge within society. It has given differential access to the sense that the world is permeable. It has sealed off communities from each other and has ranked these communities on a scale of invidious worth. We have three components, knowledge, possibility and invidious insulation. It would be a little naïve to believe that differences in knowledge, differences in the sense of the possible, combined with invidious insulation, rooted in differential *material* well-being, would not affect the forms of control and innovation in the socializing procedures of different social classes. I shall go on to argue that the deep structure of communication itself is affected, but not in any final or irrevocable way.

As an approach to my argument, let me glance at the social distribution of knowledge. We can see that the class system has affected the distribution of knowledge. Historically, and now, only a tiny percentage of the population has been socialized into knowledge at the level of the meta-languages of control and innovation, whereas the mass of the population has been socialized into knowledge at the level of context-tied operations.

A tiny percentage of the population has been given access to the principles of intellectual change, whereas the rest have been denied such access. This suggests that we might be able to distinguish between two orders of meaning. One we could call universalistic, the other particularistic. Universalistic meanings are those in which principles and operations are made linguistically explicit, whereas particularistic orders of meaning are meanings in which principles and operation are relatively linguistically implicit. If orders of meaning are universalistic, then the meanings are less tied to a given context. The meta-languages of public forms of thought as these apply to objects and persons realize meanings of a universalistic type. Where meanings have this characteristic then individuals have access to the grounds of their experience and can change the grounds. Where orders of meaning are particularistic, where principles are linguistically implicit, then such meanings are less context independent and *more* context bound, that is, tied to a local relationship and to a local social structure. Where the meaning system is particularistic, much of the meaning is embedded in the context and may be restricted to those who share a similar contextual history. Where meanings are universalistic, they are in principle available to all because the principles and operations have been made explicit, and so public.

I shall argue that forms of socialization orient the child towards speech codes which control access to relatively context-tied or relatively context-independent meanings. Thus I shall argue that elaborated codes orient their users towards universalistic meanings, whereas restricted codes orient, sensitize, their users to particularistic meanings: that the linguistic realizations of the two orders are different, and so are the social relationships which realize them. Elaborated codes are less tied to a given or local structure and thus contain the potentiality of change in principles. In the case of elaborated codes the speech may be freed from its evoking social structure and it can take on an autonomy. A university is a place organized around talk. Restricted codes are more tied to a local social structure and have a reduced potential for change in principles. Where codes are elaborated, the socialized has more access to the grounds of his own socialization, and so can enter into a reflexive relationship to the social order he has taken over. Where codes are restricted, the socialized has less access to the grounds of his socialization, and thus reflexiveness may be limited in range. *One of the effects of the class system is to limit access to elaborated codes.*

I shall go on to suggest that restricted codes have their basis in condensed symbols, whereas elaborated codes have their basis in articulated symbols; that restricted codes draw upon metaphor, whereas elaborated codes draw upon rationality; that these codes constrain the contextual use of language in critical socializing contexts and in this way regulate the orders of relevance and relation which the socialized takes over. From this point of view, change in habitual speech codes involves changes in the means by which object and person relationships are realized.

I want first to start with the notions of elaborated and restricted speech variants. A variant can be considered as the contextual constraints upon grammatical–lexical choices.

Sapir, Malinowski, Firth, Vygotsky and Luria have all pointed out from different points of view that the closer the identifications of speakers the greater the range of shared interests, the more probable that the speech will take a specific form. The range of syntactic alternatives is likely to be reduced and the lexis to be drawn from a narrow range. Thus, the form of these social relations is acting selectively on the meanings to be verbally realized. In these relationships the intent of the other person can be taken for granted as the speech is played out against a back-drop of common assumptions, common history, common interests. As a result, there is less need to raise meanings to the level of explicitness or elaboration. There is a reduced need to make explicit through syntactic choices the logical structure of the communication. Further, if the speaker wishes to individualize his communications, he is likely to do this by varying the expressive associates of the speech. Under these conditions, the speech is likely to have a strong metaphoric element. In these situations the speaker may be more concerned with how something is said, when it is said; silence takes on a variety of meanings. Often in these encounters the speech cannot be understood apart from the context, and the context cannot be read by those who do not share the history of the relationships. Thus the form of the social relationship acts selectively in the meanings to be verbalized, which in turn affect the syntactic and lexical choices. The unspoken assumptions underlying the relationship are not available to those who are outside the relationship. For these are limited, and restricted to the speakers. The symbolic form of the communication is condensed, yet the specific cultural history of the relationship is alive in its form. We can say that the roles of the speakers are communalized roles. Thus, we can make a relationship between restricted social relationships based upon communalized roles and the verbal realization of their meaning. In the language of the earlier part of this paper, restricted social relationships based upon communalized roles evoke particularistic, that is, context-tied, meanings, realized through a restricted speech variant.

Imagine a husband and wife have just come out of the cinema, and are talking about the film: 'What do you think?' 'It had a lot to say.' 'Yes, I thought so too – let's go to the Millers, there may be something going there.' They arrive at the Millers, who ask about the film. An hour is spent in the complex, moral, political, aesthetic subtleties of the film and its place in the contemporary scene. Here we have an elaborated variant; the meanings now have to be made public to others who have not seen the film. The speech shows careful editing, at both the grammatical and lexical levels. It is no longer context-tied. The meanings are explicit, elaborated and individualized. Whilst expressive channels are clearly relevant, the burden of meaning inheres predominantly in the verbal channel. The experience of the listeners cannot be taken for granted. Thus each member of the group is on his own as he offers his interpretation. Elaborated variants of this kind involve the speakers in particular role relationships, and *if you cannot manage the role, you can't produce the appropriate speech*. For as the speaker proceeds to individualize his meanings, he is differentiated from others like a figure from its ground.

The roles receive less support from each other. There is a measure of isolation. *Difference* lies at the basis of the social relationship, and is made verbally active, whereas in the other context it is *consensus*. The insides of the speaker have become psychologically active through the verbal aspect of the communication. Various defensive strategies may be used to decrease potential vulnerability of self and to increase the vulnerability of others. The verbal aspect of the communication becomes a vehicle for the transmission of individuated symbols. The 'I' stands over the 'we'. Meanings which are discrete to the speaker must be offered so that they are intelligible to the listener. Communalized roles have given way to individualized roles, condensed symbols to articulated symbols. Elaborated speech variants of this type realize universalistic meanings in the sense that they are less context-tied. Thus individualized roles are realized through elaborated speech variants which involve complex editing at the grammatical and lexical levels and which point to universalistic meanings.

Let me give another example. Consider the two following stories which Peter Hawkins, Assistant Research Officer in the Sociological Research Unit, University of London Institute of Education, constructed as a result of his analysis of the speech of middle-class and working-class five-year-old children. The children were given a series of four pictures which told a story and they were invited to tell the story. The first picture showed some boys playing football; in the second the ball goes through the window of a house; the third shows a woman looking out of the window and a man making an ominous gesture, and in the fourth the children are moving away.

Here are the two stories:

1 Three boys are playing football and one boy kicks the ball and it goes through the window the ball breaks the window and the boys are looking at it and a man comes out and shouts at them because they've broken the window so they run away and then that lady looks out of her window and she tells the boys off.

2 They're playing football and he kicks it and it goes through there it breaks the window and they're looking at it and he comes out and shouts at them because they've broken it so they run away and then she looks out and she tells them off.

With the first story the reader does not have to have the four pictures which were used as the basis for the story, whereas in the case of the second story the reader would require the initial pictures in order to make sense of the story. The first story is free of the context which generated it, whereas the second story is much more closely tied to its context. As a result the meanings of the second story are implicit, whereas the meanings of the first story are explicit. It is not that the working-class children do not have in their passive vocabulary the vocabulary used by the middle-class children. Nor is it the case that the children differ in their tacit understanding of the linguistic rule system. Rather, what we have here are differences in the use of language arising out of a specific context. One child makes explicit the meanings which he is realizing through language for the person he is telling the story to, whereas the second child does not to the same extent. The first child takes very little for granted, whereas the second child takes a great deal for granted. Thus for the first child the task was seen as a context in which his meanings were required to be made explicit, whereas the task for the second child was not seen as a task which required such explication of meaning. It would not be difficult to imagine a context where the first child would produce speech rather like the second. What we are dealing with here are differences between the children in the way they realize in language-use apparently the same context. We could say that the speech of the first child generated universalistic meanings in the sense that the meanings are freed from the context and so understandable by all, whereas the speech of the second child generated particularistic meanings, in the sense that the meanings are closely tied to the context and would be fully understood by others only if they had access to the context which originally generated the speech.

It is again important to stress that the second child has access to a more differentiated noun phrase, but there is a restriction on its *use*. Geoffrey Turner, Linguist in the Sociological Research Unit, shows that working-class, five-year-old children in the same contexts examined by Hawkins, use fewer linguistic expressions of uncertainty when compared with the middle-class children. This does not mean that working-class children do *not* have access to such expressions, but that the eliciting speech context did not provoke them. Telling a story from pictures, talking about scenes on cards, *formally framed* contexts, do not encourage working-class children to consider the possibilities of alternate meanings and so there is a reduction in the linguistic expressions of uncertainty. Again, working-class children have access to a wide range of syntactic choices which involve the use of logical operators, 'because', 'but', 'either', 'or', 'only'. The constraints exist on the conditions for their *use*. Formally framed contexts used for eliciting context-independent universalistic meanings may evoke in the working-class child, relative to the middle-class child, restricted speech variants, because the working-class child has difficulty in managing the role relationships which such contexts require. This problem is further complicated when such contexts carry meanings very much removed from the child's cultural experience. In the same way we can show that there are constraints upon the middle-class child's use of language. Turner found that when middle-class children were asked to role-play in the picture story series, a higher percentage of these children, when compared with working-class children, initially refused. When the middle-class children were asked 'What is the man saying?' or linguistically equivalent questions, a relatively higher percentage said 'I don't know'. When this question was followed by the hypothetical question 'What do you think the man might be saying?' they offered their interpretations. The working-class children role-played without difficulty. It seems then that middle-class children at five need to have a very precise instruction to *hypothesize in that particular* context. This may be because they are more concerned here with getting their answers right or correct. When the children were invited to tell a story about some doll-like figures (a little boy, a little girl, a sailor and a dog) the working-class children's stories were freer, longer and more imaginative than the stories of the middle-class children. The latter children's stories were tighter, constrained within a strong narrative frame. It was as if these children were dominated by what they took to be the *form* of a narrative and the content was secondary. This is an example of the concern of the middle-class child with the structure of the contextual frame. It may be worthwhile to amplify this further. A number of studies have shown that when working-class black children are asked to associate to a series of words, their responses show considerable diversity, both from the meaning and form-class of the stimulus word. Our analysis suggests this may be because the children for the following reasons are less constrained. The form-class of the stimulus word may have reduced associative significance and this would less constrain the selection of potential words *or* phrases. With such a weakening of the grammatical frame there is a greater range of alternatives as possible candidates for selection. Further, the closely controlled, middle-class, linguistic socialization of the young child may point the child towards both the grammatical significance of the stimulus word and towards a tight logical ordering of semantic space. Middle-class children may well have access to deep interpretative rules which regulate their linguistic responses in certain formalized contexts. The consequences may limit their imagination through the tightness of the frame which these interpretative rules create. It may even be that with *five*-year-old children, the middle-class child will innovate *more* with the arrangement of objects (i.e. bricks) than in his linguistic usage. His linguistic usage is under close supervision by adults. He has more *autonomy* in his play. [...]

Now, all children have access to restricted codes and their various systems of condensed meaning, because the roles the code presupposes are universal. But there may well be selective access to elaborated codes because there is selective access to the role system which evokes its use. Society is likely to evaluate differently the experiences realized through these two codes. I cannot here go into details, but the different focusing of experience through a restricted code creates a major problem of educability only where the school produces discontinuity between its symbolic orders and those of the child. Our schools are not made for these children; why should the children respond? To ask the child to switch to an elaborated code which presupposes different role relationships and systems of meaning without a sensitive understanding of the required contexts may create for the child a bewildering and potentially damaging experience.

So far, then, I have sketched out a relationship between speech codes and socialization through the organization of roles through which the culture is made psychologically active in persons. I have indicated that access to the roles and thus to the codes is broadly related to social class. However, it is clearly the case that social class groups today are by no means homogeneous groups. Further, the division between elaborated and restricted codes is too simple. Finally, I have not indicated in any detail how these codes are evoked by families, and how the family types may shape their focus.

What I shall do now is to introduce a distinction between family types and their communication structures. These family types can be found empirically within each social class, although any one type may be rather more modal at any given historical period.

I shall distinguish between families according to the strength of their boundary maintaining procedures. Let me first give some idea of what I mean by boundary maintaining procedures. I shall first look at boundary maintenance as it is revealed in the symbolic ordering of space. Consider the lavatory. In one house, the room is pristine, bare and sharp, containing only the necessities for which the room is dedicated. In another there is a picture on the wall, in the third there are books, in the fourth all surfaces are covered with curious postcards. We have a continuum from a room celebrating the purity of categories to one celebrating the mixture of categories, from strong to weak boundary maintenance. Consider the kitchen. In one kitchen, shoes may not be placed on the table, nor the child's chamber pot – all objects and utensils have an assigned place. In another kitchen the boundaries separating the different classes of objects are weak. The symbolic ordering of space can give us indications of the relative strength of boundary maintaining procedures. Let us now look at the relationship between family members. Where boundary procedures are strong, the differentiation of members and the authority structure is based upon clear-cut, unambiguous definitions of the status of the member of the family. The boundaries between the statuses are strong and the social identities of the members very much a function of their age, sex and age-relation status. As a short-hand, we can characterize the family as *positional*.

On the other hand, where boundary procedures are weak or flexible, the differentiation between members and the authority relationships are less on the basis of position, because here the status boundaries are blurred. Where boundary procedures are weak, the differentiation between members is based more upon *differences between persons*. In such families the relationships become more egocentric and the unique attributes of family members are made more and more substantive in the communication structure. We will call these *person-centred* families. Such families do not reduce but increase the substantive expression of ambiguity and ambivalence. In person-centred families, the role system would be continuously evoking, accommodating and assimilating the different interests and attributes of its members. In such families, unlike positional families, the members would be making their roles rather than stepping into them. In a person-centred family, the child's developing self is differentiated by continuous adjustment to the verbally realized and elaborated intentions, qualifications and motives of others. The boundary between self and other is blurred. In positional families, the child takes over and responds to the formal pattern of obligation and privilege. It should be possible to see, without going into details, that the communication structures within these two types of family are somewhat differently focused. We might then expect that the reflexiveness induced by positional families is sensitized to the general attributes of persons, whereas the reflexiveness produced by person-centred families is more sensitive towards the particular aspects of persons. Think of the difference between Dartington Hall or Gordonstoun public schools in England, or the difference between West Point and a progressive school in the USA. Thus, in person-centred families, the insides of the members are made public through the communication structure, and thus more of the person has been invaded and subject to control. Speech in such families is a major medium of control. In positional families, of course, speech is relevant but it symbolizes the boundaries given by the formal structure of the relationship. So far as the child is concerned, in positional families he attains a strong sense of social identity at the cost of autonomy; in person-centred families, the child attains a strong sense of autonomy but his social identity may be weak. Such ambiguity in the sense of identity, the lack of boundary, may move such children towards a radically closed value system.

If we now place these family types in the framework of the previous discussion, we can see that although the code may be elaborated, it may be differently focused according to the family type. Thus, we can have an elaborate code focusing upon persons or an elaborated code in a positional family may focus more upon objects. We can expect the same with a restricted code. Normally, with code restriction we should expect a positional family; however, if it showed signs of being person-centred, then we might expect the children to be in a situation of potential code switch.

Where the code is elaborated, and focused by a person-centred family, then these children may well develop acute identity problems concerned with authenticity, with limiting responsibility – they may come to see language as phony, a system of counterfeit masking the absence of belief. They may move towards the restricted codes of the various peer group sub-cultures, or seek the condensed symbols of affective experience, or both.

One of the difficulties of this approach is to avoid implicit value judgments about the relative worth of speech systems and the cultures which they symbolize. Let it be said immediately that a restricted code gives access to a vast potential of meanings, of delicacy, subtlety and diversity of cultural forms, to a unique aesthetic the basis of which in condensed symbols may influence the form of the imagining. Yet, in complex industrialized societies its differently-focused experience may be disvalued and humiliated within schools, or seen, at best, to be irrelevant to the educational endeavour. For the schools are predicated upon elaborated code and its system of social relationships. Although an elaborated code does not entail any specific value system, the value system of the middle class penetrates the texture of the very learning context itself.

Elaborated codes give access to alternative realities, yet they carry the potential of alienation, of feeling from thought, of self from other, of private belief *from role obligation.*

References and further reading

BERNSTEIN, B. (1970) 'Education cannot compensate for society', *New Society* No. 387, February.

BERNSTEIN, B. (1962) 'Family role systems, socialisation and communication', manuscript, Sociological Research Unit, University of London Institute of Education; also in 'A socio-linguistic approach to socialisation' in Gumperz, J. J. and Hymes, D. (eds) *Directions in Sociolinguistics* New York, Holt, Rinehart and Winston.

BERNSTEIN, B. and COOK, J. (1965) 'Coding grid for maternal control', available from Department of Sociology, University of London Institute of Education.

BERNSTEIN, B. and HENDERSON, D. (1969) 'Social class differences in the relevance of language to socialisation', *Sociology*, 3, No. 1.

BRIGHT, N. (ed.) (1966) *Sociolinguistics*, Mouton Press.

CARROLL, J. B. (ed.) (1956) *Language, Thought and Reality: selected writings of Benjamin Lee Whorf* New York, Wiley.

CAZDEN, C. B. (1969) 'Sub-cultural differences in child language: an interdisciplinary review', *Merrill-Palmer Quarterly*, 12.

CHOMSKY, N. (1965) *Aspects of Linguistic Theory* Cambridge, M.I.T.

COOK, J. (1971) 'An enquiry into patterns of communication and control between mothers and their children in different social classes', Ph.D. Thesis, University of London.

COULTHARD, M. (1969) 'A discussion of restricted and elaborated codes', *Educ. Rev.*, 22, No. 1.

DOUGLAS, M. (1970) *Natural Symbols*, Barrie and Rockcliff, The Cresset Press.

FISHMAN, J. A. (1960) 'A systematization of the Whorfian hypothesis', *Behavioral Science*, 5.

GUMPERZ, J. J. and HYMES, D. (eds) (1971) *Directions in Sociolinguistics* New York, Holt, Rinehart and Winston.

HALLIDAY, M. A. K. (1969) 'Relevant models of language', *Educ. Rev.*, 22, No. 1.

HAWKINS, P. R. (1969) 'Social class, the nominal group and reference', *Language and Speech*, 12, No. 2.

HENDERSON, D. (1970) 'Contextual specificity, discretion and cognitive socialisation: with special reference to language', *Sociology*, 4, No. 3.

HOIJER, H. (ed.) (1954) 'Language in Culture', *American Anthropological Association Memoir* No. 79; also published by Univ. of Chicago Press.

HYMES, D. (1966) 'On communicative competence', Research Planning Conference on Language Development among Disadvantaged Children, Ferkauf Graduate School, Yeshiva University.

HYMES, D. (1967) 'Models of the interaction of language and social setting', *Journal of Social Issues*, 23.

LABOV, W. (1965) 'Stages in the acquisition of standard English', in Shuy, W. (ed.) *Social Dialects and Language Learning* Champaign, Illinois, National Council of Teachers of English.

LABOV, W. (1966) 'The social stratification of English in New York City', Washington D.C. Centre for Applied Linguistics.

MANDELBAUM, D. (ed.) (1949) *Selected Writings of Edward Sapir* Univ. of California Press.

PARSONS, T. and SHILS, E. A. (eds) (1962) *Toward a General Theory of Action* Harper Torchbooks (Chapter 1, especially).

SCHATZMAN, L. and STRAUSS, A. L. (1955) 'Social class and modes of communication', *Am.J.Soc.*, 60.

TURNER, G. and PICKVANCE, R. E. (1971) 'Social class differences in the expression of uncertainty in five-year-old children', *Language and Speech*.

WILLIAMS, F. and NAREMORE, R. C. (1969) 'On the functional analysis of social class differences in modes of speech, *Speech Monographs*, 36, No. 2.

36 The logic of nonstandard English

W. Labov

In the past decade, a great deal of research has been devoted to the educational problems of children in ghetto schools. In order to account for the poor performance of children in these schools, educational psychologists have attempted to discover what kind of disadvantage or defect they are suffering from. The viewpoint which has been widely accepted, and used as the basis for large-scale intervention programmes, is that the children show a cultural deficit as a result of an impoverished environment in their early years. Considerable attention has been given to language. In this area, the deficit theory appears as the concept of 'verbal deprivation': Negro children from the ghetto area receive little verbal stimulation, are said to hear very little well-formed language, and as a result are impoverished in their means of verbal expression: they cannot speak complete sentences, do not know the names of common objects, cannot form concepts or convey logical thoughts.

Unfortunately, these notions are based upon the work of educational psychologists who know very little about language and even less about Negro children. The concept of verbal deprivation has no basis in social reality: in fact, Negro children in the urban ghettos receive a great deal of verbal stimulation, hear more well-formed sentences than middle-class children, and participate fully in a highly verbal culture; they have the same basic vocabulary, possess the same capacity for conceptual learning, and use the same logic as anyone else who learns to speak and understand English. [...]

I will attempt to explain how the myth of verbal deprivation has arisen, bringing to bear the methodological findings of sociolinguistic work, and some substantive facts about language which are known to all linguists. I will be particularly concerned with the relation between concept formation on the one hand, and dialect differences on the other, since it is in this area that the most dangerous misunderstandings are to be found. [...]

Here is a complete interview with a Negro boy, one of hundreds carried out in a New York City school. The boy enters a room where there is a

---

LABOV, W. (1969) from 'The logic of nonstandard English' in *Georgetown Monographs on Language and Linguistics*, vol. 22, 1–22, 26–31.

large, friendly white interviewer, who puts on the table in front of him a block or a fire engine, and says 'Tell me everything you can about this'. (The interviewer's further remarks are in parentheses.)

[*12 seconds of silence*]
(What would you say it looks like?)
[*8 seconds of silence*]
A space ship.
(Hmmmm.)
[*13 seconds of silence*]
Like a je-et.
[*12 seconds of silence*]
Like a plane.
[*20 seconds of silence*]
(What colour is it?)
Orange. [*2 seconds*] An' whi-ite. [*2 seconds*] An' green.
[*6 seconds of silence*]
(An' what could you use it for?)
[*8 seconds of silence*]
A je-et.
[*6 seconds of silence*]
(If you had two of them, what would you do with them?)
[*6 seconds of silence*]
Give one to some-body.
(Hmmm. Who do you think would like to have it?)
[*10 seconds of silence*]
Cla-rence.
(Mm. Where do you think we could get another one of these?)
At the store.
(Oh ka-ay!)

We have here the same kind of defensive, monosyllabic behaviour which is reported in Bereiter's work. What is the situation that produces it? The child is in an asymmetrical situation where anything he says can literally be held against him. He has learned a number of devices to *avoid* saying anything in this situation, and he works very hard to achieve this end. One may observe the intonation patterns of which Negro children often use when they are asked a question to which the answer is obvious. The answer may be read as 'Will this satisfy you?'

If one takes this interview as a measure of the verbal capacity of the child, it must be as his capacity to defend himself in a hostile and threatening situation. But unfortunately, thousands of such interviews are used as evidence of the child's total verbal capacity....

The verbal behaviour which is shown by the child in the test situation quoted above is not the result of the ineptness of the interviewer. It is rather the result of regular sociolinguistic factors operating upon adult and child in this asymmetrical situation. In our work in urban ghetto areas, we have often encountered such behaviour. Ordinarily we worked with boys 10–17 years old; and whenever we extended our approach downwards to 8- or 9-year-olds, we began to see the need for different techniques to explore the verbal capacity of the child. At one point we began a series of interviews with younger brothers of the 'Thunderbirds' in 1390 5th Avenue. Clarence Robins returned after an interview with 8-year-old Leon L., who showed the following minimal response to topics which arouse intense interest in other interviews with older boys.

CR: What if you saw somebody kickin' somebody else on the ground, or was using a stick, what would you do if you saw that?
LEON: Mmmm.
CR: If it was supposed to be a fair fight—
LEON: I don' know.
CR: You don't know? Would you do anything . . . huh? I can't hear you.
LEON: No.
CR: Did you ever see somebody got beat up real bad?
LEON: ... Nope???
CR: Well – uh – did you ever get into a fight with a guy?
LEON: Nope.
CR: That was bigger than you?
LEON: Nope.
CR: You never been in a fight?
LEON: Nope.
CR: Nobody ever pick on you?
LEON: Nope.
CR: Nobody ever hit you?
LEON: Nope.
CR: How come?
LEON: Ah 'on' know.
CR: Didn't you ever hit somebody?
LEON: Nope.
CR: [*incredulous*] You never hit nobody?

LEON: Mhm.
CR: Aww, ba-a-a-be, you ain't gonna tell me that. [...]

This nonverbal behaviour occurs in a relatively *favourable* context for adult–child interaction; since the adult is a Negro man raised in Harlem, who knows this particular neighbourhood and these boys very well. He is a skilled interviewer who has obtained a very high level of verbal response with techniques developed for a different age level, and he has an extraordinary advantage over most teachers or experimenters in these respects. But even his skills and personality are ineffective in breaking down the social constraints that prevail here.

When we reviewed the record of this interview with Leon, we decided to use it as a test of our own knowledge of the sociolinguistic factors which control speech. We made the following changes in the social situation: in the next interview with Leon, Clarence

1 brought along a supply of potato chips, changing the 'interview' into something more in the nature of a party;
2 brought along Leon's best friend, 8-year-old Gregory;
3 reduced the height imbalance (when Clarence got down on the floor of Leon's room, he dropped from 6 ft. 2 in. to 3 ft. 6 in.);
4 introduced taboo words and taboo topics, and proved to Leon's surprise that one can say anything into our microphone without any fear of retaliation.

The result of these changes is a striking difference in the volume and style of speech.

CR: Is there anybody who says *your momma drink pee*?
{LEON: [*rapidly and breathlessly*] Yee-ah!
{GREG: Yup!
LEON: And your father eat doo-doo for breakfas'!
CR: Ohhh!! [*laughs*]
LEON: And they say *your father – your father eat doo-doo for dinner*!
GREG: When they sound on me, I say *C. B. M.*
CR: What that mean?
{LEON: Congo booger-snatch! [*laughs*]
{GREG: Congo booger-snatcher! [*laughs*]
GREG: And sometimes I'll curse with *B. B.*
CR: What that?
GREG: Black boy! [*Leon – crunching on potato chips*] Oh that's a *M. B. B.*
CR: M. B. B. What's that?
GREG: 'Merican Black Boy!
CR: Ohh...

GREG: Anyway, 'Mericans is same like white people, right?
LEON: And they talk about Allah.
CR: Oh yeah?
GREG: Yeah.
CR: What they say about Allah?
LEON: Allah – Allah is God.
GREG: Allah—
CR: And what else?
LEON: I don' know the res'.
GREG: Allah i – Allah is God, Allah is the only God, Allah—
LEON: Allah is the *son* of God.
GREG: But can he make magic?
LEON: Nope.
GREG: I know who can make magic.
CR: Who can?
LEON: The God, the *real* one.
CR: Who can make magic?
GREG: The son of po' – [CR: Hm?] I'm sayin' the po'k chop God![1] He only a po'k chop God! [*Leon chuckles*]

The 'nonverbal' Leon is now competing actively for the floor; Gregory and Leon talk to each other as much as they do to the interviewer. [...]

The same pattern can be seen on other local topics, where the interviewer brings neighbourhood gossip to bear on Leon and Gregory acts as a witness.

CR: ... Hey Gregory! I heard that around here ... and I'm 'on' tell you who said it, too ...
LEON: Who?
CR: about you ...
LEON: Who?
GREG: I'd say it!
CR: They said that – they say that the only person you play with is David Gilbert.
LEON: Yee-ah! yee-ah! yee-ah! ...
GREG: That's who you play with!
LEON: I 'on' play with him no more!
GREG: Yes you do!

1 The reference to the *pork chop God* condenses several concepts of black nationalism current in the Harlem community. A *pork chop* is a Negro who has not lost traditional subservient ideology of the South, who has no knowledge of himself in Muslim terms, and the *pork chop God* would be the traditional God of Southern Baptists. He and his followers may be pork chops, but he still holds the power in Leon and Gregory's world.

LEON: I 'on' play with him no more!
GREG: But remember, about me and Robbie?
LEON: So that's not—
GREG: and you went to Petey and Gilbert's house, 'member? *Ah haaah*!!
LEON: So that's – so – but I would – I had came back out, an' I ain't go to his house no more . . .

The observer must now draw a very different conclusion about the verbal capacity of Leon. The monosyllabic speaker who had nothing to say about anything and cannot remember what he did yesterday has disappeared. Instead, we have two boys who have so much to say they keep interrupting each other, who seem to have no difficulty in using the English language to express themselves. And we in turn obtain the volume of speech and the rich array of grammatical devices which we need for analyzing the structure of black English vernacular (BEV): negative concord [*I 'on' play with him no more*], the pluperfect [*had came back out*], negative perfect [*I ain't had*], the negative preterite [*I ain't go*], and so on.

One can now transfer this demonstration of the sociolinguistic control of speech to other test situations – including IQ and reading tests in school. It should be immediately apparent that none of the standard tests will come anywhere near measuring Leon's verbal capacity. On these tests he will show up as very much the monosyllabic, inept, ignorant, bumbling child of our first interview. The teacher has far less ability than Clarence Robins to elicit speech from this child; Clarence knows the community, the things that Leon has been doing, and the things that Leon would like to talk about. But the power relationships in a one-to-one confrontation between adult and child are too asymmetrical. This does not mean that some Negro children will not talk a great deal when alone with an adult, or that an adult cannot get close to any child. It means that the social situation is the most powerful determinant of verbal behaviour and that an adult must enter into the right social relation with a child if he wants to find out what a child can do; this is just what many teachers cannot do. [. . .]

Verbosity

There are undoubtedly many verbal skills which children from ghetto areas must learn in order to do well in the school situation, and some of these are indeed characteristic of middle-class verbal behaviour. Precision in spelling, practice in handling abstract symbols, the ability to state explicitly the meaning of words, and a richer knowledge of the Latinate vocabulary, may all be useful acquisitions. But is it true that *all* of the middle-class verbal habits are functional and desirable in the school situation? Before we impose middle-class verbal style upon children from other cultural groups, we should find out how much of this is useful for the main work of analyzing and generalizing, and how much is merely stylistic – or even dysfunctional. In high school and college middle-class children spontaneously complicate their syntax to the point that instructors despair of getting them to make their language simpler and clearer. In every learned journal one can find examples of jargon and empty elaboration – and complaints about it. Is the 'elaborated code' of Bernstein really so 'flexible, detailed and subtle' as some psychologists believe? (Jensen 1969, p. 119). Isn't it also turgid, redundant, and empty? Is it not simply an elaborated *style*, rather than a superior code or system? [2]

Our work in the speech community makes it painfully obvious that in many ways working-class speakers are more effective narrators, reasoners and debaters than many middle-class speakers who temporize, qualify, and lose their argument in a mass of irrelevant detail. Many academic writers try to rid themselves of that part of middle-class style that is empty pretension, and keep that part that is needed for precision. But the average middle-class speaker that we encounter makes no such effort; he is enmeshed in verbiage, the victim of sociolinguistic factors beyond his control.

I will not attempt to support this argument here with systematic quantitative evidence, although it is possible to develop measures which show how far middle-class speakers can wander from the point. I would like to contrast two speakers dealing with roughly the same topic – matters of belief. The first is Larry H., a 15-year-old core member of the Jets, being interviewed by John Lewis. Larry is one of the loudest and roughest members of the Jets, one who gives the least recognition to the conventional rules of politeness.[3] For most readers of this paper, first contact with Larry would produce some fairly negative reactions on both sides: it is probable that you would not *like* him any more than his teachers do. Larry causes trouble in and out of school; he was put back from the eleventh grade to the ninth, and has been threatened with further action by the school authorities.

2 The term *code* is central in Bernstein's description of the differences between working-class and middle-class styles of speech. The restrictions and elaborations of speech observed are labelled as 'codes' to indicate the principles governing selection from the range of possible English sentences. No rules or detailed description of the operation of such codes are provided as yet, so that this central concept remains to be specified.

3 A direct view of Larry's verbal style in a hostile encounter is given in Labov, Cohen, Robins and Lewis (1968), Vol. II, pp. 39–43. Gray's Oral Reading Test was being given to a group of Jets on the steps of a brown-stone house in Harlem, and the landlord tried unsuccessfully to make the Jets move.

JL: What happens to you after you die? Do you know?
LARRY: Yeah, I know.
JL: What?
LARRY: After they put you in the ground, your body turns into – ah – bones, an' shit.
JL: What happens to your spirit?
LARRY: Your spirit – soon as you die, your spirit leaves you.
JL: And where does the spirit go?
LARRY: Well, it all depends...
JL: On what?
LARRY: You know, like some people say if you're good an' shit, your spirit goin' t'heaven... 'n' if you bad, your spirit goin' to hell. Well, bullshit! Your spirit goin' to hell anyway, good or bad.
JL: Why?
LARRY: Why? I'll tell you why. 'Cause, you see, doesn' nobody really know that it's a God, y'know, 'cause I mean I have seen black gods, pink gods, white gods, all colour gods, and don't nobody know it's really a God. An' when they be sayin' if you good, you goin' t'heaven, tha's bullshit, 'cause you ain't goin' to no heaven, 'cause it ain't no heaven for you to go to.

Larry is a paradigmatic speaker of black English vernacular (BEV) as opposed to standard English (SE).... [who] provides a paradigmatic example of the rhetorical style of BEV: he can sum up a complex argument in a few words, and the full force of his opinions comes through without qualification or reservation....

It is the logical form of this passage which is of particular interest here. Larry presents a complex set of interdependent propositions which can be explicated by setting out the SE equivalents in linear order.... His argument may be outlined as follows:

1 Everyone has a different idea of what God is like.
2 Therefore nobody really knows that God exists.
3 If there is a heaven, it was made by God.
4 If God doesn't exist, he couldn't have made heaven.
5 Therefore heaven does not exist.
6 You can't go somewhere that doesn't exist.
Therefore you can't go to heaven.
Therefore you are going to hell.

Part of the argument is implicit. [...]

Despite the fact that Larry H. does not believe in God, and has just denied all knowledge of him, John Lewis advances the following hypothetical question:

JL: . . . But, just say that there is a God, what colour is he? White or black?
LARRY: Well, if it is a God . . . I wouldn' know what colour, I couldn' say, – couldn' nobody say what colour he is or really *would* be.
JL: But now, jus' suppose there was a God –
LARRY: Unless'n they say . . .
JL: No, I was jus' sayin' jus' suppose there is a God, would he be white or black?
LARRY: . . . He'd be white, man.
JL: Why?
LARRY: Why? I'll tell you why. 'Cause the average whitey out here got everything, you dig? And the nigger ain't got shit, y'know? Y'understan'? So – um – for – in order for *that* to happen, you know it ain't no black God that's doin' that bullshit.

No one can hear Larry's answer to this question without being convinced that they are in the presence of a skilled speaker with great 'verbal presence of mind', who can use the English language expertly for many purposes. [. . .]

Let us now turn to the second speaker, an upper-middle-class, college educated Negro man being interviewed by Clarence Robins in our survey of adults in Central Harlem.

CR: Do you know of anything that someone can do, to have someone who has passed on visit him in a dream?
CHARLES M: Well, I even heard my parents say that there is such a thing as something in dreams some things like that, and sometimes dreams do come true. I have personally never had a dream come true. I've never dreamt that somebody was dying and they actually died, (Mhm) or that I was going to have ten dollars the next day and somehow I got ten dollars in my pocket. (Mhm.) I don't particularly believe in that, I don't think it's true. I do feel, though, that there is such a thing as – ah – witchcraft. I do feel that in certain cultures there is such a thing as witchcraft, or some sort of *science* of witchcraft; I don't think that it's just a matter of believing hard enough that there is such a thing as witchcraft. I do believe that there is such a thing that a person can put himself in a state of *mind* (Mhm), or that – er – something could be given them to intoxicate them in a certain – to a certain frame of mind – that – that could actually be considered witchcraft.

Charles M. is obviously a 'good speaker' who strikes the listener as well-educated, intelligent and sincere. He is a likeable and attractive person – the kind of person that middle-class listeners rate very high on a scale of 'job suitability' and equally high as a potential friend. His language is more moderate and tempered than Larry's; he makes every effort to qualify his opinions, and seems anxious to avoid any misstatements or over-statements. From these qualities emerge the primary characteristic of this passage – its *verbosity*. Words multiply, some modifying and qualifying, others repeating or padding the main argument. The first half of this extract is a response to the initial question on dreams, basically:

1 Some people say that dreams sometimes come true.
2 I have never had a dream come true.
3 Therefore I don't believe (1).

Some characteristic filler phrases appear here: *such a thing as, some things like that, particularly*. Two examples of dreams given after (2) are afterthoughts that might have been given after (1). Proposition (3) is stated twice for no obvious reason. Nevertheless, this much of Charles M.'s response is well-directed to the point of the question. He then volunteers a statement of his beliefs about witchcraft which shows the difficulty of middle-class speakers who (a) want to express a belief in something but (b) want to show themselves as judicious, rational and free from superstitions. The basic proposition can be stated simply in five words:

But I believe in witchcraft.

However, the idea is enlarged to exactly 100 words, and it is difficult to see what else is being said. [. . .]

Without extra verbiage and the OK words like *science, culture* and *intoxicate*, Charles M. appears as something less than a first-rate thinker. The initial impression of him as a good speaker is simply our long-conditioned reaction to middle-class verbosity: we know that people who use these stylistic devices are educated people, and we are inclined to credit them with saying something intelligent. Our reactions are accurate in one sense: Charles M. is more educated than Larry. But is he more rational, more logical, or more intelligent? Is he any better at thinking out a problem to its solution? Does he deal more easily with abstractions? There is no reason to think so. Charles M. succeeds in letting us know that he is educated, but in the end we do not know what he is trying to say, and neither does he. [. . .]

References

JENSEN, A. (1969) 'How much can we boost IQ and scholastic achievement?' *Harvard Educational Review*, 39, no. 1.

LABOV, W., COHEN, P., ROBINS, C. and LEWIS, J. (1968) *A Study of the non-Standard English of Negro and Puerto Rican Speakers in New York City*. Final Report, Cooperative Research Project no. 3288, Office of Education, Washington, D.C., vols. 1 and 2.

37 Non-verbal communication in human social interaction

Michael Argyle

The discovery of the importance of non-verbal communication (NVC) has transformed the study of human social behaviour. Until quite recently social psychologists were baffled by the subtleties and intricacies of social interaction, and often analyzed it in terms of how long encounters lasted, or who spoke most often. Now a new level of analysis has been opened up – the level of head-nods, shifts of gaze, fine hand-movements, bodily posture, etc. (as well as a similar detailed analysis of the verbal component). This kind of research started in the early 1960s: rather later we realized that ethologists, especially those doing field studies of primates, were using very similar variables. It looked as if human NVC was similar to animal social behaviour, and perhaps conveyed similar messages. Humans also have a verbal channel of communication, but other research showed that speech is accompanied by an intricate set of vocal and gestural non-verbal signals, which affect meaning, emphasis, and other aspects of utterances. This kind of research has led to fruitful collaboration with linguists.

Research methods

There are several different research strategies, corresponding to the conceptual assumptions of different groups of investigators.

1 Those who think that non-verbal communication is a kind of language have tried to discover its elements and structure, rather than look for empirical laws and cause-effect relations. They have analyzed short sequences of tape or film in great detail, but without statistical treatment (e.g. Scheflen 1965).

2 A second group of investigators has been concerned with the rules (i.e. implicit cultural conventions) governing verbal and non-verbal behaviour in different situations: this has been linked with an interest in the way people perceive or define situations and interpret NVC. This has led to rather informal studies of particular field situations and the analysis of etiquette books (Goffman 1963), as methods of discovering the underlying,

---

ARGYLE, MICHAEL (1972) 'Non-verbal communication in human social interaction' in Hinde, R. (ed.) *Non-verbal Communication* Cambridge, Cambridge University Press, 243–69.

often unstated, rules. Another approach has been the deliberate breaking of conventions to show that they are there – for example students behaved at home as if they were lodgers, and moved their opponents' pieces at chess (Garfinkel 1963). It is possible to do this kind of thing in a more rigorous way: Felipe and Sommer (1966) carried out experiments in which personal space was invaded – an experimenter sat down close to 'subjects' on a park bench without explanation – the subjects all left very rapidly. Systematic research on the subjective interpretation of NVC has been done by social psychologists working on person perception.

3 Social psychologists have developed a tradition of experimentation which consists of very well-controlled studies, conducted under very artificial conditions. Subjects may sit in cubicles by themselves, watch flashing lights and press buttons; often there is no verbal communication, no NVC, no real motivation, and there are no situational rules. Single cues are isolated, and their causes or effects studied, in extremely elegant experimental designs. However, the results obtained may be misleading in a number of ways. First, the results may be exaggerated. Argyle and McHenry (1970) replicated the previous finding that when people are seen briefly, the wearing of spectacles adds about 13 points to their judged IQ; however when they were seen talking for 5 minutes, spectacles made no difference to the judged IQ. Secondly, the results may be wrong: some results which have been obtained under laboratory conditions have not been confirmed under more realistic conditions. For example, the reinforcing of amount of speech or other aspects of verbal behaviour by means of head-nods and smiles has been found to work in the laboratory *only* when subjects become aware of what is wanted, but under field conditions learning takes place without subjects being aware of what is going on (Argyle 1969). Another example is research on the perception of non-verbal cues, which has often been conducted under extremely artificial conditions. Subjects may be shown photographs of faces with different facial expressions and asked to judge emotions. Such experiments overlook the fact that facial expression is normally carefully controlled, and that changes in expression during interaction are often not due to emotions, but are part of the non-verbal signalling system that accompanies speech. There is a dilemma about experimental research which it is sometimes impossible to evade: in order to test certain hypotheses it is necessary to set up peculiar experimental conditions, but if this is done the results obtained may not be true to real-life behaviour. It may be impossible to achieve both internal validity and external validity at the same time.

The approach which is recommended here is to carry out rigorously-designed experiments, which test hypotheses, but which are carried out in realistic settings with clear meanings and conventions, and which contain all the main ingredients of ordinary social behaviour. There are a number of research procedures which meet these criteria.

Field experiments on unsuspecting subjects

Here one or more trained stooges approach a member of the public, who may be walking down the street, sitting in the park, etc. The stooges behave according to a standard procedure, and the subjects' behaviour is either recorded by them or an observer, or is filmed. Experimental variations are introduced by varying the behaviour or appearance of the stooges or features of the setting. Sissons (1970) for example made films of an actor who asked ninety people at Paddington station the way to Hyde Park; in half the interviews he was dressed and spoke in an upper-middle class manner, in half he appeared to be working class; the social class of the respondents was ascertained from a second interview.

Laboratory experiments which replicate real-life situations

Subjects are invited to the laboratory to take part in an experiment. They are then asked to take part in an interview or discussion or some other social situation, whose conventions are familiar to them. They meet real people, and real motivations can be aroused. One version is for them to meet a programmed confederate, as in the previous design. Another is for two or more genuine subjects to meet, and for some other feature of the situation to be varied, such as the distance between them, or the topic of conversation or the task. Rather more realism can be introduced by the 'waiting room' technique – subjects encounter programmed stooges in the waiting room.

Role-played laboratory experiments

There is no sharp line between the experiments just described, and those in which subjects are asked to pretend or imagine that they are in a certain social situation. In perceptual experiments they may be shown a video-tape and asked to imagine that they are meeting the person shown on the monitor. Other versions are less acceptable – when subjects are shown photographs, drawings or stick figures and are asked about the emotional states of those portrayed or the relations between them.

Statistical analysis of interaction sequences

These were discussed earlier. While such studies cannot always involve the manipulation of experimental variables, it is possible to test hypotheses from the data obtained – though the direction of causation may be ambiguous. Kendon (1967) for example found that speakers looked up at the end of utterances. This led him to make a further analysis of what happened when speakers did *not* look up in this way: he found, as predicted, that there was a long pause before the other replied.

We will now describe the basic arrangements for those investigations which can be done in a laboratory. A typical observation room plan is shown in figure 1.

The experimental room is decorated to be appropriate for whatever situation is to be replicated; it should not be a white 'laboratory room'. Observations are made either by (1) TV camera and video-tape recorder, (2) ciné-camera, (3) observers pressing buttons attached to some kind of recording equipment, such as a Rustrak recorder, or electronic counters to record number and duration of gazes, or other observable events, or by

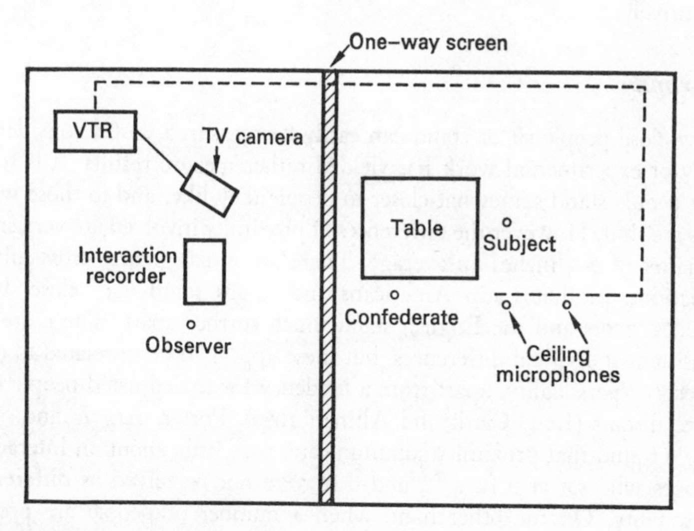

Fig. 1 Observation room arrangements.

(4) audio-tape-recorder attached to ceiling microphones, to record length and duration of utterances. (See figure 1.)

The main non-verbal signals used by man

Men use a number of different kinds of NVC, and it is convenient to classify them under ten headings. Each plays a distinctive role in social interaction; brief notes will be given on how each of them functions, with illustrative experiments. More details may be found in Argyle (1969).

Bodily contact

This may take a number of forms – hitting, pushing, stroking, etc. – most of which may involve a variety of areas of the body. There are great cross-cultural variations in the extent to which bodily contact occurs; in Britain and Japan there is very little, whilst amongst Africans and Arabs there is a lot. The most common bodily contact to occur in public settings in Britain is that involved in greetings and farewells. In most cultures bodily contact is far more common inside the family, between husband and wife and between parents and children. Even here there are tight restrictions on which part of the body may be touched by whom: Jourard (1966) found that male American white students were touched by their fathers only on the hands, though they were touched by opposite sex friends much more extensively.

Proximity

How close people sit or stand can easily be measured, but a considerable body of experimental work has yielded rather meagre results. It is found that people stand somewhat closer to people they like, and to those whose eyes are shut. However the differences of proximity involved are very small, a matter of 2–3 inches on average. There are much greater cross-cultural variations, in that Latin Americans and Arabs stand very close, while Swedes, Scots and the English stand much further apart. There are also consistent individual differences, but these appear to be unrelated to other aspects of personality, apart from a tendency for maladjusted people to be more distant (Lott, Clark and Altman 1969). Porter, Argyle and Salter (1970) found that proximity communicates very little about an interactor: stooges who sat at 2 ft, 4 ft, and 8 ft were not perceived as different in personality. On the other hand when a number of people are present, proximity is found to reflect and probably communicate the relations between them (Kendon, pers. comm.). *Changes* in proximity communicate the desire to initiate or terminate an encounter: if *A* wants to start an encounter with *B* he will move closer, though this must be accompanied by appropriate gaze and conversation.

Orientation

This is the angle at which people sit or stand in relation to each other. The normal range is from head-on to side-by-side, and orientation can be assessed by asking a subject to meet a stooge or by asking two people to meet. Orientation has been found to vary with the nature of the situation – those who are in a cooperative situation or who are close friends adopt a side-by-side position; in a confrontation, bargaining or similar situation, people tend to choose head-on; while in other situations 90° is most common in England and the USA (Sommer 1965, Cook 1970). The main exception to this is that two close friends will sit head-on when eating. There are cross-cultural variations in that Arabs prefer the head-on position (Watson and Graves 1966), and Swedes avoid the 90° position (Ingham 1971).

Appearance

Many aspects of personal appearance are under voluntary control – clothes, hair and skin, while other aspects are partly so – physique and bodily condition. Furthermore much time, money and effort is put into the control of appearance, and this can be regarded as a special kind of NVC. The main purpose of manipulating appearance seems to be self-presentation, i.e. sending messages about the self. Thus people send messages about their social status, their occupation, or the social group they belong to, by wearing the appropriate costume – bank managers do not dress up like hippies. Appearance also conveys information about personality and mood – euphoric extroverts do not wear dark suits with black ties. Young women use all these signals, but their main concern is probably rather a different one – maximizing their attractiveness as sexual objects. Appearance is meaningful only within a particular social setting where the significance of details of dress, hair or cosmetics is generally understood. Within modern cultures these fashions change extremely fast, so that simply being up to date becomes itself a main dimension of appearance.

Posture

In any given culture, many different ways of standing, sitting or lying are possible. To some extent posture has a universal meaning, like facial expression, but it also has a culturally defined meaning. There are conventions about the posture to be adopted in particular situations, such as church, dinner parties, etc. Posture is used to convey interpersonal attitudes: Mehrabian (1968) found that distinctive postures were adopted for friendly, hostile, superior, and inferior attitudes, and that these were perceived accordingly. Thus posture can be a signal for status; someone who is going to take charge sits in an upright posture (and in a central position, facing the others). Posture varies with emotional state, especially along the dimension tense–relaxed. This is of some importance since posture is less well controlled than face or voice, and there may be 'leakage', as, for example, when anxiety does not affect the face, but can be seen in posture (Ekman 1969*a*).

Head-nods

We now come to the faster-moving non-verbal signals. A simple and seemingly minor signal is the head-nod, which plays a very important role in connection with speech. It usually acts as a reinforcer, in that when a piece of *A*'s behaviour is followed by a head-nod from *B*, *A* tends to increase the frequency of that behaviour. Head-nods also play a crucial role in 'floor-apportionment', in that a head-nod gives the other permission to carry on speaking. On the other hand, rapid head-nods indicate that the nodder wishes to speak. Lastly, head-nods, like other bodily movements, are coordinated between two interactors, so that they appear to be taking part in a 'gestural dance'.

Facial expression

The face is a specialized communication area, which in non-human primates is used to communicate inter-individual attitudes and emotions. Much facial expression of emotion in humans appears to be culturally universal and largely independent of learning (Ekman 1969*b*). However there are considerable restraints on the expression of negative attitudes or emotions, so that spontaneous expressions are often concealed. However, some aspects of emotional expressions are very difficult to control – expansion of the pupils during arousal, perspiration during anxiety, and 'micro-momentary' expression of concealed feelings (Haggard and Isaacs 1966).

Facial expression is also used in close combination with speech. A listener provides a continuous commentary of his reactions to what is being said by small movements of the eyebrows and mouth, indicating puzzlement, surprise, disagreement, pleasure, etc. A speaker accompanies his utterances with appropriate facial expressions, which are used to modify or 'frame' what is being said, showing whether it is supposed to be funny, serious, important, etc. (Vine 1971).

Gestures

The hands are able to communicate a great deal: movements of head, feet and other parts of the body may also be used, but are much less expressive than those of the hands. Some gestures may indicate general emotional arousal, which produces diffuse bodily activity, while others appear to be expressions of particular emotional states, e.g. clenching the fists in anger. Gestures are also closely coordinated with speech and are made by a speaker to illustrate what he is saying, particularly when his verbal powers fail, or when objects of special shapes or sizes are being described. Hand (and head) movements may be closely coordinated with speech to indicate the internal structure of utterances, and to control the synchronizing of utterances. Gestures can even replace speech, as in gesture languages.

Looking

During conversations each participant looks intermittently at the other, for periods of 1 to 10 seconds, for 25 per cent to 75 per cent of the time: periods of mutual gaze, or eye-contact, are rather shorter. It is found that people look about twice as much while listening as while talking.

Looking plays an important role in communicating interpersonal attitudes and establishing relationships. The act of looking sends a signal to the other that a certain amount of interest is being taken in him, and interest of a kind which is signalled by the accompanying facial expression. Argyle and Dean (1965) postulated that amount of looking is a signal for intimacy, and found that people look more when another person is more distant, suggesting that looking and proximity can substitute for each other as signals for intimacy. This has been confirmed by later experiments; the effects of distance on individual gaze and eye contact are shown in figure 2.

Exline and Winters (1965) found that subjects looked more at people they liked. However, looking can be accompanied by quite different facial expressions, and can signal aggression (as is common in animals), sexual attraction, or clinical interest for example.

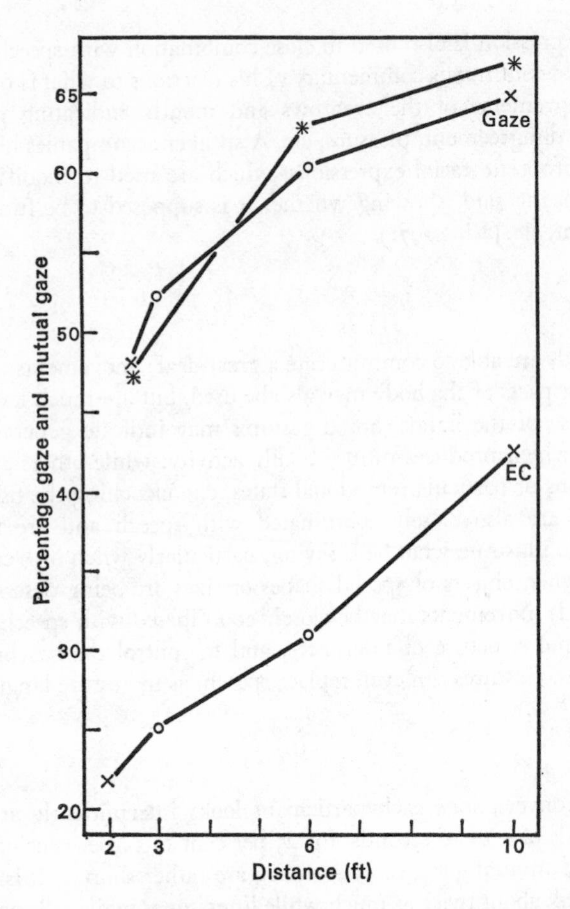

Fig. 2 Amounts of gaze at different distances from another person; gaze=individual gaze; EC=eye contact. (* From Argyle and Dean 1965; x, o from Argyle and Ingham, in press.)

Looking is closely coordinated with verbal communication. In the first place it is used to obtain information: feed-back on the other's responses while talking, extra information about what is being said while listening. In addition, shifts of gaze are used to regulate the synchronizing of speech (p. 459). Gaze is used as a signal in starting encounters, in greetings, as a reinforcer, and to indicate that a point has been understood.

Non-verbal aspects of speech

The same words can be delivered in quite different ways by variations in pitch, stress and timing. Linguists distinguish between prosodic sounds which affect the meaning of utterances, and 'paralinguistic' sounds which convey other kinds of information (Crystal 1969). Prosodic signals are pitch pattern, stress pattern, and juncture (pauses and timing) which affect the meaning of sentences, and are regarded as true parts of the verbal utterance (Lyons 1972). Paralinguistic signals include emotions expressed by tone of voice, group membership expressed by accent, personality characteristics expressed by voice quality, speech errors, etc. These non-verbal signals are not closely linked with language, do not have a complex structure, and are similar to other expressions of attitudes and emotions. The emotional state of a speaker reading a neutral passage can be recognized from a tape-recording (Davitz 1964). Thus anxious people speak fast and in a breathy way, i.e. with a high frequency distribution and with speech errors. A dominant or angry person speaks loudly, slowly and with a lower frequency distribution (Eldred and Price 1958). There are speech styles which consist of other combinations of the same variables – the speech of surly adolescents, bright hostesses, etc.

The different functions of NVC

NVC in man is used to manage the immediate social situation, to support verbal communication and to replace verbal communication.

Managing the immediate social situation

Animals conduct their entire social life by means of NVC, and it appears that humans use rather similar signals to establish a similar set of relationships.

Interpersonal attitudes. These are attitudes towards others present – the main dimensions are found to be inferior–superior, and like–dislike. A superior attitude can be conveyed by (*a*) *posture* – body erect, head raised, (*b*) *facial expression* – unsmiling, 'haughty', (*c*) *tone of voice* – loud, resonant, 'commanding', (*d*) *appearance* – clothes indicating high status and (*e*) *looking* – staring the other down. The author and his colleagues compared the effects of verbal and non-verbal signals for communicating interpersonal attitudes. Typed messages were prepared indicating that the speaker was superior, equal or inferior; video-tapes of a performer counting (1, 2, 3 . . .) were made, conveying the same attitudes; the verbal and non-verbal signals

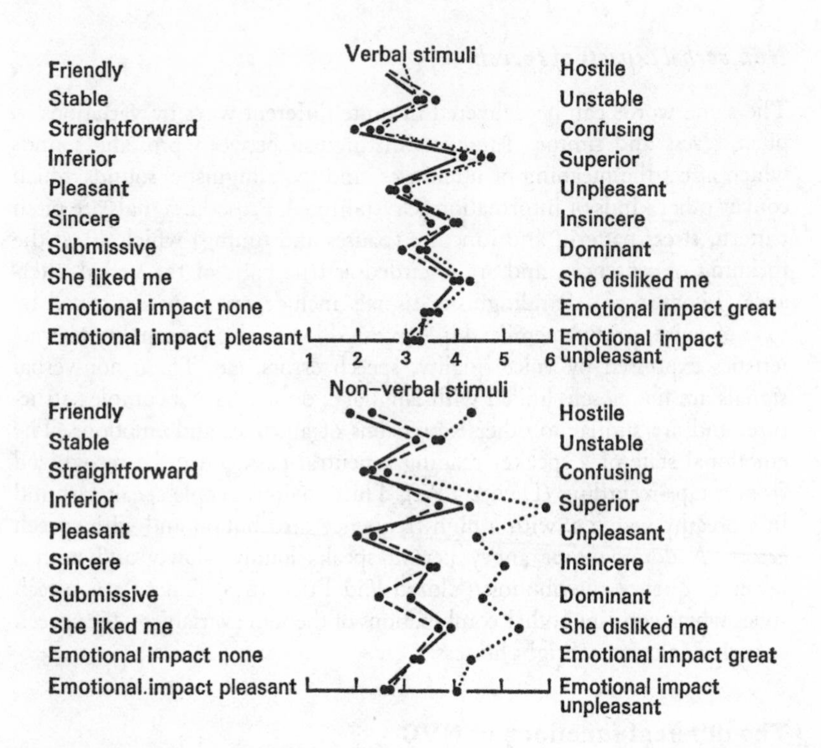

Fig. 3 Ratings of initially equated verbal and non-verbal cues for interior and superior attitudes when combined (Argyle et al. 1970). ——— = inferior, - - - - = equal, · · · · = superior.

were rated by subjects as very similar in superiority, etc. The combined signals were presented to further subjects on video-tape – superior (verbal), inferior (non-verbal) etc., nine combinations in all, and rated for superiority. It was found that the variance due to non-verbal cues was about 4½ times the variance due to verbal cues, in effecting judgments of inferior–superior (Argyle et al. 1970). The results of this experiment are shown in figure 3. Similar results were obtained in later experiments using friendly–hostile messages (Argyle, Alkema and Gilmour 1971).

Emotional states. These can be distinguished from interpersonal attitudes in that emotions are not directed towards others present, but are simply states of the individual. The common emotions are anger, depression, anxiety, joy, etc. An anxious state, for example, can be shown by (*a*) *tone of voice* (see p. 455), (*b*) *facial expression* – tense, perspiring, expanded pupils, (*c*) *posture* – tense and rigid, (*d*) *gestures* – tense clasping of objects, or general bodily activity, (*e*) *smell* – of perspiration, and (*f*) *gaze* – short glances, aversion of gaze. Interactors may try to conceal their true emotional state, or to convey that they are in some different emotional condition, but it is difficult to control all of these cues, and impossible to control the more autonomic ones. Emotional states can be conveyed by speech – 'I am feeling very happy' – but probably statements will not be believed unless supported by appropriate NVC, and the NVC can convey the message without the speech.

Self-presentation. Information can be sent about an interactor's status, group membership, occupation, personality, or sexual availability. A person might want to be seen as an eccentric, upper-class, inventor, or as an important, left-wing, intellectual. This can be done by (*a*) *appearance* – especially clothes, (*b*) *NV aspects of speech* – especially accent, loudness, speed, etc. and (*c*) *general style* of verbal and non-verbal performance. A lot of self-presentation is concerned with role-distance i.e. showing there is more to a person than can be seen from his present role performance (Goffman 1961). Again self-presentation *can* be done in words – 'look here young man, I've written more books about this than you have read' – but common experience suggests that it is not very effective. Self-presentation by NVC is basically a matter of using signals that are understood to stand for the real thing (Goffman 1956), though it is clearly better to display the actual qualities where this is possible.

Thus in this context it may be suggested that NVC and verbal communication normally play two contrasted roles. NVC is used to manage the immediate social relationship – in much the same way as in animals; verbal communication is used to convey information connected with shared tasks and problems – though it is also used to give orders and instructions. However NVC *can* convey information, as in gesture languages, and the verbal channel *can* sustain interpersonal relations, as in informal chat, and it can communicate attitudes and emotions by the words chosen.

Sustaining verbal communication

Speech plays a central role in most human social behaviour, but many linguists do not always appreciate the importance of the role played by NVC in conversation. However Abercrombie says 'We speak with our vocal organs, but we converse with our whole body' (1968:55), and Crystal (1969) and Lyons (1972) recognize clearly the importance of non-verbal signals.

Vocal and kinesic NVC which affects the meaning of utterances

A person would not be accepted as speaking a language properly, indeed he would scarcely be understood, if he did not deliver his sentences in the pitch-pattern, stress-pattern and temporal pattern of grouping and pausing, proper for that language. We showed above that the meaning of sentences depends on their prosodic features. Similar considerations apply to kinesic signals, which can affect the meaning of a sentence by (1) providing the punctuation, displaying the grouping of phrases and the grammatical structure, (2) pointing to people or objects, (3) providing emphasis, (4) giving illustrations of shapes or movements, (5) commenting on the utterance, e.g. indicating whether it is supposed to be funny or serious (Ekman and Friesen 1967).

Birdwhistell (1952) provided a system for recording 'kinesics' (bodily movements) on the analogy of the transcription methods used in phonetics; and Scheflen (1965) postulated that NVC has a hierarchical, three-level, structure corresponding to sentences, paragraphs, and longer sequences of speech. The method used by these investigators was to take a film or tape-recording of a fairly short sample of behaviour, and to make a very detailed but non-statistical study of what was happening.

Table 1 Equivalent verbal and non-verbal units

Verbal	*Non-verbal*
1. paragraph, or long unit of speech	postural position
2. sentence	head or arm position
3. words, phrases	hand movements, facial expressions, gaze shifts, etc.

(Cf. Condon and Ogston 1966.)

It has been found that speech is accompanied by bodily movements; these are coordinated with speech in that a sentence may be accompanied by related hand or head positions. These movements also have a hierarchical structure, in which smaller verbal and bodily signals are organized into larger, and coordinated, groupings of both (see Table 1). Frame-by-frame analyses of small movements of hands, head, eyes, etc. in relation to speech, have provided evidence of 'interactional synchrony', i.e. coordination of bodily movements between speaker and listener over periods of time corresponding to sentences, and even words (Kendon 1970, 1971 a, b). However these movements are somewhat idiosyncratic, though there are cultural uniformities. Since most of them can be seen only in peripheral vision, their function is rather mysterious. Kendon (1971 b) suggests that in addition to displaying the structure of utterances they (1) make the speaker more interesting, and hold the listeners' attention, and (2) give advance warning of the kind of utterance that is to come.

Floor-apportionment. When two or more people are conversing, they take it in turns to speak, and usually manage to achieve a fairly smooth 'synchronizing' sequence of utterances, without too many interruptions and silences. When people first meet, it is unlikely that their spontaneous styles of speaking will fit together, and there is a period during which adjustments are made – one person has to speak less, another has to speak faster, and so on. This is all managed by a simple system of non-verbal signalling, the main cues being nods, grunts, and shifts of gaze. For example, at a grammatical pause a speaker will look up, to see if the others are willing for him to carry on speaking – if they are they will nod and grunt. Just before the end of an utterance a speaker gives a rather more prolonged gaze at the others as is shown in figure 4. This shows the average amount of other-directed gaze by each person just before and after *A* stops speaking and *B* starts speaking, in a number of conversations analyzed by Kendon. If this system fails, interruptions will take place, and there is a struggle for the floor (Kendon 1967).

Feedback. When someone is speaking he needs intermittent, but regular, feed-back on how others are responding, so that he can modify his utterances accordingly. He needs to know whether the listeners understand, believe or disbelieve, are surprised or bored, agree or disagree, are pleased or annoyed. This information could be provided by *sotto voce* verbal muttering, but is in fact obtained by careful study of the other's face: the eyebrows signal surprise, puzzlement, etc., while the mouth indicates pleasure and displeasure. When the other is invisible, as in telephone conversation, these visual signals are unavailable, and more verbalized 'listening behaviour' is used – 'I see', 'really?', 'how interesting', etc. (Argyle, Lalljee and Cook 1968).

Signalling attentiveness. For a conversation to be sustained, those involved must provide intermittent evidence that they are still attending to the others. If an interactor turns his back, or falls asleep, the others will assume that he has withdrawn from the encounter. To signal attentiveness interactors use (*a*) *proximity* – they are within the conventionally prescribed range, (*b*) *orientation* – they are appropriately oriented for the

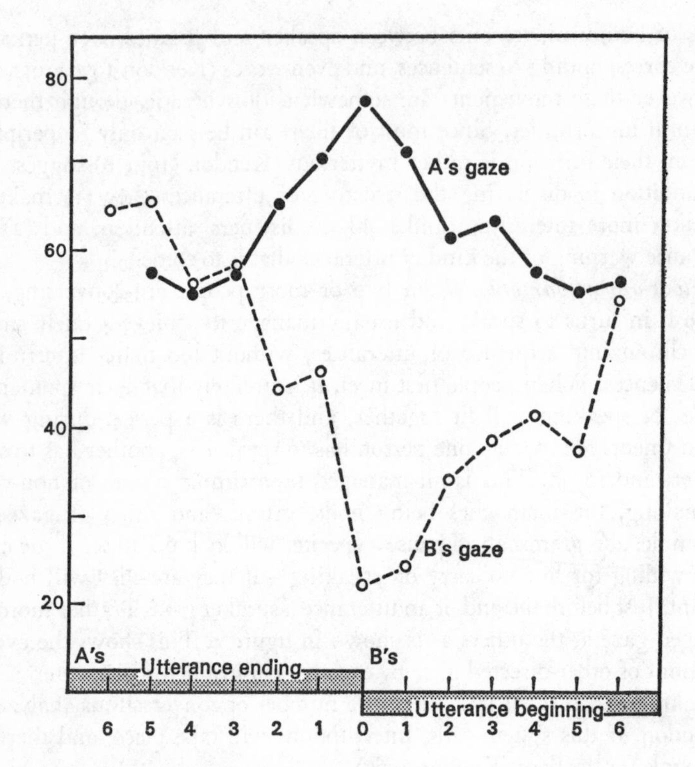

Fig. 4 Direction of gaze at the beginning and ending of long utterances. Frequency of other-directed gazes at half-second intervals before and after the beginning (broken line) and ending (continuous line) of long utterances. Pooled data from ten individuals, based on a total of sixty-eight long utterances (from Kendon 1967).

encounter in question, (*c*) *gaze* – they look at each other frequently, (*d*) *head-nods* – are used frequently by listeners, (*e*) *posture* – a listener adopts an alert, congruent posture, with slightly cocked head, or (*f*) *bodily movements* – these reflect the verbal and non-verbal signals of the speaker.

Replacing verbal communication

Verbal communication may be impossible, or fail to work, for one reason or another, in which case NVC may take over.

Sign languages. The deaf-and-dumb language is a well known example. Simpler sign languages have been developed in a number of other settings when speech is impossible e.g. in broadcasting, on racecourses, in noisy factories, and between under-water swimmers. Some Australian aboriginal tribes have developed a gesture language, based on signs for objects and actions, that enables rapid communication and is used under certain ritual conditions (Brun 1969). While English deaf-and-dumb language is based on letters of the alphabet, the American deaf-and-dumb language learned by the chimpanzee Washoe [see pp. 106–26, this volume] is based on words.

Neurotic symptoms. Some clinicians believe that the symptoms of certain mental patients are a kind of NVC, used when speech has failed. Thus psychosomatic symptoms may be signals seeking attention, love and sympathy, or may be intended to control the behaviour of others (Szasz 1961; Grant 1972).

The perception of NVC

For NVC to have any effect it must be perceived, though it need not be consciously perceived. The term is used here to refer to more than the perception of size, brightness, etc., and to include cognitive activities of interpretation. Research here is concerned with the perceptual and cognitive activities of the *perceiver*, rather than the signalling of the sender. There has been a great deal of experimental work on social perception, but much of it has unfortunately been of a very artificial kind, so that rather little is known about perception during real social interaction. Another's NVC can be interpreted in at least four ways, which we will consider separately.

1 Interpretation as personality

Since different people need to be treated differently, interactors try to categorize each other. They categorize one another in terms of age, sex, social class, occupations, and also in terms of personality traits. Individuals differ in the traits which they regard as important, and which will affect the way they treat others. Some people want to know primarily whether another is a Catholic or a Protestant, or whether he is Jewish, or how intelligent he is. All these categorizations are made on the basis of verbal and non-verbal cues, but NVC is of particular importance. The research findings in this area are of questionable validity, since they were obtained by such methods as looking at still photographs – e.g. in the studies of the effects of spectacles on judged IQ discussed above (p. 447). Physical cues which are used in this way include skin colour, hair colour and length, size of forehead, height, eye wrinkles, make-up, thickness of lips, size of nose, and shape of chin (Allport 1961). These features may be taken as evidence of category-membership (e.g. being Jewish), or as a basis for inferring personality qualities (e.g. intelligence). It seems fairly clear, however, that individuals concentrate on certain categories or dimensions, and then assume that another possesses all the other stereotyped qualities associated with the race, class or other category indicated thereby.

2 *Interpretation as emotions*

Information is needed on another's emotional state, and this can be inferred from his facial expression, tone of voice, and posture, as described above (p. 457). Whether or not a smile, for example, will be interpreted as an emotional state depends on the situation, the usual state of the person observed, and how well the observer knows him. Davitz (1964) found that there are considerable individual differences in the ability to judge emotions from tone of voice alone when neutral passages are read.

3 *Interpretation as interpersonal attitudes*

(The same distinction from emotions is being made as before.) Whether another is friendly or hostile, or feels inferior or superior, can be judged from his posture, tone of voice, facial expression. . . . Tagiuri (1958) found that perceptions of liking–disliking were quite accurate – members of a group on the whole knew who chose them as friends, though 4 per cent of others who chose them were seen as rejecting, and 9 per cent who in fact rejected were seen as choosing: the difference is probably because negative attitudes are often concealed. *A* may be more concerned with perceiving how *B* perceives *A*, than with perceiving anything else about *B* – if *A* is a candidate being interviewed, or a performer in front of an audience for example. Argyle and Williams (1969) set up a variety of social situations and asked subjects 'To what extent did you feel that you were mainly the observer or the observed?', the answers being recorded on a seven-point scale. It was found that people felt observed when (a) being interviewed or assessed, (b) the other was older, (c) young females met young males; in addition some people felt observed most of the time e.g. insecure and submissive males. However, feeling observed was not increased when others looked more, though it was greater for those who themselves looked least.

4 Perception during on-going interaction

As we have seen, during verbal communication each interactor needs intermittent information about the other's reactions, both for feed-back and to control floor-apportionment. The main cues are the other's shifts of gaze, head-nods, and small movements of the eyebrows and of other parts of the face. Most people are not consciously aware that they are receiving this information, but it is clear that they are making use of it from the lawful relationships found between these cues and other aspects of performance. This perceptual information is obtained mainly by means of intermittent visual scanning of the other's face.

There is a lot of research into the processes involved in the perception of non-verbal cues. Any of the kinds of interpretation listed above involves inference from a number of cues. When the cues are contradictory the observer does not normally average them, but rather opts for one and re-interprets the others. Individuals vary in the dimensions of personality they use, and in their sensitivity to various kinds of cue. While the recognition of emotional states is probably partly independent of specific experience, most of these perceptions depend on learning, and they can be improved by quite brief training (e.g. Jecker, Maccoby and Breitrose 1965).

NVC in social interaction

In social interaction there are streams of verbal and non-verbal signals which are closely inter-twined, and go in both directions. We shall discuss in this section some of the main kinds of sequential linkage involving non-verbal cues in the interaction process. Most human social interaction involves verbal as well as non-verbal communication, and most of the studies in this area have been concerned with both kinds of communication. We shall concentrate on sequences involving NVC here, though as shown above the two kinds of signalling are very closely related.

Response sequences

One approach is to study the statistical probability that some response of *A*'s will be followed by some response of *B*'s. One of the most common kinds of sequence is where *B* produces a similar response to *A*. It is found that if *A* smiles or nods his head *B* is likely to do the same (Rosenfeld 1967); the same applies to posture, gesture, and to various aspects of verbal performance. Such rapid responses are unthinking and can be described as unconscious 'imitation': if an interactor becomes aware of what is happening he is liable to prevent himself from doing it. If this is a case of imitation, it should occur under the usual conditions for imitation, e.g. imitating people of higher status, who possess similar attributes, etc. (Bandura 1962). This does not apply to 'reciprocity', which is quite a different kind of response-matching – the carefully thought-out and timed exchange of gifts or invitations, that is largely governed by the social norms about different kinds of relationship (Sahlins 1965). Reciprocity is important in primitive societies, and differences have been found between social classes and cultures in the extent to which helping behaviour depends on reciprocity (Berkowitz 1968).

Another important response sequence is that produced by reinforcement. Most research has concentrated on the non-verbal reinforcement of verbal behaviour, e.g. the effect of head-nods on frequency of expressing opinions. The following non-verbal signals have been found to act as reinforcers – head-nods, smiling, leaning forward, looking interested, gazing at the other, and making encouraging noises (Williams 1964). As argued above, it seems that, in the experiments conducted under real-life conditions, reinforcement was effective without awareness of what was going on (e.g. Verplanck 1955). Other experiments suggest that interactors are not aware that they are giving reinforcements. Thus during interaction, all interactors are constantly giving and receiving reinforcement without much awareness.

We described earlier how a listener provides feed-back on what is being said. Careful study of the fine movements of listeners shows that they often make a continuous facial and gestural commentary on what is being said – what Kendon (1971a) has called 'speech analogous movement'. Listeners may also produce 'movement mirroring', i.e. imitation of a speaker's bodily movements; this has been observed to occur intermittently, mainly at the beginning and end of utterances (Kendon 1970).

It has been observed by Kendon (1971a) that interactors coordinate their bodily movements in another way. For example if *A* turns towards *B*, *B* may turn slightly towards *A*; *A* has initiated a shift of attention towards *B*, or a desire for interaction with *B*, which *B* has recognized, and is indicating willingness to take part in. Another variety of this sequence is for *A* to look *B* in the eye, and for *B* to hold the gaze.

Skilled sequences of response

Social interaction cannot be analyzed wholly in terms of *S–R* sequences, since each interactor has goals he is trying to attain: these consist of desired behaviour by others, or particular types of relationship or interaction. If the other does not behave in the desired way, continuous corrective action, directed towards eliciting the desired responses, is taken. For example if *B* is too dominant for *A*'s liking, *A* may sit more upright, tilt his head back slightly, and speak more loudly. These sequences of responses have some of the characteristics of motor skills, such as driving a car. We have seen above how feed-back is sought at certain points e.g. at the ends of utterances. When another's face is invisible, interaction is found to be very difficult (Argyle, Lalljee and Cook 1968). Another way in which social performance resembles a motor skill is in the integration of lower-order sequences, complete with feed-back loops, into larger units. Social performance thus has a hierarchical structure, where the smaller elements are habitual, while the larger units are subject to cognitive control and are influenced by rules, plans (in the sense used by Miller, Galanter and Pribram 1960) and strategic considerations (Argyle and Kendon 1967).

Equilibrium processes

However there is more to interaction than individuals responding to one another – those present must behave in a highly coordinated way for there to be an interaction at all. There must be coordination over (1) the content of interaction, i.e. the nature of the activity, (2) the role-relations e.g. whether a candidate is being interviewed for a job or whether he is assessing the firm, (3) how intimate the encounter is (warm–cold), (4) the dominance relations (inferior–superior), (5) the emotional tone (anxious, serious, happy etc.), (6) the proper sequence of acts (questions should lead to answers, gestures should be responded to), and (7) the timing and amounts of speech (who shall talk most, and when). To work out a pattern of interaction between two or more people where such synchronizing occurs requires some rapid group problem-solving; this problem-solving is carried out mainly by the use of minor NV cues. Small attempts may be made at intimacy or dominance, with careful study of how the other reacts, so that these can be withdrawn if his reaction is too negative. To sustain the interaction a sufficient supply of rewards must be delivered to the other in order to keep him in the situation. Encounters often begin with a period of informal chat, the purpose of which is probably to enable some degree of synchronizing to be established. Little information is exchanged during this period, but the interactors are able to emit signals conveying interpersonal attitudes and other NVC and to begin building up an equilibrium.

Once equilibrium has been established it proves very resistant to change, as is found in interaction between psychotherapists and patients over long series of sessions (Lennard and Bernstein 1960). For some combinations of people, equilibrium is very difficult or impossible, e.g. if all want to dominate, or one wants to be intimate and others want to be formal and distant (Schutz 1958).

Sources of variation in NVC

Interaction in different group settings

We mentioned earlier that there are different rules of behaviour in different situations – for eating, at seminars, in church, etc. Here the tasks to be performed are quite different, and lead to totally different patterns of NVC. The social conventions about each of these situations specify what NVC may be used. A further source of variation is between such basically different forms of grouping as families, groups of friends and work groups. Sociological data suggest a number of differences in the communication systems of these groups (Argyle 1969). Surveys by Argyle and Little (1971) have found great differences between the kinds of NVC and social interaction in these settings.

The family has a biological basis and is found in some form in birds and mammals. The parents are drawn together originally by sexual motivation, children depend on them for food and protection, and are socialized by them. The family is a group with a definite social structure in that the behaviour and relations between the main members are similar in all cultures with some inter-cultural variation; there is a standard pattern of behaviour between father, mother, older and younger sons, older and younger daughters. The members of the family live together and have joint tasks to perform in connection with eating, sleeping, care of children and maintenance of the home. Social interaction has a special quality – there is more intimacy, aggression and affection; there is more bodily contact, less formality and politeness than in most other groups; the members know each other extremely well, and every act is loaded with meanings and associations.

Work-groups are found in all men and some animals. Work is done in groups because cooperation and complementary skills are needed for many tasks. There are also social satisfactions in work, and a great deal of purely sociable verbal and NVC occurs. The pattern of social interaction however is very much determined by the technological arrangements, and the formal ways in which men are related in the work-flow system. The main forms of NVC for work purposes are (a) the rate or method of working acting as a signal to others; (b) in coordinated task activity such as two-man sawing, physical movements are also social acts; (c) helping;

(d) guiding, by means of bodily contact; (e) gesture language, where noise or distance prevents speech; (f) non-verbal commentary on work performance, by raised eyebrows, or physical blows and (g) non-verbal accompaniments of verbal messages, indicating for example whether they are to be received as 'advice' or as 'orders'. The non-verbal signals for sociable purposes are as described earlier – communicating interpersonal attitudes, etc. (Argyle 1971).

Friendship groups are one of the main forms of human groups and also occur in some of the primates; the members are brought together solely by interpersonal motivations, rather than to perform any particular task. Adolescent groups play an important role in socialization; adults spend some of their leisure with friends. Non-human primates play with and groom their friends; humans may have common interests to pursue or they have to invent activities which will generate the desired form of interaction – dancing, eating, drinking, walking, etc. There is more self-presentation than in the home, there is more attention to appearance, behaviour is more formal and polite, greater efforts are made to preserve a synchronizing flow of interaction, and clearer signals of positive interpersonal attitudes are communicated.

Individual differences in NVC

There are of course individual differences in the use of non-verbal signals. For example people vary in their preferred *proximity*: this can be measured by asking subjects to talk to the same person, or even to a hatrack, and the variations are found to be consistent across different situations (Mehrabian 1968). There are also characteristic expressive styles in the use of *bodily movements* (Allport and Vernon 1932), and in *looking* behaviour, lengths of utterances, etc. (Kendon and Cook 1969). The same is probably true of all the other non-verbal signals, though the variation in their use between different types of situation must be borne in mind.

Certain groups of non-verbal signals are commonly found to occur together. For example, there is the pattern of warm, friendly, affiliative behaviour which includes looking a lot at the other, close proximity, smiling, leaning towards, etc. An individual with strong affiliative motivation will seek out situations where he can behave in this way, and will try to establish friendly relations in many situations.

However any individual will use quite different non-verbal behaviour patterns in different situations, and may be friendly, hostile, inferior or superior, on different occasions, just as he is able to play a number of different games. An individual's performance in different situations is not very consistent (Mischel 1969). The behaviour he emits does not depend on his personality alone, it also depends on (1) the rules governing particular situations, (2) the role-relations of those present, i.e. he will behave differently to males and females, and to those who are older and younger, and (3) the personalities of the others. We have recently found that an individual has a limited number of social performances, each of which is used for a range of social situations and relationships: 'personality' could be regarded as the sum of these performances (Argyle and Little 1971).

Theory and explanation

Three main theoretical approaches to the explanation of human NVC can be distinguished, though each is concerned with rather different aspects. We shall outline a fourth approach, which incorporates features of the other three, and adds considerations from social psychology.

First we must refer again to the three main functional types of human NVC (see pp. 455–61). (1) *Signals used to manage the immediate social situation*. These are similar to the signals used by animals: they have no reference to specific objects but only to the state and intentions of the organism. (2) *Signals used to sustain verbal communication*. These do not occur in animals, are used in close coordination with speech, are fast-moving, and probably have a complex temporal structure. (3) *Replacing verbal communication*. Gesture languages are developed when language is inconvenient, are often based on language, but may be independent of it. These three kinds of NVC are different in a number of ways, for example on Hockett's 'design features' (cf. Thorpe 1972), and a different kind of theory will probably be required for each.

Biological evolution

Social behaviour in the lower animals consists of the stereotyped production of non-verbal responses; in mammals and especially the higher primates the system is more 'open' and has to be completed by socialization experiences. In either case social behaviour consists of the emission of non-verbal signals, using parts of the anatomy adapted for the purpose, in order to achieve ends of biological importance – collective defence of territory, mating, rearing offspring, gathering food and so on. It may be safely assumed that this entire pattern of non-verbal signalling and social behaviour has emerged in the course of evolution because it contributed to the survival of individuals or groups. There is evidence that the signals for different emotional states are much the same in all human societies and occur also in blind children, so they are presumably little affected by experience [Eibl-Eibesfeldt, Chapter 10, this volume]. It is likely that the same is true of the signals for interpersonal attitudes. We have argued above that NVC in humans is used to control the immediate social situation, and shown that it is more effective than speech for doing this.

Several authors have stressed the similarities between human and animal social behaviour (Morris 1967). How far can this type of explanation be pressed? There are two main limitations to it, corresponding to the next two theories. (a) Despite the similarities between cultures in emotional expression, there are extensive differences between cultures in other aspects of NVC. Particular interest has been taken in the Japanese and Arabs, whose signalling systems are very different from those in Europe or the USA. For example Arabs stand closer, touch each other, face head-on, use a lot of eye-contact, and speak louder (Watson and Graves 1966). A given signal can mean quite different things in different cultures e.g. hissing in Japan is a sign of deference. As Darwin recognized (1872), while the expression of the emotions in man appears to be unaffected by experience, many other non-verbal signals that we use, such as nodding and shaking the head, clearly are not. (b) One of the main differences between men and apes is our use of language: most of our social behaviour involves language. Some animal gestural signs are used to send messages of a similar kind, and much of human NVC is used in close connection with the emission, reception, or control of speech. This is particularly true of head-nods, shifts of gaze, and hand movements, which are used quite differently from the way animals use them.

The structural–linguistic approach

A number of investigators have studied NVC in a similar way to that in which linguists study a language. They have tried to find out whether there is a hierarchical structure, in which smaller units are grouped to make larger ones, and if there are rules of sequence and composition.

We have seen that prosodic vocal signals and certain kinesic signals are closely coordinated with language, affect the meaning of utterances, and form part of a total communication system with a definite structure. Other non-verbal signals, such as direction of gaze, also operate in a structural way, for example in governing the synchronization of speech and in negotiating greetings. Language, in order to communicate at all, must follow certain grammatical rules; the meaning of a word depends partly on the other words with which it is grouped: similar considerations may apply to NVC, and NVC may have some kind of syntax, governing both its own sequences, and the links with language. The detailed syntax for this kind of NVC has yet to be worked out in detail, and it may not be so strict or detailed as the syntax of language itself. While no explicit theory of the origin of this aspect of NVC has been offered, it seems to be assumed that it is part of a wider system of communication and social behaviour which also includes language proper; thus it could be based on the same neural structures and have evolved at the same time as language. An alternative explanation might be that the verbal communication system and its accompanying physical structures are primary, and that non-verbal signals are inevitably acquired in order to make communication feasible – to control synchronizing, provide feedback, etc.

Sociological approaches (Symbolic interactionism and ethnomethodology)

In many situations there are definite rules governing what shall happen, for example at committee meetings, in church. In other situations there are implicit rules which are less obvious, but which become obvious when they are broken. In its emphasis on rule-following this approach is similar to the previous one: however where the structural–linguistic approach is concerned with the rules which NVC must follow to coordinate with speech and to communicate, the sociological approaches are concerned with the rules, at a more macroscopic level, governing styles of behaviour and sequences of events in particular situations and settings. This explanation in terms of rules is quite different from explanations by empirical laws: behaviour is rule-governed when people think that this is the proper thing to do, or if they are shocked when the rule is broken. There are different rules, in a given culture, for behaviour at a lecture, a seminar and a party. Barker and Wright (1954) carried out a sociological study of a small Midwest town, and concluded that there were 884 'behavior settings'. Goffman (1963) has analyzed in detail some of the rules governing NVC in American middle-class society, and suggests that all or most of social behaviour can be explained in terms of these rules. These rules have developed slowly, as part of cultural history, because they are useful. Their explanation would lie in showing how they had been useful to particular groups. There would thus be no universal laws of behaviour, merely a large number of arbitrary rules for particular situations. An alternative approach is to look for universal laws that are affected by dimensional aspects of situations – the number of people present, their formality, etc.

Sociologists have also emphasized the subjective meanings given to non-verbal signals by the culture and by particular groups. For example, in his account of 'self-presentation' Goffman (1956) maintains that people manipulate the impressions others form of them by clothes and gestures which have certain meanings. In his account of 'body-gloss' he observes how people make their behaviour comprehensible to bystanders by sending signals which indicate the motivation of their behaviour (Goffman 1971). The importance of non-verbal acts which have culturally defined and publicly shared meanings is shown in rituals and ceremonies, such as marriage. While this approach emphasizes the meanings given in a particular culture, there is no reason why it should not be able to accommodate meanings of a universal biological origin. On the other hand Goffman has tended to emphasize the *different* meanings which the same act may have in different social settings.

A social psychological approach

The contribution of the biological approach must be recognized – there is an unlearnt basis to emotional expression, and there is a basic physiological equipment on which all NVC depends. It must be accepted that most human social behaviour involves speech, that much NVC is used to accompany speech, and that this NVC may depend on similar structures to speech or have been learnt as part of the skill of verbal communication. The contribution of the sociological approach must also be recognized – there are considerable cultural variations in many aspects of NVC, and the same signal can have different meanings depending on the culture and the situation. To all this however a social psychological dimension may be added.

1 Systems of interaction build up in particular social settings, groups, and cultures, to deal with particular communication needs.

(a) *Managing the immediate social situation*. Interpersonal attitudes and emotions are expressed freely in the family, but are carefully restrained outside, where more fragile relationships have to be sustained. On the other hand there is virtually no self-presentation in the family, where it is pointless. In some situations it is prevented or controlled by the wearing of uniforms.

(b) *Sustaining verbal communication*. Non-verbal signals play a number of important roles in sustaining verbal communication under normal conditions. If these conditions are changed in any way there are adjustments in the NVC: for example when visual cues are removed, as on the telephone, auditory cues replace them for purposes of feed-back and floor-apportionment. When the videophone becomes available, a different set of adjustments will have to be devised and learnt.

(c) *Replacing speech.* Systems of gestures are developed in situations where speech is impossible.

2 When a system of communication has been established in a culture or a social group, it has to be learned by new members. This may take place through imitation, combined with the reinforcement of successful performance (Mischel 1969). There may also be trial-and-error learning: McPhail (1967) found that adolescents engage in a lot of 'experimental' behaviour, much of which is awkward, aggressive and quite unsuccessful, but that this is replaced by more effective 'mature' behaviour after the age of 17 to 18. Learning by explanation and understanding is not common in the case of NVC, which is usually emitted and received in a spontaneous manner, below the conscious threshold. However, in groups of adolescents there is often discussion of such minutiae of social performance, and in social skills training and in psychotherapy insight is given into NVC, so that it is brought more under conscious control.

Conclusion

NVC in humans consists of signals similar to those used by animals. However human social behaviour uses a second channel – language. We have suggested that there are three distinct kinds of human NVC, which have different origins and modes of functioning. (1) Some NVC is used to communicate attitudes and emotions and to manage the immediate social situation. This appears to be very similar to animal communication, though there are cultural variations in the signals used, and situational rules governing their use. (2) NVC is also used to support and complement verbal communication. This is found only in man, is coordinated with speech in a complex way, and appears to be part of an overall system of communication, with complex rules of sequence and structure. (3) NVC is also developed to replace language, as in gesture languages. Some animal communication is of a similar character, and human gesture language can be taught to chimpanzees. The outstanding problems in the study of human NVC are: (1) further understanding of the functioning of particular non-verbal signals, and how they are perceived; (2) the elucidation of the second kind of NVC, how exactly it is fitted to speech, and whether there is some kind of overall grammar; (3) further analysis of cultural differences and similarities, and the conditions under which NVC is learnt; (4) further knowledge of the processes under which new systems of NVC develop in a group or culture.

References

ABERCROMBIE, K. (1968) 'Paralanguage', *Br. J. dis. Comm.*, 3, 55–9.

ALLPORT, G. W. (1961) *Pattern and Growth in Personality* New York, Holt Rinehart and Winston.

ALLPORT, G. W. and VERNON, P. E. (1932) *Studies in Expressive Movement* New York, Macmillan.

ARGYLE, M. (1969) *Social Interaction* London, Methuen; New York, Atherton.

ARGYLE, M. (1971) *The Social Psychology of Work* London, The Penguin Press.

ARGYLE, M., ALKEMA, F. and GILMOUR, R. (1971) 'The communication of friendly and hostile attitudes by verbal and non-verbal signals', *Europ. J. soc. Psychol.*, 3, 385–402.

ARGYLE, M. and DEAN, J. (1965) 'Eye-contact, distance and affiliation', *Sociometry*, 28, 289–304.

ARGYLE, M. and KENDON, A. (1967) 'The experimental analysis of social performance', *Adv. exp. soc. Psychol.*, 3, 55–98.

ARGYLE, M., LALLJEE, M. G. and COOK, M. (1968) 'The effects of visibility on interaction in a dyad', *Hum. Relat.*, 21, 3–17.

ARGYLE, M. and LITTLE, B. R. (1971) 'Do personality traits apply social behaviour?' Paper to B.P.S., unpublished.

ARGYLE, M. and MCHENRY, R. (1970) 'Do spectacles really affect judgements of intelligence?' *Br. J. soc. clin. Psychol.*, 10, 27–9.

ARGYLE, M., SALTER, V., NICHOLSON, H., WILLIAMS, M. and BURGESS, P. (1970) 'The communication of inferior and superior attitudes by verbal and non-verbal signals', *Br. J. soc. clin. Psychol.*, 9, 221–31.

ARGYLE, M. and WILLIAMS, M. (1969) 'Observer or observed? A reversible perspective in person perception', *Sociometry*, 32, 396–412.

BANDURA, A. (1962) 'Social learning through imitation' in Nebraska Symposium on *Motivation*, Jones, M. R. (ed.), Lincoln, Nebraska University Press.

BARKER, R. G. and WRIGHT, H. F. (1954) *Midwest and its children: the Psychological Ecology of an American Town* Evanston, Ill., Row, Peterson.

BERKOWITZ, L. (1968) 'Responsibility, reciprocity and social distance in help-giving: an experimental investigation of English social class differences', *J. exp. soc. psychol.*, 4, 46–63.

BIRDWHISTELL, R. L. (1952) *Introduction to Kinesics* Louisville University Press.

BRUN, T. (1969) *The International Dictionary of Sign Language* London, Wolfe.

CONDON, W. S. and OGSTON, W. D. (1966) 'Sound film analysis of normal and pathological behaviour patterns', *J. Nerv. ment. Dis.*, 143, 338–47.

COOK, M. (1970) 'Experiments on orientation and proxemics', *Hum. Relat.*, 23, 61–76.

CRYSTAL, D. (1969) *Prosodic Systems and Intonation in English* London, Cambridge University Press.

DARWIN, C. R. (1872) *The Expression of the Emotions in Man and Animals* London, John Murray.

DAVITZ, J. R. (1964) *The Communication of Emotional Meaning* New York, McGraw-Hill.

EKMAN, P. (1969a) 'Non-verbal leakage and clues to deception', *Psychiatry*, **32**, 88–106.

EKMAN, P. (1969b) 'Pan-cultural elements in facial displays of emotion', *Science, N.Y.*, **164**, 86–8.

EKMAN, P. and FRIESEN, W. V. (1967) 'Origin, usage, and coding: the basis for five categories of non-verbal behaviour', *Semiotica* (in press).

ELDRED, S. H. and PRICE, D. B. (1958) 'Linguistic evaluation of feeling states in psychotherapy', *Psychiatry*, **21**, 115–21.

EXLINE, R. V. and WINTERS, L. C. (1965) 'Affective relations and mutual gaze in dyads' in *Affect, Cognition and Personality* Tomkins, S. and Izzard, C. (eds) New York, Springer.

FELIPE, N. J. and SOMMER, R. (1966) 'Invasions of personal space', *Social Problems*, **14**, 206–14.

GARFINKEL, H. (1963) 'Trust and stable actions' in *Motivation and Social Interaction* Harvey, O. J. (ed.) New York, Ronald.

GOFFMAN, E. (1956) *The Presentation of Self in Everyday Life* Edinburgh, Edinburgh University Press.

GOFFMAN, E. (1961) *Encounters* Indiana, Bobbs-Merrill.

GOFFMAN, E. (1963) *Behavior in Public Places* Glencoe, Ill., Free Press.

GOFFMAN, E. (1971) *Relations in Public* Harmondsworth, Allen Lane.

GRANT, E. C. (1972) 'Non-verbal communication in the mentally ill' in Hinde, R. A. (ed.) *Non-verbal Communication* Cambridge, Cambridge University Press.

HAGGARD, E. A. and ISAACS, K. S. (1966) 'Micromomentary facial expressions as indicators of ego mechanisms in psychotherapy' in *Methods of Research in Psychotherapy* Gottschalk, L. A. and Auerback, A. H. (eds), New York, Appleton Century.

HUTT, S. J. and HUTT, C. (1970) *Direct Observation and Measurement of Behavior* Springfield, Ill., Thomas.

INGHAM, R. (1971) *Cultural differences in social behaviour* D.Phil thesis, Oxford University.

JECKER, J. D., MACCOBY, N. and BREITROSE, H. S. (1965) 'Improving accuracy in interpreting non-verbal cues of comprehension', *Psych. in the Schools*, **2**, 239–44.

JOURARD, S. M. (1966) 'An exploratory study of body-accessibility', *Br. J. soc. clin. Psychol.*, **5**, 221–31.

KENDON, A. (1967) 'Some functions of gaze direction in social interaction', *Acta psychol.*, **26**, 1–47.

KENDON, A. (1970) 'Movement coordination in social interaction: some examples considered', *Acta psychol.*, **32**, 1–25.

KENDON, A. (1971a) 'The role of visible behaviour in the organization of social interaction' in *Symposium on Human Communication* von Cranach, M. and Vine, I. (eds) London and New York, Academic Press.

KENDON, A. (1971b) 'Some relationships between body motion and speech: an analysis of an example' in *Studies in Dyadic Communication* Siegman, A. and Pope, B. (eds) Elmsford, N.Y., Pergamon.

KENDON, A. and COOK, M. (1969) 'The consistency of gaze patterns in social interaction', *Br. J. Psychol.*, **60**, 481–94.

LENNARD, H. L. and BERNSTEIN, A. (1960) *The Anatomy of Psychotherapy* Columbia University Press.

LOTT, E. E., CLARK, W. and ALTMAN, I. (1969) 'A propositional inventory of research on interpersonal space', *Naval Medical Research Institute Research Report*.

LYONS, J. (1972) 'Human Language' in Hinde, R. (ed.) *Non-verbal Communication* Cambridge, Cambridge University Press, chapter 3.

MCPHAIL, P. (1967) 'The development of social skill in adolescents'. Paper to B.P.S. Oxford Department of Educational Studies.

MEHRABIAN, A. (1968) 'The inference of attitudes from the posture, orientation, and distance of a communicator', *J. Consult. Psychol.*, **32**, 296–308.

MILLER, G. A., GALANTER, E. and PRIBRAM, K. H. (1960) *Plans and the Structure of Behaviour* New York, Holt Rinehart and Winston.

MISCHEL, W. (1969) *Personality and Assessment* New York, Wiley.

MORRIS, D. (1967) *The Naked Ape* London, Cape.

PORTER, E. R., ARGYLE, M. and SALTER, V. (1970) 'What is signalled by proximity?' *Perc. Motor Skills*, **30**, 39–42.

ROSENFELD, H. M. (1967) 'Non-verbal reciprocation of approval: an experimental analysis', *J. exp. soc. Psychol.*, **3**, 102–11.

SAHLINS, M. D. (1965) 'On the sociology of primitive exchange' in *The Relevance of Models for Social Anthropology*. A.S.A. monographs I. London, Tavistock Publications.

SCHEFLEN, A. E. (1965) *Stream and Structure of Communicational Behavior* Commonwealth of Pennsylvania, Eastern Pennsylvania Psychiatric Institute.

SCHUTZ, W. C. (1958) *FIRO: A Three Dimensional Theory of Interpersonal Behavior* New York, Holt Rinehart and Winston.

SISSONS, M. (1970) 'The psychology of social class' in *Money, Wealth and Class* London, Oxford University Press.

SOMMER, R. (1965) 'Further studies of small group ecology', *Sociometry*, 28, 337–48.

SZASZ, T. S. (1961) *The Myth of Mental Illness* London, Secker and Warburg.

TAGIURI, R. (1958) 'Social performance and its perception' in *Person Perception and Interpersonal Behavior* Tagiuri, R. and Petrullo, L. (eds) Stanford University Press.

THORPE, W. H. (1972) 'The comparison of vocal communication in animal and man' in Hinde, R. A. (ed.) *Non-verbal Communication* Cambridge, Cambridge University Press.

VERPLANCK, W. S. (1955) 'The control of the content of conversation: reinforcement of statements of opinion', *J. abnorm. soc. Psychol.*, **51**, 668–76.

VINE, I. (1971) 'Communication by Facial-Visual Signals' in *Social Behaviour in Animals and Man* Crook, J. H. (ed.) New York and London, Academic Press.

WATSON, O. M. and GRAVES, T. D. (1966) 'Quantitative research in proxemic behavior', *Amer. Anthrop.*, **68**, 971–85.

WILLIAMS, J. H. (1964) 'Conditioning of verbalization: a review', *Psychol. Bull.*, **62**, 383–93.

Section 12
Personal relationships

Introduction

In the study of social behaviour and experience, as we have seen, there is the continual problem of deciding at which level and in which way to study the phenomena in question. The three papers in this section represent very different approaches to the study of personal relationships. The first paper is in the tradition of experimental psychology. Aronson and Linder demonstrate the interesting finding that one person's feelings towards another will be affected not only by whether he thinks that the other likes or dislikes him but also by whether any shift has been perceived in the other's attitude. A shift in evaluation from an originally negative to a more positive view, for example, generates a more favourable reaction than when a positive attitude is expressed from the beginning. This study shows clearly the ingenuity, care and attention to detail required in good research. It is also interesting for the way in which it shows investigators assiduously searching out and exploring possible reasons for their results by further experimental manipulations and analysis of data. Characteristic problems of laboratory experimentation in social psychology are also thrown into relief. The subjects, for example, had to be deceived as to the true purpose of the experiment. As part of the procedure, some subjects received negative evaluations about themselves which they thought represented the genuine view of another subject. They later learned that the judgments were not genuine, but at the time many subjects may well have found them distressing. Although the results were carefully obtained and evaluated, the question also arises as to how far they can be generalized. How far do they apply to people other than American female undergraduates and in the contexts of everyday life outside the laboratory setting?

The extract by Eric Berne, taken from his best-selling book, *Games people play*, is a contribution of a very different nature. We are not offered empirical evidence bearing on a specific proposition but one man's analysis of the different ways in which people relate to each other. Berne's account is amusing and, perhaps, slightly tongue in cheek but it does bring out effectively the way in which our social interactions are structured in sequences and governed by rules and conventions. In his analysis of 'games',

Berne also shows how relationships may operate at more than one level. The overt content of a transaction between people may be merely a spurious structure which disguises and yet serves to support the underlying intentions and feelings of the participants.

Hopefully, not all our relationships take the form of 'games' and 'pastimes'. In the extract 'The theory of love' Erich Fromm analyses man's need to relate to others and the different ways in which he seeks to do this. Fromm's account is speculative but it is based on his extensive experience as a psychoanalyst and deep knowledge of sociological and psychoanalytic literature. Although, like the excerpt from Berne, it lacks the precision of formulation and the empirical backing found in the experimental study, it focuses on an important topic and provides an interesting and thought-provoking conceptualization which can be tested against the reader's own experience.

38 Gain and loss of esteem as determinants of interpersonal attractiveness

Elliot Aronson and Darwyn Linder

One of the major determinants of whether or not one person (*P*) will like another (*O*) is the nature of the other's behaviour in relation to the person. Several investigators have predicted and found that if *P* finds *O*'s behaviour 'rewarding', he will tend to like *O* (Newcomb 1956, 1961, Thibaut and Kelley 1959, Homans 1961, Byrne 1961, Byrne and Wong 1962). One obvious source of reward for *P* is *O*'s attitude regarding him. Thus, of *O* expresses invariably positive feelings and opinions about *P*, this constitutes a reward and will tend to increase *P*'s liking for *O*.

Although this has been demonstrated to be true (Newcomb 1956, 1961), it may be that a more complex relationship exists between being liked and liking others. It is conceivable that the sequence of *O*'s behaviour towards *P* might have more impact on *P*'s liking for *O* than the total number of rewarding acts emitted by *O* towards *P*. Stated briefly, it is our contention that the feeling of gain or loss is extremely important specifically, that a gain in esteem is a more potent reward than invariant esteem, and similarly, the loss of esteem is a more potent 'punishment' than invariant negative esteem. Thus, if *O*'s behaviour towards *P* was initially negative but gradually became more positive, *P* would like *O* more than he would had *O*'s behaviour been uniformly positive. This would follow even if, in the second case, the sum total of rewarding acts emitted by *O* was less than in the first case.

This 'gain–loss' effect may have two entirely different causes. One is largely affective, the other cognitive. First, when *O* expresses negative feelings towards *P*, *P* probably experiences some negative effect, e.g. anxiety, hurt, self-doubt, anger, etc. If *O*'s behaviour gradually becomes more positive, his behaviour is not only rewarding for *P* in and of itself, but it also serves to reduce the existing negative drive state previously aroused by *O*. The total reward value of *O*'s positive behaviour is, therefore, greater. Thus, paradoxically, *P* will subsequently like *O* better *because* of *O*'s early negative, punitive behaviour.

This reasoning is similar to that of Gerard and Greenbaum (1962). Their

---

ARONSON, ELLIOT and LINDER, DARWYN (1965) 'Gain and loss of esteem as determinants of interpersonal attractiveness' in *Journal of Experimental Social Psychology*, vol. 1, 156–71.

experiment involved an Asch-type situation in which they varied the behaviour of the stooge whose judgments followed those of the subject. In one condition the investigators varied the trial on which the stooge switched from disagreeing with the judgment of the subject (and agreeing with that of the majority) to agreeing with the judgment of the subject. The results showed a curvilinear relationship between the point at which the stooge switched and his attractiveness for the subjects – the subjects liked him best if he switched either very early or very late in the sequence of judgments. The investigators predicted and explained the high degree of liking for the 'late-switcher' as being due to the fact that he was reducing a greater degree of uncertainty. Our reasoning is also consistent with that of Walters and Ray (1960) who, in elaborating on an experiment by Gewirtz and Baer (1958), demonstrated that prior anxiety arousal increases the effectiveness of social reinforcement on children's performance. In their experiment social approval had a greater effect on performance in the anxiety conditions because it was reducing a greater drive.

We are carrying this one step further. What we are suggesting is that the existence of a prior negative drive state will increase the attractiveness of an individual who has both created and reduced this drive state. The kind of relationship we have in mind was perhaps best expressed by Spinoza (1955) in proposition 44 of *The Ethics*: 'Hatred which is completely vanquished by love passes into love: and love is thereupon greater than if hatred had not preceded it. For he who begins to love a thing, which he has wont to hate or regard with pain, from the very fact of loving feels pleasure. To this pleasure involved in love is added the pleasure arising from aid given to the endeavour to remove the pain involved in hatred, accompanied by the idea of the former object of hatred as cause.'

The same kind of reasoning (in reverse) underlies the 'loss' part of our notion. Here, *P* will like *O* better if *O*'s behaviour towards *P* is invariably negative than if *O*'s initial behaviour had been positive and gradually became more negative. Although in the former case *O*'s behaviour may consist of a greater number of negative acts, the latter case constitutes a distinct loss of esteem and, therefore, would have a greater effect upon reducing *P*'s liking for *O*. When negative behaviour follows positive behaviour, it is not only punishing in its own right but also eradicates the positive affect associated with the rewarding nature of *O*'s earlier behaviour. Therefore, *P* dislikes the positive–negative *O* more than the entirely negative *O* precisely because of the fact that, in the first case, *O* had previously rewarded him.

The predicted gain–loss effect may also have a more cognitive cause. By changing his opinion about *P*, *O* forces *P* to take his evaluation more seriously. If *O* expresses uniformly positive or uniformly negative feelings about *P*, *P* can dismiss this behaviour as being a function of *O*'s style of response, i.e., that *O* likes everybody or dislikes everybody, and that is *his* problem. But if *O* begins by evaluating *P* negatively and then becomes more positive, *P* must consider the possibility that *O*'s evaluations are a function of *O*'s perception of him and not merely a style of responding. Because of this he is more apt to be impressed by *O* than if *O*'s evaluation had been invariably positive. It is probably not very meaningful to be liked by a person with no discernment or discrimination. *O*'s early negative evaluation proves that he has discernment and that he's paying attention to *P* – that he's neither blind nor bland. This renders his subsequent positive evaluation all the more meaningful and valuable.

By the same token, if *O*'s evaluation of *P* is entirely negative, *P* may be able to write *O* off as a misanthrope or a fool. But if *O*'s initial evaluation is positive and then becomes negative, *P* is forced to conclude that *O* can discriminate among people. This adds meaning (and sting) to *O*'s negative evaluation of *P* and, consequently, will decrease *P*'s liking for *O*.

The present experiment was designed to test the major prediction of our gain–loss notion, that is, the primary intent of this experiment was to determine whether or not *changes* in the feelings of *O* towards *P* have a greater effect on *P*'s liking for *O* than the total number of rewarding acts emitted by *O*. A secondary purpose was to shed some light on the possible reasons for this relationship. The specific hypotheses are (1) *P* will like *O* better if *O*'s initial attitude towards *P* is negative but gradually becomes more positive, than if his attitude is uniformly positive; (2) *P* will like *O* better if his attitude is uniformly negative than if his initial attitude towards *P* is positive and becomes increasingly negative.

Method

Subjects and design

In order to provide a test of the hypotheses, it was necessary to design an experiment in which a subject interacts with a confederate over a series of discrete meetings. During these meetings the confederate should express either a uniformly positive attitude towards the subject, a uniformly negative attitude towards the subject, a negative attitude which gradually becomes positive, or a positive attitude which gradually becomes negative. It was essential that the interactions between subject and confederate be

1 Actually, 84 subjects were run in these four conditions. Four of the subjects were unusable because they were able to guess the real purpose of the experiment.

constant throughout experimental conditions except for the expression of attitude. At the close of the experiment, the subject's liking for the confederate could be assessed.

The subjects were 80 female students [1] at the University of Minnesota. Virtually all of them were sophomores; they were volunteers from introductory classes in psychology, sociology, and child development. All subjects were randomly assigned to one of the four experimental conditions.

Procedure

The experimenter greeted the subject and led her to an observation room which was connected to the main experimental room by a one-way window and an audio-amplification system. The experimenter told the subject that two students were scheduled for this hour, one would be the subject and the other would help the experimenter perform the experiment. He said that since she arrived first, she would be the helper. He asked her to wait while he left the room to see if the other girl had arrived yet. A few minutes later, through the one-way window, the subject was able to see the experimenter enter the experimental room with another female student (the paid confederate). The experimenter told the confederate to be seated for a moment and that he would return shortly to explain the experiment to her. The experimenter then returned to the observation room and began the instructions to the subject. The experimenter told the subject that she was going to assist him in performing a verbal conditioning experiment on the other student. The experimenter explained verbal conditioning briefly and told the subject that his particular interest was in the possible generalization of conditioned verbal responses from the person giving the reward to a person who did not reward the operant response. The experimenter explained that he would condition the other girl to say plural nouns to him by rewarding her with an 'mmm hmmm' every time she said a plural noun. The experimenter told the subject that his procedure should increase the rate of plural nouns employed by the other girl. The subject was then told that her tasks were: (1) to listen in and record the number of plural nouns used by the other girl, and (2) to engage her in a series of conversations (not rewarding plural nouns) so that the experimenter could listen and determine whether generalization occurred. The experimenter told the subject that they would alternate in talking to the girl (first the subject, then the experimenter, then the subject) until each had spent seven sessions with her.

The experimenter made it clear to the subject that the other girl must not know the purpose of the experiment lest the results be contaminated. He explained that, in order to accomplish this, some deception must be used. The experimenter said that he was going to tell the girl that the purpose of the experiment was to determine how people form impressions of other people. He said that the other girl would be told that she was to carry on a series of seven short conversations with the subject, and that between each of these conversations both she and the subject would be interviewed, the other girl by the experimenter and the subject by an assistant in another room, to find out what impressions they had formed. The experimenter told the subject that this 'cover story' would enable the experimenter and the subject to perform their experiment on verbal behaviour since it provided the other girl with a credible explanation for the procedure they would follow. In actuality, this entire explanation was, in itself, a cover story which enabled the experimenter and his confederate to perform their experiment on the formation of impressions.

The independent variable was manipulated during the seven meetings that the experimenter had with the confederate. During their meetings the subject was in the observation room, listening to the conversation and dutifully counting the number of plural nouns used by the confederate. Since the subject had been led to believe that the confederate thought that the experiment involved impressions of people, it was quite natural for the experimenter to ask the confederate to express her feelings about the subject. Thus, without intending to, the subject heard herself evaluated by a fellow student on seven successive occasions.

There were four experimental conditions: (1) Negative–Positive, (2) Positive–Negative, (3) Negative–Negative, and (4) Positive–Positive. In the Negative–Positive condition the confederate expressed a negative impression of the subject during the first three interviews with the experimenter. Specifically, she described her as being a dull conversationalist, a rather ordinary person, not very intelligent, as probably not having many friends, etc. During the fourth session she began to change her opinion about her. The confederate's attitude became more favourable with each successive meeting until, in the seventh interview, it was entirely positive. In the Positive–Positive condition the confederate's stated opinions were invariably positive. During the seventh interview her statements were precisely the same as those in the seventh meeting of the Negative–Positive condition. In the Negative–Negative condition the confederate expressed invariably negative feelings about the subject throughout the seven interviews. The Positive–Negative condition was the mirror image of the Negative–Positive condition. The confederate began by stating that the subject seemed interesting, intelligent, and likeable, but by the seventh session she described the subject as being dull, ordinary, etc.

In the Positive–Positive condition the confederate made 28 favourable statements about the subject and zero unfavourable statements. In the Negative–Negative condition the confederate made 24 unfavourable statements about the subject and zero favourable ones. In both the Negative–Positive and Positive–Negative conditions the confederate made 14 favourable and 8 unfavourable statements about the subject.

At the opening of the first interview, the experimenter informed the confederate that she should be perfectly frank and honest and that the subject would never be told anything about her evaluation. This was done so that the subject, upon hearing favourable statements, could not readily believe that the confederate might be trying to flatter her.

Interactions between subjects and confederate

Prior to each interview with the experimenter, the confederate and the subject engaged in a 3-minute conversation. This provided a credible basis upon which the confederate might form and change her impression of the subject. During these sessions it was essential that the confederate's conversations with the subject be as uniform as possible throughout the four experimental conditions. This was accomplished by informing the subject, prior to the first session, of the kind of topics she should lead the confederate into. These included movies, teachers, courses, life goals, personal background information, etc. Once the subject brought up one of these topics, the confederate spewed forth a prepared set of facts, opinions, and anecdotes which were identical for all experimental subjects. Of course, since a social interaction was involved, it was impossible for the confederate's conversations to be entirely uniform for all of the subjects. Occasionally the confederate was forced to respond to a direct question which was idiosyncratic to a particular subject. However, any variations in the statements made by the confederate were minor and nonsystematic.

The subject and confederate met in the same room but they were separated at all times by a cardboard screen which prevented visual communication. This was done for two reasons. First, it made it easier for the confederate to play the role of the naive subject. We feared that the confederate, after saying negative things about the subject, might be reluctant to look her squarely in the eye and engage in casual conversation. In addition, the use of the screen allowed for a more precise control of the conversation of the confederate by enabling her to read her lines from a prepared script which was tacked to the screen. The use of the screen was easily explained to the subject (in terms of the verbal reinforcement cover story) as a necessary device for eliminating inadvertant nonverbal reinforcement, like nods and smiles.

The confederate carried on her end of the conversation in a rather bland, neutral tone of voice, expressing neither great enthusiasm nor monumental boredom. The same girl (an attractive 20-year-old senior) was used as the confederate throughout the experiment. In order to further convince the subject of the validity of the cover story, the confederate used increasingly more plural nouns throughout the course of the experiment.

The dependent variable

At the close of the experiment the experimenter told the subject that there was some additional information he needed from her, but that it was also necessary for him to see the other girl to explain the true nature of the experiment to her. He said that, since he was pressed for time, the subject would be interviewed by his research supervisor while he, the experimenter, explained the experiment to the other girl. The experimenter then led the subject into the interviewer's office, introduced them, and left.

A separate interviewer [2] was used in order to avoid bias, the interviewer being ignorant of the subject's experimental condition. The purpose of the interview was to measure the subject's liking for the confederate; but this could not be done in any simple manner because the bare outlines of this experiment were extremely transparent: the confederate evaluated the subject, then the subject evaluated the confederate. Unless the interviewer could provide the subject with a credible rationale (consistent with the cover story) for asking her to evaluate the other girl, even the most naive of our subjects might have guessed the real purpose of the experiment. Therefore, the interviewer took a great deal of time and trouble to convince the subject that these data were essential for an understanding of the other girl's verbal behaviour. The essence of his story was that the attitudes and feelings that the 'helpers' in the experiment had for the 'subjects' in the experiment often found expression in such subtle ways as tone of voice, enthusiasm, etc. 'For example, if you thought a lot of the other girl you might unwittingly talk with warmth and enthusiasm. If you didn't like

2 It should be reported that in an earlier attempt to test this hypothesis, a questionnaire was administered instead of an interview. This was a more economical procedure, but it proved to be less effective. Although the results in the four experimental conditions were in the predicted order, the variance was extremely large. Postexperimental discussions with the subjects led us to suspect that one reason for the large variance might be due to the fact that the subjects were treating the questionnaires in a rather casual manner, believing that this aspect of the experiment was of little importance. It was primarily for this reason that we decided to use a high-status interviewer, whose earnest presence forced the subjects to treat the interview seriously and to respond in an honest and thoughtful manner.

her you might unwittingly sound aloof and distant.' The interviewer went on to explain that, much to his chagrin, he noticed that these subtle differences in inflection had a marked effect upon the gross verbal output of the other girls, that is, they talked more when they were conversing with people who seemed to like them than when they were conversing with people who seemed not to like them. The interviewer said that this source of variance was impossible to control but must be accounted for in the statistical analysis of the data. He explained that if he could get a precise indication of the 'helpers' feelings towards the 'subject' he could then 'plug this into a mathematical formula as a correction term and thereby get a more or less unbiased estimate of what her gross verbal output would have been if your attitude towards her had been neutral.'

The interviewer told the subject that, in order to accomplish this, he was going to ask her a number of questions aimed at getting at her feelings about the other girl. He emphasized that he wanted her *feeling,* her 'gut response', i.e., that it was essential that she give her frank impression of the other girl regardless of whether or not she had solid, rational reasons for it.

After the subject indicated that she understood, the interviewer asked her whether she liked the other girl or not. After she answered, the interviewer showed her a card on which was printed a 21-point scale, from – 10 to +10. The interviewer asked her to indicate the magnitude of her feeling as precisely as possible. He verbally labelled the scale: '+10 would mean you like her extremely, – 10 that you dislike her extremely. Zero means that you are completely indifferent. If you liked her a little, you'd answer +1, +2, or +3; if you liked her moderately well, you'd answer +4, +5, or +6; if you liked her quite a bit, you'd answer with a higher number. What point on the scale do you feel reflects your feeling towards the girl most accurately?'

This was the dependent measure. In addition, the interviewer asked the subjects to rate the confederate on 14 evaluative scales including intelligence, friendliness, warmth, frankness, etc. Most of these were asked in order to ascertain whether or not general liking would manifest itself in terms of higher ratings on specific attributes; a few were asked as possible checks on the manipulations.

Finally, the interviewer asked the subject if it bothered, embarrassed, annoyed, or upset her to hear the other girl evaluate her to the experimenter. After recording her answer, the interviewer probed to find out whether or not the subject suspected the real purpose of the experiment. He then explained, in full, the true nature of the experiment and the necessity for the deception. The subjects, especially those who had been negatively evaluated, were relieved to learn that it was not 'for real'. Although several of the girls admitted to having been quite shaken during the experiment, they felt that it was a worthwhile experience, inasmuch as they learned the extent to which a negative evaluation (even by a stranger) can affect them. They left the interview room in good spirits.

In most cases the interviewer remained ignorant of which of the four experimental conditions the subject was in until the conclusion of the interview. On a few occasions, however, a subject said something casually, in the midst of the interview, from which the interviewer could infer her experimental condition. It should be emphasized, however, that the dependent variable was the first question asked; in no case was the interviewer aware of a subject's experimental condition before she responded to that question.

Results and discussion

Our hypotheses were that the confederate would be liked better in the Negative–Positive condition than in the Positive–Positive condition and that she would be liked better in the Negative–Negative condition than in the Positive–Negative condition. To test these hypotheses we compared the subjects' ratings of their liking for the confederate across experimental conditions. The significance of the differences were determined by *t*-test.[3] Table 1 shows the means, *SDs*, *t*-values, and significance levels. An examination of the table reveals that the means are ordered in the predicted direction. Moreover, it is clear that the confederate was liked significantly more in the Negative–Positive condition than in the Positive–Positive condition ($p < 0.02$, two-tailed). The difference between the Negative–Negative condition and the Positive–Negative condition showed a strong trend in the predicted direction, although it did not reach an acceptable level of significance ($p < 0.15$, two-tailed). There is a great deal of variability in these two conditions. This large variability may be partly a function of the well-known reluctance of college students to express negative feelings about their fellow students, even when the behaviour of the latter is objectively negative (e.g. Aronson and Mills 1959). Typically, in social psychological experiments, regardless of how obnoxiously a stooge

3 A *t*-test was used because it is the most direct statistical technique and it also allowed us to perform an internal analysis to be described later. However, it is not the most powerful method of analyzing the data. An analysis of variance was also performed, and the results were slightly more significant than those of the *t*-test. The difference between Negative–Positive and Positive–Positive conditions reached the 0·02 level of significance; the difference between the Negative–Negative and the Positive–Negative conditions reached the 0·07 level of significance. The over-all treatment effect was highly significant ($p < 0.0005$).

behave towards a subject, many subjects find it difficult to verbalize negative evaluations of the stooge. In these two conditions the behaviour of the stimulus person would seem to have brought forth a negative evaluation; although most of the subjects were able to do this, several came out with highly positive evaluations. Thus, the range for the Negative–Negative and Positive–Negative conditions was 15 scale units (from +7 to −7). In the other two conditions negative evaluations were *not* in order; thus, this difficulty was not encountered. The range for these two conditions was only seven scale units (from +9 to +3). Therefore, although the mean difference between the Positive–Negative and Negative–Negative conditions was actually larger than the mean difference between the Positive–Positive and Negative–Positive conditions, it fell short of statistical significance.

Table 1 Means and standard deviations for liking of the confederate

Experimental condition	*Mean*	*SD*		*t-values*
1. Negative–Positive	+7·67	1·51	1 vs. 2	2·71†
2. Positive–Positive	+6·42	1·42	2 vs. 3	7·12‡
3. Negative–Negative	+2·52	3·16	3 vs. 4	1·42*
4. Positive–Negative	+0·87	3·32		

* $p < 0{\cdot}15$.
† $p < 0{\cdot}02$.
‡ $p < 0{\cdot}001$ (all p levels are two-tailed).

Table 1 also indicates that there is a very large difference between those conditions in which the confederate ended by expressing a positive feeling for the subject and those in which she ended with a negative feeling for the subject. For example, a comparison of the Positive–Positive condition with the Negative–Negative condition yields a t of 7·12, significant at far less than the 0·001 level. As predicted, the widest mean difference occurs between the Negative–Positive condition (M = +7·67) and the Positive–Negative condition (M = +0·87). This is interesting in view of the fact that the confederate made the same number of positive and negative statements in these two conditions; only the sequence was different.

It will be recalled that the subjects were asked to rate the confederate on 14 evaluative scales in order to ascertain whether or not greater liking would manifest itself in terms of higher ratings on specific attributes. No evidence for this was found; e.g. although the subjects liked the confederate better in the Negative–Positive condition than in the Positive–Positive condition, they did not find her significantly more intelligent or less conceited. In fact, the only ratings that reached an acceptable level of significance showed a reverse effect: In the Positive–Positive condition the confederate was rated more friendly ($p < 0{\cdot}01$), nicer ($p < 0{\cdot}01$), and warmer ($p < 0{\cdot}01$) than in the Negative–Positive condition. Our failure to predict this effect may be attributable to a naive belief in generalization which served to blind us to more obvious factors. Thus, although we did not predict this result, it is not startling if one considers the simple fact that in the Positive–Positive condition the confederate's evaluations of the subject, because they were entirely positive, *did* reflect greater friendliness, niceness, and warmth. That is, when forced to consider such things as friendliness, niceness, and warmth, the subjects in the Negative–Positive condition could not give the confederate a very high rating. The confederate, here, is not the kind of person who exudes niceness; by definition she is capable of saying negative things. Nevertheless, when asked for their 'gut-response' regarding how much they liked the confederate, the subjects in the Negative–Positive condition tended to give her a high rating. To speculate, we might suggest the following: When one is asked to rate a person on a particular attribute, one tends to sum the person's relevant behaviour in a rather cognitive, rational manner. On the other hand, when one is asked how much one likes a person, one tends to state a current feeling rather than to add and subtract various components of the person's past behaviour.

Degree of liking as a function of 'upset'

The major results are consistent with the hypotheses derived from the gain–loss notion. Although, in this experiment, it was not our intention to test the underlying assumptions of this notion, there are some data which may be of relevance. Recall that one of the suggested causes of the gain–loss effect is that, in the negative conditions, the subjects experienced negative feelings such as anxiety, anger, self-doubt, etc. That is, it was predicted that the subjects in the Negative–Positive condition would like the confederate better than would the subjects in the Positive–Positive condition because in the Negative–Positive condition the confederate's behaviour was reducing a negative drive state. If this assumption is correct, the effect should not occur if, for some reason, the confederate's negative behaviour did not produce a negative drive state in the subjects. For example, in the Negative–Positive condition, if the subjects did not take the negative evaluation personally there would be no negative drive state to be reduced. Similarly, in the Positive–Negative condition, loss would not be experienced if the confederate's negative behaviour, for some reason, were not taken personally by the subject. As mentioned earlier, near the end of the experiment the interviewer asked the subject if it bothered, embarrassed, or upset her to listen to herself being evaluated by the other girl. As one might expect, in the Positive–Positive condition none of the subjects were at all bothered, upset, or embarrassed by the situation. In the Negative–Positive condition, however, 11 subjects admitted to having been somewhat upset when the other girl was evaluating them negatively; similarly, nine girls in the Negative–Negative condition and nine in the Positive–Negative condition admitted that they were upset by the negative evaluation. In these latter conditions the subjects who claimed that they were not upset by the negative evaluation tended to explain this by saying that the situation was so restricted that they lacked the freedom and relaxation to 'be themselves' and 'make a good impression' on the other girl. Typically, they felt that it was reasonable for the other girl to think of them as dull and stupid – the situation *forced* them to appear dull. Thus, many of the girls refused to take a negative evaluation personally; instead, they felt that the confederate would have liked them better if the situation had been freer, allowing them to express their usual, loveable personalities.

For what it is worth, let us compare those who were upset by a negative evaluation with those who were not in terms of how much they liked the confederate. Within the Negative–Positive condition those subjects who were upset by the negative evaluation liked the confederate *more* than those who were not upset ($t = 3{\cdot}36$, $p < 0{\cdot}01$, two-tailed). Similarly, within the Positive–Negative condition those who were upset by the negative evaluation liked the confederate *less* than those who were not upset ($t = 4{\cdot}44$, $p < 0{\cdot}01$). In the Negative–Negative condition, as might be expected, there was a tendency for those who were not upset to like the confederate better than those who were upset ($t = 1{\cdot}26$, N.S.). We can also compare degree of liking across experimental conditions, eliminating those subjects who were not upset by a negative evaluation. The difference between the Negative–Positive and Positive–Positive conditions is highly significant ($t = 4{\cdot}57$, $p < 0{\cdot}005$, two-tailed). When the 'upset' subjects only are compared, the difference between the Negative–Negative and Positive–Negative conditions approaches significance ($t = 1{\cdot}91$, $p < 0{\cdot}08$, two-tailed).

These data are consistent with the affective assumption of the gain–loss notion inasmuch as they suggest that a feeling of upset is a necessary precondition for the great liking in the Negative–Positive condition and the great dislike in the Positive–Negative condition. However, since these data are based on an internal analysis, they are not unequivocal; those subjects who were upset (strictly speaking, those who admitted to being upset) by a negative evaluation may be different kinds of animals from those who did not admit to being upset. The differences in their liking for the stimulus person may be a reflection of some unknown individual differences rather than of the manipulated differences in the independent variable. For example, considering the explanations given by those subjects who were not upset, it is conceivable that these individuals may be extreme on 'ego-defensiveness'; or, conversely, those subjects who *were* upset may be extremely 'hypersensitive'. From our data it is impossible to judge whether or not such individual differences could be correlated with the dependent variable. In sum, although the results from the internal analysis are suggestive, they are equivocal because they do not represent a systematic experimental manipulation.

A neutral–positive condition

If, for the moment, one ignores the internal analysis, the possibility exists that *any* increase in the confederate's positive evaluation of the subject would have produced an increase in the subject's liking for the confederate, even if pain had not been involved. For example, suppose the confederate's initial evaluation of the subject had been neutral rather than negative, and then had become increasingly positive; would the subject like the confederate as much in this condition as in the Negative–Positive condition? If so, then, clearly, pain and suffering are not necessary factors. To test this possibility, 15 additional subjects were run in a Neutral–Positive condition. This condition is identical to the Negative–Positive condition except that during the first three meetings, instead of expressing negative evaluations of the subject, the confederate was non-committal, saying such things as 'She seems to be pretty intelligent, but perhaps just a little on the dull side. . . .' 'I'm not sure; she kind of strikes me both ways. . . .' 'I just can't make up my mind about her. My feelings are rather neutral'. The subjects were randomly assigned to this condition, although assignment did not commence until after two or three subjects had been run in each of the other four conditions. In this condition the mean liking score was 6·66. This is almost identical with the mean in the Positive–Positive condition. The difference between the Neutral–Positive and Negative–Positive conditions approaches statistical significance ($t=1{\cdot}96$, $p<0{\cdot}07$, two-tailed).

These data, coupled with the data from the internal analysis, suggest that some upset on the subject's part increased her liking for the stimulus person. However, other factors may contribute to the effect. One such contributing factor has already been discussed as the cognitive assumption underlying the gain–loss notion. Specifically, when *O* changes his evaluation of *P*, it is indicative of the fact that he (*O*) has some discernment and that his evaluation is a considered judgment. Consequently, his evaluation of *P* should have greater impact on *P* than an invariably positive or invariably negative evaluation. This would lead to greater liking in the Negative–Positive condition and less liking in the Positive–Negative condition. We made no great attempt to investigate the validity of this assumption in the present experiment. We did ask the subjects to rate the degree of discernment of the stimulus person. Here, we found a faint glimmer of support. There was some tendency for the subjects in the Negative–Positive condition to rate the stimulus person higher (M = 6·75) than did the subjects in the Positive–Positive condition (M = 5·35), but this difference was not statistically significant ($t = 1{\cdot}40$, $p < 0{\cdot}15$). There was no difference in the ratings made by the subjects in the other two conditions.

Alternative explanations

Flattery. Recent work by Jones (1964) on flattery and ingratiation suggests the possibility that a person who makes exclusively positive statements might be suspected of using flattery in order to manipulate the subject, and therefore might be liked less than someone whose evaluations include negative statements. However, this is not a compelling explanation of the results of the present experiment because the subject was led to believe that the confederate was unaware that she (the subject) was eavesdropping during the evaluation. One cannot easily attribute these ulterior motives to a person who says nice things about us in our absence.

Contrast. Another possible alternative explanation involves the phenomenon of contrast (Helson 1964). After several negative and neutral statements, a positive evaluation may seem more positive than the same statement preceded by other positive statements. Similarly, a negative evaluation following several positive and neutral statements may appear to be more negative than one that formed part of a series of uniformly negative statements. Thus, a contrast effect, if operative, could have contributed to our results. At the same time, it should be noted that in the Neutral–Positive condition, where some degree of contrast should also occur, there is little evidence of the existence of this phenomenon. Specifically, the mean liking score in the Neutral–Positive condition was almost identical to that in the Positive–Positive condition and quite different from that in the Negative–Positive condition ($p < 0{\cdot}07$). These data suggest that, although a contrast effect could conceivably have contributed to the results, it is doubtful that such an effect was strong enough, in this experimental situation, to have generated the results in and of itself.

Competence. In the Negative–Positive condition the subject has succeeded in showing the confederate that he (the subject) is not a dull clod but is, in fact, a bright and interesting person. This is no mean accomplishment and therefore might lead the subject to experience a feeling of competence or efficacy (White 1959). Thus, in this condition, part of the reason for *O*'s great attractiveness may be due to the fact that he has provided the subject with a success experience. Indeed, during the interview many subjects in this condition spontaneously mentioned that, after hearing *O* describe them as dull and stupid, they tried hard to make interesting and intelligent statements in subsequent encounters with *O*. It is reasonable to suspect that they were gratified to find that these efforts paid off by inducing a change in *O*'s evaluations. This raises an interesting theoretical question; it may be that the feeling of competence is not only a contributing factor to the 'gain' effect but may actually be a necessary condition. This possibility could be tested in future experimentation by manipulating the extent to which the subject feels that *O*'s change in evaluation is contingent upon the subject's actual behaviour.

Possible implications

One of the implications of the gain–loss notion is that 'you always hurt the one you love', i.e., once we have grown certain of the good will (rewarding behaviour) of a person (e.g., a mother, a spouse, a close friend), that person may become less potent as a source of reward than a stranger. If we are correct in our assumption that a gain in esteem is a more potent reward than the absolute level of the esteem itself, then it follows that a close friend (by definition) is operating near ceiling level and therefore cannot provide us with a gain. To put it another way, since we have learned to expect love, favours, praise, etc. from a friend, such behaviour cannot possibly represent a gain in his esteem for us. On the other hand, the constant friend and rewarder has great potential as a punisher. The closer the friend, the greater the past history of invariant esteem and reward, the more devastating is its withdrawal. Such withdrawal, by definition, constitutes a loss of esteem.

An example may help clarify this point. After 10 years of marriage, if a doting husband compliments his wife on her appearance, it may mean very little to her. She already knows that her husband thinks she's attractive. A sincere compliment from a relative stranger may be much more effective, however, since it constitutes a gain in esteem. On the other hand, if the doting husband (who used to think that his wife was attractive) were to tell his wife that he had decided that she was actually quite ugly, this would cause a great deal of pain since it represents a distinct loss of esteem.

This reasoning is consistent with previous experimental findings. Harvey (1962) found a tendency for subjects to react more positively to a stranger than a friend when they were listed as sources of a relatively positive evaluation of the subject. Moreover, subjects tended to react more negatively to a friend than a stranger when they were listed as sources of negative evaluations of the subject. Similarly, experiments with children indicate that strangers are more effective as agents of social reinforcement than parents, and that strangers are also more effective than more familiar people (Shallenberger and Zigler 1961, Stevenson and Knights 1962, Stevenson, Keen and Knights 1963). It is reasonable to assume that children are accustomed to receiving approval from parents and familiar people. Therefore, additional approval from them does not represent much of a gain. However, approval from a stranger *is* a gain and, according to the gain–loss notion, should result in a greater improvement in performance. These latter results add credence to our speculations regarding one of the underlying causes of the gain–loss effect. Specifically, children probably experience greater social anxiety in the presence of a stranger than a familiar person. Therefore, social approval from a stranger may be reducing a greater drive than social approval from a friend. As previously noted, this reasoning is identical to that of Walters and his colleagues regarding the effect of prior anxiety on subsequent performance (Walters and Ray 1960, Walters and Foote 1962).

Summary

In a laboratory experiment, coeds interacted in two-person groups over a series of brief meetings. After each meeting the subjects were allowed to eavesdrop on a conversation between the experimenter and her partner in which the latter (actually a confederate) evaluated the subject. There were four major experimental conditions: (1) the evaluations were all highly positive; (2) the evaluations were all quite negative; (3) the first few evaluations were negative but gradually became positive; (4) the first few evaluations were positive but gradually became negative.

The major results showed that the subjects liked the confederate best when her evaluations moved from negative to positive and least when her evaluations moved from positive to negative. The results were predicted and discussed in terms of a 'gain–loss' notion of interpersonal attractiveness.

References

ARONSON, E., and MILLS, J. (1959) 'The effect of severity of initiation on liking for a group', *J. abnorm. soc. Psychol.*, **59**, 177–81.

BYRNE, D. (1961) 'Interpersonal attraction and attitude similarity', *J. abnorm. soc. Psychol.*, **62**, 713–15.

BYRNE, D., and WONG, T. J. (1962) 'Racial prejudice, interpersonal attraction, and assumed dissimilarity of attitudes', *J. abnorm. soc. Psychol.*, **65**, 246–53.

GERARD, H. B., and GREENBAUM, C. W. (1962) 'Attitudes toward an agent of uncertainty reduction', *J. Pers.*, **30**, 485–95.

GEWIRTZ, J. L., and BAER, D. M. (1958) 'The effect of brief social deprivation on behaviors for a social reinforcer', *J. abnorm soc. Psychol.*, **56**, 49–56.

HARVEY, O. J. (1962) 'Personality factors in resolution of conceptual incongruities', *Sociometry*, **25**, 336–52.

HELSON, H. (1964) 'Current trends and issues in adaptation-level theory', *Amer. Psychologist*, **19**, 26–38.

HOMANS, G. (1961) *Social behavior: Its elementary forms* New York, Harcourt, Brace, and World.

JONES, E. E. (1964) *Ingratiation: A social psychological analysis* New York, Appleton, Century, Crofts.

NEWCOMB, T. M. (1961) *The acquaintance process* New York, Holt, Rinehart, and Winston.

NEWCOMB, T. M. (1956) 'The prediction of interpersonal attraction', *Amer. Psychologist*, **11**, 575–86.

SHALLENBERGER, PATRICIA, and ZIGLER, E. (1961) 'Rigidity, negative reaction tendencies and cosatiation effects in normal and feebleminded children', *J. abnorm. soc. Psychol.*, **63**, 20–26.

SPINOZA, B. (1955) *The ethics* New York, Dover Press, Prop. *44*, p. 159.

STEVENSON, H. W., KEEN, RACHEL and KNIGHTS, R. M. (1963) 'Parents and strangers as reinforcing agents for children's performance', *J. abnorm. soc. Psychol.*, **67**, 183–85.

STEVENSON, H. W. and KNIGHTS, R. M. (1962) 'Social reinforcement with normal and retarded children as a function of pretraining, sex of *E*, and sex of *S*', *Amer. J. ment. Defic.*, **66**, 866–71.

THIBAUT, J. and KELLEY, H. H. (1959) *The social psychology of groups* New York, Wiley.

WALTERS, R. H. and FOOTE, ANN (1962) 'A study of reinforcer effectiveness with children', *Merrill-Palmer quart. Behav. Develpm.*, **8**, 149–57.

WALTERS, R. H. and RAY, E. (1960) 'Anxiety, social isolation, and reinforcer effectiveness', *J. Pers.*, **28**, 258–67.

WHITE, R. W. (1959) 'Motivation reconsidered: the concept of competence', *Psychol. Rev.*, **66**, 297–334.

39 Games people play

Eric Berne

The simplest forms of social activity are procedures and rituals. Some of these are universal and some local, but all of them have to be learned. A *procedure* is a series of simple complementary transactions directed towards the manipulation of reality. . . . A *ritual* is a stereotyped series of simple complementary transactions programmed by external social forces. An informal ritual, such as social leave-taking, may be subject to considerable local variations in details, although the basic form remains the same. A formal ritual, such as a Roman Catholic Mass, offers much less option. The form of a ritual is parentally determined by tradition, but more recent influences may have similar but less stable effects in trivial instances. [. . .]

In borderline cases it is sometimes difficult to distinguish between a procedure and a ritual. The tendency is for the laymen to call professional procedures rituals, while actually every transaction may be based on sound, even vital experience, but the layman does not have the background to appreciate that. Conversely, there is a tendency for professionals to rationalize ritualistic elements that still cling to their procedures, and to dismiss sceptical laymen on the ground that they are not equipped to understand. And one of the ways in which entrenched professionals may resist the introduction of sound new procedures is by laughing them off as rituals. . . .

Individuals who are not comfortable or adept with rituals sometimes evade them by substituting procedures. They can be found, for example, among people who like to help the hostess with preparing or serving food and drink at parties.

A simple *pastime* may be defined as a series of semi-ritualistic, simple, complementary transactions arranged around a single field of material, whose primary object is to structure an interval of time. The beginning and end of the interval are typically signalled by procedures or rituals. The transactions are adaptively programmed so that each party will obtain the maximum gains or advantages during the interval. The better his adaptation, the more he will get out of it.

Pastimes are typically played at parties ('social gatherings') or during the

---

BERNE, ERIC (1968) 'Games people play' from *Games people play* Harmondsworth, Penguin, 33–34, 36–37, 38–39, 44–56.

waiting period before a formal group meeting begins; such waiting periods before a meeting 'begins' have the same structure and dynamics as 'parties'. Pastimes may take the form described as 'chit-chat' or they may become more serious, e.g., argumentative. A large cocktail party often functions as a kind of gallery for the exhibition of pastimes. In one corner of the room a few people are playing 'PTA', another corner is the forum for 'Psychiatry', a third is the theatre for 'Ever Been' or 'What Became', the fourth is engaged for 'General Motors', and the buffet is reserved for women who want to play 'Kitchen' or 'Wardrobe'. The proceedings at such a gathering may be almost identical, with a change of names here and there, with the proceedings at a dozen similar parties taking place simultaneously in the area. At another dozen in a different social stratum, a different assortment of pastimes is underway.

Pastimes may be classified in different ways. The external determinants are sociological (sex, age, marital status, cultural, racial or economic). 'General Motors' (comparing cars) and 'Who Won' (sports) are both 'Man Talk'. 'Grocery', 'Kitchen', and 'Wardrobe' are all 'Lady Talk' – or, as practised in the South Seas, 'Mary Talk'. 'Making Out' is adolescent, while the onset of middle age is marked by a shift to 'Balance Sheet'. Other species of this class, which are all variations of 'Small Talk', are: 'How To' (go about doing something), an easy filler for short airplane trips; 'How Much' (does it cost), a favourite in lower middle-class bars; 'Ever Been' (to some nostalgic place), a middle-class game for 'oldhands' such as salesmen: 'Do You Know' (so-and-so) for lonely ones; 'What Became' (of good old Joe), often played by economic successes and failures: 'Morning After' (what a hangover) and 'Martini' (I know a better way), typical of a certain kind of ambitious young person. [...]

A *game* is an ongoing series of complementary ulterior transactions progressing to a well-defined, predictable outcome. Descriptively it is a recurring set of transactions, often repetitious, superficially plausible, with a concealed motivation; or, more colloquially, a series of moves with a snare, or 'gimmick'. Games are clearly differentiated from procedures, rituals, and pastimes by two chief characteristics: (1) their ulterior quality and (2) the pay-off. Procedures may be successful, rituals effective, and pastimes profitable, but all of them are by definition candid; they may involve contest, but not conflict, and the ending may be sensational, but it is not dramatic. Every game, on the other hand, is basically dishonest, and the outcome has a dramatic, as distinct from merely exciting, quality.

It remains to distinguish games from the one remaining type of social action which so far has not been discussed. An *operation* is a simple transaction or set of transactions undertaken for a specific, stated purpose. If someone frankly asks for reassurance and gets it, that is an operation. If someone asks for reassurance, and after it is given turns it in some way to the disadvantage of the giver, that is a game. Superficially, then, a game looks like a set of operations, but after the payoff it becomes apparent that these 'operations' were really *manoeuvres*; not honest requests but moves in the game.

In the 'insurance game', for example, no matter what the agent appears to be doing in conversation, if he is a hard player he is really looking for or working on a prospect. What he is after, if he is worth his salt, is to 'make a killing'. The same applies to 'the real estate game', 'the pajama game' and similar occupations. Hence at a social gathering, while a salesman is engaged in pastimes, particularly variants of 'Balance Sheet', his congenial participation may conceal a series of skilful manoeuvres designed to elicit the kind of information he is professionally interested in. [. . .]

What we are concerned with here, however, are the unconscious games played by innocent people engaged in duplex transactions of which they are not fully aware, and which form the most important aspect of social life all over the world. Because of their dynamic qualities, games are easy to distinguish from mere static *attitudes*, which arise from taking a position.

The use of the word 'game' should not be misleading. As explained in the introduction, it does not necessarily imply fun or even enjoyment. Many salesmen do not consider their work fun, as Arthur Miller made clear in his play, *The Death of a Salesman*. And there may be no lack of seriousness. Football games nowadays are taken very seriously, but no more so than such transactional games as 'Alcoholic' or 'Third-Degree Rapo'.

The same applies to the word 'play', as anyone who has 'played' hard poker or 'played' the stock market over a long period can testify. The possible seriousness of games and play, and the possibly serious results, are well known to anthropologists. The most complex game that ever existed, that of 'Courtier' as described so well by Stendhal in *The Charterhouse of Parma*, was deadly serious. The grimmest of all, of course, is 'War'.

A typical game

The most common game played between spouses is colloquially called 'If It Weren't For You', and this will be used to illustrate the characteristics of games in general.

Mrs White complained that her husband severely restricted her social activities, so that she had never learned to dance. Due to changes in her attitude brought about by psychiatric treatment, her husband became less sure of himself and more indulgent. Mrs White was then free to enlarge the scope of her activities. She signed up for dancing classes, and then discovered to her despair that she had a morbid fear of dance floors and had to abandon this project.

This unfortunate adventure, along with similar ones, laid bare some important aspects of the structure of her marriage. Out of her many suitors she had picked a domineering man for a husband. She was then in a position to complain that she could do all sorts of things 'if it weren't for you'. Many of her women friends also had domineering husbands, and when they met for their morning coffee, they spent a good deal of time playing 'If It Weren't For Him'.

As it turned out, however, contrary to her complaints, her husband was performing a real service for her by forbidding her to do something she was deeply afraid of, and by preventing her, in fact, from even becoming aware of her fears. This was one reason [why she] had shrewdly chosen such a husband.

But there was more to it than that. His prohibitions and her complaints frequently led to quarrels, so that their sex life was seriously impaired. And because of his feelings of guilt, he frequently brought her gifts which might not otherwise have been forthcoming; certainly when he gave her more freedom, his gifts diminished in lavishness and frequency. She and her husband had little in common besides their household worries and the children, so that their quarrels stood out as important events; it was mainly on these occasions that they had anything but the most casual conversations. At any rate, her married life had proved one thing to her that she had always maintained: that all men were mean and tyrannical. As it turned out, this attitude was related to some daydreams of being sexually abused which had plagued her in earlier years.

There are various ways of describing this game in general terms. . . . At the present time the scheme given below has been found the most useful one for theoretical game analysis. No doubt it will be improved as further knowledge accumulates. The first requisite is to recognize that a certain sequence of manoeuvres meets the criteria of a game. As many samples as possible of the game are then collected. The significant features of the collection are isolated. Certain aspects emerge as essential. These are then classified under headings which are designed to be as meaningful and instructive as possible in the current state of knowledge. The analysis is undertaken from the point of view of the one who is 'it' – in this case, Mrs White.

Thesis

This is a general description of the game, including the immediate sequence of events (the social level) and information about their psychological background, evolution and significance (the psychological level). In the case of 'If It Weren't For You', Marital Type, the details already given will serve (pages 498–9). For the sake of brevity, this game will henceforth be referred to as IWFY. [...]

The antithesis to IWFY is permissiveness. As long as the husband is prohibitive, the game can proceed. If instead of saying 'Don't you dare!' he says 'Go ahead!' the underlying phobias are unmasked, and the wife can no longer turn on him, as demonstrated in Mrs White's case.

For clear understanding of a game, the antithesis should be known and its effectiveness demonstrated in practice.

Aim

This states simply the general purpose of the game. Sometimes there are alternatives. The aim of IWFY may be stated as either reassurance ('It's not that I'm afraid, it's that he won't let me') or vindication ('It's not that I'm not trying, it's that he holds me back'). The reassuring function is easier to clarify and is more in accord with the security needs of the wife; therefore IWFY is most simply regarded as having the aim of reassurance.

Roles

Games may be described as two-handed, three-handed, many-handed, etc., according to the number of roles offered. . . . IWFY is a two-handed game and calls for a restricted wife and a domineering husband. . . .

Dynamics

There are alternatives in stating the psychodynamic driving forces behind each case of a game. It is usually possible, however, to pick out a single psychodynamic concept which usefully, aptly and meaningfully epitomizes the situation. Thus IWFY is best described as deriving from phobic sources.

Examples

Since the childhood origins of a game, or its infantile prototypes, are instructive to study, it is worth-while to search for such cognates in making a formal description. It happens that IWFY is just as frequently played by little children as by grown-ups, so the childhood version is the same as the later one, with the actual parent substituted for the restricting husband.

Transactional paradigm

The transactional analysis of a typical situation is presented, giving both the social and psychological levels of a revealing ulterior transaction. In its most dramatic form IWFY at the social level is a Parent–Child game.

Mr White: 'You stay home and take care of the house.'

Mrs White: 'If it weren't for you, I could be out having fun.'

At the psychological level (the ulterior marriage contract) the relationship is Child–Child, and quite different.

Mr White: 'You must always be here when I get home. I'm terrified of desertion.'

Mrs White: 'I will be if you help me avoid phobic situations.'

Moves

The moves of a game correspond roughly to the strokes in a ritual. As in any game, the players become increasingly adept with practice. Wasteful moves are eliminated, and more and more purpose is condensed into each move. 'Beautiful friendships' are often based on the fact that the players complement each other with great economy and satisfaction, so that there is a maximum yield with a minimum effort from the games they play with each other. Certain intermediate, precautionary or concessional moves can be elided, giving a high degree of elegance to the relationship. The effort saved on defensive manoeuvres can be devoted to ornamental flourishes instead, to the delight of both parties and sometimes of the onlookers as well. The student observes that there is a minimum number of moves essential to the progress of the game, and these can be stated in the protocol. Individual players will embellish or multiply these basic moves according to their needs, talents or desires. The framework for IWFY is as follows.

(1) Instruction–Compliance ('You can stay home' – 'All right').

(2) Instruction–Protest ('You stay home again' – 'If it weren't for you').

Advantages

The general advantages of a game consist in its stabilizing (homeostatic) functions. . . . Hence the biological gain from IWFY is derived from belligerence–petulance exchanges: a distressing but apparently effective way to maintain the health of nervous tissues.

Confirmation of the wife's position – 'All men are tyrants' – is the *existential advantage*. This position is a reaction to the need to surrender that is inherent in the phobias, a demonstration of the coherent structure which underlies all games. The expanded statement would be: 'If I went out alone in a crowd, I would be overcome by the temptation to surrender; at home I don't surrender: he forces me, which proves that all men are tyrants.' Hence this game is commonly played by women who suffer from feelings of unreality, which signifies their difficulty in keeping the Adult in charge in situations of strong temptation. The detailed elucidation of these mechanisms belongs to psychoanalysis rather than game analysis. In game analysis the end product is the chief concern.

Internal psychological advantage of a game is its direct effect on the psychic economy (libido). In IWFY the socially acceptable surrender to the husband's authority keeps the woman from experiencing neurotic fears. At the same time it satisfies masochistic needs, if they exist, using masochism not in the sense of self-abnegation but with its classical meaning of sexual excitement in situations of deprivation, humiliation or pain. That is, it excites her to be deprived and dominated.

External psychological advantage is the avoidance of the feared situation by playing the game. This is especially obvious in IWFY, where it is the outstanding motivation: by complying with the husband's strictures, the wife avoids the public situations which she fears.

Internal social advantage is designated by the name of the game as it is played in the individual's intimate circle. By her compliance, the wife gains the privilege of saying 'If it weren't for you'. This helps to structure the time she must spend with her husband; in the case of Mrs White, this need for structure was especially strong because of the lack of other common interests, especially before the arrival of their offspring and after the children were grown. In between, the game was played less intensively and less frequently, because the children performed their usual function of structuring time for their parents, and also provided an even more widely accepted version of IWFY, the busy-housewife variation. The fact that young mothers in America often really are very busy does not change the analysis of this variation. Game analysis only attempts to answer this question without prejudice: given that a young woman is busy, how does she go about exploiting her busyness in order to get some compensation for it?

External social advantage is designated by the use made of the situation in outside social contacts. In the case of the game 'If It Weren't For You', which is what the wife says to her husband, there is a transformation into the pastime 'If It Weren't For Him' when she meets with her friends over morning coffee. Again, the influence of games in the selection of social companions is shown. The new neighbour who is invited for morning coffee is being invited to play 'If It Weren't For Him'. If she plays, well and good, she will soon be a bosom friend of the old-timers, other things being equal. If she refuses to play and insists on taking a charitable view of her husband, she will not last long. Her situation will be the same as if she kept refusing to drink at cocktail parties – in most circles, she would gradually be dropped from the guest lists. [...]

The genesis of games

From the present point of view, child rearing may be regarded as an educational process in which the child is taught what games to play and how to play them. He is also taught procedures, rituals and pastimes appropriate to his position in the local social situation, but these are less significant. His knowledge of and skill in procedures, rituals and pastimes determine what opportunities will be available to him, other things being equal; but his games determine the use he will make of those opportunities, and the outcomes of situations for which he is eligible. As elements of his script, or unconscious life-plan, his favoured games also determine his ultimate destiny (again with other things being equal): the payoffs on his marriage and career, and the circumstances surrounding his death.

While conscientious parents devote a great deal of attention to teaching their children procedures, rituals and pastimes appropriate to their stations in life, and with equal care select schools, colleges and churches where their teachings will be reinforced, they tend to overlook the question of games, which form the basic structure for the emotional dynamics of each family, and which the children learn through significant experiences in everyday living from their earliest months. Related questions have been discussed for thousands of years in a rather general, unsystematic fashion, and there has been some attempt at a more methodical approach in the modern orthopsychiatric literature; but without the concept of games there is little possibility of a consistent investigation. Theories of internal individual psychodynamics have so far not been able to solve satisfactorily the problems of human relationships. These are transactional situations which call for a theory of social dynamics that cannot be derived solely from consideration of individual motivations.

Since there are as yet few well-trained specialists in child psychology and child psychiatry who are also trained in game analysis, observations on the genesis of games are sparse. Fortunately, the following episode took place in the presence of a well-educated transactional analyst.

Tanjy, age seven, got a stomach-ache at the dinner table and asked to be excused for that reason. His parents suggested that he lie down for a while. His little brother Mike, age three, then said, 'I have a stomach-ache too,' evidently angling for the same consideration. The father looked at him for a few seconds and then replied, 'You don't want to play that game, do you?' Whereupon Mike burst out laughing and said, 'No!'

If this had been a household of food or bowel faddists, Mike would also have been packed off to bed by his alarmed parents. If he and they had repeated this performance several times, it might be anticipated that this game would have become part of Mike's character, as it so often does if the parents cooperate. Whenever he was jealous of a privilege granted to a competitor, he would plead illness in order to get some privileges himself. The ulterior transaction would then consist of: (social level) 'I don't feel well' + (psychological level) 'You must grant me a privilege, too.' Mike, however, was saved from such a hypochondriacal career. Perhaps he will end up with a worse fate, but that is not the issue. The issue is that a game *in statu nascendi* was broken up right there by the father's question and by the boy's frank acknowledgement that what he proposed was a game.

This demonstrates clearly enough that games are quite deliberately initiated by young children. After they become fixed patterns of stimulus and response, their origins become lost in the mists of time and their ulterior nature becomes obscured by social fogs. Both can be brought into awareness only by appropriate procedures: the origin by some form of analytic therapy and the ulterior aspect by antithesis. Repeated clinical experience along these lines makes it clear that games are imitative in nature, and that they are initially set up by the Adult (neopsychic) aspect of the child's personality. If the Child ego state can be revived in the grown-up player, the psychological aptitude of this segment (the Adult aspect of the Child ego state) is so striking, and its skill in manipulating people so enviable, that it is colloquially called 'The Professor' (of Psychiatry). Hence in psychotherapy groups which concentrate on game analysis, one of the more sophisticated procedures is the search for the little 'Professor' in each patient, whose early adventures in setting up games between the ages of two and eight are listened to by everyone present with fascination and often, unless the games are tragic, with enjoyment and even hilarity, in which the patient himself may join with justifiable self-appreciation and smugness. Once he is able to do that, he is well on his way to relinquishing what may be an unfortunate behaviour pattern which he is much better off without.

Those are the reasons why in the formal description of a game an attempt is always made to describe the infantile or childhood prototype.

The function of games

Because there is so little opportunity for intimacy in daily life, and because some forms of intimacy (especially if intense) are psychologically impossible for most people, the bulk of the time in serious social life is taken up with playing games. Hence games are both necessary and desirable, and the only problem at issue is whether the games played by an individual offer the best yield for him. In this connexion it should be remembered that the essential feature of a game is its culmination, or payoff. The principal function of the preliminary moves is to set up the situation for this payoff, but they are always designed to harvest the maximum permissible satisfaction at each step as a secondary product. Thus in 'Schlemiel' (making messes and then apologizing) the payoff, and the purpose of the game, is to obtain the forgiveness which is forced by the apology; the spillings and cigarette burns are only steps leading up to this, but each such trespass yields its own pleasure. The enjoyment derived from the spilling does not make spilling a game. The apology is the critical stimulus that leads to the denouement. Otherwise the spilling would simply be a destructive procedure, a delinquency perhaps enjoyable. [...]

Beyond their social function in structuring time satisfactorily, some games are urgently necessary for the maintenance of health in certain individuals. These people's psychic stability is so precarious, and their positions are so tenuously maintained, that to deprive them of their games may plunge them into irreversible despair and even psychosis. Such people will fight very hard against any antithetical moves. This is often observed in marital situations when the psychiatric improvement of one spouse (i.e. the abandonment of destructive games) leads to rapid deterioration in the other spouse, to whom the games were of paramount importance in maintaining equilibrium. Hence it is necessary to exercise prudence in game analysis.

Fortunately, the rewards of game-free intimacy, which is or should be the most perfect form of human living, are so great that even precariously balanced personalities can safely and joyfully relinquish their games if an appropriate partner can be found for the better relationship.

On a larger scale, games are integral and dynamic components of the unconscious life-plan, or script, of each individual; they serve to fill in the time while he waits for the final fulfilment, simultaneously advancing the action. [...]

40 The theory of love

Erich Fromm

Any theory of love must begin with a theory of man, of human existence. While we find love, or rather, the equivalent of love, in animals, their attachments are mainly a part of their instinctual equipment; only remnants of this instinctual equipment can be seen operating in man. What is essential in the existence of man is the fact that he has emerged from the animal kingdom, from instinctive adaptation, that he has transcended nature – although he never leaves it he is a part of it – and yet once torn away from nature, he cannot return to it; once thrown out of paradise – a state of original oneness with nature – cherubim with flaming swords block his way, if he should try to return. Man can only go forward by developing his reason, by finding a new harmony, a human one, instead of the prehuman harmony which is irretrievably lost.

When man is born, the human race as well as the individual, he is thrown out of a situation which was definite, as definite as the instincts, into a situation which is indefinite, uncertain and open. There is certainty only about the past – and about the future only as far as that it is death.

Man is gifted with reason; he is *life being aware of itself*; he has awareness of himself, of his fellow man, of his past, and of the possibilities of his future. This awareness of himself as a separate entity, the awareness of his own short life span, of the fact that without his will he is born and against his will he dies, that he will die before those whom he loves, or they before him, the awareness of his aloneness and separateness, of his helplessness before the forces of nature and of society, all this makes his separate, disunited existence an unbearable prison. He would become insane could he not liberate himself from this prison and reach out, unite himself in some form or other with men, with the world outside.

The experience of separateness arouses anxiety; it is, indeed, the source of all anxiety. Being separate means being cut off, without any capacity to use my human powers. Hence to be separate means to be helpless, unable to grasp the world – things and people – actively; it means that the world can invade me without my ability to react. Thus, separateness is the source of intense anxiety. Beyond that, it arouses shame and the feeling of guilt. . . .

The deepest need of man, then, is the need to overcome his separateness,

FROMM, ERICH (1962) 'The theory of love' in *The Art of Loving* London, Unwin, 13–21.

to leave the prison of his aloneness. The *absolute* failure to achieve this aim means insanity, because the panic of complete isolation can be overcome only by such a radical withdrawal from the world outside that the feeling of separation disappears – because the world outside, from which one is separated, has disappeared.

Man – of all ages and cultures – is confronted with the solution of one and the same question: the question of how to overcome separateness, how to achieve union, how to transcend one's own individual life and find at-one-ment. The question is the same for primitive man living in caves, for nomadic man taking care of his flocks, for the peasant in Egypt, the Phoenician trader, the Roman soldier, the medieval monk, the Japanese samurai, the modern clerk and factory hand. The question is the same, for it springs from the same ground: the human situation, the conditions of human existence. The answer varies. The question can be answered by animal worship, by human sacrifice or military conquest, by indulgence in luxury, by ascetic renunciation, by obsessional work, by artistic creation, by the love of God, and by the love of Man. While there are many answers – the record of which is human history – they are nevertheless not innumerable. On the contrary, as soon as one ignores smaller differences which belong more to the periphery than to the centre, one discovers that there is only a limited number of answers which have been given, and only could have been given by man in the various cultures in which he has lived. The history of religion and philosophy is the history of these answers, of their diversity, as well as of their limitation in number.

The answers depend, to some extent, on the degree of individuation which an individual has reached. In the infant I-ness has developed but little yet; he still feels one with mother, has no feeling of separateness as long as mother is present. His sense of aloneness is cured by the physical presence of the mother, her breasts, her skin. Only to the degree that the child develops his sense of separateness and individuality is the physical presence of the mother not sufficient any more, and does the need to overcome separateness in other ways arise.

Similarly, the human race in its infancy still feels one with nature. The soil, the animals, the plants are still man's world. He identifies himself with animals, and this is expressed by the wearing of animal masks, by the worshipping of a totem animal or animal gods. But the more the human race emerges from these primary bonds, the more it separates itself from the natural world, the more intense becomes the need to find new ways of escaping separateness.

One way of achieving this aim lies in all kinds of *orgiastic states*. These may have the form of an auto-induced trance, sometimes with the help of drugs. Many rituals of primitive tribes offer a vivid picture of this type of solution. In a transitory state of exaltation the world outside disappears, and with it the feeling of separateness from it. Inasmuch as these rituals are practised in common, an experience of fusion with the group is added which makes this solution all the more effective. Closely related to, and often blended with this orgiastic solution, is the sexual experience. The sexual orgasm can produce a state similar to the one produced by a trance, or to the effects of certain drugs. Rites of communal sexual orgies were a part of many primitive rituals. It seems that after the orgiastic experience, man can go on for a time without suffering too much from his separateness. Slowly the tension of anxiety mounts, and then is reduced again by the repeated performance of the ritual.

As long as these orgiastic states are a matter of common practice in a tribe, they do not produce anxiety or guilt. To act in this way is right, and even virtuous, because it is a way shared by all, approved and demanded by the medicine men or priests; hence there is no reason to feel guilty or ashamed. It is quite different when the same solution is chosen by an individual in a culture which has left behind these common practices. Alcoholism and drug addiction are the forms which the individual chooses in a non-orgiastic culture. In contrast to those participating in the socially patterned solution, such individuals suffer from guilt feelings and remorse. While they try to escape from separateness by taking refuge in alcohol or drugs, they feel all the more separate after the orgiastic experience is over, and thus are driven to take recourse to it with increasing frequency and intensity. Slightly different from this is the recourse to a sexual orgiastic solution. To some extent it is a natural and normal form of overcoming separateness, and a partial answer to the problem of isolation. But in many individuals in whom separateness is not relieved in other ways, the search for the sexual orgasm assumes a function which makes it not very different from alcoholism and drug addiction. It becomes a desperate attempt to escape the anxiety engendered by separateness, and it results in an ever-increasing sense of separateness, since the sexual act without love never bridges the gap between two human beings, except momentarily.

All forms of orgiastic union have three characteristics: they are intense, even violent; they occur in the total personality, mind *and* body; they are transitory and periodical. Exactly the opposite holds true for that form of union which is by far the most frequent solution chosen by man in the past and in the present: the union based on *conformity* with the group, its customs, practices and beliefs. Here again we find a considerable development.

In a primitive society the group is small; it consists of those with whom one shares blood and soil. With the growing development of culture, the group enlarges; it becomes the citizenry of a *polis*, the citizenry of a large state, the members of a church. Even the poor Roman felt pride because he could say '*civis romanus sum*'; Rome and the Empire were his family, his home, his world. Also in contemporary Western society the union with the group is the prevalent way of overcoming separateness. It is a union in which the individual self disappears to a large extent, and where the aim is to belong to the herd. If I am like everybody else, if I have no feelings or thoughts which make me different, if I conform in custom, dress, ideas, to the pattern of the group, I am saved; saved from the frightening experience of aloneness. The dictatorial systems use threats and terror to induce this conformity; the democratic countries, suggestion and propaganda. There is, indeed, one great difference between the two systems. In the democracies non-conformity is possible and, in fact, by no means entirely absent; in the totalitarian systems, only a few unusual heroes and martyrs can be expected to refuse obedience. But in spite of this difference the democratic societies show an overwhelming degree of conformity. The reason lies in the fact that there *has* to be an answer to the quest for union, and if there is no other or better way, then the union of herd conformity becomes the predominant one. One can only understand the power of the fear to be different, the fear to be only a few steps away from the herd, if one understands the depths of the need not to be separated. Sometimes this fear of non-conformity is rationalized as fear of practical dangers which could threaten the non-conformist. But actually, people *want* to conform to a much higher degree than they are *forced* to conform, at least in the Western democracies.

Most people are not even aware of their need to conform. They live under the illusion that they follow their own ideas and inclinations, that they are individualists, that they have arrived at their opinions as the result of their own thinking – and that it just happens that their ideas are the same as those of the majority. The consensus of all serves as a proof for the correctness of 'their' ideas. Since there is still a need to feel some individuality, such need is satisfied with regard to minor differences; the initials on the handbag or the sweater, the name plate of the bank teller, the belonging to the Democratic as against the Republican party, to the Elks instead of to the Shriners become the expression of individual differences. The advertising slogan of 'it is different' shows up this pathetic need for difference, when in reality there is hardly any left. [. . .]

Union by conformity is not intense and violent; it is calm, dictated by routine, and for this very reason often is insufficient to pacify the anxiety of separateness. The incidence of alcoholism, drug addiction, compulsive sexualism, and suicide in contemporary Western society are symptoms of this relative failure of herd conformity. Furthermore, this solution concerns mainly the mind and not the body, and for this reason too is lacking in comparison with the orgiastic solutions. Herd conformity has only one advantage: it is permanent, and not spasmodic. The individual is introduced into the conformity pattern at the age of three or four, and subsequently never loses his contact with the herd. Even his funeral, which he anticipates as his last great social affair, is in strict conformance with the pattern.

In addition to conformity as a way to relieve the anxiety springing from separateness, another factor of contemporary life must be considered: the role of the work routine and of the pleasure routine. Man becomes a 'nine to fiver', he is part of the labour force, or the bureaucratic force of clerks and managers. He has little initiative, his tasks are prescribed by the organization of the work; there is even little difference between those high up on the ladder and those on the bottom. They all perform tasks prescribed by the whole structure of the organization, at a prescribed speed, and in a prescribed manner. Even the feelings are prescribed: cheerfulness, tolerance, reliability, ambition, and an ability to get along with everybody without friction. Fun is routinized in similar, although not quite as drastic ways. Books are selected by the book clubs, movies by the film and theatre owners and the advertising slogans paid for by them; the rest is also uniform: the Sunday ride in the car, the television session, the card game, the social parties. From birth to death, from Monday to Monday, from morning to evening – all activities are routinized, and prefabricated. How should a man caught in this net of routine not forget that he is a man, a unique individual, one who is given only this one chance of living, with hopes and disappointments, with sorrow and fear, with the longing for love and the dread of the nothing and of separateness?

A third way of attaining union lies in *creative activity,* be it that of the artist, or of the artisan. In any kind of creative work the creating person unites himself with his material, which represents the world outside of himself. Whether a carpenter makes a table, or a goldsmith a piece of jewellery, whether the peasant grows his corn or the painter paints a picture, in all types of creative work the worker and his object become one, man unites himself with the world in the process of creation. This, however, holds true only for productive work, for work in which *I* plan, produce, see the result of my work. In the modern work process of a clerk, the worker on the endless belt, little is left of this uniting quality of work. The worker becomes an appendix to the machine or to the bureaucratic organization. He has ceased to be he – hence no union takes place beyond that of conformity.

The unity achieved in productive work is not interpersonal; the unity achieved in orgiastic fusion is transitory; the unity achieved by conformity is only pseudo-unity. Hence, they are only partial answers to the problem of existence. The full answer lies in the achievement of interpersonal union, of fusion with another person, in *love*.

This desire for interpersonal fusion is the most powerful striving in man. It is the most fundamental passion, it is the force which keeps the human race together, the clan, the family, society. The failure to achieve it means insanity or destruction – self-destruction or destruction of others. Without love, humanity could not exist for a day. Yet, if we call the achievement of interpersonal union 'love', we find ourselves in a serious difficulty. Fusion can be achieved in different ways – and the differences are not less significant than what is common to the various forms of love. Should they all be called love? Or should we reserve the word 'love' only for a specific kind of union, one which has been the ideal virtue in all great humanistic religions and philosophical systems of the last four thousand years of Western and Eastern history?

As with all semantic difficulties, the answer can only be arbitrary. What matters is that we know what kind of union we are talking about when we speak of love. Do we refer to love as the mature answer to the problem of existence, or do we speak of those immature forms of love which may be called *symbiotic union*? In the following pages I shall call love only the former. I shall begin the discussion of 'love' with the latter.

Symbiotic union has its biological pattern in the relationship between the pregnant mother and the foetus. They are two, and yet one. They live 'together', (*sym-biosis*), they need each other. The foetus is a part of the mother, it receives everything it needs from her; mother is its world, as it were; she feeds it, she protects it, but also her own life is enhanced by it. In the *psychic* symbiotic union, the two bodies are independent, but the same kind of attachment exists psychologically.

The *passive* form of the symbiotic union is that of submission, or if we use a clinical term, of *masochism*. The masochistic person escapes from the unbearable feeling of isolation and separateness by making himself part and parcel of another person who directs him, guides him, protects him; who is his life and his oxygen, as it were. The power of the one to whom one submits is inflated, may he be a person or a god; he is everything, I am nothing, except inasmuch as I am part of him. As a part, I am part of greatness, of power, of certainty. The masochistic person does not have to make decisions, does not have to take any risks; he is never alone – but he is not independent; he has no integrity; he is not yet fully born. In a religious context the object of worship is called an idol; in a secular context of a masochistic love relationship the essential mechanism, that of idolatry, is the same. The masochistic relationship can be blended with physical, sexual desire; in this case it is not only a submission in which one's mind participates, but also one's whole body. There can be masochistic submission to fate, to sickness, to rhythmic music, to the orgiastic state produced by drugs or under hypnotic trance – in all these instances the person renounces his integrity, makes himself the instrument of somebody or something outside of himself; he need not solve the problem of living by productive activity.

The *active* form of symbiotic fusion is domination or, to use the psychological term corresponding to masochism, *sadism*. The sadistic person wants to escape from his aloneness and his sense of imprisonment by making another person part and parcel of himself. He inflates and enhances himself by incorporating another person, who worships him.

The sadistic person is as dependent on the submissive person as the latter is on the former; neither can live without the other. The difference is only that the sadistic person commands, exploits, hurts, humiliates, and that the masochistic person is commanded, exploited, hurt, humiliated. This is a considerable difference in a realistic sense; in a deeper emotional sense, the difference is not so great as that which they both have in common: fusion without integrity. If one understands this, it is also not surprising to find that usually a person reacts in both the sadistic and the masochistic manner, usually towards different objects. Hitler reacted primarily in a sadistic fashion towards people, but masochistically towards fate, history, the 'higher power' of nature. His end – suicide among general destruction – is as characteristic as was his dream of success – total domination.

In contrast to symbiotic union, mature *love* is *union under the condition of preserving one's integrity*, one's individuality. *Love is an active power in man*; a power which breaks through the walls which separate man from his fellow men, which unites him with others; love makes him overcome the sense of isolation and separateness, yet it permits him to be himself, to retain his integrity. In love the paradox occurs that two beings become one and yet remain two. [...]

In the most general way, the active character of love can be described by stating that love is primarily *giving*, not receiving. . . . The most important sphere of giving is not that of material things, but lies in the specifically human realm. What does one person give to another? He gives of himself, of the most precious he has, he gives of his life. This does not necessarily mean that he sacrifices his life for the other – but that he gives him of that which is alive in him; he gives him of his joy, of his interest, of his understanding, of his knowledge, of his humour, of his sadness – of all expressions and manifestations of that which is alive in him. In thus giving of his life, he enriches the other person, he enhances the other's sense of aliveness by enhancing his own sense of aliveness. He does not give in order to receive; giving is in itself exquisite joy. But in giving he cannot help bringing something to life in the other person, and this which is brought to life reflects back to him; in truly giving, he cannot help receiving that which is given back to him. Giving implies to make the other person a giver also and they both share in the joy of what they have brought to life. In the act of giving something is born, and both persons involved are grateful for the life that is born for both of them. Specifically with regard to love this means: love is a power which produces love; impotence is the inability to produce love. This thought has been beautifully expressed by Marx: 'Assume,' he says, '*man* as *man*, and his relation to the world as a human one, and you can exchange love only for love, confidence for confidence, etc. If you wish to enjoy art, you must be an artistically trained person; if you wish to have influence on other people, you must be a person who has a really stimulating and furthering influence on other people. Every one of your relationships to man and to nature must be a definite expression of your *real*, *individual* life corresponding to the object of your will. If you love without calling forth love, that is, if your love as such does not produce love, if by means of an *expression of life* as a loving person you do not make of yourself a *loved person*, then your love is impotent, a misfortune.'[1] But not only in love does giving mean receiving. The teacher is taught by his students, the actor is stimulated by his audience, the psychoanalyst is cured by his patient – provided they do not treat each other as objects, but are related to each other genuinely and productively.

It is hardly necessary to stress the fact that the ability to love as an act of giving depends on the character development of the person. It presupposes the attainment of a predominantly productive orientation; in this orientation the person has overcome dependency, narcissistic omnipotence, the wish to exploit others, or to hoard, and has acquired faith in his own human powers, courage to rely on his powers in the attainment of his goals. To the degree that these qualities are lacking, he is afraid of giving himself – hence of loving.

Beyond the element of giving, the active character of love becomes evident in the fact that it always implies certain basic elements, common to all forms of love. These are *care*, *responsibility*, *respect* and *knowledge*.

That love implies *care* is most evident in a mother's love for her child.

1 'Nationalökonomie und Philosophie', 1844, published in Karl Marx' *Die Frühschriften*, Alfred Kröner Verlag, Stuttgart, 1953, pp. 300, 301. (My translation, E. F.)

No assurance of her love would strike us as sincere if we saw her lacking in care for the infant, if she neglected to feed it, to bathe it, to give it physical comfort; and we are impressed by her love if we see her caring for the child. It is not different even with the love for animals or flowers. If a woman told us that she loved flowers, and we saw that she forgot to water them, we would not believe in her 'love' for flowers. *Love is the active concern for the life and the growth of that which we love.* Where this active concern is lacking, there is no love....

Care and concern imply another aspect of love; that of *responsibility*. Today responsibility is often meant to denote duty, something imposed upon one from the outside. But responsibility, in its true sense, is an entirely voluntary act; it is my response to the needs, expressed or unexpressed, of another human being. To be 'responsible' means to be able and ready to 'respond'. . . . Cain could ask: 'Am I my brother's keeper?' The loving person responds. The life of his brother is not his brother's business alone, but his own. He feels responsible for his fellow men, as he feels responsible for himself. This responsibility, in the case of the mother and her infant, refers mainly to the care for physical needs. In the love between adults it refers mainly to the psychic needs of the other person.

Responsibility could easily deteriorate into domination and possessiveness, were it not for a third component of love, *respect*. Respect is not fear and awe; it denotes, in accordance with the root of the word (*respicere*, to look at), the ability to see a person as he is, to be aware of his unique individuality. Respect means the concern that the other person should grow and unfold as he is. Respect, thus, implies the absence of exploitation. I want the loved person to grow and unfold for his own sake, and in his own ways, and not for the purpose of serving me. If I love the other person, I feel one with him or her, but with him *as he is*, not as I need him to be as an object for my use. It is clear that respect is possible only if *I* have achieved independence; if I can can stand and walk without needing crutches, without having to dominate and exploit anyone else. Respect exists only on the basis of freedom: 'l'amour est l'enfant de la liberté' as an old French song says; love is the child of freedom, never that of domination.

To respect a person is not possible without *knowing* him; care and responsibility would be blind if they were not guided by knowledge. Knowledge would be empty if it were not motivated by concern. There are many layers of knowledge; the knowledge which is an aspect of love is one which does not stay at the periphery, but penetrates to the core. It is possible only when I can transcend the concern for myself and see the other person in his own terms. I may know, for instance, that a person is angry, even if he does not show it overtly; but I may know him more deeply than that; then I know that he is anxious, and worried; that he feels lonely, that he feels guilty. Then I know that his anger is only the manifestation of something deeper, and I see him as anxious and embarrassed, that is, as the suffering person, rather than as the angry one.

Knowledge has one more, and a more fundamental, relation to the problem of love. The basic need to fuse with another person so as to transcend the prison of one's separateness is closely related to another specifically human desire, that to know the 'secret of man'. While life in its merely biological aspects is a miracle and a secret, man in his human aspects is an unfathomable secret to himself – and to his fellow man. We know ourselves, and yet even with all the efforts we may make, we do not know ourselves. We know our fellow man, and yet we do not know him, because we are not a thing, and our fellow man is not a thing. The further we reach into the depth of our being, or someone else's being, the more the goal of knowledge eludes us. Yet we cannot help desiring to penetrate into the secret of man's soul, into the innermost nucleus which is 'he'.

There is one way, a desperate one, to know the secret: it is that of complete power over another person; the power which makes him do what we want, feel what we want, think what we want; which transforms him into a thing, our thing, our possession. The ultimate degree of this attempt to know lies in the extremes of sadism, the desire and ability to make a human being suffer; to torture him, to force him to betray his secret in his suffering. In this craving for penetrating man's secret, his and hence our own, lies an essential motivation for the depth and intensity of cruelty and destructiveness. In a very succinct way this idea has been expressed by Isaac Babel. He quotes a fellow officer in the Russian civil war, who has just stamped his former master to death, as saying: 'With shooting – I'll put it this way – with shooting you only get rid of a chap. . . . With shooting you'll never get at the soul, to where it is in a fellow and how it shows itself. But I don't spare myself, and I've more than once trampled an enemy for over an hour. You see, I want to get to know what life really is, what life's like down our way.'[2]

In children we often see this path to knowledge quite overtly. The child takes something apart, breaks it up in order to know it; or it takes an animal apart; cruelly tears off the wings of a butterfly in order to know it, to force its secret. The cruelty itself is motivated by something deeper: the wish to know the secret of things and of life.

The other path to knowing 'the secret' is love. Love is active penetration of the other person, in which my desire to know is stilled by union. In the

2 I. Babel, *The Collected Stories*, Criterion Books, New York, 1955.

act of fusion I know you, I know myself, I know everybody – and I 'know' nothing. I know in the only way knowledge of that which is alive is possible for man – by experience of union – not by any knowledge our thought can give. Sadism is motivated by the wish to know the secret, yet I remain as ignorant as I was before. I have torn the other being apart limb from limb, yet all I have done is to destroy him. Love is the only way of knowledge, which in the act of union answers my quest. In the act of loving, of giving myself, in the act of penetrating the other person, I find myself, I discover myself, I discover us both, I discover man. [. . .]

Section 13
Group dynamics and group experience

Introduction

Small face-to-face groups are a ubiquitous feature of our lives: families, leisure groups, committees, teams, etc. We join some groups voluntarily, but often find ourselves in others contrary to our inclinations or better judgment. In presenting material related to the study of human groups there are essentially two tactics: one could be called the 'traditional' approach in which specific processes are abstracted from group experience in general and studied in relative isolation, for example, power, group-structure, leadership or norms. The other tactic, and the one adopted here, is to look at specific groups and see what processes seem to be operating in them.

The groups here chosen for comparison are a therapeutic group brought together and led by a psychoanalyst (W. R. Bion), a delinquent gang (Lewis Yablonsky) and juries (A. P. Sealy). Membership of these groups varies widely and so do ways of joining or escaping them. They have different norms, rules and structures and their members adopt different roles on joining them. The object of including these three examples is not only to illustrate the diversity of group experience but also to demonstrate different approaches to studying groups. These range from participant observation by a member (leader) of a group in therapy, the observations of a delinquent gang in the real life situation and the experimental simulations of decision-taking by juries.

The therapeutic group is characterized by having a voluntary membership, indeed people often make considerable sacrifices of time, money and convenience to join. They do so with a very specific objective and yet, as Bion shows in our first extract, the mere fact of being a group of people produces dynamics of behaviour and feeling that can effectively negate the group's activities. The dynamics are seen as pervasive and powerful influences on group behaviour and, hence, on its effectiveness as a therapeutic agent.

In our second paper, Yablonsky in his study of the gang analyses three influences on group behaviour: the social structure of the neighbourhood, the personalities of the members of the group and of its leader and the structure of the group. Determinants within the group as well as in the wider social context are seen as necessary to explain its violent behaviour. Situational and personal variables are therefore closely meshed. This may be contrasted with some of the findings of our third paper. Here, Sealy in his study of decision-taking by groups of jurors, demonstrates the preponderant impact of situational factors at the expense of personal ones. Jurors could be said to adopt a role appropriate to the situation and, on analysis, personality characteristics were not found to influence decisions to any great extent. The scientific study of juries is perhaps particularly fascinating. Despite many controversies, the jury, as a means of making certain types of judicial decisions, has survived for many centuries. Until recently, its decision could result in a defendant's execution; today, the freedom of the accused may hinge on the verdict of these twelve people. The ways in which jurors reach their decision, the factors that influence them, the role of their own personal experiences and opinions, are not directly ascertainable as the jury's deliberations are secret. However, as Sealy shows in his paper (which was specially written for this volume) the jury can be studied experimentally, using simulated trials. This study, then, in addition to the interest of the actual findings, is also particularly rewarding from a methodological point of view. It illustrates how a complex phenomenon of everyday life can be taken into the social psychologist's laboratory and systematically studied under controlled conditions whilst yet retaining some of the flavour of the real situation.

We have focused in this section on three group situations among the many that make up our social life. How typical of group behaviour in general are these three groups? How do they work? Can general statements be made about 'group processes' or can statements be made only about how certain types of groups tend to behave in certain types of situations? The papers in this section are presented, not to provide answers, but to stimulate questions.

41 Experiences in groups

W. R. Bion

. . . Let us first consider a few group situations.

As we sit round in a rough circle, the room softly lit by a single standard lamp, a woman patient in the group complains angrily:

> You [that is, the group] always say I am monopolizing, but if I don't talk you just sit there like dumb things. I'm fed up with the whole damn lot of you. And you [pointing to a man of twenty-six who raises his eyebrows in a smoothly efficient affectation of surprise] are the worst of the lot. Why do you always sit there like a good little boy – never saying anything, but upsetting the group? Dr Bion is the only one who is ever listened to here, and he never says anything helpful. All right, then, I'll shut up. Let's see what you do about it if I don't monopolize.

Now another one: the room is the same, but it is a sunlit evening in summer; a man is speaking:

> This is what I complain about here. I asked a perfectly simple question. I said what I thought was happening because I don't agree with Dr Bion. I said it would be interesting to know what other people thought, but do any of you reply? Not a bloody one. And you women are the worst of the lot – except Miss X. How can we get anywhere at all if people won't answer you? You smile when I say except Miss X, and I know what you're thinking, but you're wrong.

Here is another: a woman patient says:

> Everyone seems to agree absolutely with what Dr Bion has just said, but I said the same thing five minutes ago, and because it was only me no one took the slightest notice.

And yet another; a woman says:

> Well, since nobody else is saying anything, I may as well mention my dream. I dreamed that I was on the seashore, and I was going to bathe. There were a lot of seagulls about . . . There was a good deal more like that.
> *A member of the group:* Do you mean that that is all you can remember?
> *Woman:* Oh, no, no. But it's all really rather silly.

The group sits about glumly, and each individual seems to become rapt

---

BION, W. R. (1961) 'Experiences in groups' in *Experiences in Groups* London, Tavistock, 41–58.

in his thoughts. All contact between members of the group appears to have broken.

> *Myself:* What made you stop talking about your dream?
> *Woman:* Well, nobody seemed very interested, and I only said it to start the ball rolling.

I will draw attention only to one aspect of these episodes. The first woman patient said: 'You [the group] always say I am monopolizing'. . . . In actual fact, only one person had said this, and that on only one occasion, but her reference was to the whole group, and clearly indicated that she thought the whole group always felt this about her. The man in the second example said: 'You smile when I say except Miss X, and I know what you're thinking.' . . . In the third example the woman said: '. . . because it was only me no one took the slightest notice.' In the fourth example the woman felt that the group was not interested, and that she had better abandon her initiative. . . . Anyone who has any contact with reality is always consciously or unconsciously forming an estimate of the attitude of his group towards himself. These examples taken from groups of patients show, if there is really any need for demonstrations, that the same kind of thing is going on in the patient group. For the time being I am ignoring obvious facts, such as that there is something in the speaker which colours his assessment of the situation in which he finds himself. Now, even if it is still maintained that the individual's view of the group attitude to himself is of no concern to anybody but himself, I hope that it is clear that this kind of assessment is as much a part of the mental life of the individual as is his assessment, shall we say, of the information brought to him by his sense of touch. Therefore, the way in which a man assesses the group attitude to himself is, in fact, an important object of study even if it leads us to nothing else.

But my last example, of a very common occurrence, shows that, in fact, the way in which men and women in a group make these assessments is a matter of great importance to the group, for on the judgments that individuals make depends the efflorescence or decay of the social life of the group.

What happens if I use this idea of group attitude to the individual as a basis for interpretation? We have already seen some of the reactions in the first section. In the examples I gave, there could be seen, though I did not stress them, some results of this sort of interpretation; but one common reaction I shall mention now. The group will tend to express still further its preoccupation with myself, and then a point seems to be reached where, for the time being, the curiosity of the group is satisfied. This may take two or three sessions. Then the group begins the thing all over again, but this time with some other member of the group. What happens is that another member is the object of the forces that were previously concentrated on myself. When I think enough evidence has accumulated to convince the group, I say that I think this has happened. One difficulty about doing this is that the transition from a preoccupation with myself to a preoccupation with another member of the group is marked by a period during which the preoccupation with the other member shows unmistakable signs of containing a continued preoccupation with myself....

Many people dispute the accuracy of these interpretations. Even when the majority of members in the group have had unmistakable evidence that their behaviour is being affected by a conscious or unconscious estimate of the group attitude to themselves, they will say they do not know what the rest of the group thinks about them, and they do not believe that anyone else does either. This objection to the accuracy of the interpretations must be accepted, even if we modify it by claiming that accuracy is a matter of degree; for it is a sign of awareness that one element in the individual's automatic assessment of the attitude of the group towards himself is doubt. If an individual claims he has no doubt at all, one would really like to know why not. Are there occasions when the group attitude is utterly unmistakable? Or is the individual unable to tolerate ignorance about a matter in which it is essential to be accurate if his behaviour in a society is to be wise? In a sense, I would say that the individual in a group is profiting by his experience if at one and the same time he becomes more accurate in his appreciation of his position in the emotional field, and more capable of accepting it as a fact that even his increased accuracy falls lamentably short of his needs.

It may be thought that my admission destroys the foundations of any technique relying on this kind of interpretation; but it does not. The nature of the emotional experience of interpretation is clarified, but its inevitability as part of human mental life is unaltered, and so is its primacy as a method. That can only be attacked when it can be demonstrated that some other mental activity deals more accurately with matters of greater relevance to the study of the group.

Here is an example of a reaction where the accuracy of the interpretation is questioned; the reader may like to bear the preceding passages in mind when he considers the conclusions I draw from this and the associated examples.

For some time I have been giving interpretations which have been listened to civilly, but conversation has been becoming more and more desultory, and I begin to feel that my interventions are not wanted; I say so in the following terms: 'During the past half hour the group has been discussing the international situation, but I have been claiming that the conversation was demonstrating something about ourselves. Each time I have done this I have felt my contribution was jarring and unwelcome. Now I am sure I am the object of your hostility for persisting in this kind of contribution.'

For a moment or two after I have spoken there is a silence, and then a man member of the group says very civilly that he has felt no hostility at all to my interpretations, and has not observed that anybody else has either. Two or three other members of the group agree with him. Furthermore, the statements are made with moderation, and in a perfectly friendly manner, except possibly for what one might think was an excusable annoyance at having to give a reassurance that ought to have been unnecessary. In some respects I might say again that I feel I am being treated like a child who is being patiently dealt with in spite of his tiresomeness. However, I do not propose to consider this point just now, but rather to take perfectly seriously the statement made by these members of the group who seem to me to represent the whole group very fairly in denying any feeling of hostility. I feel that a correct assessment of the situation demands that I accept it as a fact that all individuals in the group are perfectly sincere and accurate when they say they feel no hostility towards myself.

I recall another episode of a similar kind.

Besides myself, three men and four women are present in the group; a man and a woman are absent. One of the men says to a woman:

How did your affair go last week?

The woman: You mean my party? Oh, that went all right. Very well, really. Why?

The man: Well, I was just wondering. You were rather bothered about it if you remember.

The woman [rather listlessly]: Oh, yes. I was really.

[After a slight pause the man starts again.]

He says: You don't seem to want to say very much about it.

She replies: Oh, yes, I do really, but nothing much happened. It really went all right.

Another woman now joins in and tries to carry the conversation further, as if she felt aware that it was faltering, but in a minute or two she also gives up. There is a pause, and then another woman comes forward with an experience she had during the week. She starts off quite briskly, and then comes to a stop. One or two members attempt to encourage her by their questions, but I feel that even the questioners seem to be oppressed by some preoccupation. The atmosphere of the group is heavy with fruitless effort. Nothing could be clearer to me than the determination of the individuals to make the session what they would consider to be a success. If only it were not for the two absentees, I think, I believe this group would be going very well. I begin myself to feel frustrated, and I remember how much the last two or three sessions have been spoilt because one or more members of the group have been absent. Three of the people present at this session have been absent at one or other of the last two sessions. It seems too bad that the group should be spoilt like this when all are prepared to do their best. I begin to wonder whether the group approach to problems is really worth while when it affords so much opportunity for apathy and obstruction about which one can do nothing. In spite of the effort that is being made, I cannot see that the conversation is anything but a waste of time. I wish I could think of some illuminating interpretation, but the material is so poor that there is nothing I can pick up at all. Various people in the group are beginning to look at me in a hopeless sort of way, as much as to say that they have done all they can – it is up to me now – and, indeed, I feel they are quite right. I wonder if there would be any point in saying that they feel like this about me, but dismiss this because there seems to be no point in telling them what they must know already.

The pauses are getting longer, comments more and more futile, when it occurs to me that the feelings which I am experiencing myself – in particular, oppression by the apathy of the group and an urge to say something useful and illuminating – are precisely those which the others present seem to have. A group whose members cannot attend regularly must be apathetic and indifferent to the sufferings of the individual patient.

When I begin to wonder what I can say by way of interpretation I am brought up against a difficulty that will have already occurred to the reader: what is this group which is unsympathetic and hostile to our work? I must assume that it consists of these same people that I see struggling hard to do the work, but, as far as I am concerned at any rate, it also includes the two absentees. I am reminded of looking through a microscope at an overthick section; with one focus I see, not very clearly perhaps, but with sufficient distinctness, one picture. If I alter the focus very slightly I see another. Using this as an analogy for what I am doing mentally, I shall now have another look at this group, and will then describe the pattern that I see with the altered focus.

The picture of hard-working individuals striving to solve their psychological problems is displaced by a picture of a group mobilized to express its hostility and contempt for neurotic patients and for all who may wish to approach neurotic problems seriously. This group at the moment seems to me to be led by the two absentees, who are indicating that there are better ways of spending their time than by engaging in the sort of experience with which the group is familiar when I am a member of it. At a previous session this group was led by one of the members now absent. As I say, I am inclined to think that the present leaders of this group are not in the room; they are the two absentees, who are felt not only to be contemptuous of the group, but also to be expressing that contempt in action. The members of that group who are present are followers. I wonder as I listened to the discussion if I can make more precise the facts that give me this impression.

At first, I must confess, I see little to confirm me in my suspicions, but then I notice that one of the men who is asking the questions is employing a peculiarly supercilious tone. His response to the answers he receives appears to me, if I keep my mental microscope at the same focus, to express polite incredulity. A woman in the corner examines her fingernails with an air of faint distaste. When a silence occurs it is broken by a woman who, under the former focus, seemed to be doing her best to keep the work of the group going, with an interjection which expresses clearly her dissociation from participation in an essentially stupid game.

I do not think I have succeeded very well in giving precision to my impressions, but I think I see my way to resolving the difficulty in which I found myself in the first example. On that occasion, it will be remembered, I felt quite positive that the group was hostile to myself and my interpretations, but I had not a shred of evidence with which to back my interpretation persuasively. Truth to tell, I found both experiences very disconcerting; it seemed as if my chosen method of investigation had broken down, and broken down in the most obvious kind of way. Anyone used to individual therapy might have foretold that a group of patients would deny an interpretation, and anyone could have foretold that the group would present a heaven-sent opportunity for denying it effectively. It occurs to me, however, that if a group affords splendid opportunities for evasion and denial, it should afford equally splendid opportunities for observation of the way in which these evasions and denials are effected. Before investigating this, I shall examine the two examples I have given with a view to formulating some hypothesis that will give form to the investigation.

It can be seen that what the individual says or does in a group illumines both his own personality and his view of the group; sometimes his contribution illumines one more than the other. Some contributions he is prepared to make as coming unmistakably from himself, but there are others which he would wish to make anonymously. If the group can provide means by which contributions can be made anonymously, then the foundations are laid for a successful system of evasion and denial, and in the first examples I gave it was possibly because the hostility of the individuals was being contributed to the group anonymously that each member could quite sincerely deny that he felt hostile. We shall have to examine the mental life of the group closely to see how the group provides a means for making these anonymous contributions. I shall postulate a group mentality as the pool to which the anonymous contributions are made, and through which the impulses and desires implicit in these contributions are gratified. Any contribution to this group mentality must enlist the support of, or be in conformity with, the other anonymous contributions of the group. I should expect the group mentality to be distinguished by a uniformity that contrasted with the diversity of thought in the mentality of the individuals who have contributed to its formation. I should expect that the group mentality, as I have postulated it, would be opposed to the avowed aims of the individual members of the group. If experience shows that this hypothesis fulfils a useful function, further characteristics of the group mentality may be added from clinical observation.

Here are some experiences that seem to me to be to the point.

The group consists of four women and four men, including myself. The ages of the patients are between thirty-five and forty. The prevailing atmosphere is one of good temper and helpfulness. The room is cheerfully lit by evening sunlight.

Mrs X: I had a nasty turn last week. I was standing in a queue waiting for my turn to go to the cinema when I felt ever so queer. Really, I thought I should faint or something.

Mrs Y: You're lucky to have been going to a cinema. If I thought I could go to a cinema I should feel I had nothing to complain of at all.

Mrs Z: I know what Mrs X means. I feel just like that myself, only I should have had to leave the queue.

Mr A: Have you tried stooping down? That makes the blood come back to your head. I expect you were feeling faint.

Mrs X: It's not really faint.

Mrs Y: I always find it does a lot of good to try exercises. I don't know if that's what Mr A means.

Mrs Z: I think you have to use your will-power. That's what worries me – I haven't got any.

Mr B: I had something similar happen to me last week, only I wasn't even standing in a queue. I was just sitting at home quietly when ...

Mr C: You were lucky to be sitting at home quietly. If I was able to do that I shouldn't consider I had anything to grumble about.

Mrs Z: I can sit at home quietly all right, but it's never being able to get out anywhere that bothers me. If you can't sit at home why don't you go to a cinema or something?

After listening for some time to this sort of talk, it becomes clear to me that anybody in this group who suffers from a neurotic complaint is going to be advised to do something which the speaker knows from his own experience to be absolutely futile. Furthermore, it is clear that nobody has the least patience with any neurotic symptom. A suspicion grows in my mind, until it becomes a certainty, that there is no hope whatever of expecting cooperation from this group. I am led to ask myself what else I expected from my experience as an individual therapist. I have always been quite familiar with the idea of a patient as a person whose capacity for cooperation is very slight. Why, then, should I feel disconcerted or aggrieved when a group of patients demonstrates precisely this quality? It occurs to me that perhaps this very fact will afford me an opportunity for getting a hearing for a more analytical approach. I reflect that from the way in which the group is going on its motto might be: 'Vendors of quack nostrums unite.' No sooner have I said this to myself than I realize that I am expressing my feeling, not of the group's disharmony, but of its unity. Furthermore, I very soon become aware that it is not accidentally that I have attributed this slogan to the group, for every attempt I make to get a hearing shows that I have a united group against me. The idea that neurotics cannot cooperate has to be modified.

I shall not multiply examples of teamwork as a characteristic of the group mentality, chiefly because I cannot, at present, find any method of describing it. I shall rely upon chance instances as they occur in the course of these papers to give the reader a better idea of what I mean, but I suspect that no real idea can be obtained outside a group itself. For the present I shall observe that in the group mentality the individual finds a means of expressing contributions which he wishes to make anonymously, and, at the same time, his greatest obstacle to the fulfilment of the aims he wishes to achieve by membership of the group.

It may be thought that there are many other obstacles to the fulfilment of the individual's aims in a group. . . . It is clear that when a group forms the individuals forming it hope to achieve some satisfaction from it. It is also clear that the first thing they are aware of is a sense of frustration produced by the presence of the group of which they are members. It may be argued that it is quite inevitable that a group must satisfy some desires and frustrate others, but I am inclined to think that difficulties that are inherent in a group situation, such, for example, as a lack of privacy which must follow from the fact that a group provides you with company, produce quite a different sort of problem from the kind of problem produced by the group mentality.

I have often mentioned the individual in the course of my discussions of the group, but in putting forward the concept of a group mentality, I have described the individual, particularly in the episode in which the two absentees played a big part in the emotional orientation of the group, as being in some way opposed to the group mentality although a contributor to it. It is time now that I turned to discuss the individual, and in doing so I propose to take leave of the neurotic and his problems.

Aristotle said man is a political animal, and, in so far as I understand his Politics, I gather that he means by this that for a man to lead a full life the group is essential. I hold no brief for what has always seemed to me an extremely dreary work, but I think that this statement is one that psychiatrists cannot forget without danger of achieving an unbalanced view of their subject. The point that I wish to make is that the group is essential to the fulfilment of a man's mental life – quite as essential to that as it is to the more obvious activities of economics and war. . . . The point that emerges in all the groups from which I have been drawing examples is that the most prominent feeling which the group experiences is a feeling of frustration – a very unpleasant surprise to the individual who comes seeking gratification. The resentment produced by this may, of course, be due to a naïve inability to understand the point that I made above, that it is the nature of a group to deny some desires in satisfying others, but I suspect that most resentment is caused through the expression in a group of impulses which individuals wish to satisfy anonymously, and the frustration produced in the individual by the consequences to himself that follow from this satisfaction. In other words, it is in this area, which I have temporarily demarcated as the group mentality, that I propose to look for the causes of the group's failure to afford the individual a full life. The situation will be perceived to be paradoxical and contradictory, but I do not propose to make any attempt to resolve these contradictions just now. I shall assume that the group is potentially capable of providing the individual with the gratification of a number of needs of his mental life which can only be provided by a group. I am excluding, obviously, the satisfactions of his mental life which can be obtained in solitude, and, less obviously, the satisfactions which can be obtained within his family. The power of the group to fulfil the needs of the individual is, I suggest, challenged by the group mentality. . . . It will be seen that, in the scheme I am now putting forward, the group can be regarded as an interplay between individual needs, group mentality, and culture. To illustrate what I mean by this triad, here is another episode taken from a group.

For a period of three or four weeks in a patient group I was in very bad odour – my contributions were ignored, the usual response being a polite silence, and then a continuation of the conversation which, as far as I could see, showed no sign of having been deflected by any comments of my own. Then suddenly a patient began to display what the group felt to be symptoms of madness, making statements that appeared to be the products of hallucination. Instantaneously I found I had been readmitted to the group. I was the good leader, master of the situation, fully capable of dealing with a crisis of this nature – in short, so outstandingly the right man for the job that it would have been presumption for any other member of the group to attempt to take any helpful initiative. The speed with which consternation was changed into bland complacency had to be seen to be believed. Before the patient began to alarm the group my interpretations might have been oracular pronouncements for all the ceremonious silence with which they were received; but they were the pronouncements of an oracle in decay – nobody would dream of considering their content as worthy of note. After the group had become alarmed I was the centre of a cult in its full power. Looked at from the point of view of an ordinary man attempting to do a serious job, neither situation was satisfactory. A group structure in which one member is a god, either established or discredited, has a very limited usefulness. The culture of the group in this instance might almost be described as a miniature theocracy. I do not attach importance to this phrase as a description, except in so far as it helps to define what on that occasion I would have meant by culture. Having done that, the proper employment of my hypothesis of individual, group mentality, and culture, requires an attempt to define the qualities of the other two components in the triad. Before the turning-point, the group mentality had been of such a nature that the needs of the individual were being successfully denied by the provision of a good friendly relationship between the patients, and a hostile and sceptical attitude towards myself. The group mentality operated very hardly upon this particular patient, for reasons into which it is unnecessary to go. It was possible on this occasion, by exhibiting something of the culture of the group, to effect a change in the group without elucidating either the group mentality or the effect upon the individual that the group mentality was having. The group changed and became very like school-children in the latency period in its outlook and behaviour. The seriously disturbed patient, outwardly at least, ceased to be disturbed. Individuals then attempted again to state their cases, but put forward only such problems as were of a trivial or painless nature. I was then able to suggest that the group had adopted a cultural pattern analogous to that of the playground, and that while this must be presumed to be coping fairly adequately with some of the difficulties of the group – I meant coping with the group mentality but did not say so – it was a culture which only permitted of the broaching of the kind of problem one might well expect a school-child to help with. The group again changed, and became one in which all members, including myself, seemed to be more or less on a level. At the same time a woman mentioned for the first time in six months quite serious marital difficulties that were troubling her.

These examples, I hope, give some idea of what I mean by culture, and also some idea of what I consider to be the need to attempt to elucidate, if possible, two of the three components in the triad.

My attempt to simplify, by means of the concepts I have adumbrated, will prove to be very misleading unless the reader bears in mind that the group situation is mostly perplexing, and confused; operations of what I have called the group mentality, or of the group culture, only occasionally emerge in any strikingly clear way. Furthermore, the fact that one is involved in the emotional situation oneself makes clear-headedness difficult. There are times, such as the occasion I described when two members of the group were absent, when it is clear that the individuals are struggling against the apathy of the group. On that occasion I attributed behaviour to the group on the strength of the behaviour of one or two individuals in it. There is nothing out of the ordinary about this: a child is told that he or she is bringing disgrace upon the school, because it is expected that the behaviour of one will be interpreted as the behaviour of all; Germans are told that they are responsible for the behaviour of the Nazi government; silence, it is said, gives consent. Nobody is very happy about insisting on collective responsibility in this way, but I shall assume, nevertheless, that unless a group actively disavows its leader it is, in fact, following him. In short, I shall insist that I am quite justified in saying that the group feels such and such when, in fact, perhaps only one or two people would seem to provide by their behaviour warrant for such a statement, if, at the time of behaving like this, the group show no outward sign of repudiating the lead they are given. I dare say it will be possible to base belief in the complicity of the group on something more convincing than negative evidence, but for the time being I regard negative evidence as good enough.

42 The violent gang as a near group

Lewis Yablonsky

Normal groups are constellations of roles and norms defining prescribed ways in which members may interact effectively and harmoniously. The normal group may be viewed partially as a projected model for behaviour towards the accomplishment of the mutually agreed-upon goals of its members. A dominant characteristic of such a group is the fact that most members are in consensual agreement about the important norms and reciprocal expectations that regulate and determine each group member's behaviour. Thus an essential element in a normal group is that its members agree upon and are able to fulfil certain prescribed norms or standards of behaviour.

. . . On the daily level of group interaction, relevant others validate the individual's group participation at a minimal level of social expectation. However, 'under certain circumstances individuals with socially inadequate development fail progressively to maintain such a level, with the result that they become socially disarticulated and very often have to be set aside from the rest of their community to live under artificially simplified conditions' (Cameron 1943). *The violent gang in this context serves as a 'simplified' withdrawal for the sociopathic youth from the more demanding community.*

The type of person who requires this forced or sometimes voluntary disassociation from the general community has sociopathic characteristics. . . . His essential limitation in his ineffectuality in taking the role of another, except for egocentric purposes. He lacks a social conscience. In an oversimplified fashion this type of individual tends to become paranoid and have interchangeable delusions of persecution and excessive grandeur. These emotions result from an essentially correct assessment of his personal-social inability – an inability developed in a vacuum of effective socializing agents and processes. The paranoids' reactions of illusion and persecution are useful in fooling themselves that they are powerful and at the same time blaming their social inability upon a world that unfairly persecutes them. Both paranoid devices ('grandeur' and 'persecution') tend temporarily to take the pressure off of blaming their already battered ineffectual selves for their problem.

YABLONSKY, LEWIS (1962) 'The violent gang as a near group' in *The Violent Gang* New York, Macmillan, 243–54.

This delusional process is at first internal and on the personal thought level; however, in time it tends to become projected on to and involved with the surrounding community. According to Cameron:

> The paranoid person, because of poorly developed role-taking ability, which may have been derived from defective social learning in earlier life, faces his real or fancied slights and discriminations without adequate give-and-take in his communication with others and without competence in the social interpretation of motives and intentions. (p. 33)

This type of person, whose role-taking skills are impaired, lacks the ability adequately to assess the 'other' in interaction. He begins to take everything the wrong way and, because of his social inabilities to think as others do, he becomes increasingly alienated and disassociated from the 'real world'. His delusional fantasies become hardened and he begins to see and experience things not consensually validated or similarly felt by others. As Cameron specifies, he 'becomes prejudiced with regard to his social environment.' His responses tend first to select reactions from his surroundings that fit into such an interpretation and then to reshape in retrospect things that seemed innocent enough when they occurred, in such a way that they support the trend of his suspicions. Partially because of his already incipient disturbance, and particularly if the individual is evolving in a defective socializing community (for example, the disorganized slum), he is unable to get relevant responses from others to counteract a developing reaction formation, which finally hardens into what Cameron has termed a 'paranoid pseudo-community':

> As he begins attributing to others the attitudes which he has towards himself, he unintentionally organizes these others into a functional community, a group unified in their supposed reactions, attitudes, and plans with respect to him. He in this way organizes individuals, some of whom are actual persons and some only inferred or imagined, into a whole which satisfies for the time being his immediate need for explanation but which brings no reassurance with it and usually serves to increase his tensions. The community he forms not only fails to correspond to any organization shared by others but actually contradicts the consensus. More than this, the actions and attitudes ascribed by him to its personnel are not actually performed or maintained by them; they are united in no common undertaking against him. What he takes to be a functional community is only a pseudo-community created by his own unskilled attempts at interpretation, anticipation, and validation of social behavior.
>
> This pseudo-community of attitude and intent which he succeeds in thus setting up organizes his own responses still further in the direction they have been going; and these responses in turn lead to greater and greater systema-

> tization of his surroundings. The pseudo-community grows until it seems to constitute so grave a threat to the individual's integrity or to his life that, often after clumsy attempts to get at the root of things directly, he bursts into defensive or vengeful activity. This brings out into the open a whole system of organized responses to a supposed functional community of detractors or persecutors which he has been rehearsing in private. The real community, which cannot share in his attitudes and reactions, counters with forcible restraint or retaliation. (p. 35)

The fact of the real community's response and retaliation only serves to strengthen the individual's suspicions and distorted intepretations. He utilizes this as further evidence of the unfair discrimination to which he is being subjected. He comes out into the open with overt action against his supposed enemies and manages to bring down actual social retaliation upon himself. This new phase makes the paranoid pseudo-community more objective and real to him. 'The reactions of the real community in now uniting against him are precisely those which he has been anticipating on the basis of his delusional beliefs.' (Cameron 1943). The pseudo-community calcifies, becomes more articulate and real to the person caught in this whirlpool of processes. He begins after a while to live in 'it' almost to the exclusion of other social alternatives.

The processes through which an individual becomes enmeshed in a paranoid pseudo-community closely parallel the processes that 'hook' a sociopathic youth into the violent gang. The sociopathic youth 'growing up' in the disorganized slum has a personality syndrome that easily interlocks with the paranoid pseudo-community of the violent gang.

The sequence of events

Summarily the pseudo-community processes as they apply to the violent gang show the following sequential pattern of development:

Step I: Defective socialization. The socialization vacuum of the disorganized slum, with its many inconsistencies, produces sociopathic youths with limited social conscience or ability to relate. This asocial milieu is fertile for negative conditioning.

Step II: Alienation and disassociation. Owing to their sociopathic tendencies, these youths are further disconnected and alienated from the more consensually real and constructive community. Their negative self-feelings of 'difference', social ineffectiveness, and rejection become reinforced and hardened by the disorganized and callous world to which they are exposed.

Step III: Paranoid reactions – delusions of grandeur and persecution. Two paranoid patterns, delusions of grandeur and persecution, become articulated out of self-defence in reaction to the world around them. These patterns become functional in shifting the responsibility from themselves to others and take the pressure off an already weak and suffering self. Delusions of grandeur, 'gang leadership', 'control of large divisions', 'being part of a vast youth gang army', and a violent rep give the depressed youth some illusory ego strength. Indications of being persecuted, 'enemy gangs', 'getting kicked out of school', and so on, are seized upon and enable the sociopathic youth to shift the responsibility from himself to 'society'. His prejudice towards the community hardens and he selectively perceives the outside world's behaviour to fit his emotional needs.

Step IV: The pseudo-community of the violent gang. The violent gang of both reality and unreality becomes, for this type of youth, a convenient pseudo-community, one that is functional in at least temporarily alleviating his personal inadequacies and problems. The structure of the violent gang, with its flexibility of size, power roles and delusionary possibilities, makes it a most convenient and socially acceptable escape-hatch for the sociopathic youth.

The 'legitimate' quality of violent-gang structure

The worship of the 'hoodlum' as a 'hero' and the acceptance of violent-gang behaviour as normal by the larger society help to harden the gang's arteries. Most pathological behaviour is stigmatized and/or sympathized with – not so the violent gang. The general community response of intrigue, and in some fashion, covert aggrandizement, reinforces the violent gang as a most desirable, stigma-free pseudo-community for the sociopathic youth. The community's almost positive response to this pattern of pathology may be partially accounted for by a traditional American worship of aggressive, adventuresome, sociopathic heroes who 'go it alone', unencumbered by social restraints or conscience.[1]

Another possible speculation about the seeming public acceptance of the violent-gang syndrome may be related to an assumption that pathological behaviour is restricted only to individual behaviour; that is, the argument that if one individual commits a bizarre act he is considered disturbed; however, the same act committed in a group provides the individual actor with a degree of immunity from being considered pathological. The ap-

1 To some extent the competitive, successful, aggressive salesman, unencumbered by conscience, serves as a positive role model. Other models of sociopathic heroes include many mass-media leading men (i.e., Marlon Brando as 'The Wild One', George Raft as a 'hood', etc.). In the criminal tradition, John Dillinger, Al Capone, and Frank Costello have served as idealized figures for many youths. (Frank Costello when released from prison was mobbed by a crowd of autograph hunting hero-worshippers of all ages.)

praisal of collective behaviour patterns gives some clue to this element of group legitimization and sanction for bizarre and pathological group action. Lang and Lang (1961) make this point in a discussion of 'crowds'. They comment that certain aspects of a group situation help to make pathological acts and emotions acceptable:

> . . . The principle that expressions of impulses and sentiments are validated by the social support they attract extends to collective expressions generally. The mere fact that an idea is held by a multitude of people tends to give it credence.
>
> The feeling of being anonymous sets further limits to the sentiment of responsibility. The individiual in the crowd or mass is often unrecognized; hence, there is a partial loss of critical self-control and the inhibitions it places on precipitate action. There is less incentive to adhere to normative standards when it appears to the individual that his behaviour is not likely to provoke sanctions against him personally.
>
> . . . each person sees himself acting as part of a larger collectivity which, by inference, shares his motives and sentiments and thereby sanctions the collective action. In this sense the crowd is an *excuse* for people all going crazy together (p. 35).

In the violent gang when all the boys 'go crazy' together their behaviour tends, at least in the public view, to have greater rationality. Gang '*legitimacy*' therefore partially derives from the fact that group behaviour, however irrational, is generally not considered truly bizarre. Although society may disapprove, the gang remains as a rational social group in the public mind. Thus, public agencies give recognition to the violent gang and try to redirect it as an entity. (In 'detached street gang worker' projects, for example, the violent gang is viewed as a legitimate, non-pathological entity suffering only from misguided activities that need to be redirected into 'constructive channels'.)

Another clue to the legitimation of gang violence as non-pathological behaviour may be its uncomfortable closeness to the behaviour of the overall society. The 'crazy machination' of the violent gang and its 'military structure' are bizarre replicas of current structures of international violence and warfare. Using the social context of the current international scenes as a 'normal' reference point, violent-gang machinations do not appear too pathological. Although many gang adjustments require closer examination, the violent gang interestingly caricatures many patterns of the upper world. The gang president (even if he doesn't really lead), drafting new soldiers (even if they are not really members), grand alliances (even if they do not fully cooperate), 'summit peace meetings' (even if they are only for propaganda and solve nothing) are all constructs that bear some resemblance to the international climate of violence.

The gang thus emerges as a desirable pseudo-community reaction for many sociopathic youths. Different degrees of 'membership' participation are a function of the individual's momentary emotional needs. The gang leader and the core gang member are more closely identified with the violent-gang paranoid pseudo-community than are more marginal members. Of considerable significance is the fact that the nature of the violent gang's pathological membership produces an unusual pattern of group structuring. Stated in reverse, group organization in the pathological pseudo-community has a quality and arrangement different from the structure usually found in normal groups.

The near-group conception

The organization of human collectives may be viewed on a continuum of organization factors. At one extreme, an organized, cohesive collection of persons interacting around shared functions and goals for some period of time form a normal group. At the other extreme of human organization a collection of individuals generally characterized by anonymity, spontaneous leadership, motivated and ruled by momentary emotion (for example, lynch mob, youth riots, people in panic, and so on), forms a mob or crowd. Although the term *mob* fits a youth riot, and *group* fits a cohesive delinquent gang, neither the conception of *group* nor that of *mob* seems especially appropriate in describing violent-gang structure. (See Figure 1, 'Collective structures', as a guide to this discussion.)

'Groups' that emerge midway on an organized–unorganized continuum are distorted in one or the other direction by most perceivers. It appears as if there is a psychological (autistic) need to consolidate one's view of the

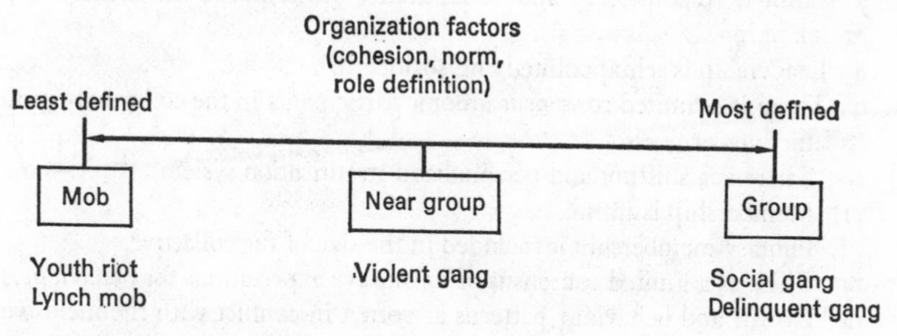

Fig. 1 Collective structures.

world. Violent-gang organization, therefore, despite considerable evidence to the contrary, is often mistakenly perceived by observers as a cohesive group. And in some youth riots no organization is seen despite the fact that in most cases a degree of organization exists.

Because no existing 'group conceptions' seem suitable for describing the violent gang, the following formulation is constructed to delineate its organization correctly. *The sociological category will be referred to as a* NEAR GROUP. The *near group* stands midway on the mob–group (organized–unorganized) continuum. It is differentiated from other collectivities that are temporarily midway because it has some degree of *permanence* or *homeostasis* as a *near group*. A cohesive group may be partially disorganized for a period of time but it is in a state of 'becoming' either organized or disorganized. The violent gang as a *near group*, however, consistently maintains its partial state of organization. (Figure 1 illustrates the location of these relevant collective structures and makes reference to such organizational elements as cohesion, norm, and role definition.)

The violent gang as an ideal-type *near-group* structure includes most of the following characteristics:

1 Participants in the *near-group* violent gang are generally sociopathic personalities. The most sociopathic are core participants or leaders, and the less sociopathic are more marginal members.

2 The *near-group* gang to these individuals is a compensatory paranoid pseudo-community, and serves as a more socially desirable adjustment pattern than other pathological syndromes available in the community.

3 Individualized roles are defined to fit emotional needs of the participant.

4 The definition of membership is diffuse, and varies for each participant.

5 Behaviour is essentially emotion-motivated within loosely defined boundaries.

6 Group cohesiveness decreases as one moves from the centre of the collectivity to the periphery.

7 Limited responsibility and social ability are required for membership or belonging.

8 Leadership is self-appointed and sociopathic.

9 There is a limited consensus among participants in the collectivity as to its functions or goals.

10 There is a shifting and personalized stratification system.

11 Membership is in flux.

12 Fantasy membership is included in the size of the collective.

13 There is a limited consensus of normative expectations for behaviour.

14 Norms and behaviour patterns are often in conflict with the inclusive social system's prescriptions.

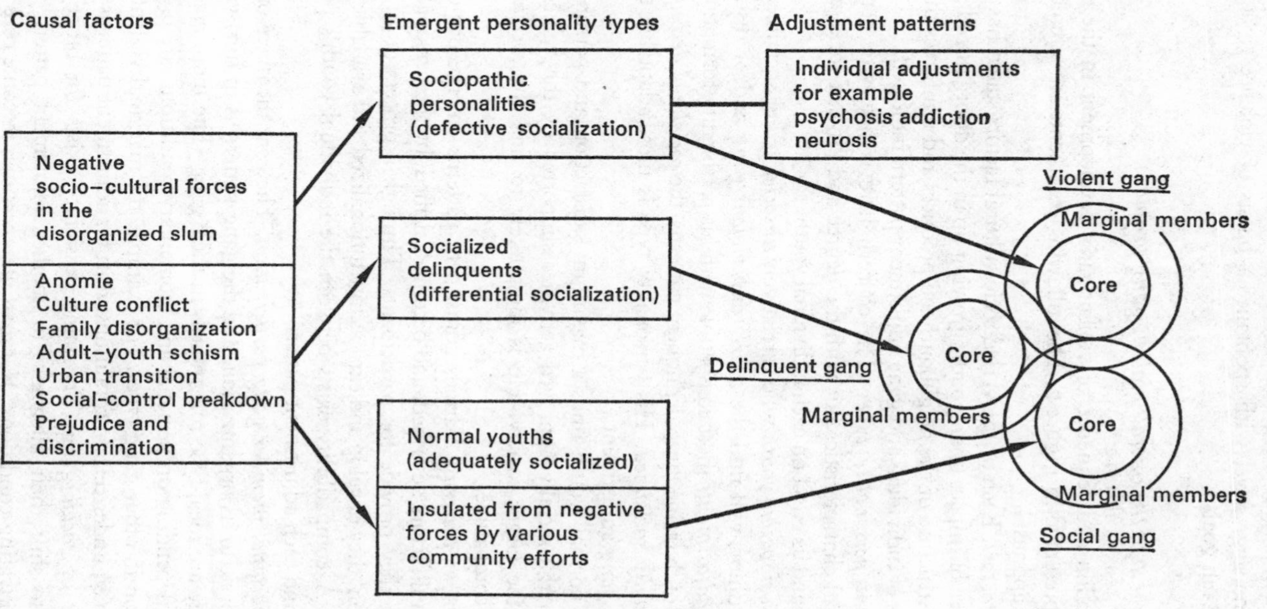
Causal factors
Emergent personality types
Adjustment patterns
Negative socio-cultural forces in the disorganized slum
Anomie
Culture conflict
Family disorganization
Adult–youth schism
Urban transition
Social-control breakdown
Prejudice and discrimination
Sociopathic personalities (defective socialization)
Socialized delinquents (differential socialization)
Normal youths (adequately socialized)
Insulated from negative forces by various community efforts
Individual adjustments for example psychosis addiction neurosis
Violent gang
Marginal members
Core
Delinquent gang
Core
Marginal members
Core
Marginal members
Social gang

Fig. 2

15 Interaction within the collectivity and towards the outer community is hostile and aggressive, with spontaneous bursts of violence to achieve impulsively felt goals.

A capsule view of the overall violent-gang problem

The conception and sequence of violent-gang development in the entire analysis is presented in Figure 2. The following comments are offered as a guide to its appraisal.

1 *Causal factors*. Each of the varied socio-cultural factors stated has a different degree of impact upon youths growing up in the disorganized slum. The social structure of the neighbourhood produces and reinforces the different types of individual and gang adjustment pattern indicated.

2 *Emergent personality types*. The concern here is not with personal psychological characteristics but with the degree and kind of *socialization* that occurs and its effect on each individual youth.

(A) The *sociopathic youth* who is relatively *unsocialized* or socialized in a distorted fashion will find the *near-group violent gang* and/or disturbed *individual adjustments* most compatible with his personality formation.

(B) The youth trained into delinquent patterns, the *socialized delinquent*, is *differentially socialized*. His personality type is most adaptable to the *delinquent gang* adjustment.

(C) The 'normal' youth finds a maximum satisfaction and personal expression in the socially approved activities supported by the values and norms of the larger society. He is most likely to find the *social gang* personally compatible.

3 *Adjustment patterns*. Various adjustment patterns emerge out of the socio-cultural factors described, and become 'calcified' by the personal-need satisfaction they provide for participants. Through a process of 'cultural transmission' they develop and exist as institutionalized and available social structures. A compatibility exists between the individual youth's personality type and each adjustment pattern.

4 *Core-marginal member gang participation*. The *core* members of each gang are basic to its organization, and the gang pattern is in turn vital to them. They are ideal-type role models in their gang. The more *marginal* members, depending on personal and momentary conditions, are prone to participation in other gang types. For example, the marginal violent-gang member may, under certain conditions, shift his adjustment patterns to the *delinquent* or *social* gang. The same possibility exists for other gang members to shift their allegiance to another adjustment pattern under certain motivating conditions. *Marginal members* may become *core mem-*

bers of their gang if they find this direction compatible with their shifting personal needs. Thus, as indicated, the individual and the adjustment pattern generally make a satisfactory fit. For the sociopathic youth, the structure of the violent gang serves as a most amenable and appropriate adjustment pattern.

References

CAMERON, N. (1943) 'The paranoid pseudo-community', *American Journal of Sociology*, 49, 32–8.

LANG, K. and LANG, GLADYS E. (1961) *Collective Dynamics* New York, Thomas Y. Crowell Co.

43 The jury: decision-making in a small group

A. P. Sealy

Introduction

Throughout much of its history the jury has been a centre of controversy, attracting, as Kalven and Zeisel (1966) say 'at once the most extravagant of praise, and the most harsh criticism' (Kalven and Zeisel 1966, p. 4).

For Blackstone (1791) it was the 'palladium of justice', for Sebille (1924) it was an 'effete and sterile . . . system'. In recent years the clamour of argument has been increased by new, and somewhat discordant voices demanding 'relevant scientific research' expressed amongst others by Sir Robert Mark (1973) who recently stated: 'If exposing the truth about the Jury would destroy the public's belief in its value, then surely it's high time that belief was destroyed' (Mark 1973, p. 615).

There is, contrary to the implications in Mark's lecture, much research on the jury, some devoted to its effectiveness, some to its social and political relevance, and some to aspects of its activities believed to exemplify important psychological and social processes. Finally, many writers have probed into its actual functioning within the legal system. The present essay is an attempt to look at these issues from a different perspective – that of the theory and research on small groups – and to explore how far this approach may illuminate the processes of trial by jury and help in evaluating its contribution to the legal system. In presenting this point of view, the results of a number of researches on the jury will be considered, but particularly those from the London School of Economics Jury project, in which lawyers and psychologists cooperated in an experimental study using simulated juries.[1]

Much of the previous research has either missed this perspective or dealt with it in only limited ways. Kalven and Zeisel's (1966) classic study hardly touched on this aspect of their research, since they report only the results of an inquiry of judges as to why disagreements arose between them and

1 The project was run jointly by the present author, Professor W. R. Cornish, Department of Law, LSE, Mr D. H. Thomas, Institute of Criminology, Cambridge, and Mr D. G. Harper, Imperial College, London, with Mrs C. M. Wain as research assistant.

SEALY, A. P. (1975) 'The jury: decision-making in a small group'. (Commissioned for this volume.)

their juries. Two aspects of their findings are germane to the present topic, however. First, agreement occurred in 75 per cent of the 3576 trials considered, whilst of the remainder the jury wished to acquit 16·9 per cent of cases the judge wanted to convict, but wished to convict in only 2·2 per cent of cases against the judge's own inclinations. The jury also failed to agree in 4·4 per cent of the cases the judge wished to convict. Thus, where there were disagreements, they were largely in the direction of the jury being more cautious about conviction, a finding not in accord with some of the experimental literature on group behaviour.

The second point of interest is the reasons the judges give for disagreements in these cases. Since the judges may give several such reasons, it was necessary to weight the answers. Kalven and Zeisel state that the reasons given were as follows:

	%
feelings about the law	29
attitude to the defendant	11
issues of evidence	54
facts judge alone knew	2
disparity of counsel	4

Overwhelmingly, the reasons judges give for their disagreements with juries are concerned with matters of substance, rather than factors of bias or incompetence. Of course their results apply only to what judges *think* were the reasons why they disagreed with the jury's verdict. Simon (1967) and Cornish and Sealy (1973) have presented results relating to the effectiveness of the rules that constrain juries. Simon shows some interesting results in her cases of housebreaking and incest, in which there was a defence plea of insanity. Two types of plea were used, based on the McNaughton rules and the Durham rules. The former stress that an insanity plea would apply where the defendant did not know what he was doing or, if he did, he did not know it was wrong. The Durham rules apply if the defendant's action was the product of mental disease or disorder. Table 1 contains Simon's results, in terms of the percentage of jurors voting Not Guilty by reason of insanity in her two trials.

These results, it must be stressed, apply to the decisions jurors make *prior* to the discussion, after hearing the trial; they show that the greatest use of the category 'not guilty through reasons of insanity' occurred in the conditions in which no instructions were given on this matter. This might be interpreted as lending support to the view that many jurors have a quite sophisticated sense of their role as jurors, which may or may not be modi-

Table 1 Pre-deliberation verdicts of individual jurors in Simon's two cases: percentage voting Not Guilty through insanity (NGI).

	Housebreaking Total N	% NGI	*Incest* Total N	%
No instructions	120	76	264	34
McNaughton	119	59	240	24
Durham	119	65	312	36

fied by specific instructions given in the trial. Perhaps even more interesting is the fact that these differences disappeared as a result of discussion.

One further aspect of the literature on juries is worthy of consideration: the effect of group size. Zeisel (1975) and Davis (1973) have reviewed many studies and presented some interesting findings. The research emerges out of the American Supreme Court's decision to permit six-man juries. Davis argues that in most juries initial majority predicts final verdict, and increasingly so as the size of the initial majority increases. From this he arrives at a predictive model for twelve-man juries which, when applied to six-man juries, allows one to compute the approximate proportion of cases in which varying the size of the jury would result in a different verdict, and this proportion is surprisingly small, perhaps less than 10 per cent. Davis applies his model to twelve, eight and six-person juries, using students as jurors in a simulated trial of rape. The model works well, although the limitations of type of case and selection of jurors compel caution. Zeisel and Diamond (1975) criticize much of the work in this area and quote some evidence of the differences in average settlement in civil cases between six-person and twelve-person juries:

six-person juries:	average settlement	$5,800
twelve-person juries:	average settlement	$15,800

However, since large juries tended to have more complex cases (three out of four of their cases are so described) and since they take longer on average to come to a decision (on average twice as long), it is clear that the results do not permit an unequivocal statement about the effects of group size.

Another aspect of group dynamics frequently studied in the past concerns that of participation and social status. Strodtbeck (1957) and others have shown how social class, education level and sex are all related to participation, with higher status, better educated males saying most and being more likely to act as foreman. The research fails to tease out the variable of majority–minority status in a particular jury. Since the working class, women, and the less educated are usually in a minority in any given jury, it is not clear how far social status and majority status within a given jury are compounded.

Juries have been used as exemplars of many social psychological processes, such as the primacy–recency effect in attitude change, but in most of these cases the trial is used in very skeletal form and the results bear more on psychological controversies than on jury functioning. In summary, then, several themes have emerged from previous research on the jury as a small group. First, the movement towards leniency and, if the legal philosophy is accepted, towards caution, is fairly common; secondly, in cases where complex instructions are involved, jurors without these instructions behave in much the same way as jurors who have been given them; and finally, the size of the jury makes relatively little difference to its verdict, although here important compounding effects are often ignored. The rest of this essay will consider selective results from the LSE jury project in the light of small group processes. In this connection three main aspects will be considered in succession: membership and its consequences, norms and rules and their effects, and finally, some comments on the role of juror. First, however, it is necessary briefly to describe the methods.

LSE jury project

Methods

Two trials,[2] one of theft and one of rape, were tape recorded from the trial transcripts, altering only names of participants and locations. Trials were then played to jurors recruited from the general population, initially in a rather ad hoc manner but later using strict quota sampling techniques. Jurors heard the trials as far as possible as they occurred in court and, after recording a private verdict by questionnaire, proceeded on their own, though observed by closed circuit television and tape recorder, to attempt to reach a verdict. The trials varied systematically in a factorial design co-varying four conditions related to the previous record of the defendant and three concerned with instructions on burden of proof. These conditions are set out in the table on page 544.

These conditions are described more fully in Cornish and Sealy (1973). In the theft case two juries were completed in each condition and in addition four were run in slight variants of these conditions and six with different

2 The Appendix provides a brief synopsis.

	Conditions on previous record
X	Previous record for similar offences allowed
Y	Previous record for dissimilar offences allowed
Z	Previous record for similar offences disallowed by judge
Co	Control – no previous record presented
	Conditions on burden of proof
A	'Reasonable Doubt'
B	'Sure and Certain'
C	'Balance of Probabilities'

procedures for sampling, making thirty-four in all. In the rape case eighteen juries were run in an incomplete version of the main design with four additional juries on two further variations. In all cases the experimental variations were incorporated into the trial material in a manner consistent with current legal practice. All jurors were paid for their services.

Membership and its implications

There are many ways of becoming a member of a particular group, from personal choice to enforcible selection. By the same token membership itself can mean different things in different groups, from that of representative delegate to that of freely participating individual. The jury has, as a group, certain unique characteristics: first, membership is not voluntary, although people may attempt, with varying success, to evade membership; secondly, jurors are chosen from a wide spectrum of society and there is an implicit hope that they will not be known to one another; thirdly, jurors are not expected to share common interests, indeed, diversity of interest is another implicit hope; fourthly, juries are thought of as representative of the wider society from which they are selected, without any intention that they should represent any particular interest, for example, it may be the aim to see that men and women should be fairly equally represented on juries but it is not expected that a woman, say, should be regarded as representing women's interests; fifthly a jury is anonymous, not only in the sense that the names of jurors serving on a particular case are kept secret from the public, but also in the sense that jurors rarely go through an introduction phase (e.g. my name is Brian Smith, you are . . . ?); finally, a jury has to make a very important decision but is not held responsible for it, since in the cases of miscarriage of justice where it is later proved that an incorrect decision had been reached, it is the judge or the police who can be held responsible. A jury, then, is a group characterized by being involuntary, representative but not representing, anonymous, not held responsible for its decisions and impermanent. The question, therefore, is how far and in what ways do these characteristics affect the behaviour of individual jurors?

It would seem to follow from the non-representative, anonymous, not-responsible and impermanent nature of the jury that individual factors ought to play a large role in decision-making, and in this context three broad hypotheses can be made: first jurors' decisions should be predictable from their personalities and personal characteristics, secondly, this bias should be more pronounced before discussion than after it, thirdly, this bias should be more marked in more doubtful cases. The precise variables to be analyzed are the personality dimensions of dogmatism, rigidity and authoritarianism all of which should produce some leaning towards decisions of guilty, and the personal characteristics of age, sex, social class and educational level. For these variables it was predicted that the social class would be biasing in the case of theft, as would sex, in the case of rape.

The results concerning the major sources of bias in the final verdicts, that is, after discussion, have been presented elsewhere (Sealy and Cornish 1973). The relevant results will be presented here in a different and more extensive form. Table 2 shows the correlations between background factors and verdict.

Table 2 Correlations between background factors and verdict for the theft case

Factors	*Initial verdict* $n = 319$	*Final verdict*
Age	−0·04	0·04
Sex	0·01	0·11
Education level	−0·12	−0·02
Social class	−0·04	−0·00

None of these correlations approaches an acceptable level of significance ($r=0{\cdot}13$, $p < 0{\cdot}01$), and so from these results it can be concluded, contrary to our expectations, that basic life experiences do not produce a bias in verdict, as measured by these correlations. The reasons for this absence of correlation could be any of the following: first, no correlation in fact exists, secondly, a non-linear correlation occurs and, thirdly, the background data were inadequately sampled. Only replications of the experiment can answer the first question; the second possibility has been investigated, but so far no significant non-linearities have been discovered. An attempt was made to examine the third possibility by running six juries with a sample recruited from the general population on a quota sample basis, considering social class and, less stringently, sex and age. This did not produce any results contradicting the conclusions reached previously, although the small number of subjects (n=70) and the high frequency of decisions to acquit make the results from this set of juries undependable.

Similar correlations were computed for the rape case, in which there are two defendants: 'Harrison', who admits a good deal of the evidence against him, and 'Bryce' who denies everything. These are set out in the next table:

Table 3 Correlations between background factors and verdicts for the rape case

Factor	*'Harrison'*		*'Bryce'*	
	Before discussion	*Final*	*Before discussion*	*Final*
	n = 249			
Age	0·04	0·15*	0·22*	0·27*
Sex	0·03	−0·11	−0·11	−0·03
Educational level	−0·10	−0·11	−0·04	0·04
Social Class	0·04	0·01	0·04	0·05

* Significantly different from zero with a probability of less than $p_r = <$ 0·01.

These results again fail to support our expectations: it is only age that correlates with verdict – younger jurors tending towards acquittal – and this bias appears in the case of Harrison only after discussion, whereas it was expected that discussion would attenuate bias. It is noteworthy that sex and social class were unrelated to verdicts in both cases except for the final verdict on Bryce, where women were more likely to convict.

The next set of variables to be considered relate to the personalities of jurors: in terms both of the underlying theories, and the content of the measures, rigid, dogmatic and authoritarian people should be more punitive and more prone to reach verdicts of guilty especially in doubtful cases. The results are set out in Table 4.

Table 4a Personality and verdicts in the theft trial

Variable	*Test*	*n*	*Correlation with initial verdict*	*Correlation with final verdict*
Rigidity	Gough (1957)	201	−0·02	0·03
Dogmatism	Rokeach	201	−0·04	−0·05
Punitiveness	Sealy[1] (1960)	200	0·01	−0·03
Pro-Jury	Sealy[2]	200	0·05	0·13

Table 4b Personality and verdict in the rape trial

			Correlation for Harrison		Bryce	
Variable	*Test*	*n*	*1st verdict*	*Final verdict*	*1st verdict*	*Final verdict*
Rigidity	Gough	197	0·02	0·01	0·03	0·10
Dogmatism	Rokeach	196	−0·05	0·04	0·08	0·16
Authoritarianism	(a)[3]	197	+0·15	+0·20*	0·14	0·16
	(b)[3]	195	0·05	0·02	0·02	0·03
	(c)[3]	197	0·01	0·09	0·10	0·17*

* Significantly different from zero with a probability of 0·01 or less.
[1] A Likert scale developed especially for the present research measuring people's attitudes of punitiveness within the legal system, e.g. belief that sentences for criminal offences should be severe, etc.
[2] A Likert scale measuring the view that the jury is a just and socially valuable system.
[3] The traditional F-scale measure of authoritarianism (Adorno *et al.* 1950) was scored in terms of
(a) Submission to authority;
(b) Authoritarian attitudes to sexual matters;
(c) Authoritarian aggressiveness to others.

One overwhelming conclusion emerges from these results: relevant personality dimensions, as measured by well established scales, are almost totally uncorrelated with the decisions the jurors make.

It is unusual to present non-significant results in such detail, but they are presented here because they require some explanation. The first, and most obvious, explanation is that the measures are inadequate. In view of this possibility, the responses to these questionnaires were carefully factor-analyzed and the factors correlated with verdicts: this should clarify the personality dimensions measured by the tests and hence improve their predictive value. No such result occurred. A second explanation is that personality affects the style of decision-making in this setting, not the decision itself: in other words, some people may acquit or convict dogmatically, rigidly or in an authoritarian manner. At present no way has been found to analyze the qualitative problem. Thirdly, it is possible that personality plays virtually no role in the decisions people make in jury-like situations: their verdicts are, in fact, the genuine outcome of their perception of the evidence, their argument with their co-jurors, and their interpretation of the instructions they receive from the judge. The analysis of the latter interpretation is the next task.

Norms and rules in the jury

The jury is a very rule-bound group: the judge, in his role as interpreter of the legal system, explains what evidence they should consider, how they should use such evidence, what levels of uncertainty they should tolerate in making a decision, as well as other much more abstruse points of law. In 'Juries and the rules of evidence' (Cornish and Sealy 1973) details of the final verdicts were presented. These will now be amplified by comparing them with verdicts given privately prior to the discussion. Results for the theft case are set out in Table 5.

Table 5a Verdicts in the theft case by instructions on burden of proof

	Initial			*Final*		
Condition	G	NG	%G	G	NG	%G
A (Reasonable Doubt)	66	71	48	43	94	31
B (Sure and Certain)	44	46	49	32	58	37
C (Balance of Probabilities)	50	42	54	42	50	46
	$X^{2}_{2} = 1{\cdot}00$ n.s.			$X^{2}_{2} = 4{\cdot}57$ $p_r < 0{\cdot}20$		

Table 5b Verdicts by conditions relating to previous record

	Initial			*Final*		
	G	NG	%G	G	NG	%G
X (Similar PC's)	50	40	56	51	39	57
Y (Dissimilar PC's)	35	33	51	17	51	33
Z (PC's disallowed)	36	33	52	24	45	35
Co (No PC's)	39	53	42	25	67	27
	$X\,2^{2}_{3} = 3{\cdot}36$ n.s.			$X^{2}_{3} = 23{\cdot}29$ $p_r < {\cdot}001$		

The most noteworthy feature of these results is that the information relating to the previous record of the defendant had no effect on verdicts recorded privately at the end of the trial but a highly significant effect after discussion, in the expected direction as a result of the discussion: where a record of previous similar convictions is revealed the likelihood of guilty verdicts increases. All other conditions produce a movement towards acquittal.

The results for the case of rape are presented in Tables 6a and 6b.

Table 6a Verdicts in rape case by instructions on burden of proof

Condition	*Harrison*						*Bryce*					
	Initial			*Final*			*Initial*			*Final*		
	G	NG	% G	G	NG	% G	G	NG	% G	G	NG	% G
A	103	39	74	94	48	66	67	75	47	46	96	32
B	48	23	68	39	32	55	25	46	35	13	58	18
C	29	15	66	30	14	68	24	20	55	18	26	41
	$X^2_2 = 1{\cdot}24$ ns			$X^2_2 = 2{\cdot}34$ ns			$X^2_2 = 4{\cdot}50$ ns			X^2_2 7·59 $p_r < 0{\cdot}05$		

Table 6b Verdicts in rape case by previous record of defendant

Condition	*Harrison*						*Bryce*					
	Initial			*Final*			*Initial*			*Final*		
	G	NG	% G	G	NG	% G	G	NG	% G	G	NG	% G
X	52	17	75	55	14	80	34	35	49	25	44	36
Y	29	17	63	26	20	57	20	26	43	4	42	9
Z	14	10	58	9	16	33	9	15	37	7	17	29
Co	85	33	72	74	44	63	53	65	45	41	77	48
	$X^2_3 = 4{\cdot}19$ ns			$X^2_3 = 18{\cdot}39$ 0·01			$X^2_3 = 1{\cdot}29$			$X^2_3 = 18{\cdot}39 < p_r 0{\cdot}01$		

In this case, as indicated in the Appendix, there were two defendants, one of whom (Harrison) virtually convicts himself and one (Bryce) who denies every charge. In the case itself jurors could choose verdicts of not guilty, guilty of attempted rape or guilty of rape for both cases; here only the distinction of guilty (on either charge) or not guilty is considered. Several things stand out in these results. None of the experimental variables differentially affected private verdicts of jurors prior to discussion; in this sense the results are very similar to those of the theft case. After discussion however, several significant findings emerged: first, the instructions of burden of proof significantly affected the proportion of jurors wishing finally to convict Bryce with the 'reasonable doubt' instructions producing intermediate levels of conviction, as compared with the more stringent instructions of 'Sure and Certain' (which produced lowest levels of conviction) and the more lenient instructions of 'Balance of Probabilities'.

The second effect of note was that for Bryce, the introduction of his previous record had significant but odd effects: the highest rate of conviction was where no record was produced (35 per cent), and, where a record of a similar offence was described (36 per cent); where a different type of offence was described, the defendant was most likely to be acquitted (91 per cent of jurors wishing to do so). Thus for Bryce there is a 'boomerang' effect with two interesting contrasting sides: firstly, give the man a previous record of different offences and his likelihood of acquittal increases greatly, but, secondly, the record for similar offences has no more effect in producing verdicts of guilty than complete silence on the issue.

A third effect is even more surprising: after discussion there are significant differences between the various experimental conditions for the defendant Harrison: when Bryce has a record for similar offences, and no mention is made of Harrison's record, then the likelihood of Harrison being convicted increases greatly (80 per cent of jurors wishing to convict him). The lowest level of convictions for Harrison (33 per cent) is where

Table 7 Guilty verdicts against Harrison: rape or attempted rape in final verdicts

	Verdicts of *rape*	*attempted rape*	*Total*	*% Rape*
X	8	47	55	14
Y	2	24	26	8
Z	2	6	8	25
Co	21	27	48	44

$X + Y + Z$ *vs* Co $\quad X^2_2 = 14{\cdot}05 \quad p_r < {\cdot}001$

the judge instructs the jury not to pay any attention to Bryce's previous record. This curious result is still further compounded if the distinction between rape and the lesser charge of attempted rape is considered. Table 7 shows whether those jurors who wanted to convict Harrison preferred the more or less serious charges.

Again these results show an effect after discussion that was not present before. A number of general points can be made on the basis of these results: the first is that quite significant variations in the information jurors receive, for instance, an account of the defendant's previous record, may have little or no effect on the verdicts people arrive at privately, but may have considerable effect on the results of discussion; the second point is that information about one defendant may have serious effects on the verdicts given for a co-defendant both negative (as in the X condition) and positive (as in the Y condition), but again, only after group discussion; finally, within a decision category (in the present case, guilty of rape or guilty of attempted rape) the presentation of the co-defendant's previous record may result in considerable attenuation of the verdict for those jurors who wished to convict.

It might be argued that both the rules and the norms governing the behaviour of a group of jurors only become effective as a result of interaction within the groups. The principal rule referred to here is the use of evidence of a previous record in a direct way, but, to a much lesser extent, this conjecture also applies to the rule relating to general confidence and certainty of mind necessary for a guilty verdict. Variations in these rules in our experimental simulations produced results *only* after discussion. The principal norm under consideration here relates to the jurors' role as standing between the law and the defendant, giving allowances to the latter as their common sense dictates. The 'boomerang' effects are particularly relevant here, for they seem to represent, both in terms of overall statistics and in terms of things jurors say in argument, a tendency for jurors, once they get into discussion, to respond to the norms of the situation: for instance, in the situation in which a previous record for dissimilar offences is described comments like these emerged: 'If they had to bring that up, their case must have been weak, which makes me lean towards not guilty' or 'If they bring up things like his previous record they must be gunning him: he needs somebody on his side'.

The important point, though, is that the application of the rules – rigidly enunciated by the judge, or the application of norms – the jury as standing somewhere between the individual and the Law, both emerge only in discussion, not in the individual's own procedures for processing information.

The role of juror

'The evidence is for you, the law is for me.' That is how Devlin (1956) characterizes the charge to the jury from a Judge. The problem, however, is more complex than this: the evidence presented to the juror is often constrained by the 'rules of evidence' (see Cornish 1968): only certain types of evidence are admissible; some evidence is admissible only for certain purposes, e.g. admitting the complaints of a victim of an alleged assault only as adding consistency to his or her complaint, not as evidence of assault in itself.

One thing is evident from listening to the discussions of simulated juries: jurors arrive in the discussion room with a fairly well organized set of ideas about how the law works and what they should do. They spend considerable proportions of their time discussing the criteria of proof; they discuss the relevance of a defendant's previous record irrespective of whether they have direct evidence for it, as, for example, in one of our control juries, where the jury talked about the relevance of the defendant's previous convictions for from ten to fifteen minutes. Some jurors said you could not avoid using it as evidence, others that you had to ignore the idea rigorously. After a while this discussion was intercepted by one juror who said, 'But they didn't actually mention a previous record, did they?'

The jury is operating at two levels: first, the common-sense level, often urged on them by the Judge, where they may make inferences that are sometimes sensible but often technically irrelevant; secondly, the legalistic level in which they try to use arguments about legal procedure, without necessarily understanding them fully. An example of the latter is the use of the term 'circumstantial evidence'. Sometimes it is used in an attempt to exempt certain facts from consideration; sometimes it is used to try to permit dubious material into serious consideration, and sometimes this definition is used appropriately. In these cases, the juror is adopting a role, pretending, as Garfinkel (1973) suggests, that he is being a sort of lawyer. This role-taking behaviour may be the reason for the relative unimportance of personality and background variables in predicting the verdicts of jurors: such personal bias is suppressed by the role demands of the particular situation. Likewise, this role-taking behaviour may account for the failure of our variations in the instructions on burden of proof to affect verdicts: jurors already knew that you had to be sure 'beyond reasonable doubt' and any other instruction gets assimilated into this idea, as in the case of the juror in Condition B who reported that he was told to be 'sure and certain, beyond reasonable doubt', thereby incorporating accurately the actual instructions he received into what he expected to receive.

Conclusion

In this essay, a number of researches on juries have been cited and our own described in some detail, with the intention of showing the dynamics of such a group. It was argued that the nature of people's membership of a jury ought to predicate a high level of personal bias in decision-making. This prediction was shown to be totally invalid: rather it is the rules and norms of the group itself which dominate the group's activities, even to the extent that jurors adopt a very particular role – that of juror, with many judicial overtones – when they find themselves in the particular situation. Of course, it is possible that a person may adopt a particular personal role in a given jury, but, on the basis of the present results, it seems that jurors are in fact more likely in general to adopt this rather legalistic style of reaction. This conclusion, of course, requires more substantial support than that presented here, but further analyses of discussions and responses to questionnaires should elucidate this issue.

Appendix

Cases used in the LSE experiments

The case of theft concerned a porter in a meat market, named 'Taylor' who is accused of stealing meat. A suspicious bag of meat is seen on his barrow and, according to the evidence of the salesman, marked in pencil with a cross. After leaving the market, Taylor is stopped by the police, who have been summoned by the salesman. He is brought back to the saleroom where a policeman searches his barrow. The marked bag of meat is not found in his barrow, but it 'appears', inexplicably, on a previously empty shelf below the meat barrow. The prosecution claim that Taylor must surreptitiously have pushed the bag of meat off his barrow without anyone engaged in the search noticing. The defence claims that since no one actually saw him move the meat, there is no direct evidence against him.

The case of rape concerned two youths named, by us, 'Harrison' and 'Bryce'. They chased some girls unsuccessfully around the fires on bonfire night. Later they chased the victim of the alleged rape 'Mary'. Harrison admits catching her, leading her to some waste land and attempting to have intercourse with her. He agrees under cross-examination that he did not actually ask her consent. The girl alleges that Harrison hit her and used force, and that after he had left her Bryce did the same thing. Afterwards she was seen bruised and distressed by a number of people. For the defendant Harrison the case hinges on the interpretation of the term 'without her consent' and on whether he actually achieved penetration (rape or attempted rape). For Bryce the case hinges on whether the girl's allegations are accepted, as against his total denial that he had anything to do with her.

References

ADORNO, R. W. *et al.* (1950) *The Authoritarian Personality* New York, Harper and Row.

BLACKSTONE, (1791) *Commentaries* Vol. IV, p. 350.

CORNISH, W. R. (1968) *The Jury* Harmondsworth, Penguin.

CORNISH, W. R. and SEALY, A. P. (1973) 'Juries and the rules of evidence', *Crim. Law Rev.*, 36, pp. 496–508.

DAVIS, J. H. (1973) 'Social decision schemes', *Psych. Review*, **80.**

DEVLIN (1956) *Trial by Jury* London, Methuen.

GARFINKEL, H. (1973) in Turner, D. K. (ed.) *Ethnomethodology* Harmondsworth, Penguin.

GOUGH, H. C. (1957) *Manual for the California Psychological Inventory* Consulting Psych. Press, Palo Alto.

KALVEN, H. and ZEISEL, H. (1966) *The American Jury* Boston, Little Brown.

MARK, SIR ROBERT (1973) *The Listener*, **90,** no. 2328, p. 613 ff.

ROKEACH, M. (1960) *The Open and Closed Mind* New York, Basic Books.

SEALY, A. P. and CORNISH, W. R. (1973) 'Jurors and their verdicts', *Crim. Law Rev.*, vol. X, pp. 208–223.

SEBILLE (1924) 'Trial by Jury: an ineffective survival', *Amer. Bar Assoc. Journal*, **10,** p. 53.

SIMON, R. J. (1967) *The jury and defence of insanity* Boston, Little Brown.

STRODTBECK, F. L., JAMES, R. J. and HAWKINS, C. (1957) 'Social status and jury deliberations', *Amer. Social Rev.*, **22,** p. 713.

ZEISEL, H. (1975) *The American jury on the defensive: Proceedings of the Cropwood Conference 1974*, Institute of Criminology, Cambridge.

ZEISEL, H. and DIAMOND, S. (1975) 'Convincing empirical evidence on the six-member jury', *Univ. Chicago Law. Rev.*, **41,** p. 280.

Section 14
Persuasion and coercion

Introduction

The theme of this section, persuasion and coercion, may not on initial reflection seem to warrant a separate collection of empirical studies or theoretical concepts. Much of what has already been covered in the sections on attitudes, communications or groups may quite rightly be said to be relevant to persuasion and coercion. Nevertheless there is a case to be made for treating this as an area in its own right. In the first place, isolating persuasion and coercion from other social psychological processes alerts us to the difference between accidental or spontaneous influence processes which go on routinely in social life and those more deliberate and systematic efforts at changing people which tend to generate public debate and to call for emotional and ethical arguments.

Another reason for singling out this area is that it reminds us of the difficulty of drawing a hard and fast distinction between the individual and his society. It is simply not possible to study the effects of mass communications or of 'brainwashing' without taking into account both social and psychological factors.

In our first article, Elihu Katz points out that research on mass communications has demonstrated that new information is 'filtered' not only by the individual's values and knowledge but by his interpersonal relationships. Whilst television, radio and newspapers have made it possible to reach a 'mass' audience, this audience is found not to be a mass of isolated, unrelated people, each one individually vulnerable to persuasive communications. The sociological evidence concerning the diffusion of innovation as well as psychological research points, on the contrary, to the fact that the group affiliations of members of the audience affect their selection, perception of and response to mass communications.

In our second paper, which is an extract from a longer article, Edward Shils and Morris Janowitz discuss the impact of Allied psychological warfare on members of the German Army during the second world war. Here, too, we see demonstrated (on the basis of interviews with prisoners of war) the importance of primary group membership. Allied propaganda became more effective in inducing German soldiers to surrender when primary groups were disintegrating in a worsening military situation. But conversely, appeals to surrender were also more effective when allied leaflets specifically encouraged men to talk to each other about their military situation, the threat to their families and the need to survive.

Both these articles suggest that information, propaganda or advertising may be effective in limited ways if what is advocated broadly meets the needs or expectations of individuals and their social groups. But can people's attitudes and values or their behaviour be changed more drastically? If a change does occur, is it likely to last?

In 1954 Robert Lifton, a psychiatrist, studied in Hong Kong Western and Chinese intellectuals who had fled from China or who had been expelled. They had been subjected to what is variously translated from Chinese as thought reform or brainwashing. These processes go beyond what one would normally refer to as persuasion and the term 'coercion' in the title to this section refers to them.

Our third paper is one of the case studies from Lifton's book *Thought Reform and the Psychology of Totalism*. This moving account clearly shows that for drastic changes in belief to be possible, deliberate steps must be taken to strip the individual of his selfhood and assault his identity. This is achieved by taking him away from his normal setting and normal group memberships, weakening him by lack of sleep and food and by humiliating him to the point of breakdown. A new set of beliefs is then built on the foundations which remain and by providing new (and compulsory) group membership. In this way pressures from the environment are manipulated to force a new identity on the individual. The experiences of the people interviewed by Lifton are more extreme perhaps but not dissimilar to those Erving Goffman (1968)[1] describes as happening in a mental hospital or other 'total' institutions. It is likely that no one will emerge unscathed from the experiences of thought control and the insights he glimpsed into parts of his mind which he previously did not know existed. Nevertheless in terms of the adoption of political views the extract here reproduced (and other evidence) suggests that they are not maintained once the individual returns to an environment in which these new views are no longer supported.

Quite often research on the way in which people respond when under pressure to modify their beliefs or behaviour invokes the concept of conformity. While this term is frequently used in common sense explanations of behaviour, Marie Jahoda in the concluding article warns us against adopting too simplistic a definition of this process. After reviewing the empirical work on this topic, she arrives at the conclusion that conformity and independence do not represent opposite ends of a continuum but rather they can be broken down into eight distinguishable processes.

[1] GOFFMAN, E. (1968) *Asylums* Harmondsworth, Penguin.

44 Communication research and the image of society: convergence of two traditions

Elihu Katz

Research on mass communications has concentrated on persuasion, that is, on the ability of the mass media to influence, usually to change, opinions, attitudes, and actions in a given direction. This emphasis has led to the study of campaigns – election campaigns, marketing campaigns, campaigns to reduce racial prejudice, and the like. Although it has been traditional to treat audience studies, content analysis, and effect studies as separate areas, there is good reason to believe that all three have been motivated primarily by a concern with the effective influencing of thought and behaviour in the short run.[1]

Other fields of social research have also focused on the effectiveness of campaigns, a prominent example being the twenty-year-old tradition of research by rural sociologists on the acceptance of new farm practices. Yet, despite this shared concern, the two traditions of research for many years were hardly aware of each other's existence or of their possible relevance for each other. Indeed, even now, when there is already a certain amount of interchange between them, it is not easy to conceive of two traditions that, ostensibly, seem more unrelated. Rural sociology suggests the study of traditional values, of kinship, primary relations, *Gemeinschaft*; research on mass communications, on the other hand, is almost a symbol of urban society.

The recognition that these two traditions of research have now begun to accord each other is, in large measure, the product of a revision of the image of society implicit in research on mass communications. Thus, although the convergence now taking place has surely proceeded from both directions, this paper attempts to present the story from one side only.[2]

Communication research and the image of society

Until very recently, the image of society in the minds of most students of communication was of atomized individuals, connected with the mass media but not with one another.[3] Society – the 'audience' – was conceived of as aggregates of age, sex, social class, and the like, but little thought

---

KATZ, ELIHU (1960) 'Communication research and the image of society' in *American Journal of Sociology*, vol. 65. no. 5.

was given to the relationships implied thereby or to more informal relationships. The point is not that the student of mass communications was unaware that members of the audience have families and friends but that he did not believe that they might affect the outcome of a campaign; informal interpersonal relations, thus, were considered irrelevant to the institutions of modern society.

What research on mass communications has learned in its three decades is that the mass media are far less potent than had been expected. A variety of studies – with the possible exception of studies of marketing campaigns – indicates that people are not easily persuaded to change their opinions and behaviour.[4] The search for the sources of resistance to change, as well as for the effective sources of influence when changes *do* occur, led to the discovery of interpersonal relations.[5] The shared values in groups of family, friends, and co-workers and the networks of communication which are their structure, the decision and the networks of members to accept or resist a new idea – all these are interpersonal processes which 'intervene' between the campaign in the mass media and the individual who is the ultimate target. These recent discoveries, of course, upset the traditional image of the individual audience upon which the discipline has been based. Moreover, there is good reason to believe that the image of society in the minds of students of popular culture needs revision in other dimensions as well.[6] But these remarks are concerned only with the discovery that the mass audience is not so atomized and disconnected as had been thought.

Interpersonal relations and mass communications

Given the need to modify the image of the audience so as to take account of the role of interpersonal relations in the process of mass communications, researchers seem to have proceeded in three directions. First of all, studies were designed so as to characterize individuals not only by their individual attributes but also by their relationship to others. At the Bureau of Applied Social Research of Colombia University, where much of this work has gone on, a series of successive studies examined the ways in which influences from the mass media are intercepted by interpersonal networks of communication and made more or less effective thereby. These were studies of voters, of housewives to try a new kind of food, of doctors to adopt a new drug, and so on.[7] Elsewhere, studies have focused on the relevance of such variables as relative integration among peers or membership in one kind of group rather than another.[8] These studies are rapidly multiplying.

A second strategy is the study of small groups; indeed, a number of links have been forged between macroscopic research on the mass media and the microscopic study of interpersonal communication.[9]

But, while research on small groups can provide many clues to a better understanding of the role of interpersonal relations in the process of mass communications, it focuses almost exclusively on what goes on *within* a group. The third strategy of research, then, was to seek leads from research concerned with the introduction of change from *outside* a social system. Here the work of the rural sociologists is of major importance.[10] For the last two decades the latter have been inquiring into the effectiveness of campaigns to gain acceptance of new farm practices in rural communities while taking explicit account of the relevant channels of communication both outside and inside the community.[11] Yet, despite the obvious parallel between rural and urban campaigns, it was not until after the 'discovery' of interpersonal relations that the student of mass communications had occasion to 'discover' rural sociology.

Interpersonal relations and rural communication

If the assumption that interpersonal relations were irrelevant was central to the research worker on mass communications, the opposite was true of the student of rural campaigns. And the reasons are quite apparent: rural sociologists never assumed, as students of mass communications had, that their respondents did not talk to each other. How could one overlook the possible relevance of farmers' contacts with one another to their response to a new and recommended farm practice? The structure of interpersonal relations, it was assumed, was no less important for channeling the flow of influence than the farm journal or the country agent.[12]

Why did relationships among members of the audience figure so much more prominently in research on new farm practices than in research on marketing campaigns, campaigns to reduce prejudice, and the like? Consider the following explanations.

It is obvious, in the first place, that rural sociologists define their arena of research, at least in part, by contrast with the allegedly impersonal, atomized, anomic life of the city. If urban relationships are 'secondary', rural life must be somewhere near the other end of the continuum. Hence primary, interpersonal relations – their location, their sizes and shapes, and their consequences – are of central concern.[13]

Second, research on mass communications, linked as it is to research on opinions and attitudes, is derived more directly from individual psychology than sociology. Students of rural change, on the other hand, have a sociological heritage and a continuing tradition of tracing the relations of cliques, the boundaries of neighbourhoods, the web of kinship and the like.[14]

Only recently has sociological theory begun to have a cumulative impact upon research on mass communications.

Rural sociologists, moreover, who study the adoption of new farm practices are, typically, in the employ of colleges of agriculture, which, in turn, are associated with state colleges and universities. The locale of operations is somewhat more circumscribed, as a result, than it is in the case of the student of urban mass media. The student of the adoption of new farm practices is not interested in, say, a representative national sample. Sometimes, therefore, he will interview all the farmers in a given county or a very large proportion of them, and this makes it possible to collect data on the relations among individual respondents, which, obviously, is impossible in random cross-sectional sampling where respondents are selected as 'far apart' from each other as possible. By the same token, the investigator of rural communication is more a part of the situation he is studying; it is more difficult for him to overlook interpersonal influence as a variable.

Finally, a fact, related in part to the previous one, is that the rural sociologist has been primarily interested in the efficacy of the local agricultural agency's programme, and, while the local agent employs the mass media as well as personal visits, demonstrations, and other techniques, his influence is plainly disproportionately effective among the more educated and those enjoying prestige in the community and considerably less so among others. Research workers soon were able to suggest, however, that the county agent's effectiveness for a majority of the population may be indirect, for the people he influences may influence others. This idea of a 'two-step' flow of communication also suggested itself as a promotional idea to magazines and other vehicles of mass communications, but it was not actually studied – perhaps because it was more difficult to define operationally – until rather recently.[15]

Some consequences of convergence

That research of mass communications and on the diffusion and acceptance of new farm practices have 'discovered' each other is increasingly evident from the references and citations in recent papers in both fields.[16] The realization of the shared interest in the problem of campaigns – or, more accurately now, in the shared problems of diffusion – has evidently overcome academic insulation. From the point of view of students of mass communications, it took a change in the image of the audience to reveal that the two traditions were studying almost exactly the same problem.

Now that the convergence has been accomplished, however, what consequences are likely to follow? First of all, the two will be very likely to affect each other's design of research. The problem of how to take account of interpersonal relations and still preserve the representativeness of a sample is paramount in studies of mass communications, while that of rural sociologists is how to generalize from studies of neighbourhoods, communities, and counties. What is more, despite their persistent concern with interpersonal relations, students of rural diffusion have never mapped the spread of a particular innovation against the sociometric structure of an entire community; paradoxically, a recent study deriving from the tradition of research on mass communications has attempted it.[17] Clearly, both fields can contribute to the refinement of research design, and their contributions, moreover, would have implications not only for each other but for a growing number of substantive fields which are interested in tracing the spread of specific innovations through social structures. This includes the work of students of technical assistance programmes, of health campaigns, of marketing behaviour, of fads and fashions, and the like.

Second, the convergence has already revealed a list of parallel findings which strengthen theory in both. Several findings that seem most central are:

1 In both urban and rural settings personal influence appears to be more effective in gaining acceptance for change than are the mass media or other types of influence. A number of studies – but by no means all – have found that there is a tendency for adopters of an innovation to credit 'other people' with having influenced their decisions.[18] What is of interest, however, is not the precise ranking of the various sources of influence but the undeniable fact that interpersonal communication plays a major role in social and technical change both in the city and on the farm.

2 When decision-making is broken down into phases (e.g. becoming aware of an innovation, becoming interested in it, evaluating it, deciding to try it, etc.), the mass media appear relatively more influential in the early informational phases, whereas personal influences are more effective in the later phases of deliberation and decision. The tendency in both traditions is no longer to look at the media as competitive but, rather, as complimentary by virtue of their function in various phases of an individual's decision.[19]

3 The earliest to accept the innovation are more likely than those who accept later to have been influenced by agricultural agencies, mass media, and other formal and/or impersonal sources, whereas the latter are more likely to be influenced by personal sources (presumably, by the former).[20] Furthermore, the personal sources to which early adopters respond are likely to be outside their own communities, or at a greater distance, than are the personal sources influencing later adopters.[21] The orientation of early

adopters – 'cosmopolitan', 'secular', 'urbanized', 'scientific' (to choose from among the terms that have been employed) – also reveals an openness to the rational evaluation of a proposed change and a willingness for contact with the world outside their communities.[22] Many of the studies support the notion of a 'two-step' flow of communication in which innovators are influenced from outside and in which they, in turn, influence others with whom they have personal contact.

This is not to claim that there are no differences between communication in urban and rural society or that the direction of the difference between the two kinds of communities may not be essentially as originally perceived by social theorists. Nor is it claimed that all research findings are mutually compatible. Instead, the purpose of this paper is to call attention to the image of society implicit in two fields of research on communication, pointing to the influence of such images on the design of research and on 'interdisciplinary' contacts, and to call attention to a few remarkably similar findings in these heretofore unrelated fields, suggesting that the study of communication will surely profit from their increasing interchange.

Notes

1 This point is elaborated in Elihu Katz and Paul F. Lazarsfeld, *Personal Influence: The Part Played by People in the Flow of Mass Communication*, Free Press, New York, 1955.

2 It would be interesting if a rural sociologist would tell it from his point of view. In any case, this meeting of traditions is timely, in view of the pessimism expressed by C. Arnold Anderson's 'Trends in Rural Sociology', in Robert K. Merton et al. (eds), *Sociology Today*, Basic, New York, 1959, p. 361. Anderson regards research on diffusion as the most sophisticated branch of rural sociology.

3 Cf. similar conclusions of Eliot Freidson, 'Communications Research and the Concept of the Mass', in Wilbur Schramm (ed.), *The Process and Effects of Mass Communication*, U. of Illinois Press, Urbana, 1954, pp. 380–8, and Joseph B. Ford, 'The Primary Group in Mass Communication', *Sociology and Social Research*, 1954, 38, pp. 152–8.

4 For a review of such studies see Joseph T. Klapper, *The Effects of the Mass Media*, Bureau of Applied Social Research, New York, 1949; relevant excerpts from this document appear in Schramm (ed.), *op. cit.*, pp. 289–320. G. D. Wiebe suggests reasons why marketing campaigns fare better than others, in 'Merchandising Commodities and Citizenship on Television', *Public Opinion Quarterly*, 1951–52, 15, pp. 679–91. See also Paul F. Lazarsfeld and Robert K. Merton, 'Mass Communication, Popular Taste and Organized Social Action', in Wilbur Schramm (ed.), *Mass Communications*, U. of Illinois Press, Urbana, 1949, pp. 459–80.

5 This parallels the discovery of the relevance of interpersonal relations in other modern institutions, especially in mass production.

6 See Edward A. Shils, 'Mass Society and Its Culture', *Daedalus*, 1960, 89, pp. 288–314, for a critique of the common tendency among students of communication to conceive of mass society as disorganized and anomic.

7 For a review of these studies see Elihu Katz, 'The Two-Step Flow of Communication: An Up-to-Date Report on an Hypothesis', *Public Opinion Quarterly*, 1957, 21, pp. 61–78.

8 For a systematic exposition of a number of these studies see John W. Riley, Jr., and Matilda W. Riley, 'Mass Communication and the Social System', in Merton et al. (eds), *op.*

cit., pp. 537–78, and Joseph T. Klapper, 'What We Know about the Effects of Mass Communication: The Brink of Hope', *Public Opinion Quarterly*, 1957–58, **21**, pp. 453–74.
9 E.g., Carl I. Hovland, Irving L. Janis, and Harold H. Kelley, *Communication and Persuasion*, Yale U. P., New Haven, 1953, chap. V, 'Group Membership and Resistance to Influence', and John W. C. Johnstone and Elihu Katz, 'Youth Culture and Popular Music', *American Journal of Sociology*, 1957, **62**, pp. 563–8. For a review of the implications of research on the small group for the design of research on mass communication see Katz and Lazarsfeld, *op. cit.*, Part I.
10 Relevant also is the anthropological study of underdeveloped areas where social structure may sometimes be taken into account along with culture in explaining the acceptance of chance; e.g., see Benjamin D. Paul (ed.), *Health, Culture and Community: Case Studies of Public Reactions to Health Programs*, Russell Sage Foundation, New York, 1955.
11 For reviews of research in this field see Subcommittee on the Diffusion and Adoption of New Farm Practices of the Rural Sociological Society, *Sociological Research on the Diffusion and Adoption of New Farm Practices*, Lexington: Kentucky Agricultural Experiment Station, 1952, and Eugene A. Wilkening, 'The Communication of Information on Innovations in Agriculture', in Wilbur Schramm (ed.), *Communicating Behavioral Science Information*, Stanford U. P., Stanford, Calif. A bibliography on *Social Factors in the Adoption of Farm Practices* was prepared by the North Central Rural Sociology Subcommittee on Diffusion, Iowa State College, Ames, 1959.
12 Yet rural sociologists have justifiably berated their colleagues for not taking more *systematic* account of interpersonal structures (e.g., Herbert F. Lionberger, 'The Diffusion of Farm and Home Information as an Area of Sociological Research', *Rural Sociology*, 1952, **17**, pp. 132–44.
13 See the propositions concerning the systems of social interaction in rural, as contrasted with urban, society in Pitirim Sorokin and Carle C. Zimmerman, *Principles of Rural-Urban Sociology*, Holt, New York, 1929, pp. 48–58.
14 The work of Charles P. Loomis is outstanding in this connection; on his approach to the relationship between interpersonal structures and the introduction of change see Loomis and J. Allan Beegle, *Rural Sociology: The Strategy of Change*, Prentice-Hall, Englewood Cliffs, N.J., 1957, Sociometry has played an important role in this development.
15 For mention of the claims of communicators that members of their audiences are influential for others see one of the earliest pieces of research on opinion leaders: Frank A. Stewart, 'A Sociometric Study of Influence in Southtown', *Sociometry*, 1947, **10**, pp. 11–31.
16 E.g., Everett M. Rogers and George M. Beal, 'The Importance of Personal Influence in the Adoption of Technological Changes', *Social Forces*, 1958, **36**, pp. 329–35, and Herbert Menzel and Elihu Katz, 'Social Relations and Innovation in the Medical Profession', *Public Opinion Quarterly*, 1955–56, **19**, pp. 337–53. More important, perhaps, is the 'official' recognition of the relevance of research on mass communications in the 1959 bibliography of the North Central Rural Sociology Subcommittee, *op. cit.*
17 See James S. Coleman, Elihu Katz, and Herbert Menzel, 'The Diffusion of an Innovation among Physicians', *Sociometry*, 1957, **20**, pp. 253–70. See also the reports of 'Project Revere', e.g., Stuart C. Dodd, 'Formulas for Spreading Opinions', *Public Opinion Quarterly*, 1958–59, **22**, pp. 537–54, and Melvin L. DeFleur and Otto N. Larsen, *The Flow of Information*, Harper, New York, 1958. Extensive work on informal cliques as facilitators and barriers to interpersonal communication in rural communities has been reported by Herbert F. Lionberger and C. Milton Coughenor, *Social Structure and the Diffusion of Farm Information*, University of Missouri Agricultural Experiment Station, Columbia, 1957.
18 Typically, the respondent is asked to recall the sources influencing him, arrange them chronologically, and then select the one which was 'most influential'. The shortcomings of this are obvious. There are many exceptions, but a sizeable number of studies have reported that the influence of 'other people' is more influential than other sources. See, e.g., Herbert F. Lionberger, *Information-seeking Habits and Characteristics of Farm Operators*, Missouri Agricultural Experiment Station Research Bull. 581, Columbia, 1955; E. A. Wilkening, *Adoption of Improved Farm Practices as Related to Family Factors*, Wisconsin Agricultural

Experiment Station Research Bull. 183, Madison, 1953; Marvin A. Anderson, 'Acceptance and Use of Fertilizer in Iowa', *Croplife*, II, 1955; George Fisk, 'Media Influence Reconsidered', *Public Opinion Quarterly*, 1959, 23, pp. 83–91; and Katz and Lazarsfeld, *op. cit.*, Part II. The more important question, however, is under what conditions certain sources of influence are more or less likely to be influential. Different innovations, different social structures, and different phases of the process of decision and of diffusion have been shown to be associated with variations in the role of the media. The latter two factors are treated below.

19 Cf. James S. Coleman, Elihu Katz, and Herbert Menzel, *Doctors and New Drugs*, Free Press, New York, 1960, with such recent rural studies as Rogers and Beal, *op. cit.*; James H. Copp, Maurice L. Sill, and Emory J. Brown, 'The Function of Information Sources in the Farm Practice Adoption Process', *Rural Sociology*, 1958, 23, pp. 146–57; and Eugene A. Wilkening, 'Roles of Communicating Agents in Technological Change in Agriculture', *Social Forces*, 1956, 34, pp. 361–67. Earlier formulations tended to *infer* the psychological stages of decision-making from the typical sequence of the media reported by respondents, but more recent formulations define the phases of decisions and the media employed in each phase independently. The studies cited above representing the most advanced approach to this problem are also considering the consequences of the use of media 'appropriate' or 'inappropriate' to a given stage of decision.

20 This, of course, is the 'two-step' flow of communication, a conception which finds support in the studies reviewed by Katz, *op. cit.*; Rogers and Beal, *op. cit.*; Lionberger, *op. cit.*; and F. E. Emery and O. A. Oeser, *Information, Decision and Action: Psychological Determinants of Changes in Farming Techniques*, University of Melbourne Press, Melbourne, Australia 1958.

21 Cf. Coleman, Katz, and Menzel, *op. cit.*, with E. A. Wilkening, *Acceptance of Improved Farm Practices in Three Coastal Plain Counties*, North Carolina Agricultural Experiment Station Technical Bull. 98, Chapel Hill, 1952, and James Copp, *Personal and Social Factors Associated with the Adoption of Recommended Farm Practices*, Kansas State College, Agricultural Experiment Station Research Bull., Manhattan, 1956.

22 See Bryce Ryan and Neal Gross, *Acceptance and Diffusion of Hybrid Seed Corn in Two Iowa Communities*, Iowa State College, Agricultural Experiment Station Bull. 372, Ames, 1950, and Emery and Oeser, *op. cit.* The latter, however, suggest that, under certain conditions, personal contact may be more important for early adopters even though they, in turn, are primary sources of influence for those who follow their lead.

45 The impact of allied propaganda on Wehrmacht solidarity

Edward A. Shils and Morris Janowitz

The system of controls which the social structure of the Wehrmacht exercised over its individual members greatly reduced those areas in which symbolic appeals of the Allies could work. But the millions of leaflets which were dropped weekly and the 'round-the-clock' broadcasts to the German troops certainly did not fail to produce some reactions.

The very first German prisoners of war who were interrogated directly on their reactions to Allied propaganda soon revealed a stereotyped range of answers which could be predicted from their degree of Nazification. The fanatical Nazi claimed, 'No German would believe anything the enemy has to say,' while an extreme attitude of acceptance was typified by a confirmed anti-Nazi who pleaded with his captors: 'Now is the moment to flood the troops with leaflets. You have no idea of the effect sober and effective leaflets have on retreating troops.' But these extreme reactions of soldiers were of low frequency; Nazi soldiers might admit the truth of our leaflets but usually would not accept their conclusions and implications.

The fundamentally indifferent reaction to Allied propaganda was most interestingly shown in an intensive study of 150 prisoners of war captured in October 1944 of whom 65 per cent had seen our leaflets and for the most part professed that they believed their contents. This was a group which had fought very obstinately, and the number of active deserters, if any, was extremely small. Some forty of these prisoners of war offered extended comments as to what they meant when they said they believed the contents of Allied leaflets.

Five stated outright that they believed the messages and that the leaflets assisted them and their comrades to surrender.

Seven declared they believed the leaflets, but were powerless to do anything about appeals to surrender.

Eight stated that they believed the contents, but nevertheless as soldiers and decent individuals would never think of deserting.

Twenty-two declared that events justified belief in the leaflets, but they

---

SHILS, EDWARD A. and JANOWITZ, MORRIS (1948) 'The impact of allied propaganda on Wehrmacht solidarity' from 'Cohesion and disintegration in the Wehrmacht in World War II' in *Public Opinion Quarterly*, vol. 12, 280–315.

clearly implied that this had been of little importance in their battle experiences.

In Normandy, where the relatively small front was blanketed with printed material, up to 90 per cent of the prisoners of war reported that they had read Allied leaflets, yet this period was characterized by very high German morale and stiff resistance.

Throughout the Western campaign, with the exception of periods of extremely bad weather or when the front was fluid, the cumulative percentage of exposure ranged between 60 and 80 per cent. (This cumulative percentage of exposure was based on statements by prisoners of war that they had seen leaflets sometimes while fighting on the Western front after D-Day. A few samples indicated that penetration during any single month covered about 20 per cent of the prisoners.) Radio listening among combat troops was confined to a minute fraction due to the lack of equipment; rear troops listened more frequently. In the case of both leaflets and radio it was found that there was widespread but desultory comment on the propaganda, much of which comment distorted the actual contents.

Not only was there wide penetration by Allied leaflets and newssheets, but German soldiers frequently circulated them extensively among their comrades. A readership study of *Nachrichten für die Truppe*, a daily newssheet published by the Allied Psychological Warfare Division, showed that each copy which was picked up had an average readership of between four and five soldiers – a figure which is extremely large in view of the conditions of combat life. Not only were leaflets widely circulated, but it became a widespread practice for soldiers to carry Allied leaflets on their person, especially the 'safe conduct pass' leaflets which bore a statement by General Eisenhower guaranteeing the bearer swift and safe conduct through Allied lines and the protection of the Geneva convention. There is evidence that in certain sectors of the front, German soldiers even organized black-market trading in Allied propaganda materials.

It is relevant to discuss here the differences in effectiveness between tactical and strategic propaganda. By tactical propaganda, we refer to propaganda which seeks to promise immediate results in the tactical situation. The clearest example of this type of propaganda is afforded by 'cross the lines' loudspeaker broadcasts, which sometimes facilitated immediate capture of the prisoners of war – not by propaganda in the ordinary sense, but by giving instructions on how to surrender safely, once the wish to surrender was present.

No sufficiently accurate estimate is available of the total number of prisoners captured by the use of such techniques, but signal successes involving hundreds of isolated troops in the Normandy campaign have been credited to psychological warfare combat teams. Even more successful were the loud-speaker-carrying tanks employed in the Rhine River offensive, when the first signs of weakening resistance were encountered. For example, the Fourth Armoured Division reported that its psychological warfare unit captured over 500 prisoners in a four-day dash from Kyll River to the Rhine. Firsthand investigation of these loudspeaker missions, and interrogation of prisoners captured under such circumstances, establish that Allied propaganda was effective in describing the tactical situation to totally isolated and helpless soldiers and in arranging an Allied cease fire and thereby presenting an assurance to the German soldier of a safe surrender. The successful targets for such broadcasts were groups where solidarity and ability to function as a unit were largely destroyed. Leaflets especially written for specific sectors and dropped on pin point targets by fighter-bombs were used instead of loudspeakers where larger units were cut off. This method proved less successful, since the units to which they were addressed were usually better integrated and the necessary cease fire conditions could not be arranged.

Less spectacular, but more extensive, was strategic propaganda. Allied directives called for emphasis on four themes in this type of propaganda: (1) ideological attacks on the Nazi Party and Germany's war aims, (2) the strategical hopelessness of Germany's military and economic position, (3) the justness of the United Nations war aims and their unity and determination to carry them out (unconditional surrender, although made known to the troops, was never stressed), (4) promises of good treatment to prisoners of war, with appeals to self-preservation through surrender.

Although it is extremely difficult, especially in view of the lack of essential data, to assess the efficacy of these various themes, some tentative clues might be seen in the answers given to the key attitude questions in the monthly Psychological Warfare opinion poll of captured German soldiers.[1] Thus, there was no significant decline in attachment to Nazi ideology until February and March 1945. In other words, propaganda attacks on Nazi ideology seem to have been of little avail, and attachment to secondary symbols, e.g., Hitler, declined only when the smaller military units began to break up under very heavy pressure.

Since the German soldier was quite ignorant of military news on other fronts, it was believed that a great deal of printed material should contain factual reports of the military situation, stressing the strategical hopelessness of the German position. As a result, the third most frequently recalled items of our propaganda were the military news reports. It seems reasonable to

1 See Gurfein, M. I., and Janowitz, Morris (1946) 'Trends in Wehrmacht Morale', *The Public Opinion Quarterly*, 10, no. 1, 78.

believe that the emphasis on these subjects did contribute to the development of defeatist sentiment.

Despite the vast amount of space devoted to ideological attacks on German leaders, only about five per cent of the prisoners of war mentioned this topic – a fact which supported the contention as to the general failure of ideological or secondary appeals. Finally, the presentation of the justness of our war aims was carried out in such a way as to avoid stressing the unconditional surrender aspects of our intentions, while emphasizing post-war peace intentions and organizational efforts; much was made of United Nations unity. All this fell on deaf ears, for of this material only a small minority of prisoners of war (about 5 per cent) recalled specific statements about military government plans for the German occupation.

As has been pointed out previously, the themes which were most successful, at least in attracting attention and remaining fixed in the memory, were those promising good treatment as prisoners of war. In other words, propaganda referring to immediate concrete situations and problems seems to have been most effective in some respects.

The single leaflet most effective in communicating the promise of good treatment was the 'safe conduct pass'. Significantly, it was usually printed on the back of leaflets which contained no elaborate propaganda appeals except those of self-preservation. The rank and file tended to be favourably disposed to its official language and legal, document-like character. In one sector where General Eisenhower's signature was left off the leaflet, doubt was cast on its authenticity.

Belief in the veracity of this appeal was no doubt based on the attitude that the British and the Americans were respectable law-abiding soldiers who would treat their captives according to international law. As a result of this predisposition and the wide use of the safe conduct leaflets, as well as our actual practices in treating prisoners well, the German soldier came to have no fear of capture by British or American troops. The most that can be claimed for this lack of fear was that it may have decreased or undercut any tendency to fight to the death; it produced no active opposition to continued hostilities.

As an extension of the safe-conduct approach, leaflets were prepared instructing non-commissioned officers in detailed procedures by which their men could safely be removed from battle so as to avoid our fire and at the same time avoid evacuation by the German field police. If the Germans could not be induced to withdraw from combat actively, Allied propaganda appealed to them to hide in cellars. This in fact became a favourite technique of surrender, since it avoided the need of facing the conscience-twinging desertion problem.

As a result of psychological warfare research, a series of leaflets was prepared whose attack was aimed at primary group organization in the German Army, without recourse to ideological symbols. Group organization depended on the acceptance of immediate leadership and mutual trust. Therefore this series of leaflets sought to stimulate group discussion among the men and to bring into their focus of attention concerns which would loosen solidarity. One leaflet declared, 'Do not take our (the Allies) word for it; ask your comrade; find out how he feels.' Thereupon followed a series of questions on personal concerns, family problems, tactical consideration and supply problems. Discussion of these problems was expected to increase anxiety. It was assumed that to the degree that the soldier found that he was not isolated in his opinion, to that degree he would be strengthened in his resolve to end hostilities for himself at least.

At the beginning of the second world war, many publicists and specialists in propaganda attributed almost supreme importance to psychological warfare operations. The legendary success of Allied propaganda against the Germany Army at the end of the first world war and the tremendous expansion of the advertising and mass communications industries in the ensuing two decades had convinced many people that human behaviour could be extensively manipulated by mass communications. They tended furthermore to stress that military morale was to a great extent a function of the belief in the rightness of the 'larger' cause which was at issue in the war; good soldiers were therefore those who clearly understood the political and moral implications of what was at stake. They explained the striking successes of the German Army in the early phases of the war by the 'ideological possession' of the German soldiers, and they accordingly thought that propaganda attacking doctrinal conceptions would be defeating this army.

Studies of the German Army's morale and fighting effectiveness made during the last three years of the war throw considerable doubt on these hypotheses. The solidarity of the German Army was discovered by these studies – which left much to be desired from the standpoint of scientific rigour – to be based only very indirectly and very partially on political convictions or broader ethical beliefs. Where conditions were such as to allow primary group life to function smoothly, and where the primary group developed a high degree of cohesion, morale was high and resistance effective or at least very determined, regardless in the main of the political attitudes of the soldiers. The conditions of primary group life were related to spatial proximity, the capacity for intimate communication, the provision of paternal protectiveness by NCOs and junior officers, and the gratification of certain personality needs, e.g., manliness, by the military organization and its activities. The larger structure of the army served to maintain morale through the provision of the framework in which potentially individuating physical threats were kept at a minimum – through the organization of supplies and through adequate strategic dispositions.

The behaviour of the German Army demonstrated that the focus of attention and concern beyond one's immediate face-to-face social circles might be slight indeed and still not interfere with the achievement of a high degree of military effectiveness. It also showed that attempts to modify behaviour by means of symbols referring to events or values outside the focus of attention and concern would be given an indifferent response by the vast majority of the German soldiers. This was almost equally true under conditions of primary group integrity and under conditions of extreme primary group disintegration. In the former, primary needs were met adequately through the gratifications provided by the other members of the group; in the latter, the individual had regressed to a narcissistic state in which symbols referring to the outer world were irrelevant to his first concern – 'saving his own skin'.

At moments of primary group disintegration, a particular kind of propaganda less hortatory or analytical, but addressing the intensified desire to survive and describing the precise procedures by which physical survival could be achieved, was likely to facilitate further disintegration. Furthermore, in some cases aspects of the environment towards which the soldier might hitherto have been emotionally indifferent were defined for him by prolonged exposure to propaganda under conditions of disintegration. Some of these wider aspects, e.g., particular strategic consideration, then tended to be taken into account in his motivation and he was more likely to implement his defeatist mood by surrender than he would have been without exposure to propaganda.

It seems necessary, therefore, to reconsider the potentialities of propaganda in the context of all the other variables which influence behaviour. The erroneous views concerning the omnipotence of propaganda must be given up and their place must be taken by much more differentiated views as to the possibilities of certain kinds of propaganda under different sets of conditions.

It must be recognized that on the moral plane most men are members of the larger society by virtue of identifications which are mediated through the human beings with whom they are in personal relationships. Many are bound into the larger society only by primary group identifications. Only a small proportion possessing special training or rather particular kinds of personalities are capable of giving a preponderant share of their attention and concern to the symbols of the larger world. The conditions under which these different groups will respond to propaganda will differ, as will also the type of propaganda to which they will respond.

46 Re-education: Dr Vincent

Robert J. Lifton

I first heard of Dr Charles Vincent through a newspaper article announcing his arrival in Hong Kong by ship after three and one-half years of imprisonment and twenty previous years of medical practice in China. I was put in touch with him through another subject of mine who had known him in the past. When I telephoned him at the boarding house where he was staying, he readily agreed to talk with me; but when I began to describe to him the location of my office, he showed some hesitation and then made it clear that he wanted me to come and pick him up. I consented to this arrangement and met him in the lobby of his rooming house just five days after he crossed the border. Dr Vincent was a short, dark-complexioned, muscular Frenchman in his early fifties. He was not emaciated, but he did look pale; and in his eyes was that characteristic combination of fear and distance which has been aptly labelled 'the thousand-mile stare'.

He said little during the brief automobile ride, but in response to my inquiries about how he was getting on in Hong Kong, he described feeling frightened and nervous. Upon entering my study, he sat down hesitantly, and listened without comment to my few sentences of explanation about my research. When I had finished, he looked at me directly for the first time and asked a quick series of questions: How old was I? How long had I been in Hong Kong doing this work? And then, with particular emphasis, 'Are you standing on the "people's side", or on the "imperialists' side"?' I told him I was part of the non-Communist world, but that I tried as much as possible to take no side in order to gain an understanding of the process of thought reform. He went on to explain that this was important because

> From the imperialistic side we are not criminals; from the people's side we are criminals. If we look at this from the imperialists' side, re-education is a kind of compulsion. But if we look at it from the people's side, it is to die and be born again.

Having expressed both his fear and his dilemma – and, indeed, the paradox of thought reform itself – he needed no more prompting to go into the

---

LIFTON, ROBERT J. (1961) 'Re-education: Dr Vincent' in *Thought Reform and the Psychology of Totalism. A Study of 'Brainwashing' in China* London, Victor Gollancz, 19–31.

details of his ordeal. I said little during this first three-hour interview, and not much more during the remaining fifteen hours (five additional meetings) which we spent together, for Dr Vincent had a great need to talk about what he had been through, and he did so in an unusually vivid fashion.

As one of the few remaining foreign physicians in Shanghai, he had been conducting a lucrative practice which included several Communist officials – until suddenly confronted on the street one afternoon by five men with revolvers. They produced a warrant for his arrest and took him to the 'detention house' (or 're-education centre') where he was to spend the next three and a half years.

Interrogation and 'struggle'

After a few preliminaries he was placed in a small (8′ × 12′) bare cell which already contained eight other prisoners, all of them Chinese. They were a specially selected group, each of them 'advanced' in his personal 'reform', each eager to apply himself enthusiastically to the reform of others as a means of gaining 'merits' towards his own release. Their greeting was hardly a friendly one: the 'cell chief' identified himself, and addressing Vincent in Chinese [1] by his newly-acquired prison number, instructed him to sit in the centre of the cell while the other prisoners formed a circle around him. Each in turn then shouted invectives at Vincent, denouncing him as an 'imperialist' and a 'spy', demanding that he 'recognize' his 'crimes' and 'confess everything' to the 'government'. Vincent protested: He was not a spy. He was a doctor. He had worked as a doctor in China for twenty years. But this only resulted in more vehement accusations: 'The government has all the proof. They have arrested you and the government never makes a mistake. You have not been arrested for nothing.' Then his cellmates went on to question him further about all the activities in which he engaged as a physician to 'cover up' his 'spy personality'. This procedure in the cell was known as a 'struggle', conducted for the purpose of 'helping' a prisoner with his 'confession', and it was an experience which Vincent had to undergo frequently, particularly during the early phases of his imprisonment.

After several hours of this disturbing treatment, Vincent was called for his first interrogation. He was taken to a small room with three people in it: the interrogator or 'judge',[2] an interpreter, and a secretary. The judge opened the session with a vague accusation and an emphatic demand: 'You have committed crimes against the people, and you must now confess everything.' Vincent's protestations of innocence were countered with the angry declaration: 'The government never arrests an innocent man.' The judge went on to ask a series of general questions concerning Vincent's activities, professional associations, organizational contacts, friends, and acquaintances during his entire twenty years in China. He answered these as accurately as he could, but was unable to satisfy his interrogator. The judge's demands always contained a tantalizing combination of hint, threat and promise: 'The government knows all about your crimes. That is why we arrested you. It is now up to you to confess everything to us, and in this way your case can be quickly solved and you will soon be released.'

After a few hours of this interrogation, questions began to focus more and more upon alleged connections with people from several groups: his own embassy, American government officials, and Catholic, Japanese, and Nationalist Chinese agencies. By 6 am, after ten successive hours of interrogation, he had produced much information; but he still asserted his innocence, denied that he was a spy or had any subversive relationship with these organizations, and again said that he did not understand why he had been arrested. This angered the judge, who ordered handcuffs applied to Vincent's wrists, holding his arms behind his back. He dismissed the prisoner from the room, demanding that he 'think over' his 'crimes'. But when he was returned ten minutes later, Vincent still stated that he could not recognize crimes of any kind. The judge again became incensed, ordered chains placed about Vincent's ankles, and sent him back to his cell. His return there was the occasion for continuous struggle and humiliation.

> When you get back with your chains, your cellmates receive you as an enemy. They start 'struggling' to 'help you'. The 'struggle' goes on all day to 8 pm that night. You are obliged to stand with chains on your ankles and holding your hands behind your back. They don't assist you because you are too reactionary . . . You eat as a dog does, with your mouth and teeth. You arrange the cup and bowl with your nose to try to absorb broth twice a day. If you have to make water they open your trousers and you make water in a little tin in the corner . . . In the WC someone opens your trousers and after you are finished they clean you. You are never out of the chains. Nobody pays any attention to your hygiene. Nobody washes you. In the room they say you are in chains only because you are a reactionary. They continuously tell you that, if you confess all, you will be treated better.

Towards the end of the second day, Vincent was concerned only with finding some relief ('You start to think, how to get rid of these chains. *You must get rid of the chains*'[3]). That night, when called for interrogation, he made what he called a 'wild confession' – a description of espionage activities which he knew to be non-existent. As he explained it:

> We see in the judge someone who wants to press something on us. And if we show we are a big criminal, maybe we will get better treatment . . . Everyone of us tries to cheat the government this way. We know they are angry with the Americans . . . so we become a member of an American spy ring . . . I invented a whole organization.

But when he was pressed for details, he could not substantiate his story, and inconsistencies appeared. The confession was rejected, and he was once more summarily dismissed by the judge. The round of interrogation and struggle continued.

On the third night, he changed his tactics. Aware that the officials were greatly interested in his activities and contacts, he began to reconstruct and confess every detail of every conversation with friends and associates which he could remember from the whole of his twenty years in China. He did this because 'I thought they were trying to prove I gave intelligence to friends'.

Now that he was talking freely, his captors began to press home their advantage. Interrogations, ever more demanding, took up the greater part of each night; these were interrupted every two or three hours for a rapid and painful promenade (in chains) which served to keep the prisoner awake, to increase his physical discomfort, and to give him a sense of movement ('in order to convince you to speed up your confession'). During the day, he was required to dictate to another prisoner everything he had confessed the night before, and anything additional he could think of. When he was not dictating the confessions or making new ones, he was being struggled. Every activity in the cell seemed to be centred around him and his confession. He soon realized that the cell chief was making daily reports to prison officials and receiving regular instructions on how to deal with him. Everything he did or said – every word, movement, or expression – was noted and written down by other prisoners, then conveyed to the prison authorities.

For eight days and nights, Vincent experienced this programme of alternating struggle and interrogation, and was permitted no sleep at all.[4] Moreover, he was constantly told by his cellmates that he was completely responsible for his own plight. ('You want the chains! You want to be shot! . . . Otherwise, you would be more "sincere" and the chains would not be necessary.') He found himself in a Kafka-like maze of vague and yet damning accusations: he could neither understand exactly what he was guilty of ('recognize his crimes') nor could he in any way establish his innocence. Overwhelmed by fatigue, confusion, and helplessness, he ceased all resistance.

> You are annihilated . . . exhausted . . . you can't control yourself, or remember what you said two minutes before. You feel that all is lost . . . From that moment, the judge is the real master of you. You accept anything he says. When he asks how many 'intelligences' you gave to that person, you just put out a number in order to satisfy him. If he says, 'Only those?', you say, 'No, there are more.' If he says, 'One hundred,' you say, 'One hundred' . . . You do whatever they want. You don't pay any more attention to your life or to your handcuffed arms. You can't distinguish right from left. You just wonder when you will be shot – and begin to hope for the end of all this.

A confession began to emerge which was still 'wild' – full of exaggerations, distortions, and falsehoods – but at the same time closely related to real events and people in Vincent's life. Every night Vincent would sign a written statement of his newly confessed material with a thumbprint, as his hands were not free for writing. He was so compliant by this time that he made no attempt to check upon the accuracy of what he was signing.

After three weeks, the emphasis again shifted; now he was required to report on others, to make exhaustive lists of all of the people he had known in China, and to write out their addresses, their affiliations, and anything at all which he knew about their activities. Vincent complied, again supplying a mixture of truths, half-truths, and untruths. But after two weeks of this, under the continuing pressures of his captors, these descriptions became exposés and denunciations; friends, associates became drawn into the web. Still the clamour from the judge, officials, and cellmates was the same as it had been since the moment of imprisonment: 'Confess! . . . Confess all! . . . You must be frank! . . . You must show your faith in the government! . . . Come clean! . . . Be sincere! . . . Recognize your crimes! . . .'

At this point – about two months from the date of his arrest – Vincent was considered to be ready for a beginning 'recognition' of his 'crimes'. This required that he learn to look at himself from the 'people's standpoint' – to accept the prevailing Communist definition of criminal behaviour, including the principle that 'the people's standpoint makes no distinction between news, information, and intelligence'. He described two examples of this process:

> For instance, I was the family physician and friend of an American correspondent. We talked about many things, including the political situation . . . The judge questioned me again and again about my relationship with this man. He asked me for details about everything we had talked about . . . I admitted that at the time of the 'liberation', when I saw the horsedrawn artillery of the Communist army, I told this to my American friend . . . The

> judge shouted that this American was a spy who was collecting espionage material for his spy organization, and that I was guilty of supplying him with military intelligence . . . At first I did not accept this, but soon I had to add it to my confession . . . This is adopting the people's standpoint . . .
>
> I knew a man who was friendly with an American military attaché. I told him the price of shoes and that I couldn't buy gasoline for my car. I had already agreed that this was economic intelligence. So I wrote that I gave economic intelligence to this man. But they made it clear that I must say that I received an espionage mission from the American military attaché through the other person, to collect economic intelligence . . . This was the people's standpoint.

'Leniency' and 'study'

Just as Vincent was beginning to express himself from the 'people's standpoint' – but in a dazed, compliant, and unenthusiastic manner – he was suddenly surprised by a remarkable improvement in his status: the handcuffs and chains were removed, he was permitted to be comfortably seated when talking to the judge, and he was in turn addressed in friendly tones. He was told that the government regretted that he had been having such a difficult time, that it really wanted only to help him, and that in accordance with its 'lenient policy' it would certainly treat him kindly and soon release him – if only he would make an absolutely complete confession, and then work hard to 'reform' himself. And to help things along, pressures were diminished, and he was permitted more rest. This abrupt reversal in attitude had a profound effect upon Vincent: for the first time he had been treated with human consideration, the chains were gone, he could see a possible solution ahead, there was hope for the future.

Now he was offered more friendly 'guidance' in rewriting (not once but many times) his entire confession, including descriptions and denunciations of other people; and his change of fortune gave him added incentive in applying himself to the task. But he soon found that this guidance was not to be taken lightly, and on three occasions when he expressed some measure of resistance, saying, 'This I didn't do', the chains were reapplied for two or three days, accompanied by a return to the harsh treatment of previous weeks.

Once 'leniency' had been initiated, however, Vincent was never again to experience anything as overwhelming as the assaults of his early prison period. Given the luxury of eight hours of sleep a night, of relatively calm and restrained interrogations (he was even permitted to sit on a chair), of practically no harassment in the cell, Vincent spent the next two or three weeks doing nothing but developing in even greater detail his confession material. During his sessions with the judge, he received further instructions upon the proper way to apply the 'people's standpoint' to all that he was writing and saying.

Meanwhile, he was initiated into the regular cell routine: carefully regimented arrangements for sleeping and awakening, for eating and for relieving oneself. Freed of the chains, he could join the others on the two daily excursions to the toilet (everyone running head down, to an area with two open toilets, each permitted about forty-five seconds to attend to his needs with sharp criticism directed at anyone who took longer than this), and in the use of the urine bucket in the cell. He was still addressed only by prison number, and continued to receive food adequate for survival but poor in quality. And the sores and infections caused by his chains and handcuffs were given more attention, including local applications and penicillin injections.

Then, three weeks after the beginning of 'leniency', he began to take part in the cell's organized 're-education' procedures. This meant active involvement in the group study programme – the *hsüeh hsi* – whose sessions took up almost the entire waking existence of the prisoners, ten to sixteen hours a day. Led by the cell chief, its procedure was simple enough: one prisoner read material from a Communist newspaper, book, or pamphlet; and then each in turn was expected to express his own opinion and to criticize the views of others. Everyone was required to participate actively, and anyone who did not was severely criticized. Each had to learn to express himself from the 'correct' or 'people's standpoint' – applied not only to personal actions, but to political, social, and ethical issues. With each of the prisoners feeling that his freedom or even his life might be at stake, the zeal of the participants was overwhelming.

For a long time after Dr Vincent joined the group (and probably because of his presence), discussions centred upon past Western insults to China: territorial aggrandizement, infringements upon sovereignty, special privileges demanded for Western nationals. And the message was conveyed to him personally that 'under the cloak of medicine' he was nothing but a representative of 'exploitation', an agent of the 'imperialists', a lifelong 'spy', whose actions were from the beginning 'harmful to the Chinese people'.

Discussions starting at an intellectual level would quickly become concerned with personal analysis and criticism. When Dr Vincent was found wanting in his adoption of the 'people's standpoint' or when his views were considered 'erroneous', it became necessary for him to 'examine himself' and look into the causes of these 'reactionary' tendencies. He had to search out the harmful 'bourgeois' and 'imperialistic' influences from his past for further evaluation and self-criticism. Every 'question' or 'problem' had to be 'solved', according to the 'facts', in order to get to the 'truth', viewing everything, of course, from the 'people's standpoint'.

Special 'movements' would take place, jolting the prisoners from the ordinary routine into renewed emotional efforts. Sometimes these were part of broad, all-China campaigns, sometimes related to national prison movements, and sometimes locally initiated; but whether directed at 'thought attitude', prison discipline, hygiene problems, or personal confessions, they always served to plunge each prisoner into a more thorough and compelling self-examination. Everyone was intent upon demonstrating his own 'reform' and 'progressive viewpoint'. The atmosphere came to resemble that of a great moral crusade.

Dr Vincent was still receiving more personal attention than anyone else in the cell. At first he simply gave lip-service to what he knew to be the 'correct' point of view, but over a period of weeks and months, he began to accept these judgments inwardly, and to apply them to himself.

> In the cell, you work in order to recognize your crimes. . . . They make you understand your crimes are very heavy. You did harm to the Chinese people. You are really a spy, and all the punishment you received was your own fault. . . . In the cell, twelve hours a day, you talk and talk – you have to take part – you must discuss yourself, criticize, inspect yourself, denounce your thought. Little by little you start to admit something, and look to yourself only using the 'people's judgment'.

At times, the prison would take on a highly academic atmosphere. Vincent and his fellow prisoners would focus their attention on applying Marxist theory to Chinese and international problems; prisoners would be referred to as 'schoolmates', prison officials would be called 'instructors', and all would emphasize that only 'discussion' and 'persuasion' should be used to teach the ignorant. As Vincent became more and more involved in the process, he began to experience its impact.

> They put in evidence, in a compulsory way, the progress of the people. The people have a future. The theories of Marx about history teach us that imperialism is condemned to be destroyed. . . . They put in evidence all the examples of repression by the imperialists in China, the missions, their charity, helping landlords, helping the KMT [Kuomintang, or Nationalist Party] – all against the people. . . . They put in evidence the development of the Soviet Union – its industries, re-education, culture, uplifting of the people, the friendly help of the Soviet to China. They told us of the victory against imperialism in the Korean war, the gradual remoulding of Chinese society, the three- and five-year plans in order to arrive at socialist society,

> the transformation of agriculture, the development of heavy industries, military improvement to defend the people, peace movement. . . . Living conditions of the Soviet state are very high; we see it in the movies, magazines, newspapers. We see the better conditions of Chinese people in comparison with pre-liberation times – the hygiene movement in China, the cultural, the economic movement, the rights for minorities, rights between man and woman, free elections, the difference between freedom in the socialist and the imperialist worlds. . . . They solve every problem through discussion – the Korean war, the Indo-Chinese war. . . . They never use force; every question is solved through conference.

But always, the emphasis would shift back to the individual emotional experience – to the 'thought problems' which prevented prisoners from making progress. Dr Vincent learned to express 'spontaneously' all of his reactions and attitudes during the discussions and especially to bring out his 'wrong thoughts'. And as he did so, he became ever more enmeshed in the special problem-solving techniques of this ideological world.

> You have to get rid of and denounce all your imperialist thoughts, and you must criticize all of your own thoughts, guided by the official. If not, they will have someone else solve your problem and criticize you more profoundly. . . . You have a problem – you have to denounce it – a schoolmate has to help you – his help has to have 'proper standpoint'. . . . I am quiet – they say, 'You have a problem'; I say, 'I wonder why the Chinese didn't confiscate all of the capitalist properties like the Soviets. I think it might be better to do it like the Russians – this is my problem.' They have schoolmates to solve my problems, to demonstrate I am on the wrong side because the Chinese Communists have to proceed in another way. Their way is reform rather than compulsion. He demonstrates that the Soviet revolution was different from the Chinese revolution – that the Chinese capitalists suffered through the imperialists because we imperialists never gave them the opportunity to develop their industries. Now the Chinese capitalists have to be useful to the Chinese government and undergo reform. If they follow the government they will have a bright future. . . . They have to explain the facts until I am convinced. If I am not convinced I must say I don't understand, and they bring new facts. If I am still not satisfied, I have the right to call an inspector – but I wouldn't, I would just accept, otherwise there might be a struggle. . . . You are all day under the compulsion of denouncing your thoughts and solving your problems. . . . You understand the truth of the people – day by day, moment by moment – and you cannot escape, because from your external manifestation they say they can understand your internal situation. If you continually denounce your thoughts, you can be happy denouncing yourself. You are not resisting. But they keep a record, and after one week if you are not saying anything, they tell you you are resisting your re-education. . . . If you think out five or

> six problems it is a good manifestation; you are progressing because you like to discuss your imperialist thoughts. This is necessary, because if you don't get rid of these thoughts, you can't put in new ones.

When Vincent was too quiet and did not produce enough 'wrong thoughts', he was criticized for not being 'sincere' – for not taking an active enough part in thought reform. When his views showed the slightest deviation from Communist orthodoxy, he was told that he was 'too subjective', 'individualistic', or that he retained 'imperialist attitudes'. When it was felt that he was not wholeheartedly involved in his reform – but was merely going through the motions – he was accused of 'spreading a smokescreen', 'window dressing', 'finding a loophole', or 'failing to combine theory with practice'. And after a while he followed the others' lead in seeking out these faults in himself through self-criticism, and analyzing their cause and their significance.

A portion of the study hours each day were devoted to 'daily-life criticisms': general conduct, attitudes towards others, willingness to do one's share of work in the cell, eating and sleeping habits. Where Vincent was found wanting in any of these, this was attributed to 'imperialist' or 'bourgeois' greed and exploitation, in contrast to the 'people's attitude' of sharing and co-operation. When considered lax in his work, he was criticized for lacking the 'correct labour point of view'; when he dropped a plate, this was wasting the people's money; if he drank too much water, this was 'draining the blood of the people'; if he took up too much room while sleeping, this was 'imperialistic expansion'.

Vincent would still hear talk of men who were shot because 'they resisted'; and on the other hand he heard of the 'bright future' – early release or happy existence in China – for those who 'accepted their re-education'.

Advanced standing

After more than a year of this continuous 're-education', Vincent was again subjected to a series of interrogations aimed at once more reconstructing his confession – 'because after one year the government hopes you understand a little better your crimes'. Now from among the great mass of material which he had already produced, the judge focused upon a few selected points, all of which had some relationship to actual events. And thus, 'from a wild confession, you go to a more concrete confession'. Then, eight 'crimes' emerged – including membership in a right-wing French political organization, several forms of 'espionage' and 'intelligence' in association with American, Catholic, and other 'reactionary' groups, other anti-Communist activities, and 'slanderous insults to the Chinese people'. But now Vincent was more deeply immersed in the 'people's standpoint', and the confession had a much greater sense of reality for him than before.

> You have the feeling that you look to yourself on the people's side, and that you are a criminal. Not all of the time – but moments – you think they are right. 'I did this, I am a criminal.' If you doubt, you keep it to yourself. Because if you admit the doubt you will be 'struggled' and lose the progress you have made. . . . In this way they built up a spy mentality. . . . They built up a criminal. . . . Then your invention becomes a reality. . . . You feel guilty, because all of the time you have to look at yourself from the people's standpoint, and the more deeply you go into the people's standpoint, the more you recognize your crimes.

And at this point he began, in the 'correct' manner, to relate his own sense of guilt to the Communist world view:

> They taught us what it means to be a capitalist . . . to enslave and exploit the people so that a small group of persons can enjoy life at the expense of the masses, their capital coming from the blood of the people, not from labour . . . . that all property comes from the blood of the peasant . . . . that we helped this bad policy, that our minds are the capitalistic minds . . . and in our profession we exploited everyone. We used our profession to exploit people, as we can see from our crimes.

Then came another fourteen months of full-time re-education. Vincent continued to concentrate upon applying Communist theory to his personal situation, demonstrating an ever-expanding 'recognition' of his 'crimes'.

> After two years, in order to show that you are more on the people's side, you increase your crimes. . . . I said I wasn't frank before, there were really more intelligences. . . . This is a good point. It means that you are analyzing your crimes. . . . It means that you realize your crimes are very big, and that you are not afraid to denounce yourself . . . . that you trust the people, trust your re-education, and that you like to be reformed.

By this time his activities were no longer limited to his own case; he had by now become active – and skilful – in criticizing others, 'helping' them to make progress in confession and reform. He had become an experienced prisoner, and was beginning to be looked upon as a true progressive. He even came to believe a great deal of what he was expressing – although not in a simple manner:

> You begin to believe all this, but it is a special kind of belief. You are not absolutely convinced, but you accept it – in order to avoid trouble – because every time you don't agree, trouble starts again.

During his third year of imprisonment, he was once more called in for a revision of his confession. The document became even more brief, concrete, 'logical', and convincing. Now Vincent began to think of his sentence, estimating it from the 'people's standpoint' which had become so much a part of him.

> You have the feeling that your sentence is coming and that you will be sent somewhere else . . . and you are waiting. . . . You think, 'How long – maybe twenty, twenty-five years' . . . . You will be sent to reform through labour . . . to a factory or to a field. . . . They are very generous about this. . . . The government is very generous. The people are very generous. . . . Now you know that you cannot be shot. . . . But you are thinking that your crimes are very heavy.

Now Vincent was told that his 'attitude' had greatly improved. He was transferred to a different wing of the prison – and given treasured privileges, such as an hour of outdoor exercise a day and additional recreation periods in the cell. He found himself living in harmony with his captors, and during the last few months of his imprisonment was even permitted to give French lessons to other prisoners and to conduct medical classes for students brought to the prison for this purpose. All of this was not without its effect:

> They used this as a premium in order to show me that they weren't against my work or my profession, but were only against my reactionary mind. To show that my work was well accepted, that they accepted my theories. . . . To show what it means to live among the people, if I become one of the people. . . . To put in my mind that life among the people is good.

Soon he was called in for a formal signing of his confession – both a French version in his own handwriting, and a Chinese translation. Photographers and moving-picture cameramen were on hand, and he also read it for sound recording. With many others like it, it was widely disseminated throughout China and other parts of the world. A short time later he was called before the judge, and after three years of 'solving' his case, he was read both the charges and the sentence: for 'espionage' and other 'crimes' against the people, three years of imprisonment – this considered to be already served. He was expelled immediately from China, and within two days, he was on a British ship heading for Hong Kong.

Freedom

From his story, Dr Vincent might appear to be a highly successful product of thought reform. But when I saw him in Hong Kong, the issue was much more in doubt. He was a man in limbo, caught between the two worlds.

In his confusion and fear he felt that he was being constantly observed and manipulated. Much of this paranoid content was an internal extension to his prison environment:

> I have a certain idea that someone is spying on me – an imperialist spying on me because I came from the Communist world – interested to look and see what I think. . . . When I am doing something I feel someone is looking at me – because from external manifestation he is anxious to look at what is going on inside of me. We were trained this way in our re-education.

And thinking out loud about me, he said:

> I have a feeling he is not just a doctor. He is connected with some imperialist organization which will bring me danger. . . . I think maybe someone else is telling you the questions to ask me. . . . But I give you everything, and if tomorrow something happens, I could say, 'This is the truth. I have endeavoured to tell the truth.'

He expressed distrust towards the friend who had arranged for him to see me:

> I opened myself with him and told him my ideas. But then I thought, perhaps he will use this against me. We were both re-educated, taught to denounce everybody and not to trust anybody, that it is your duty to denounce.

He later explained the reason for his request that I pick him up at his boarding house:

> When you telephoned me . . . I thought maybe he is a Communist. . . . Perhaps an enemy. . . . I refused to come here alone, because I didn't have a witness. . . . This way you come, you are seen, and if I disappear there is a witness.

In this borderline psychotic state, Vincent graphically described his split identity:

> When I left China I had this strange feeling: Now I am going to the imperialistic world. No one will take care of me. I'll be unemployed and lost. . . . Everyone will look at me as a criminal. . . . Still, I thought, there is a Communist Party in my country. I am coming out of a Communist

world; they must know I have had reform training. Perhaps they will be interested in keeping me. Maybe they can help me, and I will not be really lost. I will go to the Communists, tell them where I came from, and I'll have a future....

But when I came to Hong Kong, the situation changed completely. The Consulate sent a man right away on board with a special motorboat. They took care of me and asked me if I am in need. They told me they wired my government and my family. They brought me to a boarding house, nice room, nice food – and gave me money to spend. The capitalist world is more friendly than I thought it would be.

In his struggle to achieve some sense of reality, his perceptions of his new environment were faulty. He wavered between beliefs, always influenced by his fears:

I had dinner last night at the home of Mr. Su [a wealthy, retired Hong Kong Chinese merchant]. I had the feeling that Mr. Su was a pro-Communist. I had this manifestation. Every time he spoke, I wanted to say, 'Yes'. I thought he was a judge – I was sympathizing with Mr. Su because he had a court. He asked me my crimes. I told him all of them in order. He said, 'Do you feel guilty about this?' I said, 'Yes, I feel guilty about this.' I had the impression he was a judge in contact with the Communists and can report everything....

But this morning I wrote a letter to my wife, and I went into detail about my crimes. In this letter I denied completely my crimes. I know my wife – I know her well – she can't do anything to me, so I wrote, 'How cruel they were to make a criminal out of someone like me' – and yet last night I admitted guilt. Why? Because there was a judge there....

Today at lunch with the Jesuit Fathers, I know them well – I denied everything because they are my friends. When I feel safe I am on one side. when I have the feeling I am not safe, right away I jump on the other side.

In his constant testing of his new environment, he began to call into question many of the teachings of his thought reform:

When I arrived in Hong Kong, another foreigner coming out of China put me in this difficult position. He told me about the situation in North China – that it was impossible to get meat there, and that there is rationing because everything is going to the Soviet Union. I said – 'Impossible! A foreigner likes to exaggerate' – because we never heard about this rationing in jail. I said, 'How can it be possible that the Soviet Union needs food from China when they are making such progress?' .... In prison we saw their food lists – butter, meat, whatever they like – but now I hear that food is not enough in the Soviet Union. I ask myself. 'Where is the truth?'

He found that what he was experiencing more and more came into conflict with his reform, and he felt that this reality-testing was beneficial to him:

> They say there is no progress in my country. But I was surprised to see a new steamer from there here in the harbour. I hear that it is an air-conditioned steamer, built since the war. I thought then that my country is not a colony of America – they can have a steamer line come to Hong Kong. I started little by little to come to reality – bit by bit to make comparison of what they told me. The reality is quite good for me. I am thinking that if a school partner [cellmate] could have the possibility of seeing what I have seen in eight days – what could he believe of his re-education? . . .

And similarly when he read in an American magazine about immense new railroad machinery developed in the United States, he questioned the precepts that 'the imperialists are interested in only light industry – to exploit the people' and that 'Soviet heavy industry is leading everybody'. He commented:

> When I saw these, I thought that the Communists were cheating me – cheating everybody.

Midway through the series of interviews, he began to feel restless, neglected, and increasingly hostile to his new surroundings. He reversed the previous trend, and again became suspicious of ulterior motives in his new environment:

> Every day I read the Hong Kong paper I see children are receiving milk and eggs through the help of America. . . . But in prison they are all the time saying that the American imperialists are giving things to people in order to cover up – to show that they take an interest. I see this as a political point – a feeling I have which is strictly connected with re-education.

He became markedly critical of what he saw around him, and more favourable in his references to his prison experience – looking back upon it almost longingly.

> Since coming out, arguments and conversation are terribly uninteresting. There are no concrete things. Time is very superficial – people don't solve any problems. They are just going on – spending four hours for nothing – between one drink and another smoke and wait for tomorrow. In re-education we solved every problem . . . we were given texts to use and had to read them – then new discussions until the moment when there were no more problems. . . . I went to a film last night. I was disturbed by it. Disturbed because it wasn't an educational film – it was just a lot of shooting and

> violence. I was thinking how much more comforting to have an education film as in the prison – never a film like this there. So brutal – so much fighting and killing....
>
> When we came out of the movie, a Chinese child touched the handbook of a Western lady who was with us. She was very disturbed and kicked the child. I thought, 'Why violence, why not just explain to the child that he shouldn't do it?' This has a connection with re-education – because all of the time they told us that relations in society should be on a logical basis, not on a forced basis.

He expressed the loneliness of his new freedom:

> There is this kind of freedom here – if you want to do something, you can do it. But there is not the collective way of progress – just an individual way of going on. Nobody pays any attention to you and your surroundings.

Referring back to his prison experience, he said:

> It is not that I miss it, but I find that it was more easy.

At this time he also began to feel that I was 'exploiting' him for my own professional gain; he 'confessed' these feelings to me:

> I had a very bad thought about you. I thought that Americans are all the same – when they have need of you they use you, and after that you are a forgotten man.

But during the last two interviews, he became more cheerful and optimistic, more concerned about arrangements for his future. He was now more definite in his conviction that the Communists had wronged him cruelly throughout his imprisonment.

His views on Communist methods became more sharply critical, and more interpretive.

> My impression is that they are cruel and that there is no freedom. There is compulsion in everything, using Marxism and Leninism in order to promise to the ignorant a bright future.... I was really accepting things in order to make myself more comfortable – because I was in great fear.... In this situation your willpower completely disappears.... You accept because there is a compulsion all the time – that if you don't go on their road, there is no escape.... To avoid argument you become passive....

He described his post-imprisonment change of heart towards his former captors – from toleration to condemnation:

> My first few days out I recognized that they were cruel with us – but not

in a strong way. There was a religious belief playing on me: if someone does bad to you, don't keep your hate; and another feeling – what I pass through there would be useful for me in the next life. I looked upon it as bad versus good, and I felt I suffered for something. . . . Now my resentment is stronger than it was the first few days. I have the feeling that if I meet a Communist in my country, my first reaction towards him will be violent.

Before leaving for Europe, he began to seek contacts and letters of introduction which he felt could help him in the future. He again wished to do medical work in an underdeveloped Asian setting, but he noted a significant change in the type of position which he sought:

Before I would never accept a nine-to-five job, because it means that you are busy all the time with no time to do what you want. Now – it is very strange – I would like to have such an engagement. I have the feeling that with this kind of job, everything is easy. I don't have to think of what happens at the end of the month. It would give me security, a definite feeling for the future because I have nothing definite in the future.

But Dr Vincent knew himself well enough to recognize that this quest for regularity and security would not last.

This is not one hundred per cent of my feeling . . . You see the contradiction – I am just out from the door of the cell – only one step out. But if I take some more steps – and consider what is best for my character – perhaps I will again decide to be by myself. . . . In a Communist country everybody does the same thing – and you accept. Here it is different: you are still the master of yourself.

He felt that the most significant change which he had undergone as a result of his reform was his increased willingness to 'open myself to others'. And in regard to our talks together, he said:

This is the first time a foreigner knows my character. I believe this comes through re-education – because we were instructed to know our internal selves . . . I have never talked so frankly. I have a feeling I left part of myself in Hong Kong.

Notes

1 Vincent, like many of my Western subjects, knew enough spoken Chinese so that most of his reform could be conducted in that language; and his fluency greatly improved during his ordeal. A bilingual fellow prisoner (or during interrogations, an official translator) was always available for Chinese–English interpretation, however.

2 The judge is actually a high-ranking prison official, and the interrogations which he presides over are official court proceedings; other prison officials of less exalted rank may conduct ordinary interrogations. These distinctions do not always hold.

3 The italics used in quotations from subjects during this and subsequent chapters are, of course, my own.

4 Here I could not be sure that the recollection of sleep-deprivation was completely accurate; I believe that it was reasonably so, although the subjects may have neglected to report brief periods of dozing. The officials always allowed prisoners to get sleep enough to be able to participate in the interrogations, but sometimes during this early period of imprisonment they were permitted little more.

47 Conformity and independence – a psychological analysis

Marie Jahoda

The rapidly growing psychological literature on conditions producing conformity raises a major new question: How is non-conformity possible? Curiosity about this question sets the stage for this paper.

To be curious about the conditions under which independence occurs presupposes a belief in its existence. I admit to this belief, even though it receives small support from the literature. Not only is there widespread consensus among many diagnosticians of the climate of our times that this is an age of conformity; the relevant psychological literature is almost unanimous in its emphasis on conditions accounting for conformity. Actually, there is, of course, ample evidence for the existence of independence not only in common-sense observations but also in every single experiment which rejects the null-hypothesis of independence on statistically impressive levels of confidence. There is a tacit implication in many of these experiments that those insubordinate subjects who are outside the hypothesis-confirming majority are a nuisance. The fewer there are of them, the less said about them, the better. Unless, of course, one can think of an additional experimentally manipulable variable which will bring the recalcitrants into line. Concern with statistical significance, has, to be sure, helped to increase immeasurably the level of rigour in psychological thought; but it also has at least one undesirable consequence: It threatens to interfere with the general task of psychology which is to understand human behaviour, and not merely the behaviour of majorities, however large or significant.

In any case, I submit that it makes psychological sense to speak of non-conformity, and hence to inquire into the conditions which make it possible....

Is the distinction between conformity and non-conformity valid?

There is an easy general answer to this question: It all depends on what is meant by conformity. No doubt. But as one looks into the meaning given

JAHODA, MARIE (1959) 'Conformity and independence – a psychological analysis' in *Human Relations*, vol. 12, 99–120.

to the term in various contexts, matters become more difficult. In the current debate on political conformity, confusion is great because the term 'conformity' is contaminated by value judgments on the issue with regard to which conformity is diagnosed. On that level 'good' and 'bad' or 'right' and 'wrong' are often used synonymously with 'independent' and 'conforming'.

On a barely more sophisticated level, those who agree with the majority are called conformists, those who agree with the minority independents. For example, we learn from Stouffer's study (1955) that the majority of the adult population think that a communist should not be permitted to be a sales clerk. Personally, I am convinced that most of the people adhering to this opinion actually are conformists, at least in this respect. But to prove the point by reference to the size of the majority is committing 'high treason: to be right for the wrong reason'.

On a higher level of insight, conformity is regarded as the reduction of diversity through social influence processes. But it is on this more sophisticated level where value and majority views are discarded as criteria that serious doubts arise about the wisdom of the distinction between independence and conformity. In the political and cultural debate Trilling has used gentle but none the less devastating mockery to show that when value judgments and deviations from majority opinions are rejected as criteria of non-conformity, nothing much but conformity remains. In his essay on *Freud and the Crisis of our Culture* (1955) he says:

> The American educated middle class is firm in its admiration of non-conformity and dissent. The right to be non-conformist, the right to dissent, is part of our conception of community. Everybody says so: in the weekly, monthly, quarterly magazines, and in the *New York Times*, at the cocktail party, at the conference of psychiatrists, at the conference of teachers. How good that is, and how right! And yet, when we examine the contents of our idea of nonconformity, we must have been dismayed at the smallness of the concrete actuality this very large idea contains. The rhetoric is as sincere as it is capacious, yet we must sometimes wonder whether what is being praised and defended is anything more than the right to have had some sympathetic connection with Communism ten or twenty years ago. Men of principle have opposed reactionary tendencies in our society and some have taken risks in their opposition, but for most of us our settled antagonism to that instance of reactionary tendency we call McCarthyism is simply the badge of our class. Our imagination of dissent from our culture can scarcely go beyond this. We cannot really imagine non-conformity at all, not in part, not in moral or social theory, certainly not in the personal life – it is probably true that there never was a culture which required so entire an eradication of

> personal differentiation, so bland a uniformity of manner. Admiring non-conformity and living community, we have decided that we are all non-conformists together.

Trilling exempts from the general charge of conformity 'men of principle'. There is no doubt that Trilling approves of them; or that they are in a small minority; or that they are not just conforming to non-conformity. There is a mere suggestion in the passage that some crucial other factor is involved in their behaviour. If we can identify this crucial factor in a man of principle, we may be nearer to a useful distinction between independence and conformity. Perhaps an example will help. I have chosen one from John F. Kennedy's book *Profiles in Courage* (1955).

It is the case of Senator Edmund G. Ross of Kansas. In 1868 in the frenzied aftermath of the Civil War, impeachment proceedings were brought against President Andrew Johnson. A two-thirds majority of the Senate was necessary to confirm the impeachment vote of the House of Representatives. The Republicans – Ross was a Republican – had brought the charges. They needed 36 votes; they were sure of 35. Ross's vote was to be decisive. Every conceivable pressure was brought to bear on him. His residence was watched; his social associations were suspiciously scrutinized; his political career was at stake; a fearful avalanche of telegrams came from his constituents and from people in other parts of the country; his party and the press cajoled, bribed and threatened. Senator Ross later on described the moment of voting: 'I almost literally looked down into my open grave. Friendships, position, fortune, everything that makes life desirable to an ambitious man were about to be swept away by the breath of my mouth, perhaps forever. It is not strange that my answer was carried waveringly over the air and failed to reach the limits of the audience, or that repetition was called for by distant Senators on the opposite side of the Chamber'. But the answer was 'not guilty'. Several others who had been undecided when impeachment proceedings first started had also been exposed to severe pressures. Their vote was 'guilty'.

Senator Edmund Ross manifested what most people would regard as independent behaviour. What is the psychological variable which distinguishes him from others who started off with the same hesitation and were subjected to the same pressures, but yielded in the end?

To say that other forces were stronger than the external pressure is certainly not a satisfactory answer. What other forces? Two types of explanatory concepts come to mind: the impact of an absent reference group and some enduring personality characteristic. Let us consider the adequacy of each.

The unsatisfactory nature of the reference group concept lies in the fact that, unless we are very careful it leads to a sort of reductionist thinking which can do away with the distinction between Ross and his colleagues. At least, this can be concluded from Cooley's discussion, some 50 years ago, of conformity and non-conformity (1909). The non-conformist, he says, is the one who seems to be out of step with the procession because he is keeping time to another music. Cooley calls this behaviour 'remote conformity', and concludes that 'There is, therefore, no definite line between conformity and non-conformity: there is simply a more or less characteristic and unusual way of selecting and combining accessible influences.' In other words, we are back at assuming fundamentally similar events in conformist and independent behaviour. This is not to imply that this reduction of independence to conformity is illogical or impossible; on the contrary it is tantamount to asserting that all human behaviour is determined. Nor do I deny the valuable sensitizing function that the more current term 'reference group behaviour' has for social-psychological work. All I want to emphasize is that if one is interested in specifying the *difference* between Ross and his colleagues, one does not want to commit oneself too readily to a viewpoint which may lead to the conclusion that they are basically alike.

What about personality characteristics as a decisive variable to account for the difference? Terms like 'ego-strength', 'superego', 'sense of security', or more superficially 'stubbornness' and the like suggest themselves. To be sure, it would be of great help to have a Rorschach, an MMPI, or a TAT of Ross, or of somebody committing an equally independent action, just as it would be useful to know his reference groups. But I am doubtful whether such personality measures would give us a fully satisfactory answer. On the most concrete level my doubt stems from what Kennedy says about Ross's personality which he presents, of course, not in psychological terms. Ross's own description of his faltering voice at the dramatic moment does not suggest a personality free from anxiety or happy in defying the world. In other less dramatic situations he occasionally demonstrated independence, occasionally conformity.

In more general terms, the problem then is, which among the numerous possible approaches to personality yields the best tool for predicting conforming behaviour? The very fact that one and the same person conforms on some occasions but not on others, even though the results of psychodiagnostic testing must be assumed to be identical on both occasions, raises doubt as to the help such tests can provide for the task. Again, I should limit my heresy: This is not to say that psychodiagnostic measures are invalid. All I wish to say is that as far as I understand their rationale they are after more or less enduring attributes of a person. These attributes are modifiable by external factors, and do not necessarily win the day, as Tolstoy already sensed when he wrote in *Resurrection*:

> One of the most widespread superstitions is that every man has his own special qualities; that a man is kind, cruel, wise, stupid, energetic, apathetic, etc. Men are not like that. We may say of a man that he is more often kind than cruel, more often wise than stupid, more often energetic than apathetic, or the reverse. . . . Every man carries in himself the germs of every human quality, and sometimes one manifests itself; sometimes another, and the man often becomes unlike himself, while still remaining the same man.

Tolstoy implies that situational factors can prove so powerful that they break through habitual response patterns. To be sure, Tolstoy did not deny the power of enduring attributes of the personality either. He explicitly recognizes it in the phrase 'remaining the same man'. But remaining the same man in what respect? Surely not only as a physical organism; and equally surely not in overt behaviour. Tolstoy suggests it is not traits. Is it the psychodynamics underlying behaviour and traits? Is the basic organization of motives, as Chein (1943) suggests, or are cognitive controls, as George Klein (1954) suggests, the best indicator of what remained the same in Senator Ross while he was first a respected member of the Republican party and then a rebel? Clinical psychology will have to teach us in what the identifiable sameness consists which a person carries from one situation to the other.

But the possible types of answer to the question as to what remains the same in a man as he moves from one situation to the other do not yet promise help in predicting conforming behaviour. For none of the alternatives mentioned above promises to discriminate between the situations in which persons like Senator Ross choose to conform or not to conform.

R. Bendix (1952) draws attention to this power of a person to make choices. People can respond to an external factor, he states, either because or in spite of their personality predisposition. On both counts one and the same enduring personality attribute may – under unspecified conditions – be related either to acceptance or to resistance of external influences. A person with a strong ego, for example, may conform to a majority view of his colleagues but not to the political climate of his times. If his job is at stake he may act in accordance with his convictions, or against them.

Thus far the explanatory concepts which I have examined as possible major determinants of independent or conforming behaviour have not proved adequate. But, perhaps, the difficulty lies less with these concepts than with the fact that the phenomenon which they are supposed to explain has not been sufficiently clarified. Let us consider Senator Ross again for a lead as to the characteristics of the special type of behaviour in which he engaged.

From Kennedy's description (only briefly summarized here) it becomes clear that *the most significant matter in his action was that he cared very much about the issue at stake*. To be sure, he had a reference group, he was a 'remote conformist', or, if you will, he conformed to his own conscience. To be sure, he had a strong ego. But these enduring personality attributes came into play against overwhelming pressures only because he really cared about the impeachment issue. This condition – the close link between a person and an object in the external world (object, because the issue existed independent of Senator Ross's existence) – permitted him to act as he did. For this process, the term 'ego-involvement' suggests itself. Some of its connotations, however, make it not entirely appropriate: The emphasis on ego implies a contrast to, or an exclusion of, other aspects of the personality. As one reconstructs in imagination Senator Ross's experience it becomes quite clear that the entire personality organization of the man was related to the issue. Not only his mind or his ego; but intense emotional forces and conflicts were involved. For this affective and rational link between a person and an object, psychoanalysis uses the term 'cathexis'.

Recently the term 'cathexis' has been introduced into systematic social-science thinking. In the introductory statement to the book *Toward a General Theory of Action*, all the contributors to the volume agree to call the 'tendency to react positively or negatively to objects the cathectic mode of orientation. Cathexis, the attachment to objects which are gratifying and rejection of those which are noxious, lies at the root of the selective nature of action.' And somewhat later: 'The term cathexis is broader . . . than effect. It is affect plus object.'

In the psychoanalytic literature the term is used in various ways, and the underlying concept not clearly defined. This is why I shall only note in passing the similarity to cathexis of what I regard as a crucial and critical attribute of independent behaviour. Here, I shall rather use the term 'emotional and intellectual investment in the issue'.

One advantage of regarding such central investment in an issue as a necessary attribute of what is widely but vaguely meant by independent behaviour, lies in the fact that it immediately helps us to clarify the universal diagnosis of conformity in our public life. There, the question should perhaps be reformulated to the effect of asking: Have people lost the ability to develop such investments in issues or is the general diagnosis based on the fact that the types of issue which provoke investment have changed? Both questions could be empirically answered without leading to a confusion about implicit value judgments or to the untenable oversimplification that independent behaviour is identical with agreeing with a minority, conforming behaviour with agreeing with a majority.

To regard emotional and intellectual investment in an issue as an attribute of independence, and its absence as an attribute of conformity, implies a shift from a unidimensional description of the phenomenon to a more complex notion, which I will elaborate later on. Before doing so, it is appropriate to turn to the experimental literature on conformity.

To the extent that the experimental literature is largely limited to manipulating conditions of influence with regard to matters in which the individual has no investment, it now becomes understandable why we know in psychology so much more about conformity than about independence. What actually do we know about conformity?

A survey of research on some aspects of conformity

The operational criterion of conformity which underlies most empirical research on the topic is the private and/or public agreement of an individual with an opinion which he had not held before it was presented to him. The existence of this phenomenon is, of course, the basis of all human society and undoubtedly accounts for the direction of the overwhelming majority of all human behaviour. Sherif's early experiment on the autokinetic effect (1936) and Blake's experiments (1954), which ingeniously use real-life settings in a controlled manner, have demonstrated that when people are exposed to social influences they tend to yield to them. Whether you want to call this conformity or trust in others is a terminological question which I want to avoid at this point. The ubiquity of conforming behaviour has also been demonstrated from a different point of view by Barker and Wright (1955) in their ecological studies of the behaviour of children in the Middle West. Barker and Wright state that 95 per cent of the behaviour of children during an ordinary day is determined by behaviour settings in which they find themselves. They define a behaviour setting as a locale for role performance which has the quality of eliciting largely similar responses from persons who find themselves in that locale; the corner drugstore, for example, is a behaviour setting. It is reasonable to expect that a similar proportion of adult behaviour is also regulated.

These demonstrations that conformity is indeed the rule make, at least by implication, another point of interest: Persons who do not thus conform show some deficiency or deviation from the normal. The point has been made explicitly in a number of recent experimental studies with psychoneurotics and schizophrenics. Such persons do not show the general trend toward conforming behaviour that others demonstrate. Hovland, Janis and Kelley (1953), for example, say that 'persons with acute psychoneurotic symptoms are predisposed to be resistant to persuasive communications'. Levine and colleagues (1954) repeated the autokinetic experiments with neurotics, whom they found to be less influenced by group judgments than non-neurotics. Sarbin and Hardyck (1955) found perceptual conformance negatively correlated with schizophrenia. Anybody who has ever visited a mental hospital will find his observations there in complete accord with these experimental findings. Non-conformity in this sense is sometimes indeed the first indication of incipient mental disease.

The point to be kept in mind here is that it may be reasonable to distinguish first between ability and inability to conform. Those who are able to conform may then be further studied as to whether they also have the ability not to conform – for example, whether their conforming behaviour expresses a compulsive need to go along with the opinions of others or whether the ability can be used discriminatingly in a variety of circumstances. The experimental literature is mainly concerned with specifying these circumstances.

It is convenient to discuss the available empirical research under the following headings: *inducing agents; situational context; reference group behaviour and group membership; personality predispositions; variations in issues; types of response.*

Inducing agents

By inducing agent I mean both the source of the opinion to which experimental subjects finally agree and the nature and manner of presentation of this opinion. The most systematic series of studies here are the Yale studies. Among other things we learn from them that sources of high credibility have a greater immediate effect in producing conformity of opinion than sources of low credibility: the difference tends to disappear, however, with time.

As to the nature of the communication the Yale group distinguishes between arguments on the one hand, and rewards or punishment on the other. Their published experiments, as far as I know, have not tried to combine these two types of variable in one experiment. Rather, variations have been tested within each type. With regard to the arguments, they have established that if the conclusions of an argument are explicitly presented, the communication will result in greater conformity if the issue is very complex and if the audience is on an intellectually relatively low level.

With regard to the reward–punishment variables their experiments on different degrees of fear-arousing appeals are relevant. They suggest that a moderate amount of fear-appeal is probably more successful in producing conformity than high amount.

Other studies on the inducing agent have frequently utilized group opinions as the agent. Goldberg (1954), for example, experimented with the size of the group which presents the opinion to which subjects conform. He found that 'the degree of conformity to groups of four is not different from the degree of conformity to groups of two'. Asch (1952) likewise found that the conformity effect was not increased by enlarging the number of group members. Both authors also varied the number of exposures to group opinion divergent from individual opinion and found, by and large, that conformity occurs within the first few exposures. Additional exposures do not increase the conformity effect significantly.

Kelman (1953) used an authority figure with seventh-grade students in an effort to get them to conform. Two conditions were compared: high and low pressure to conform. In the high-pressure group it was made clear to the children that they were to write an essay agreeing with the authority figure. In the low-pressure group it was explained that although the best agreeing essays would be rewarded, non-agreement was quite permissible. He found that the high-pressure group showed more immediate conformity in their essays, but less attitude change as separately ascertained. Here, we come across for the first time the important distinction between private and public conformity which has been made in many other experiments. The finding that low pressure from the inducing agent has more enduring conformity effects than high pressure agrees with the Yale fear-appeal studies, as well as with a number of other investigations. Jerome Frank (1944), for example, also came to the conclusion that low pressure and a step-by-step approach were more effective than high pressure in having people accept the demand of the experimenter.

In the light of such consensus it is particularly interesting that some studies show greater conformity effects in response to high pressure. Festinger, for example (1954), reports high pressure as being most effective. There are, of course, many nonexperimental observations and studies which support Festinger. Galileo would certainly not have yielded to anything but the stake. Some federal employees in their excessive self-imposed restrictions (Grodzins 1956) would not have yielded to anything but the threat of loss of their jobs and the danger of not finding new ones. The whole notion of a 'breaking-point' for all stress experiences is in line with the statement that the higher the pressure, the higher the degree of conformity. I believe that these apparently contradictory results could be reconciled if we distinguished behaviour on an issue according to the degree of cathexis of that issue, and in terms of several other qualifications which will be introduced later.

Another variable that has been used when groups are the inducing agent is the attractiveness of the group to the member or the liking he has for it. Bovard (1951), for example, finds that leader-centred groups are less effective in inducing conformity than group-centred groups. Since liking for the group was greater in the latter, he suggests that this is a major factor in producing conformity to group norms. Back (1951) confirms this point explicitly: the more cohesive a group, the greater its influence on opinions of members. In the same vein, the Yale studies conclude that 'persons who are most highly motivated to maintain their membership (in groups) tend to be most susceptible to influence by other members within the group'.

There are many other studies demonstrating the power of the group to induce conformity. Deutsch and Gerard (1955) criticize some of this work in pointing out that in several of these experiments the presence of others is regarded as tantamount to the existence of a group. They distinguish conceptually between inducing agents which exercise a normative social influence, i.e., an influence to conform with the positive expectations of another, and those which exercise an informational social influence, i.e., the acceptance of information from another as evidence. Their experimental work does not actually compare the relative impact of these two types of influence. On the basis of their theorizing, however, they hypothesize and find that social influences produce more conformity in individuals forming a group than in an aggregation of unrelated persons; that the effect will be less under conditions of anonymity or when no pressure from others is perceived; that social influence to conform to one's own judgment will reduce the impact of influence to conform to that of others; and that a personal commitment to conform to one's own judgment is strengthened when supported by another person.

Situational context

Most experimental studies are, as we all know and deplore, conducted among college students. But some have made efforts to use groups of other kinds: high-school students, youth groups, airmen, navy draftees, officers, industrial managers, etc. The effort of many investigators goes in the direction of working in 'realistic' situational contexts. But there is relatively little comparative work on conformity behaviour of the same individual in different situations. Situational contexts vary mostly in the degree of artificiality of the situation used for experimental purposes. Comparisons here are difficult because of the difference in methodology and criteria used.

It might be pointed out here that survey-type research has used the most realistic settings. Stouffer's study on *Conformity, Communism and Civil Liberties* (1955) shows, for example, a higher degree of conformity with regard to current political pressures in the population at large than in the leadership of voluntary organizations. Jahoda and Cook (1956), in their exploratory study of the impact of the loyalty and security measures on federal employees, also suggest a high degree of conformity to current pressures; in addition they raise the hypothesis that situations in which there is emotional and factual support from colleagues and superiors, and where the group atmosphere is frank and trusting, lead to *less* conformity with the general climate of opinion than do reverse conditions. Altogether, however, we know less about variations in situational contexts than about variations in the inducing agent.

Reference group behaviour and group membership

A number of investigators have drawn attention to the importance of an individual's reference groups as a factor related to the tendency to conform. The Yale group (Hovland, et al. 1953), for example, mentions the salience of group norms as a matter of importance in producing conformity. The findings among Catholic high-school students, for whom Catholicism was made salient by giving them pre-experimentally Catholic material to read, suggest 'that the use of contents which arouse awareness of a reference group can have a marked effect on the audience's tendency to accept or reject the recommended opinion'. However, the authors add: 'The absence of a similar effect for the college students raises some question as to whether the phenomenon is a general one or occurs only for persons who are strongly attached to a group but have relatively little understanding of its norms.' In his analysis of juvenile delinquency among lower-class gangs, Albert K. Cohen (1955) uses – at least by implication – also the power of a reference group as an explanatory factor for conformity. Delinquency becomes a possible solution to the juvenile's life problems only to the extent that his gang, i.e., his reference group, shares his values and norms. The same point has been made fifteen hundred years ago by St Augustine when he explains a pear-stealing episode he was involved in as a lad in terms of his membership in a group.

In general, these findings raise the question as to the conditions under which different reference groups become factors in determining opinions.

As far as I know, this central question of reference group theory has not yet been tackled in research. As a rule, the concept is used as if the individual had only one group with whom he shared norms, namely the one deliberately built into the research design.

Kelley and Woodruff (1956) indicate that opinions that were perceived as being expressed by a reference group, even when these opinions contradicted the expected norms of the group, had a profound influence on an individual's stand. The investigators are careful to point out that conforming to such opinions is only one way of dealing with the situation: Another is to reinterpret the unexpected opinion of the reference group.

In a sense, the status of an individual in a group can also be regarded under this heading. Kelley and Shapiro (1954) have experimented with this variable in a group situation where conformity was detrimental to the goals of the group. They found that the persons most secure in their group membership, that is those who were liked best by the others, were more likely to deviate from the norm than members who were less acceptable to the others.

Personality predispositions

There are a number of studies dealing with personality predispositions to conformity. Janis (1954) states that persons with low self-esteem tend to be more readily influenced than others. On the other hand, he finds, in line with what was previously described as inability to conform, that persons with acute symptoms of neurotic anxiety tend to conform less. Hoffman (1953) finds that conformity has an anxiety-reducing function for compulsive conformists, i.e., those whose conformity is based on non-rational needs to agree with one's peer group. He distinguishes from this compulsive conformity based on such realistic factors as external pressure, greater task-relevant information or skills on the part of other group members, etc. Interestingly he finds no difference in the frequency of conformity behaviour, whether compulsive or realistic conformity is involved. Hoffman's findings on the anxiety-reducing function of conformity are in line with Riesman's idea that anxiety is the self-inflicted punishment for non-conformity in other-directed persons (1950).

Crutchfield's (1955) findings on personality correlates of conformity show authoritarian attitudes and behaviour to be positively correlated with conformity, a conclusion which agrees with those in *The Authoritarian Personality*. The independent person he finds to have more intellectual effectiveness, ego-strength, leadership ability, and maturity in social relations, together with a conspicuous absence of inferiority feelings, of rigid and excessive self-control, and of authoritarian attitudes. More elaborate is Barron's list of personality differences between conformists and non-conformists (1950): 'Independents and Yielders were found to be equally stable in personality, but *do* differ in their values and self-descriptions. Independents see themselves primarily as original, emotional, and artistic; Yielders characterize themselves as obliging, optimistic, efficient, determined, patient, and kind. Yielders tend to be practical-minded, somewhat physicalistic in their thinking, and group-oriented; Independents placed higher values on creativity, close inter-personal relations, and the individual as opposed to the group.' Goldberg (n.d.) suggests a hypothesis on cognitive functioning to account for variations in conformity. He assumes that the individual performs some sort of probability calculation as to the likelihood that one's own or the other person's judgment is correct, and acts in the light of the outcome.

On the perceptual level, Harriet Linton finds certain styles of perception related to a tendency to conform (1955). She says: 'The tendency for behaviour to be modified by an external stimulus regardless of whether the external stimulus is personal or impersonal in nature, is a function of enduring attributes of the person; consequently, subjects whose performance in perceptual tasks is highly affected by the perceptual field will be those whose behaviour in other situations is most likely to be modified so as to conform to an external standard.'

It is beyond question that all these results are meaningful on some level of human functioning. But in the light of the preceding analysis of the distinction between independence and conformity, it is still an open question how they bear on our central problem here, i.e., on the relation of independence and conformity to the significance of the issue for a person. It is interesting to note that hardly any of the studies reported so far concern themselves with the nature of the issue on which independence or conformity is observed apart from mentioning it in the description of procedures, let alone with the relation of the individual to that issue, emotionally and intellectually invested or otherwise. It is hence with particular curiosity that one turns to what is known from current research about the effects of variation in the issue.

Variations in the issue

Crutchfield (1955), in his elaboration of the Asch experiments, varied systematically the nature of the problem on which conformity or independence was observed. He used perceptual judgments, logical solutions, vocabulary, attitudes, opinions, preferences for ornamental designs, etc. In the course of his experiments he told the group immediately after each judgment what the 'right' answer was. Actually, the experimenter reinforced as 'right' the pretended group consensus on the wrong answer. The effect of this additional pressure was striking in increasing the group's conformity behaviour. But there is an exception to this regularity. As Crutchfield states: 'The enhanced power of the group does *not* carry over to increase the influence on expression of opinions and attitudes. The subjects exposed to this correction method (the experimenter's false announcement of the right answer) do not exhibit greater conformity to group pressure on opinion and attitudes than that found in other subjects.' In other words, the information about the 'right' answer was effective only on those items where 'right' answers were possible. Crutchfield's speculation on this result is interesting, even though I question whether his emphasis on the rational element alone gives the full picture. He says:

> This crucial finding throws some light on the nature of the psychological processes involved in the conformity situation. For it seems to imply that conformity behaviour under such group pressure, rather than being solely an indiscriminate and irrational tendency to defer to the authority of the group, has in it important rational elements. There is something of a reasonable differentiation made by the individual. He may be led to accept the superiority of the judgment of the group on matters where there is an objective frame of reference against which the group can be checked. But he does not, thereby, automatically accept the group's superiority on matters of a less objective sort. To some degree, therefore, it can be argued that the individual is functioning with respect to his group in a manner which strikes a sensible balance, by sometimes making relevant use of the group's judgments as a resource in his own judgments, without at the same time becoming indiscriminately dependent upon the group's judgments in all matters.

'The sensible balance' which the individual sometimes strikes between his own judgment and the judgment of the group raises a crucial question: When is 'sometimes'? Surely 'sometimes' cannot mean when attitudes and opinions are involved. Most other studies have, after all, established conformity with regard to attitudes and opinions. Unless we can find an approach to an answer to this question, this important qualification makes us doubt whether we actually know as much about conformity as the literature suggests.

It should be noted that Luchins (1945) in a relatively early study already pointed to related ideas. He used children 11 to 13 years of age as subjects in the interpretation of ambiguous drawings. A confederate's answer preceded the subject's response. The children tended to see what the confederate said when the drawing left enough scope for ambiguity. But when the drawing presented a clearly structured object, subjects tended to remain independent of the confederate's pronouncement.

The Asch experiments themselves (1952) implicitly make a contribution to the question 'When is sometimes?' This series of experiments is outstanding in several ways, but particularly in relation to one point which, perhaps, Asch himself has not sufficiently emphasized. In addition to the conventional statistical treatment of the variations in his basic design, there is hidden in his data a perfect correlation of +1, a result of 100 per cent, which it will be admitted, is a rarity in psychological research. The implicit result I refer to is the creation of intense conflict in all his experimental subjects. The evidence for this result comes from the interviews Asch conducted with all his subjects after the experiment.

But how is this related to the question of the issue on which conformity and independence were observed? As you know, the issue in the Asch experiments was a perceptual judgment on length of lines. Disagreement by the group on these judgments produced intense conflicts in the individuals because reliance on one's perceptual judgment is the deeply anchored basis of all our relations to the world around us. Woodworth, as quoted by Hilgard (1951), has made the point: 'To see, to hear – to see clearly, to hear distinctly – to make out what it is one is seeing or hearing – moment by moment, such concrete, immediate motives dominate the life of relation with the environment.' And Hilgard conjectures 'that perceptual goals are intimately related to the other goals of the learner. The basic reason for achieving a stable world is that such a world is the most convenient one in which to satisfy our needs'. Much in line with these statements is Festinger's (1954) statement on a basic human motive, to know one's environment and to know oneself. He speaks of 'a motivation in the human organism to hold *correct* opinions, beliefs and ideas about the world in which he lives and to know *precisely* what his abilities enable him to to do in this world'.

In any case, these statements demonstrate that there is reason to believe that the Asch situation attacked an immensely cathected issue for the individual. Hence the universality of deep conflict in his subjects and the curious fact that, notwithstanding the strength of the pressure, only about one-third of all subjects yielded, though the percentage of yielders is as a rule much greater in other experiments on other issues. Nevertheless, there are, even under these conditions, differences in responses.

Occasionally, the judgment as to the relevance or importance of an issue is made in terms of the investigator's judgment rather than in psychological terms from the point of view of the acting person. This leads to confusions of the following kind. In discussing the psychology of voting, Lipset and colleagues (1954) say: 'We do know, in a general way, that decisions which are not ego-involved are more easily influenced from the outside, a fact which explains the great success of commercial advertising as compared with the failure of many compaigns to improve race relations or attitudes towards international issues.' The implication is clear that the general population is assumed to be ego-involved with international issues and not with the goods offered in advertising campaigns. Of course, the opposite is the case. Housewives care very much about coffee and very little about our relations with China. I shall try to clear up this confusion later on.

Types of response

Many investigators have, of course, been aware of the variety of behaviours which are commonly called conformity, and have accordingly tried to distinguish between them. The most frequent distinction is that between private and public conformity. On a basis of statements by Lewin (1951) and research by French (1944), Festinger (1953) has conceptualized this distinction. He summarizes the major points of a theory of compliant behaviour thus: '(1) Public compliance without private acceptance will occur if the person in question is restrained from leaving the situation and if there is a threat of punishment for noncompliance. (2) Public compliance with private acceptance will occur if there is a desire on the part of the person to remain in the existing relationship with those attempting to influence him.' These generalizations are true for some people in some circumstances. Not for all, of course. It is easy enough to imagine a situation where public compliance without private acceptance occurs where one wishes to remain in the existing relation with those attempting to influence one. For example, a person may wish to remain on good terms with a friend. Just because of this wish he complies publicly with a statement by his friend, even though he privately regards it as unsound.

This is, of course, not to say that the distinction between private and public acceptance is unimportant. On the contrary: it is of crucial significance. But its importance derives more from viewing it in conjunction with cathexis to the issue than in conjunction with group membership. Note, for example, the remarkable challenge to social psychologists offered by such historical episodes as that of the Marrano Jews in Spain who, for almost five centuries, maintained secret adherence to Judaism while publicly adhering to the Roman Catholic faith – a situation which, to say the least, gives us some perspective about the magnitude of the effects we are able to create experimentally.

Another distinction made by Hoffman (n.d.) between compulsive and realistic conformity has already been mentioned. Brodbeck and colleagues (1956) also speak of two kinds of conformity: conformity to the individual's standards and conformity to others. This distinction within the concept of conformity leads to a reductionism unsuitable for our purposes here, as suggested earlier in connection with Cooley's 'remote conformity'.

More recently another type of distinction has been introduced, which is based on the realization that one and the same outcome of a social influence can be the result of a variety of processes. Kelley (1954), for example, has developed a scheme to deal with the fact of resistance to efforts of persuasion. Using as an example Kendall and Wolf's (1949) ingenious analysis of resistance to the message in the Mr Biggot's cartoon series, he has suggested that resistance can come about through distortion or misunderstanding of content, through cognitive restructuring (in line with Asch's position in his discussion of the suggestion literature), or through changing interpretations of the inducing agent or his social prestige.

When the phenomenon to be explained is not resistance but conformity several authors have also distinguished separate processes. Asch speaks of conformity to a rule, either because a person is convinced that the rule is right, or because it is the thing that everybody does, or because it is dangerous not to observe that rule. Kelman (1954) has elaborated on three processes which he calls internalization, identification and compliance. In an earlier paper I (1956) have distinguished four processes, three of which correspond to Asch's and Kelman's distinctions: consentience, roughly corresponding to Asch's conviction and Kelman's internalization; conformance, corresponding to Asch's 'what-everybody-does' and Kelman's identification; compliance, corresponding to Asch's 'it-is-dangerous-not-to-conform' and Kelman's identical term. The fourth, convergence, is a sort of strategy an individual uses in going along for the sake of other related consequences.

All three authors have made it clear that the distinctions between these processes are necessary for understanding the different meaning of conformity behaviour. Kelman and Jahoda have stated that the consequences of conformity vary for each process, as do the conditions under which they can be changed.

Conformity and independence: a complex criterion

In the light of the foregoing remarks it must be obvious that I have some doubts whether the customary operational criterion by which independence is distinguished from conformity – agreement or disagreement with a presented opinion not previously held by the individual – is the best possible criterion in efforts to extend our knowledge in the area. This criterion is at the root of the confusion in the public debate on the subject. It has led only to partial understanding, and, I believe, cannot stand up under logical or psychological scrutiny. I have tried to show that the inadequacy of the agreement criterion stems from the fact that one and the same position taken by different individuals can have completely different meanings, that is, different antecedents, different contexts, and different consequences. If this is correct, the classification of persons according to this unidimensional criterion or the study of factors related to it must lead into a blind alley. Position-taking on an issue in which the individual has intellectual and emotional investment is psychologically so different a process from position-taking on an issue which is not so invested, that they must be assumed to manifest different regularities. If this is granted, then the first task, obviously, is to specify the dimensions which have to enter into a criterion distinguishing these different processes.

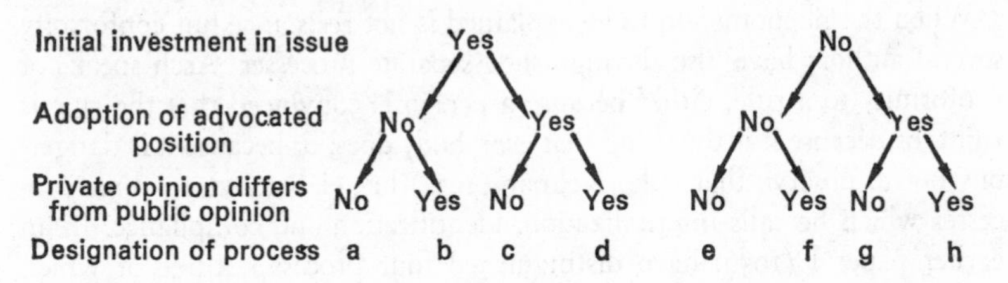

Fig. 1 Types of conformity and independence.

Though I have particularly emphasized the investment in an issue, a relatively neglected aspect in research, the review of the literature makes it clear that at least two further dimensions need to be taken note of: the actual position arrived at by an individual under the impact of social influences, and a qualification of this position corresponding to the distinction between private and public opinion on the issue.

Let us keep a concrete example in mind, say the position of people on the issue of capital punishment. Let us assume that, before some external influence is brought to bear, the people we are interested in all take the position implied in the law of the land that capital punishment is proper punishment for certain crimes. After some influence has been brought to bear on these people, some adhere to their old position, some have changed. What has happened?

A combination of these three dimensions – dichotomized for purposes of simplicity – yields eight distinguishable processes, as shown in Figure 1.

It remains to be seen whether these eight logical possibilities are also psychological possibilities. Processes *a-d* occur in persons who have an emotional and intellectual investment in the issue of capital punishment. It had a place in their life space with some salience even before the campaign started. Process *a* designates a person who, though reached by the campaign, does not change his mind, and is at ease with himself about the final position he takes. This is *independent dissent*.

Process *b* implies a person who adheres to his original position but feels less comfortable with it than he used to be. Publicly he gives the impression of independence; but privately the influence process has undermined his stand. He experiences conflict. The non-yielders in the Asch experiment who continued to say what they saw but developed doubts about their eyesight are an example to the point. This position may be called *undermined independence*. . . .

Process *c* describes a person who changed his mind as a result of the pressures in the campaign. He emerges from the internal turmoil in which the realization that others disagree with him may have thrown him into a changed position with which he is again completely at ease. To make this plausible in the light of his investment in the issue we must assume that he has restructured the manner in which he sees the issue. For example, he may have thought about capital punishment in relation to the nature of the crime. Challenged by public pressure, he may have re-examined the arguments against capital punishment in relation to the punisher and the morality of society. Given investment in the issue, nothing but such a restructuring of the issue could result in a conflict-free change of mind. I suspect that Senator Cain[1] has undergone exactly this process in his recent change of opinion on the effects of the internal security procedures. This position may be termed *independent consent*.

Process *d* implies taking a stand against one's own conviction; there is no cathexis to the new position. Private opinion remains what it was. Galileo is the prime example for this sort of *compliance*. To undergo this process presupposes extremely strong pressures on a person, ordinarily severe threats.

The next four positions are taken by persons for whom the issue of capital punishment was either very much on the periphery of their life space or never in it. Process *e* is one where such a person does not change his

1 Senator Cain had originally supported the security measures, but in the course of investigating one or two cases among his own constituents he became convinced of their detrimental effect and changed his position on the issue.

position, and does not feel any conflict about it. This position appears unreasonable. One would expect this type of behaviour in those who lack the essential ability to respond to external pressure, or in those who reject a stand just because it is demanded by others. Such people show *compulsive resistance.*

Process *f* – no investment in the issue, no change, and conflict – is psychologically not immediately plausible within the present scheme. The process becomes conceivable if one enters into the complex relationship which other issues bear to the one under discussion.

An ordinary American liberal may serve as an example. He has never given the matter much thought when he is reached by the Rosenberg campaign. He feels that an example should be set in view of what he regards as the overwhelming threat of communism. He may also think that the campaign has been organized by communists. Both these factors touch on issues in which he has considerable intellectual and emotional investment, but which are different from the issue of capital punishment. His apparent independence of efforts to get him to oppose capital punishment results from considerations related to other issues. A shift in frame of reference has occurred. His is *expedient resistance* [Editor's italics].

Process *g* may well be the most frequent one when there is no involvement with the issue, and the position is changed without creating conflict. It is a very reasonable type of behaviour which goes with a certain amount of trust in other people. This is *conformity* in the narrow sense of the word. These people may be involved with other persons rather than have investments in the issue under consideration. No strong influence is necessary to move them to another position.

Finally, process *h* is again not immediately plausible. With little, if any, investment the position is changed, but conflict results. A person sympathetic to communism may serve as an example in his attitude to the Rosenberg campaign. He gives in to pressures to change his opinion because of incidental special issues in the Rosenberg case. Here again a shift in the frame of reference occurs. He can see great advantage in using the counterarguments in this particular case, for obvious reasons. Emotional and intellectual investment in his system of political beliefs makes it expedient to go along with social pressures. His agreement is *expedient conformity.*

The empirical identification of these eight patterns will not be easy. But I cannot see a simpler scheme within which it makes sense to talk about political independence and conformity. It remains to be demonstrated through experimental work that our understanding of social influence processes will be advanced by the adoption of this multi-dimensional criterion.

Let me briefly demonstrate the usefulness of thinking in these terms to clear the confusion about why commercial advertising is successful though the same methods fail in efforts to influence opinions on international relations. What happens, I believe, is that advertising compaigns concerned with heavily invested matters such as cosmetics, result in type *c* responses, independent consent. Women want to be beautiful. When confronted with a pressure to use X to soften their skin they deliberately decide to comply. Advertising campaigns concerned with matters in which people have little investment, such as international relations, result in type *g* responses, conformity. That is, people do not deliberately relate themselves to the issue. Everything goes that is suggested. The confusion arises from the value judgment of the observer who understandably prefers independent consent to conformity. An additional point, often made implicitly in the literature, accounts for the difference in the two responses: It is apparently easier to reach persons in a public campaign on an issue in which they have emotional and intellectual investment than on one which is of no significance to them. Advertising campaigns on cosmetics are followed with intelligent interest; campaigns on international problems are not.

We now turn finally to the central question with which this paper started.

How is independence possible?

The scheme I have outlined defines eight distinguishable acts. It is in the nature of these definitions that one and the same person can perform any one of these acts, depending on the subject-matter with regard to which social influence processes are exercised and on the conditions under which this occurs. At this stage, then, it does not make sense to speak of independent persons; only of independent actions of a person. Even the term 'independent action' may be a misleading oversimplification in view of the distinction made between independent dissent, independent consent, and undermined independence.

To take actions rather than persons as the unit of study does certainly not imply an underrating of the personality factor in response to social influence processes. On the contrary. The concept of investment, or cathexis, is a personality concept, referring, as it does, to the habitual relationship to an idea or issue of a total personality, not just of his ego or conscious knowledge.

Research on social influence processes resulting in one or the other of the eight types of action depends, then, on the possibility of identifying the three components of the multidimensional criterion we have established. Two of these components – position-taking and correspondence between private and public opinion – have often been used in research and do not present special difficulties. The identification of degrees of investment, however, is a major problem. It is necessary to develop methods which permit one to locate an issue in a person's life space.

The term 'life space' has become a shibboleth in social psychology. We all use it freely, but we know very little about it. It is mainly referred to as a boundary condition without much concern for its content and structure. Lewin has spoken of the growing differentiation of the life space from infancy both in terms of content and in terms of its time dimension. If we are to discover whether a given political or social issue is cathected for an individual we ought to investigate his life space before he is exposed to any influence, be that influence nothing more than the direct question by an interviewer with regard to the issue, a question which, of course, introduces the issue into the life space. With some such notion in mind, a number of studies concerned with independence and conformity in political and social matters have appropriately started the interview with general and open-ended questions. Thus the Stouffer study began with questions designed to find out what kind of things people worry about, and what problems they discussed with their friends. Stouffer found that communism, conformity, and civil liberties were mentioned spontaneously by only 1 per cent of the population. Similarly in a study of attitudes towards blacklisting in the entertainment industry (1956), questions about satisfactions and frustrations preceded questions about the topic proper. Here 6 per cent of the people interviewed mentioned blacklisting spontaneously.

These techniques go undoubtedly in the right direction. But in both cases, I now feel uncertain whether the existence or the absence of investment can be safely inferred from this rather crude effort. First of all, existence of an issue in the life space does not necessarily imply emotional and intellectual investment; and second, not everything that is so invested will come out into the open in response to such questions. When it comes down to it, we do not know what people really care about; nor have we sharpened our methodological tools to find this out. Somewhere in the social science literature – but I cannot recall where – I remember a statement to the effect that the majority of people know only two activities which elicit total investment because they are immediately gratifying; ends in themselves, not means to an end: sex among adults and play among children. Whether or not this pessimistic view of the world is justified, I do not know. However, I have less doubt that ideas are a relatively rare occurrence as objects of investment, and, hence, that the conformity in political and social matters of our times is largely a result of lack of such investment.

The difficulty in empirically identifying whether an issue is cathected by an individual lies largely in the fact that reasonably normal human beings do not invest all their emotional and intellectual energies in one object. Material things, human relations, other ideas, life itself can be cathected. The relationship of such diverse investments to each other needs to be explored empirically and broadly before more standardized measures of the degree of investment in an issue can be designed. At present, I can only speculate on the nature of measurable variables which may prove helpful in identifying investment in an issue. Two such variables come to mind: (1) the degree of compartmentalization of interconnectedness of factors in the life space, in other words, its spatial organization; and (2) the time-span of the space with regard to the issue, in other words, its temporal organization. I am about to explore the usefulness of a free-association method, starting from the issue, with regard to both organizational principles. Here, I only want to add a remark about the time dimension of the life space. We know as an empirical generalization from research that the narrow present situation tends to dominate the life space for persons relatively free from neurosis. To be able to meet a current situation on its own terms, and not with the obsolete and infantile cathexes acquired in early life, is actually the goal of psychotherapy and one relatively clear distinction between neurosis and absence of neurosis. Yet Heinz Hartmann (1947) speaks of another tendency in human behaviour:

> In stressing the importance of factors like anticipation, postponement of gratification, and the like, in the development of action, we at the same time give action its place in a general trend of human development, the trend toward a growing independence from the immediate impact of present stimuli, the independence from the 'hic et nunc'. This trend can also be described as one toward 'internalization' ... a process of inner regulation replaces the reaction and actions due to fear of the social environment.

It is possible to think of this longer time-span of which Hartmann speaks as characteristic for behaviour with regard to cathected issues. For only to the extent that the scope of the life space extends beyond the physically given present situation can past experiences, absent reference groups, anticipations of consequences of one's actions, shifts in frame of reference, and other such factors support the position on a cathected issue. When the life space is dominated by the past to the exclusion of present and future, we have the inability to conform which early in this paper was deliberately excluded from consideration. When the present dominates to the exclusion of past and future, independent dissent will be unlikely, conformity the rule. When the time dimension of the life space is balanced between past, present, and future, independent action is most likely.

Tentatively, then, I suggest that the interconnectedness of an issue with other matters in the life space, and the large time-span of the life space with regard to an issue should be regarded as criteria for investment.

What does all this mean for research? As I see it, the first task is the development of methods for the identification of investment in an issue. If and when such methods are developed, the experiments on conformity in the literature must be repeated, replacing the unidimensional criterion with the more complex definition I have attempted. Doing so will, I am confident, increase our knowledge of social influence processes, and sharpen the diagnosis of what is now all too easily called an 'age of conformity'.

References

ASCH, S. (1952) *Social psychology* New York, Prentice-Hall.

BACK, K. W. (1951) 'Influence through social communication', *Journal of Abnormal and Social Psychology*, **64**, 9–23.

BARRON, F. K. (1953) 'Some personality correlates of independence of judgment,', *Journal of Consulting Psychology*, **21**, 287–97.

BARKER, R. G. and WRIGHT, H. T. (1955) *Midwest and its children; The psychological ecology of an American town* Evanston, Ill., Row, Peterson.

BENDIX, R. (1952) 'Compliant behaviour and individual personality', *American Journal of Sociology*, **58**, 292–363.

BERENDA, RUTH (1950) *The influence of the group on the judgments of children; An experimental investigation* New York, King's Crown Press.

BLAKE, R. R. and MOUTON, J. S. (1954) 'Present and future implications of social psychology for law and lawyers', *Journal of Public Law* Boston, Emory University.

BOVARD, E. W., JR. (1951) 'Group structure and perception', *Journal of Abnormal Social Psychology*, **46**, 398–405.

BRODBECK, A. J., NOGEE, P. and DIMASCIO, A. 'Two kinds of conformity: A study of the Riesman typology applied to standards of parental discipline', *Journal of Psychology*, **41**, 23–45.

CHEIN, I. (1943) 'Personality and typology', *Journal of Social Psychology*, **18**, 89–109.

COHEN, A. K. (1955) *Delinquent boys: The culture of the gang* New York, Free Press.

COOLEY, H. (1909) *Social organization* New York, Scribner's.

CRUTCHFIELD, R. (1955) 'Conformity and character', *American Psychologist*, **10**, 191–8.

DEUTSCH, M. and GERARD, H. B. (1955) 'A study of normative and informational social influences upon individual judgment', *Journal of Abnormal and Social Psychology*, **51**, 629–36.

FESTINGER, L. (1953) 'An analysis of compliant behaviour' in Sherif, M. and Wilson, M. O. (eds) *Group relations at the crossroads* New York, Harper.

FESTINGER, L. (1954) 'Motivation leading to social behaviour' in Jones, M. R. (ed.) *Nebraska symposium on motivation* Lincoln, Neb., University of Nebraska Press.

FESTINGER, L., BACK, K., SCHACHTER, S., KELLEY, H. H. and THIBAUT, J. (1950) *Theory and experiment in social communication* Research Centre for Group Dynamics, Institute for Social Research, University of Michigan.

FRANK, J. D. (1944) 'Experimental studies of personal pressure and resistance', *Journal of General Psychology*, 30, 43–56.

FRENCH, J. R. P., JR. (1944) 'Organized and unorganized groups under fear and frustration', *Studies in topological and vector psychology, III* Iowa City, University of Iowa.

GOLDBERG, S. C. (n.d.) *Some cognitive aspects of social influence; a hypothesis.*

GOLDBERG, S. C. (1954) 'Three situational determinants of conformity to social norms', *Journal of Abnormal and Social Psychology*, 49, 325–9.

GRODZINS, M. (1956) *The loyal and the disloyal: Social boundaries of patriotism and treason* Chicago, University of Chicago Press.

HARTMAN, H. (1947) 'On rational and irrational action' in *Psychoanalysis and the social sciences*, I.

HARTMANN, H. (1955) 'Notes on a theory of sublimation' in Eissler, Ruth (ed.) *The psychoanalytic study of the child, X* New York, International Universities Press, pp. 9–29.

HILGARD, E. R. (1951) 'The role of learning in perception' in Blake, R. R. and Ramsey, G. V. (eds) *Perception, an approach to personality* New York, Ronald.

HOCH, P. and ZUBIN, J. (eds) *Psychiatry and the law.*

HOFFMAN, M. L. (n.d.) *Compulsive conformity as a mechanism of defense and a form cf resistance to group influence.* Manuscript.

HOFFMAN, M. J. (1953) 'Some psychodynamic factors in compulsive conformity', *Journal of Abnormal and Social Psychology*, 48, 383–93.

HOVLAND, J. C., JANIS, I. L. and KELLEY, H. H. (1953) *Communication and persuasion* New Haven, Conn., Yale University Press.

JAHODA, MARIE (1956) In *Report on blacklisting, II.* Meridian Books, July 1956.

JAHODA, MARIE (1956) 'Psychological issues in civil liberties', *American Psychologist*, 11, 234–340.

JAHODA, MARIE and COOK, S. W. (1952) 'Security measures and freedom of thought', *Yale Law Journal*, March 1952.

JANIS, I. (1954) 'Personality correlates of susceptibility to persuasion', *Journal of Personality*, 22, 504–18.

KELLEY, H. H. (1954) *Resistance to change and the effects of persuasive communications.* Manuscript.

KELLEY, H. H. and SHAPIRO, M. M. (1954) 'An experiment on conformity to group norms where conformity is detrimental to group achievement', *American Sociological Review*, 19, 667–77.

KELLEY, H. H. and WOODRUFF, C. I. (1956) 'Members' reactions to apparent group approval of a counter-norm communication', *Journal of Abnormal and Social Psychology*, 52, 167–74.

KELMAN, H. C. (1954) *A discussion of three processes of opinion change.* Manuscript.

KELMAN, H. C. (1953) 'Attitude change as a function of response restriction', *Human Relations*, 6, 185–214.

KELMAN, H. C. (1955) *Individual liberties in an atmosphere of conformity.* Manuscript.

KENDALL, P. L. and WOLF, K. M. (1949) 'The analysis of deviant cases in communications research' in Lazarsfeld, P. F. and Stanton, F. N. (eds) *Communications research, 1948–49* New York, Harper.

KENNEDY, J. F. (1955) *Profiles in Courage* New York, Harper.

KLEIN, G. S. (1954) 'Need and regulation' in Jones, M. R. (ed.) *Nebraska symposium on motivation* Lincoln, Neb., University of Nebraska Press.

LEVINE, J., LAFFAL, J., BERKOWITZ, M., LINDEMANN, J. and DREVDAHL, J. (1954) 'Conforming behaviour of psychiatric and medical patients', *Journal of Abnormal and Social Psychology*, 49, 251–5.

LEWIN, K. (1951) 'Behaviour and development as a function of the total situation', in Cartwright, D. (ed.) *Field theory in social science* New York, Harper (London, Tavistock, 1952).

LINTON, HARRIET B. (1955) 'Dependence upon external influences: Correlates in perception attitudes and judgment', *Journal of Abnormal and Social Psychology*, 51, 502–7.

LIPSET, S. M., LAZARSFELD, P. F., BONTON, A. B. and LINZE, J. (1954) 'The psychology of voting: An analysis of political behaviour' in Lindzey, G. (ed.) *Handbook of social psychology* Reading, Mass., Addison-Wesley.

LUCHINS, A. S. (1945) 'Social influence on perception of complex drawings', *Journal of Social Psychology*, 21, 257–73.

MCBRIDE, D. (1955) in 'An experimental study of overt compliance without private acceptance'. PhD. thesis, University of Minnesota.

PARSONS, T. and SHILS, E. A. (eds) (1951) *Toward a general theory of action* Cambridge, Mass., Harvard University Press.

RIESMAN, D. (1950) *The Lonely Crowd* New Haven, Conn., Yale University Press.

ST AUGUSTINE *Confessions* New York, Sheed and Ward.

SARBIN, T. R. and HARDYCK, C. D. (1955) 'Conformance in role perception as a personality variable', *Journal of Consulting Psychology*, 19, 109–11.

SCHACHTER, S. (1951) 'Deviation, rejection and communication', *Journal of Abnormal and Social Psychology*, 46, 190–207.

SHERIF, M. (1936) *The psychology of social norms* New York, Harper.

Social science and freedom; A report to the people. Social Science Research Center of the Graduate School, University of Minnesota, 1955.

STOUFFER, S. A. (1955) *Communism, conformity and civil liberties* New York, Doubleday.

TRILLING, L. (1955) *Freud and the crisis of our culture* Boston, Beacon Press.
WALLACE, M. (1956) 'Future time perspective in schizophrenia', *Journal of Abnormal and Social Psychology*, 52, 240–5.
WYLIE, RUTH (1956) *Pressure towards uniformity as a variable in making evaluations of self*. Manuscript.

Index of People, Places and Publications

Page numbers in *italics* following a title indicate that a substantial passage has been reprinted from that book or periodical.

Index of Main Subjects